Global Issues

Local Arguments

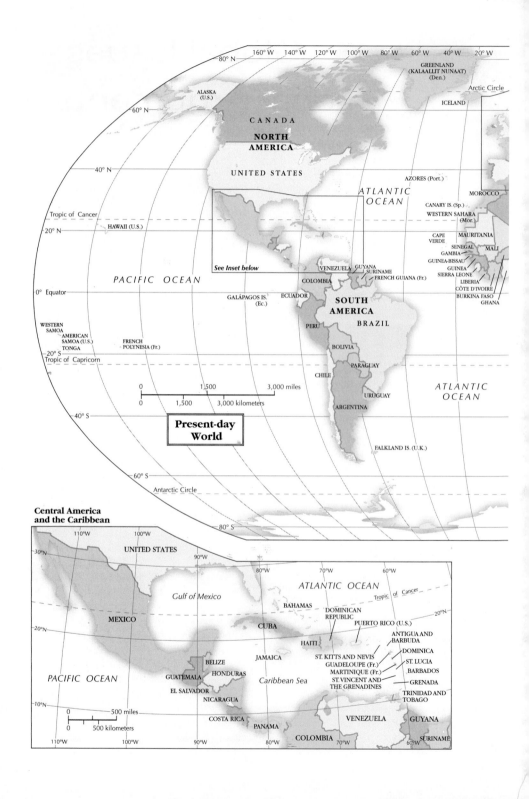

Present-day World

Central America and the Caribbean

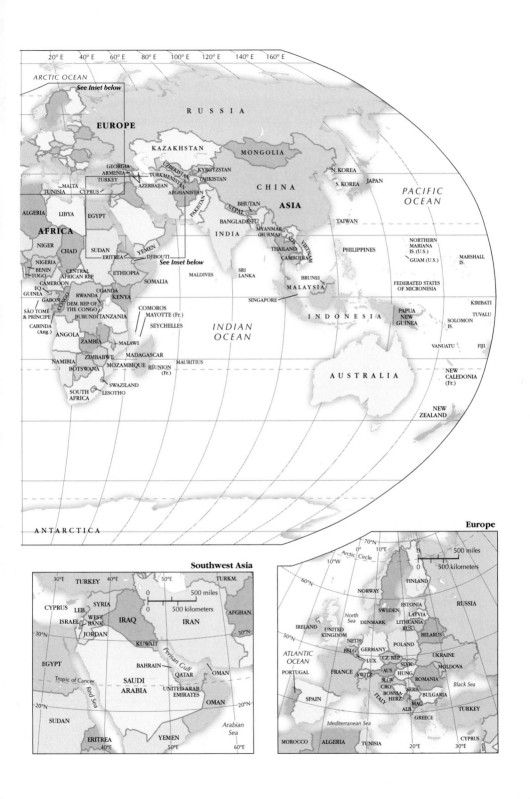

20° E   40° E   60° E   80° E   100° E   120° E   140° E   160° E

ARCTIC OCEAN

See Inset below

EUROPE

RUSSIA

KAZAKHSTAN

MONGOLIA

GEORGIA
ARMENIA
TURKEY   UZBEKISTAN   KYRGYZSTAN   N. KOREA
MALTA   AZERBAIJAN   TURKMENISTAN   TAJIKISTAN   S. KOREA   JAPAN
TUNISIA   CYPRUS   AFGHANISTAN   PACIFIC
                                                                            OCEAN
ALGERIA   LIBYA   EGYPT   BHUTAN   ASIA
                                      NEPAL
AFRICA   BANGLADESH   TAIWAN
                                    INDIA   MYANMAR
NIGER   SUDAN   YEMEN   (BURMA)   LAOS VIETNAM
CHAD   ERITREA   DJIBOUTI   THAILAND   PHILIPPINES   NORTHERN
NIGERIA   See Inset below   CAMBODIA   MARIANA
BENIN   CENTRAL   ETHIOPIA   IS. (U.S.)   MARSHALL
TOGO   AFRICAN REP   SOMALIA   SRI   BRUNEI   GUAM (U.S.)   IS.
CAMEROON   MALDIVES   LANKA
EQ.   UGANDA   MALAYSIA   FEDERATED STATES
GUINEA   RWANDA   KENYA   OF MICRONESIA
SÃO TOMÉ   DEM. REP OF   SINGAPORE   KIRIBATI
& PRÍNCIPE   THE CONGO   COMOROS   PAPUA   TUVALU
CABINDA   BURUNDI TANZANIA   MAYOTTE (Fr.)   INDONESIA   NEW   SOLOMON
(Ang.)   ANGOLA   SEYCHELLES   GUINEA   IS.
ZAMBIA   INDIAN   VANUATU   FIJI
                MALAWI   OCEAN
NAMIBIA   ZIMBABWE   MADAGASCAR   MAURITIUS   NEW
BOTSWANA   MOZAMBIQUE   RÉUNION   AUSTRALIA   CALEDONIA
                        (Fr.)   (Fr.)
SWAZILAND
SOUTH   LESOTHO   NEW
AFRICA   ZEALAND

ANTARCTICA

Europe

70°N
Arctic Circle   0°   10°E   0   500 miles
10°W   0   500 kilometers
60°N   FINLAND
        NORWAY   RUSSIA
        NORTH   SWEDEN   ESTONIA
        Sea   DENMARK   LATVIA
IRELAND   UNITED   LITHUANIA
        KINGDOM   RUS.
50°N   NETH.   BELARUS
        BELG.   GERMANY   POLAND
ATLANTIC   LUX.   CZ. REP   UKRAINE
OCEAN   FRANCE   SWITZ.   AUS.   SLVK.
PORTUGAL   SLOV.   HUNG.   MOLDOVA
                CRO.   ROMANIA
        SPAIN   BOSNIA-   SERB.   Black Sea
                HERZ.   ITALY   BULGARIA
                        MAC.   TURKEY
                Mediterranean Sea   ALB.   GREECE
MOROCCO   ALGERIA   TUNISIA   20°E   CYPRUS
                                    30°E

Southwest Asia

30°E   TURKEY   40°E   50°E   TURKM.
CYPRUS   LEB.   SYRIA   0   500 miles
ISRAEL   WEST   IRAQ   IRAN   AFGHAN.   0   500 kilometers
        BANK
        JORDAN
                KUWAIT
30°N   30°N
EGYPT   BAHRAIN   Persian Gulf
                QATAR   OMAN
        Tropic of Cancer   SAUDI   UNITED ARAB
Red Sea   ARABIA   EMIRATES
20°N   OMAN   20°N
                                    Arabian
SUDAN   Sea
        ERITREA   YEMEN
        40°E   50°E   60°E

Global Issues, Local Arguments

Readings for Writing

June Johnson
Seattle University

PEARSON
Longman

New York   San Francisco   Boston
London   Toronto   Sydney   Tokyo   Singapore   Madrid
Mexico City   Munich   Paris   Cape Town   Hong Kong   Montreal

Publisher: Joseph Opiela
Acquisitions Editor: Lauren A. Finn
Senior Marketing Manager: Sandra McGuire
Supplements Editor: Donna Campion
Production Manager: Savoula Amanatidis
Project Coordination, Text Design, and Electronic Page Makeup: Elm Street Publishing
Services, Inc.
Cover Designer Manager: Wendy Ann Fredericks
Cover Designer: Kay Petronio
Cover Photos: *Clockwise from top left:* © Shutterstock; © AP Photo/Ruth Fremso;
© Getty Images, Inc.; © Shutterstock; and © Corbis
Photo Researcher: Marcy Lunetta, Page to Page
Manufacturing Buyer: Roy Pickering
Printer and Binder: R. R. Donnelley and Sons Company—Crawfordsville
Cover Printer: Phoenix Color Corporation

For permission to use copyrighted material, grateful acknowledgment is made to the
copyright holders on pp. 570–571, which are hereby made part of this copyright page.

Library of Congress Cataloging-in-Publication Data
Johnson, June.
    Global issues, local arguments: readings for writing/June Johnson.
        p. cm.
    Includes index.
        Contents: Defining and exploring globalization—Consumerism, free trade, and
    sweatshops—Trading jobs: outsourcing and employment in a global economy—
    Crossing borders: immigration—Cultural rights: global tensions over media,
    technology, film, food, music, and sports—Human rights: trafficking in women and
    children and forced child labor—Environmental resources and rights: global conflicts
    over water and climate change—Feeding global populations—Spreading diseases in the
    global community.
    ISBN 0-321-24423-0
        1. History, Modern—21st century—Sources. I. Title.

D861.4.J65 2007
320.6—dc22

                                                                        2006045388

Please visit us at http://www.ablongman.com

ISBN 0-321-24423-0

1 2 3 4 5 6 7 8 9 10–DOC–09 08 07 06

Brief Contents

Contents

  Discussion   120
Writing Assignments   122

CHAPTER 4   Crossing Borders
          Immigration   125
          Context for a Network of Issues   125
          Stakes and Stakeholders   127
          Student Voice: Experiencing Immigration Issues
            (Esperanza Borboa)   130
          International Voices
            Residents of a Small Town in Mexico Responding
              to Immigration   132
          Global Hot Spot: Mexico   133

     Readings   133

          Jagdish Bhagwati, "Borders Beyond Control"   133
          Kofi Annan, "Lecture on International Flows of Humanity"   139
          Clay Bennett, "Offer May Vary" (cartoon)   147
          Ruben Navarrette, Jr., "America's Mixed Messages to
            Foreigners at the Gate"   148
          Mexico's Ministry of Foreign Relations, From *Guide for the
            Mexican Migrant*   150
          Linda Chavez, "Guest Worker Visas"   153
          John Laughland, "Immigration Is Turning Britain
            into a Sweatshop"   155
          Brian Fairrington, "Illegal Immigrant Economy" (cartoon)   159
          Don Melvin, "When Guest Workers Opt Not to Go Home;
            German Example Shows Some Migrant Policies Lead to
            Isolation, Poverty"   160
          Anti-Immigration Bumper Stickers   163
          Samuel P. Huntington, "The Special Case of Mexican
            Immigration"   164
          Mexican American Legal Defense and Educational Fund
            (MALDEF) and League of United Latin American Citizens
            (LULAC), "MALDEF and LULAC Rebuke Samuel Huntington's
            Theories on Latino Immigrants and Call on America to Reaffirm
            Its Commitment to Equal Opportunity and Democracy"   169
          Yasmin Alibhai-Brown, "No Room at the Inn"   175
          Faisal Mahmood, Pakistanis Protesting France's Ban
            on the Hijab (photograph)   179
          Francis Fukuyama, "Our Foreign Legions"   181

CHAPTER 5 Cultural Rights

Global Tensions Over Media, Technology,
Music, Film, and Food 191

Readings 200

CHAPTER 6 Human Rights

Trafficking of Women and Children and Forced Child Labor   271

Readings   501

Preface

Why should writing instructors bring global issues into the writing classroom? Global issues belong in writing courses because we are bumping into these issues more frequently and because global issues spark students' interest in learning and lead them to produce good writing.

Daily, the media bombard us with stories and images that remind us that our states, regions, and country are part of the larger world. Controversies over free trade, outsourcing, immigration, climate change, and bird flu increasingly demand our attention. In my writing classes, I have found that students welcome the opportunity to study these controversies, to discuss and write about them. Some of these issues are new and intriguing to students: How does our shopping at the local mall affect workers in clothing factories in China? How does lack of safe water in Africa threaten global security? Some are immediately relevant: How will sending businesses and jobs to Mexico and India affect the number of jobs available to young adults in the United States and Canada? Some have urgency: Should each country create an emergency plan for containing outbreaks of diseases such as bird flu that can spread in hours around the world and can kill millions? From working with global issues in my writing and argument classes, I have discovered that these issues, connecting "over there" with "home here," appeal to today's students, whose generation has been shaped by media images from around the world.

Global Issues, Local Arguments is based on two main ideas: first, seeing how global issues touch us and how our decisions as consumers and voters have far-reaching consequences is very important in today's world, and second, studying the public arguments on these issues in the writing classroom has great value. Unlike multicultural texts that have for years featured readings about the world, this text is an argument reader that introduces students to global controversies and their local connections. It helps students think their way through these issues and enter into them in their writing.

WHAT *GLOBAL ISSUES, LOCAL ARGUMENTS* OFFERS WRITING INSTRUCTORS AND STUDENTS

Global Issues, Local Arguments has grown directly out of my experiences as a writing instructor grappling with the ongoing challenge of teaching my students to be successful writers. I have designed *Global Issues, Local Arguments* with the following goals in mind: reaching a wide range of students with current, high-interest material; encouraging students to be involved citizens; fostering critical thinking; and most of all, helping students develop as writers and arguers.

Reaching a Wide Range of Students Many instructors are looking for ways to teach college reading and writing to students heading for diverse fields and are seeking accessible, stimulating, current issues to explore in their courses. This text has grown out of my work in writing classrooms with students whose interests range widely, from nursing to engineering, from environmental science to international business. The public controversies in this book provide significant, complex, and lively readings that span fields. The arguments in each chapter stimulate active reading and motivate students to respond with their own writing.

Encouraging Students to Be Involved Citizens The local and global issues in this book exemplify argument as an active, productive instrument to build communities of supporters and bring about change. Understanding stakeholders' investments in issues—why they care—and how they try to change their readers' thinking and move them to action can help students find their own investment in arguments they write. In its chapter introductions, readings, discussion questions, and writing assignments, this text pushes students to ponder their local connection to global issues and in doing so forges fruitful links between academic writing and civic engagement. Instructors can see that probing global problems that have roots or repercussions locally can propel students into local action. Grappling with issues that are at this very moment shaping our world will help equip students to be responsible citizens and professionals.

Helping Students Develop as Critical Thinkers Issues that bridge local and global communities are ideal for teaching critical thinking because these issues are complex, layered, and multifaceted. In preparation for writing about these issues, students are forced to examine and weigh multiple perspectives. Recognizing the controversial nature of these issues, in selecting readings for this text I focused on representing multiple political perspectives and including international views. This book encourages students to explore how diverse stakeholders such as individual citizens around the world, national and international advocacy groups, businesses, think tank analysts, and policymakers are invested in these issues. As students wrestle with multisided arguments and seek to sort out, analyze, and synthesize viewpoints on these issues, they develop key critical thinking skills.

Helping Students Develop as Writers and Arguers Most importantly, this book functions as a tool to teach writing in three main ways. First, it helps students analyze the readings as arguments as they examine the rhetorical power of arguments and think about how to infuse that power into their own arguments. Chapter introductions, headnotes to readings, discussion questions, and writing assignments direct students' attention to the way that the structure, content, and depth of arguments are shaped by the target audience and the genre and publication. The multisided arguments in each chapter demonstrate the importance of rhetorical context: Is the writer speaking at a global conference, writing for an advocacy Web site, or contributing to a local newspaper? These arguments on global issues are particularly good at showing how writers tailor their claims, reasons, evidence, and emotional and imaginative appeals to move their readers to think from new perspectives. In addition, each chapter's readings represent diverse argument genres for students to analyze and respond to in writing: op-ed pieces, researched arguments, policy analyses from news commentary magazines, advocacy Web site policy statements, book critiques, speeches, fliers, posters, and editorial cartoons.

Second, *Global Issues, Local Arguments* also is based on the idea that students write best when their knowledge of issues has depth. Each chapter is structured to help students work their way through the complexity of the issues: chapter introductions, headnotes, and questions provide context for the readings, help students understand the controversies and the stakeholders invested in them, and lead students to make their own connections. These local and global arguments and the suggestions for writing assignments growing out of them provide prime opportunities for teaching students how to use writing to learn and how to use analysis of print and visual texts as preparation for writing their own arguments. The text is designed to prepare students to produce perceptive, idea-rich arguments.

Finally, *Global Issues, Local Arguments* helps students advance as arguers by moving them beyond thinking of argument as pro-con debate, seeking quick closure, or simply choosing a side on issues. Featuring global-local issues that do not have simple solutions, this book emphasizes the intellectual work involved in reading and writing arguments and shows how argument is connected to problem solving as well as persuasion. In studying multisided issues, students work their way toward more complex, informed views and toward writing richer arguments.

STRUCTURE OF *GLOBAL ISSUES, LOCAL ARGUMENTS*

This text is modularly structured for use in multiple writing courses. It offers a rich variety of readings for analysis and discussion and a range of writing assignments to foster intellectual engagement and quality writing. Both the readings and suggestions for writing assignments can be easily incorporated into numerous different writing courses. The following overview of the features of this global argument reader shows how it can bring relevance, liveliness, and rigor to the writing classroom.

Chapter 1, "Introduction: Defining and Exploring Globalization" This introductory chapter equips students with a big-picture understanding of globalization and eases them into the significant issues in the text's readings by showing how the term *globalization* itself is a subject of debate; it briefly sketches the major controversies that underlie global issues. It invites students to begin thinking about the relationship between their local space—city, region, country—and global issues through two challenging but fun exploration activities: "Exploration One: How Wide Is Your Global View?" is an informal trivial pursuit–type quiz that asks students to see how much they know about other countries and cultures; and "Exploration Two: Picturing the Globe" is an activity that focuses on visual representations of the globe, their symbolic meaning, and the stakes involved in these representations.

Eight Chapters of Readings on Important Global Issues The eight chapters of readings present a rich array of print and visual texts (political cartoons, posters, and photos) on global-local issues. All of these readings are nonfiction—arguments—representing many stakeholders and argument genres, from op-ed pieces to longer policy statements, white papers, and scholarly arguments. These readings vary in complexity and level of difficulty, with each chapter including several challenging pieces. Most importantly, the print and visual texts in each chapter exemplify multisided arguments. The chapters focus on eight main global topics, each a network of issues with local dimensions:

• **Chapter 2, "Consumerism, Free Trade, and Sweatshops"** How does the consumerism in developed countries—indeed our own shopping habits and purchasing decisions—nurture sweatshop conditions in poorer countries? Can free trade bring prosperity to these developing nations?

• **Chapter 3, "Trading Jobs: Outsourcing and Employment in a Global Economy"** Is the outsourcing of jobs from the United States to developing nations beneficial for the United States and for these other countries?

• **Chapter 4, "Crossing Borders: Immigration"** How can the movement of people around the world be managed to the benefit of all countries?

• **Chapter 5, "Cultural Rights: Global Tensions Over Media, Technology, Music, Film, and Food"** How can all cultures have a say in cross-cultural exchanges of music, food, and film? Is globalization enriching cultures or making them blandly alike?

• **Chapter 6, "Human Rights: Trafficking of Women and Children and Forced Child Labor"** How has globalization advanced human rights throughout the world? Conversely, how has it facilitated the illicit trade in humans?

• **Chapter 7, "Environmental Resources and Rights: Global Conflicts Over Water and Climate Change"** How can rich and poor nations work together to preserve safe water supplies and curb the damage to the environment?

- **Chapter 8, "Feeding Global Populations"** Should the world focus on producing more food to combat world hunger? Do organically-grown crops or genetically modified crops offer more promise for feeding the world's growing population?

- **Chapter 9, "The Spread of Disease in the Global Community"** What should the global community do to combat pandemics like AIDS and the spread of diseases like SARS and bird flu? What responsibility as world citizens do countries have to manage their national public health?

Many of these chapters' issues intersect, creating even richer conversations and fuller pictures of these complex problems. For example, the chapters on consumerism and free trade, outsourcing, immigration, and cultural rights all involve global movements of goods, people, jobs, and cultural products across national borders, all of which are related to controversies over free trade. The questions and writing projects at the ends of chapters as well as ideas in the *Instructor's Manual* help students make connections among the chapters' issues.

PEDAGOGICAL FEATURES OF *GLOBAL ISSUES, LOCAL ARGUMENTS*

The pedagogical features of the text are designed to provide students with background information, help them read the arguments analytically, and help them synthesize and evaluate what they have read by writing.

Chapter Introductions That Give Background Information and Context
The introduction that opens each chapter has three main objectives: (1) to spark students' intellectual curiosity about each chapter's topic; (2) to make these global issues appealing and accessible to instructors and students; and (3) to provide historical information, explanations, and definitions of terms to equip students with the knowledge they will need to understand the readings and write about the issues. To provide instructors and students with this background, each chapter introduction includes the following features:

- A "Question to Ponder" asks students to think about their connections to the chapter's global issues.

- "Context for a Network of Issues" sketches the current status of the issues, provides brief historical information, and explains key terms such as *free trade, nongovernmental organizations (NGOs),* and *offshore outsourcing.*

- "Stakes and Stakeholders" illuminates some of the main controversies and issue questions that people are arguing about, starts students thinking about the global and local ties, and prepares students to analyze how people's investments in these issues shape their arguments.

- "Student Voice" presents a student's personal narrative response to or reflection on the issue to convey its experiential reality and to inspire students to look for their own connections with global issues.

- "International Voices" presents brief views from another part of the world in interviews and newspaper articles, bringing a concrete, human dimension to these issues.

- "Global Hot Spot" uses an excerpt from a foreign newspaper or Web site to zoom in on one of the main regions or countries grappling with this global issue to show its complexity and to engage students emotionally and intellectually.

Context and Discussion Questions for Each Reading Brief introductory headnotes with preview questions and follow-up questions for discussion accompany each visual and verbal text to help students analyze the rhetorical context and the rhetorical features of these arguments. These "For Class Discussion" items focus students' attention on how each piece works as an argument, how each contributes to the global conversation on the issue, and often how readings talk to each other. Rhetorical terms are intentionally generic (for example, "author's reliability and credibility" instead of "appeals to *ethos*") to enable instructors to use this text in a range of writing courses.

Questions Concluding Each Chapter Each chapter's "Chapter Questions for Reflection and Discussion" pose questions that encourage students to see relationships among readings, to explore points of agreement and disagreement among these arguments, and to frame their own questions for further research. These questions mention subissues and often Web sites for students to investigate and research on their own or in groups.

Chapter Suggestions for Multiple Writing Assignments To give instructors maximum flexibility in using this text, the writing assignments at the end of each chapter offer options for instructors and students who are using the chapter's material early in the course as well as those using it later. "Brief Writing Assignments" include suggestions for short, informal writing; for writing-to-learn pieces; and for writing that can help students generate ideas for their longer, more formal writing assignments. These writing assignments also lead students to find their own local stakes in these global matters and to think out their own views.

The suggestions for "Writing Projects" also offer a range of writing assignments:

- analysis and synthesis prompts that ask students to rethink one reading in light of another and to draw their own conclusions based on both arguments

- argument assignments that ask students to construct their own arguments on one of the chapter's subissues for different audiences

- argument assignments that foster civic engagement through letters to political representatives or op-ed pieces directed to university or regional newspapers

• community-based assignments that lend themselves to service learning and that call for fieldwork, interviews, surveys, and research into local conditions

• research projects that broaden or deepen the chapter's issues, often through Web research on international and local organizations or advocacy groups

Glossary and Films List The Glossary of this text provides brief definitions of key economic and political terms related to globalization. A list of films related to each chapter's issues provides ideas for further individual and class exploration. The *Instructor's Manual* discusses ways to incorporate these films.

STRATEGIES FOR USING THIS TEXT

Global Issues, Local Arguments can be used in conjunction with any rhetoric text or writer's handbook. Instructors may choose to use the readings in the chapters in a number of ways: (1) as texts to analyze for their views on global issues; (2) as models of arguments that students can examine for their rhetorical features, argument genres, and argumentative strategies; and (3) as conversations about controversial issues that students can join with their own writing.

The modular structure of *Global Issues, Local Arguments* as well as the multiple thematic threads running throughout the chapters enable this text to support many different course designs. The following approaches sketch three possible ways to use this text in writing courses.

Approach 1 Instructors might choose three to five chapters of readings for the class to read and examine together, and then ask students to use the readings from other chapters for individual research and writing projects and for class presentations. This approach uses other chapters as research resources.

Approach 2 Instructors might choose a thematic approach, centering the course on two or three chapters of readings and then pursuing thematic connections in three to four other chapters, assigning chapter introductions and a few readings from the other chapters to set up more complex conversations. Many readings throughout the text touch on major umbrella issues: for example, the power of consumers in rich countries, human rights, and threats to global security.

Approach 3 Instructors might select three or four readings from each chapter to illustrate argument genres and argumentative strategies and to explore multiple issues. Depending on the reading and writing abilities of their students, instructors might lean the course toward the shorter and simpler or longer and more complex readings in each chapter. Because each chapter includes several subissues, instructors might choose a subissue in each chapter.

The *Instructor's Manual* suggests ideas for course designs in more detail with sample syllabi, examines the many local-to-global connections in the readings, provides rhetorical approaches to the articles, and discusses how issues have potential for local community involvement. Answers to questions in the text are provided, along with suggestions for class discussion, in-class activities, and research activities out of class.

Global Issues, Local Arguments invites students and instructors—all of us—to broaden and deepen our perspectives on the world and to use argument to think together about the opportunities before us and the problems that now pervade our own local spaces and others' local spaces around the globe.

ACKNOWLEDGMENTS

First, I want to thank Eben Ludlow, my first Longman editor, now retired, who urged me to undertake a global argument reader and inspired me with his enthusiasm for the global and local connections that became the theme of this book.

I am especially appreciative of my academic institution, Seattle University, and its commitment to social justice. With its emphasis on global citizenship and its frequent speakers and workshops on global issues, the university provided a wonderfully stimulating environment for this project. In particular, I want to thank my colleagues Gary Chamberlain and Cynthia Moe-Lobeda in the department of theology and religious studies and Richard Young in the department of history for sharing their disciplinary perspectives on global issues. I also want to thank John Bean, my friend and coauthor on other texts, and Edwin Weihe, my English department chair, for being enormously supportive during the months of intensive work it took to create this book. My Seattle University students' insights and writing on global topics influenced every part of this text. I am grateful to my students who shared their narratives of the way global issues have touched their lives—eight of them provided the "Student Voices" in this text—and to all my students for helping me explore ways to teach global issues in my writing classes.

Several very capable students worked closely with me on this book. I owe special thanks to Terrence Thornburgh for sending newspaper articles and photos of garment factories from Saipan; to Malia Burns-Rozycki for reporting on water shortage and AIDS in Benin, Africa; to Jean Bessette, who did research and worked on the readings' headnotes for several chapters; to A. J. Chavez for researching the films listed at the end of the text; and to Tiffany Anderson, who did research and applied her background in political science and English to writing definitions for the terms in the Glossary.

I am very grateful to other colleagues who made substantial intellectual contributions to this book. Joan Thompson, of Normandale Community College, Minnesota, helped me launch and shape this project with her keen understanding of global issues and her expert research. Arlene Plevin, of Olympic College, author of the *Instructor's Manual,* shared her broad reading, her expertise on environmental issues, and her local and national contacts with people working for global justice. Bill Lalicker of West Chester University, Pennsylvania, shared his knowledge of contemporary China and his photos showing China's fusion of Eastern and Western culture, several of which appear in Chapter 5.

I have the deepest respect for the pedagogical experience of the people who reviewed this book at various stages of development. Whenever I could, I followed their insightful and very useful suggestions, and I am grateful to these scholars and teachers:

Shelley Aley, *James Madison University*
James Allen, *College of DuPage*
Gwen S. Argersinger, *Mesa Community College at Red Mountain*
Greg Barnhisel, *Duquesne University*
Shanti Bruce, *Indiana University of Pennsylvania*
Farrah M. Cato, *University of Central Florida*
James D'Agostino, *Southeast Missouri State University*
Chitralekha Duttagupta, *Arizona State University*
Judith G. Gardner, *University of Texas at San Antonio*
David Gold, *Ensworth High School*
Collin Hutchison, *San Jacinto College South*
Jennifer Liethen Kunka, *Francis Marion University*
Joshua J. Mark, *Marist College*
Patricia Roberts Miller, *University of Texas–Austin*
Meg Morgan, *University of North Carolina–Charlotte*
James M. Mullins, *University of Texas at El Paso*
Christine Norris, *University of Nevada–Reno*
Michael Pennell, *University of Rhode Island*
Avantika Rohatgi, *Butler University*
Robert A. Schwegler, *University of Rhode Island*
Tim N. Taylor, *St. Louis Community College at Meramec*
Mark L. Wiley, *California State University–Long Beach*
Justin Young, *University of Oklahoma*

My big thanks go to Joe Opiela, Longman publisher, who urged this project along when Eben Ludlow retired; and to Lauren Finn, my inspirational new editor, who has supported this project in every way. I am grateful to Marcy Lunetta, who worked skillfully on the permissions for this text and to Martha Beyerlein, who provided excellent guidance at the production stage.

I owe special thanks to Marion Castellucci, my development editor, for her expertise and personal encouragement during the final shaping and revising of this text.

Finally, I want to thank my parents and my brother, a novelist and poet, who heartily advised me to pursue my passion for this project. My deepest gratitude goes to my husband, Kenneth Bube, who has been a wonderful intellectual and domestic partner, standing by me at every step of this project, and my daughter, Jane Ellen, who has also continuously cheered me on.

JUNE JOHNSON
Seattle University

CHAPTER

Introduction

Defining and Exploring Globalization

Almost overnight, globalization has become the most pressing issue of our time, something debated from boardrooms to op-ed pages and in schools all over the world.*

—Joseph E. Stiglitz, Nobel Prize-winning economist

In this statement, Joseph E. Stiglitz succinctly articulates the immediacy, scope, and importance of globalization. Globalization—the increasing interconnectedness of all parts of the world in terms of communication, trade, business, politics, travel, and culture—affects us every day although its presence may often be masked. Globalization affects what we eat, what we wear, what jobs are available to us, what the population of our cities is, and so on.

This text invites you to join worldwide conversations about globalization by reading, examining, and discussing eight of the major global issues that people are arguing about, and by adding your own voice to the public dialogue through your writing about these issues. As you read and enter into these conversations, this text will continuously draw your attention to its overall thesis: that global issues affect us locally and that local matters have global consequences. For example, think about these hypothetical but realistic problems:

- The payroll department of an oil company is moved overseas, causing your mother to lose her job, yet this outsourcing has brought new career opportunities and vital income to some workers in India.

- You have just discovered that your little brother's toys were made in a factory in China where workers toil seven days a week in rooms filled with poisonous fumes; without medical benefits, they struggle with serious illnesses contracted on the job.

**Globalization and Its Discontents* (New York: W. W. Norton & Company, 2002), 4.

- You have learned that some of the fruits and vegetables you regularly eat were grown by chemical-using agribusinesses in Nicaragua that have displaced and impoverished small subsistence farmers. You wonder if you should investigate produce grown organically by local farmers.

- Your city has experienced an influx of immigrants from different parts of the world. You are interested in the new international restaurants, but you wonder what forces are driving these people to leave their countries and how the United States will integrate these people into life here, for instance, into the schools.

What do these experiences have in common? They are instances of the increasingly apparent global connections that link the everyday lives of Americans with the lives of people around the world: in short, they are examples of globalization. They also suggest problems of globalization that call on us to be informed, to seek solutions, and to make decisions.

Before embarking on your exploration of the global issues presented in each of the following chapters in this text, this introductory chapter invites you to begin thinking about the relationship between your local space and global concerns by doing two exploration activities. The first, a series of questions, resembles those informal, playful quizzes, often about global geography, that newspapers sometimes run. The second activity asks you to think about how visual images of the globe are used rhetorically in public controversies and corporate ads. Both of these exercises suggest significant questions about perception and about the mental, cultural, and geographical locations we inhabit and introduce the idea of multiple perspectives. Both are intended to stimulate and expand your thinking about globalization and to be an enjoyable challenge.

Finally, this introduction asks you to consider what people mean by the term *globalization.* It briefly sketches the major controversies surrounding the concept of globalization itself and the big-picture questions that underlie global issues. Thinking about what scholars, journalists, and activists are saying about globalization will prepare you to explore the issues and arguments presented in the chapter readings.

EXPLORATION ONE: HOW WIDE IS YOUR GLOBAL VIEW?

As Americans, we sometimes forget that people living in other countries view the world differently from the way we do. Globalization draws all parts of the world closer together, and yet reduced transportation time and rapid communication should not fool us into believing that there is only one perspective on events, people, and problems. This first exploration activity resembles a newspaper quiz or Trivial Pursuit game with global subject matter. As you seek to answer the questions that follow, explore how wide your global view is. Try to think beyond an American or Western-dominated perspective of the world. Working individually, with a partner, or with a group, you may want to search for answers to some of these questions by using the Web and by checking general reference books in a library.

Global Pursuit

1. If we consider only the city proper, what are the top-three most populous cities in the world?

2. Tae kwon do is one of the world's most popular martial arts. What country does it come from?

3. What is the world's most popular (consumed by the most people) brand of alcoholic beverage?
   a. an American bourbon
   b. a French wine
   c. a Russian vodka
   d. a Chinese beer

4. In what cities would you find these buildings, the two tallest buildings in the world?

(© AP Photo/Wally Santana)   (© Petroliam Nasional Berhad, 2005)

5. Which continent produces the largest amount of the world's coffee?

6. George W. Bush, Bill Clinton, and Ronald Reagan have been U.S. presidents during the last twenty years. What are the names of comparable heads of state in Canada and Mexico during this time?

7. What is the most popular international team sport?

8. The countries with the least access to information and communication technology (computers and Internet connections) are found in which region of the world?
   a. South America
   b. Oceania, a group of Pacific Islands including Polynesia (New Zealand), Melanesia, and Micronesia
   c. Africa
   d. Eastern Europe

9. What countries are these popular singers and musical groups from?
   a. Shonen Knife
   b. Thalia
   c. Lebo Mathosa
   d. Los Lobos

10. What is the currency used by the European Union?

11. How many provinces and territories does Canada have?

12. When American companies choose to move their customer service, accounting, data analysis, and software development and maintenance to countries outside the United States (called "outsourcing") to cut costs, which country is the first choice for these relocated jobs?
   a. China
   b. India
   c. Ireland
   d. Philippines

13. What do Megawati Sukarnoputri, Helen Clark, and Aung San Suu Kyi have in common?

14. After weapons and drugs, what is the most profitable commodity in illegal global trade?

15. What is the world's largest Muslim nation?

16. Why is the Indian film industry known as "Bollywood"?

17. According to predictions, which language will have the greatest number of speakers by the year 2050?
   a. Arabic
   b. Hindu-Urdu
   c. Spanish
   d. Chinese

18. Which country in South America has the largest gross national product (GNP)?

19. Identify and match capital cities with countries: Harare, Samoa, Wellington, Port-au-Prince, Bulgaria, Kabul, North Korea, Sofia, Haiti, Apia, Colombo, Beijing, Afghanistan, Asmara, Pyongyang, China, New Zealand, Eritrea, Sri Lanka, Zimbabwe.

20. Which country has the fastest train in the world?
   a. France
   b. Japan
   c. China
   d. Germany

After you have located answers for the quiz, write informally for ten to fifteen minutes in response to these questions:

1. Which quiz questions and answers surprised you the most?
2. Why was (or was not) this information part of your regular cultural knowledge?
3. Have these questions made you think of other parts of the world as familiar or unknown, as close to home or far away?
4. How did searching for answers to these questions affect your thinking about the importance of being knowledgeable about the world?

After you have responded to these self-reflection questions, your class might discuss your quiz answers, where you found them, and what insights this activity has given you about other parts of the world.

EXPLORATION TWO: PICTURING THE GLOBE

The phenomenon of globalization has also influenced the way we literally *see* the world. Scholar Wolfgang Sachs argues that "the image of the blue planet" has become a rich symbol adopted by diverse stakeholders who put it to very different uses. In fact, he asserts that the "photography of the globe contains the contradictions of globalization."* He says that the image of the blue and green globe reminds environmentalists that the earth is a finite place, a planet with limited water, air, livable land, and natural resources. Environmentalists want to convey that because the earth is all we have, we must wisely work together to preserve it. However, for another group of stakeholders—the corporations who do business in countries all over the world—the image of the globe symbolizes the expansive potential of business territory and trade. Depicting the world in its entirety as a blue and

---

*"Globalization and Sustainability," in *The Globalization Reader*, ed. Frank J. Lechner and John Boli, 2nd ed. (Malden, MA: Blackwell, 2004), 398.

green ball of continents and oceans with no country borders enables the business community to communicate the message that the world is open and available for economic growth.

When we see images of the globe in ads and on the Internet, it is interesting to speculate how the globe is depicted and how each image is being used rhetorically to shape our thinking. The following activity asks you to examine two images of the globe. One appears on the Web page of a government organization concerned with environmental protection (www.state .tn.us/environment/earthday/), and the second is an image from a stock photography Internet site, (www.fotosearch.com/), in the category "global business." After looking at these images in Figures 1.3 and 1.4, test out Sachs's claim and think creatively on your own, using the following questions as departure points:

1. How would you describe the image of the earth as the globe in each figure? (In color, Figure 1.3 is deep blue and green.) What text or objects are shown with the globe?

2. How is the image of the globe being used on the Tennessee Web page?

3. To test out Wolfgang Sachs's theory, investigate by doing a Google search for environmental depictions of the globe. You might search with the key words "global environmentalism," "climate change," "global warming,"

FIGURE 1.3 Tennessee Department of Environment and Conservation Earth Day 2005 Home Page *(Courtesy of the Department of Environment and Conservation, State of Tennessee)*

FIGURE 1.4 Global Business Image

and "conservation." Also investigate corporate depictions of the globe by skimming such magazines as the *Harvard Business Review, Forbes Magazine, Fortune, TIME Magazine,* and *U.S. News & World Report,* looking especially at ads for international travel, communication technology, and computers. How well do the images in these two main contexts fit Sachs's theory of environmental respect for global limitations and global business' celebration of expanded opportunity? What do the images of the globe symbolize?

4. Think of a business, a product, and an audience for which you might use the image in Figure 1.4. What words would you use in your ad? What message about the globe would you seek to convey through this image?

The following sections offer several different definitions of globalization, introduce you to the disagreements over these definitions, and prepare you to think about arguments over global issues.

WHAT DOES THE TERM *GLOBALIZATION* MEAN?

When people argue about globalization "from boardrooms to op-ed pages and in schools all over the world," what exactly are they arguing about? On the most general level, people are debating the meaning of globalization itself.

Disagreements may focus on any or all of these major underlying questions about globalization:

Underlying Controversies about Globalization

- Is globalization a new phenomenon? Or is it simply an accelerated stage in a centuries-long process?
- What forces are driving globalization?
- Is globalization inevitable and uncontrollable? Or is it the product of human decisions and therefore controllable?
- Is globalization harmful or beneficial, a problem or the solution to problems?
- Are there clear winners and losers in globalization?
- How is globalization changing our perceptions and behavior, and most other aspects of our lives?
- Should we welcome, applaud, encourage, resist, protest, or seek to change globalization?

These questions are the foundation of all the global issues explored in this reader. As you discuss the global-to-local connections in the chapters' readings, think about how specific issues and individual arguments tap into these foundational questions.

Three Competing Definitions of Globalization

Most books about globalization begin with the author's definition of globalization as both a process and a phenomenon. Indeed, the term *globalization* has sparked intense discussion and argument. Let's look at three definitions from three different spokespeople.

One common definition of globalization envisions it as the new, defining phenomenon of our historical moment. Thomas L. Friedman, foreign affairs journalist and editorialist for the *New York Times* and Pulitzer Prize winner, articulates this vision of globalization:

Thomas L. Friedman's Definition of Globalization

". . . it is the inexorable integration of markets, nation-states and technologies to a degree never witnessed before—in a way that is enabling individuals, corporations and nation-states to reach around the world farther, faster, deeper and cheaper than ever before and in a way that is enabling the world to reach into individuals, corporations and nation-states farther, faster, deeper, and cheaper than ever before."*

Note that Friedman emphasizes "integration" and pervasive, expansive, and accelerated connections. In his view, all parts of the world are being drawn ever closer together by unstoppable historical processes.

Another common definition of globalization zeros in on the *economic* features and forces of globalization. Jagdish Bhagwati, a professor of international economics and a former special advisor to the United Nations on globalization, distinguishes between cultural globalization, the revolution in communication of the recent past and present, and the profound, powerful economic changes referred to as "economic globalization":

Jagdish Bhagwati's Definition of Economic Globalization

"Economic globalization constitutes integration of national economies into the international economy through trade, direct foreign investment (by corporations and multinationals), short-term capital flows, international flows of workers and humanity generally, and flows of technology. . . ."†

Still other prominent voices in the globalization debate emphasize the *problems of defining globalization.* Cynthia Moe-Lobeda, a professor of theology and ethics, argues that it is crucial that we distinguish between two main definitions of globalization: (1) the "intercontinental connections," the way that transportation, communication, and technology have facilitated the movement of materials, goods, and ideas around the world and among continents and countries (basically Friedman's definition), and (2) the dominant model and system of economic globalization (Bhagwati's definition). Moe-Lobeda asserts that the first kind of globalization describes a process of modernization and technological change that is inevitable and beneficial in many ways, whereas economic globalization is not inevitable and not universally beneficial. She contends that it matters *how* we define globalization because Friedman's definition of globalization masks the power dynamics driving global economic forces while Bhagwati's definition downplays who has control of economic forces and who is benefiting the most from the increased connections around the world. Moe-Lobeda and other opponents of economic globalization believe that it needs to be described in terms that reveal how it distributes economic and political power.‡ David Korten, a scholar, activist, and one of the most vocal and well-known critics of economic globalization, provides such a description:

---

* *The Lexus and the Olive Tree* (New York: Random House, 1999), 9.

† *In Defense of Globalization* (New York: Oxford University Press, 2004), 3.

‡ "Defining Globalization: A Faculty Roundtable," in "Debating Globalization: An Interdisciplinary Dialogue" (conference, Seattle University, April 16–17, 2004).

David Korten's Definition of Economic Globalization

"[Economic globalization refers to] the forces of corporate globalization advanced by an alliance between the world's largest corporations and the most powerful governments. This alliance is backed by the power of money, and its defining project is to integrate the world's national economies into a single, borderless global economy in which the world's mega-corporations are free to move goods and money anywhere in the world that affords an opportunity for profit, without governmental interference."*

Economic globalization as an economic model and system is sometimes called "corporate globalization" or "neoliberalism." Among its main principles, neoliberalism as a political-economic philosophy maintains that governments should stay out of trade and give markets free rein; that resources and services such as railroads, electricity, and water should be controlled by private companies; and that the benefits of capitalism and unregulated trade will lead to beneficial economic and social development.

However, some people around the world are questioning and protesting the practical results of following these principles; it is this economic globalization that people are challenging. These people believe that economic globalization is not inevitable and that because it is the product of economic and political decisions made by international trade organizations, multinational corporations, and politicians, this global economic system can be changed.

In this text, the term *globalization* refers to both Friedman's definition of a technologically advanced, increasingly interconnected world and to economic globalization. While many of the chapters and their readings delve into issues of economic globalization, also keep in mind the broader definition as you are reading and discussing.

Promoting and Protesting Globalization

One reason that globalization is so controversial is that the lived experience of it differs depending on people's country, economic class and status, race, gender, age, and even religion.

Supporters praise globalization's sharing of knowledge and technologies. They point to the growth of industries and new markets and the rate at which developing countries are being integrated into the international economy. They argue that globalization in all its forms has brought an improvement in the standard of living and longer lives for many.

Moderate critics of globalization acknowledge the gains and benefits of globalization but voice objections as well, mainly about the unequal distribution of benefits and about problems with the global market. For example, George Soros, an entrepreneur, billionaire, activist, philanthropist, and author,

---

*When Corporations Rule the World (San Francisco: Berrett-Koehler Publishers, 2001), 4.

sees globalization as an opportunity for greater freedom for everyone; however, he argues that the public good and social well-being of people in developing countries, especially, have been overrun by market forces. Similarly, Joseph E. Stiglitz asserts that economic globalization favors the industrialized nations over developing nations, which lack the economic advantages to compete. Stiglitz also argues that global institutions such as the International Monetary Fund (IMF), the World Bank, and the World Trade Organization (WTO) put decision-making power into the hands of an elite financial community that is not accountable to the people whose lives are most directly affected by its decisions.

Still others vehemently challenge economic globalization as the ruling economic system in the world today. Environmentalists, advocates for social justice, representatives of indigenous peoples and developing countries, political activists, and some economists see economic globalization as a warping of the market itself. Furthermore, Cynthia Moe-Lobeda, David Korten, Indian activist Vandana Shiva, and others believe that economic globalization, with its emphasis on immediate profits, is, in Korten's words, "enriching the few at the expense of the many, replacing democracy with rule by corporations and financial elites, destroying the real wealth of the planet and society to make money for the already wealthy. . . ."* In short, they see economic globalization in its current form as strongly antidemocratic and harmful to people and the environment.

How Should We Make Decisions and Act in Response to Globalization?

The responses to globalization that writers are advocating differ as dramatically as their definitions of globalization and their perception of its value. Knowing about these divergent definitions, perceptions, and responses, briefly described here, will help you examine how they are embedded in the readings throughout this text.

Proponents of globalization primarily campaign for the extension and continuation of the globalization process.

• Many enthusiasts argue that most of the problems countries are experiencing with globalization are related to the current stage of globalization and are temporary setbacks for the global trade system. They say that global trade must continue to grow and that developing nations must continue to push toward full economic and industrialized maturity. Advocates of globalization such as Jagdish Bhagwati argue that the problems people attribute to globalization such as world poverty and hunger will diminish and that more people will benefit from globalization as these developing countries participate more in the international global economy.

---

*When Corporations Rule the World, 5.

• Other supporters of globalization argue that the problems come from people, institutions, and countries that try to interfere with globalization. They warn developing countries, as well as developed countries such as the United States, not to erect barriers to international trade that would interrupt the process of globalization but instead to welcome more open exchanges of culture, goods, and people.

Critics of globalization offer a range of responses.

• Some, such as George Soros and Joseph E. Stiglitz, want to revise the system. Soros calls for new international institutions to balance market forces, to provide for the public good, and to protect the social well-being of people in developing countries and poorer people everywhere. Stiglitz believes that we need to change economic globalization to create more equitable benefits, beginning with transforming the global institutions of the IMF and the WTO.

• Others such as Cynthia Moe-Lobeda, David Korten, and Vandana Shiva maintain that corporate globalization, with its distribution of economic and political power, is inherently flawed. They believe that people everywhere must reject the principle of economic growth, reduce consumption, and commit to preserving the environment and working for social justice in order to end world hunger and poverty.

• Still other opponents of globalization such as Gustavo Esteva and Madhu Suri Prakash focus on the way that global forces have threatened "local spaces." They claim that it is arrogant and impossible to think "globally" because "[w]e can only think wisely about what we can know well." They say that global policies represent small groups foisting their local views and interests on other places and peoples. Esteva and Prakash envision an antiglobalization movement composed of "people thinking and acting locally, while forging solidarity with other local forces."* They urge all of us to resist global policies and forces at the local level as we make our decisions about what we eat, what we buy, and how we live.

Navigating the Controversies

As you read the arguments in this text about global issues and their local connections, try to place the issues in the context of these big-picture questions about globalization: What assumptions have the writers made about the meaning of globalization? Are they assuming that globalization is inevitable? Do they believe that globalization is basically a good thing? Also examine the way their arguments pursue solutions to global problems and strive to win adherents to their views. After reading the multisided arguments in each chapter, consider how they have expanded and clarified your own views and your thoughts about the way these issues influence your life.

---

*"From Global to Local: Beyond Neoliberalism to the International of Hope," in *The Globalization Reader*, 2nd ed. (Malden, MA: Blackwell, 2004), 412–16.

CHAPTER 2

Consumerism, Free Trade, and Sweatshops

QUESTION TO PONDER

We may find it difficult to comprehend that buying a latte at Starbucks is an action that makes us "players in the global economy" who "influence livelihoods and government policies around the world."* Coffee pickers in Latin America struggle to make a living wage as the price of a pound of coffee fluctuates under free trade conditions and agreements. However, coffee that is Fair Trade Certified guarantees to pay coffee pickers $1.26 a pound compared to the free trade price of as little as 10¢ a pound. As coffee drinkers, you and your friends are wondering if you should buy only fair trade coffee to help coffee workers. Should Americans and people in rich countries factor into our consumer choices the working conditions under which products were grown or made?

CONTEXT FOR A NETWORK OF ISSUES

Free trade affects us every day—what we eat, wear, and buy—and we hear the term "free trade" almost as frequently as we hear the term "globalization" itself. Basically, "free trade" refers to the economic philosophy and practice of reducing barriers such as tariffs, taxes, subsidies, and quotas so that raw materials, goods, and services can move unhampered across national borders. Supporters of free trade point out that facilitating the movement of goods around the world enlarges the variety of available products, for example, bringing American consumers a choice of cars from South Korea, Japan, and Germany; a choice of wine from Australia, Italy, and

---

*Jake Baatsell, "Cup by Cup, Coffee Fuels World Market," *Seattle Times*, September 19, 2004.

France; and a choice of kiwis and apples from New Zealand when it is winter in the United States. Free trade also helps to lower the cost of goods so that consumers can buy more things and have a higher standard of living.

However, even as we enjoy bargains on DVDs, jeans, and household wares at nearby superdiscount stores, we are gradually becoming aware that there are some hidden costs of free trade. (One cost of free trade is the loss of American jobs to other countries, discussed in Chapter 3 on outsourcing.) The media and advocacy groups are making us more conscious of the production processes that create the goods that make our lives comfortable. While advances in technology play a part in cheaper prices, we learn more about where our televisions, clothing, and toys are made when we look at the labels on these items: men's shirts made in Cambodia and Taiwan, sheets made in India, jeans made in Mexico, women's sweaters made in the Philippines, fleece jackets made in Jordan, women's blouses made in Sri Lanka, and athletic shoes made in China. Even more importantly, news stories increasingly give us glimpses of the exploitation, injustices, and abuses experienced by workers in factories throughout Mexico, Central America, East Asia, the Middle East, and Southeast Asia: twelve- to eighteen-hour shifts; minimal or no overtime pay; housing in stark, barricaded dormitories; working amid poisonous chemical waste; dangerous, poorly maintained equipment; minimal or no compensation for occupational injuries; and firing in response to unionization efforts. These reports of "sweatshop" conditions in factories in developing countries raise questions for us as citizens and consumers in the world's richest country. How are we to interpret and respond to the contradictory views, experiences, and consequences of free trade?

Free Trade Theory in Brief. First we need a basic understanding of free trade as a philosophy and a global economic system. Free trade theory emphasizes continuous economic growth and believes that this growth is the solution to world poverty; in metaphoric terms, the "pie" of global wealth-earning potential needs to grow bigger so that more countries can have a piece. Proponents of free trade regularly cite the theories of eighteenth-century Scottish economist Adam Smith (author of the 1776 book *The Wealth of Nations*) and David Ricardo, a nineteenth-century British economist. Smith argued that if government stays out of trade, then wealth created by private businesses and trade will benefit the public. Ricardo asserted that countries need to specialize in the goods that they can produce most efficiently and cheaply and that when countries trade their specialties, all will benefit (a principle called "comparative advantage"). Free trade theory claims that economic competition with minimal government intervention will lead to greater efficiency, productivity, and innovation; will reduce costs for consumers; and will free up more capital for further investment. Free trade's removal of barriers such as tariffs should promote economic growth, foster a cooperative spirit among nations, help developing nations become independent economies, and end poverty around the world.

Some Key Free Trade Agreements and Institutions. As citizens and consumers, we also need a basic understanding of how free trade has become the global trading system. In 1944, the global economic institutions and agreements—the International Monetary Fund, the World Bank, and the General Agreement on Tariffs and Trade—that have implemented this theory of free trade were launched. The International Monetary Fund and World Bank were intended to further economic progress in poorer countries by lending them money to help them through economic crises and help them build the systems (called "infrastructure") such as roads, power plants, ports, and education that provide the foundation for economic development. In 1947, the General Agreement on Tariffs and Trade (GATT), accepted by developed countries (also called "industrialized" or "first world" countries) and developing countries (also called "unindustrialized" or "third world" countries), sought to shape international trade by minimizing trade barriers, especially tariffs. In 1994, this agreement became an institution, the World Trade Organization (WTO). By removing barriers to trade, the WTO seeks to create "a level playing field"—that is, equal opportunity for businesses in all countries. Additionally, free trade agreements provide many benefits for large corporations, including the establishment of Export Processing Zones (EPZs) that are tax-free locations for factories producing goods for big retailers.

Besides the WTO, other free trade agreements create free trade zones and regional partnerships among groups of countries. The European Union is a trading bloc among twenty-five countries throughout Europe that was formed to coordinate these countries' political and economic affairs. Another trading bloc, the North American Free Trade Agreement among the United States, Canada, and Mexico, took effect in 1994.

STAKES AND STAKEHOLDERS

People throughout the world, businesses and multinational corporations, national and local governments, whole countries, and individual citizens and consumers have much to gain or lose from the way that conflicts over free trade's principles and practices are argued and resolved. Here are some of the significant issue questions that show how the interests of different global citizens are pitted against each other.

Is Free Trade a Universally Good Global Economic System? This major controversy over who benefits from free trade is complex partly because the information used to measure growth and success varies. Economists, politicians, and free trade supporters hold up the economic growth of South Korea, India, and now China as examples of the positive effects of free trade, yet critics point out that wealth may be accumulating in the hands of a small group of privileged elites.

Some political analysts and social activists representing workers and indigenous peoples around the world argue that free trade is creating winners (in particular, big corporations) and losers (indigenous peoples and poor workers in developing countries) because both the theory and practice of free trade are flawed. Environmentalists and social activists challenge free trade's goal of continuous economic growth with its drain on the earth's resources. Political analysts such as David Korten believe that free trade theory misinterprets and misapplies the theories of Adam Smith and David Ricardo. For instance, Korten asserts that Smith disliked corporations and believed in local investment and production so that business owners and managers would be responsible to the people most affected. Many critics contend that free trade enables powerful corporations called "transnationals" or "multinationals" to exploit poor developing countries' resources and workers. Furthermore, critics point out that much of the increased trade that appears to be among nations is actually intrafirm—one part of a corporation located in one country trading with another part of the same corporation located in another country.

Should Free Trade Be Freer?   Some leaders and citizen groups in developing countries accept the model and goals of free trade but argue that the rules and agreements currently favor rich countries and large corporations. How can newer and smaller companies compete with the adaptability, efficiency, and mass-produced goods of larger companies and with fluctuations in the world market? Farmers in developing countries protest that they cannot compete with U.S. and European farmers, whose governments give them tax cuts and financial support. Furthermore, rich countries put high tariffs on competing foreign goods (called "protectionism") while at the same time demanding that developing countries lower their tariffs on American and European products. For small farmers and factories in developing countries such as Mexico, free trade can mean losing out to the low-priced goods from the United States and Europe, going bankrupt, and falling into poverty. Many developing countries are arguing that the economic playing field needs to be leveled further.

Should National, Regional, and Local Governments or Global Organizations Have More Power?   Both those who favor free trade and those who oppose it recognize that free trade agreements mean a loss of power and political control at the national, regional, and local levels of government; however, they disagree whether dissolving national borders and powers is good or detrimental. Should countries be able to make laws to meet their own needs? Opponents of free trade agreements argue that standardizing trade rules (in economic terms, "harmonizing" regulations) often leads to minimal protection of the environment, workers, and consumers.

Many citizens want their government to be able to make laws covering inspection procedures, package and labeling requirements, and product content to protect consumers' health.

Should Free Trade Agreements Be Extended and Enlarged or Restricted and Reconceived? Particularly now as the expansion of free trade agreements is under consideration around the world, politicians, economic leaders, and social activist groups are debating the expansion of free trade agreements. For example, should the North American Free Trade Agreement linking the United States, Canada, and Mexico expand and develop to become the Free Trade Agreement of the Americas, linking thirty-four countries of the Western Hemisphere in a free trade bloc? Currently, Argentina, Brazil, and Venezuela—as well as labor unions, consumer groups, and the Catholic Church in Latin America—are protesting what they see as economic domination by largely U.S. transnational corporations.

Does the Employment That Derives from the Current Free Trade System Benefit Global Workers? If we move from the big picture of free trade controversies to examine the well-being of workers, we find analysts, businesses, and activists arguing about sweatshops and foreign factories. Supporters of free trade claim that these low-paid jobs are a necessary and inevitable road to economic progress and that even exploitive jobs are better than no jobs. However, other analysts, social activists, and workers say that market competition and corporate greed are creating sweatshop conditions in foreign factories. They claim that free trade has enabled corporations to move their factories to the countries with the cheapest labor and fewest regulations on worker health and safety. Labor activists and workers argue that when transnational corporations like Wal-Mart pressure subcontracting factories to reduce costs or when they shift their manufacturing from Nicaragua to China, where workers will work longer hours for less pay, these corporations are forcing workers to compete against each other in a "race to the bottom." Furthermore, free trade has cost Americans jobs. As manufacturing has left the United States, where unions ensure fair wages, benefits, and conditions for workers, to go to developing countries with a much lower cost of living, few regulations, and no unions, some Americans have been left without comparable-paying jobs. (Chapter 3, "Trading Jobs," examines these issues.) Anticorporate advocates view this worldwide competition among workers for jobs as a shift in the global distribution of wealth, dividing the workers everywhere from corporations, managers, owners, and stockholders.

What Role Do and Should Consumers Play in Free Trade? Advocates of the free market and corporations believe that consumers are *helping* the workers in developing countries when they buy the products these workers make. Corporations argue that to meet the demands of their stockholders for profits and the demands of their customers for the lowest prices, they must seek the cheapest labor and the most favorable free trade agreements. Do the consumer habits of developed nations drive the global competition of corporations? Anticorporate activists and labor supporters say we need to use our consumer power to influence the improvement of factory conditions around the world. However, these human rights advocates, union supporters, workers organizations, and consumer groups disagree about *how* to use consumer power and *how* to change consumer habits: should we boycott abusive companies, demand corporate accountability, buy only union-made goods, and/or be willing to pay higher prices for goods to ensure fair wages for workers?

What Are Alternatives to Free Trade? As free trade creates many corporations that are wealthier and more powerful than countries, some critics, activists, and consumer groups are arguing that corporate-driven free trade needs to be replaced with an alternative trade system built on an equitable relationship among producers, sellers, and consumers. This new approach, called "fair trade," seeks to connect farmers, artisans, and workers in developing regions to markets in developed nations in direct, long-term relationships. Proponents of fair trade want to establish dependable markets and a living wage and actively campaign to reduce poverty. Some of the main fair trade organizations and advocacy groups are SERRV International Fair Trade, the Fair Trade Federation, Global Exchange, and TransFair USA. While fair trade supporters urge consumers to buy only fair trade goods, skeptics argue that fair trade networks are unrealistic and unfeasible because the fair trade system can't hope to compete with the powerful corporate globalization that has money, technological advances, scope, size, and efficiency on its side.

The three sections that follow—"Student Voice," "International Voices," and "Global Hot Spot,"—help you explore ways that your life and other people's lives are being touched by consumerism, free trade, and factory production.

STUDENT VOICE: EXPERIENCING CONSUMERISM AND SWEATSHOPS

Some Americans, as Tiffany Anderson shows, are beginning to question our participation in the unequally distributed benefits of free trade.

Tiffany Anderson

I spent the summer of my sophomore year of college working stock at the Gap Outlet in the nearby mall. Although I complained of the early morning hours, the stifling heat of the back room, and the physical labor it required, I was secretly proud to be a part of our all-girl stock team. We worked hard, but our shifts resembled the ambiance of sleepovers; we gossiped, joked around, and blasted the top-40 station as we unpacked boxes of clothing and accessories. On days when shipments of new products came in, we each took turns passing snap judgments on the cuteness of the new items. On this particular day, I knew it was going to be rough because we were getting one of the biggest shipments for the Back to School season. I pulled on my black apron and searched for my exacto-knife, eyeing the seemingly endless stacks of boxes. There was nothing to do but start.

I hummed along to the new Christina Aguilera song as I pulled corduroy pants from their protective plastic wrapping, wrinkling my nose at the sour smell of newness that clung to them. I finished unpacking the box, broke it down, threw it onto the garbage heap, and ripped open the next box on my stack. I tore off the lid and froze as a numbing chill enveloped my perspiring body, and I yelled, "Oh, you guys. Look."

My co-workers gathered around, anticipating my horror at an atrocious sweater or some ill-advised pants. Instead, I pointed to a few lines scrawled across the inside lid of my box in navy blue pen and in a foreign language that I couldn't translate or decipher. The language looked Thai, or maybe Vietnamese . . . something Asian, I was sure. The tags on the clothing were of little help. In the one box alone, there were tags from Indonesia, China, Vietnam, and Thailand.

"What do you think it says?" asked Amy.

Each of us knew The Gap had been cited repeatedly as a major employer of sweatshop labor, although we rarely acknowledged this fact to each other.

"Do you think it's a cry for help?" I sensed the author's presence, as if the sight of the blue right-slanting writing had freed the author from her prison, like the rubbing of a lamp releases a genie. I pictured a woman, my age but skinny, with sunken eyes and black hair, locked into a blindingly hot factory until she met her daily quota. I thought about her family of five she had to feed on a skimpy wage, children raised by a mother who was practically absent as she tried to provide for them. We went through the possible scenarios, embarrassed by our frequent references to our own jobs as "sweatshop labor." An unsettling silence descended on the room, and all you could hear was the tearing of plastic and cardboard. Before I recycled the box, however, I tore off the piece with the message and put it in my locker, hoping to find a translation although I never did.

As the day progressed, I couldn't shake the feeling that I had been chosen to open that box, that I now had a responsibility to my friend overseas, trapped in a situation she couldn't free herself from. Maybe I was being melodramatic, but the problem was I had very little information on the actual working conditions of the people who made my clothes. Now I could no longer ignore the fact that I didn't know.

As an American, I realized that I had the privilege to listen to the radio at work and chatter with my co-workers. My biggest complaints consisted of feeling tired after a six- or seven-hour day, or of having to drive home sweaty and dust-covered. I worked to make money so I could go out dancing during the school year and get a discount on Gap jeans. I now felt guilty that my $30 pair of jeans paid a marginal fraction of the profit to the person who had made them. It slowly began to occur to me that I had a choice of which companies to support and that I had responsibility as a consumer to know what sort of practices my money supported. While research only problematized these issues further for me, I at least think now that consumer consciousness is encouraging. Nothing will change if I continue to ignore the problem, unwrapping khakis and singing along with the radio, as if I'm the only person in the world.

INTERNATIONAL VOICES

One problem American consumers have in trying to understand how free trade competition affects foreign workers is the contradictory messages we receive from workers. To investigate the workers' situation, we could focus on any of the Export Processing Zones (also called Export Trade Zones) in Central America and Southeast Asia or any place where multinational corporations have subcontracted their manufacturing work. While some workers would agree with Candida Rosa Lopez, an employee in a Nicaraguan garment factory, who told a *Miami Herald* reporter, "I wish more Americans would buy the clothes we make,"* others convey their distress over the exploitive factory conditions. For example, Isabel Reyes, a worker in Honduras, reported her experience of the pressure to produce more goods at lower prices. This passage comes from an article entitled "Wal-Mart Wrings Efficiency from Third World Factories" by Nancy Cleeland, Evelyn Iritani, and Tyler Marshall that appeared on November 28, 2003, in the *Seattle Times*:

Comments from a Factory Worker Producing Clothing for Wal-Mart

San Pedro Sula, Honduras—When Wal-Mart Stores demands a lower price for the shirts and shorts it sells by the millions, the consequences are felt in a remote Chinese industrial town, at a port in Bangladesh and in Honduras, under the corrugated metal roof of the Cosmos clothing factory.

---

*David R. Henderson, "The Case for Sweatshops," *Miami Herald*, February 7, 2000.

Isabel Reyes, who has worked at the plant for 11 years, pushes fabric through her sewing machine 10 hours a day, struggling to meet the latest quota scrawled on a blackboard.

She now sews sleeves onto shirts at the rate of 1,200 garments a day. That's two shirts a minute, one sleeve every 15 seconds.

"There is always an 'acceleration,'" said Reyes, 37, who can't lift a cooking pot or hold her infant daughter without the anti-inflammatory pills she gulps down every few hours. "The goals are always increasing, but the pay stays the same."

Reyes, who earns the equivalent of $35 a week, says her bosses blame the long hours and low wages on big U.S. companies and their demands for ever-cheaper merchandise. Wal-Mart, the biggest company of them all, is the Cosmos factory's main customer.

Reyes is skeptical. Why, she asked, would a company in the richest country in the world care about a few pennies on a pair of shorts?

The answer: Wal-Mart has built its empire on bargains.

The company's size and obsession with shaving costs have made it a global economic force. Its decisions affect wages, working conditions and manufacturing practices—even the price of a yard of denim—around the world.

GLOBAL HOT SPOT: CHINA

The news about China's rapid industrialization is also full of contradictions. Recently, China has been the recipient of many factories relocated from Mexico and has become the largest exporter of goods to the United States. On the one hand, China exemplifies substantial growth toward market capitalism, modernization, and economic prosperity. The following passage from an article entitled "Factory Labor Runs Short in China" by Peter S. Goodman from the *Seattle Times*, September 26, 2004, supports the positive picture of free trade economic development.

Dongguan, China—. . . . Where once a paycheck, even under harsh conditions, was enough to entice tens of millions of people to leave their villages in China's interior and flock to factories on the coast, workers are beginning to turn their backs on the prospect of laboring in 100-degree heat, living in rat-infested dormitories and being cheated out of their earnings.

They are instead staying in their home villages to take advantage of rising farm wages—up from 15 to 40 percent in the past year as the government streamlines taxes and as growing domestic spending power raises the price of vegetables and meat.

Or they are finding jobs closer to home in inland cities along China's expanding road and rail networks.

At bus and train stations here, migrant workers carry belongings in plastic sacks, headed back to villages in the interior. "The wages are too low and the work is too hard," said a 21-year-old man from Guangxi province as he waited to board an all-night bus home. "It's a waste of time."

"Manufacturing wages are going up, and they are going to keep going up," said Jonathan Anderson, a former International Monetary Fund official and now chief economist at UBS Investment Research in Hong Kong.

That refutes a theory that as more of the world's manufacturing shifts to this country of 1.3 billion people, China's peasant labor force would force global wages lower for decades, particularly given that independent labor unions are banned and even the threat of organization meets with stiff prison sentences.

On the other hand, China also illustrates the economic dependence and exploitation found in developing countries. The pressures of global free trade to cut costs and to treat workers as dispensable parts of the production process have made economic progress costly to many workers. The following excerpt from a *Detroit Free Press* article entitled "Savage Form of Capitalism: Chinese Factory Workers Risk Limbs to Hold Jobs" by Tim Johnson, published on April 17, 2004, reveals some of these costs:

Shenzhen, China— . . . . In a grim replay of the industrial revolution in the United States and other countries, industrial machinery will crush or sever the arms, hands and fingers of some 40,000 Chinese workers this year, government-controlled news media report. Some experts privately say the true number is higher.

A majority of accidents occurs in metalworking and electronics plants with heavy stamping equipment, shoe and handbag factories with leather-cutting equipment, toy factories and industrial plastics plants with blazing hot machinery.

In Shenzhen's hospital wards, maimed factory workers nurse mangled hands and forearm stumps. They tell of factory managers who've removed machine safety guards that slowed output and of working on decrepit, unsafe machinery. Workers toiling 100 hours a week grow dazed from fatigue, then lose their fingers to machines.

Local officials routinely overlook appalling safety conditions, worried that factory owners will relocate. They send mutilated migrant workers back to distant rural villages, shunting the burden of workplace injuries onto poorer inland provinces.

. . . But labor monitors say that foreign companies that relentlessly demand lower prices and U.S. consumers who gobble up low-cost goods contribute to the problem.

Zhou Litai, a lawyer who represents hundreds of workers maimed or killed on the job, said foreign consumers should be aware that some "Made in China" products are "tainted with blood from cut-off fingers or hands."

As these news stories suggest, free trade, global factory production, and consumerism meet in complex economic and ethical ways. The readings in this chapter present arguments on the benefits and drawbacks of free trade for developing countries, on consumers' responsibility to the workers who make our goods, and on the value and ethics of Wal-Mart, a big corporate player in the global economy.

READINGS

AXT Workers' Rights
Khalil Bendib

Khalil Bendib is a sculptor, artist, and political cartoonist originally from Morocco and Algeria. He is known around the United States and abroad for his political cartoons and public artworks. This cartoon about American corporations and worker exploitation appears on his Web site http://www.bendib.com/index.html for March 29, 2004.

> Silicon Valley in California is the site of many leading U.S. technology companies. OSHA is the Occupational Safety and Health Administration, a U.S. governmental agency that establishes regulations for workplace safety. What would the businessman in this cartoon say are the advantages of free trade?

FIGURE 2.1 AXT Workers' Rights (© Khalil Bendib, 2004)

For Class Discussion

1. Who are the characters in this cartoon and what story does the cartoon tell?

2. What is the main claim of this political cartoon? Who is the target of this cartoon's attack?

3. What questions for further investigation does this cartoon raise about U.S. industries, manufacturing, and use of factories abroad?   ■

Poor Man's Hero
[Interview with Johan Norberg]
Nick Gillespie

This article appeared in the December 2003 issue of *Reasononline,* the Web version of *Reason,* a monthly magazine dedicated to "free minds and free markets." *Reason* states its libertarian perspective and purpose: to provide "a refreshing alternative to right-wing and left-wing opinion magazines by making a principled case for liberty and individual choice in all areas of human activity" (http:reason.com/aboutreason.shtml). Nick Gillespie is editor in chief of this libertarian publication and a widely published journalist who has written for the *New York Times, The Washington Post, Slate,* and *Salon.* Johan Norberg, the focus of this interview, is a Swedish political writer and activist best known for his 2001 book *In Defense of Global Capitalism.*

> How does Norberg try to make his libertarian pro-free trade views understandable and persuasive in this interview? What view of protectionism versus open borders do libertarians hold?

1   If there is any moral certainty underpinning today's antiglobalization movement, it's that desperate actions—from sometimes violent street demonstrations to public crop burnings to dressing up as giant sea turtles—are needed to protect the traditions, forests, and human rights of the Third World against the rapacious greed to the First. The anti-globo left has little doubt that anyone who favors international free trade, open markets, and the cultural mongrelization they foster must be a greedy corporate bastard hellbent on plundering the world's poor and chopping down the last tree left on the planet. On the right, if George W. Bush is any indication, a different sort of blindness is at work: It's OK to pass nakedly protectionist legislation as long as you talk a good game about favoring free trade.

2   This is why Johan Norberg, a 30-year-old Swede with roots in the anarchist left, is so important. He is the author of *In Defense of*

Global Capitalism, which makes a powerful moral and economic case for globalization. Norberg throws rhetorical Molotov cocktails both at left-wing critics who would condemn developing countries to poverty by insisting on First World workplace and environmental standards as a prerequisite for trade and at Western governments whose free market rhetoric is shamefully undercut by draconian tariffs on textiles and agriculture, the two areas in which the developing world can actually compete.

3   Norberg focuses on the human dimension of globalization, how increased and freer trade is the best way to help the wretched of the earth. A bestseller in Sweden when it appeared there in 2001, *In Defense of Global Capitalism* is a richly detailed and nuanced brief in favor of globalization. It was translated for British audiences by the influential London free market think tank the Institute of Economic Affairs. The Cato Institute has just released a new and updated American translation by Roger Tanner (with help from Reason Associate Editor Julian Sanchez, who previously worked at Cato).

4   A fellow at the Stockholm think tank Timbro, Norberg is the author of several previous books, including *State, Individual, and Market* (2000), *A History of Swedish Liberalism* (1998), and *The Resistance Man* (1997), a study of the Swedish writer Vilhelm Moberg.

5   *In Defense of Global Capitalism* is a compelling book on what is arguably the major economic issue of our time. In Johan Norberg, globalization has found a persuasive and passionate spokesman who may well reshape the terms of debate. If he succeeds in doing so, it won't be his first such success. In the early 1990s, as part of a libertarian group called the Freedom Front, Norberg helped to organize speakeasies that illegally sold liquor to protest Sweden's restrictive licensing laws. After the group grew to 30,000 members—and after more than a dozen raids by the police—Swedish politicians realized they couldn't contain what was becoming a broad-based social movement. Instead, they liberalized their laws, allowing drinking establishments to maintain longer hours. "That's my biggest political success to date," jokes Norberg.

6   Editor-in-Chief Nick Gillespie interviewed Norberg in Washington, D.C., in early September.

7   REASON: Your book is titled *In Defense of Global Capitalism*. Can you summarize your case?

8   JOHAN NORBERG: The core is that capitalism and globalization—by which I basically mean free and open markets and the liberal political, economic, and social institutions that support them—bring freedom of choice to people in countries that have never experienced this before. If we want to defend globalization—and we should—our focus must be on developing countries, not our own Western countries. Global capitalism means that people are

no longer confined by the decisions of national elites. These could be the local monopolies, the local powers, politicians, and so on.

9   By making local powers compete or by bypassing them altogether, globalization gives people more freedom to decide over their own consumption, to buy things from abroad, to get the cultural influences they want, to travel, to meet friends, and to cross borders.

10   REASON: What's the evidence that global capitalism benefits people in poor countries?

11   NORBERG: Take just about any statistic, any indicator of living standards in the world, and you can see the progress that has been made over the exact period that worries globalization critics. In the last 30 years we've seen chronic hunger and the extent of child labor being halved. In the last 40 years, we've seen life expectancy going up to 64 years in developing countries. We've seen literacy levels approaching the maximum in most countries in the world. According to World Bank statistics, 200 million people have left absolute poverty—defined as living on the equivalent of less than $1 a day—over the past 20 years. What's more, the most progress is found in the countries that increased trade and contacts with the outside world.

12   Globalization has also helped extend rights to women that had long been confined to men. These include being able to go into business, get an education, inherit money, and so on. One reason for this is simple economics. In a globalized, competitive economy, women are a potential resource. They are able to have new ideas, to produce, and to work. If you discriminate against women—or anyone else—you lose opportunities as a society or as an employer. Take the discussion that's going on now in Saudi Arabia about whether women should be allowed to drive, which they can't legally do now. While it's unlikely the situation there will change anytime soon, it's progress just to have the discussion. People are saying it's extremely costly to hire drivers, often from other countries, to drive women around. You can see how basic economics, basic capitalism, creates the incentive to give women more rights.

13   A second reason is that all the goods, ideas, and people that cross borders under globalization allow people to see more alternatives, to see other ways of living. When women and other oppressed groups in poor countries see how their counterparts in Western societies are treated, they begin to have ideas about how they want to be treated. Globalization is a great influence because people everywhere get all sorts of new ideas. They say, "Wow, things can be very different than I'm used to."

14   This isn't to say everything is rosy. Most things are getting better in the developing world, but there are new problems,

including AIDS. Yet we can see the old scourges, the old diseases, being abolished. Life expectancy wouldn't be getting longer if things were getting worse in terms of health, hunger, and the environment. We have the few exceptions in sub-Saharan Africa, which also happens to consist of the very countries that are the least globalized. They have the least foreign investment and, generally speaking, the least political and economic liberty. More than anything, they need the sort of economic growth that will allow them to buy not simply relatively expensive AIDS drugs but penicillin and vaccines for more basic sorts of illnesses.

15   REASON: Can you give a specific example of a developing nation that has benefited from globalization?

16   NORBERG: Look at Vietnam, which I visited recently. It had the benefit that when the Communists took power there, they actually implemented their ideas. They collectivized agriculture and they destroyed private property, which meant that in the mid-1980s people were starving there. The Communists' own ideas managed to do what the American bombs never did: destroy communism. In the wake of such failure, the government began to look for other examples, and they saw that Taiwan had succeeded by globalizing. The Communists in China were liberalizing trade and ownership laws and were seeing fast progress. The contrast is especially clear on the Korean peninsula. It's the same population, with the same culture, just having two very different political and economic systems. In 50 years, one of them went from hunger and poverty to Southern European living standards. The other one is still starving.

17   Looking at all this, the Vietnamese chose to go global. They began to price land and they began to open up for investments and for trade, which led to quick results. Agricultural production took off and has made them one of the world's biggest exporters of rice. But they also took in investments for manufacturing production. They've received tons of foreign investments and factories that gave people new opportunities and new resources that have increased their standard of living.

18   REASON: Critics would say that what Vietnam really imported were sweatshops.

19   NORBERG: Sweatshops are a natural stage of development. We had sweatshops in Sweden in the late 19th century. We complained about Japanese sweatshops 40 years ago. You had them here. In fact, you still do in some places. One mistake that Western critics of globalization make is that they compare their current working standards to those in the developing world: "Look, I'm sitting in a nice, air-conditioned office. Why should people in Vietnam really have to work in those terrible factories?" But you've got to compare things with the alternatives that people

actually have in their own countries. The reason why their workplace standards and wages are generally lower is the lack of productivity, the lack of infrastructure, the lack of machinery, and so on. If workers were paid U.S. wages in Vietnam, employers wouldn't be able to hire them. The alternative for most workers would be to go back to agriculture, where they could work longer hours and get irregular and much lower wages.

20   Sweatshops are the way poor countries tap into their competitive advantage, which is cheap labor. Multinational corporations bring in more modern technology, including things like training and management systems, that actually increase productivity. When workers are more productive, they tend to earn more. That's why in a typical developing nation, if you're able to work for an American multinational, you make eight times the average wage. That's why people are lining up to get these jobs. When I was in Vietnam, I interviewed workers about their dreams and aspirations. The most common wish was that Nike, one of the major targets of the anti-globalization movement, would expand so that a worker's relatives could get a job with the company.

21   When unions, when protectionists, when uncompetitive corporations in the U.S. say that we shouldn't buy from countries like Vietnam because of it's labor standards, they've got it all wrong. They're saying: "Look, you are too poor to trade with us. And that means that we won't trade with you. We won't buy your goods until you're as rich as we are." That's totally backwards. These countries won't get rich without being able to export goods. . . .

22   REASON: If the benefits of globalization are so obvious, why is there so much opposition to it, especially in the West? Vietnamese workers may be clamoring for more Nike factories, but protesters in Europe and North America are tossing bricks through the windows of McDonald's and Starbucks.

23   NORBERG: The further you get from the West, the more positive people are toward globalization, toward more business and trade ties with the rest of the world. The most vocal opponents of globalization in poor countries are often funded by critics from wealthier countries. For instance, Vandana Shiva [director of the New Delhi-based Research Foundation for Science, Technology, and Ecology] is a very vocal opponent of economic liberalization and biotechnology, and she's funded by a lot of different Western groups. Actual farmers in the developing world mostly would like these new crops to actually get something done.

24   There are the old groups that have always been scared of foreign competition. Corporations that wouldn't be able to beat competition from other countries are one of them. In the U.S.,

that includes the textile industry, which has funded a lot of the anti-sweatshop propaganda. You see the same thing when it comes to unions that are trying to educate people against free trade, trying to block the NAFTA agreements, the World Trade Organization negotiations, and similar things. But there are newer pressure groups too. These include nongovernmental organizations that have been mostly interested in domestic issues, which could be anything from workplace safety to opposing privatization and outsourcing. In a globalized world, it makes sense for these groups to make their case in front of international bodies. Probably more than most, environmental groups understood that they have an interest in challenging the new globalization forces. They are used to being able to lobby their own governments to stop certain substances, to stop genetically modified crops and the like. They understand that they have to take their issues to the WTO and to be able to fight for them there.

25   All these groups may have different agendas—the unions are interested in domestic jobs and the greens in air quality—but they're willing to collaborate. They don't have the same views, and they don't have the same goals. But they do have the same enemy.

26 REASON: Let's talk about the environmental groups a bit. In your book, you convincingly demonstrate that economic development is a boon to the environment because richer countries tend to pollute less. You point to research suggesting that economic growth correlates positively with cleaner air and water once countries reach around $10,000 per capita GDP—the level of South Korea, Argentina, and Slovenia. You argue that the best way to clean the environment is to get the developing world to move as quickly as possible from a pre-industrial to a post-industrial economy. Why would environmental groups not buy that argument?

27 NORBERG: I think that there are two basic reasons that lead environmentalists to oppose globalization and the industrial development that goes along with it. The first is a real concern about the environment. Many environmentalists care about green forests, clean air, clean water, and so on. What they don't appreciate is that attitude is itself a result of industrial development. In our countries, people didn't care about these things 100 years ago. Preferences shift when you can feed your children and give them an education. That's when you begin to care about these sorts of things. Environmentalists in this camp merely project a contemporary sense of these issues onto developing countries that are at the place where the West was a century ago. It's an intellectually honest mistake, one that new

information and data can change. So can talking with people in developing countries.

28   But there's another motivation at work among some environmentalists. I don't think this viewpoint represents the majority, but it often includes the intellectual leaders of environmental groups. These are people who are bothered not by environmental degradation per se. Rather, they reject the modern project altogether. They are skeptical of the lifestyles and societies that we have created. They think we are alienated from nature compared to the past and that it is wrong to see nature as a tool that human beings can use for their own convenience and benefit. It's a fundamentally aesthetic understanding of the world that is reminiscent of early 19th century German romanticism. It paints a very distorted view of the pre-industrial world as a utopia. In reality, that world was a place in which starvation was the rule and not the exception.

29   I was extremely skeptical towards modern industrial society for a long time, so I understand these sentiments. If you live in an urban, developed area and your main experience of rural areas is secondhand, they're quite understandable. You feel very sad about countries that are modernizing and building factories, and about people who will be buying espresso machines that make loud noises instead of, I don't know, sitting around listening to the birds singing.

30   My attitude changed as I began to read history and understood what kind of circumstances my ancestors lived in. The world they lived in was far from ideal. It was starvation, it was children dying in the first year of their lives. And of course, backbreaking labor, including child labor, was everywhere. I think the best way to rebut this romantic, aesthetic challenge to globalization, to our modern project, is by actually looking at the circumstances of pre-industrial society.

31   REASON: In your book, you really lay into Western governments, many of which talk out of both sides of their mouths when it comes to liberalizing trade. They want unfettered access to new markets, but they routinely employ protectionist tariffs against developing countries. You call this "the white man's shame" and point out that "Western duties on export commodities from the developing world are 30 percent above the global average."

32   NORBERG: Since the end of the Second World War, we've liberalized trade in most areas. Ironically, the main places where we haven't done so are textiles and agriculture—the very two areas where poor countries can compete.

33   In the developed world, the textile and agricultural sectors are very strong special interest groups with a lot of political

resources. They can make a lot of noise in the public debate. We know that if we open these markets to competition, we'll have to restructure those parts of our economies. People will have to change jobs and go into something else. That would be painful, of course, but it's outrageous, since those are precisely where poor countries would be able to do well.

34 REASON: This opens up a larger question about increasing globalization. If trade laws come down to special interest politics, how do you defeat those interests? How do we get to a point where the U.S. and the European Union finally give up on protectionism for textiles and agriculture?

35 NORBERG: I think the first thing that is necessary is moral outrage. We need to explain what's on the line, what the cost is to poor people in the least developed countries. People are *dying* because we in the West are unwilling to change and to actually live by the free market rhetoric we often spout. We also have to explain to the public that it's not merely developing countries that lose out by these policies. We do too.

36 REASON: How do we lose out?

37 NORBERG: We deny ourselves access to better goods at cheaper prices from other countries. We lose out because we have to pay billions in tax-funded subsidies to these special interest groups so that they don't have to face competition. Agricultural subsidies cost something on the order of $1 billion a day in Western countries. We have to explain to people, "Look, if we have real free trade, we'll make another $1 billion every day, simply because we abolished our agricultural subsidies." One study I cite in the book estimates that the world would gain about $70 billion annually from a 40 percent tariff reduction on manufactures—and that 75 percent of that gain would go to developing nations.

38 REASON: The WTO is meeting in Cancun as we're talking. What do you think of the WTO, which is a major target both of anti-globalizers and many free market advocates?

39 NORBERG: It's a good thing that it exists, but it's rightly been called the free traders' deal with the devil. The best solution for all of us would be unilateral free trade: Just open our borders. We don't need *protection* from cheap goods; they're exactly what we want!

40   Unfortunately, we don't live in a perfect world, and in that case I think that the WTO is important for two reasons. One is that it's hard to combat the special interests that are against opening up market access for other countries. But if we do it in multilateral negotiations, we can face the special interests and say: "OK, we might lose jobs in those sectors that we open up to competition. But in exchange we get access to new markets

over here." That helps convince people in the export business. It helps get, say, unions on our side for free trade, and that's a good thing. The other reason that the WTO is important is that [it] helps create a rule of law in the international trade system. We lock in free trade reform so that politicians can't backtrack every time there's a failure or a downturn in their national or local economy.

41   Those are reasons the WTO is important, but it really is a deal with the devil, if only because it gives the impression constantly that when we open up markets, when we give ourselves the opportunity to buy a wider variety of goods at better prices, we are giving up something. I think that's one of the reasons why we have a backlash against free trade. The president of the U.S. and everybody else always act as if free trade is some sort of concession.

42   REASON: In the wake of the 9/11 attacks and the rationale offered for them by bin Laden, many observers in the West suggested that there was something intrinsic to the Arab world and Islam that makes them particularly uncomfortable with the creative destruction that accompanies what you've called "global capitalism." What do you think?

43   NORBERG: . . . Although I'm glad Saddam has been toppled—it's a good day whenever a tyrant is dethroned—I don't think that war and occupation are the way to do this. The best way is through globalization, through the introduction of new ideas, of Western influences, into these countries. You can see that happening even in Iran. You can see it happening in Jordan and Qatar and in many other countries that have more access to Western goods and media.

44   Because of globalization, it's easier for people to watch and read about Western societies, and more and more do. As we mentioned, Arab women see that Western women have the same rights and opportunities as men. That sort of contact is a great source of inspiration. The same thing happens when they see that we can express our own beliefs in a general way, in culture and in music. That's the big hope, I think, for the region. But we have to be very patient because it's going to take a long time. It took a long time for Japan to turn into a peaceful, productive country; it took nearly 50 years for South Korea to become something like a liberal democracy.

45   But I see the rise of fundamentalist forces in the Middle East not as a sign of the strength of their ideas. It's more a sign that they are terrified of the globalization that is already occurring. The fundamentalists can see that there's a new middle class growing in these countries and that these people are interested more in living the good life, in choosing their own lives, and not

in following the literal teachings of the Koran. Critics of global-ization worry about the Disneyfication or McDonaldization of culture, of standardization replacing "authentic" traditions. But it's more correct to say that no single culture is becoming domi-nant. Instead, it's pluralism, the freedom to choose among many different paths and destinations, that is gaining ground due to globalization and greater exchange.

For Class Discussion

1. This interview has two "writers" in that Nick Gillespie introduces Johan Norberg, and then Norberg presents his argument as answers to Gillespie's questions. In his introduction, how does Gillespie identify different groups and their views on globalization? How does he characterize the antiglobalization movement? How does Gillespie's choice of words contribute to readers' sense of his authority on the subject and to the persuasiveness of his views?

2. According to Johan Norberg, what are the advantages of global capitalism for developing countries?

3. What is Norberg's view of sweatshops and how does he justify his views?

4. Which of Norberg's points about the benefits of global free trade or the problems of global free trade as it is currently conducted do you think he most effectively supports with evidence? How could you confirm or dispute his use of numerical evidence?

5. *Reason* is a widely read and well-respected nonpartisan publication that often discusses the libertarian case for free trade. What audi-ence besides libertarians do you think would find Norberg's argu-ment persuasive and why? ■

Twelve Reasons to Oppose the World Trade Organization
Global Exchange

This policy statement is taken from the Web site for Global Exchange, "an in-ternational human rights organization dedicated to promoting political, social, and environmental justice globally" (www.globalexchange.org/about/index. html). Global Exchange seeks to stir up public awareness about injustices and elicit support for fair trade. This policy statement was downloaded October 24, 2004.

This flier focuses on laying out a case against the World Trade Organi-zation in broad, sweeping points. For what purpose and for what audience would this flier be particularly effective?

TWELVE REASONS TO OPPOSE
THE WORLD TRADE ORGANIZATION

The World Trade Organization is writing a constitution for the entire globe. The trade ministers and corporate CEOs who control the WTO would like you to believe thats its purpose is to inspire growth and prosperity for all. In reality, the WTO has been the greatest tool for taking democratic control of resources out of our communities and putting it into the hands of corporations. An international movement is growing to oppose the corporate rule of the WTO and replace it with a democratic global economy that benefits people and sustains the communities in which we live. And importantly, we are winning!

1. The WTO Is Fundamentally Undemocratic

The policies of the WTO impact all aspects of society and the planet, but it is not a democratic, transparent institution. The WTO rules are written by and for corporations with inside access to the negotiations. For example, the US Trade Representative gets heavy input for negotiations from 17 "Industry Sector Advisory Committees." Citizen input by consumer, enviornmental, human rights and labor organizations is consistently ignored. Even simple requests for information are denied, and the proceedings are held in secret. Who elected this secret global government?

2. The WTO Will Not Make Us Safer

The WTO would like you to believe that creating a world of "free trade" will promote global understanding and peace. On the contrary, the domination of international trade by rich countries for the benefit of their individual interests fuels anger and resentment that make us feel less safe. To build real global security, we need international agreements that respect people's rights to democracy and trade systems that promote global justice.

3. The WTO Tramples Labor and Human Rights

WTO rules put the "rights" of corporations to profit over human and labor rights. The WTO encourages a 'race to the bottom' in wages by pitting workers against each other rather than promoting internationally recognized labor standards. The WTO has ruled that it is illegal for a government to ban a product based on the way it it produced, such as with child labor. It has also ruled that governments cannot take into account "non commercial values" such as human rights, or the behavior of companies that do business with vicious dictatorships such as Burma when making purchasing decisions. The WTO has more power to punish countries that violate its rules than the United Nations has to sanction violators of international human rights standards.

4. The WTO Would Privatize Essential Services

The WTO is seeking to privatize essential public services such as education, health care, energy and water. Privatization means the selling off of public assets—such as radio airways or schools—to private (usually foreign) corporations, to run for profit rather than the public good. The WTO's General Agreement on Trade in Services, or GATS, includes a list of about 160 threatened services including elder and child care, sewage, garbage, park maintenance, telecommunications, construction, banking, insurance, transportation, shipping, postal services, and tourism. In some countries, privatization is already occurring. Those least able to pay for vital services—working class communities and communities of color—are the ones who suffer the most.

5. The WTO Is Destroying the Environment

The WTO is being used by corporations to dismantle hard-won local and national environmental protections, which are attacked as "barriers to trade." The very first WTO panel ruled that a provision of the US Clean Air Act, requiring both domestic and foreign producers alike to produce cleaner gasoline, was illegal. The WTO declared illegal a provision of the Endangered Species Act that requires shrimp sold in the US to be caught with an inexpensive device allowing endangered sea turtles to escape. The WTO is attempting to deregulate industries including logging, fishing, water utilities, and energy distribution, which will lead to further exploitation of these natural resources.

6. The WTO Is Killing People

The WTO's fierce defense of 'Trade Related Intellectual Property rights (TRIPs)—patents, copyrights and trademarks—comes at the expense of health and human lives. The WTO has protected pharmaceutical companies' 'right to profit' against governments seeking to protect their people's health by providing lifesaving medicines in countries in areas like subsaharan Africa, where thousands die every day from HIV/AIDS. Developing countries won an important victory in 2001 when they affirmed the right to produce generic drugs (or import them if they lacked production capacity), so that they could provide essential lifesaving medicines to their populations less expensively. Unfortunately, in September 2003, many new conditions were agreed to that will make it more difficult for countries to produce those drugs. Once again, the WTO demonstrates that it favors corporate profit over saving human lives.

7. The WTO Is Increasing Inequality

Free trade is not working for the majority of the world. During the most recent period of rapid growth in global trade and investment (1960 to 1998) inequality worsened both internationally and within countries. The UN Development Program reports that the richest 20 percent of the world's population consume 86 percent of the world's resources while the poorest 80 percent consume just 14 percent. WTO rules have hastened these trends by opening up countries to foreign investment and thereby making it easier for production to go where the labor is cheapest and most easily exploited and evironmental costs are low.

8. The WTO Is Increasing Hunger

Farmers produce enough food in the world to feed everyone—yet because of corporate control of food distribution, as many as 800 million people worldwide suffer from chronic malnutrition. According to the Universal Declaration of Human Rights, food is a human right. In developing countries, as many as four out of every five people make their living from the land. But the leading principle in the WTO's Agreement on Agriculture is that market forces should control agricultural policies—rather than a national commitment to guarantee food security and maintain decent family farmer incomes. WTO policies have allowed dumping of heavily subsidized industrially produced food into poor countries, undermining local production and increasing hunger.

9. The WTO Hurts Poor, Small Countries in Favor of Rich Powerful Nations

The WTO supposedly operates on a consensus basis, with equal decision-making power for all. In reality, many important decisions get made in a process whereby poor countries' negotiators are not even invited to closed door meetings—and then 'agreements' are announced that poor countries didn't even know were being discussed. Many countries do not even have enough trade personnel to participate in all the negotiations or to even have a permanent representative at the WTO. This severely disadvantages poor countries from representing their interests. Likewise, many countries are too poor to defend themselves from WTO challenges from the rich countries, and change their laws rather than pay for their own defense.

10. The WTO Undermines Local Level Decision-Making and National Sovereignty

The WTO's "most favored nation" provision requires all WTO member countries to treat each other equally and to treat all corporations from these countries equally regardless of their track record. Local policies aimed at rewarding companies who hire local residents, use domestic materials, or adopt environmentally sound practices are essentially illegal under the WTO. Developing countries are prohibited from creating local laws that developed countries once pursued, such as protecting new, domestic industries until they can be internationally competitive. California Governor Gray Davis vetoed a "Buy California" bill that would have granted a small preference to local businesses because it was WTO-illegal. Conforming with the WTO required entire sections of US laws to be rewritten. Many countries are even changing their laws and constitutions in anticipation of potential future WTO rulings and negotiations.

11. There Are Alternatives to the WTO

Citizen organizations have developed alternatives to the corporate-dominated system of global economic governance. Together we can build the political space that nurtures a democratic global economy that promotes jobs, ensures that every person is guaranteed their human rights to food, water, education, and health care, promotes freedom and security, and preserves our shared environment for future generations.

12. The Tide Is Turning Against Free Trade and the WTO!

International opposition to the WTO is growing. Massive protests in Seattle in 1999 brought over 50,000 people together to oppose the WTO—and succeeded in shutting the meeting down. When the WTO met in 2001, the Trade negotiators were unable to meet their goals of expanding the WTO's reach. The WTO met in Cancún, Mexico this past September 10–14, and met thousands of activists in protest and scored a major victory for democracy. Developing countries refused to give in to the rich countries' agenda of WTO expansion—and caused the talks to collapse!

GET INVOLVED!!

EDUCATE your community and connect with local corporate issues through bringing speakers, videos, and books like GX's *Globalize This! The Battle Against the World Trade Organization and Corporate Rule*, available on our website.

*TRAVEL to Miami to protest the proposed Free Trade Area of the Americas. Contact us at 415-255-7296 or deborah@globalexchange.org to order an Action Pack and check out www.globalexchange.org for more information.

For Class Discussion

1. What goals and principles of free trade policy does Global Exchange challenge in this flier? Or to put it another way, what alternative views does it articulate and rebut?
2. What policies and course of action does this piece advocate?
3. What are the strengths and limitations of this genre of argument?
4. How effective is this piece in influencing your view of free trade? ∎

Garment Factory in Saipan

This photo, taken in 2004, shows workers in a garment factory in Saipan, part of the U.S. Commonwealth of the Northern Mariana Islands in the Pacific Ocean and an Export Processing Zone. Workers come from China, Thailand, the Philippines, Vietnam, and other Asian countries to make garments in some thirty factories for big-name retailers such as Abercrombie & Fitch, Calvin Klein, the Gap, J. Crew, The Limited, Liz Claiborne, and Tommy Hilfiger. Recent lawsuits have yielded improvements in the sweatshop conditions in these factories: better dormitories, improved water and food, overtime pay for work over forty hours a week, protection from sexual abuse, and payment of back wages.

What are your first impressions of the scene depicted in this photo?

FIGURE 2.2 Garment Factory in Saipan *(© June Johnson)*

For Class Discussion

1. How would a journalist who wanted to use this photo in an article criticizing the treatment of workers in factories in Export Processing Zones (EPZs) interpret this photo? What features of the scene would lend themselves rhetorically to an antisweatshop article?

2. Imagine a different rhetorical use of this photo. What do you think a journalist who wanted to praise improved conditions in foreign factories would emphasize?

3. Consult these Web sites to investigate the lawsuits brought against companies' exploitation of factory workers: Global Exchange (www.globalexchange.org) and Clean Clothes Campaign (www.cleanclothes.org). With this background information, examine the photo again. What features of the scene draw your attention now?

Fight over Free Trade Worth Having and Losing

George F. Will

George F. Will is an internationally known conservative journalist and a syndicated columnist with the Washington Post Writers' Group. He has won many of the most prestigious journalism awards, including the Pulitzer Prize for commentary in 1977. A former editor of the *National Review,* he authors a biweekly column for *Newsweek* and is currently a contributing analyst for *ABC News.* This editorial appeared in the Utah newspaper *Deseret News* on February 12, 2004.

> What features of the way this piece is written might make it difficult for the general reader to understand? What features make this piece engaging?

1 WASHINGTON—Saturday, Valentine's Day, sweets will be showered on sweethearts—a bonanza for candymakers. But the very next day all 242 Fannie May and Fanny Farmer chocolate candy stores will be closed.

2 They and many jobs—625 of them at the firm's 75-year-old Chicago manufacturing plant—are, in part, casualties of that outdated facility, bad business decisions and high U.S. labor and other costs. But jobs in America's candy industry also are jeopardized by protectionism, which is always advertised as job-protection. In this case, the protectionism is an agriculture subsidy—sugar import quotas.

3   Chicago is no longer Carl Sandburg's wheat stacker and hog butcher, but it remains America's candy capital, home of Tootsie Rolls and many other treats. But in 1970, employment by the city's candy manufacturers was 15,000. Today it is under 8,000, and falling.

4   Alpine Confections Inc., the Utah-based candy company, has bought Fannie May and Fanny Farmer and may continue some products. This is partly because the price of sugar is less important in soft chocolates than in hard candies.

5   But the end of 2003 brought the end of Brach's production of hard candy on the city's west side. A decade ago, Brach's employed about 2,300. Until recently, many of the remaining Teamster jobs paid $19 an hour. Many signs in the abandoned Chicago facility were in Spanish, Polish and Greek for the immigrant work force, most of whose jobs have gone to Mexico. Labor is cheaper there, but so is 92 percent of the raw material for hard candy—sugar. By moving outside the United States, Branch's can pay the world market price of sugar, which is one-half to one-third of the U.S. price as propped up by import quotas.

6   Life Savers, which for 90 years were made in America, are now made in Canada, where labor costs are comparable to those in the United States, but the yearly cost of sugar is $10 million less. Chicago's Ferrara Pan Candy Company, makers of Jaw Breakers, Red Hots and Boston Baked Beans, has moved much of its production to Mexico and Canada.

7   Dueling economic studies, few of them disinterested, purport to demonstrate that more American jobs are saved or—much more plausibly—lost because protectionist quotas raise the price of sugar for 280 million Americans. In the life of this republic, in which rent-seeking—bending public power for private advantage—is pandemic, sugar quotas are symptomatic.

8   It was to a North Dakota radio station that Robert Zoellick, U.S. trade representative, vowed that he would stand like Horatius at the bridge to block Australian sugar. The quotas can be considered among the bearable transaction costs of democracy, keeping North Dakota's, Minnesota's and other states' growers of sugar beets and Florida's, Louisiana's and other state's growers of sugar cane from starving.

9   Or seceding. Or—heaven forfend—being forced to grow something else. But protectionism is unconservative, unseemly and unhealthy—indeed, lethal.

10   Unconservative? Protectionism is a variant of what conservatives disparage as "industrial policy" when nonconservatives do it. It is government supplanting the market as the picker of economic winners. Another name for industrial policy is lemon socialism—survival of the unfit.

11   Unseemly? America has no better friend than Australia. Yet such is the power of American sugar interests, the Bush administration has forced Australia to acquiesce in continuing quotas on its sugar exports to America. That was a price for achieving the not-exactly "free trade" agreement signed last weekend. But look on the bright side: Restrictions on beef imports will be phased out over 18 years.

12   Is protectionism lethal? Promoted by Democrats hawking their compassion, protectionism could flatten somewhat the trajectory of America's rising prosperity. But protectionism could kill millions in developing nations by slowing world growth, thereby impeding those nations from achieving prosperity sufficient to pay for potable water, inoculations, etc. Developed nations spend $1 billion a day on agriculture subsidies that prevent poor nations' farmers from competing in the world market.

13   Sugar quotas, although a bipartisan addiction, are worst when defended by Republicans who actually know better, and who lose their ability to make a principled argument against the Democrats' protectionist temptation. Fortunately, splendid trouble may be on the horizon.

14   Last September's collapse of the World Trade Organization's ministerial meeting in Cancun meant that the pernicious "peace clause" was not renewed. For nine years it has prevented the WTO from treating agricultural subsidies as what they obviously are— market distortions incompatible with free trade. For Americans, a fight over that is worth having, and losing.

For Class Discussion

1. What connections does George F. Will make between free trade, protectionism, jobs, and consumers' interests? Where does he stand on free trade?

2. What is Will's argument against subsidizing and protecting the U.S. sugar industry?

3. What evidence does Will offer to support his claim? Why do you think a general newspaper audience would or would not find this evidence compelling?

4. Identify where Will's use of labels, sentence fragments, and other word choices reveal his sarcasm and his criticism of political parties' positions on free trade. What audience would most likely be receptive to Will's language and tone in this piece?

5. How has Will expanded your view of the domestic impact of free trade?

■

Appetite for Destruction
Mike Shanahan

Mike Shanahan holds a doctorate in tropical ecology. He is an environmental and human rights activist who has recently become the news editor for
SciDev.Net, which features science and technology news. This article was
published in the March 2003 edition of *The Ecologist*, an activist publication considered "the world's most widely-read environmental magazine"
(www.theecologist.org/about_us.html).

> What harmful relationship among free trade, consumers in developed
> countries, and workers in developing countries does Shanahan ex-
> pose in this piece?

1   Susan, a middle-aged cashier in a London high street bank, has developed a penchant for prawns. Ten years ago tiger prawns (also called
shrimp) were beyond her budget—a rare treat reserved for birthdays
and other celebrations. Nowadays, she finds them more affordable
and consumes them with gusto at every given opportunity. In contrast, Sri Lankan fisherman Anil caught enough fish to sell and feed
his family a decade ago. Today, he struggles to fill his nets and often
goes to bed hungry. His eight-year-old son regularly misses school to
help his mother find drinking water or his father catch fish. Although the lives of Susan and Anil could hardly be more different
they are, of course, closely linked.

SHRIMP: CRUSTACEAN OF DEVASTATION

2   Last year diners in the industrialised nations of Europe, North
America and Japan peeled, chewed and dribbled their way through
over a million tonnes of farmed shrimps worth over $7 billion.
Shrimp, it would seem, is manna from heaven. It's abundant, pro-
tein-rich, eminently tasty and readily adaptable to the full range of
the world's cuisines. But, as new research by the Environmental
Justice Foundation reveals, the true costs of consuming shrimp are
dangerously high.

3   Shrimp has traditionally been trawled from the ocean in arguably the most inefficient fisheries practice on the planet. The effect of trawl nets on ecological communities on the ocean floor is
the underwater equivalent of clear-cutting forests. Although shrimp
trawlers provide only 2 per cent of the world's seafood, they haul in
a third of all the global fishing industry's 'by-catch'. In that by-catch
over 400 marine species have been identified. Nonetheless it is all
discarded—most of it dead—because of its low economic value relative to that of shrimp. In some shrimp fisheries, by-catch levels of

up to 20 kg for every 1 kg of shrimp have been recorded. The species affected include rare turtles, 150,000 of which are estimated to be caught as by-catch annually.

4   To the uninitiated, the concept of farming shrimp might be quite idyllic—perhaps conjuring images of rosy-cheeked, straw-sucking pastoralists leaning over fences to watch their shell-bound charges grow until sufficiently sized to take to market. The reality is less bucolic. In fact, shrimp farming is more of an industrial than an agricultural phenomenon. Having been responsible for widespread clearance of productive land and mangrove forests, shrimp farming is also heavily reliant upon the use of water pumps, aerators and chemical inputs of pesticides, disinfectants, steroid hormones and antibiotics—including chemicals banned for use in food production by the EU and US. Many of these chemicals are hazardous to human health. The wider environment is also threatened by the release of effluent from shrimp farms into surrounding waters.

5   The effects of shrimp farming can be swift and devastating for coastal communities. Livelihoods that have sustained communities for generations have been disrupted, and human rights abuses widespread. As a result, a brutal struggle is being waged on the coasts of some of the world's poorest countries, with grassroots campaigners lining up against the giant shrimp-farming industry.

DYING FOR OUR DINNER?

6   In April 2002, father of four Sebastião Marques de Souza became the latest casualty in this struggle. Sebastião was a community activist protesting the expansion of shrimp farms into the mangrove forests of Brazil. One night, two men—alleged by local campaigners to be connected to the country's burgeoning shrimp-farming industry—approached him under the pretence of needing to buy some petrol. They shot him dead.

7   Worldwide, opponents of the industry claim that shrimp farming destroys lives and livelihoods of coastal communities and that it causes significant environmental damage. Worldwide, those who have voiced opposition to the industry have been threatened, intimidated, beaten or silenced for good by bullets, bombs and machete blades. People have been murdered in at least 11 countries.

8   In Honduras, murders in the mangroves are no longer a cause of surprise—12 small-scale fishermen have been killed in as many years. Jorge Varela, director of a local human rights and environmentalist group who has himself received death threats on numerous occasions, has said: 'With the complicity of our government, we have given away our people's patrimony to a few national and foreign individuals, and we have deprived thousands of persons of their livelihoods. We have turned the blood of our people into an appetiser.'

9　　These sentiments are common to poor, vulnerable and often landless communities that have risen up in protest at the way shrimp farms have blocked access to the coast, reduced local fish catches, and destroyed mangrove forests that for generations have supplied food, medicines, fuel and building materials.

10　　It is not only fishing communities that have an axe to grind about the impacts of shrimp farming. Rice and cattle farmers have found their land rendered infertile and their livestock prone to disease because of the infiltration of salt water pumped in and out of shrimp ponds. In Bangladesh farmland has been seized by force or deliberately polluted to ensure its cheap sale to shrimp-farm owners. The country's coast has become a hot spot of violence and intimidation. Local advocacy group Nijera Kori estimates that over 150 people have died in incidents directly related to the industry's expansion. Frequently implicated in these murders are Bangladesh's 'musclemen'—hired enforcers paid by shrimp farmers to protect their interests and further their ambitions. At demonstrations clashes have occurred between landless protestors and police or these musclemen. Shrimp-farm guards have caught and beaten to death innocent people wrongly suspected of coming to steal shrimp. Witnesses in legal cases linked to the industry have been murdered.

11　　Profits for shrimp-farm owners can be spectacular, and such is the avarice associated with the industry that the practice of intimidating or eliminating opponents has become widespread. A culture of impunity is typical of the major shrimp-farming countries, which are characterised by corruption, cronyism and gross inequity. The widespread lack of organisational and economic equality between the industry and the communities opposing it means that while the latter often have no recourse to the law, the former often has little to fear from it.

12　　In many countries, politicians and military figures either have vested interests in, or own, shrimp farms. It is less surprising, then, that army or police personnel have been used to violently suppress protests or to seize land on which to build shrimp ponds. A peaceful protest against illegal land seizures by shrimp farmers in Bangladesh was brutally quelled when police personnel opened fire. Four people were killed—including Peasant Women's Association leader Zaheda Begum—and 250 were wounded.

PROFIT AND LOSS IN A CULTURE OF CORRUPTION

13　The farming of marine species was initially promoted as a 'blue revolution', supposedly capable of producing large volumes of food without impacting marine stocks, and thereby increasing availability of food for the hungry. International finance institutions like the World Bank and the Asian Development Bank have actively endorsed shrimp farming as a means of speeding development and alleviating poverty in the developing countries where most shrimp farming occurs. However, while some players in the industry have made vast profits, the external costs are not borne by those who reap the benefits. Rather, these costs are displaced onto some of the poorest and most vulnerable communities. Furthermore, the financial benefits of shrimp production often fail to trickle down to these communities.

14   As land has been seized or rendered unusable, hundreds of thousands of rural poor have been displaced—often to cities or to other countries. 'If the mangroves disappear, we shall eat garbage in the outskirts of the city; we shall become prostitutes,' said one traditional shellfish collector in Ecuador, where a single hectare of mangrove forest can provide food and livelihoods for 10 families. By contrast, an Ecuadorian shrimp farm of 110 hectares employs just six people during the preparation of shrimp and a further five during the harvest. Likewise, in Sri Lanka's Puttlam district nearly 20,000 lagoon fishers have been obliged to move to the city in search of work as shrimp farming has wiped out their traditional livelihoods. Civil society groups have reported Sri Lankan refugees citing the spread of shrimp farming as a factor contributing to their flight to the UK. Anil the fisherman and Susan the bank clerk may yet meet.

15   For those who do not migrate to cities or overseas, employment must be sought in the very industry that deprived them of their livelihoods in the first place. Shrimp fry are needed to stock the ponds and are harvested directly from the sea. In Bangladesh, women work in the water for eight to 10 hours each day. Illness is common. Some collect shrimp fry near to the farms, where polluted water causes internal damage and skin diseases. Gloves are not provided and hands begin to rot.

16   Conditions in processing plants also leave much to be desired. Many female workers in Indian shrimp-peeling factories are reportedly held virtual captives by the owners. They may sleep above the processing units, where the inhalation of odours and ammonia refrigerants is unavoidable. Common complaints include skin problems and backache from standing for prolonged periods. Urinary tract infections are linked to inadequate toilet facilities. Handling ice-cold food for long hours has also been linked to arthritis. In 2000, there were widespread reports of processing plant workers having half their $30 monthly salary deducted to pay for a daily meal of thin watery soup.

17   In a number of countries the salinisation of water supplies and the reduced availability of food resources associated with shrimp farming forces children to miss school to help find food and water for their families. Children also risk their health by working in the

same unsanitary shrimp farm and factory conditions as their elders. Shrimp industry child labour has been reported in Sri Lanka,
India, Bangladesh, Thailand, Cambodia, Indonesia, Peru, Ecuador
and Burma.

THE FUTURE

18   Industrial shrimp farming has experienced massive growth since its
advent in the 1970s. Shrimp is now farmed in over 50 largely tropical
and sub-tropical countries. Today nearly a third of shrimp eaten
comes from these farms. Shrimp recently overtook tuna as the top
seafood in the US, where an average of 1.9 kg of shrimp is consumed
per person per year. The industry's expansion is relentless, and new
areas of Africa's coastline are currently being targeted by investors.

19   Like so many activities that result in resource-use conflict,
shrimp farming is destined to continue causing serious social problems. The roll call of martyrs will keep growing unless the industry
undergoes radical change. Just as logging and oil exploration have
become the focus of international attention following exposure of
their human rights and environmental consequences, so there is an
urgent need for scrutiny of shrimp farming.

20   Whether stir-fried, barbecued or curried, our passion for this
tender crustacean is undeniable. However, to sate our appetites,
communities worldwide are becoming hungrier, thirstier and less
empowered to determine their own lives. This is not a model of development of which to be proud.

21   The late Shri Banke Behary Das was a prominent Indian environmental campaigner. His words, which resonate with passion
and poignancy, neatly encapsulate the essence of shrimp farming's
negative effects and identify the players most capable of forcing a
change—us, the consumers. 'I say to those who eat shrimp—and
only the rich people from industrialised countries eat shrimp—I
say they are eating the blood, sweat and livelihoods of the poor
people of the Third World.'

Environmental Justice Foundation was established by Juliette Wilson and Steve
Trent in 1999.

WHAT YOU CAN DO

As a consumer, you have considerable power and responsibility.
With your help, unsustainable methods of shrimp production can
be eradicated.

1. Read more about the problems of shrimp production at www.
   ejfoundation.org/shrimp

2. Spread the word

3. Cut down on eating shrimp—or cut it out altogether

4. Tell your supermarket/favourite restaurant/fishmonger that you only want to buy shrimp that is produced in a way that does not involve human rights abuses or environmental devastation

5. Sign the Environmental Justice Foundation petition online at www.ejfoundation.org/shrimp/prawn_stop_it.html. The petition will be delivered to leading shrimp importers, distributors and retailers in Europe and North America

For Class Discussion

1. How does Mike Shanahan establish and support his claim that consumers of shrimp in wealthy countries are directly connected to people in developing nations? What other global connections does he assert?

2. Part of the impact of this argument on readers derives from Shanahan's ability to present the radically different views of shrimp held by different groups of people. What views do the different stakeholders have?

3. Shanahan employs narrative techniques and graphic word choices and images such as this one—"We have turned the blood of our people into an appetiser"—to convey the seriousness of the problems he is discussing and to tap his audience's sympathy and values. List other similar word choices and images and explain which ones work particularly well for you.

4. What do Shanahan's use of terms such as "by-catch," "effluent," "a culture of impunity," "blue revolution," "external costs," "salinisation of water supplies," and "resource-use conflict" and his use of numerical data contribute to the persuasiveness of his argument?

5. How has this argument changed your view of foreign industrial labor, of what you buy, and of what you eat?   ∎

Harnessing Our Power as Consumers: Cost of Boycotting Sweatshop Goods Offset by the Benefits

Ed Finn

This piece was first published in the June 2003 edition of the *Canadian Centre for Policy Alternatives Monitor*, a progressive monthly journal focusing on social and economic justice. According to its Web site, this organization's motto is "Think again," and it seeks to inform people of alternatives "to the message that we have no choice about the policies that affect our lives" (www.policyalternatives.ca/aboutus/). Ed Finn is the senior editor of this publication.

> In this proposal argument, what is the link that Finn posits between our purchasing decisions as consumers and sweatshops in developing countries?

1   Being follicly challenged, I can't venture out in the noonday sun without a cap. So I went looking for one. My shopping foray took nearly two weeks. Not because headgear was hard to find in Ottawa, but because I wanted a cap made by workers who were fairly paid and well-treated—and that kind of headgear is hard to find.

2   Had I been content to buy a cap made in a sweatshop in China, Haiti, Malaysia, or some other Third World nation, it would have been easy. The stores were full of them. But I wanted a cap made preferably by a unionized worker in Canada, or, failing that, in another country with decent labour standards.

3   After visiting a score of clothing shops, I finally located such a cap. It was made in England. I had to pay nearly $40 for it, four or five times more than a comparable cap from an Asian sweatshop would have cost. But the Brit beanie was far more comfortable and durable. It comes out of the washing machine looking as good as new. I bought it four years ago and it still shows no sign of wearing out. So, even from an economic standpoint, I didn't suffer for sticking to my "buy non-sweatshop" principles.

4   Most Canadians, sad to say, don't make any effort to find domestic apparel. Or they give up after visiting their third or fourth clothing store, where the racks are crammed with shirts, pants, sweaters and jackets sewn by underpaid and abused workers in Asia or Latin America.

5   Imported outfits do cost less. They appeal to anyone looking for the cheapest item and indifferent to how and where it was made. Even when reminded that millions of children under the age of 14—the UN estimates they number at least 25 million—are being inhumanly exploited in Third World sweatshops, most Canadians find the lure of a "bargain" irresistible.

6   They should be more concerned—not just because they want to help mistreated workers overseas, but because they want to help themselves. The exploitation of cheap foreign labour is part of a vast global strategy designed ultimately to force wages down in Canada and other Western nations. This strategy is already well advanced. Freed from national restrictions by free trade, deregulation, and instant global communications systems, the transnational corporations can now relocate production to countries and regions where wages, taxes, and environmental laws are the lowest.

7   This corporate mobility has eroded the power of Canadian workers and their unions to protect their jobs, benefits, and working conditions.

8   As consumers, however, we are far from powerless. We can refuse to buy the products of child labour, prison labour, and sweatshop labour in the Third World. In the short term, this will unavoidably increase our living expenses, but in the long term it could save our jobs and prevent our wages from plummeting further.

9   The corporations are counting on us to keep our needs as consumers entirely separate from our needs as workers. And, unfortunately, up to now, most of us have done just that—in the process unthinkingly worsening our own financial security. The more sweatshop goods we buy, the more we reward the corporations for their downsizing here and their cheap labour strategy abroad. And—contrary to some right-wing pundits—we aren't doing any favours to oppressed foreign workers, either. We are in effect perpetuating their serfdom.

10   Some politicians, business leaders and academics argue that, if we boycotted goods made by underpaid foreign workers, we would be depriving them of their livelihood, as meagre as it may be.

11   But this claim is as spurious today as it was in Victorian times, when it was advanced to rationalize the use of child labour. ("Take away these kids' jobs and they'll starve to death or turn to lives of crime.")

12   The same flawed reasoning was trotted out by conservatives to oppose the economic boycott of the apartheid regime in South Africa. Had their arguments been heeded, that country would still be ruled by a brutal and racist government, and Nelson Mandela would still be in prison.

13   The leaders of opposition movements in developing nations ruled by dictators know that boycotts of sweatshop goods would temporarily add to their people's woes. But they also know that, in the long run, such boycotts offer the best hope of toppling the dictators and thereby vastly improving their people's lives.

14   One such leader is Nobel Peace Prize winner Aung San Suu Kyi, who heads the National League for Democracy in Burma. Like Mandela, she too was jailed by that country's ruthless military rulers and still endures their harassment. She favours the same kind of economic sanctions that finally got rid of apartheid in South Africa, even if they temporarily cause more hardship for Burma's sweatshop workers.

15   "All profits from business enterprises in my country," she said recently, "go to a small privileged elite. Companies that continue to invest here only serve to prolong the agony of my country and its people by encouraging the military regime to persevere in its atrocities."

16   She could have said the same thing about consumers in Canada and other developed nations, who also prop up Burma's dictatorship when they buy made-in-Burma merchandise.

17   It's time for us to look at the labels of the goods we buy. If we stopped buying sweatshop products, we would accomplish three things: 1) we would be helping to slow down and eventually stop the export of jobs from Canada; 2) we would be helping the oppressed people in the Third World to throw off the yoke of military and corporate tyranny; and 3) we would be effectively challenging the corporations' global low-wage strategy.

18   Granted, such a change in our shopping habits would involve some additional costs to us as consumers. But these costs would eventually be offset by the gains we would derive as workers—and the gains that would be made by brutally mistreated workers in the Third World.

For Class Discussion

1. What is Ed Finn's claim in this article? How does he connect the purchasing decisions of Canadian consumers with Canadian jobs and the political and economic advance of developing countries?

2. What does Finn's personal experience as a consumer contribute to his argument? Have you had similar shopping experiences to Finn's?

3. Where does Finn acknowledge and respond to alternative views?

4. What strengths and weaknesses do you see in Finn's reasoning and evidence in this argument? What points does he not develop in this argument?

5. How has Finn's argument affected your thinking as a consumer?

Comment and Analysis: The Price of Dignity: Business Is Imposing Virtual Slavery in the Developing World—and Only We, the Consumers, Can Stop It

Anita Roddick

In 1976, Anita Roddick, a dedicated environmentalist and activist for human rights, founded The Body Shop, an international health and beauty products business devoted to "the pursuit of social and environmental change" (www.anita.roddick.com). A leader in showing how running a business based on social justice can lead to enormous financial success, The Body Shop practices fair trade through its forty-two trade relationships with specific communities in twenty-six countries (www.the-body-shop. com). In addition, Roddick's new communications company has published two books, *A Revolution in Kindness* and *Brave Heart, Rebel Spirits: A Spiritual Activists Handbook* (both in 2003). This article appeared in *The Guardian*, a Manchester newspaper in the United Kingdom, on September 22, 2003.

How does Roddick frame the problems of the free trade system and sweatshops and what solutions does she propose?

1   In the past two years, 500 export assembly factories have shut down in Mexico, throwing 218,000 workers onto the street. Their crime was the $1.26-an-hour base wage they were paid by companies such as Alcoa Fujikura to produce auto parts for export to the US. Those wages are now "too high" in the global economy.

2   Never mind that the Alcoa workers in Acuna live in makeshift cardboard huts that lack potable water. Never mind that many of the workers in nearby Piedras Negras were selling their blood plasma twice a week to Baxter International for $30 in order to survive. Those same auto parts are now being made in Honduras by workers earning 59 cents an hour, in Nicaragua for 40 cents an hour and in China for 27 cents an hour.

3   Right now, in Nicaragua and Honduras, factory workers report that management is telling them to get ready to work harder and longer for lower wages, because there are 1,000 people in China lined up and ready to take each of their jobs. If they don't like it, the company will just have to shut down the plant and leave.

4   Multinational companies sourcing production in China are having an enormous impact on the global economy, lowering wages and rolling back labour rights. Workers in China assembling healthcare products for companies such as Viva and Sport-Elec are being forced to work 16 hours a day, seven days a week (with just 12 days off a year) for 16 cents an hour. There is no overtime premium. The workers have no health insurance and no pensions. If they try to organise, they will be fired, perhaps even beaten and imprisoned.

5   It does not have to be like this. But what happens when workers dare to stand up to ask that their basic rights be respected? When young women in Bangladesh, being paid just five cents for every $17.99 Disney shirt they sewed, asked for one day a week off, the Walt Disney Company responded by pulling its work from the factory. These women needed these jobs, but they also wanted to be treated as human beings. The message Disney is delivering to

workers across the developing world is that if you dare to raise your voice, you too will be fired and thrown out on the street with nothing.

6   One thing is certain in the new global economy: workers struggling for their rights cannot succeed if there is not also simultaneous pressure on the corporations in their marketplaces. I am not talking about a boycott. It must be the very opposite: what is needed are campaigns to keep jobs in the developing world while at the same time working to guarantee respect for worker rights.

7   This is where the consumer comes in. We in the developed world hold the key to ending child labour and sweatshop abuses. If enough of us care, and if enough of us act, the squeaky wheel gets the grease.

8   Corporations continue to hide the factories they use around the world to make the goods we purchase. Wal-Mart, for example, uses 4,400 factories in one Chinese province alone. As a first step, we need full public disclosure of all factory names and locations. Such transparency will make it much harder to hide abuses.

9   Corporations have long demanded all sorts of enforceable laws, such as intellectual property and copyright laws, to defend their products and trademarks. Corporations tell us that there must be a level playing field in the economy, or they cannot function and everything descends into chaos. However, when you say to the companies, "that sounds reasonable, but can't we also protect the fundamental rights of the 16-year-old who made the product?", these same companies say that would be an impediment to free trade. So, in today's global economy, the product is protected but not the human being who made it. We must not let this stand. We need enforceable laws to defend workers' rights—laws every bit as strong as those currently afforded to products.

10   In the short run, there is plenty we can do. We need to draw up a "preferred companies" list, made up of corporations which may not be perfect but are far better than average and moving in the right direction. We need to reward companies that are doing the right thing.

11   I would suggest the following standards for companies on the preferred list: full public disclosure of factory names and addresses; adoption of a code of conduct which calls for strict adherence to all local laws and core International Labour Organisation-recognised rights; release at least once a year of monitoring reports regarding the conditions in their factories; an agreement to respond to allegations of worker rights' violations.

12   At this very moment, while the Bush administration is pressing to impose the free trade agreement of the Americas, unions across central America are being wiped out as part of a campaign by companies seeking to roll back any rights workers have won.

13   The US-based national labour committee is about to release dozens of documented reports of worker rights struggles in Honduras, Nicaragua, El Salvador, Costa Rica, Haiti, Bangladesh and China. These are not just academic reports—they are calls to action to support these workers in their struggle for dignity and justice. Are we listening?

For Class Discussion

1. In this proposal argument, Anita Roddick devotes a large part of her argument to establishing the problem. What evidence does she use to make a case that a problem exists? How does Roddick seek to elicit her audience's sympathy for factory workers in developing countries?

2. What is Roddick's proposed solution and her justification of it?

3. What effect might knowing that Roddick is the founder of a skin care products business that is both very successful *and* committed to social justice have on readers' response to her call to consumers to take action against sweatshops?

4. What contribution does this argument make to the controversy surrounding consumer choices and sweatshops? What influence might this piece have on your consumer habits?   ■

Help Is on the Way, Dude
Chip Bok

Chip Bok is a prominent editorial cartoonist whose work appears in the *Chicago Tribune*, *The Washington Post*, the *New York Times*, the *Los Angeles Times*, *Newsweek*, and *TIME Magazine*. He has won awards from the National Cartoonist Society, the Ohio Associated Press, and the National Press Association. This cartoon (p. 52) appeared in *Reason* magazine, a publication committed to the free market and individual freedom.

What does the cartoonist want viewers to think about the practice of moving factories to developing countries?

For Class Discussion

1. What groups of people do the two characters in this cartoon represent?

2. Whom is this cartoon criticizing and why?

FIGURE 2.3 Help Is on the Way, Dude *(© Chip Bok, 2000)*

3. What arguments about free trade and sweatshops in this chapter is this cartoon refuting? What readings in this chapter might it support?

4. What features make this cartoon persuasive?

The New Colossus: Wal-Mart Is America's Store, and the World's, and Its Enemies Are Sadly Behind

Jay Nordlinger

Jay Nordlinger, a reporter and critic, is a managing editor of the *National Review*, a conservative weekly news commentary magazine. He has written for *The New Criterion*, the *New York Sun*, and *The Weekly Standard*. During the 2000 election, he worked as a speechwriter for George W. Bush. This article appeared in the April 19, 2004, edition of the *National Review*.

> How has Nordlinger tailored his defense of Wal-Mart to the conservative readers of the *National Review*?

1   Who's the biggest, baddest company of them all? Wal-Mart, of course, leader of the Fortune 500 list and the largest employer in America (next to the government, that is). Wal-Mart is also the largest employer in Mexico (again, next to the government). The company has

1.4 million employees worldwide, and it has made its investors a ton of money. In short, this is a classic American success story, and free-market success story. Therefore, the company has a lot of enemies.

2   In fact, Wal-Mart is featuring in Democratic campaign rhetoric, and other rhetoric, as a villain, along with Enron and Halliburton. Is this wise of politicians, considering that 100 million people shop at Wal-Mart every week? We'll leave that to the political strategists.

3   The roster of Wal-Mart foes includes the following: Democratic politicians, particularly those trying to impress unions; union leaders (while we're on the subject); left-wing pundits; a handful of right-wing pundits, concerned for localism; and arbiters of taste (mainly soi-disant).

4   In the Democratic primaries, John Kerry knocked Wal-Mart on a number of fronts, particularly that of health care: He denounced the company's provisions for its employees as "disgraceful" and "unconscionable." He also said, "They throw a lot of money around, they get a lot of things happening, but it ain't necessarily good for the community." (Here, he is attempting a little populism—he did not learn that language in his Swiss boarding school.) Kerry continued, "We need to stand up and demand they behave corporately responsibly." (That's more like it.) The candidate suggested that the company be punished by loss of tax deductions.

5   Howard Dean, too, was a fighter against Wal-Mart. (His Vermont was the very last state to accept a Wal-Mart store.) In the presidential primaries, Dean took the usual line that Wal-Mart "kills small towns." Somewhat refreshingly, however, he promised audiences that if he got the chance to "do what I want to do on trade agreements, you are going to pay higher prices at Wal-Mart"—he would crack down on the Chinese, for one thing.

6   John Edwards, before he bit the dust, slammed the company for "driving down the pay scale for everybody." Richard Gephardt—the most unionized of the candidates—offered the opinion that the company was ripe for an anti-trust suit. And Dennis Kucinich, bless him, warned that someday Wal-Mart might "take over" Iraq. (The *New York Sun* caught that last nugget, and others.)

7   The tale of Kerry and Wal-Mart has a nice twist: Part of his fortune rests on the company, because his wife owns between $1 million and $5 million in Wal-Mart stock. That may be chump change for the Kerry-Heinzes, but it counts. And a Wal-Mart spokesman noted cheekily that Wal-Mart sells Heinz soup—made in Muscatine, Iowa—to the good people of South Korea. How's that for globalization?

8   The Democrats aren't through with their anti-Wal-Marting. Rep. George Miller, the veteran lefty from California, ordered what might be called a hit study on Wal-Mart, through the Committee on

Education and the Workforce, on which he is the senior Democrat. The study was drawn up by his staff. Released in February, it maintained that Wal-Mart actually costs taxpayers money, because—so mean is the company to its employees—all the rest of us have to subsidize their health care, child care, and so on. It is the Democratic aim to paint Wal-Mart as an awful machine both Dickensian and Orwellian, gobbling up towns, people, and souls. This portrait is ridiculous—but many enjoy it.

AN ALL-PURPOSE BOGEYMAN

9 What, exactly, are the complaints against Wal-Mart? They are numerous—it is almost blamed for the common cold—but the main ones appear to be these: that it is too big. That it is too impersonal. That it "drains the life out of Main Street." That it is "Sprawl Mart." That it pays its employees too little. That it denies them health care. That it is un-unionized (that much is true). That it employs illegal aliens (about that, more later). That it relies on foreign goods. That it is square (banning racy magazines, for instance). That it is crassly American. That it is vulgar.

10 Frankly, more than a bit of snobbery goes into Wal-Mart bashing. This is a store that sells every product under the sun at very low prices to Middle America. (It is the biggest seller of groceries, toys, and furniture. It sells 30 percent of all disposable diapers purchased in the U.S., 30 percent of hair products, etc.) Wal-Mart is gloriously, unabashedly, star-spangledly American. I hope it's not too McCarthyite to suggest that those who dislike Wal-Mart are those who may not be so crazy about America *tout court.*

11 Daniel Mindus of the Center for Consumer Freedom points out that Wal-Mart has become, for the Left, like the SUV, or the oil and gas industry, or the gun—a simple hate object. Wal-Mart fires the passions of anti-globalism, anti-consumerism, and anti-corporatism (along with snobbery). This company may be considered the most flagrant expression of democratic capitalism, loud testimony to the size, scope, entrepreneurialism, and efficiency of America. That doesn't sit well with a good many people.

12 As can be seen from the remark about Heinz soup and Korea, the company is pretty adept at responding to critics. This is not a patsy company, not a "suicidal corporation," to borrow Paul H. Weaver's memorable phrase. It invests heavily in PR, and it invests heavily in politicians: Wal-PAC is a formidable political action committee, the number-two such giver in the country (next to Goldman Sachs). And if someone blasts the company on television or in print, Wal-Mart is likely to respond—nimbly and tartly, too.

13 The company says, basically, that it does the service of employing over a million people, and of supplying high-quality goods at

rock-bottom prices to many millions more. That is a bad thing? Critics like to contend that Wal-Mart employees live "paycheck to paycheck"; that is not true. But what is true—certainly truer—is Wal-Mart's rejoinder: "We are the store of countless people who live paycheck to paycheck, wanting and needing decent products at decent prices." Touché.

14   Many object to a Wal-Mart in their community, but most people welcome it—they are just not the activist type, and seldom write articles for the newspaper or deliver commentaries on public television. Some of us have a romantic feeling about Mom-'n'-Pop stores: but people vote with their feet, and they are not, most of them, voting for Mom 'n' Pop. Besides which, how many people did Mom 'n' Pop employ, and what sort of benefit package did they offer *them*?

15   About health insurance: More than 90 percent of Wal-Mart employees have it. Fifty percent of those employees get their insurance through the company; and the rest get it through . . . Well, teenagers get it through their parents; others are covered by their spouse's plan; senior citizens have Medicare, or benefits from a previous employer. There are options. Wal-Mart is a huge employer of the young—those wanting their first jobs—and the old (those in retirement, or semi-retirement, wanting to keep a hand in, to mingle with the folks). A company spokesman says, hard-headedly, "If we weren't a desirable employer, we wouldn't be able to fulfill our growth potential. We have competitive wages and benefits in every community we serve. We don't start at minimum wage anywhere in the country—unlike our unionized competitors."

16   Ah, yes, the unions. It is an ongoing affront to organized labor that Wal-Mart, the biggest and baddest, remains un-unionized. The United Food & Commercial Workers has a whole department devoted to Wal-Mart—to targeting it, unionizing it. The UFCW campaigns as though its very existence, as a union, depended on success.

17   No one should suppose that a Wal-Mart job is a demeaning or a dead-end job. Two-thirds of Wal-Mart managers come from the ranks of hourly employees. The company constantly stresses that it is a place of opportunity, and this is not mere corporate propaganda. Interestingly, the accusations now hurled at Wal-Mart are exactly those once hurled at McDonald's. Remember "McJobs"? That phrase had a life in the 1988 presidential campaign, as Governor Dukakis went on about "good jobs at good wages." (Since employment was so high, one could hardly complain about the raw number of jobs.) It took Thomas Sowell and other smart people to explain that McDonald's was important for those wanting to reach the first rung of the job ladder—they could then climb, within McDonald's or elsewhere.

18   A word, now, about illegal aliens—this is one of the Wal-Mart "scandals." Last October, the feds staged some well-publicized raids on Wal-Mart stores; they busted a bevy of illegals. According to the company—and there is no reason to doubt it—Wal-Mart had worked for three years with the government, which was investigating some of the cleaning contractors used by the company. Wal-Mart "continued to employ the contractors long after we would have brought those services in house, at a cost savings to us." (So says a company spokesman.) The federal investigation continues. Wal-Mart is not off the hook. But the company can't help pointing out that many of those whose hearts usually bleed for illegals, and their right to work, go positively jingo when it comes to Wal-Mart—and Wal-Mart alone.

19   And, yes, the company is a heavy importer of foreign goods, including from China. This is a noteworthy development, as Wal-Mart started out with a "Made in America" theme. It was quasiprotectionist. Now the Wal-Mart theme is, "Made Anywhere, So What?" A company vice president told *Business Week*, "The mindset around here is, we're agents for our customers." Critics who never breathe a word about Laogai, in other circumstances, get all human-rightsy when discussion turns to Wal-Mart. (Laogai is the Chinese gulag.)

THE *TIMES* NO LIKE

20   In the field of Wal-Mart sniping, the *New York Times* is pretty much champion. It has not exactly crusaded against Wal-Mart—not like it did against Augusta National Golf Club, in the time of editor Howell Raines. But the paper emits a steady stream of stories casting Wal-Mart in the worst possible light.

21   One story—published on March 6—began in almost comical fashion: "Alexander Luten's grandfather did well for a man born into slavery." A right-wing parodist could not improve on that. What story against Wal-Mart *wouldn't* begin with an evocation of slavery? The *Times's* article, headlined "In a Historic Black Hamlet, Wal-Mart Finds Resistance," concerned Sandfly, Ga., and the arrival of a Wal-Mart Supercenter there. The writer, Andrew Jacobs, did not cite any particular offense, but said that opponents "see Wal-Mart's coming as disrespectful to a community that feels intense pride in its past and its roots in West African culture." One local was quoted as saying, "Our culture and values were passed down from our parents and great-grandparents, and we are trying to pass them down to our kids." How Wal-Mart might impede this process is a mystery. But Wal-Mart is seen, by some, as a sinister force, with a magical capacity to destroy almost anything.

22   And did you read this, last December? "The annual celebration of the American consumer economy—the holiday shopping season—is just underway, and Wal-Mart, the juggernaut of retailing, already seems to have claimed its first victim." That would be F. A. O. Schwarz, the old-line (and pricey) toy seller, which was on the verge of going under—Wal-Mart had cut severely into its business, selling the same toys at much lower prices. *Time* magazine went the *Times* one better, however, with the headline "Will Wal-Mart Steal Christmas?" (The newspaper itself noted this.) Everyone knows that Christmas isn't *really* Christmas unless you overpay for toys.

23   The *Times* had the good grace to quote a Federal Reserve economist who said, "Wal-Mart is the greatest thing that ever happened to low-income Americans."

24   Editorially, the paper has decried "the Wal-Martization of America," claiming that the company's effect on the national workforce "threatens to push many Americans into poverty." This betrays a strange understanding of economics, and it is the same understanding that has defamed McDonald's for years. Wal-Mart has done McDonald's this favor: It has replaced the hamburger chain as Bogeyman No. 1 in the mind and rhetoric of the Left. The fact is, Wal-Mart is held—by many economists—to have single-handedly kept American unemployment down, and productivity up or steady, in lean times.

25   Of course, the left-wing magazines have been hard on Wal-Mart for many a moon. Listen to a recent "comment" in *The Nation*: "The Los Angeles area remains one of the few urban centers that Wal-Mart has yet to penetrate. But having gained a foothold in suburbia, the chain is now furiously pummeling the gates of the urban core, whose potential consumer base is disproportionately immigrant and poor—and therefore primed to respond to Wal-Mart's discount appeal."

26   Bear in mind: This is considered a bad thing.

A COMPANY LIKE NO OTHER

27   Because Wal-Mart is so big—and so important—it attracts endless flak. According to *Fortune*, the company was sued 6,087 times in 2002 alone, "or about once every 90 minutes every day of the year." And surely Wal-Mart is guilty here and there. As a company spokesman remarked for this same *Fortune* article, "When you have one million people working for you, there are always going to be a couple of knuckleheads out there who do dumb things." The company adjusts, adapts, copes, even to the point of a little PC: A major Wal-Mart executive has grumped about the number of white men working as Wal-Mart managers. (Too many.) And the company's

detractors may be interested to know that its anti-discrimination policies cover gays.

28   Moreover, Wal-Mart has hired a "reputation consultant" and aired TV ads touting the company as a friendly, nurturing place to work. As it was morning in America, it is morning at Wal-Mart.

29   But warmth and fuzziness aside, Wal-Mart is a bracing, historic enterprise. As Larry Kudlow—the economist, TV personality, and enthusiast for capitalism—says, "They have invented the modern company. They are really the first Internetized, globalized company, engaged in real-time inventories, real-time pricing—everything. They are the model for everyone else." Brink Lindsey, the Cato Institute trade guru, calls Wal-Mart "an agent of dynamism," meaning, naturally, that "others have an interest in demonizing it." Furthermore, "Wal-Mart is a distinctly American phenomenon, and therefore an anti-European phenomenon." Euros and their like-nesses in America have no patience for Wal-Mart. "The Europeans sniff at our job creation," says Lindsey, "while their job market is stagnant. They say, 'Oh, America just has Wal-Mart-type jobs.' Actually, the percentage of managerial and professional jobs in our country has climbed steadily. Yes, we have a lot of low-end jobs, but we have a lot of young people and older people in our workforce, unlike Europe. There, they don't let people get hired, they don't let industries move fast, they don't create jobs"—they just snort at America and Wal-Mart, unwilling to dent their own double-digit unemployment.

30   None of this is to say that brave new economic worlds are al-ways comfortable, for everybody. In a column, Thomas Sowell quoted Judge Robert Bork to the effect that "somebody always gets hurt in a courtroom." Added Sowell, "Somebody always gets hurt in an economy that is growing. You can't keep on doing things the old way and still get the benefits of the new way." Or, as a lady from Sandfly, Ga., put it to the *New York Times*, "Change is here. Sometimes you just have to accept it and move on." Only in this in-stance, change is overwhelmingly good: Wal-Mart employs masses of workers, has made investors piles of money, has saved con-sumers a fortune. How many other companies do as well? How many politicians contribute as much?

For Class Discussion

1. What is Jay Nordlinger's main claim in this argument?

2. In this article, Nordlinger carries on a lively exchange with Wal-Mart opponents. According to Nordlinger, why do critics "demonize" Wal-Mart and what are the criticisms leveled at this company? How does Nordlinger rebut these criticisms?

3. Part of the liveliness of this piece comes from Nordlinger's mocking treatment of Wal-Mart's enemies. Find some examples and discuss how much Nordlinger's making fun of Wal-Mart opponents contributes to the persuasiveness of his argument for his target audience, the conservative readers of the *National Review*. If he wanted to publish this article in a liberal magazine, what changes would he have to make?

4. Nordlinger cites a Wal-Mart executive saying that "we're agents for our customers," meaning that Wal-Mart acts in the consumers' interest by manufacturing and selling products in ways that best suit its consumers. From the argument in this article and your own experience, how reasonable is this belief in consumer responsibility?

5. In what ways has Nordlinger changed your view of Wal-Mart and why?

Calculating the Real Cost of "Everyday Low Prices"
Froma Harrop

Froma Harrop writes regularly for the *Providence Journal*. She is a well-known syndicated columnist with a liberal bent and a lively, forthright style. This op-ed piece appeared in the *Seattle Times* on October 23, 2003.

> According to Froma Harrop, what connections exist among American consumer habits, sweatshops, free trade, and American jobs?

1   America worships at the altar of Everyday Low Prices. That's how Wal-Mart can get away with ravaging American wages, benefits and the jobs themselves. That's how Wal-Mart can go on hollowing out America's downtowns—and with taxpayer subsidies, to boot.

2   Wal-Mart is not the only big-box discounter turning the American countryside into a "crudscape" and its working people into paupers. But the monster leads the pack in terms of size and its holy crusade to cut costs. With $245 billion in revenues last year, Wal-Mart is the world's largest company. Sales at the Bentonville, Ark.-based giant are bigger than the combined total of Home Depot, Target, Sears and Kroger.

3   *Business Week* described the "everyday low prices" slogan as the core value of "a cult masquerading as a company." All those yellow smiley faces and front-door "greeters" are part of a bigger strategy: to get rich off America's workers, while undercutting them at every turn. What am I talking about? Here are the particulars:

4   • Wal-Mart likes to call its sales clerks "associates," but "serfs" would be more like it. The company paid its salespeople an average $8.23 an hour in 2001. At that wage, a full-time worker made only $13,861 a year. The poverty level for a family of three was $14,630. Only 38 percent of Wal-Mart's workers have health coverage. It should surprise no one that nearly half of Wal-Mart's employees quit every year. (Before the recession, the annual turnover rate was 70 percent.)

5   • Wal-Mart is destroying factory jobs in America. Example: Levi Strauss was one of the last apparel makers to actually produce stuff in the United States. But the made-in-America label means zip to Wal-Mart, which scours the globe's sweatshops for the sweetest prices. Demands for the cheapest jeans have forced Levi Strauss to shut down about a dozen U.S. plants. A factory in San Antonio is about to become the latest casualty.

6   Wal-Mart lobbies furiously in Washington for free-trade deals that guarantee a flood of goods made by pennies-an-hour labor ($12 billion worth from China alone last year). Small wonder America's manufacturers call Wal-Mart the Beast from Bentonville.

7   • To Wal-Mart, unions are the devil and must be destroyed. Three years ago, meat cutters in Jacksonville, Texas, tried to establish the first Wal-Mart union. Eleven days after they joined the United Food and Commercial Workers, Wal-Mart closed all the meat-cutting departments at its stores and started buying pre-cut meat.

8   Wal-Mart is now on a rampage to devour the nation's supermarkets, and so threatens workers everywhere. Its Supercenter stores, which sell groceries, have already sent more than 20 national supermarket chains into bankruptcy. Wal-Mart has plans for 1,000 new Supercenters.

9   Terrified of a Wal-Mart invasion, California's three biggest supermarket chains have tried to lower their own costs by demanding concessions from their unionized employees. The result is a strike by 70,000 workers at supermarkets in Southern California.

10   • Wal-Mart is paving over America and destroying our communities. Its ugly boxes, plopped down on the edge of town, vacuum up business from local shopkeepers. (So much for any notion of customer loyalty.)

11   A group named Sprawl-Busters was formed 10 years ago to block Wal-Mart from forcing itself onto Greenfield, Mass. Every day, five or six towns from across the country contact Sprawl-Busters for advice on stopping a Wal-Mart, according to the group's founder, Al Norman. "It's not even about shopping," Norman says. "It's about how we relate to the places we live in. These towns are being changed economically, physically and socially."

12   • Wal-Marts hurt surrounding communities. Iowa State University economist Kenneth Stone has studied the impact of Wal-Mart on rural Iowa. He found that some business districts benefited from a Wal-Mart but other towns within 20 miles suffered badly, with retail sales plummeting 25 percent after five years. Having lost their local merchants, the people in surrounding areas find themselves driving long distances to the Wal-Mart.

13   The line of groups calling for boycotts of Wal-Mart and its Sam's Club subsidiary grows by the week. As a former Wal-Mart customer, your author appreciates the lure of a good price. But there are competing values. When we understand the real cost of these "everyday low prices," they don't seem much of a bargain at all.

For Class Discussion

1. What is Froma Harrop's purpose in this op-ed piece and what is her central claim?

2. What are her main rhetorical strategies for achieving that purpose? Try to find the most up-to-date figures for Wal-Mart wages and the poverty line in the United States. How much do these numbers support Harrop's argument?

3. How effective is her conclusion in wrapping up her argument?

4. How does Harrop's view of Wal-Mart differ from Nordlinger's? Where does she dispute his claims about Wal-Mart?

5. How has Harrop influenced the way you think about bargains and buying? ∎

Wal-Martian Invasion
Barbara Ehrenreich

Barbara Ehrenreich is a biologist, eminent author, social activist, feminist, and journalist. In addition to publishing numerous books, among them the acclaimed *Nickel and Dimed* (2001) about America's working poor, she has written for *Time*, *Harper's*, *The Nation*, and the *New York Times Magazine*, among other well-regarded publications. This piece appeared in the *Baltimore Sun* on July 27, 2004.

Why do you think that Ehrenreich chooses a fanciful way to protest the growth of the giant discount retailer Wal-Mart?

1   It's torn cities apart from Inglewood, California, to Chicago, and engulfed the entire state of Vermont. Now the conflict's gone national as a presidential campaign issue, with John Kerry hammering the

mega-retailer for its abysmally low wages and Dick Cheney praising it for its "spirit of enterprise, fair dealing and integrity." This could be the central battle of the 21st century: Earth people vs. the Wal-Martians.

2 No one knows exactly when the pod landed on our planet, but it seemed normal enough during its early years of gentle expansion. Almost too normal, if you thought about it, with those smiley faces and that red-white-and-blue bunting, like the space invaders in a 1950s sci-fi flick when they put on their human suits.

3 Then it began to grow. By 2000, measures of mere size— bigger than General Motors! Richer than Switzerland!—no longer told the whole story. It's the velocity of growth that you need to measure now: two new stores opening and $1 billion worth of U.S. real estate bought up every week; almost 600,000 American employees churned through in a year (that's at a 44 percent turnover rate). My thumbnail calculation suggests that by the year 4004, every square inch of the United States will be covered by supercenters, so that the only place for new supercenters will be on top of existing ones.

4 Wal-Mart will be in trouble long before that, of course, because with everyone on the planet working for the company or its suppliers, hardly anyone will be able to shop there. Wal-Mart is frequently lauded for bringing consumerism to the masses, but more than half of its own "associates," as the employees are euphemistically termed, cannot afford the company's health insurance, never mind its Faded Glory jeans.

5 With hourly wages declining throughout the economy, Wal-Mart—the nation's largest employer—is already seeing its sales go soft.

6 In my own brief stint at the company in 2000, I worked with a woman for whom a $7 Wal-Mart polo shirt, of the kind we had been ordered to wear, was an impossible dream: It took us an hour to earn that much.

7 Some stores encourage their employees to apply for food stamps and welfare; many take second jobs. Critics point out that Wal-Mart has consumed $1 billion in public subsidies, but that doesn't count the government expenditures required to keep its associates alive. Apparently the Wal-Martians, before landing, failed to check on the biological requirements for human life.

8 But a creature afflicted with the appetite of a starved hyena doesn't have time for niceties. Wal-Mart is facing class-action lawsuits over sex discrimination and nonpayment for overtime work (meaning no payment at all), as well as accusations that employees have been locked into stores overnight, unable to get help even in medical emergencies. These are the kinds of conditions we associate

with Third World sweatshops, and in fact Wal-Mart fails at least five out of ten criteria set by the Worker Rights Consortium, which monitors universities' sources of logoed apparel—making Wal-Mart the world's largest sweatshop.

9   Confronted with its crimes, the folks at the Bentonville, Ark., headquarters whimper that the company has gotten too "decentralized"—meaning out of control—which has to be interpreted as a cry for help. But who is prepared to step forward and show Wal-Mart how to coexist with the people of its chosen planet? Certainly not the enablers, such as George Will and *National Review*'s Jay Nordlinger, who smear the company's critics as a "liberal intelligentsia" that favors Williams-Sonoma. (Disclosure: I prefer Costco, which pays decent wages, insures 90 percent of its employees and is reputedly run by native-born humans.)

10   No, Wal-Mart's only hope lies with its ostensible opponents, such as Madeline Janis-Aparicio, who led the successful fight against a new superstore in Inglewood.

11   "The point is not to destroy them," she told me, "but to make them accountable."

12   Andy Stern, president of the Service Employees International Union, will soon begin a national effort to "bring Wal-Mart up to standards we can live with." He envisions a nationwide movement bringing together the unions, churches, community organizations and environmentalists who are already standing up to the company's recklessly metastatic growth.

13   Earth to Wal-Mars, or wherever you come from: Live with us or go back to the mothership.

For Class Discussion

1. Ehrenreich has embedded a number of serious criticisms of Wal-Mart within this humorous science fiction piece, among them that Wal-Mart is "the world's largest sweatshop." List her reasons for discrediting Wal-Mart. What evidence does she offer to support her criticisms?

2. How does Ehrenreich use her personal experience to support her argument?

3. Ehrenreich has chosen to take a fanciful and satirical approach in this critique of Wal-Mart. Where do you find this approach effective for a general audience? For you, particularly?

4. Where do the economics of free trade, sweatshops, and consumerism fit into the big picture of Ehrenreich's argument against Wal-Mart?

5. How does this piece speak back to Jay Nordlinger's defense of Wal-Mart? How do Ehrenreich's and Harrop's views and rhetorical approaches compare?   ∎

CHAPTER QUESTIONS FOR REFLECTION AND DISCUSSION

1. Some of the arguments in this chapter explore the big issue of free trade as a global economic system—its benefits, costs, successes, and problems. Now that you have read these arguments, how many specific ways can you identify that free trade affects your life? Try to list five to ten specific ways.

2. Several of this chapter's arguments discuss the way that free trade is affecting workers in developing countries; however, writers Johan Norberg, Anita Roddick, and Mike Shanahan disagree about these facts. Imagine a debate between Norberg and Roddick or between Norberg and Shanahan. What would they say to each other about the way that free trade benefits workers in developing countries? What counterarguments, reasons, and evidence would each enlist to refute the other's points?

3. Free trade and fair trade as economic philosophies and systems share some goals: achieving justice, ending world poverty, and bringing prosperity to countries around the world. However, these two approaches to international trade differ radically in other ways. After reading this chapter, what do you see as the major differences between free trade and fair trade?

4. Johan Norberg and George F. Will argue that free trade is beneficial to countries and consumers. What specific points do they agree on? Where do they disagree?

5. Mike Shanahan's article "Appetite for Destruction" focuses on the way that the eating habits of rich nations affect shrimp farmers and fishermen in developing countries. How does Shanahan's argument support Global Exchange's points in "Twelve Reasons to Oppose the World Trade Organization"?

6. Ed Finn and Anita Roddick share a concern for the economic and social injustice that foreign workers are experiencing. How do their proposals for action differ?

7. After thinking about the readings in this chapter, your own experiences, and other articles you have read about Wal-Mart, which view of Wal-Mart do you find the most persuasive: Wal-Mart as the exploitive and greedy megacorporation or Wal-Mart as the global employer and consumers' friend? Why? You might want to consult Wal-Mart's Web sites (www.walmartstores.com and www.walmart.com) as well as anti-Wal-Mart sites. As an alternative, you might want to investigate the number of Wal-Mart stores in your area and survey consumers' reasons for shopping there.

8. The following items are some of the main commodities currently exchanged through fair trade agreements: coffee, cocoa, tea, chocolate, bananas, rice, toys, handicrafts, and jewelry. Use the Web to help you answer these questions:

   - What items of clothing that you regularly wear could you buy as fair trade or union-made products and where would you buy them?

   - What food products that you regularly eat could you buy as fair trade or union-produced goods and where would you buy them?

9. Controversies over free trade, consumerism, and sweatshops intersect with issues presented in other chapters of this text such as the outsourcing of jobs (Chapter 3), immigration (Chapter 4), human rights and child labor (Chapter 6), environmental resources (Chapter 7), and food for the world (Chapter 8). For instance, George F. Will and Froma Harrop mention the way that global trade and consumerism are affecting the loss of American jobs in candy manufacturing and apparel manufacturing, respectively, as these jobs move to countries where labor is cheaper—an issue that is examined in more depth in Chapter 3's readings on outsourcing. Identify an issue or subissue in this chapter and pursue it in a related chapter. What do you see as the main connections? For example, what are some ways that free trade affects child labor?

WRITING ASSIGNMENTS

Brief Writing Assignments

1. Write a brief narrative in which you describe a moment that made you think in a new way about your consumer habits. You could describe (1) a personal experience when you became aware of the consumer benefits of free trade; (2) a personal experience that made you aware of some of the production problems of free trade; or (3) a personal experience when you discovered how you could buy fair trade products.

2. Choose one of the following controversial claims and write informally for twenty minutes, supporting or contesting this claim. Use examples from your reading, personal experience, and knowledge to provide evidence to support your views. As a variation on this assignment, your instructor might ask you to write a short response in favor of the claim and then a short response arguing against it.

   A. The free trade global system is inherently flawed and favors rich nations.

   B. The first priority of American consumers is bargain prices.

   C. All corporations should be required to tell consumers where and how their products are manufactured.

D. The rewards and benefits of free trade will eventually be more evenly distributed among nations.

E. Fair trade is not a realistic trading system.

3. Write a short response to this question: How have the readings in this chapter affected the way you think about the connection between your buying habits and global economic justice? Which argument moved you the most?

Writing Projects

1. Choose one of the following claims about free trade, sweatshops, and consumerism and construct a well-developed argument in favor or against this claim. Write for a neutral or indifferent audience of your peers who have not thought much about this issue.

   A. Free trade benefits developing countries.

   B. Consumers in rich nations hold major responsibility for the competitive business conditions that lead to worker exploitation in developing countries.

   C. Americans need to think beyond bargain prices when they shop.

   D. American consumers should actively pursue alternatives to free trade such as fair trade.

   E. Superdiscount stores such as Wal-Mart are good for the international global economic system.

2. In groups or individually, investigate the price and availability of a product produced under fair trade or union conditions versus the price of that product not produced by a union or under fair trade conditions. Choose a product such as coffee, bananas, workout clothes, or baseball caps. You may need to go to several supermarkets, grocery stores, or discount department stores to compare prices. Read the labels and any manufacturing information carefully. Present your findings as a short informative report. You might use a table, chart, or graph as part of your report to present some of your findings visually.

3. Role-play this situation. Suppose a friend says to you, "I really feel bad that workers are laboring under life-threatening conditions to produce the jeans (or sneakers, sweaters, CD player) I buy. However, practically, I don't have time right now to figure out how to be a college student, prepare for a career, work at my part-time job, *and* change my consumer habits." Write an argumentative response to your friend in which you either agree and elaborate on the difficulties of changing our consumer habits, or disagree and propose some concrete ways to learn about manufacturing processes and the treatment of workers. For evidence to build your argument, you might use these sources: the affordable prices of superdiscount stores; the

good sales at local malls; the convenience of retail catalogs; personal experience; the readings in this chapter; other research you have done; and the following Web sites, which explore the ways that goods are produced:

Responsible Shopper (www.responsibleshopper.org)
American Apparel (www.americanapparel.net/)
No Sweat Apparel (www.nosweatapparel.com)
Ethical Threads (www.ethicalthreads.co.uk)

4. A number of the readings in this chapter question what consumers in rich nations should do about the exploitation of workers in sweatshops around the world. The social justice advocacy group Corporation Watch broadly defines sweatshops in these terms: "Extreme exploitation, including the absence of a living wage or benefits; poor working conditions, such as health and safety hazards; and arbitrary discipline, such as physical and psychological abuse" (www.corpwatch.org/article .php?id=11304). However, some scholars and researchers, such as David R. Henderson in his article "The Case for Sweatshops," published on Stanford University's Hoover Institution Web site (www.hoover .stanford.edu/), argue that "sweatshops in third-world countries are a good deal for the people who work in them" and that consumers can help the workers in these factories most by continuing to buy the goods that they produce. Considering these views and consumer responsibility, write a policy proposal for a consumer group, expressing your informed view of sweatshops and consumerism. Argue your case for boycotting irresponsible companies, for pressuring companies to make their manufacturing practices transparent, for rewarding socially responsible companies with your business, or for some other course of action.

5. Choose one of your favorite clothing companies or brands of clothing such as Nike Inc., Eddie Bauer, the Gap, Levi Strauss & Co., Reebok International Ltd., and J. Crew Group Inc., and conduct an investigation of this company's manufacturing practices and treatment of workers using the company's Web site and annual report and one of the following Web sites: Responsible Shopper (www.responsibleshopper.org); Maquila Solidarity Network (www.maquilasolidarity.org); Corporation Watch (www.corpwatch.org); Fair Labor Association (www.fairlabor.org/); or United Students against Sweatshops (www.studentsagainstsweatshops.org). These sites or your company's Web site can give you the name and address of the company's CEO. Write a letter to the CEO of the company, praising the company for its social responsibility, fair labor practices, or recent improvements in factory conditions and treatment of workers *or* expressing your disapproval of its violation of labor rights. Try to be specific about what you admire or what you

find reprehensible. The following Web sites have sample letters that show how consumer and citizen power can be used to expose and protest companies' exploitive labor practices.

- Clean Clothes Campaign: Improving Working Conditions in the Garment Industry (www.cleanclothes.org)
- CorpWatch: Sweatshops (www.corpwatch.org)
- United Students against Sweatshops (www.studentsagainstsweatshops .org)

6. Some companies are using fair trade or responsible manufacturing practices to avoid exploiting growers, producers, and workers. Research the companies listed here and others you find on your own. Write an upbeat editorial for your university newspaper in which you encourage your readers to buy products from these companies and to promote a new consumer awareness. As an alternative, you could create a directory of "preferred companies" that value the just treatment of workers and the environment.

The Body Shop (www.the-body-shop.com)
Juan Valdez Café de Colombia (www.juanvaldez.com)
Indigenous Designs (www.indigenousdesigns.com)
American Apparel (www.americanapparel.com)

CHAPTER **3**

Trading Jobs
Outsourcing and Employment in a Global Economy

QUESTION TO PONDER

Your older sister is graduating from college this year with a degree in computer science. She was hoping to start her career with a job as a computer programmer, but the companies she wanted to work for are now sending their programming work to India ("offshore outsourcing" these jobs). Should Americans support or oppose the movement of "white-collar" jobs and manufacturing jobs to developing countries?

CONTEXT FOR A NETWORK OF ISSUES

Tlalpujahua, Mexico, faces a major crisis in the next few years. The factories in this town, which make Christmas tree ornaments mostly for the United States, are employing many fewer workers because Mexico is losing business to Chinese factories. In the last two years, hundreds of factories and hundreds of thousands of manufacturing jobs have moved from Mexico to China and other Asian countries that offer one-third the labor costs, greater output of work, and lower labor and environmental standards. A parallel transformation has been taking place in the last few years in the IT (information technology) industry, where many companies have subcontracted their work to vendor companies in English-speaking developing countries such as India. What do Mexican factory workers and American computer programmers have in common? They are experiencing what N. Gregory Mankiw, former chairman of President George W. Bush's Council of Economic Advisors, has called a "new way of doing international trade": trading jobs, or as opponents of this trend say, trading *away* jobs.

As part of free trade's global movement of money and goods, since the 1980s an increasing number of manufacturing jobs and whole auto plants and clothing factories have been moved to developing countries. Today many of the garments, toys, footwear, computer components, electronic equipment, appliance parts, and plastic goods that Americans buy are made in factories located in countries such as Mexico, Nicaragua, the Philippines, Indonesia, Pakistan, and China. In the late 1980s and 1990s, call centers (customer service departments of companies such as help desks for computer software that are accessed by phone) and business processing also moved to other countries with lower wages. More recently, corporations, especially high-tech companies, have transferred some of their departments to developing countries such as India, the Philippines, Hong Kong, Taiwan, South Korea, and Singapore, where a qualified labor force can do the same work for much lower wages than American workers.

To reduce overhead costs and gain efficiency, American companies for years have been "outsourcing" some of their work: that is, moving it out of the companies' central office to subcontracted individuals and other companies elsewhere in the United States. However, "offshore outsourcing"—the name given to the movement of white-collar jobs to other countries—has been gaining momentum and publicity in the last few years. Substantial advances in the Internet, technology, and communication have made it possible for all kinds of work to be conducted in real time from the other side of the world. According to A. T. Kearney, a global management consulting firm, in choosing an offshoring site, American firms look for low costs; availability of people with the necessary skills in mathematics, science, and reading; English-speaking workers with an understanding of American culture; economic and political stability; and good tax rates. Based on these criteria, in 2004 A. T. Kearney's Offshore Location Attractiveness Index gave countries this ranking:

1. India
2. China
3. Malaysia
4. Czech Republic
5. Singapore
6. Philippines
7. Brazil
8. Canada
9. Chile
10. Poland
11. Hungary
12. New Zealand

The fact that global management firms have established criteria and publicize such lists indicates the corporate world's acceptance of offshore outsourcing as a common practice and important trend.

STAKES AND STAKEHOLDERS

From the perspective of many people, global relations appear to be thriving, and yet trading jobs to other countries has ignited much heated, anxious debate. Offshore outsourcing is a complex and multilayered controversy in which many people in the United States, other developed nations, and developing nations have high stakes. They are voicing arguments on a number of major issue questions.

Is Offshore Outsourcing a New Economic Phenomenon or Simply the Latest Phase of an Ongoing Process of Corporate Development and Globalization? Advocates of free trade, some economists, and some corporations as well as some politicians argue that offshore outsourcing is nothing new to be alarmed about. In its tapping of the cheap labor resources of developing countries, offshore outsourcing is merely the latest phase in the corporate search for efficiency and the integration of the world economy. In opposition, free trade skeptics and critics of corporate globalization as well as many workers disagree, arguing that the large number and range of jobs being sent out of the country and moved from country to country is something new that calls for immediate critical analysis and reconsideration. In their eyes, offshore outsourcing demonstrates corporations' priority of short-term profits over the well-being of people at home and abroad and over long-term economic stability.

Does the Increase in Offshore Outsourcing of Jobs from the United States Pose Major Economic Threats to American Workers? Advocates of free trade and corporations acknowledge that some Americans have found themselves out of work when their jobs have gone overseas. However, advocates along with some economists claim that offshore outsourcing will spur innovation in business and prompt the creation of new jobs (a principle called "creative destruction"). In disagreement with this economy theory, some policymakers, analysts, economists, and worker organizations are saying that offshore outsourcing is harmful to workers in the United States and asking how much outsourcing is contributing to the high unemployment rate in the United States and the increase in the number of Americans living in poverty. They further wonder if displaced American workers will be able to find other, comparable jobs that use their expertise and pay as well. Many stakeholders are questioning how many new jobs are being created. With the outsourcing of jobs as diverse as customer call center operators, technical support for computer companies, software and data management, medical transcription, and reading X-rays and CAT scans, some people are wondering if any jobs in the U.S. are secure. As the following table indicates, hiring workers in other countries yields substantial savings for American corporations.

Job	United States: Average Yearly Salary	India: Average Yearly Salary
Software engineer	$66,100	$10,000
Mechanical engineer	$55,600	$ 5,900
Information technology manager	$55,000	$ 8,500
Accountant	$41,000	$ 5,000

Numerical data from the International Labour Organisation.

Analysts and many groups of Americans are asking the question, When a number of developing countries have educated people willing and able to work for far less than people in the United States, will education and training be any insurance that Americans can find and maintain jobs? Furthermore, many are wondering what will happen to the tax base for local, state, and federal governments when businesses are relocated abroad.

Social activists and labor advocates also point out the ongoing problem with the loss of U.S. jobs in manufacturing. Some factory towns and communities are protesting the loss of factories that were the primary means of employment for most of their residents. For instance, what will the effect of the recent closing of Ford and General Motors plants be?

In response, however, some leaders in small and large businesses contend that their companies need to capitalize on the savings from outsourcing to remain competitive in the market. They claim they have to lower costs and raise profits to meet demands of American consumers who want inexpensive goods and of stockholders who want maximum gain on their investments.

How Does the Offshore Outsourcing of Jobs Influence the Global Economy and Affect Global Politics and Workers in Other Countries?
Many proponents of free trade and supporters of offshore outsourcing argue that outsourcing jobs to other countries helps the United States establish strong political alliances. Economists and policymakers assert that providing employment in developing countries will substantially enhance the economic development of those countries, create new markets for goods from developed countries, and help these countries to be more politically stable: in other words, trading jobs can improve global relations, even nurture peace.

However, many stakeholders are questioning the benefits that outsourcing brings to developing countries and the global economy. Some advocacy groups and workers' organizations claim that free trade agreements' moving businesses, especially factories, abroad has enabled corporations to lower the standards of working conditions, creating sweatshops, to increase profits at the expense of foreign workers.* Analysts and anticorporate activists also are questioning what happens to the countries' economies and to the workers' lives when factories move from one developing country to another that offers lower wages.

The three sections that follow—"Student Voice," "International Voices," and "Global Hot Spot"—take you deeper into local and global connections to offshore outsourcing and its effects on people's lives in the United States and abroad.

 ## STUDENT VOICE: EXPERIENCING OFFSHORE OUTSOURCING

For some Americans, as student Nicole Neumiller indicates, the offshore outsourcing of jobs has created crises for their families. Nicole reports on her Seattle community, near Microsoft, that has had a significant loss of jobs in the computer field.

Nicole Neumiller

I live in Redmond, Washington, home to many of the United States' computer programming, software and hardware companies, and it seems every time I see my aunt she is telling us about lay-offs happening in her department as more and more work is outsourced to India. The result? Those families are struggling to make house payments and using up their savings to make it through a hopefully short unemployed period. However, those laid off aren't finding new jobs. One family friend confessed to me that the place where she was applying had over fifty applicants for only three open programming positions. In my high school graduating class, it was startlingly common for students to choose a two-year community college over a four-year university because their upper-middle-class families were still trying to cope with one or both parents being laid off over a year ago. While American business may be flourishing by utilizing the outsourcing option that has come from economic globalization, I think many people are suffering and the loss of income to the middle-class American worker will be more devastating to our economy than people looking at corporate gains realize.

---

*Chapter 2 explores questions about sweatshops from the angles of consumerism and free trade.

INTERNATIONAL VOICES

Although jobs are being outsourced around the globe, India is the recipient of many jobs in computer technology, and many Americans are frustrated and angry that their jobs are now being done in India. Meanwhile, their Indian counterparts are frustrated that American workers blame them for the loss of jobs. Furthermore, the idea that is sometimes promoted by American corporations, that the United States is farming out the less-skilled jobs, conveys an attitude of American superiority and condescension that does not build positive international relations. Are Indian call center workers and Indian computer programmers simply cheaper than their American counterparts? What roles do efficiency, talent, and expertise play in the job market? Gaurav Sabnis from Mumbai, India, wrote this blog (short for "Web log," a medium on which individuals can post journal-like entries and other people can respond) on DialogNow on January 30, 2004, to show the pride that Indians take in their abilities. Sabnis protests the idea that "the only reason we are getting their [American] jobs is because we are cheaper, not because we are better."

Comment from an Indian Working in the Information Technology Field

It is my humble opinion that we are no less innovative and entrepreneurial, given the right conditions. It is not America alone that can give birth to Steve Jobses and Bill Gateses. What Laxmi Mittal has achieved is no less. It is just that in this silly socialistic "state-led-industrialisation" model, most entrepreneurs ran out of steam. Would Steve Jobs have been able to make Apple what it is, if he had to wait five years for a simple factory license? We are GOOD. Especially at IT because it is so mathematical and logical in nature. It is not the racial characteristics that make us good at this, but our culture. There is a lot of glamour attached to math in India, whereas in the West math or science geniuses are termed "nerds" or "geeks," with no one dating them. In general mathematics has a very important status in the East. Look at the countries that always do well in the Math Olympiad— China, Russia, Iran, India, etc. My best friend in school was a math genius, and he was every bit as popular among girls as the football team captain.

GLOBAL HOT SPOT: INDIA

To see how the movement of jobs from country to country is changing the lives of individuals and groups of people, we could look at manufacturing towns in Mexico and China; towns in the American South; U.S. communities like Silicon Valley (home of many computer companies) near San Jose, California; Bangalore, India; and Mumbai, India's largest city and the home to its major software and computer development companies. Because India is currently the favored location for much of the offshore outsourcing of white-collar jobs, this section takes a closer look at India. The article excerpts that follow provide insight into the way that the offshore outsourcing of jobs is affecting Indian employment opportunities, work conditions, and quality of life.

The following passage is from an article entitled "India Tastes the Good Life" by John Lancaster. It appeared in the September 30, 2003, edition of the *Seattle Times*.

Calcutta, India—For a man living the Indian dream, Saubir Chakrabarty could use a little more closet space.

A manager at a local firm that designs Web sites and software for clients in India and abroad, Chakrabarty, 34, comes home each night to a cramped, two-bedroom apartment he shares with his parents, wife and 2-year-old daughter. The family makes do with a single small bathroom and swelters through summer nights without air conditioning. Their living room looks out on an air shaft.

But Chakrabarty and his wife, a customer representative at a financial-services firm, are nothing if not upwardly mobile. They recently bought their first car, a used Maruti compact, watch movies on a new video-compact-disc player and regularly visit the malls and chain stores springing up all over town.

Chakrabarty's success story echoes throughout India. Twelve years after the government began liberalizing the economy, service industries such as banking, insurance, health care—and, most visibly, anything related to information technology—are booming in the world's second-most populous nation, driving an unprecedented and long-awaited expansion in the ranks of the middle and upper classes.

While Lancaster's article suggests that the standard of living is improving for a number of Indians profiting from the influx of jobs, the passage from the next article by Kranti Kumara, "India Reacts with Dismay to Recent US Legislation on Outsourcing," raises doubts about the optimistic picture that Lancaster paints. First published on the World Socialist Web Site (www.wsws.org) on March 16, 2004, Kumara's piece takes a pro-worker stance against the world's "financial elite."

With an estimated 50 million to 100 million workers unemployed in India, call centers are among the only jobs open to young educated workers. The long and irregular working hours as well as continuous monitoring of performance make these jobs especially stressful and have resulted in a high job turnover rate.

The Indian IT industry has a huge pool of engineering and computer science graduates from which to recruit. The salary of an Indian graduate with an advanced engineering degree from a top university such as the Indian Institutes of Technology does not exceed $12,000 per year. India annually churns out up to 151,000 engineering graduates and around 100,000 information technology graduates from its 900 colleges affiliated with 250 universities.

Given this huge pool of graduates, the competition for technology jobs in India is fierce, and Indian companies exploit this gratuitous gift fully.

Most of the entry-level graduates are paid as little as $300 per month and are frequently expected to work longer hours without compensation for six days a week. During job interviews, these young workers are bluntly informed that they are expected to put in extra hours despite having been hired for eight-hour workdays. If they demur, they are informed that others will take their place. Many of these young workers log in more than 16 hours a day and frequently burn out in a few years, requiring hospitalization. Once uncommon, depression now afflicts many young workers, whose average age is only 26.5 years.

As you read the arguments in this chapter, think about the ways they confirm or refute the ideas in these testimonies and news articles and the network of issues they explore related to the benefits and changes that off-shore outsourcing is bringing to the global community.

READINGS

30 Little Turtles
Thomas L. Friedman

This op-ed piece appeared in the *New York Times* on February 29, 2004. Thomas L. Friedman, a well-known journalist, is the foreign affairs columnist for the *New York Times*. He has authored two books, *The World Is Flat: A Brief History of the Twenty-First Century* (2005) and *The Lexus and the Olive Tree: Understanding Globalization* (1999), that trace the emergence of globalization after the Cold War. In *The Lexus and the Olive Tree*, Friedman analyzes globalization as a new phenomenon: ". . . what is new today is the degree and intensity with which the world is being tied together into a single globalized marketplace and village. What is also new is the sheer number of people and countries able to partake of today's globalized economy and information networks, and to be affected by them." *

> How does Friedman's approach to the subject suit his broad, educated audience and draw on his identity as a world traveler and journalist of international affairs?

1   Indians are so hospitable. I got an ovation the other day from a roomful of Indian 20-year-olds just for reading perfectly the following paragraph: "A bottle of bottled water held 30 little turtles. It didn't matter that each turtle had to rattle a metal ladle in order to get a little bit of noodles, a total turtle delicacy. The problem

---

The Lexus and the Olive Tree: Understanding Globalization (New York: Random House, 1999), xvii.

was that there were many turtle battles for less than oodles of noodles."

2   I was sitting in on an "accent neutralization" class at the Indian call center 24/7 Customer. The instructor was teaching the would-be Indian call center operators to suppress their native Indian accents and speak with a Canadian one—she teaches British and U.S. accents as well, but these youths will be serving the Canadian market. Since I'm originally from Minnesota, near Canada, and still speak like someone out of the movie *Fargo*, I gave these young Indians an authentic rendition of "30 Little Turtles," which is designed to teach them the proper Canadian pronunciations. Hence the rousing applause.

3   Watching these incredibly enthusiastic young Indians preparing for their call center jobs—earnestly trying to soften their t's and roll their r's—is an uplifting experience, especially when you hear from their friends already working these jobs how they have transformed their lives. Most of them still live at home and turn over part of their salaries to their parents, so the whole family benefits. Many have credit cards and have become real consumers, including of U.S. goods, for the first time. All of them seem to have gained self-confidence and self-worth.

4   A lot of these Indian young men and women have college degrees, but would never get a local job that starts at $200 to $300 a month were it not for the call centers. Some do "outbound" calls, selling things from credit cards to phone services to Americans and Europeans. Others deal with "inbound" calls—everything from tracing lost luggage for U.S. airline passengers to solving computer problems for U.S. customers. The calls are transferred here by satellite or fiber optic cable.

5   I was most taken by a young Indian engineer doing tech support for a U.S. software giant, who spoke with pride about how cool it is to tell his friends that he just spent the day helping Americans navigate their software. A majority of these call center workers are young women, who not only have been liberated by earning a decent local wage (and therefore have more choice in whom they marry), but are using the job to get M.B.A.'s and other degrees on the side.

6   I gathered a group together, and here's what they sound like: M. Dinesh, who does tech support, says his day is made when some American calls in with a problem and is actually happy to hear an Indian voice: "They say you people are really good at what you do. I am glad I reached an Indian." Kiran Menon, when asked who his role model was, shot back: "Bill Gates—[I dream of] starting my own company and making it that big." I asked C. M. Meghna what she got most out of the work: "Self-confidence," she said, "a lot of self-confidence, when people come to you with a problem and you can solve it—and having a lot of independence." Because the call center teams work through India's night—which

corresponds to America's day—"your biological clock goes haywire," she added. "Besides that, it's great."

7   There is nothing more positive than the self-confidence, dignity and optimism that comes from a society knowing it is producing wealth by tapping its own brains—men's and women's—as opposed to one just tapping its own oil, let alone one that is so lost it can find dignity only through suicide and "martyrdom."

8   Indeed, listening to these Indian young people, I had a deja vu. Five months ago, I was in Ramallah, on the West Bank, talking to three young Palestinian men, also in their 20's, one of whom was studying engineering. Their hero was Yasir Arafat. They talked about having no hope, no jobs and no dignity, and they each nodded when one of them said they were all "suicide bombers in waiting."

9   What am I saying here? That it's more important for young Indians to have jobs than Americans? Never. But I am saying that there is more to outsourcing than just economics. There's also geopolitics. It is inevitable in a networked world that our economy is going to shed certain low-wage, low-prestige jobs. To the extent that they go to places like India or Pakistan—where they are viewed as high-wage, high-prestige jobs—we make not only a more prosperous world, but a safer world for our own 20-year-olds.

For Class Discussion

1. What is Friedman's view on the outsourcing of American jobs to India?

2. How does personal experience support Friedman's argument? What other kinds of evidence does he use to make his view persuasive?

3. What specific contributions does this op-ed piece make to the public's understanding of the offshoring controversy?

4. What gaps, contradictions, or weaknesses might readers criticize in this argument?   ■

Re: "30 Little Turtles," by Thomas L. Friedman
Paritosh Bansal

This letter to the editor, written by Paritosh Bansal of Los Angeles, appeared in the *New York Times* on March 4, 2004.

How does Paritosh Bansal's view of the jobs that have come to India from the United States differ from Friedman's?

1   The avenues of consumption have increased in India, not jobs. The developing world stays primarily a market, not an investment destination, for Western corporations. And attrition of traditional jobs comes as a condition of globalization.

2   For the educated, English-speaking Indian elite, the alternative is worse. They have traded jobs for more wants.

3   Call center work, in particular, offers neither a career nor growth. A salary of $200 a month is not enough to fulfill middle-class aspirations, even in India. The 20-year-olds who work there are not adding to family income; they are being subsidized by it.

4   As Americans debate outsourcing, then, they might want to focus on the cause rather than the effect. The question is, Are Americans prepared to stay wedded to the global economy in good times and bad? The problem is that it is too late to ask that.

For Class Discussion

1. What holes or problems does Paritosh Bansal point out in Friedman's argument?

2. How do you interpret the question that concludes Bansal's letter?

3. If Bansal were to present his views in a genre of argument that allowed for more development of points, what ideas would you like him to elaborate?

4. What important perspective does Bansal's letter contribute to the outsourcing controversy?   ∎

Some Job Angst Flies Against Experience
Missoulian.com News Online

This editorial was first published on Missoulian.com News Online (Western Montana's News Online) on March 14, 2004. Montana is well known for its beautiful western scenery, its mountain sports, and especially its fishing.

How does this piece connect globalization, consumerism, and outsourcing in terms that are meaningful, particularly to its Montana audience?

1   The "outsourcing" of U.S. jobs to places like India has become a hot topic, garnering a lot of attention in the news media and figuring prominently in the early presidential election campaign. The issue really flared recently after White House chief economist Gregory

Mankiw said exporting jobs is just another form of international trade and "is probably a plus for the economy in the long-run."

2   That's not an especially savvy way of putting it, but he's probably right. To understand why, let's cast our attention to a small and early example of job outsourcing—one that strikes particularly close to home for many Montanans: fly tying.

3   Flies, of course, are the edible-looking things fly fishermen tie on the end of a line to catch fish—in these parts, mostly trout.

4   Fly-tying is a skill-based, labor-intensive endeavor that involves wrapping fur, feathers and other materials around a tiny hook to produce something that resembles an insect or minnow. The process defies automation. Flies must be tied one at a time by hand, each one following a particular design. A well-tied fly is a piece of art, as well as utillitarian device.

5   Up until, say, the early 1970s, most of the artificial flies used for fishing in America were tied in the United States. A generation ago, we recall walking into Dan Bailey's Fly Shop in Livingston to see a whole room full of workers tying flies. More commonly, the flies fishermen bought in sporting goods stores were tied by independent contractors working out of their homes.

6   People still make a living tying flies today, but a large percentage of flies sold in the United States are tied overseas in places like Sri Lanka, Thailand, China and, yes, India. Great improvements in the quality of materials and workmanship have contributed to an easing of the traditional aversion fly fishermen had to imported flies. Better fishing shops clearly identify the origins of imported flies, but an awful lot of fishermen undoubtedly buy their flies without knowing or caring who tied them or where.

7   It takes instruction and years of experience before most people can tie flies of commercial quality. What's more, with bargain flies retailing for less than $1 apiece and very few flies selling for more than $2 apiece (wholesaling for perhaps half that), it's the rare American craftsman who can make a livable wage tying flies— especially when you factor in the cost of materials, such as hooks, thread, feathers and fur. It's more economical to hire low-wage workers in other countries to tie flies and import them.

8   According to the U.S. Commerce Department's International Trade Administration, the United States last year imported nearly 137 million flies and "artificial baits," which also includes fishing lures. That translates into thousands of jobs shipped overseas. And that's bad for the United States, right? Not really.

9   At the same time that fly-tying jobs were outsourced to Asia and elsewhere, the American fishing industry blossomed. According to the American Sportfishing Association, anglers today spend $41.5 billion in retail sales and generate $116 billion in overall

economic activity annually—making fishing the equivalent of 32nd on the Fortune 500 list of America's largest companies. Nearly 1.07 million Americans find work in fishing-related jobs. The ASA says fishing-related businesses support more than 7,000 jobs in Montana, accounting for over $136 million in wages and a total economic impact of $544 million annually.

10   Fewer Montanans may be working as commercial fly tiers than a generation ago, but more are working as guides, boatbuilders, rod makers, sales clerks, hoteliers, outdoor writers, biologists and such—all jobs that pay more than most people ever could earn tying flies.

11   What's more, if you were to compare today's average fisherman's fly box with that of his grandfather's, what you'd see is a much larger and more diverse selection of flies in today's box. That and a whole lot more equipment and more expensive tackle in general. Lower-cost imported flies make it affordable to stock up on more flies. Money not spent on flies very likely gets spent on more expensive rods or clothing or services. And all of that generally translates into greater fishing success, greater satisfaction and even greater demand for goods and services.

12   And now look: Finding it tough to compete with imports on the basis of price, American fly tiers are finding ways to compete on the basis of quality and creativity. Many tiers carve out a niche by specializing in flies especially suited for local waters. Others come up with innovative new designs that catch more fish—or at least capture fishermen's imagination. Walk into any upscale fishing shop in America and you'll find such value-added, locally tied flies selling for a premium.

13   Meanwhile, halfway around the globe, people are buying food, shelter and clothing with the money they earn tying the run-of-the-mill flies that so many American fishermen use. Their productivity contributes to other economic activity that, as it spreads across the vast array of manufacturing and service jobs we might consider outsourced from the United States, ultimately, leads to the purchase of machines, grain, medicine, computer software, music CDs and myriad other products created by workers in the United States.

14   They sell us stuff they make cheaper or better, and we sell them stuff that we make cheaper or better. Over time, we all fare better than we would with self-sufficient economies. That's the lure of free trade.

For Class Discussion

1. What reasoning and evidence does this editorial use to justify its stand on outsourcing the fly-tying industry?

2. How has outsourcing fly tying benefited fishermen? How has it benefited Montanans specifically? Who else has benefited?

3. How does this argument explain the gains of free trade?

4. How successful is this argument at connecting local and global issues?   ■

Jobs Terror Alert
Larry Wright

Larry Wright has worked as the editorial cartoonist for the *Detroit News* since 1976. In addition to producing three cartoons a week for the op-ed page, he also draws a daily cartoon strip called *Kit 'N' Carlyle*. He has served as president of the Association of American Editorial Cartoonists. This cartoon was originally published in the *Detroit News* on May 20, 2003, and appears on Daryl Cagle's Professional Cartoonists Index Web site, affiliated with the online political and cultural commentary magazine *Slate*.

In its basic image and main idea, what current events and background knowledge about the United States does this cartoon draw on?

For Class Discussion

1. What is the main claim this cartoon makes?

2. Following the ongoing trend of moving American manufacturing jobs abroad, in the last five years the rate at which jobs in computer

FIGURE 3.1   Jobs Terror Alert *(© Larry Wright)*

programming, software development, data processing, accounting, insurance claims processing, and answering phones at company help desks have moved abroad has increased. The character in this cartoon is a college graduate, probably heading for a "white-collar" job. Why do you think the outsourcing issue has exploded in the media and the public sphere in the last five years?

3. What readings in this chapter support the alarm expressed in this cartoon? Which readings refute it?

4. What thoughts about your own future does this cartoon spark?

The Outsourcing Bogeyman
Daniel W. Drezner

This article appeared in the May/June 2004 issue of *Foreign Affairs*. Published by the Council on Foreign Relations since 1922, this journal describes itself as "America's most influential publication on international affairs and foreign policy" and "the international forum of choice for the most important new ideas, analysis, and debate on the most significant issues in the world" (www.foreignaffairs.org). Daniel W. Drezner is an assistant professor of political science at the University of Chicago. A monthly contributor to the *New Republic Online*, he has also published several books and has written for the *New York Times*, *Foreign Policy*, and *Slate*.

> According to Daniel W. Drezner, what is the economic and political position in favor of the free trade movement of jobs abroad? Whom is Drezner trying to persuade?

THE TRUTH IS OFFSHORE

1   When a presidential election year coincides with an uncertain economy, campaigning politicians invariably invoke an international economic issue as a dire threat to the well-being of Americans. Speechwriters denounce the chosen scapegoat, the media provides blanket coverage of the alleged threat, and legislators scurry to introduce supposed remedies.

2   The cause of this year's commotion is offshore outsourcing— the alleged migration of American jobs overseas. The depth of alarm was strikingly illustrated by the firestorm of reaction to recent testimony by N. Gregory Mankiw, the head of President George W. Bush's Council of Economic Advisers. No economist really disputed Mankiw's observation that "outsourcing is just a new way of doing international trade," which makes it "a good thing."

But in the political arena, Mankiw's comments sparked a furor on both sides of the aisle. Democratic presidential candidate John Kerry accused the Bush administration of wanting "to export more of our jobs overseas," and Senate Minority Leader Tom Daschle quipped, "If this is the administration's position, I think they owe an apology to every worker in America." Speaker of the House Dennis Hastert, meanwhile, warned that "outsourcing can be a problem for American workers and the American economy."

3   Critics charge that the information revolution (especially the Internet) has accelerated the decimation of U.S. manufacturing and facilitated the outsourcing of service-sector jobs once considered safe, from backroom call centers to high-level software programming. (This concern feeds into the suspicion that U.S. corporations are exploiting globalization to fatten profits at the expense of workers.) They are right that offshore outsourcing deserves attention and that some measures to assist affected workers are called for. But if their exaggerated alarmism succeeds in provoking protectionist responses from lawmakers, it will do far more harm than good, to the U.S. economy and to American workers.

4   Should Americans be concerned about the economic effects of outsourcing? Not particularly. Most of the numbers thrown around are vague, overhyped estimates. What hard data exist suggest that gross job losses due to offshore outsourcing have been minimal when compared to the size of the entire U.S. economy. The outsourcing phenomenon has shown that globalization can affect white-collar professions, heretofore immune to foreign competition, in the same way that it has affected manufacturing jobs for years. But Mankiw's statements on outsourcing are absolutely correct; the law of comparative advantage does not stop working just because 401(k) plans are involved. The creation of new jobs overseas will eventually lead to more jobs and higher incomes in the United States. Because the economy—and especially job growth—is sluggish at the moment, commentators are attempting to draw a connection between offshore outsourcing and high unemployment. But believing that offshore outsourcing causes unemployment is the economic equivalent of believing that the sun revolves around the earth: intuitively compelling but clearly wrong.

5   Should Americans be concerned about the political backlash to outsourcing? Absolutely. Anecdotes of workers affected by outsourcing are politically powerful, and demands for government protection always increase during economic slowdowns. The short-term political appeal of protectionism is undeniable. Scapegoating foreigners for domestic business cycles is smart politics, and protecting domestic markets gives leaders the appearance of taking direct, decisive action on the economy.

6   Protectionism would not solve the U.S. economy's employment problems, although it would succeed in providing massive subsidies to well-organized interest groups. In open markets, greater competition spurs the reallocation of labor and capital to more profitable sectors of the economy. The benefits of such free trade—to both consumers and producers—are significant. Cushioning this process for displaced workers makes sense. Resorting to protectionism to halt the process, however, is a recipe for decline. An open economy leads to concentrated costs (and diffuse benefits) in the short term and significant benefits in the long term. Protectionism generates pain in both the short term and the long term.

THE SKY IS FALLING

7   Outsourcing occurs when a firm subcontracts a business function to an outside supplier. This practice has been common within the U.S. economy for some time. (Witness the rise of large call centers in the rural Midwest.) The reduction of communication costs and the standardization of software packages have now made it possible to outsource business functions such as customer service, telemarketing, and document management. Other affected professions include medical transcription, tax preparation, and financial services.

8   The numbers that are bandied about on offshore outsourcing sound ominous. The McKinsey Global Institute estimates that the volume of offshore outsourcing will increase by 30 to 40 percent a year for the next five years. Forrester Research estimates that 3.3 million white-collar jobs will move overseas by 2015. According to projections, the hardest hit sectors will be financial services and information technology (IT). In one May 2003 survey of chief information officers, 68 percent of IT executives said that their offshore contracts would grow in the subsequent year. The Gartner research firm has estimated that by the end of this year, 1 out of every 10 IT jobs will be outsourced overseas. Deloitte Research predicts the outsourcing of 2 million financial-sector jobs by 2009.

9   At first glance, current macroeconomic indicators seem to support the suspicion that outsourcing is destroying jobs in the United States. The past two years have witnessed moderate growth and astonishing productivity gains, but overall job growth has been anemic. The total number of manufacturing jobs has declined for 43 consecutive months. Surely, many observers insist, this must be because the jobs created by the U.S. recovery are going to other countries. Morgan Stanley analyst Stephen Roach, for example, has pointed out that "this is the first business cycle since the advent of the Internet—the enabler of a new real-time connectivity to low-cost offshore labor pools." He adds, "I don't think it's a coincidence that this jobless recovery has occurred in such an environment."

Those who agree draw on anecdotal evidence to support this assertion. CNN's Lou Dobbs routinely harangues U.S. companies engaged in offshore outsourcing in his "Exporting America" series.

10   Many IT executives have themselves contributed to this perception. When IBM announced plans to outsource 3,000 jobs overseas this year, one of its executives said, "[Globalization] means shifting a lot of jobs, opening a lot of locations in places we had never dreamt of before, going where there's low-cost labor, low-cost competition, shifting jobs offshore." Nandan Nilekani, the chief executive of the India-based Infosys Technologies, said at this year's World Economic Forum, "Everything you can send down a wire is up for grabs." In January testimony before Congress, Hewlett-Packard chief Carly Fiorina warned that "there is no job that is America's God-given right anymore."

11   That last statement chills the blood of most Americans. Few support the cause of free trade for its own sake, out of pure principle. The logic underlying an open economy is that if the economy sheds jobs in uncompetitive sectors, employment in competitive sectors will grow. If hi-tech industries are no longer competitive, where will new jobs be created?

INSIDE THE NUMBERS

12   Before answering that question, Americans need to separate fact from fiction. The predictions of job losses in the millions are driving the current outsourcing hysteria. But it is crucial to note that these predictions are of gross, not net, losses. During the 1990s, offshore outsourcing was not uncommon. (American Express, for one, set up back-office operations in India more than a decade ago.) But no one much cared because the number of jobs leaving U.S. shores was far lower than the number of jobs created in the U.S. economy.

13   Similarly, most current predictions are not as ominous as they first sound once the numbers are unpacked. Most jobs will remain unaffected altogether: close to 90 percent of jobs in the United States require geographic proximity. Such jobs include everything from retail and restaurants to marketing and personal care— services that have to be produced and consumed locally, so outsourcing them overseas is not an option. There is also no evidence that jobs in the high-value-added sector are migrating overseas. One thing that has made offshore outsourcing possible is the standardization of such business tasks as data entry, accounting, and IT support. The parts of production that are more complex, interactive, or innovative—including, but not limited to, marketing, research, and development—are much more difficult to shift abroad. As an International Data Corporation analysis on trends in IT services concluded, "the activities that will migrate offshore are

predominantly those that can be viewed as requiring low skill since process and repeatability are key underpinnings of the work. Innovation and deep business expertise will continue to be delivered predominantly onshore." Not coincidentally, these are also the tasks that generate high wages and large profits and drive the U.S. economy.

14   As for the jobs that can be sent offshore, even if the most dire-sounding forecasts come true, the impact on the economy will be negligible. The Forrester prediction of 3.3 million lost jobs, for example, is spread across 15 years. That would mean 220,000 jobs displaced per year by offshore outsourcing—a number that sounds impressive until one considers that total employment in the United States is roughly 130 million, and that about 22 million new jobs are expected to be added between now and 2010. Annually, outsourcing would affect less than .2 percent of employed Americans.

15   There is also reason to believe that the unemployment caused by outsourcing will be lower than expected. Gartner assumed that more than 60 percent of financial-sector employees directly affected by outsourcing would be let go by their employers. But Boston University Professor Nitin Joglekar has examined the effect of outsourcing on large financial firms and found that less than 20 percent of workers affected by outsourcing lose their jobs; the rest are repositioned within the firm. Even if the most negative projections prove to be correct, then, gross job loss would be relatively small.

16   Moreover, it is debatable whether actual levels of outsourcing will ever match current predictions. Despite claims that the pace of onshore and offshore outsourcing would quicken over time, there was no increase in 2003. In fact, TPI Inc., an outsourcing advisory firm, even reports that the total value of business process outsourcing deals in the United States fell by 32 percent in 2003.

17   There is no denying that the number of manufacturing jobs has fallen dramatically in recent years, but this has very little [to] do with outsourcing and almost everything to do with technological innovation. As with agriculture a century ago, productivity gains have outstripped demand, so fewer and fewer workers are needed for manufacturing. If outsourcing were in fact the chief cause of manufacturing losses, one would expect corresponding increases in manufacturing employment in developing countries. An Alliance Capital Management study of global manufacturing trends from 1995 to 2002, however, shows that this was not the case: the United States saw an 11 percent decrease in manufacturing employment over the course of those seven years; meanwhile, China saw a 15 percent decrease and Brazil a 20 percent decrease. Globally, the figure for manufacturing jobs lost was identical to the U.S. figure—11 percent.

The fact that global manufacturing output increased by 30 percent in that same period confirms that technology, not trade, is the primary cause for the decrease in factory jobs. A recent analysis of employment data from U.S. multinational corporations by the U.S. Department of Commerce reached the same conclusion.

18   What about the service sector? Again, the data contradict the popular belief that U.S. jobs are being lost to foreign countries without anything to replace them. In the case of many low-level technology jobs, the phenomenon has been somewhat exaggerated. For example, a Datamonitor study found that global call-center operations are being outsourced at a slower rate than previously thought—only five percent are expected to be located offshore by 2007. Dell and Lehman Brothers recently moved some of their call centers back to the United States from India because of customer complaints. And done properly, the offshore outsourcing of call centers creates new jobs at home. Delta Airlines outsourced 1,000 call-center jobs to India in 2003, but the $25 million in savings allowed the firm to add 1,200 reservation and sales positions in the United States.

19   Offshore outsourcing is similarly counterbalanced by job creation in the high-end service sector. An Institute for International Economics analysis of Bureau of Labor Statistics employment data revealed that the number of jobs in service sectors where outsourcing is likely actually increased, even though total employment decreased by 1.7 percent. According to the Bureau of Labor Statistics Occupation Outlook Handbook, the number of IT-related jobs is expected to grow 43 percent by 2010. The case of IBM reinforces this lesson: although critics highlight the offshore outsourcing of 3,000 IT jobs, they fail to mention the company's plans to add 4,500 positions to its U.S. payroll. Large software companies such as Microsoft and Oracle have simultaneously increased outsourcing and domestic payrolls.

20   How can these figures fit with the widespread perception that IT jobs have left the United States? Too often, comparisons are made to 2000, an unusual year for the technology sector because Y2K fears and the height of the dot-com bubble had pushed employment figures to an artificially high level. When 1999 is used as the starting point, it becomes clear that offshore outsourcing has not caused a collapse in IT hiring. Between 1999 and 2003, the number of jobs in business and financial operations increased by 14 percent. Employment in computer and mathematical positions increased by 6 percent.

21   It is also worth remembering that many predictions come from management consultants who are eager to push the latest business fad. Many of these consulting firms are themselves reaping commissions from outsourcing contracts. Much of the perceived

boom in outsourcing stems from companies' eagerness to latch onto the latest management trends; like Dell and Lehman, many will partially reverse course once the hidden costs of offshore outsourcing become apparent.

22   If offshore outsourcing is not the cause of sluggish job growth, what is? A study by the Federal Reserve Bank of New York suggests that the economy is undergoing a structural transformation: jobs are disappearing from old sectors (such as manufacturing) and being created in new ones (such as mortgage brokering). In all such transformations, the creation of new jobs lags behind the destruction of old ones. In other words, the recent recession and current recovery are a more extreme version of the downturn and "jobless recovery" of the early 1990s—which eventually produced the longest economic expansion of the post-World War II era. Once the structural adjustments of the current period are complete, job growth is expected to be robust. (And indeed, current indicators are encouraging: there has been a net increase in payroll jobs and in small business employment since 2003 and a spike in IT entrepreneurial activity.)

23   Offshore outsourcing is undoubtedly taking place, and it will likely increase over the next decade. However, it is not the tsunami that many claim. Its effect on the U.S. economy has been exaggerated, and its effect on the U.S. employment situation has been grossly exaggerated.

THE UPSIDE OF OUTSOURCING

24   To date, the media's coverage of outsourcing has focused on its perceived costs. This leaves out more than half of the story. The benefits of offshore outsourcing should not be dismissed.

25   The standard case for free trade holds that countries are best off when they focus on sectors in which they have a comparative advantage—that is, sectors that have the lowest opportunity costs of production. Allowing countries to specialize accordingly increases productivity across all countries. This specialization translates into cheaper goods, and a greater variety of them, for all consumers.

26   The current trend of outsourcing business processes overseas is comparative advantage at work. The main driver of productivity gains over the past decade has been the spread of information technology across the economy. The commodification of simple business services allows those benefits to spread further, making growth even greater.

27   The data affirm this benefit. Catherine Mann of the Institute for International Economics conservatively estimates that the globalization of IT production has boosted U.S. GDP by $230 billion over the past seven years; the globalization of IT services should lead to a similar increase. As the price of IT services declines, sectors that

have yet to exploit them to their fullest—such as construction and health care—will begin to do so, thus lowering their cost of production and improving the quality of their output. (For example, cheaper IT could one day save lives by reducing the number of "adverse drug events." Mann estimates that adding bar codes to prescription drugs and instituting an electronic medical record system could reduce the annual number of such events by more than 80,000 in the United States alone.)

28   McKinsey Global Institute has estimated that for every dollar spent on outsourcing to India, the United States reaps between $1.12 and $1.14 in benefits. Thanks to outsourcing, U.S. firms save money and become more profitable, benefiting shareholders and increasing returns on investment. Foreign facilities boost demand for U.S. products, such as computers and telecommunications equipment, necessary for their outsourced function. And U.S. labor can be reallocated to more competitive, better-paying jobs; for example, although 70,000 computer programmers lost their jobs between 1999 and 2003, more than 115,000 computer software engineers found higher-paying jobs during that same period. Outsourcing thus enhances the competitiveness of the U.S. service sector (which accounts for 30 percent of the total value of U.S. exports). Contrary to the belief that the United States is importing massive amounts of services from low-wage countries, in 2002 it ran a $64.8 billion surplus in services.

29   Outsourcing also has considerable noneconomic benefits. It is clearly in the interest of the United States to reward other countries for reducing their barriers to trade and investment. Some of the countries where U.S. firms have set up outsourcing operations— including India, Poland, and the Philippines—are vital allies in the war on terrorism. Just as the North American Free Trade Agreement (NAFTA) helped Mexico deepen its democratic transition and strengthen its rule of law, the United States gains considerably from the political reorientation spurred by economic growth and interdependence.

30   Finally, the benefits of "insourcing" should not be overlooked. Just as U.S. firms outsource positions to developing countries, firms in other countries outsource positions to the United States. According to the Bureau of Labor Statistics, the number of outsourced jobs increased from 6.5 million in 1983 to 10 million in 2000. The number of insourced jobs increased even more in the same period, from 2.5 million to 6.5 million.

POLITICAL ECONOMY

31   When it comes to trade policy, there are two iron laws of politics. The first is that the benefits of trade diffuse across the economy, but

the costs of trade are concentrated. Thus, those made worse off by open borders will form the more motivated interest group. The second is that public hostility toward trade increases during economic downturns. When forced to choose between statistical evidence showing that trade is good for the economy and anecdotal evidence of job losses due to import competition, Americans go with the anecdotes.

32   Offshore outsourcing adds two additional political pressures. The first stems from the fact that technological innovation has converted what were thought to be nontradeable sectors into tradeable ones. Manufacturing workers have long been subject to the rigors of global competition. White-collar service-sector workers are being introduced to these pressures for the first time—and they are not happy about it. As Raghuram Rajan and Luigi Zingales point out in "Saving Capitalism From the Capitalists," globalization and technological innovation affect professions such as law and medicine that have not changed all that much for centuries. Their political reaction to the threat of foreign competition will be fierce.

33   The second pressure is that the Internet has greatly facilitated political organization, making it much easier for those who blame outsourcing for their troubles to rally together. In recent years, countless organizations—with names such as Rescue American Jobs, Save U.S. Jobs, and the Coalition for National Sovereignty and Economic Patriotism—have sprouted up. Such groups have disproportionately focused on white-collar tech workers, even though the manufacturing sector has been much harder hit by the recent economic slowdown.

34   It should come as no surprise, then, that politicians are scrambling to get ahead of the curve. During the Democratic primary in South Carolina—a state hit hard by the loss of textile jobs—billboards asked voters, "Lost your job to free trade or offshore outsourcing yet?" Last Labor Day, president Bush pledged to appoint a manufacturing czar to get to the bottom of the outflow of manufacturing positions. In his stump speech, John Kerry bashes "Benedict Arnold CEOs [who] send American jobs overseas."

35   Where presidential candidates lead, legislators are sure to follow. Senator Charles Schumer (D-N.Y.) claimed in a January *New York Times* op-ed authored with Paul Craig Roberts that because of increased capital mobility, the law of comparative advantage is now null and void. Senator Tom Daschle (D-S.D.) has observed, "George Bush says the economy is creating jobs. But let me tell you, China is one long commute. And let me tell you, I'm tired of watching jobs shift overseas." Senator Christopher Dodd (D-Conn.) and Representative Nancy Johnson (R-Conn.) are sponsoring the USA Jobs Protection Act to prevent U.S. companies from hiring foreign

workers for positions when American workers are available. In February, Senate Democrats announced their intentions to introduce the Jobs for America Act, requiring companies to give public notice three months in advance of any plan to outsource 15 or more jobs. In March, the Senate overwhelmingly approved a measure banning firms from federal contracts if they outsource any of the work overseas. In the past two years, more than 20 state legislatures have introduced bills designed to make various forms of offshore outsourcing illegal.

SPLENDID ISOLATION?

36   There are clear examples of jobs being sent across U.S. borders because of U.S. trade policy—but not for the reasons that critics of outsourcing believe. Consider the example of candy-cane manufacturers: despite the fact that 90 percent of the world's candy canes are consumed in the United States, manufacturers have sent much of their production south of the border in the past five years. The attraction of moving abroad, however, has little to do with low wages and much to do with protectionism. U.S. quotas on sugar imports have, in recent years, caused the domestic price of sugar to become 350 percent higher than world market prices. As candy makers have relocated production to countries where sugar is cheaper, between 7,500 and 10,000 workers in the Midwest have lost their jobs—victims not of outsourcing but of the kind of protectionism called for by outsourcing's critics.

37   A similar story can be told of the steel tariffs that the Bush administration foolishly imposed from March 2002 until December 2003 (when a ruling by the World Trade Organization prompted their cancellation). The tariffs were allegedly meant to protect steelworkers. But in the United States, steel users employ roughly 40 times more people than do steel producers. Thus, according to estimates by the Institute for International Economics, between 45,000 and 75,000 jobs were lost because higher steel prices made U.S. steel-using industries less competitive.

38   These examples illustrate the problem with relying on anecdotes when debating the effects of offshore outsourcing. Anecdotes are incomplete narratives that fail to capture opportunity costs. In the cases of steel and sugar, the opportunity cost of using protectionism to save jobs was the much larger number of jobs lost in sectors rendered less productive by higher input prices. Trade protectionism amounts to an inefficient subsidy for uncompetitive sectors of the economy, which leads to higher prices for consumers and a lower rate of return for investors. It preserves jobs in less competitive sectors while destroying current and future jobs in sectors that have a comparative advantage. Thus, if barriers are

erected to prevent offshore outsourcing, the overall effect will not be to create jobs but to destroy them.

39 So if protectionism is not the answer, what is the correct response? The best piece of advice is also the most difficult for elected officials to follow: do no harm. Politicians never get credit for inaction, even when inaction is the best policy. President George H.W. Bush, for example, was pilloried for refusing to follow Japan's lead by protecting domestic markets—even though his refusal helped pave the way for the 1990s boom by letting market forces allocate resources to industries at the technological frontier. Restraint is anathema to the political class, but it is still the most important response to the furor over offshore outsourcing. As Robert McTeer, president of the Federal Reserve Bank of Dallas, said when asked about policy responses to outsourcing, "If we are lucky, we can get through the year without doing something really, really stupid."

40 The problem of offshore outsourcing is less one of economics than of psychology—people feel that their jobs are threatened. The best way to help those actually affected, and to calm the nerves of those who fear that they will be, is to expand the criteria under which the Trade Adjustment Assistance (TAA) program applies to displaced workers. Currently, workers cannot apply for TAA unless overall sales or production in their sector declines. In the case of offshore outsourcing, however, productivity increases allow for increased production and sales—making TAA out of reach for those affected by it. It makes sense to rework TAA rules to take into account workers displaced by offshore outsourcing even when their former industries or firms maintain robust levels of production.

41 Another option would be to help firms purchase targeted insurance policies to offset the transition costs to workers directly affected by offshore outsourcing. Because the perception of possible unemployment is considerably greater than the actual likelihood of losing a job, insurance programs would impose a very small cost on firms while relieving a great deal of employee anxiety. McKinsey Global Institute estimates that such a scheme could be created for as little as four or five cents per dollar saved from offshore outsourcing. IBM recently announced the creation of a two-year, $25 million retraining fund for its employees who fear job losses from outsourcing. Having the private sector handle the problem without extensive government intervention would be an added bonus.

THE BEST DEFENSE

42 Until robust job growth returns, the debate over outsourcing will not go away—the political temptation to scapegoat foreigners is simply too great.

43   The refrain of "this time, it's different" is not new in the debate over free trade. In the 1980s, the Japanese variety of capitalism—with its omniscient industrial policy and high nontariff barriers—was supposed to supplant the U.S. system. Fifteen years later, that prediction sounds absurd. During the 1990s, the passage of NAFTA and the Uruguay Round of trade talks were supposed to create a "giant sucking sound" as jobs left the United States. Contrary to such fears, tens of millions of new jobs were created. Once the economy improves, the political hysteria over outsourcing will also disappear.

44   It is easy to praise economic globalization during boom times; the challenge, however, is to defend it during the lean years of a business cycle. Offshore outsourcing is not the bogeyman that critics say it is. Their arguments, however, must be persistently refuted. Otherwise, the results will be disastrous: less growth, lower incomes—and fewer jobs for American workers.

For Class Discussion

1. At the beginning of his article, Drezner lays out the main opposing perspectives on offshore outsourcing. According to Drezner, what do opponents of outsourcing claim and how do they want to combat the problem?

2. How does he define and employ some key economic terms such as *comparative advantage, protectionism,* and *subsidy*? On what economic principles does he build his argument?

3. What reasons and evidence does Drezner offer to support his claim that offshore outsourcing is not a major economic problem for Americans? How does Drezner's use of numerical data support his claim?

4. Drezner believes the issue of sending jobs abroad has been exaggerated and misrepresented. According to him, (a) What is the main cause of job loss in the United States? (b) What is the cause of minimal job growth? (c) Who is distorting the real situation?

5. Why is protecting certain industries economically harmful? What examples does Drezner offer?

6. What is the political case in favor of outsourcing jobs to other countries?

7. What is Drezner's proposal for managing the American economy in its current state? (If you read the Johan Norberg interview in Chapter 2, what connections do you see between Drezner's and Norberg's economic ideas?)

Educated, Experienced, and Out of Work: Long-Term Joblessness Continues to Plague the Unemployed

Sylvia Allegretto and Andy Stettner

This article was posted on the Economic Policy Institute Web site as an Issue Brief on March 4, 2004. On its Web site, the EPI says it was founded in 1986 "to broaden the discussion about economic policy to include the interests of low- and middle-income workers" (www.epinet.org). Its mission is "to provide high-quality research and education in order to promote a prosperous, fair, and sustainable economy. The Institute stresses real world analysis and a concern for the living standards of working people, and it makes its findings accessible to the general public, the media, and policy makers." Sylvia A. Allegretto is an economist working for the EPI who specializes in labor markets, income and wage inequality, and unions and collective bargaining. Andy Stettner, who focuses on unemployment insurance, is a policy analyst for the National Employment Law Project.

> This piece, written by think tank researchers and analysts, is intended to be a rich source of data for policymakers and the general public and consequently is detailed. What is the gist of Allegretto and Stettner's claim about the current state of jobs and unemployment in the United States?

1   Long-term unemployment—when unemployed workers have been seeking work for six months or more—is the most severe form of joblessness. The consequences of extended periods of joblessness are significant: the long-term unemployed often face financial, personal, and health care hardships as well as the loss of their unemployment insurance benefits. An analysis of long-term unemployment from 2000 to 2003 (a period spanning the recession that occurred between March and November 2001) shows that the number of people without work for six months or more has risen at the extraordinarily high rate of 198.2% over this period.[1] Job seekers with college degrees and those age 45 and older have had an especially difficult time finding work, with long-term unemployment for those groups rising by 299.4% and 217.6%, respectively.

2   Since the recession ended in November 2001, elevated rates of long-term joblessness among the unemployed have persisted longer than during any similar period in the past 30 years. The long-term unemployment situation continued to worsen between 2001 and 2003 as job creation lagged. A number of important trends

emerge from the data on long-term unemployment across this time period:

• **In 2003, 22.1% of all unemployed workers had been out of work for more than six months, an increase from 18.3% in 2002.** This proportion is higher than at comparable points in the recovery periods of the four most recent recessions, and it is the highest annual rate of long-term unemployment since 1983. Despite the continued need for help beyond the regular six months of state unemployment insurance, Congress cut off federal jobless benefits in December 2003, leaving the long-term unemployed without a safety net at a time when prolonged joblessness is at its highest rate in 20 years (see Table 1).

• **College graduates represent 15.3% of total unemployment, but 19.1% of long-term unemployment.** Long-term unemployment among college-educated workers increased by 299.4% between 2000 and 2003, a much faster rate than the increase of 156.1% for workers with a high school degree or less.

TABLE 1 Percent of all unemployed out of work for more than six months

Year	Long-term unemployed	Year	Long-term unemployed
1966	8.3%	1985	15.4%
1967	5.9	1986	14.4
1968	5.5	1987	14.0
1969	4.7	1988	12.1
1970	5.8	1989	9.9
1971	10.4	1990	10.0
1972	11.6	1991	12.9
1973	7.9	1992	20.3
1974	7.4	1993	20.1
1975	15.2	1994	20.3
1976	18.2	1995	17.3
1977	14.7	1996	17.4
1978	10.5	1997	15.8
1979	8.7	1998	14.1
1980	10.7	1999	12.3
1981	14.0	2000	11.4
1982	16.6	2001	11.8
1983	23.9	2002	18.3
1984	19.1	2003	22.1

Source: Bureau of Labor Statistics.

- **While long-term unemployment hit all age and occupational groups, more experienced jobless workers had a disproportionately difficult time getting back to work in 2003.** Although job seekers age 45 and older made up 25.7% of the total unemployed population, the rate of long-term unemployment for this group was 35.4%.

- **Workers in the manufacturing industry are the largest share of the long-term unemployed (19%).** In comparison, they represent 13% of total unemployment. The ranks of long-term unemployed manufacturing workers grew by 259% from 2000 to 2003. Workers laid-off from the well-paid professional and business services sector suffered along with those in manufacturing, posting the second highest long-term unemployment share, at 14% (see Table 2).

3   In this persistent jobless recovery, anemic job creation has caused increased long-term unemployment in all employment sectors. The data indicate that the long-term jobless face significant hardship, not because they lack skills, experience, or motivation, but for a reason beyond their control—the absence of available jobs.

THE HARSH CONSEQUENCES OF A JOBLESS RECOVERY

4   The long-term unemployed face a particularly daunting array of hardships: after six months of unemployment, many workers have eroded their savings, increased their levels of family stress, and even been forced to move out of their homes. Simply put, unemployment lasting six months or more is a prolonged burden on job seekers that detrimentally affects all areas of life, even more so than short spells of joblessness. While the prospect of any period of unemployment is disconcerting for many workers, the threat of long-term unemployment during the current economy's failure to generate the necessary number of jobs has elevated anxiety levels among U.S. workers.

5   In 2001 alone, at a time when the United States was in the midst of a recession, the economy lost about 1.8 million jobs. The subsequent recovery period that began in November 2001 has been referred to as a "jobless" recovery because the decline in payroll jobs continued throughout 2002 (−563,000) and 2003 (−53,000). A close examination of the long-term unemployed reveals the casualties of the jobless recovery in 2003. . . .

6   In January 2004, 22.7% of the unemployed were out of work for more than six months, higher than at other comparable points 26 months after the official end of recent recessions; previous rates of long-term unemployment had hit 19.6% in May 1993, 15.5% in January 1985, and 15.6% in May 1977. Thus, long-term unemployment has persisted longer in this post-recessionary period than

TABLE 2 Composition of long-term unemployment in 2003

	Share of total unemployed	Share of all long-term unemployed	Difference
ALL GROUPS	100.00%	100.00%	
EDUCATION			
High school or less	59.7%	55.6%	−4.1%
Some college	25.0	25.4	0.4
Bachelor's degree	15.3	19.1	3.8
AGE			
16–24	31.3%	19.3%	−12.0%
25–44	43.0	45.3	2.3
45+	25.7	35.4	9.7
OCCUPATION			
Construction and extraction	9.3%	6.8%	−2.5%
Management, business, and financial	7.2	9.9	2.7
Office and administrative support	12.3	13.5	1.2
Production	9.2	11.6	2.4
Professional and related	10.6	12.2	1.6
Sales and related	11.3	10.2	−1.1
Service	19.2	15.2	−4.0
Transportation and material moving	8.5	8.5	0.0
Other[a]	12.4	12.1	−0.3
INDUSTRY			
Construction	10.2%	7.7%	−2.5%
Educational and health services	10.6	9.0	−1.6
Financial activities	3.8	4.7	0.9
Information	3.0	4.2	1.2
Leisure and hospitality	12.2	8.9	−3.3
Manufacturing	13.4	19.0	5.6
Professional and business services	12.8	14.4	1.6
Transportation and utilities	3.7	3.9	0.2
Wholesale and retail trade	14.5	13.9	−0.6
Other[b]	15.8	14.3	−1.5
GENDER			
Women	44.1%	41.4%	−2.7%
Men	55.9	58.6	2.7
RACE			
Black	19.6%	24.5%	4.9%
Hispanic	16.4	12.2	−4.2
White	56.9	54.9	−2.0
Other	7.0	8.4	1.4

[a] Other occupations include: farming, fishing, and forestry; installation, maintenance, and repair; and armed forces.
[b] Other industries include: agriculture, forestry, fishing, and hunting; mining; other industries and services; and public administration.

Source: Author's analysis of *Current Population Survey*, 2003.

during any similar period in the past 30 years. This unprecedented level of long-term unemployment is the human consequence of the nation's job woes.

TRACKING THE RISE OF LONG-TERM UNEMPLOYMENT IN THE JOBLESS RECOVERY

7   From 2000 to 2003, long-term unemployment increased from 649,119 to more than 1.9 million, a staggering 198.2% increase (see Table 3). Across 2002 and 2003 alone, long-term unemployment swelled by 26.1%, reflecting a high level of long-term unemployment that persisted longer than in any of the three prior recovery periods. In 2000, long-term unemployment accounted for 11.4% of all unemployment. That percentage nearly doubled in 2003 to 22.1%. By 2003, long-term unemployment—measured as a proportion of all jobless workers—was higher than in any year since 1983, when long-term unemployment averaged 23.9%.

8   An analysis of microdata from the *Current Population Survey*, which is used to calculate the official unemployment numbers, illustrates the characteristics of workers who were more likely to find themselves among the ranks of the long-term unemployed in 2003. Comparing the share of long-term unemployed to the share of the total unemployed (Table 2, columns 1 and 2) indicates which subgroups of jobless workers are over-represented among the long-term unemployed. In other words, subgroups of unemployed workers that are over-represented are likely to find themselves unemployed for a period of six months or more, whereas subgroups that are under-represented as a share of the long-term unemployed are likely to be unemployed for shorter periods of time. The numbers in the third column of Table 2 indicate whether a subgroup's share of long-term unemployment is over-represented (a positive number) or under-represented (a negative number) compared to its share of total unemployment. For example, within occupational groups, service occupations are 19.2% of the total unemployed, but only 15.2% of long-term unemployed. Therefore, unemployed workers from service occupations are under-represented as a share of the long-term unemployed. Unemployed persons from management, business and financial occupations, on the other hand, are over-represented as a share of long-term unemployed (9.9%) as compared to their share of total unemployment (7.2%).

HIGHLY EDUCATED AND EXPERIENCED WORKERS ARE INCREASINGLY THE VICTIMS OF UNEMPLOYMENT

9   Perhaps the most striking conclusion shown in Table 2 is that the most educated, well-paid, and experienced workers are not insulated from the consequences of this prolonged weak labor market.

TABLE 3 Long-term unemployment growth, 2000–03

	2000 totals	2003 totals	Percent change, 2000 to 2003
ALL GROUPS	649,119	1,935,814	198.2%
EDUCATION			
High school or less	420,002	1,075,552	156.1%
Some college	136,698	491,146	259.3
Bachelor's degree or higher	92,418	369,115	299.4
AGE			
16–24	153,219	374,065	144.1%
25–44	280,085	876,362	212.9
45+	215,815	685,387	217.6
OCCUPATION			
Construction and extraction	46,147	130,774	183.4%
Management, business, financial	47,090	192,369	308.5
Office and administrative support	91,804	261,922	185.3
Production	81,647	224,619	175.1
Professional and related	53,922	236,800	339.2
Sales and related	59,549	197,196	231.1
Service	127,746	295,175	131.1
Transportation and material moving	58,728	163,637	176.6
INDUSTRY			
Construction	51,605	149,895	190.5%
Educational and health services	66,542	173,562	160.8
Financial activities	32,875	91,028	176.9
Information	17,990	81,601	353.6
Leisure and hospitality	72,058	172,042	138.8
Manufacturing	102,311	367,323	259.0
Professional and business services	72,103	277,844	285.3
Transportation and utilities	28,848	75,716	162.5
Wholesale and retail trade	83,486	268,470	221.6
GENDER			
Women	287,558	801,811	178.8%
Men	361,561	1,134,002	213.6
RACE			
Black	181,407	475,229	162.0%
Hispanic	116,054	235,402	102.8
White	309,100	1,063,284	244.0
Other	42,557	161,898	280.4

Source: Author's analysis of *Current Population Survey* data. Selected subgroups sums do not necessarily equal overall totals.

These data illuminate the nature of the current economic situation—sluggish job creation is keeping workers of all ages, education levels, and occupations from contributing to the U.S. economy.

• **Age**: The nation's most experienced workers were hit disproportionately hard by long-term unemployment in 2003. Workers age 45 and older represented more than one-third of all the long-term jobless (35%) but only one-quarter of the total unemployed. The 9.7% discrepancy between older workers' share of total and long-term unemployment is the largest of any subgroup in Table 2. This suggests that companies may be averse to investing in experienced older workers, presumably in an attempt to keep labor costs low.

• **Education**: Although they are less likely to be laid-off in the first place, educated unemployed workers encountered more trouble re-entering the labor force, with the impact most dramatic on workers who have a bachelor's degree or more. A full 19.1% of all long-term jobless were four-year college graduates, compared to just 15.3% of all unemployed workers. This 3.8% over-representation in the ranks of the long-term unemployed is more than all other educational groups (see Table 2, column 3). However, workers at all education levels saw an increase in long-term unemployment of more than 100% between 2000 and 2003: prolonged joblessness rose by 156% among workers with a high school degree or less, 259% among workers with some college education, and 299% among four-year college graduates.

• **Occupation**: As shown in Table 3, the number of long-term unemployed grew faster among high-salary occupational groups—such as management, business, and financial occupations (308%) and professional occupations (339%)—than among service occupations (131%) or office and administrative support (185%). Additionally, blue-collar production occupations show disproportionately high shares of long-term unemployment (see Table 2, column 3).

MANUFACTURING INDUSTRY IS PARTICULARLY HARD HIT

10 The United States has been losing manufacturing jobs for 43 straight months. Long-term unemployment in this sector increased by 259%, far exceeding industries such as leisure and hospitality, educational and health services, and construction (Table 3, column 3). With this growth in the jobless rate of the manufacturing industry, workers laid off from manufacturing jobs represented the largest share of the long-term unemployed (19.1%), although they comprised only 13.4% of the total unemployed. Lower-paying industries, however, were more likely to be under-represented as a share of the long-term unemployed. For example, the retail industry (combined with intermediate wholesalers) was the industry with

the largest share of the nation's jobless in 2003, but represented only the third largest share of the long-term unemployed.

11   With an average hourly wage of $15.81 in January 2004, the manufacturing industry provides better-paying opportunities than other industries to workers without a college degree. With some jobs permanently lost through trade and job growth slowing as companies delay investment or new production, more and more of these well-paid workers have found themselves without jobs for long periods of time.

12   Other industries have also been hit hard, as demonstrated by sustained long-term unemployment. In the information industry, there was a 354% increase in long-term unemployment. The second largest increase in long-term unemployment was for the professional and business industry (285%). The weak recovery has invaded every industrial sector, not only hurting the blue-collar industries that have traditionally suffered unemployment woes, but also leading to widespread joblessness among white-collar workers.

13   Workers in industries that had not been as affected by long-term unemployment through 2002 experienced significant increases in joblessness in 2003. For instance, long-term unemployment grew faster among workers from the educational and health services field (33%) than any other industry, as jobs in this sector fell victim to state and local budget cuts. Conversely, growth in long-term unemployment among workers laid off from manufacturing jobs slowed in 2003 as compared to 2000 through 2002. Due to the persistent job losses in high-tech industries, long-term unemployment in the information industry (30%) continued to grow faster than the national average of 26% (see Table 4).

LONG-TERM UNEMPLOYMENT IN 2003: THE GENDER AND RACE STORY

• **Gender**: With the male-dominated manufacturing industry hit hard by unemployment, it is not surprising that men are more susceptible to long-term joblessness. However, the gender gap was narrower in 2003 than at a similar point during the last job slump in the early 1990s. In 1992, women represented 35.7% of all of the long-term jobless and 42.5% of the total unemployed, indicating an under-representation of –6.8%. By 2003, women made up 41.4% of the long-term unemployed, but represented 44.1% of the total unemployed; while women were still under-represented as a share of the jobless population, this difference (2.7%) was much smaller than in previous years (see Table 2). Increasingly, long-term unemployment is a problem for women.

• **Race**: Both black and Asian workers experienced above average long-term unemployment in 2003. Black workers are significantly

TABLE 4 Long-term unemployment growth among selected groups, 2002–03

	Percent change, 2002 to 2003
ALL GROUPS	26.1%
EDUCATION	
High school or less	24.2%
Some college	25.9
Bachelor's degree or higher	32.5
AGE	
16–24	23.5%
25–44	26.4
45+	27.2
OCCUPATION	
Construction and extraction	20.1%
Management, business, and financial	14.3
Office and administrative support	12.2
Production	14.3
Professional and related	38.3
Sales and related	21.0
Service	31.0
Transportation and material moving	40.9
INDUSTRY	
Construction	23.6%
Educational and health services	32.6
Financial activities	24.2
Information	30.0
Leisure and hospitality	23.4
Manufacturing	25.2
Professional and business services	29.6
Transportation and utilities	11.0
Wholesale and retail trade	16.8
GENDER	
Female	20.5%
Male	30.4
RACE	
Black	28.2%
Hispanic	23.2
White	22.8
Other	50.7

Source: Author's analysis of *Current Population Survey*, 2003. Selected subgroups sums do not necessarily equal overall totals.

over-represented among both the long-term and total unemployed. Similar to other periods of economic decline, black workers have been harmed more than other racial groups.

POLICY AND LABOR MARKET IMPLICATIONS OF LONG-TERM JOBLESSNESS

14   In 2002 and 2003, college graduates, workers age 45 and older, and workers in the information and manufacturing sectors entered the ranks of the long-term unemployed at alarming rates; however, no industry or demographic group has escaped the effects of the jobless recovery. Large numbers of workers will likely not return to their previous jobs. Many companies have either reorganized production to make do with a smaller workforce or made arrangements with foreign contractors to accomplish the tasks previously done by workers in the United States. The prevalence of long-term unemployment among skilled and educated workers indicates that no group is immune from the devastating impact of this shift in business practices as the labor market responds to the lack of job growth.

15   Although the effects of the jobless recovery can be seen in nearly every industry, age, and education group, in December 2003, Congress allowed the federal extension of unemployment benefits to expire. Until that point, the Temporary Extended Unemployment Compensation (TEUC) program had provided additional unemployment benefits to those workers who had been out of work for more than six months and had thus exhausted their regular state unemployment insurance benefits. With long-term unemployment continuing to grow through the end of 2003 and persisting longer than in any recovery period in the last 30 years, there is a clear need to continue these federal benefits.

16   The characteristics of the long-term unemployed and the causes of the severe jobless rates were discussed during the debate in Congress over whether to extend TEUC. Some members of Congress argued that the long-term unemployed needed "tough love"—i.e., if their benefits were cut off they would be forced back to work. However, the data presented here strongly refute this point. The long-term unemployed have a proven record of job experience and a strong attachment to the labor market. But with only one job for every three unemployed workers, finding a job in this economy is unusually difficult. Unemployment benefits average just $265 per week and replace less than half of the average worker's prior salary. Therefore, workers accustomed to relatively high wages are unlikely to find unemployment insurance benefits generous. Rather, such benefits are a modest source of income support that these workers (and all long-term unemployed) need when the job market cannot deliver.

The National Employment Law project is a national advocacy organization for the unemployed and the working poor. NELP can be contacted at 55 John St., 7th Floor, New York, NY, 10038, (212) 285-3025. or at www.nelp.org.

Endnote

1. This time period includes the recession from March 2001 to November 2001, and a pre- and a post-recessionary period. The post-recessionary period extends two years after the economy officially moved from recession to recovery in November 2001.

For Class Discussion

1. How do Sylvia Allegretto and Andy Stettner challenge the economic theories that praise the current growth of the American economy and that claim that offshore outsourcing is good for our economy? Where do the Economic Policy Institute economists differ from conservative economists in their facts, interpretation of facts, and values?

2. Daniel W. Drezner asserts in "The Outsourcing Bogeyman" that Americans are overreacting to alarmist examples and discussions of offshore outsourcing as the cause of job loss for Americans. How do Allegretto and Stettner refute his views? What would Drezner say in response?

3. In accordance with their purpose to educate the public, Allegretto and Stettner have made a rhetorical choice to build their argument on statistics and tables. How well do the authors' use of statistics convey their authority, enhance their credibility, or drive home their points? Where have the authors clearly interpreted their data and incorporated it into their argument?

4. If you were going to write an op-ed piece for your local or university newspaper about long-term unemployment, what conclusions would you draw from the article's tables and how would you use these data in your piece?

5. How well does this article fulfill the goals presented in the Economic Policy Institute mission statement quoted in the introduction to this article? How has this article influenced your view of current unemployment in the United States?

6. This article focuses mainly on arguing for the seriousness of a problem. What, if any, solutions do Allegretto and Stettner propose? ■

Cover of *Wired* Magazine

Wired magazine is a mainstream publication that offers wide coverage of popular Internet, science, and technology topics and in-depth analyses as well as brief news reports and reviews. Its features and advertisements are known for their slick, attractive design. The February 2004 cover of *Wired* magazine provoked enormous controversy, especially within the information technology community in the United States and in India. The editor of

Wired, Chris Anderson (who also wrote an article in the February 2004 edition entitled "Why Coders and Call Centers Are Just the Beginning"), described readers' powerful response to the February cover and articles saying, "Of the record 1,000-plus letters we received, 80% expressed 'concern' about outsourcing," and "February may have been our best newsstand issue ever . . . I am happy that we stimulated debate, and this will continue" (from the March 15, 2004 *Media Industry Newsletter*).

> How do the image and writing on this magazine cover differ from the way you might expect the issue of outsourcing computer technology jobs to India to be presented? What contradictory messages does this cover send?

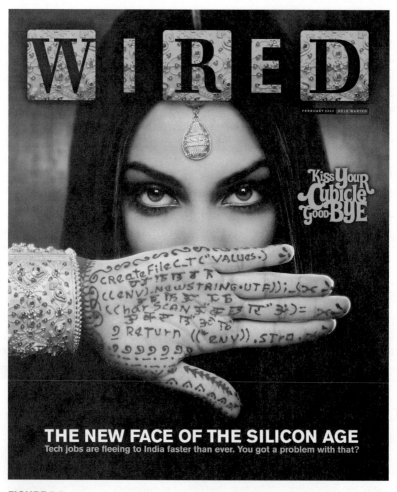

FIGURE 3.2 Cover of *Wired* Magazine *(Cover art by Ian White. © 2004 Condé Nast Publications, Inc. All rights reserved)*

For Class Discussion

1. What stands out the most about the image of the woman? What appears on her hand and what is the intended cultural reference? What is the typestyle of the phrase "Kiss Your Cubicle Good-Bye"? What 1960s associations does that typestyle have?

2. Some commentators have called the woman who appears on this cover "a Bollywood image"; in other words, she looks like an Indian movie star and not a computer programmer. What other conflicting or problematic messages does this cover send?

3. Some Indians writing on DialogNow, an online discussion community founded as a forum for conversations in South Asia, accused this cover of being "deliberately grabby," of being racist and fanning prejudice, and of "scapegoating Indians." One person wrote, "I think it's very troubling that people are getting away with blaming an entire country when it is the decisions of top managers that are the cause." What visual features of this cover support these criticisms? How does this cover promote global competition for jobs?

4. American Information Technology professionals responded angrily to this cover and the articles, some even canceling their subscriptions to *Wired*. What makes the text on this cover offensive to Americans?

5. How does this cover suggest that American workers should respond to offshore outsourcing?

6. Do you agree with *Wired* editor Chris Anderson that this cover makes a worthwhile contribution to the public dialogue about outsourcing?

Protect Workers' Rights
Bruce Raynor

This editorial was first published in *The Washington Post* on September 1, 2003. *The Washington Post* is known for its excellent, hard-hitting, and detailed coverage of national and international issues and for its widely respected columnists. Bruce Raynor is the president of UNITE, a union of 250,000 apparel, textile, laundry, and distribution workers.

> How does Bruce Raynor expose crucial differences in the way that economic prosperity is measured and explain why these differences are important to his general readership and all Americans?

1   This summer Pillowtex Corp., successor to the century-old firm Fieldcrest Cannon, the largest unionized textile company in the country, closed its 16 textile plants and let go almost 6,500 employees

in 10 states. In North Carolina, where the largest plants were located, it was the single biggest layoff in state history.

2   Pillowtex is only one of hundreds of textile mills that have closed in the past several years. For me, the Pillowtex shutdown was especially painful because for 20 years I was involved in efforts to organize a union there. In 1999 the workers finally succeeded. These workers overcame illegal threats, harassment and attempts to racially divide the workers. But the hardest-working, most dedicated workers in the world could not overcome a government policy that believes open markets and expanded trade, whatever the cost, are always justified. Problem is, the costs keep rising and the benefits never seem to trickle down.

3   The workers are now desperate. They received no severance payments. Their health insurance is gone. Mortgages, car payments and taxes aren't being paid. Kannapolis, N.C., where Pillowtex is located, has always been a textile town. There are no other jobs available. And while the union is still trying to find a buyer for the company, the local government's response for economic development is to buy an ad in USA Today or the Wall Street Journal asking Bill Gates, Oprah Winfrey or Warren Buffett to consider moving some of their business operations to Kannapolis.

4   What happened to Pillowtex workers is illustrative of destructive trends that threaten American prosperity and, indeed, the global economy.

5   Every manufacturing industry in the United States—apparel, textiles, metals, paper, electronics—has lost jobs in the past year. Over the past 36 months manufacturing employment has declined by 2.7 million. This is the longest decline since the Great Depression. The job crisis is not only in manufacturing. Since the economic recovery began, more than a million jobs have disappeared. Apparently the economy is doing well. Only workers are suffering.

6   The usual response of policymakers to manufacturing workers who have lost their jobs is to preach the virtues of education. Workers are told that if they would only acquire new skills, they would qualify for white-collar service jobs that are safe from the economic forces that have shifted millions of factory jobs to foreign countries. Perhaps that was once true.

7   Today white-collar jobs—telemarketing, accounting, claims adjusting, home loan processing, architectural practices, radiographers and even some state and local government jobs—are going offshore. In a survey of the world's 100 largest financial services firms, Deloitte Research found that these companies expect to shift $356 billion worth of operations and about 2 million jobs to low-wage countries over the next five years. These developments appear already to be affecting wages in some sectors. According to

Sharon Marsh Roberts of the Independent Computer Consultants Association, outsourcing has forced down hourly wage rates by 10 percent to 40 percent for many U.S. computer consultants.

8   These trends also affect workers in developing countries. For example, since January 2000, 520 manufacturing plants have closed in Mexico, most of them moving to China. And in 2005, when all apparel and textile quotas are to be lifted, developing countries around the globe will be faced with a massive loss of jobs as the industry moves into China. For example, a United Nations study predicts that Bangladesh will lose 1 million apparel jobs when quotas are abolished. Many other countries in Africa, Asia, the Caribbean and Eastern Europe, where the apparel industry is the largest employer, will also suffer huge job losses when quotas are lifted.

9   As low as wages are in many developing countries, they can't compete with the pennies an hour paid in China. China scholar Anita Chan describes how different regions in China seek to maintain their attractiveness to foreign capital by lowering minimum wages and not enforcing labor regulations and health and safety laws. According to Chan, "though employment in the low-wage industries in China may be expanding, the wages of the workers in these industries are not rising, and for many of them have been falling." The benefits of globalization, Chan warns, "will not trickle down to those who make products."

10   So it turns out that workers in Kannapolis, N.C., Silicon Valley, Calif.; Juarez, Mexico, and Guangdong, China, have much in common. It is becoming increasingly clear that when wages and conditions of work are undercut in one part of the globe they will eventually be cut in others as well.

11   The downward spiral of lower wages and worsening working conditions is fueling popular skepticism over globalization. A prosperous economy requires that workers be able to buy the products that they produce. That means we need rules for the global economy that protect workers' rights—and not just in China—we also need [them] in the United States.

For Class Discussion

1. How does Raynor connect specific local sites in the United States to global sites?

2. How does Raynor both enlarge and deepen the arguments against unregulated free trade and the moving of American jobs abroad?

3. For what solution to the condition and status of workers does Raynor's argument lay the foundation?

4. What is the tone of Raynor's argument? How does it contribute to the persuasiveness of his argument? ■

Our Do-It-Yourself Economy
Ellen Goodman

Ellen Goodman is a renowned columnist for the *Boston Globe* who is syndicated by the Washington Post Writers Group. Her columns regularly appear in over four hundred newspapers across the nation. She has won numerous awards including the Pulitzer Prize for Distinguished Commentary in 1980, and she has a number of books to her name: *Turning Points* (1979), about social change, and collections of her columns, among them *Keeping in Touch* (1985), *Making Sense* (1989), and *Value Judgments* (1993). Acclaimed for her influence on American journalism, she is a popular public lecturer, often speaking on the media's role in society and women's roles. Goodman's writing is valued for its blend of political and social commentary, cultural insight, personal warmth, and tempered liberal views. This op-ed piece appeared in the *Boston Globe* on February 5, 2004.

> In this editorial, what new perspective and insights about American jobs and the economy does Goodman add to the current national debates about outsourcing?

1   Have you seen those economists scratching their heads trying to understand the jobless recovery? Every time they run the numbers they end up with a question mark: How is it possible that only 1,000 new jobs were created in the past month?

2   Well, maybe it's time we let them in on our little secret. The economy has created hundreds of thousands of new jobs. Only they aren't in the manufacturing sector. They aren't even in the service economy. They're in the self-service economy.

3   Companies are coming back to life without inviting employees back to work for one simple reason: They are outsourcing the jobs to us. You and I, my fellow Americans, have become the unpaid laborers of a do-it-yourself economy.

4   It all began benignly enough a generation ago when ATMs replaced bank tellers. The average American child may know that money doesn't grow on trees; it grows out of walls.

5   The ATM followed the self-service gas station. At first in the classic bait and switch, we were offered a discount for being our own gas jockey; now we have to pay a premium to have a person fill 'er up.

6   Now gradually, we are scanning our own groceries at the supermarket, getting our own boarding passes at airport kiosks and picking up movie tickets from machines that don't call in sick, go on vacation, or require a pension.

7   People who used to have secretaries now have Microsoft Word. People who used to have travel agents now have the Internet.

People who used to drop off their film to be developed have been lured into buying new cameras for the joy of printing or not printing pictures ourselves.

8   We also serve (ourselves) by being required to wait longer for the incredible shrinking support system. When was the last time you called your health plan? The service consists of a hold button, a list of phone options, and the strategic corporate decision that sooner or later a percentage of us will give up.

9   Remember 411? If you actually want information from a phone company today, you have to pay someone in Omaha to give you the new number of a neighbor in Albany.

10   If the phone breaks, you may have to dial fix-it-yourself. A new chapter in the annals of the self-service economy comes from a friend who was told by Verizon to go find the gray box attached to her house and test the line herself. The e-mail instructions told her merrily: "You don't have to be a telephone technician or an electrical engineer." Next year they'll be telling her to climb the telephone pole.

11   Then of course there is the world of computers. We have all become our own techie. A Harvard Business School professor actually told a reporter recently that we fix them ourselves because: "There's a real love of technology and people want to get inside and tinker with them." My friends have as much of a desire to tinker with computer insides as to perform amateur appendectomies.

12   But tech support has become less reliable than child support checks from an ex-husband. Consumer Reports show that 8 million people a year contact the tech support lines at software companies, and one-third of them don't get any help. These same companies have laid off more than 30,000 support workers and replaced them with messages telling us to fix our "infrastructure migration" by performing an "ipconfig/release" and "ipconfig/renew."

13   As for online help? If my Web server was managing 911, I would still be on the floor somewhere gasping for breath. The only part of the self-help economy that keeps us aloft is a battery of teenagers fed and housed solely because they can get the family system back up.

14   Oh, and if we finally find someone to perform a so-called service call, we end up with an alleged appointment for that convenient hour known as "when the cows come home."

15   I don't know how much labor has been transferred from the paid to the unpaid economy, but the average American now spends an extraordinary amount of time doing work that once paid someone else's mortgage. The only good news is that the corporations can't export the self-help industry to Bombay. Or maybe that's the bad news.

16   People, actual human beings who work and interact, are now a luxury item. The rest of us have been dragooned into an invisible unpaid labor force without even noticing. We scan, we surf, we fix, and we rant. To which I can only add the motto of the do-it-yourself economy: Help!

For Class Discussion

1. What group of readers among her large general audience do you think Goodman specifically has in mind? Why?

2. What is Goodman's basic argument in this piece? How do her examples function in support of her claim?

3. Although Goodman is known for her liberal views, this piece does not focus on questioning the outsourcing of American jobs. How could the points and evidence in this piece be used to support either a libertarian, probusiness argument in favor of outsourcing or a liberal view that favors putting priority on domestic needs and better support for American workers?

4. What does humor contribute to this op-ed piece?

5. How does this piece complicate, enrich, or otherwise affect your understanding of the controversy over outsourcing?   ■

Interview with New Jersey State Senator Shirley Turner

Lisa Vaas

This interview with State Senator Shirley Turner of New Jersey appeared on the online source eWeek March 24, 2003. Recently, Senator Turner has gained notoriety as a vocal opponent of the practice of states' outsourcing their government jobs. Turner's bill, which follows this interview, resembles much of the proposed legislation currently under consideration by state governments as well as the federal government. ("IT" in this interview refers to information technology, a white-collar field that has been deeply affected by offshore outsourcing.)

Protectionism has been used by free trade advocates as a bad word. How does Shirley Turner reclaim protecting American workers as a politically responsible action?

1   When New Jersey State Sen. Shirley Turner was first inspired to propose legislation banning the outsourcing of IT and other state

contracts to overseas companies, she had no clue that bill No. 1349 would incite both heated lobbying by technology groups against it and a wildfire of support from laid-off technology workers. Since its introduction in March 2002, the bill has generated more response than any other piece of legislation introduced by the Democrat from Ewing in her nine-year political career.

2   But by March 6, 2003, the day the bill was scheduled to be heard by the New Jersey Legislature's State Government Committee, technology lobbying groups such as the National Association of Software and Services Companies, an association of Indian technology companies, were ready to water it down. They proposed an amendment stating that outsourcing could occur if the work cost less to do offshore or promised improved quality offshore.

3   The lobbyists succeeded in getting the bill tabled. But they didn't succeed in persuading Turner to give up. Encouraged by an outpouring of support from IT workers, Turner said she will continue to lobby for the bill. The senator recently met with eWeek Senior Writer Lisa Vaas to talk about her rationale.

4   eWEEK: Why did you propose this bill?

5   TURNER: The work in question was a Department of Human Services contract for $326,000 a month for seven years . . . dealing with [offshore] call center agents calling recipients regarding their welfare checks.

6   You can only be on welfare a given period of time before you have to get a job. If we're telling people they have to get a job, it's incumbent on us as legislators to make sure there are jobs out there for them. We've had around a 6 percent unemployment rate in New Jersey. We have people looking for work who can't find it. I have no problem if we outsource jobs because we can't find people to do the work, but [we're talking about work] that anybody can do.

7   eWEEK: How do you answer those who say offshore outsourcing makes sense because of its low costs?

8   TURNER: Some of the people who are supportive of the special-interest groups are saying we're saving taxpayer money. We're not. . . . At the time [a given offshore company] got the bid, they were paying wages to people here in this country, at around $8 to $10 an hour. They get the contract, and then they move the operations to where they're paying $1 to $2 an hour, but we didn't get any rebate on what we're paying them.

9   It's unfair. Another company could have gotten that contract themselves. So [the offshore company] probably underbid, knowing what they were going to do. If you bid the contract here, you win it here, you should perform it here.

10 eWEEK: Your interest is in protecting jobs for U.S. IT workers. Does it then make sense to disqualify companies that employ H-1B and L1 visa holders from receiving state contracts?*

11 TURNER: If the federal government is allowing this to occur, as a state legislator, I have no control over these workers who are coming in on these visas. I could not say they're not qualified to work because the federal government is saying that they are.

12 eWEEK: How much of a security risk is posed by the act of sending sensitive consumer or business information overseas?

13 TURNER: When [overseas companies are] dealing with welfare clients, those clients' whole life history and financial informa-tion is available to the people who are making those phone calls [from overseas call centers]. From what I've been told by people who've contacted me, there are situations where they've had phone calls made by credit card companies that were being made offshore. They were concerned about [those companies] having financial information available to them. They thought it was something this government should be concerned about, what with all the acts of terrorism.

14 eWEEK: Who's writing to you?

15 TURNER: People who've been laid off because of people coming in on these special visas. Those people in the computer area who've been laid off because their jobs were outsourced to for-eign countries—China, Russia, India, the Philippines.

16 It's unbelievable. I've never gotten so much e-mail on any one issue. I had no idea what I was doing when I introduced that bill. It was so narrow in terms of what I was trying to do. Now some people want it to be a panacea for other issues as-sociated with this. Others are more realistic—they see it as a step in the right direction.

17 eWEEK: Isn't this protectionism?

18 TURNER: You're right—it is protectionism. I'm protecting jobs in this country. Our economy is in a recession. We have a deficit, just like any other state. The reason is, we don't have people work-ing and paying taxes. And those people are the ones who need the jobs. They have families to support.

---

*An HIB visa is a work visa/work permit that the Immigration Bureau requires interna-tional professionals and students to have in order to work and live legally in the United States. HIB visas pertain to specialty occupations such as computing and Information Technology, health care, finance, accounting, sales, teaching, advertising, and engineer-ing, among other professions. These visas enable the foreigner to work in the United States for six years and to apply for a Green Card (permanent residency). An L1 visa enables companies in the United States and abroad to transfer their foreign managers, executives, and staff with special knowledge to U.S. branches of the companies for up to seven years.

SENATE, No. 494

STATE OF NEW JERSEY

211th LEGISLATURE

PRE-FILED FOR INTRODUCTION
IN THE 2004 SESSION

Sponsored by:
Senator SHIRLEY K. TURNER
District 15 (Mercer)
Senator JOSEPH CONIGLIO
District 38 (Bergen)

Co-Sponsored by:
Senators Palaia, Allen and Gill

SYNOPSIS

Provides that only citizens or persons authorized to work in the US pursuant to federal law may be employed in performing certain State contracts.

CURRENT VERSION OF TEXT

Introduced Pending Technical Review by Legislative Counsel.

(Sponsorship Updated As Of: 2/24/2004)

S494 TURNER, CONIGLIO

2

AN ACT concerning State contracts and supplementing chapter 34 of Title 52 of the Revised Statutes.

BE IT ENACTED *by the Senate and General Assembly of the State of New Jersey:*

1 The Director of the Division of Purchase and Property and the Director of the Division of Property Management and Construction in the Department of the Treasury shall include, in every State contract for the performance of services, provisions which specify that only citizens of the United States and persons authorized to work in the United States pursuant to federal law shall be employed in performance of services under the contract or any subcontract awarded under the contract.

2 This act shall take effect immediately.

STATEMENT

Recent published reports have indicated that telephone inquiries by welfare and food stamp clients under New Jersey's Families First Program were being handled by operators in Bombay, India, after the contractor moved its operations outside of the United States as a cost-cutting measure.

This bill directs the Director of the Division of Purchase and Property and the Director of the Division of Property Management and Construction in the Department of the Treasury to include in every State contract for the performance of services provisions which specify that only citizens of the United States and persons authorized to work in the United States pursuant to federal law may be employed in the performance of services under the contract or any subcontract awarded under the contract.

For Class Discussion

1. What reasons against sending state jobs abroad does Shirley Turner offer?

2. According to Turner, where do politics and economics intersect on this issue?

3. What perspective does Turner add to the controversy over outsourcing?

4. What formal proposal does Turner's bill make? What was the motivating occasion of this bill?

5. What is distinctive about the language and structure of a state bill?

6. How has Turner influenced your thinking about outsourcing? Is the same shipping of state government jobs abroad happening in your state? ∎

Don't Ban Outsourcing; Create Jobs

Tom Salonek

This article was published in the Minneapolis *Star Tribune* on March 22, 2004. Tom Salonek speaks as an owner of technology-related companies and articulates why companies like his need to outsource their work to survive.

> How does Salonek explain the trends and causes that have led him and other business owners and top-level executives to choose to outsource parts of their companies?

1   It must be an election year. How else to account for all the recently introduced legislation, in Minnesota and elsewhere, designed to keep U.S. jobs from being outsourced to companies overseas that can do the work for considerably less than their American counterparts?

2   With more than 3.3 million U.S. jobs projected to leave the country during the next decade, this is an issue affecting many worried voters. The temptation to offer seemingly simple legislative solutions must be overwhelming to politicians—particularly those trying to hold onto their own jobs.

3   There's only one problem with legislative solutions: They won't work. As the owner of two technology-related companies in Minnesota, I can tell you first-hand that the pressure to outsource work overseas is strong and growing. I wish it weren't the case. As a card-carrying American, I'd just as soon hire people in the United States to meet all of my clients' needs.

4   And, frankly, it's simpler to manage employees in the next cubicle or down the hall. It's more efficient to gather everyone into the same conference room for a quick daily meeting to check the status of projects. And it's infinitely easier to communicate with someone who speaks English and lives in the same time zone.

5   But as my father used to remind me, no honest man ever said that life—or business—is easy.

6   The much-ballyhooed global village is alive and well today. From your electronic equipment to the food you eat and the car you drive, many people from other countries have had a large hand in getting those goods to your home cheaply and in record time.

7   As much as Americans bemoan the jobs lost to outsourcing, most love shopping for bargains at Wal-Mart. It's no wonder that *Fortune* magazine just named Wal-Mart the "most admired company in America." It has created five of the 10 richest people in the world.

8   On the business side of the equation, it's no different. Stockholders want companies to keep earning higher profits every single

quarter. That's tough to do without finding ways to cut costs. Outsourcing offers a way to significantly lower business costs, from writing software code to answering call center phones. Something's got to give to keep our economic system humming.

9 I'm well aware that the legislation being suggested by Gov. Pawlenty and others around the country is aimed at protecting jobs being outsourced by government agencies. No self-respecting politician wants to say that government contracts help employ non-Americans overseas on his or her watch. But, as a nation that worships cost-cutting Wal-Mart, do we really buy into these initiatives?

COMPETITIVE ADVANTAGE

10 Unlike many, I don't believe that outsourcing is the scourge on the economic landscape that politicians are making it out to be in this election year. As a business owner, I'm committed to finding out what works for customers and doing right by my employees.

11 My company has experimented with outsourcing certain software projects. Our goal was to find a way to work with people who shared our work ethic, client philosophy and commitment to doing great work on time and within budget. We wanted to combine our employees in Eagan with workers in another country by linking them over the Internet into one lean, software-development machine capable of developing software 24 hours a day, five days a week, thanks to differences in the time zones.

12 It didn't quite work out that way. Cultural differences and communications challenges made it tough to manage the team and keep things moving smoothly. We've decided to put that initiative on hold, for now, while we work out the bugs. Competitive pressures leaves us no choice but to try again.

13 As Robin Vasan, managing director of Mayfield Fund, a venture-capital firm based in Menlo Park, Calif., notes in a recent issue of *TIME Magazine:* "Any start-up today, particularly a software company, that does not have an outsourcing strategy is at a competitive disadvantage."

14 It's the same story for small companies and big companies, too. The larger companies, such as Dell, are blazing the trail to find ways to make outsourcing work. They have developed different levels of support, based on the size of their customers. Higher-end customers—those that spend in the thousands, not the hundreds—automatically receive access to customer support centers based in the United States. Those customers pay more and must keep their operations running smoothly. Conversely, smaller customers enjoy lower costs on computers but must make do with offshore customer support.

15   Instead of turning outsourcing into a lose-lose political football, our leaders should get out of the way and let the market sort out the pros and cons. Instead of pointing fingers at the North American Free Trade Agreement (NAFTA), which the Labor Department estimates was responsible for the loss of more than 500,000 U.S. jobs between 1994 and 2002, we should be looking for ways to expand new businesses and encourage innovation at home.

16   For good or ill, we live in a global village. Pretending otherwise is an exercise in futility. Forcing businesses, or government agencies for that matter, to ignore competitive pressures and pay higher costs of doing business will only further hobble our economy.

For Class Discussion

1. What reasons does Salonek give against offshore outsourcing? How does recognizing these views enhance his credibility and persuasiveness?

2. How does Salonek put some of the pressure to send jobs abroad on American consumers?

3. What is Salonek's proposed solution to the current economic crisis over jobs and outsourcing?

4. What does Salonek add to your understanding of this controversy?

■

Supermart Tennis Shoes
Henry Payne

Henry Payne is a well-known conservative cartoonist and journalist. This cartoon (p. 120) appeared on the Reasononline Web site (www.reason .com/hod/cartoon.hp091903.shtml) on September 19, 2003. Reasononline is a libertarian publication, forthrightly promoting free trade.

What are the key economic ideas behind the scenario that this cartoon portrays?

For Class Discussion

1. What dimension of the pro-outsourcing perspective does this cartoon draw on? Which of the readings in this chapter could this cartoon accompany or illustrate?

2. How does the cartoon employ exaggeration to convey its claim?

3. How would you go about finding out how much tennis shoes would cost if they were made in the United States?

"THANK GOODNESS CONGRESS PASSED LEGISLATION PREVENTING MANUFACTURING JOBS FROM GOING TO CHEAP, OVERSEAS LABOR.... THAT'LL BE $1,599.99 FOR THE TENNIS SHOES."

FIGURE 3.3 Supermart Tennis Shoes *(Henry Payne: © DetroitNews/Dist. By United Feature Syndicate)*

4. Would you say that this cartoon appeals the most to an audience who agrees with the economic views underlying it, a neutral audience, or a resisting audience? Why?

5. If you have read the articles in Chapter 2 on consumerism and sweatshops, what relationships do you see among this cartoon and those readings?

CHAPTER QUESTIONS FOR REFLECTION AND DISCUSSION

1. Having read the articles in this chapter, in what direct and indirect ways do you think that the offshore outsourcing issue might affect you or your family in the future?

2. In what ways has offshore outsourcing touched your region of the country, your city, and your community? What companies have moved, what factories have closed, or what businesses have laid off employees? How do you know that offshore outsourcing was involved?

3. Using the visual and print arguments in this chapter, sort out the multi-sided perspectives on the trading of jobs in our global economy by stating the main claim of each of the following stakeholders and listing at least three major reasons in support of their claims:

   - American factory workers who have lost their jobs
   - Factory workers in Mexico who might lose their jobs to lower-wage workers in China
   - American computer programmers concerned about losing their jobs
   - College students preparing for careers
   - Newly hired computer software workers in India
   - American consumers looking for good prices on computer equipment or the latest fashions in clothing
   - American businesses investigating an offshore outsourcing location for part of their companies

4. Which of the articles in this chapter do you think makes the most compelling argument in favor of offshore outsourcing and why?

5. As with many issues, advocates tend to frame the issue in extreme or simplified terms. For instance, the main options for the United States on trading jobs seem to be for American companies to have unlimited freedom to conduct business as they see fit or for the government to intervene in the private sector and put restrictions on the American jobs that are allowed to be moved out of the country. Stated in economic terms, the options become an unregulated free market allowed to grow, self-adjust, and create new jobs versus protectionism with the government subsidizing various organizations and industries. However, some of the readings in this chapter suggest that there might be some alternatives or intermediate possibilities that would have widespread benefits. What alternatives emerge from these articles? What compromise policies or approaches to outsourcing can you imagine?

6. Some additional views that the readings in this chapter did not develop are these: by a current policy of minimal taxation on big corporations, the U.S. government is already providing subsidies to big businesses; and other countries outsource some of their work to the United States, as seen in foreign firms such as Honda Motors, DaimlerChrysler, and Matsushita Electrical Industrial Corp, which employ Americans here in the States. How would these two views factor into the national debate? From your reading outside class and your awareness of the news, can you add any other views that should be included in the national discussion?

7. Investigate your prospective career and the jobs currently available. How has this career been affected by offshore outsourcing? How might it be affected in the future?

WRITING ASSIGNMENTS

Brief Writing Assignments

1. Write a brief narrative in which you describe how a personal experience has helped you understand offshore outsourcing. For example, have you ever had your call to a business or to a helpline (about a bill, your credit, a computer malfunction, or some other customer issue) be answered by a call center in another country? Has any local business or manufacturing plant moved from your community or state to another country? If so, what public statements has this company made to explain its outsourcing decision? Have you seen any big changes first-hand in your prospective profession as a result of offshore outsourcing?

2. Explain in a short piece of writing which reading in this chapter gave you the most insight into the forces driving offshore outsourcing, into its problems, or into its benefits, or explain which reading is the most compelling argument and why.

3. Choose one of the following claims and write informally for twenty minutes supporting or contesting this claim. Try to incorporate examples from your reading, personal experience, and knowledge to provide evidence to support your views.

   A. Offshore outsourcing is best understood as a national problem that the U.S. government and businesses should try to solve.

   B. Offshore outsourcing is a problem for only certain occupations.

   C. American consumers are a main force driving offshore outsourcing.

   D. Corporations' pursuit of profits is a main force driving offshore outsourcing.

   E. For political, economic, and social justice reasons, U.S. citizens should be willing to share the benefits of steady jobs with citizens of developing countries.

4. If you were to write your own researched policy proposal on trading jobs, what questions would you want to research? What ideas in this chapter's readings would you use as departure points?

5. If you have read Chapter 2, "Consumerism, Free Trade, and Sweatshops," explain in your own words the connections you see among the issues of that chapter and the outsourcing of jobs.

Writing Projects

1. New Jersey State Senator Shirley Turner said in her interview that she has received more e-mail about the offshore outsourcing of state jobs than about any other previous issue. Write a letter to one of your legislators in which you state your informed view on the issue of government regulation of offshore outsourcing. Use the arguments and evidence from the articles in this chapter to support your own position.

You could argue any of the following positions or your own modification of them:

A. Argue that the federal or your state government should take measures to protect jobs for Americans.

B. Argue that the federal or your state government should not intervene in corporations' business and should instead let these corporations restructure themselves and create new jobs, as economists claim they will.

C. Argue that the federal or your state government should not install protectionist measures but should aid workers with better unemployment insurance or stronger retraining programs.

D. Argue that the federal or your state government should mandate that private corporations improve the way they treat workers who have lost their jobs by providing more financial aid and more help in finding new jobs.

2. Choose one of the articles in this chapter to analyze for rhetorical features and content. Summarize the article in a few sentences in your own words. Then analyze the rhetorical strategies that the author employs such as the explicitness or implicitness of the author's main claim; the author's assumptions about his/her audience and the author's beliefs or values; the kinds of evidence used (statistics, personal experience, a range of examples); the author's acknowledgment of and response to opposing views; and the formality or informality of the author's language. Analyze the content of the argument by discussing what contribution you think this piece makes to the public dialogue over outsourcing.

3. Write a comparative analysis of two articles in this chapter that present very different arguments on the U.S. outsourcing of jobs to other countries. In your comparative analysis, examine similarities and differences in how each author frames the issue in his or her thesis (which might be stated or implied); what kinds of evidence each author uses to support his or her view (facts, numerical data, personal experience, information from interviews or sources, and so forth); and what values and assumptions underlie each author's views. In your conclusion, either (a) discuss the limitations of each author's approach to the offshore outsourcing issue; or (b) discuss which article you find most persuasive, explaining how it has shaped your understanding of the outsourcing controversy.

4. Use ideas and information from the articles in this chapter to agree or disagree with Daniel W. Drezner's and the economists' claim that "Americans should not be concerned about the economic effects of outsourcing."

5. Many advocacy Web sites and policy institutes with online forums are contributing their views to the public controversy about trading jobs.

Choose one of the organizations below, and then choose one of the following writing options:

A. Write an analysis of the organization's position on the offshore outsourcing controversy: What are the organization's aims? What are the values espoused by this organization? What assumptions underlie its views? What contribution does this organization make to the public understanding of the issue?

B. Write an interpretive argument in which you praise or criticize this organization for its views on the trading jobs issue. You might consider the clarity of its main claims, the quality—sufficiency, accuracy, or relevance—of its use of evidence, and its appeal to readers.

- The Organization for the Rights of American Workers [T.O.R.A.W.] (www.toraw.org/) [Examine their theme song "Mad in America"]
- Economic Policy Institute (www.epinet.org/)
- Information Technology Association of America: Workforce & Education (www.itaa.org/workforce/index.cfm)
- McKinsey Global Institute (www.mckinsey.com)
- Institute for International Economics (www.iie.com/)
- Rescue American Jobs: American Jobs for Americans (www .rescueamericanjobs.org/)*

---

*You could also consult one of the many advocacy organizations that campaign to end exploitation of workers in sweatshops in the United States and around the world. Chapter 2 on consumerism and free trade explores issues concerning factory workers in the global economy, and some readings in Chapter 4 discuss connections between low wages, the scarcity of American jobs, and U.S. immigration policies.

CHAPTER 4

Crossing Borders
Immigration

QUESTION TO PONDER

One of the many editorials written in response to President George W. Bush's 2004 proposal for managing illegal immigrants asserts that Americans "pay the lowest prices for agricultural products in any industrialized nation in the world" because our produce is "subsidized by the poorest wage earners in America," many of whom are illegal immigrants from Mexico.* If you investigated the supermarket prices of fresh fruit grown and picked in the United States, you would find low prices like these: apples for $1.99 a pound; oranges for 99¢ a pound; grapefruit for $1.49 a pound; pears for $1.29 a pound. Realizing that this fruit was most likely picked by immigrant laborers, you are asking, "How do average Americans benefit from legal and illegal immigrants and what global forces are driving the growing immigrant population?"

CONTEXT FOR A NETWORK OF ISSUES

In some communities on Long Island, New York, tension has been building over the last few years as homeowners, politicians, and advocacy groups wrangle over what to do about the growing influx of Latino immigrants. In these long-established suburban communities with few rental properties, immigrants are crowding into houses, causing concern over health, sanitation, and residential codes. Each morning, immigrants cluster on corners waiting to be hired by contractors for a day's wages negotiated between the parties. Upset residents of these communities are embroiled in civic debates over these questions: Should communities designate town halls as hiring locations for day laborers? Should landlords be allowed to rent one-family homes to large groups of immigrants? If not, where should these people live? What can be

---

*Ricardo Sanchez, letter to the editor, *Seattle Post-Intelligencer*, January 30, 2004, http://seattlepi.nwsource.com/opinion/158609_ricardo30.html.

done about businesses employing illegal immigrants and undercutting competitors that have higher labor costs because they pay their legal immigrant workers good wages and provide medical insurance and benefits? And should the presence of large groups of immigrants be allowed to change the "character" of these communities? Like the towns on Long Island, many cities and communities around the country are wrestling with these questions.

Sites of social conflict such as these communities on Long Island are a symptom of larger U.S. issues with immigration. Known as a nation of immigrants, the United States now has a population of whom 11 percent are foreign-born, according to the 2000 census. The decades 1901–1910 and 1981–1990 were peak periods of immigration, with the greatest number of immigrants arriving between 1991 and 2000: roughly nine million. *The Statistical Yearbooks of the Immigration and Naturalization Service* reports that Mexico, India, the Philippines, China, and El Salvador—developing countries with great economic needs and large, growing populations—contributed 40 percent of the legal immigrants in 2003. The trend toward increasing numbers of immigrants raises questions about the future of U.S. immigration.

Efforts by the U.S. government to control immigration through legislation and physical restraint have proved problematic. The McCarran-Walter Act of 1952 repealed the 1924 Immigration Act and ended the ban on Asian immigration, but it established a quota system by which immigrants were limited by national origin, race, and ancestry. Then in 1965, the Immigration and Nationality Act Amendments ended the discriminatory national origins quota system. This was replaced with a first-come, first-served system, giving preference to uniting families and establishing numerical restrictions according to the Eastern and Western Hemispheres. Another significant piece of legislation was the Immigration Reform and Control Act of 1986, which attempted to fix the problem of the large number of illegal immigrants by granting permanent resident status to those who had lived and worked in the United States since 1982.

More recent governmental efforts to control the volume of immigration have been ineffective. In 1990, the Immigration Act increased the number of new immigrants allowed into the country to 700,000 a year. However, both the total number and the rate of legal and illegal immigration continue to increase. The number of illegal immigrants residing in the United States is now somewhere between eight and ten million, and that number grows by hundreds of thousands each year. Furthermore, governmental strategies to restrain immigration physically along the 1,951-mile U.S.-Mexican border—a concern that has become a heightened national security issue—have also proved unsuccessful. The millions of dollars spent on fences, helicopters, and border patrols have failed to deter illegal immigrants. Instead, because of tighter surveillance in border cities such as El Paso and Laredo, Texas, and San Diego, California, people now take more dangerous routes through the Sonora Desert, where many die of thirst, hunger, and heat.

Once in the United States, immigrants face discrimination and exploitation. Immigrants, particularly undocumented Mexicans, work under the most dangerous conditions in construction jobs and agriculture. Mexicans represent one in twenty-four workers in the United States but one in fourteen deaths on the job. According to the Occupational Safety and Health Administration, these largely preventable deaths occur because of lack of safety equipment and job training.* More recently, journalists and policymakers have been drawing attention to the huge subclass of undocumented workers who work for low wages at some of the most necessary but least appreciated jobs in manufacturing, agriculture, and the service sector. Indeed, businesses, hospitals, restaurants, and other parts of American society including American households that hire gardeners, nannies, and housecleaners have come to depend on this inexpensive labor. For example, estimates suggest that between 50 and 85 percent of agricultural workers are in the United States illegally.†

U.S. immigration issues are part of the larger, global picture of political, economic, and social forces driving immigration and of the global economic and social problems of regulating and humanely treating immigrants. The movement of masses of people across national borders continues to increase in our globally connected world. According to Susan F. Martin, director of the Institute for the Study of International Migration at Georgetown University, "150 million people or 2.5% of the world's population live outside their country of birth," a figure that has "doubled since 1965."‡ Some of these people are refugees fleeing political or ethnic persecution and extreme danger in their countries and seeking asylum; many countries such as Haiti, Bosnia, and Kosovo have had political upheavals and ethnic clashes. However, most immigrants move for economic reasons. Some college-educated persons and professionals choose to leave their poorer countries for developed countries, where they can use their training and education under better conditions for substantially higher pay, a phenomenon called the "brain drain." The main pattern of migration is from developing countries to richer, more economically stable, and prosperous developed countries. The United States, Canada, and the countries of the European Union are receiving, or destination, countries for many immigrants from sender countries, usually poorer countries.

STAKES AND STAKEHOLDERS

Citizens of developed countries as well as citizens of developing countries hold stakes in the potential gains and costs of global immigration. Policymakers, analysts, and citizens around the world are speculating about the reasons that so many people are leaving their countries of origin and are arguing about the most effective ways to manage immigration. Here are some key issue questions and some of the positions arguers are taking.

---

*Justin Pritchard, "Lethal Labor," *Seattle Times*, March 27, 2004.
†Suzanne Gamboa, "Q&A," *Seattle Times*, August 1, 2004.
‡Susan F. Martin, "Heavy Traffic: International Migration in an Era of Globalization." *Brookings Review* 19, no. 4 (Fall 2001): 41.

How Is Globalization Fueling Immigration? Some analysts emphasize "pull" factors such as the enticing lifestyle of the world's wealthiest nations that is broadcast globally by television and other media, and that insidiously suggests the superiority of these values, customs, and "good life." Other analysts, such as former U.S. Ambassador to Mexico Jeffrey Davidow, posit the dominance of "push" factors—the conditions compelling people to move from developing countries to developed countries. Davidow asserts that emigration from Mexico "will continue at high rates until the Mexican economy can provide sufficient work opportunities and decent standards of living for a far greater percentage of its population."* Some activists and citizens of developing countries fault global institutions such as the International Monetary Fund (IMF) and the North American Free Trade Agreement (NAFTA) for pressuring developing countries to pay their debts and criticize large multinational corporations for displacing the poor. For example, when giant agribusinesses buy up small subsistence farms in Mexico, they force these farmers to seek food, work, and dignity in the United States. Analysts and politicians from Latin America note that their developing nations depend on remittances—money earned by their citizens abroad and sent back to their own countries in the form of money orders, personal checks, or electronic transfers—as a key percentage of their gross domestic product.

How Much Should Receiving Countries Focus on Their National Interest and How Can Immigrants Be Integrated for the Economic and Social Benefit of All? Citizens and politicians of the rich European Union (EU) nations are debating whether to impose restrictions on immigration from the ten new EU members from Eastern Europe, who, like Slovakia and the Czech Republic, have high unemployment rates. Many British citizens, journalists, U.S. citizens, policymakers, and activists are debating how and to what degree they should restrict immigrants' access to social benefits, such as the dole (welfare) and housing in Britain and driver's licenses, welfare, food stamps, Medicaid, and financial support for higher education in the United States. In the United States, some environmental groups such as the Sierra Club are concerned about the need to limit immigration in order to reduce U.S. population growth and the drain on natural resources, whereas some European analysts and politicians are arguing that immigrants are beneficial, even necessary, to supply labor to offset Western Europe's aging population and low birthrate.

To What Extent Are the Most Urgent Problems of Immigration Economic Problems and to What Extent Are They Cultural Problems? Some analysts, politicians, and groups of citizens see immigration problems as religious and cultural differences affecting national identity and cultural

---

*"Immigration, the United States, and Mexico," Mexidata.Info, http://www.mexidata .info/id350.html.

integrity. For example, confronted with increasing numbers of Muslim immigrants from Turkey, Southeast Asia, North Africa, and the Middle East, some Europeans are speaking out in favor of preserving traditional European values. Some voices in this controversy, such as political scientist Samuel Huntington in the United States and France's president, Jacques Chirac, believe that large immigrant groups need to assimilate into the dominant culture of their receiving countries. In opposition, some immigrants, such as members of the Muslim community in Europe, have labeled these attitudes as racist and are protesting. The recent furor in France over whether Muslim girls should be allowed to wear headscarves (hijabs) in school is an example of these complex clashes over culture and religion. The killing of Dutch filmmaker Theo van Gogh by a Moroccan man because van Gogh had made a controversial film about abused Muslim women, and the recent fires and riots in France reveal the potential for violence in these cultural conflicts.

Are Guest Worker Policies Like Those Proposed by President Bush a Fair and Effective Way to Manage Legal and Illegal Immigration? The immigration reform plan that Bush announced in January 2004 focuses on regulating illegal immigration, improving homeland security, meeting the economic needs of businesses, and improving the treatment of legal and illegal immigrants. This plan—called a "guest worker plan"—would enable immigrants to apply for renewable three-year worker visas. Both illegal immigrants currently in the United States and people currently in other countries would be able to apply for these temporary visas. People already in the United States would have to show proof of employment and pay a fee to obtain a guest worker visa. Businesses and employers would have to give evidence that they couldn't fill their jobs with American workers and thus have a need for these immigrant workers. This plan proposes to bolster U.S. security by helping identify and monitor the eight to ten million illegal immigrants and to keep additional illegal immigrants out. It also proposes offering worker protection, retirement benefits, and tax savings accounts to immigrant workers, as well as temporary visas allowing workers to come and go across the U.S. border.

In favor of a guest worker plan, some U.S. owners of agriculture, manufacturing, tourist, restaurant, construction, and landscaping businesses welcome this means to fill unskilled jobs that illegal immigrants currently hold. The proconsumer position cites the benefits of inexpensive labor and the low cost of services. Thinking of national security, some policymakers and politicians like the idea of being able to identify the immigrant population who would be allowed to go openly back and forth to their home countries and see potential to decrease smuggling and drug trafficking.

Although skeptics and opponents are in favor of the legal protection and secure work environments currently denied to immigrant workers with illegal status, they argue that the proposed guest worker system with three-year renewable visas offers too few gains for these workers, empowering and benefiting employers much more than the workers. Some citizens and U.S. labor advocates maintain that a guest worker plan would create laws for employers and employees that could not be enforced and argue that the supposed "need" for unskilled immigrant workers has been created by practices that deliberately drive wages lower. In addition, some citizens and anti-immigration groups have labeled Bush's plan "backdoor amnesty" that rewards lawbreakers by granting them legal status. More extreme anti-immigration groups such as the Federation for American Immigration Reform (FAIR) want to preserve Anglo-American values and racial priorities and call for tighter control of U.S. borders and strict penalties for employers who hire illegal immigrants. In opposition, Latin American politicians and immigrant advocacy groups argue that years of work in the United States should be a qualification for applying for citizenship. If current illegal immigrants registered, they would achieve only temporary legal status and then could be expelled from the country.

What Are Some Alternatives to a Guest Worker Program? Some politicians, analysts, and policymakers believe that the way to solve U.S. immigration problems with Mexico and Latin American countries, to stop the further erosion of the U.S. workers' economic base, and to bring political stability and prosperity to these countries is to tackle the income disparity between the United States and these developing countries. Free trade proponents argue that more emphasis on free trade will bring economic improvement and greater economic equality to these countries. However, other activists contend that free trade dominated by corporations has been a major source of economic disruption—even devastation—in these Latin American countries, and are working instead for more independence and social justice in these countries.

What Existing and New Global Institutions Could Help to Guide and Regulate Immigration on a Global Level? Some analysts and policymakers do not think immigration can be controlled or restricted, while other leaders are campaigning for regional and international organizations and multilateral approaches with new policies and new laws to help deal with the patterns of global immigration. They propose that global organizations beyond the United Nations should become the overriding institutions and influential powers to govern the movement of both refugees and economic migrants.

 ## STUDENT VOICE: EXPERIENCING IMMIGRATION ISSUES

In the narrative that follows, student writer Esperanza Borboa shares her experience of the exploitation of illegal immigrants in the United States.

Esperanza Borboa

I'm from Los Angeles, California, and in 1976, I worked in the garment industry in the heart of downtown where small and large cutting rooms employed anywhere from 5 to 100 people. Gender roles were clearly marked in this industry. Men were cutters, spreaders and pattern makers. Women were seamstresses. Salaries were oftentimes below minimum wage with no benefits, and women sat at the bottom of that pay scale. I worked in the office as an assistant bookkeeper for minimum wage and no benefits. Most of the workers at our shop were Mexicans with a few Cubans. Everyone, including the boss, knew there were some who were undocumented, but we never talked about it. I was slowly becoming aware of how these people were exploited with no protection or recourse. Working and getting to know these men and women, I was learning what they were willing to risk and suffer just for the opportunity to work and provide for themselves and their children, something they couldn't do in their home countries. One day an experience made me feel the pain of their situation.

On that day I walked out to the cutting room to double–check some tickets with numbers I couldn't read. A young man came running by me, and all at once people were running in all directions. I asked Carmen, one of the lead workers, what was going on and she said the Migra (Immigration) was outside. There was a black passenger van in the alley half filled with workers from our shop and the one across the alley. One of the women being led to the van was crying and shouting to her co-worker "Vaya a mi casa y escoge a mis hijos y te llamo por teléfono!" ("Go to my house and get my children and I'll phone you!")

Although I knew they couldn't take me, a U.S. citizen, in that van, I was scared and stunned. I had known that raids were common, but this was my first experience of one. I asked Carmen what would happen to these people. She said, "They'll be deported to Mexico, and some of them will be back here by next week if they can come up with the money to pay a Coyote to cross them over the border. Their kids will stay here with friends till their mother or another family member can get here." As we watched the van pull away, my furious boss was ranting that he needed our help finding replacement workers and that we should let our friends know he was hiring. The Immigration official said they had received an anonymous call about illegal aliens working in this area. We all knew that someone always benefited from these raids, perhaps a competitor or the boss himself. Sometimes the raids would conveniently come the day before payday, enabling the boss not to have to pay "illegal" workers, even if they managed to come back.

That day my heart ached for all those picked up, and I felt powerless, voiceless and guilty for working there, but as a young single mother I needed to work. I quit that job shortly after the raid and found another job with a company in the same industry only to see it happen again, but this time, most of us were pretty sure the boss had something to do with it because it was too close to a pay period. I quit that job too.

Many years later, I moved to Washington state, and while working with farmworkers, I found out that the same practices were taking place in fields all across the country. The Migra would show up when the fields were almost completely cleared. The growers would deny they had anything to do with it just as the company owners did in Los Angeles, but we all knew better.

INTERNATIONAL VOICES

Along with a number of Latin American countries, Mexico is experiencing dramatic social and economic changes bound up with immigration. Immigration can mean economic survival, improving individuals' lives and enabling immigrants to send home money, which is then used to build up those communities. However, immigration can also cause emotional distress and major social disruption for individuals, families, communities, and regions. The following article, "Town's Fate Lies in Immigration Reform" by Mark Stevenson from the March 27, 2004, *Seattle Times*, reveals some of the repercussions of immigration: economic and social instability and importation of negative cultural influences from the United States.

Residents of a Small Town in Mexico Responding to Immigration

Santa Ana Del Valle, Mexico—

. . . Teacher Eleazar Pedro Santiago says that elsewhere in the mountains of Oaxaca state, he has seen several "ghost towns" with just a few old people and farm animals. . . .

"Everybody has the same idea—to earn money up there and start a business back here," says Aquino, the weaver. "What they don't think about is: What are they going to sell and who are they going to sell to?"

Most residents agree things can't go on as they are. The dual existence the town has led since the 1960s—one foot here, one foot in the north—has not been good for Santa Ana.

"Many of the people came back corrupted by the U.S. lifestyle," Aquino says. "They import all these fantasies from up north: the good life, total freedom, not having to answer to anyone."

The habits of U.S. inner cities have already begun to invade. Boys greet each other with a street gang-style handshake, drugs are a problem, and graffiti has begun to appear on the town's adobe walls.

Many say the town's salvation doesn't involve the United States at all.

"What we need here are more job opportunities, so people won't have to go," says Abelardo Gonzalez, the school director. "Now, there's just farmwork, and that's only when there's rain."

GLOBAL HOT SPOT: MEXICO

As the United States has increased its surveillance of the border and its pressure on cities such as San Diego and El Paso, the risks of immigrating have increased substantially. This excerpt from the article "Mexican Biologist's Desperate Dream Leads to Doom in Desert" by Richard Boudreaux from the October 20, 2004, edition of the *Seattle Times* reveals both Mexico's social acceptance of illegal immigration as a route to economic survival and the desperation and persistence of Mexican immigrants. It also points out some of the physical dangers of crossing the border illegally: the possibility of dying of heat, cold, thirst, exhaustion, and abandonment.

> Sasabe, Mexico—. . . The border's busiest migration corridor has become the 57-mile dirt road from Altar to Sasabe in the Mexican state of Sonora. Altar's 7,000 residents run guest houses, sell backpacks and work as drivers for migrants, who gather by the hundreds in the town square each day to meet with smugglers and ride north to foot trails that cross the border.
>
> Within 25 minutes on a recent afternoon, eight vans crammed with migrants out of Altar passed a checkpoint just south of Sasabe run by Grupo Beta, the humanitarian arm of Mexico's National Migration Institute. Many of the occupants were from tropical lowlands in southern Mexico, getting their first blast of desert heat.
>
> They looked bored by Julio Mallen's words of caution.
>
> "It's important to go with enough water for at least two or three days," the Beta agent emphasized, peering into each van. "Wear long sleeves to protect yourself from the sun. If anyone feels tired and cannot continue, tell your companions so they can help you find a road and get help."
>
> Grupo Beta defines its mission as minimizing harm to U.S.-bound migrants without explicitly discouraging their exodus. "Have a safe trip and God bless you," Mallen said at the end of his lecture.

The readings in this chapter will help you think about globalization and immigration from different national and global perspectives as you try to formulate your own views on how receiving and sender nations should respond to these global migration issues.

READINGS

Borders Beyond Control
Jagdish Bhagwati

Jagdish Bhagwati is a bold, articulate defender of economic globalization who has authored numerous books, including *In Defense of Globalization*, published by Oxford University Press in 2004. Bhagwati holds the title University Professor at Columbia University as well as Andre Meyer Senior Fellow in International Economics at the Council on Foreign Relations and has functioned as an advisor to the United Nations. His writing is published regularly in the *New York Times*, the *Wall Street Journal*, and the *New Republic.* This piece appeared in the January–February 2003 issue of *Foreign Affairs.* Published by the Council on Foreign Relations since 1922, this journal describes itself as "America's most influential publication on international affairs and foreign policy" and "the international forum of choice for the most important new ideas, analysis, and debate on the most significant issues in the world" (www.foreignaffairs.org/about/).

> Jagdish Bhagwati's target audience for this piece is readers who are well informed about and engaged in global issues. How does he try to make his views on immigration accessible to other readers seeking insights into global immigration problems?

A DOOR THAT WILL NOT CLOSE

1   International migration lies close to the center of global problems that now seize the attention of politicians and intellectuals across the world. Take just a few recent examples.—Prime Ministers Tony Blair of the United Kingdom and Jose Mará Aznar of Spain proposed at last year's European Council meeting in Seville that the European Union withdraw aid from countries that did not take effective steps to stem the flow of illegal emigrants to the EU. Blair's outspoken minister for development, Clare Short, described the proposal as "morally repugnant" and it died amid a storm of other protests.—Australia received severe condemnation worldwide last summer when a special envoy of the UN high commissioner for human rights exposed the deplorable conditions in detention camps that held Afghan, Iranian, Iraqi, and Palestinian asylum seekers who had landed in Australia.

2   —Following the September 11 attacks in New York City and Washington, D.C., U.S. Attorney General John Ashcroft announced several new policies that rolled back protections enjoyed by immigrants. The American Civil Liberties Union (ACLU) and Human Rights Watch fought back. So did Islamic and Arab ethnic organizations. These groups employed lawsuits, public dissent, and congressional lobbying to secure a reversal of the worst excesses.

3   —The *Economist* ran in just six weeks two major stories describing the growing outflow of skilled citizens from less developed countries to developed countries seeking to attract such immigrants. The "brain drain" of the 1960s is striking again with enhanced vigor.

4   These examples and numerous others do not just underline the importance of migration issues today. More important, they show governments attempting to stem migration only to be forced into

retreat and accommodation by factors such as civil-society activism and the politics of ethnicity. Paradoxically, the ability to control migration has shrunk as the desire to do so has increased. The reality is that borders are beyond control and little can be done to really cut down on immigration. The societies of developed countries will simply not allow it. The less developed countries also seem overwhelmed by forces propelling emigration. Thus, there must be a seismic shift in the way migration is addressed: governments must reorient their policies from attempting to curtail migration to coping and working with it to seek benefits for all.

5   To demonstrate effectively why and how this must be done, however, requires isolating key migration questions from the many other issues that attend the flows of humanity across national borders. Although some migrants move strictly between rich countries or between poor ones, the most compelling problems result from emigration from less developed to more developed countries. They arise in three areas. First, skilled workers are legally emigrating, temporarily or permanently, to rich countries. This phenomenon predominantly concerns the less developed countries that are losing skilled labor. Second, largely unskilled migrants are entering developed countries illegally and looking for work. Finally, there is the "involuntary" movement of people, whether skilled or unskilled, across borders to seek asylum. These latter two trends mostly concern the developed countries that want to bar illegal entry by the unskilled.

6   All three problems raise issues that derive from the fact that the flows cannot be effectively constrained and must instead be creatively accommodated. In designing such accommodation, it must be kept in mind that the illegal entry of asylum seekers and economic migrants often cannot be entirely separated. Frustrated economic migrants are known to turn occasionally to asylum as a way of getting in. The effective tightening of one form of immigrant entry will put pressure on another.

SOFTWARE ENGINEERS, NOT HUDDLED MASSES

7   Looking at the first problem, it appears that developed countries' appetite for skilled migrants has grown—just look at Silicon Valley's large supply of successful Indian and Taiwanese computer scientists and venture capitalists. The enhanced appetite for such professionals reflects the shift to a globalized economy in which countries compete for markets by creating and attracting technically skilled talent. Governments also perceive these workers to be more likely to assimilate quickly into their new societies. This heightened demand is matched by a supply that is augmented for old reasons that have intensified over time. Less developed

countries cannot offer modern professionals the economic rewards or the social conditions that they seek. Europe and the United States also offer opportunities for immigrant children's education and career prospects that are nonexistent at home. These asymmetries of opportunity reveal themselves not just through cinema and television, but through the immediacy of experience. Increasingly, emigration occurs after study abroad. The number of foreign students at U.S. universities, for example, has grown dramatically; so has the number who stay on. In 1990, 62 percent of engineering doctorates in the United States were given to foreign-born students, mainly Asians. The figures are almost as high in mathematics, computer science, and the physical sciences. In economics, which at the graduate level is a fairly math-intensive subject, 54 percent of the Ph.D.'s awarded went to foreign students, according to a 1990 report of the American Economic Association.

8   Many of these students come from India, China, and South Korea. For example, India produces about 25,000 engineers annually. Of these, about 2,000 come from the Indian Institutes of Technology (IITS), which are modeled on MIT and the California Institute of Technology. Graduates of IITS accounted for 78 percent of U.S. engineering Ph.D.'s granted to Indians in 1990. And almost half of all Taiwanese awarded similar Ph.D.'s had previously attended two prestigious institutions: the National Taiwan University and the National Cheng Kung University. Even more telling, 65 percent of the Korean students who received science and engineering Ph.D.'s in the United States were graduates of Seoul National University. The numbers were almost as high for Beijing University and Tsinghua University, elite schools of the People's Republic of China.

9   These students, once graduated from American universities, often stay on in the United States. Not only is U.S. graduate education ranked highest in the world, but it also offers an easy way of immigrating. In fact, it has been estimated that more than 70 percent of newly minted, foreign-born Ph.D.'s remain in the United States, many becoming citizens eventually. Less developed countries can do little to restrict the numbers of those who stay on as immigrants. They will, particularly in a situation of high demand for their skills, find ways to escape any dragnet that their home country may devise. And the same difficulty applies, only a little less starkly, to countries trying to hold on to those citizens who have only domestic training but are offered better jobs abroad.

10   A realistic response requires abandoning the "brain drain" approach of trying to keep the highly skilled at home. More likely to succeed is a "diaspora" model, which integrates present and past citizens into a web of rights and obligations in the extended

community defined with the home country as the center. The diaspora approach is superior from a human rights viewpoint because it builds on the right to emigrate, rather than trying to restrict it. And dual loyalty is increasingly judged to be acceptable rather than reprehensible. This option is also increasingly feasible. Nearly 30 countries now offer dual citizenship. Others are inching their way to similar options. Many less developed countries, such as Mexico and India, are in the process of granting citizens living abroad hitherto denied benefits such as the right to hold property and to vote via absentee ballot.

11   However, the diaspora approach is incomplete unless the benefits are balanced by some obligations, such as the taxation of citizens living abroad. The United States already employs this practice. This author first recommended this approach for developing countries during the 1960s, and the proposal has been revived today. Estimates made by the scholars Mihir Desai, Devesh Kapur, and John McHale demonstrate that even a slight tax on Indian nationals abroad would substantially raise Indian government revenues. The revenue potential is vast because the aggregate income of Indian-born residents in the United States is 10 percent of India's national income, even though such residents account for just 0.1 percent of the American population.

UNSTOPPABLE

12 The more developed countries need to go through a similar dramatic shift in the way they respond to the influx of illegal economic immigrants and asylum seekers. Inducements or punishments for immigrants' countries of origin are not working to stem the flows, nor are stiffer border-control measures, sanctions on employers, or harsher penalties for the illegals themselves.

13   Three sets of factors are behind this. First, civil-society organizations, such as Human Rights Watch, the ACLU, and the International Rescue Committee, have proliferated and gained in prominence and influence. They provide a serious constraint on all forms of restrictive action. For example, it is impossible to incarcerate migrants caught crossing borders illegally without raising an outcry over humane treatment. So authorities generally send these people back across the border, with the result that they cross again and again until they finally get in. More than 50 percent of illegals, however, now enter not by crossing the Rio Grande but by legal means, such as tourist visas, and then stay on illegally. Thus, enforcement has become more difficult without invading privacy through such measures as identity cards, which continue to draw strong protests from civil liberties groups. A notable example of both ineffectual policy and successful civil resistance is the 1986

Sanctuary movement that surfaced in response to evidence that U.S. authorities were returning desperate refugees from war-torn El Salvador and Guatemala to virtually certain death in their home countries. (They were turned back because they did not meet the internationally agreed upon definition for a refugee.) Sanctuary members, with the aid of hundreds of church groups, took the law into their own hands and organized an underground railroad to spirit endangered refugees to safe havens. Federal indictments and convictions followed, with five Sanctuary members given three- to five-year sentences. Yet, in response to a public outcry and an appeal from Senator Dennis DeConcini (D-Ariz.), the trial judge merely placed the defendants on probation.

14   Sanctions on employers, such as fines, do not fully work either. The General Accounting Office, during the debate over the 1986 immigration legislation that introduced employer sanctions, studied how they had worked in Switzerland and Germany. The measures there failed. Judges could not bring themselves to punish severely those employers whose violation consisted solely of giving jobs to illegal workers. The U.S. experience with employer sanctions has not been much different.

15   Finally, the sociology and politics of ethnicity also undercut enforcement efforts. Ethnic groups can provide protective cover to their members and allow illegals to disappear into their midst. The ultimate constraint, however, is political and results from expanding numbers. Fellow ethnics who are U.S. citizens, legal immigrants, or amnesty beneficiaries bring to bear growing political clout that precludes tough action against illegal immigrants. Nothing matters more than the vote in democratic societies. Thus the Bush administration, anxious to gain Hispanic votes, has embraced an amnesty confined solely to Mexican illegal immigrants, thereby discarding the principle of nondiscrimination enshrined in the 1965 Immigration and Nationality Act.

MINDING THE OPEN DOOR

16   If it is not possible to effectively restrict illegal immigration, then governments in the developed countries must turn to policies that will integrate migrants into their new homes in ways that will minimize the social costs and maximize the economic benefits. These policies should include children's education and grants of limited civic rights such as participation in school-board elections and parent-teacher associations. Governments should also assist immigrants in settling throughout a country, to avoid depressing wages in any one region. Greater development support should be extended to the illegal migrants' countries of origin to alleviate the poor economic conditions that propel emigration. And for the less

developed countries, there is really no option but to shift toward a diaspora model.

17   Some nations will grasp this reality and creatively work with migrants and migration. Others will lag behind, still seeking restrictive measures to control and cut the level of migration. The future certainly belongs to the former. But to accelerate the progress of the laggards, new institutional architecture is needed at the international level. Because immigration restrictions are the flip side of sovereignty, there is no international organization today to oversee and monitor each nation's policies toward migrants, whether inward or outward bound.

18   The world badly needs enlightened immigration policies and best practices to be spread and codified. A World Migration Organization would begin to do that by juxtaposing each nation's entry, exit, and residence policies toward migrants, whether legal or illegal, economic or political, skilled or unskilled. Such a project is well worth putting at the center of policymakers' concerns.

For Class Discussion

1. How would you summarize the three main global immigration patterns that Jagdish Bhagwati describes?

2. How does Jagdish Bhagwati support his claim that the migration of masses of people cannot be stopped in a globalized economy?

3. What does Bhagwati mean by the terms "brain drain," "civil-society organizations," "the politics of ethnicity," "economic immigrants," and "asylum seekers"?

4. Bhagwati proposes two solutions to the immigration problems facing the world today: the "disapora" model and a World Migration Organization. How does he support and justify these proposed solutions?

5. What strengths and weaknesses in Bhagwati's argument might general readers identify?

Lecture on International Flows of Humanity

Kofi Annan

Born in Ghana, Kofi Annan became secretary-general of the United Nations in 1997 after years of holding various leadership positions in world organizations, including the World Health Organization, and serving as the United Nations High Commissioner for Refugees and Assistant Secretary-General for Human Resources Management and Security Coordinator for the

UN System. He is currently serving his second term as secretary-general. Educated internationally and in the United States, Annan holds a master of science in management from the Massachusetts Institute of Technology. In 2001, he and the United Nations won the Nobel Peace Prize. Annan's priorities continue to be reforming the United Nations, advocating human rights and equality, and combating the HIV/AIDS epidemic. Annan delivered this speech at Columbia University on November 21, 2003, as the Emma Lazarus Lecture. (Emma Lazarus [1849–1883] was a well-known Jewish American poet and political activist. Her famous sonnet "The New Colossus" was engraved on a plaque on the Statue of Liberty's pedestal in 1903. This poem helped to enhance the Statue's role as a symbol of the United States as a welcoming place of freedom and opportunity for immigrants. Copies of this poem are readily available on the Web.)

> How does Kofi Annan make use of the specific rhetorical context of this speech and how does he try to connect with his audience in his introductory remarks?

1   There could be no place more fitting for a lecture on international flows of humanity than this great university, located as it is in a city which has been the archetypal success story of international migration.

2   And you could not have chosen a better person to name it after than Emma Lazarus, whose unforgettable lines are inscribed on the base of the Statue of Liberty, the Mother of Exiles. Just in case you have forgotten them, they are printed in your programme!

3   While Emma Lazarus's immortal words promised welcome to the tired, the poor, the wretched, and the huddled masses yearning to be free, another American poet, Walt Whitman, spoke of the vibrancy and vitality that migrants brought to the new world. He called New York the "city of the world" because, he said, "all races are here, all lands of the earth make contributions here".

4   How right he was—and still is. Today, more than one in three inhabitants of New York City was born outside the United States. The city boasts communities of 188 different national origins—only three fewer than there are Member States in the United Nations— and 47 per cent of them speak a second language at home.

5   New York, in other words, is a brilliant success story of migration, as are many other cities all around the world today. In fact, in the year 2000, some 175 million people, about 3 per cent of the world's population, lived outside their country of birth—more than at any other time in history.

6   Of these, around 16 million were recognized refugees—people who did not choose to leave home but were forced to. Another 1 million were asylum seekers—people who claimed to be refugees,

but whose claims were in the process of being verified. The remainder, some 158 million, were deemed international migrants—that is, people who have chosen to move.

7   So much mobility and diversity should be cause for celebration. But migration also gives rise to many problems, leading people to ask: Can we absorb large numbers of new people? Will they take our jobs or absorb our social services? Are they a threat to our security, our way of life or our national identity?

8   These are understandable concerns, and they must be answered. The answers are not easy. But I have come here today to say that they do not lie in halting migration—a policy that is bound to fail. I say the answer must lie in managing migration—rationally, creatively, compassionately and cooperatively. This is the only approach that can ensure that the interests of both migrant and host communities will be looked after and their rights upheld.

9   It is the only approach that can effectively address the complex issues surrounding migration—issues of human rights and economic opportunity, of labour shortages and unemployment, of brain drain and brain gain, of xenophobia and integration, of refugee crises and asylum seekers, of law enforcement and human trafficking, of human security and national security. And it is the only approach that can, if we get it right, bring advantages to all parties—sender countries, countries of transit, host countries, and migrants themselves.

10   Many migrants, while not literally forced to move, choose to do so under duress. They see no opportunity at home to improve themselves, or perhaps even to earn a living at all. Their departure may be a source of sadness for themselves and their families, and also a loss for their home countries—often poor ones, which could have benefited from their talents. They are usually not free riders looking for an easy life, but courageous men and women who make great sacrifices in search of a better future for themselves or their families.

11   Nor are their lives always to be envied once they have left home. They often face as many risks and unknowns as they do hopes and opportunities. Many fall prey to smugglers and traffickers on their journey, and many more face a surly welcome of exploitation, discrimination and prejudice once they arrive. Many have little choice but to do dirty, dangerous and difficult jobs.

12   Undoubtedly more needs to be done to create opportunities in poor countries for individual self-improvement. This is yet another reason why we must strive harder to achieve the Millennium Development Goals, including by forging a global partnership for development which, among other things, gives poor countries a fair chance to compete in the global market.

13   But migration itself can also be part of that global partnership— part of the solution to economic problems, not only in sender

countries, but also in receiving ones. Sender countries benefit enormously from migrant remittances. They bring not only vital sustenance to the migrants' families. They also bring much-needed stimulus to the national economy. Last year alone, migrant workers in developed countries sent at least $88 billion back to their countries of origin—more than those same developing countries received in official development aid. These amounts are growing fast.

14   Emigration also relieves the pressures of overpopulation and unemployment, and in time endows sender countries with an educated diaspora who often bring or send home new skills, products, ideas and knowledge.

15   In short, migration is one of the tools we have to help put more of the world's people on the right side of—and ultimately, to eliminate—the vast divides that exist today between poor and rich, and between fettered and free.

16   Host country economies, too, can reap benefits. After all, the main reason any country attracts immigrants is its need for their labour. They perform many services that the host population is eager to consume, but is either unwilling or unable to provide for itself—from highly skilled work in research or information technology to less skilled jobs tending fields, nursing the sick and elderly, working on construction sites, running corner shops that stay open all night, or looking after children and doing housework while parents are out pursuing careers.

17   Increasingly, as birth rates in many developed countries fall, and populations age, immigrant labour, taxes and spending are becoming a demographic and economic necessity. Without them, pension schemes and health-care systems will be in danger of collapse. While immigration may not by itself be the answer to all these challenges, there is no answer to them that does not include immigration.

18   So migration has a demand as well as a supply side. Migrants are rational human beings who make economic choices. Up to now, rich countries have been far too comfortable with a policy framework that allows them to benefit from immigrant labour, while denying immigrants the dignity and rights of a legal status.

19   That is not good enough. Let us remember from the start that migrants are not merely units of labour. They are human beings. They have human emotions, human families, and above all, human rights—human rights which must be at the very heart of debates and policies on migration. Among those rights is the right to family unity—and in fact families reuniting form by far the largest stream of immigration into North America and Europe.

20   The more we try to deal with migration simply by clamping down on it with tighter border controls, the more we find that human rights are sacrificed—on the journey, at the border, and inside host countries.

21   Few, if any, States have actually succeeded in cutting migrant numbers by imposing such controls. The laws of supply and demand are too strong for that. Instead, immigrants are driven to enter the country clandestinely, to overstay their visas, or to resort to the one legal route still open to them, namely the asylum system. This experience shows that stronger borders are not necessarily smarter ones. And it shows that they can create new problems of law enforcement and lead almost inevitably to human rights violations.

22   The gravest violations come at the hands of smugglers and traffickers. Smuggling occurs with the complicity of migrants, usually because they can see no legal route to migrate. Trafficking is a modern form of slavery in which migrants are coerced and exploited. All too often, people who initially collaborate with smugglers later find themselves in the hands of traffickers.

23   Asylum processes, meanwhile, become clogged with doubtful cases, with the result that bona fide refugees are often detained for long periods. They are often denied the rights accorded to accused or convicted criminals—and, when free, they are objects of suspicion and hostility. This, in turn, undermines support for migration in host countries—despite the fact that many of them need migrants.

24   Those who manage to get in, or stay, illegally become acutely vulnerable to exploitation. If they attempt to assert their rights, they can be met with a threat of exposure and deportation. Migrant women and unaccompanied children are especially vulnerable to physical, psychological, and sexual abuse, sometimes involving the risk of infection with HIV/AIDS.

25   I am not suggesting that all these problems could be solved at a stroke simply by lifting all restrictions on migration. It is vital for States to harmonize their policies and maintain networks of cooperation and information sharing on smuggling and trafficking routes and trends, and on effective practices in prevention and assistance.

26   Nor do I suggest that a society can be expected to forego any process for deciding which immigrants it will accept, and how many at a time. But I do say that those decisions need to be positive as well as negative. And I say here, in the United States, that while I understand this nation's need to ensure that those who come here are not a threat to homeland security, it would be a tragedy if this diverse country were to deprive itself of the enrichment of many students and workers and family members from particular parts of the world, or if the human rights of those who would migrate here were compromised.

27   I also believe that States need carefully thought-out policies for integrating immigrants who are allowed in. Since both migrants and host societies stand to benefit from successful integration, both must play their part in making it happen. It is reasonable for

societies to expect those who would become citizens to share certain basic values, to respect the law of the land, and to develop fluency in the local language, with assistance if they need it.

28 For their part, host societies must have effective anti-discrimination legislation and procedures, reflecting international standards and obligations, and should also take measures to promote appreciation of cultural diversity among all their citizens and residents.

29 But laws and policies are not enough. Leadership is vital too. All national leaders should be conscious that any form of discrimination against immigrants is a regression from the standards for a just society enshrined in the Universal Declaration of Human Rights and the binding treaties that derive from it.

30 Many people, in government and academia, in the private sector and in civil society as a whole, are showing the leadership that is needed to combat xenophobia and stigma. I salute them for it. But I am also disturbed by the vilification, in some quarters, of migrants—particularly of asylum seekers—often in an effort to achieve political gain.

31 Many of those vilified have fled their homelands in fear of their lives. States have a legal obligation not to return them to danger. They must establish fair procedures to determine the legitimacy of asylum claims. If, in extreme circumstances, asylum seekers must be detained, certain minimal standards must be provided, and enforced, to ensure respect for their human dignity and human rights.

32 The international regime for protecting migrant workers, set out in a host of human rights conventions that are either regional in scope or confined to particular categories of workers, should be made applicable to all categories of migrants, both regular and irregular, and to members of their families. Many States have recognized this need.

33 Recently, a step forward was taken with the entry into force of the International Convention on the Protection of the Rights of All Migrant Workers and Members of their Families—the bill of rights for migrant workers and their families in their new home countries. This step was important. But it was not enough. So far, only sender States have ratified the Convention, which means that it will have little practical effect. I call on all States, and in particular receiving States, to ratify the Convention, so that the human rights of migrant workers are protected by law.

34 The Migrant Workers Convention is but one instance of the efforts that are being made to address the issue of migration at the global level. But despite these efforts, consensus is lacking on many of the principles and policies which should be applied to the governance of international migration.

35   Internationally, we are not well organized to forge that consensus.

36   The United Nations does play an important role in dealing with many aspects of migration, and a leading role in helping refugees through the office of the High Commissioner. The International Labour Organization gives a voice to organized labour, and sets standards for fair labour practices, in conjunction with governments and the private sector. Outside the United Nations system, the International Organization for Migration (IOM) facilitates the movement of people, at the request of member States. United Nations agencies and the IOM have come together in the Geneva Migration Group to work more closely on this issue.

37   But we still lack a comprehensive institutional focus at the international level that could protect the rights of migrants and promote the shared interest of emigration, immigration and transit. No single agency works systematically across the whole spectrum of migration issues, and there is no complete legal framework in place to deal with this quintessentially global phenomenon.

38   I do not pretend that we can achieve such a framework overnight. And we should not await it before increasing bilateral and regional efforts. I am heartened by the efforts of some States— particularly those of the European Union—to find ways of coordinating their actions and harmonizing their policies.

39   Yet more and more people are coming to the conclusion that we also have to address this issue globally. Doing it regionally or bilaterally is not enough. I particularly welcome the decision taken by a core group of Member States from both North and South to form a Global Commission on International Migration to deepen our understanding of this issue and to make recommendations for improving international cooperation.

40   The Commission will have two distinguished co-Chairs in Jan Karlsson of Sweden and Mamphela Ramphele of South Africa. It has my full backing, and I hope it will receive support from States in all parts of the world and from institutions like yours. Most of all, I hope it will help us approach this issue creatively and cooperatively.

41   As the Commission's work proceeds, there are many questions I believe it should be asking, and that the rest of us should be asking too. For instance:

- Can greater cooperation be built between sender and receiver countries?
- Have the benefits of short-term and long-term temporary immigration been fully explored?
- Could more be done to work with the laws of supply and demand rather than against them?

- Might financial methods of discouraging illegal migration be more effective and more humane than some current practices?
- What are the best ways to speed up the integration of immigrants into host societies?
- Could more be done to harness the potential of migration as a force for development?
- Can developing countries do more to maintain contact with their emigrants?

42   No doubt there are numerous other equally important issues to be addressed as well.

43   Above all, I believe we must approach this issue with a strong ethical compass. The basic fairness and decency of any society can best be measured by its treatment of the weak and vulnerable. The principle of nondiscrimination has become an integral part of the universal moral code, one on which the defence of all other universal values depends. We should keep a firm hold upon it.

44   The willingness of rich countries to welcome migrants, and the way that they treat them, will be a measure of their commitment to human equality and human dignity. Their preparedness to adjust to the changes that migration brings will be an indicator of their readiness to accept the obligations as well as the opportunities of globalization, and of their conception of global citizenship. And their attitude to the issue will also be a test of their awareness of the lessons, and obligations, of history. After all, many migrants today are seeking to enter countries which not so long ago conquered and exploited their own. And many countries that are now attracting immigrants were until recently major exporters of emigrants.

45   Along with other countries, the United States falls into a third category—a nation built by immigration, a land where constant renewal and regeneration are essential elements of the national character. That character must never be lost.

46   And the hope and reality of a new future for those who would migrate must glow brighter today than ever before.

47   As Emma Lazarus wrote: "Send these, the homeless, tempest-tost to me, I lift my lamp beside the golden door."

For Class Discussion

1. Annan identifies the global stakeholders in immigration issues as "sender countries, countries of transit, host countries, and migrants themselves." According to Annan, what does each group lose and gain through migration?

2. How does Annan seek to elicit sympathy for migrants?

3. What does Annan claim are the main problems with immigration that are facing receiving countries?

4. What role in regulating immigration does Annan advocate for global institutions?
5. What features of this piece contribute to making it a persuasive argument in favor of global migration?
6. How has it affected your understanding of this subject?

Offer May Vary
Clay Bennett

Clay Bennett is a nationally known editorial cartoonist for the *Christian Science Monitor*. He is a graduate of the University of North Alabama and holds degrees in art and history. He has worked for the *Pittsburgh Post-Gazette* and the *St. Petersburg Times*. In 2002, he won a Pulitzer Prize for editorial cartooning.

How is Bennett using the contrast between the Statue of Liberty's traditional symbolism and his revised version in this cartoon to raise questions about the current U.S. immigration policies?

FIGURE 4.1 Offer May Vary *(Clay Bennett / © 2002 The Christian Science Monitor (www.csmonitor.com). All rights reserved)*

For Class Discussion

1. To understand this cartoon, what historical and cultural background information is it helpful to know about the Statue of Liberty? Why has this statue come to be a famous symbol of the United States?
2. How is Clay Bennett employing this symbol?
3. What is the main claim of this cartoon?
4. The phrase "offer may vary" echoes advertising provisos. What rhetorical effect does it have on readers? ∎

America's Mixed Messages to Foreigners at the Gate
Ruben Navarrette, Jr.

A syndicated columnist with the Washington Post Writers Group, Ruben Navarrette, Jr., publishes his editorials worldwide. He is a columnist and member of the editorial board for the *Dallas Morning News*, where this op-ed piece first appeared on February 6, 2004. A native of Fresno, California, and now a resident of Dallas, Navarrette holds a bachelor of arts and a master of arts in public administration from Harvard. He frequently speaks on public television news commentaries on Latino affairs, immigration, and politics.

> What important problem of U.S. immigration policy does this opinion piece expose?

1   Those Americans who crusade against illegal immigration often say they want to send the people of other countries a message: Come legally, or don't come at all.

2   The word isn't getting through. One reason could be that illegal immigrants—especially those from Mexico and the rest of Latin America—get tons of messages from the United States, and most are mixed.

3   I recently heard Rep. Tom Tancredo, R-Colo., a vocal opponent of illegal immigration, express concern that too many immigrants no longer seem interested in becoming U.S. citizens and involving themselves in the political process.

4   Just a few weeks earlier, I watched talk show host Bill O'Reilly of Fox News, another vocal foe of illegal immigration, express a different concern—that too many immigrants might become U.S. citizens and involve themselves in the political process.

5   So what is it that folks are really worried about—that immigrants won't become an active part of our society, or that they will and in the process change that society?

6   Mixed messages are nothing new, and they start even before the immigrants get to the United States.

7   The fences and border guards say: *Stay out. If you don't come legally, you're not welcome.*

8   But once they get here, most immigrants—even the illegal kind—never lack for jobs in the United States. The willingness of American employers to hire the undocumented and the desire of some politicians to give employers new batches of guest workers all say: *Come right in. We're glad to have you. Tell your friends.*

9   Then there is the thorny issue of language. English-only laws and the popularity of fire-breathing politicians who push linguistic homogeneity send the message: *In the United States, we speak English and we demand the same of you. Don't expect us to cater to you in your native tongue.*

10   But bilingual education, bilingual ballots and our willingness to translate everything from government documents to menus at fast-food restaurants tell people: *Don't bother learning English. Keep your native language.*

11   Demands that immigrants blend into their surroundings, and the way that many Americans cling to the fantasy that earlier waves of newcomers shed their culture when they arrived on these shores, sends the message: *You must assimilate! You have to change your ways and adapt to the ways of your new country.*

12   Yet the efficiency with which many U.S. businesses—eager to get their share of more than $600 billion in annual spending by Latino consumers—helped build the multibillion-dollar industry of Spanish-language billboards, newspapers, radio and television says: *You can come to this country and feel like you never left your own. What's important is that you buy our products.*

13   And of course, voters in various states are always threatening to deprive illegal immigrants of education, health care and other services, as if to say: *You don't deserve anything. After all, you shouldn't even be here.*

14   Yet illegal immigrants still pay their fair share of taxes—sales, property, municipal, payroll and even (for those who want to become legal residents) federal income tax. That the tax collector isn't so choosy about who pays the tax sends the message: *If you want to live here—and consume goods here—legal or not, you'll have to pay up.*

15   It's politically fashionable for Americans and those politicians who pander to them to beat their chests and demand that we get tough on illegal immigration.

16   As I have written many times, I'm all for it—as long as we begin by cracking down on the root cause: the employers without whom there would be no illegal immigration.

17   But being tough isn't enough. Americans also have to be crystal clear. First, they have to be clear in their own minds that they're prepared to live without the conveniences, bargain prices and higher standard of living afforded them by a ready abundance of cheap labor.

18   And then they have to be clear in what they communicate to immigrants themselves. After all, Americans want the people of the world to respect their authority and not question their resolve when it comes to protecting U.S. borders. That's hard to do without first being consistent, credible and clear.

19   Got the message?

For Class Discussion

1. How does Navarrette support his main claim?

2. What attitude toward his subject and his audience does Navarrette convey in this piece?

3. What is the rhetorical effect of the use of italics?

4. What contribution does this op-ed piece make to the national debate over illegal immigration?   ∎

From *Guide for the Mexican Migrant*
Mexico's Ministry of Foreign Relations

In January 2005, Mexico's Ministry of Foreign Relations issued a pamphlet entitled *Guide for the Mexican Migrant*. In this pamphlet, the Mexican government addresses the reality of steady illegal migration and tries to protect its citizens who are seeking a new life in the United States. Soon after its publication, translations of the *Guide* began appearing in U.S. newspapers. *American Renaissance*, a monthly magazine that bills itself as "a literate, undeceived journal of race, immigration and the decline of civility," printed a version of the *Guide* in English, from which this excerpt is taken (www.amren.com/). To see the entire text of the *Guide*, go to this site or others on the Web.

As its title indicates, this pamphlet falls in the genre of guidebooks. How are the function and purpose of this guidebook like and unlike those of guidebooks you have used?

INTRODUCTION

1   Esteemed Countryman:

2   The purpose of this guide is to provide you with practical advice that may prove useful to you in case you have made the

difficult decision to search for employment opportunities outside of your country.

3   The sure way to enter another country is by getting your passport from the Ministry of Foreign Affairs, and the visa, which you may apply for at the embassy or consulate of the country you wish to travel to.

4   However, in practice we see many Mexicans who try to cross the Northern Border without the necessary documents, through high risk zones that involve grave dangers, particularly in desert areas or rivers with strong, and not always obvious, currents.

FIGURE 4.2

5   Reading this guide will make you aware of some basic questions about the legal consequences of your stay in the United States of America without the appropriate migratory documents, as well as about the rights you have in that country, once you are there, independent of your migratory status.

6   Keep in mind always that there exist legal mechanisms to enter the United States of America legally.

7   In any case, if you encounter problems or run into difficulties, remember that Mexico has 45 consulates in that country whose locations you can find listed in this publication.

8   Familiarize yourself with the closest consulate and make use of it.

DANGERS IN CROSSING HIGH RISK ZONES

9   To cross the river can be very risky, above all if you cross alone and at night.

10   Heavy clothing increases in weight when wet and this makes swimming and floating difficult.

11   If you cross by desert, try to walk at times when the heat will not be too intense.

12   Highways and population centers are far apart, which means you will spend several days looking for roads, and you will not be

FIGURE 4.3

able to carry foodstuffs or water for long periods of time. Also, you can get lost.

13 Salt water helps keep liquids in your body. Although you may feel more thirst if you drink salt water, the risk of dehydration is much less.

14 The symptoms of dehydration are:

- Little or no sweat.
- Dryness in the eyes and in the mouth.
- Headache.
- Tiredness and excessive exhaustion.
- Difficulty in walking and thinking.
- Hallucinations and visions.

15 If you get lost, guide yourself by [telephone poles], train tracks, or dirt roads.

BEWARE OF HUMAN TRAFFICKERS (COYOTES, POLLEROS)

16 They can deceive you with assurances of crossing in a few hours through the mountains and deserts. This is simply not so!

17 They can risk your life taking you across rivers, drainage canals, desert areas, train tracks, or highways. This has caused the death of hundreds of persons.

18 If you decide to hire people traffickers to cross the border, consider the following precautions:

19 Do not let them out of your sight. Remember that they are the only ones who know the lay of the land, and therefore the only ones who can get you out of that place.

20 Do not trust those who offer to take you to "the other side" and ask you to drive a car or to take or carry a package for them. Normally, those packages contain drugs or other prohibited substances. For this reason, many people have ended up in jail.

For Class Discussion

1. How is this guide designed to appeal to its target audience?

2. What does the use of comic book illustrations contribute to the rhetorical effect of this pamphlet? (If you find this *Guide* on the Web, you will see the numerous illustrations in color.)

3. How do you think the genre and appearance of the *Guide* have contributed to the strong emotional responses it has evoked, especially from some advocacy groups and politicians in the United States?

4. The *Guide* includes this disclaimer by the Mexican government: "This Consular Protection Guide does not promote crossing by Mexicans without legal documentation required by the government of the United States. Its purpose is to make known the risks,

and to inform the migrants about their rights, whether they are legal residents or not." What features of the content, tone, and style of this pamphlet support this declaration? What features, if any, suggest an ambivalent attitude toward illegal migration?

5. Do a brief investigation of the *Guide* on the Web. What have people in Mexico and in the United States said about this pamphlet? ∎

Guest Worker Visas
Linda Chavez

Known for her forthright views on Latino affairs, Linda Chavez is a prominent conservative journalist who has written for the *Washington Post*, the *Wall Street Journal*, the *New Republic*, and *USA Today*. From 1977 to 1983, she served as editor of *American Educator*, the quarterly journal of the American Federation of Teachers. She has worked with the United Nations and the federal government and is currently president of the Center for Equal Opportunity in Washington, D.C. In addition, she has authored several books, including *Out of the Barrio: Toward a New Politics of Hispanic Assimilation* (1991), and appeared on television journals such as *CNN & Co.* This editorial was published in *Investor's Business Daily* on November 13, 2002, and appeared on the TownHall.com: Conservative Columnists Web site.

According to Linda Chavez, what is the rationale for a guest worker program in the United States? Whom is she trying to persuade?

1   Washington's unwillingness to deal with illegal immigration has emboldened several Latin American governments to come up with their own solutions. An estimated 9 million illegal aliens from Latin America live in the United States, so Mexico, El Salvador, Honduras and Guatemala have recently begun issuing identification cards to illegal aliens through their consular offices in the U.S. These IDs allow illegal aliens living here to open bank accounts, obtain drivers' licenses and library cards, and fly on U.S. domestic airlines.

2   While many Americans may find the practice objectionable, a number of local and state governments have been quick to embrace these new "matricula consular" IDs as a way to bring illegal aliens in their communities out of the shadows, where they are easy prey to criminals and scam artists. So far, several jurisdictions in California, Texas, Arizona, Illinois, Georgia and elsewhere have decided to accept these identification cards where official government IDs are required.

3   Now, El Salvador has gone a step further in driving U.S. immigration policy by actually lobbying its nationals to stay in the

United States—even though they came here illegally in the first place. Salvadoran President Francisco Flores recently sent recorded messages to Salvadorans living in the U.S., reminding them to re-apply for the limited amnesty they were granted two years ago in the wake of two devastating earthquakes in their home country. The emergency measure permitted Salvadorans who entered the U.S. illegally prior to February 2001 to apply for temporary work permits, which expired in September 2002. The message from the Salvadoran president was delivered via Americatel, a long-distance carrier, to some 750,000 persons in the United States who had placed calls to El Salvador previously.

4   Mexico, El Salvador and other Latin American countries are taking these unorthodox steps because illegal immigration has become a safety valve for their own struggling economies. Those unable to find jobs in their own countries simply sneak across the border to the United States, where work is relatively plentiful and wages are substantially higher than at home. What's more, these illegal aliens send literally billions of dollars home to support family members left behind. Throughout Latin America, these remittances from illegal aliens living in the United States have boosted local economies, even providing needed infrastructure in some communities—roads, schools and even sewers for remote villages. Experts estimate that remittances from family members living in the U.S. are now the chief source of foreign aid to Latin America.

5   But can the United States afford to have other countries encouraging their nationals to disobey U.S. immigration law? The fact is, these countries are simply taking advantage of the vacuum that exists in American immigration policy. Despite a lot of bombastic political rhetoric over illegal immigration, most politicians—from both parties—are unwilling to take the bull by the horns and come up with a sensible solution.

6   Like it or not, it's not possible simply to round up all the illegal aliens in the country and ship them home. Nor would it be desirable to do so. Our economy is simply too dependent on their labor to withstand a round up of illegals like the one the U.S. engaged in during the Great Depression. Most illegal aliens are gainfully employed doing dirty, often dangerous jobs that Americans won't take, at least not at wages that allow employers to keep the jobs here rather than ship the jobs overseas.

7   The only answer is a properly constructed guest worker program that regulates the flow of workers into the country, depending on economic conditions in the United States. When we face boom times and labor shortages, we should be able to bring in more workers. When the job market tightens and the economy contracts, we should be able to send them home again. Those already

living and working here, albeit illegally, ought to be able to "earn" legal status by paying a hefty fine for having broken our immigration laws, learning English and demonstrating work history and skills that make them a good bet as future workers.

8   A guest worker program may not be the perfect solution to our growing illegal immigration problem, but it's a lot better than what we have now: U.S. officials' wink and a nod to illegal immigration and foreign governments' open encouragement to their nationals to flout our laws.

For Class Discussion

1. Which of Chavez's reasons for a guest worker program in the United States strike you as particularly persuasive?

2. Chavez spends the first two-thirds of her article sketching for her readers the problem she is addressing. In the last third, she presents her solution. How effective is this rhetorical strategy?

3. How does Chavez use evidence in her argument?

4. What does this piece contribute to your understanding of immigration within a global context?   ■

Immigration Is Turning Britain into a Sweatshop
John Laughland

John Laughland has a doctorate in philosophy from the University of Oxford and currently lectures at various French universities. Laughland is a fellow of Sanders Research Associates, an independent firm formed in Ireland in 1997, which is devoted to analyzing "the global political economy for individuals and companies" and to asking critical, probing questions (found at www.sandersresearch.com). He is affiliated with the British Helsinki Human Rights Group and is an independent columnist who publishes his writing in British, European, and American newspapers. This piece appeared in the London paper *Mail on Sunday* on March 14, 2004.

What parallels between Britain and the United States does John Laughland draw in the economic problems behind the migration of people from poorer countries to richer countries?

1   The first time I visited the sinisterly named Lunik 9, a gipsy slum outside the Slovak town of Kosice, was in 1998.

2   Children, young people and adults cascaded from every door and window to throng around us.

3   They lived in terrible squalor as they had just been unceremoniously moved out of the centre of town on the orders of mayor Rudolf Schuster, now Slovakia's president.

4   I went there because there was a scare about gipsies flooding into Britain.

5   A programme on Slovak TV had told people they could come to Britain and claim benefit, and many did. Britain took emergency measures, imposing visas on all Slovaks, and the issue eventually died down.

6   But the scare discredited the government of the day, headed by Schuster's rival, because it was falsely claimed they were fleeing persecution: an example of how the gipsy issue is easily manipulated for shortterm political purposes.

7   Has anything changed? Some weeks ago the BBC, among others, started a new 'Slovak gipsies scare' by sending journalists to a gipsy camp. Other reporters followed, but Slovak journalists have complained that their British colleagues falsified their reports to claim the gipsies all intended to come to Britain on May 1, when Slovakia joins the European Union. But any gipsies who had wanted to come from Slovakia would have had little difficulty coming here in recent years as asylum seekers.

8   As a result, the British Government is to crack down on benefit scroungers.

9   But while this is welcome, it is irrelevant. Benefit tourism is being used as a smokescreen for the far more important issue of mass immigration of Eastern Europeans to Britain after May 1 for work. EU enlargement means that about 70 million people will have the right to come to work in Britain, and it is inevitable that huge numbers will.

10   The British Government has said it actively wants people to come and work here legally. As with asylum seekers, it likes to give the impression that the new arrivals will bring valuable skills.

11   Some will, but many will be unskilled or semiskilled, and this will exert an inevitable downward pressure on wages, especially for people already struggling on low pay.

12   Middleclass Government Ministers and other professionals will welcome an influx of cheap labour because they, and their friends in big business, will profit from it. It is our working classes, and those on low pay, who will lose out.

13   Supporters of immigration argue that it boosts economic growth and that everyone profits from having a healthy economy. But history does not bear this out.

14   Take America, where there was huge immigration during the late 19th and early 20th Centuries.

15   Between 1890 and 1913, the US economy grew at an annual rate of 1.9 per cent and there were more than six million

immigrants. From 1913 to 1929 more than 15 million immigrants arrived and growth fell to 1.1 per cent a year.

16   Compare that with the experience of Japan, which enjoyed huge economic growth from 1955 to 1993, yet there was virtually no immigration.

17   It is possible that economic output will go up if the population increases through immigration. This is because GDP figures are simply the aggregate of all economic activity: by definition, they go up if more people come here.

18   But this is not a measure of prosperity. What counts is income per head and this will fall especially for the poorest sections of our society if the immigrants drive down wages.

19   *The New Americans*, a book published by the U.S. National Research Council, calculated that the mass immigration of the Eighties reduced the wages of all native-born American workers competing with immigrants by about two per cent.

20   The effect of the May 1 expansion is likely to be much the same in Britain.

21   Sometimes, the last generation of immigrants suffers most. The American experience has shown that blacks remain an underclass as Hispanic immigration booms. Middleclass people may welcome Polish plumbers who are cheaper than British ones, but the main economic effect will be to ensure a fresh supply of unskilled labour in the agricultural and food sectors. In other words, immigration tends to shore up a 'sweatshop' economy, rather than making British manufacturing more sophisticated.

22   Therein lies a fundamental problem. Britain has had immigration for decades and yet we systematically see our manufacturing base seep away. This is because immigration allows employers to increase profits by driving down wages, instead of increasing productivity by investing in high-tech manufacturing. As long as there is a supply of cheap labour, there is little incentive to improve productivity.

23   Even skilled and educated Eastern European immigrants tend to take lower-paid or unskilled jobs for a host of reasons, including a lack of connections in this country and language difficulties. It is already common to find, say, Russian airline pilots working as builders in the West, or Serbian graduates working as nannies.

24   We already have a legal immigration rate of 200,000 a year, and an unknown amount of illegal immigration. As the Morecambe Bay disaster shows, illegal immigration is hardly policed at all. This flow will turn into a flood on May 1 because the Government, to please big business, has decided to keep down wages.

25   On its websites, it sells Britain to foreign 'investors', that is people who take their profits out of this country, on the basis that 'Labour market regulations in the UK, including working hours,

are the most flexible in Europe, and staffing costs are highly competitive'.

26   It even boasts that British labour law does not require a written contract.

27   In plain English, we are a low-wage economy with little labour protection.

28   The Government is trying to pretend that few will come, but Britain is the only one of the 15 existing EU states not to impose restrictions on labour from the accession countries from May 1.

29   The influx is inevitable because of the catastrophic economic situation in those countries. The president of the European Parliament, Pat Cox, has said growth in Poland is now five per cent and that Poles have more opportunities at home than here.

30   This is simply untrue. The official unemployment rate in Poland is nearly 20 per cent: more than four times our own.

31   But these figures underestimate the true level of joblessness. It is very difficult to sign on the dole in Poland, and you get only Pounds 5 a month. In fact, about half the adults in Poland, 15 million, do not have a job.

32   People get by through scrounging off their families, doing the occasional odd job, buying something here and selling something there. In western Poland, the most prosperous part of the country, unskilled work is paid at 20p per hour.

33   I know from observing elections in Eastern Europe that the main reason the people voted to join the EU is that it will allow them to work abroad.

34   The question in places such as Lithuania is not whether they are going to leave, but when.

35   Migrants will not be able to claim benefits, but they will be able to do the low-paid jobs. So business will be able to reap the profits, while poor British families will continue to be forced to live off the taxpayer. This is the equivalent of the Mexican solution in America.

36   And what do the British people think about this? We do not know, because no one has bothered to ask.

For Class Discussion

1. What is the main claim of this argument?

2. How does John Laughland support his argument? Which pieces of his evidence are the most persuasive?

3. How does he respond to opposing views?

4. What audience do you think Laughland is particularly trying to reach with this argument, which appeared in a general circulation news publication in Britain?

5. A critical reader might say that the title and the opening of this article play on sensationalism and fear. How does Laughland's argument justify or fail to justify his use of these attention-getting moves?

Illegal Immigrant Economy
Brian Fairrington

Brian Fairrington is a syndicated cartoonist with Cagle Cartoons. His cartoons have been published in hundreds of newspapers and publications including the *New York Times* and *USA Today,* and he is a regular editorial cartoonist for the *Arizona Republic.* This cartoon appeared on the online publication *Slate Magazine*'s Cagle Cartoon Index for October 17, 2003.

> What are the multiple perspectives on illegal immigrant labor portrayed in this cartoon?

For Class Discussion

1. What story does this cartoon tell? What is the setting? Who are the characters?

2. What does the vocal customer not understand about undocumented workers?

FIGURE 4.4 Illegal Immigrant Economy (© *Brian Fairrington*)

3. A key word in this cartoon is "benefit(s)." What is ironic about the use of this word in this cartoon?

4. Which articles in this chapter agree with this cartoon? Which disagree?

5. If you were to discuss the issue of benefits for illegal aliens with the customer in this cartoon, what questions might you need to research first? ■

When Guest Workers Opt Not to Go Home; German Example Shows Some Migrant Policies Lead to Isolation, Poverty

Don Melvin

Don Melvin works on the international staff of Knight-Ridder Tribune. This article was first published in Texas's *Austin American Statesman* on February 1, 2004.

How does Don Melvin try to make the problems of guest worker plans interesting, important, and relevant to general American readers?

1   Berlin—Fevzi Cakir came to Germany intending to stay a year or two. It was his plan, and that of the German government as well, that he would return shortly to his native Turkey. Thirty-nine years later he's still here. His wife is here. Two of his four children were born here. He likes his life in Berlin.

2   He came as a guest worker, and now he's a citizen. He should be a fan of guest worker programs, right?

3   Wrong. Such programs, in his view, cause serious problems.

4   "I don't understand why America is planning something like that," said Cakir, who is 62.

5   As the United States contemplates a proposal by President Bush to temporarily legalize some foreign workers with the expectation that they will eventually return to the lands of their birth, the German experience may provide a cautionary tale.

6   More than 40 years after the first Turkish guest workers arrived to help the country rebuild—World War II had left West Germany flush with Marshall Plan reconstruction money but short of manpower—a significant number are still here.

7   Many of the immigrants live in ghettos. Many, even children, do not speak German. Housing and education are substandard. Crime

is high. Unemployment, 18 percent among Berliners, is 35 percent among the city's Turks.

8   About three of every four Turks in Germany are not citizens, even after decades in the country. Many play no role in the political life of the country. They feel the sting of bigotry and keep to themselves.

9   Some, clinging to their roots in a land that remains foreign to them, practice Islam in a manner more conservative and rigid than many people in Turkey. Young people, devoid of prospects, have developed a hip hop-like culture of gold chains and aggressive behavior.

10   "I don't think the whole program is very good," "Cakir said. "It creates heavy problems, as we see here."

11   Germany's guest worker program began in 1955. At first, under treaties Germany negotiated with countries with high unemployment, the workers came from Italy. Spanish and Greek workers followed; then, in 1961, workers from Turkey began to come, followed by those from Morocco and elsewhere.

12   By 1970, 3 million foreign-born people lived in the country, nearly 5 percent of the population. The program ended in 1973, when the worldwide oil crisis slowed the German economy.

13   But as family members came to Germany to join the workers, the number swelled to 7.3 million by the beginning of 2002.

14   The largest group is the Turks. Nearly 3 million live in Germany, about 200,000 of them in Berlin. Some of the city's neighborhoods are overwhelmingly Turkish, with Turkish doctors, lawyers, shops, eateries, salons. Many apartments are fitted with satellite dishes to pick up Turkish TV.

15   Citizenship, while not impossible to obtain, is difficult. Although Germany's citizenship law was liberalized in 2000, for many years it gave preference to applicants believed to have Teutonic ancestry, required a minimum residency of 15 years and required that other citizenship be renounced, something many older Turks were reluctant to do.

16   Many of the problems are in part attributable to the guest worker concept, according to government officials, academics and members of the Turkish community. Everybody—the German government and the guest workers themselves—assumed the situation was temporary and acted accordingly. There was denial on both sides that what was taking place was immigration, said Ruth Mandel, who teaches anthropology at University College in London and is on leave writing a book about Turks in Germany.

17   For decades, the German government asserted stoutly that "Germany is not an immigration country" and the word immigrant was never used in referring to the workers. No money was spent to teach the immigrants the German language or to help them integrate into German society.

18   Nor did the migrants themselves make much effort. Cumali Kangal came to Germany 30 years ago to work in a metal factory, assuming he was staying only temporarily. It wasn't until seven or eight years later that it finally struck him that he ought to learn the language.

19   Turkish parents have often shuttled their children between countries, enrolling them in German schools for a year or two, then sending them to school in Turkey for a while.

20   "Many generations of children have grown up basically as bilingual illiterates." Mandel said.

21   "Language is one of the biggest problems we have," said Michael Ried, a high school chemistry teacher. "If a student does not speak German properly we are of course unable to teach him anything."

22   German employers, too, found a temporary program less to their liking than they had expected. They were loath to send workers away once they were trained.

23   "Economically, it's nonsense for the factories to change every year the personnel," said Safter Cinar, an official with the Turkischer Bund, or Turkish Federation, in Berlin.

24   For that reason, a temporary worker program makes sense only when the work itself is temporary, said Barbara John, who retired recently after 22 years as Berlin's commissioner for migration and integration. If the workers must leave when the crops are finished, that makes sense, she said. To hire temporary workers for industry, she said, does not.

25   In addition, she said, it is difficult to enforce temporary programs when there is great economic disparity between the new country and the country of origin. While the program proposed by President Bush is aimed primarily at workers already in the United States illegally, it would also apply to prospective workers abroad.

26   People familiar with the German experience say there are lessons for all concerned. Kangal, in addition to urging workers to learn the language earlier than he did, said the host country should enter the arrangement with open eyes.

27   If a country, needing cheap labor, hires another country's least qualified workers, it will get poorly educated and unsophisticated people ill equipped to learn the language and assimilate.

28   Though he is a Turk and experiences prejudice "every day," he also said it was not primarily Turkey's elite who had come to Germany. "In some ways," he said, "the prejudice is not wrong."

29   And Mandel said the host country should have what she called "an ethics of hospitality."

30   The German example of making citizenship very difficult to acquire should be avoided, she said. The new citizenship law enacted in Germany in 2000 lowered the minimum residency

requirement from 15 to eight years and grants dual citizenship to children born in Germany whose foreign-born parents have resided in the country for at least eight years.

31   "The worst thing is for a society to set up a new and separate economic class with a different set of rights," she said. That, she said, is a "recipe for divisiveness."

For Class Discussion

1. In this article, Don Melvin presents a precedent argument based on his claim that the United States should not establish a guest worker program like Germany's after World War II. What reasons does Melvin provide in support of this claim?

2. In this piece, written for a general newspaper audience in a casual, easy-reading journalistic style, Melvin develops his argument with examples and quotations. Which pieces of support are particularly persuasive and rhetorically effective for this audience?

3. If the United States wanted to proceed with a guest worker plan, what could it learn from Germany's experience with guest workers? In other words, what should the United States do differently?

Anti-Immigration Bumper Stickers

These bumper stickers (shown only as text here) appear on a commercial Web site directed toward people who want to express their anger and anxiety about illegal immigration (www.illegalimmigrationbumperstickers.com/).

What audience beliefs and fears do these bumper stickers speak to?

PROTECT AMERICAN WAGES! END ILLEGAL
IMMIGRATION NOW!

**DON'T GAMBLE WITH OUR HOMELAND SECURITY
SEAL OUR BORDERS!**

FIRST OUR FACTORIES LEAVE,
THEN 7,000,000 ILLEGAL ALIENS
COME TAKE THE JOBS THAT ARE LEFT!

**PROTECT
AMERICAN
WAGES!**

END ILLEGAL IMMIGRATION NOW!

(© Illegal Immigration. Used with permission.)

For Class Discussion

1. Bumper stickers are a flashy, in-your-face, abbreviated form of argument. How would you express the claims presented in these bumper stickers in more complete thoughts?

2. To whom do you think the message of these bumper stickers is directed? What group of people are they trying to influence? What actions or changes would the proponents of these bumper stickers like to see?

3. Use the Web address www.illegalimmigrationbumperstickers.com to see these bumper stickers in color with their accompanying symbolic images. How do some of these bumper stickers try to use the emotional charge of patriotism to reinforce their messages?

4. What assumptions about the American economy, American workers, and illegal immigrants would the supporters of these bumper stickers hold?

5. Numerous advocacy groups and organizations agree with these bumper stickers, among them, Immivasion (www.immivasion.us); ImmigrationsHumanCost.org; Federation for American Immigration Reform (www.fairus.org). Americans for Immigration Control (www.immigrationcontrol.com); Americans for Better Immigration (www.betterimmigration.org); and Minuteman Project (www .minutemanproject.com). After investigating some of these organizations' Web sites, list the reasons and evidence they offer to support these bumper stickers' claims. In other words, how do these organizations justify their views and what actions are they promoting to solve the problems they perceive?   ■

The Special Case of Mexican Immigration

Samuel P. Huntington

Samuel P. Huntington is a major scholarly analyst in the fields of international relations, comparative politics, and American politics. He is the chairman of the Harvard Academy for International and Area Studies, cofounder of *Foreign Policy* magazine, a vocal neoconservative, and a prolific writer. His famous book *The Clash of Civilizations and the Remaking of the World Order* (1996) posits the thesis that the main conflicts of our global age will not be economic, political, or environmental; instead they will center on the values of groups of people (civilizations) and will involve their history, culture, and religion. Huntington has sparked even more controversy with his recent argument about the threat and challenge of Mexican immigration to

U.S. national identity. He advances this position in his article entitled "The Hispanic Challenge," published in both *Foreign Affairs* and *Foreign Policy* magazines, and in his most recent book, *Who Are We? The Challenges to America's National Identity* (2004). "The Special Case of Mexican Immigration" is an adaptation of these longer writings. It appeared in 2000 in the *American Enterprise*, the online publication of the American Enterprise Institute, a conservative think tank. This publication says it seeks to appeal to a wide range of readers and to promote informed, independent thinking by offering well-reasoned and highly readable arguments.

Many of the articles in this chapter focus on economic issues related to immigration. In contrast, where does Huntington think the main U.S. problems with immigration lie?

1   America is often described as a country defined by commitment to a creed formulated in the writings of our Founders. But American identity is only partly a matter of creed. For much of our history we also defined ourselves in racial, religious, ethnic, and cultural terms.

2   Before the Revolution we thought of ourselves in religious terms: 98 percent of Americans were Protestants, and Catholic Spain and France were our enemies. We also thought of ourselves in racial and ethnic terms: 80 percent of Americans at the time of the Revolution were from the British Isles. The other 20 percent were largely German and Dutch.

3   America is also often described as a nation of immigrants. We should distinguish immigrants, however, from settlers. Immigrants are people who leave one society and move to a recipient society. Early Americans did not immigrate to an existing society; they established new societies, in some cases for commercial reasons, more often for religious reasons. It was the new societies they created, basically defined by Anglo-Protestant culture, that attracted subsequent generations of immigrants to this country.

4   Demographer Campbell Gibson has done a very interesting analysis of the evolution of the United States' population. He argues that if no immigrants had come to this country after 1790, the population of the United States in 1990 would have been just about half of what it actually was. Thus, the American people are literally only half an immigrant people.

5   There have been great efforts in our history to limit immigration. In only one decade in the nineteenth century did the annual intake of immigrants amount to more than 1 percent of the population each year. In three other decades it was slightly over eight-tenths of 1 percent, while in six decades it was less than four-tenths of 1 percent. Obviously immigration has been tremendously important to this

country, but the foreign-born population has exceeded 10 percent of our total population only in the seven census years from 1860 to 1930. (When the 2000 census results come out we will be back above the 10 percent level again.)

6   As I began to investigate the question of immigration, I came to the conclusion that our real problem is not so much immigration as assimilation. Seventy-five or 100 years ago there were great pressures to ensure that immigrants assimilated to the Anglo-Protestant culture, work ethic, and principles of the American creed. Now we are uncertain what immigrants should assimilate to. And that is a serious problem.

7   As I went further in my research, I concluded there was a still more significant problem, a problem that encompasses immigration, assimilation, and other things, too—what I will refer to as the Mexican problem. Much of what we now consider to be problems concerning immigration and assimilation really concern Mexican immigration and assimilation. Mexican immigration poses challenges to our policies and to our identity in a way nothing else has in the past.

8   There are five distinctive characteristics of the Mexican question which make it special. First, Mexican immigration is different because of contiguity. We have thought of immigration as being symbolized by Ellis Island, and perhaps now by Kennedy Airport. But Mexicans do not come across 2,000 miles of ocean. They come, often easily, across 2,000 miles of land border.

9   Our relationship with Mexico in this regard is in many respects unique in the world. No other First World country has a land frontier with a Third World country—much less one of 2,000 miles. The significance of this border is enhanced by the economic differences between the two countries. The income gap between Mexico and us is the largest between any two contiguous countries in the world.

10   The second distinctive aspect of today's Mexican immigration concerns numbers. Mexican immigration during the past several decades has been very substantial. In 1998 Mexican immigrants constituted 27 percent of the total foreign-born population in this country; the next largest two contingents, Filipinos and Chinese, each amounted to only 4 percent. Mexicans constituted two-thirds of Spanish-speaking immigrants, who in turn were over half of all new arrivals between 1970 and 1996. Our post-1965 wave of immigration differs from previous waves in having a majority from a single non-English language group.

11   A third distinguishing characteristic of this Mexican immigration is illegality. Illegal immigration is overwhelmingly a post-1965 and Mexican phenomenon. In 1995, according to one report, Mexicans made up 62 percent of the immigrants who entered the United States illegally. In 1997, the Immigration and Naturalization

Service estimated Mexican illegals were nine times as numerous as the next largest contingent, from El Salvador.

12   The next important characteristic of Mexican immigration has been its concentration in a particular region. Mexican immigrants are heavily concentrated in the Southwest and particularly in southern California. This has very real consequences. Our Founders emphasized that immigrants would have to be dispersed among what they described as the English population in this country. To the extent that we have a large regional concentration of immigrants, it is a departure from our usual pattern.

13   Now obviously we have previously had high concentrations of immigrants in particular areas, such as the Irish in Boston, but by and large the immigrants have dispersed to different cities, and those cities have simultaneously hosted many different immigrant groups. This is the case still in New York, where there are many immigrants today, but no group that dominates. In Southern California, though, two-thirds or more of all the children in school are Spanish speaking. As Abe Lowenthal and Katrina Burgess write in *The California-Mexico Connection*, "No school system in a major U.S. city has ever experienced such a large influx of students from a single foreign country. The schools of Los Angeles are becoming Mexican."

14   Finally, there is the matter of the persistence of Mexico's large immigration. Previous waves of immigration fairly soon came to an end. The huge 1840s and '50s influxes from Ireland and Germany were drastically reduced by the Civil War and the easing of the Irish potato famine. The big wave at the turn of the century came to an end with World War I and the restrictive legislation in 1924.

15   These breaks greatly helped to facilitate the assimilation of the newcomers. In contrast, there does not seem to be any prospect of the current wave, begun over three decades ago, coming to an end soon. Mexican immigration may eventually subside as the Mexican birth rate slows, and possibly as a result of long-term economic development in Mexico. But those effects will only occur over a very long term. For the time being we are faced with substantial continued immigration from Mexico.

16   Sustained high levels of immigration build on themselves. After the first immigrants come from a country, it is easier for others from that country to come. Immigration is not a self-limiting process, it is a self-enhancing one.

17   And the longer immigration continues, the more difficult politically it is to stop. Leaders of immigrant organizations and interest groups develop a vested interest in expanding their own constituency. Immigration develops political support, and becomes more difficult to limit or reshape.

18   For all these reasons Mexican immigration is unique. What are the implications of this for assimilation?

19   The answer appears uncertain. In education and economic activity, Mexicans rate much lower than other immigrant groups. The rate of intermarriage between Hispanics and other Americans appears to be decreasing rather than increasing. (In 1977, 31 percent of all Hispanic marriages were interethnic; in 1994, 25.5 percent were.) With respect to language, I suspect Mexicans will in large part follow the pattern of earlier immigrants, with the third generation being fluent in English, but quite possibly, unlike previous third generations, also fluent in their ancestral language.

20   All of the characteristics I have mentioned lead to the possibility of a cultural community evolving in the Southwest in which people could pursue their lives within an overwhelmingly Mexican community, without ever having to speak English. This has already happened with the Cubans in Miami, and it could be reproduced on a larger and more significant scale in the Southwest. We know in the coming decades people of Hispanic origin will be a majority of the people in California and eventually in other southwestern states. America is moving in the direction of becoming a bilingual and bicultural society.

21   Without Mexican immigration, the overall level of immigration to this country would be perhaps two-thirds of what it has been— near the levels recommended by Barbara Jordan's immigration commission a few years ago. Illegal entries would be relatively minor. The average skill and education level of immigrants would be the highest in American history, and the much-debated balance of economic benefits versus costs of immigration would tilt heavily toward the positive side. The bilingual education issue would fade from our agenda. A major potential challenge to the cultural, and conceivably political, integrity of the United States would disappear.

22   Mexico and Mexican immigration, however, will not disappear, and learning to live with both may become more and more difficult. President-elect Vicente Fox wants to remove all restrictions on the movement of Mexicans into the United States.

23   In almost every recent year the Border Patrol has stopped about 1 million people attempting to enter the U.S. illegally from Mexico. It is generally estimated that about 300,000 make it across illegally. If over 1 million Mexican soldiers crossed the border, Americans would treat it as a major threat to their national security and react accordingly. The invasion of over 1 million Mexican civilians is a comparable threat to American societal security, and Americans should react against it with comparable vigor.

24   Mexican immigration looms as a unique and disturbing challenge to our cultural integrity, our national identity, and potentially to our future as a country.

For Class Discussion

1. What points would you include in a summary of Huntington's ideas in this article?

2. The American Enterprise Institute is a conservative think tank. What features of this article's structure, depth of material, main points, and kinds of evidence indicate that its publication, the *American Enterprise*, seeks to reach a broad audience?

3. Many people responding to Huntington's book *Who Are We?* and his article "The Hispanic Challenge," which develop the views presented in this piece, have criticized Huntington for fostering racism and nativism (privileging native-born residents over immigrants). What ideas in this article could fuel those attitudes toward immigrants? What assumptions would an audience have to hold about Mexican immigration in order to agree with Huntington?

4. What key points about immigration, especially Mexican immigration, is Huntington *not* factoring into his argument? In your view, how would including those points affect the logic and credibility of his argument?   ∎

MALDEF and LULAC Rebuke Samuel Huntington's Theories on Latino Immigrants and Call on America to Reaffirm Its Commitment to Equal Opportunity and Democracy

Mexican American Legal Defense and Educational Fund (MALDEF) and League of United Latin American Citizens (LULAC)

This policy statement, dated April 23, 2004, is a formal response to Samuel P. Huntington's publications on Mexican immigration. The Mexican American Legal Defense and Educational Fund protects the legal rights of Latinos. It is a national, nonprofit, nonpartisan organization headquartered in

Washington, D.C. Also centered there, the League of United Latin American Citizens is a grassroots organization committed to the civil rights of Latinos. Both of these organizations are large, well established, and highly reputable. On its "About Us" link on its Web site, MALDEF states its mission "to foster sound public policies, laws and programs to safeguard the civil rights of the 40 million Latinos living in the United States and to empower the Latino community to fully participate in our society" (www.maldef.org).

How does the mission of MALDEF itself refute Huntington's underlying thesis? What impression of the Latino community does this refutation of Huntington's views convey?

1   On May 27th, Samuel P. Huntington will publish his new book, alleging that Latino immigration threatens "Anglo-Protestant values" which are the "creed" of American culture. Since the release of his article announcing his new theory in *Foreign Policy* magazine in March,[1] Huntington's methodology and conclusions have been proven wrong by experts across the board.[2] As national Latino civil rights groups, we further believe that Huntington's writing is dangerously biased against Latinos and goes against fundamental American values.

2   **Huntington's biases are un-American.** The United States is a nation of immigrants from around the world. In the U.S., individual accomplishment is valued. The very foundation of American democracy is the Bill of Rights, respecting and even guaranteeing

---

[1] S. Huntington, "José, Can You See?" Samuel Huntington on how Hispanic immigrants threaten America's identity, values, and way of life (*Foreign Policy,* March/April 2004)(cover story).

[2] *See,* e.g., D. Glenn, "Critics Assail Scholar's Article Arguing that Hispanic Immigration Threatens U.S.," *Chronicle of Higher Education* (Feb. 24, 2004)(disproving methodology/ citations); D. Brooks, "The Americano Dream," *New York Times* (Editorial, Feb. 24, 2004); A. Oppenheimer, "Racists Will Love New 'Hispanic Threat' Book," *Miami Herald* (Feb. 26, 2004)(assimilation trend); R. Navarrette, "Professor Huntington Has Short Memory of Past Immigrants," *Dallas Morning News* (Mar. 3, 2004)(immigration facts wrong); Lexington, "A Question of Identity—Despite new arguments to the contrary, Latino immigration is still good for America," *The Economist* (Mar. 6th–12th, 2004 issue); F. de Ortego y Gasca, "Something About Harvard-Dreaming in English," *Hispanic Vista* (Mar. 14, 2004); M. Casillas, D. Rocha & M. Hernandez, "The Hispanic Contribution," *Harvard Crimson* (Mar. 18, 2004); C. Fuentes, "Looking for Enemies in the Wrong Places," *Miami Herald* (Mar. 28, 2004); A. Lanier, "Stigmatization of Hispanics is Unwarranted," *Chicago Tribune* (Editorial Board Member)(April 4, 2004); M. Elliott, "New Patriots In Our Midst—A forthcoming book says Mexican Americans won't assimilate. It's wrong," *TIME Magazine* (April 12, 2004)(citations wrong and do not prove conclusions).

individual rights. By passing various civil rights laws in the 1960's, Congress re-established that our Constitution also means that not one race, religion or ethnicity should dominate another. The American dream is built upon the hard work of immigrants and the fundamental value of equal opportunity. We must not go back to a system where one's race, class or religion determines one's fate, regardless of one's intellect or willingness to work hard.

3   **Huntington has made astonishing and unsupported generalizations about Latinos.** His generalizations about Latinos being "persistent" in immigrating to the U.S., being exceedingly fertile, having less interest in education and not wanting to learn English are not based on fact and appear to emanate from a prejudice against Latinos. He has no proof that every Latino/a, or even the majority of Latinos/as and their families, fall into these stereotypes, nor any proof that Latinos are very different from other ethnic groups. This kind of analysis harkens back to the justifications for legal segregation and discriminatory policies that were commonplace prior to the civil rights laws of the 1960's.[3]

4   **Mexican-Americans and Latino immigrants are not inferior to white Anglo-Protestants.** A recent *New York Times* poll found that Latino immigrants are hard-working, have strong family values, do not take public benefits, and generally epitomize the American dream.[4] Latino immigrants are contributing billions of dollars to the economy and even creating jobs for U.S. citizens.[5] Studies consistently find that immigrants contribute far more in taxes to the government than they use in government services.[6]

---

[3] V. Ruiz, "We Always Tell Our Children They Are Americans" *Méndez v. Westminster* and the California Road to Brown v. Board of Education, Review No. 200, Fiftieth Anniversary of the Supreme Court Ruling (College Board, Fall 2003), at p. 20–23 (Detailing history of Latino school segregation, along with other forms of segregation, "justified" by racial myths alleging Mexican Americans [are] not like "Americans"; social scientists were needed to disprove these myths in a 1944 *Méndez v. Westminster* school desegregation case).

[4] S. Romero & J. Elder, "Hispanics in U.S. Report Optimism," *New York Times* (Aug. 6, 2003).

[5] D'Vera Cohn, "Immigrants Account for Half of New Workers—Report Calls Them Increasingly Needed for Economic Growth" *New York Times* (Dec. 2, 2003)(analyzing Center for Labor Market Studies report). *See also* R. Hinojosa-Ojeda, "Comprehensive Migration Policy Reform in North America: The Key to Sustainable and Equitable Economic Integration." North American Integration and Development Center, University of California, Los Angeles (2001).

[6] *See*, e.g., M. Fix & J. Passel, "Immigration and Immigrants. Setting the Record Straight." Urban Institute (1994) at [p.] 6 ("Overall, annual taxes paid by immigrants to all levels of government more than offset the costs of services received, generating a net annual surplus of $25 billion to $30 billion.").

Latina/o parents value education and encourage their children to do well in school at the same rates as Anglo parents, with more than 90 percent of Latina/o children reporting that their parents want them to go to college.[7] Moreover, studies demonstrate that Mexican Americans support American core values at least as much as Anglos.[8]

5   <u>Huntington alleges that Latinos do not want to become American, despite the fact that Latino immigrants consciously choose to leave their home countries and migrate to the U.S. in order to become American and live the American dream, especially for their children.</u> Everything that is traditionally thought of as "American," Latinos live out fully. They are family-oriented, religious, hard-working and loyal to the U.S. In fact, Latinos have won more medals of honor for their service in the U.S. military than any other ethnic group.

6   <u>Huntington fails to take into account that the significant accomplishments of Latinos have occurred in spite of the long and shameful history of discrimination specifically directed against Latinos in the U.S.</u> When Huntington alleges that Latinos have not achieved as much as whites in education, he neglects to acknowledge the history of segregation against Latinos, and Mexican Americans in particular, especially in the Southwest. Even today, when legal segregation is outlawed, Huntington does not take into account that Latinos are attending the most segregated schools in the country, which are providing a lesser quality of education as compared to majority white schools.[9] Predominantly minority schools have less-qualified teachers, more overcrowding, worse educational facilities, and less access to advanced curricula. Despite all these barriers, children of Latino immigrants are succeeding at a very high rate.

---

[7] A. Ginorio & M. Huston, *¡Si Se Puede! Yes We Can! Latinas in School,* Values, Expectations and Norms (American Assn. of Univ. Women, 2001), at pp. 22–24.

[8] R. de la Garza, A. Falcon & F. C. Garcia, "Will the Real Americans Please Stand Up: Anglo and Mexican-American Support of Core American Political Values," Vol. 40, No. 2 *American Journal of Political Science* (May 1996), pp. 335–51 (Results were that: "At all levels of acculturation, Mexican-Americans are no less likely and often more likely to endorse values of individualism and patriotism than are Anglos."). Also, 9 out of 10 Latinos new to the U.S. believe it is important to change so they can fit into American society. R. Pastor, *Toward a North American Community; Lessons from the Old World for the New World* (Wash, D.C., Institute for International Economics, 2001), pp. 164–166 (*citing* Washington Post, Kaiser Foundation and Harvard Univ. comprehensive poll).

[9] Associated Press, "Latinos Segregated 50 Years After Brown v. Board of Ed" (April 6, 2004)(also reporting that no national policies specifically address Latino school education).

7   **It is ironic that Huntington blames Latinos for segregation.**[10] Latinos and other people of color know from tough experience that such segregation is not voluntary, as it [is] still difficult for Latinos to gain equality in white communities, and there is still discrimination in jobs and housing. However, like African-Americans, Latinos have been segregated and mythologized as "different," and subject to unfair criticism, because of their ethnicity.

8   **Huntington criticizes Latinos' use of Spanish and falsely alleges that Latinos do not want to learn English.** The majority of Latinos speak English. Among Spanish-speaking Latinos, poll after poll shows that Latinos want to learn English.[11] Their ability to learn English is sometimes limited if they entered the U.S. at an older age and when they do not have access to English classes because they are working more than one job and there are limited English classes offered. As far as the ability to speak Spanish, Huntington portrays it as a negative, whereas in the global economy, many see such language capabilities are a positive.

9   **Huntington mischaracterizes the history between the U.S. and Mexico and the causes for migration patterns between the two countries.** Huntington characterizes Mexican immigration as "persistent" and a "massive influx" post-1960's civil rights laws. This characterization fails to recognize the unique, historical relationship between the two countries. In 1848, the U.S. acquired a significant portion of Mexico, which became what is now known as the Southwest in the U.S. Those people living in that region were Mexican citizens prior to the acquisition. When the U.S. experienced severe labor shortages while its soldiers were fighting in the world wars, the U.S. entered into several agreements with Mexico to bring temporary migrant laborers from Mexico who worked under abusive conditions in the agricultural fields for decades. Most of these workers did not have the opportunity to become citizens, making it difficult to exercise full political participation. During the Great Depression, the U.S. government and a number of state and

---

[10]"Majority of Americans Prefer to Live in Mixed Neighborhoods," *Diversity.com* (April 9, 2004)("According to the 'Civil Rights and Race Relations' survey conducted by Gallup, 68 percent of African Americans, 61 percent of Latinos and 57 percent of whites prefer to live in mixed neighborhoods.").

[11]Moreover, comprehensive studies demonstrate that the rate of linguistic assimilation of immigrants is just as rapid as it has been in previous generations. *See* S. Nicolan & R. Valdivieso, "The Veltman Report: What it Says, What it Means," Intro, C. Veltman, *The Future of Spanish Language in the United States* (New York, Wash. D.C.: Hispanic Policy Dev. Project, 1988) at i–x. Among first-generation native born Mexican Americans, 95% are proficient in English. K. McCarthy & R. Burciaga Valdez, *Current and Future Effects of Mexican Immigration in California* (The Rand Corp. 1985).

local governments forced repatriation of one-third of the Mexican American population to impoverished conditions in Mexico. Shockingly, most of those who were deported were U.S. citizens who happened to be of Mexican ethnicity.[12] Despite this checkered past, Mexican immigrants continued to come to the U.S. to fill U.S. economic needs and to pursue economic opportunities not available in Mexico.[13]

10   **Characterizing past non-Mexican immigration as "legal" and current Mexican immigration as "illegal" is false and misleading.** Prior to 1939, it was not illegal to enter the U.S. without the U.S. government's permission. Millions of immigrants, mostly from Western Europe, entered the U.S. without proper visas.[14] Currently, many Mexicans enter the U.S legally. The U.S. legal immigration system, however, is in need of serious overhaul. The current system is not meeting the economic or family reunification principles it was designed to meet. The backlogs in legal visa processing for the spouses and children of Mexican legal immigrants living in the U.S. are causing families to be separated for 13 years. In order to reunite with their families, some Mexican citizens do enter without proper documentation.

11   **Present high levels of migration between the U.S. and Mexico are based on geographic proximity and economic interdependence of the two countries.** Many Mexicans come here because Mexico is our close neighbor and trading partner. Mexico is closer than Europe so the voyage to America is more natural. The U.S. and Mexican fate and economies are inextricably intertwined. That is, the U.S. is just as dependent on Mexico and Mexican migration as the opposite is true.

For Class Discussion

1. This is a bare-bones argument, a policy statement structured as a rebuttal to Samuel P. Huntington's articles and book on Mexican immigration. What reasoning and evidence are persuasive? What points call for more development in order to be persuasive to a general audience?

2. What is the rhetorical effect of the extensive documentation in this argument?

---

[12]F. Balderrama & R. Rodríguez, *Decade of Betrayal: Mexican Repatriation in the 1930's* (1995).

[13]*See*, e.g., "The Hispanic Challenge? What We Know About Latino Immigration," Woodrow Wilson International Center/Migration Policy Institute Panel of Experts (R. Suro, E. Grieco, D. Gutierrez, M. Jones-Correa, R. Stanton-Salazar)(Mar. 29, 2004).

[14]D. Weissbrodt, *Immigration Law and Procedure*, Ch. 1. History of U.S. Immigration Law and Policy (West 1998).

3. In your mind, does this article incorporate key points about immigration that Huntington omits? How does MALDEF seek to reframe the controversy over cultural integration?

4. Where or how could this argument acknowledge alternative views?

■

No Room at the Inn
Yasmin Alibhai-Brown

Educated at Oxford University, Yasmin Alibhai-Brown is a British Muslim journalist from Uganda. In the 1980s, she worked for the *New Statesman* and currently writes a weekly column for the *Independent*. She has been a fellow of the Institute for Public Policy Research, a British think tank connected to the Labour Party. She has also published a number of books, among them *Who Do We Think We Are? Imagining the New Britain* (2001), *Mixed Feelings: The Lives of Mixed Race Britons* (2002), and *Some of My Best Friends Are . . .* (2004). Alibhai-Brown is considered an articulate voice in the current public controversies in Britain over cultural integration, race, and national identity. This piece was published in the October 2002 issue of the *New Internationalist*. The Web site for this group describes it as "a workers' cooperative . . . to report on the issues of world poverty and inequality; to focus attention on the unjust relationship between the powerful and powerless worldwide; to debate and campaign for the radical changes necessary to meet the basic needs of all; and to bring to life the people, the ideas and the action in the fight for global justice" ("About Us," www.newint.org).

> In her redefinition of the controversies surrounding immigration in Europe, how does Yasmin Alibhai-Brown connect global justice, immigration, cultural integration, and racism in her argument?

1   People attending a Holocaust Memorial Day in London in 2001 will never forget the appearance on stage of Kemal Pervanic, the once-emaciated Bosnian Muslim seen on the news looking through barbed wire in the Serb-built Omarska concentration camp.

2   He spoke evocatively in English about what he had been made to suffer, but this was not the same man who had been broken by starvation and humiliation. His smart suit, beautifully groomed long hair and supreme confidence symbolized the vital reclamation of a lost life. He fled to the UK in 1993 and is now a science graduate. Britain gave him a future, by letting him come here as a refugee. It is what European countries used to do.

3   Populist anti-immigration politicians now in the ascendancy across Europe are destroying this precious heritage and have embarked on a concerted project which will create a white Fortress Europe rejecting and ejecting desperate people who are not white

or Christian. These leaders may pretend that they are responding to 'illegal' immigrants but it is pernicious racism and xenophobia which is animating their zeal and policies.

4 The assertion is easily proved. Where is the hysteria in Europe about white South Africans and white Zimbabweans who flood into the continent? They end up in top jobs and yet they are not resented or despised. Spain, so troubled that immigrants are rushing in, ignores the destruction of the Spanish national character by English immigrants on the south coast who do not integrate and who have criminals and anti-social exiles nestling in their enclaves. Politicians and others may claim that they are concerned about immigration and 'culture' but this latest flare-up is all about white panic brought about by the knowledge that most of the world's refugees at present are Muslims and are black or brown.

5 In Britain in 1997 only 0.18 per cent of applications from Australian visitors were denied. The figure for Ghanaians was 30 per cent. Almost all US citizens requesting settlement rights in Britain were granted these rights but 30 per cent of Indians failed to acquire residency.

6 Those who temporarily make it are left in no doubt that they are unwanted. At a school in London this is a poem I heard recited by refugee children.

> *Sorry*
> *Sorry that we are here*
> *That we take your time*
> *Sorry*
> *Sorry that we breathe in your air*
> *That we walk on your ground*
> *That we stand in your view*
> *Sorry*
> *That my name is not David*
> *Or Catherine*
> *Or Mary*
> *But Rushed*
> *And Hotly...*
> *And sorry that we brought nothing*
> *The only thing we have is a story*
> *Not even a happy story.*

7 European Jews should know this well. In 1888 the *Manchester City News* wrote about Jews escaping pogroms in Eastern Europe: 'Their unclean habits, their wretched clothing and miserable food enables them to perpetuate existence upon a pittance ... they have flooded the market with cheap labour.' In 1905 the Aliens Act was passed by politicians eager to placate these prejudices. Some 1,378 Jews were deported soon after. In 1938 the *Express* riled against an 'influx of Jews ... who are overrunning the country'.

'CARRIERS OF CHAOS'

8   MC—the name appears Kurdish—sends me this email: 'I have no chance of warding off the emotional tauntings and assaults of some peer groups of white guys . . . How should I act in this situation and continue preserving my self-esteem and not start behaving like them? I have been beaten and called "fucking Paki".'

9   Every week I get a number of such desperate e-mails from asylum seekers who obviously use their meagre allowances in internet cafés in order to express their grief and rage at the way they are forced to live. One such young man, 22-year-old Firstat Yildez from Turkey, was murdered in an unprovoked racist attack in Sighthill, Glasgow, the city which received 4,000 asylum seekers last March. Hundreds of asylum seekers are currently in prison without being charged or convicted of any crime and many of them are picked on for 'special treatment' by inmates and officers.

10   Death of non-white immigrants evokes little sympathy. Two years ago the bodies of 58 young Chinese men and women were found in the back of an airless container on one of the hottest days of the year in Britain. Imagine the horror. The piss and vomit and clawed flesh, wild screams and fists banging on the walls. The nameless 58—after all they were only Chinese, plenty more of them in the world—vanished into the ether, ignored by politicians, even in death un-pitied as 'economic migrants'.

11   White immigrants are always seen as 'intrepid' people with 'vigorous' blood which adds to the stock of the receiving nation; similarly ambitious immigrants with darker skin or other 'alien' characteristics are always presumed to be carriers of chaos and untold problems.

12   Politicians and opinion-makers would deny that they are being racist or xenophobic. It is to do with culture, they argue, and to keep indigenous populations from feeling 'swamped' and thus prey to rabid extremists.

13   Once more the underpinning xenophobia becomes evident. The murder of Pim Fortuyn, the gay, so-called 'liberal' yet vehemently anti-immigrant politician, brought this agenda out in the open. He became a hero overnight for being the first to 'dare' to bring up cultural protectionism as a reason for his policies.

14   In the wake of this killing, nearby Denmark brought in the most punitive asylum laws of any developed country, mainly because the population does not want more Muslims entering the country. France and Germany only take people who can prove persecution by the State. This means that Algerians fleeing unidentified murder squads or Palestinians trying to escape the wretched battles between their militants and the hard-line Israeli Government would have no case at all in those countries. These policies are tailor-made to exclude people whose lives are destroyed by a

number of forces and almost all these people are from poorer or Muslim countries.

MONGREL CONTINENT

15   The assumption is that the European nations have superior mono-cultural identities which are threatened by dark hordes who will destroy the democratic heart of the continent. But Europe has always been a mongrel continent, made and remade by outsiders who come in and change the countries and themselves. Most non-white Europeans would not return to their countries because they now value democracy, freedom and rights which they have acquired through migration.

16   And in time many give their adopted country much more than they ever take from it, as a British government report *Migration, an Economic and Social Analysis* confirms. Levels of entrepreneurship, self-employment and education are high. At present 33 per cent of asylum seekers to Britain have a degree or professional qualifica-tions compared with 15 per cent of the British population; 65 per cent speak at least two languages in addition to their first language; 66 per cent had jobs in their own countries.

17   Those unquantifiable benefits count for far more than the plain economics of course, in sports, the arts, pop music, food. The best selling author of *White Teeth* Zadie Smith and top heart-transplant surgeon Sir Magdi Yacoub are products of the searing and creative interactions and exchanges which migration forces both on those who move and the inhabitants of the places they move to.

18   Immigration brings new blood and extraordinary advantages. There are challenges to be met. Integration and disintegration are real problems as is civic unrest and social disorder. When people with diverse values share spaces, there is inevitable internal compe-tition. As immigration debates get ever more emotive, settled migrants and citizens of colour react with animosity towards new arrivals whatever the push factors. Politicians from the main par-ties and sections of the media have convinced British people of all races that their good lives are in jeopardy, threatened by newcom-ers who are mostly liars, thugs, thieves, with contrived sob stories about human-rights abuses which they use as illegal passports to enter and settle down in a country which patently does not want or believe them.

19   Societies, too, have the right to reject values which are directly inimical to human rights and social democracy. Some hard ongoing bargaining on just what is appropriate and acceptable in terms of cultural and religious rights should be part of the process of settle-ment. In many European countries there is understandable rejec-tion of oppressive practices against young people and women

within some migrant groups. Forced marriages, denials of personal autonomy or rights to education cannot be 'tolerated' in the name of multiculturalism. Governments have the right to question and marginalize immigrants who operate as an enemy within or those who ask to be allowed to operate as states within states. Most European Muslims—who do feel themselves to be just that and not Muslims who are just camped in Europe—find it intolerable to be associated with militant haters of Jews, Christians and others and they would welcome a more prominent role in defining immigration and integration policies.

20   In Canada, which has one of the more intelligent, compassionate and less racist immigration policies, it is stated up-front that all arrivals should be bound by a set of non-negotiable principles and values in exchange for equal and fair treatment. Sure, racism exists but a clear policy and well-resourced public education campaigns reduce its impact. It is a model Europe would do well to emulate.

For Class Discussion

1. According to Alibhai-Brown, why should European countries value their immigrants? What is her main claim?

2. How does Alibhai-Brown seek to tap into her readers' values and emotions? What connections do you see between the mission of the *New Internationalist*, its target audience, and the approach Alibhai-Brown has taken in writing about her subject?

3. What is the meaning of the title of the article and how does it function rhetorically?

4. What details of European history does she relate to the current cultural problems in Britain and Europe?

5. In what part of her argument does she acknowledge and respond to opposing views?

6. Alibhai-Brown devotes most of her argument to identifying a problem. What solutions does she suggest?

7. How has this piece influenced your views of immigration?   ■

Pakistanis Protesting France's Ban on the Hijab

Faisal Mahmood

In 2004, France passed a law upholding secularism and prohibiting the wearing of Christian crosses, Jewish skullcaps, and Muslim headscarves (hijabs) in schools. Critics of the law say it is mainly directed at Muslim girls

FIGURE 4.5 Pakistanis Protesting France's Ban on the Hijab (© *FAISAL MAHMOOD/ Reuters/Corbis*)

and their wearing of the hijab. The law has sparked intense debate, particularly in the older European Union countries of Germany, France, and England. In addition to touching on human rights and feminist issues, it is perceived by its critics to be an act of exclusion and control of the Muslim religion and Muslims themselves. The countries of the European Union have substantial, growing communities of Muslims from Turkey, North Africa, Southwest Asia, and the Middle East and are wrestling with issues of integration, assimilation, and tolerance of these immigrant groups. This photo was taken on January 28, 2004 outside the French Embassy in Islamabad, the capital of Pakistan. It shows supporters of Jamat-e-Islami Pakistan, the country's major political party, protesting France's ban on students wearing the hijab (headscarf).

What features of this photo stand out for you? What impressions does this photo convey?

For Class Discussion

1. After researching the meaning of the hijab to Muslim culture and religion and investigating the protests that took place in January of 2004 against France's ban on girls wearing the hijab in school (especially the International Day of Solidarity with the Hijab), what do you think are the many different reasons protesters want to protect

the right to wear the hijab in school? What threats to traditional European culture does the wearing of these headscarves pose?

2. How is this controversy both a big issue itself in Europe and a symbolic one?

3. What ideas about globalization can you draw from the fact that Muslims and Muslim supporters around the world joined protests against France's ban?

4. Not all Muslims oppose the hijab ban. From your research, what reasons do some Muslims give for not insisting that women wear the hijab?

5. What comparable problems over the cultural integration and assimilation of immigrants has the United States had?   ■

Our Foreign Legions
Francis Fukuyama

Francis Fukuyama is a professor at the Paul H. Nitze School of Advanced International Studies at Johns Hopkins. He is the author of numerous books on politics, democracy, the international political economy, and culture's effect on the economy; among his most recent books are *The End of History and the Last Man* (1992) and *State-Building: Governance and World Order in the 21st Century* (2004). Fukuyama has served on various political boards, including the President's Council on Bioethics. This article was first published in the *Wall Street Journal* on January 26, 2004, and then posted on the Web site for the World Security Network the same day. According to its "About Us" link, the World Security Network strives to prevent war by offering valuable analytical insights to journalists, political leaders, and academics. It seeks to remedy "the lack of pubic awareness about imminently threatening crises and conflicts, a lack of analytical judgment and crisis management, but above all, a lack of targeted action before the situation explodes" (www.worldsecuritynetwork.com/corp/index3.cfm).

In its approach to cultural conflicts, how does this article suit the purpose and audience of the World Security Network?

1   We have seen demonstrations all over Europe and the Middle East to protest the French government's proposed prohibition of Muslim girls from wearing headscarves in public schools. This ban is part of a larger struggle taking place throughout Europe over the continent's cultural identity. France and other European countries are host to Muslim minorities that constitute upward of 10% of their populations, minorities that are becoming increasingly active politically. European Muslims are primarily responsible for the rise

in anti-Semitic incidents over the past three years, and their perceptions heavily color European media reporting of the Israeli-Palestinian conflict. This demographic shift has already affected foreign policy: the French government's stance against the Iraq war and U.S. foreign policy more generally seeks in part to appease Muslim opinion.

2   But while the French government is publicly supportive of Arab causes, it and other European governments are privately worried about future trends. Sept. 11 revealed that assimilation is working very poorly in much of Europe: terrorist ringleaders like Mohamed Atta were radicalized not in Saudi Arabia or Afghanistan, but in Western Europe. In a revealing incident that took place shortly after the attack on the World Trade Center, a crowd of mostly second- and third-generation French North Africans booed the Marseillaise during a soccer match between the French and Algerian national teams and chanted Osama bin Laden's name. Third-generation British Muslims have traveled to the West Bank to martyr themselves in suicide operations.

3   Europeans differ among themselves in the way that they approach assimilation. The Germans for many years never tried; until their citizenship law was changed in 2000, a third-generation Turk who grew up in Germany and spoke no Turkish often had a harder time getting citizenship than an ethnic German from Russia who spoke no German. The German state, moreover, recognizes the communal rights of religious groups, collecting taxes on behalf of the Protestant and Catholic churches. The issue there, as in the Netherlands, is whether to add an Islamic pillar to the existing Christian ones, one that would have control over education and other issues. Such a policy would tend, of course, to enshrine rather than diffuse cultural differences over time.

4   The French by contrast have always accepted the principle of assimilation. French citizenship, like ours, is not based on ethnicity but is universal. The republican tradition recognizes only the rights of individuals, not groups, and its commitment to laicite or secularism remains strong. French schoolteachers in particular are heirs to an anticlerical tradition stemming from the French Revolution, and have looked askance at expressions of religiosity in public schools.

5   The new French policy on headscarves should thus be seen as a type of forced assimilation. Previously it had been up to individual schools and teachers whether to ban headscarves or not; the new policy takes this burden off their shoulders by making it a national policy. Whether the ban will work is a delicate tactical issue: it may create a counterproductive backlash, driving observant Muslims out of the public school system and into their own Islamic schools.

But the ultimate goal of the policy is not to crush religious freedom but to promote assimilation, one that American opponents of multiculturalism should appreciate.

6   Europeans have only recently begun to confront the problem of assimilation, and continue to suffer from a stifling political correctness in talking honestly about the issue of immigration. In 2001 the German Christian Democrats gingerly floated the concept of leitkultur, or "leading culture," the idea that immigrants would be accepted as Germans but only if they in turn accepted certain German cultural values. The idea was immediately batted down as racist, and never raised again.

7   There is a strong correlation in Europe between immigrants and crime, just as there is between race and crime in the U.S., but mainstream politicians have been loath to acknowledge this. This explains the meteoric rise of the openly gay Dutch politician Pim Fortuyn, who was the first to argue that Muslim immigration should be limited because Muslims did not accept traditional Dutch tolerance. Only with the national soul-searching that followed his assassination in 2002 did discussions in Holland become more open about the immigration-crime nexus. And only when Jean-Marie Le Pen, leader of the extreme right-wing National Front, came in second behind Jacques Chirac in the 2002 French Presidential election, did the government begin to get serious about dealing with crime and immigration through appointing the tough interior minister Nicolas Sarkozy. The headscarf policy is simply part of this new line.

8   The ultimate success of assimilation depends not just on policy, but on the cultural characteristics of the immigrant group being assimilated as well. Europeans are right to say that they face a bigger problem with their Muslim immigrant populations than Americans do with their Hispanic immigrants.

9   The speed with which an immigrant group assimilates in the second and third generations after arrival has very much to do with that group's rate of outmarriage, which in turn is a byproduct of the degree to which immigrant families can control their daughters' sexuality. In the U.S., rates of outmarriage correlate strongly with both assimilation and upward socioeconomic mobility on the part of different racial and ethnic groups. In many Middle Eastern countries, there is a strong emphasis on cousin marriage, in which daughters are urged to marry not just within their ethnic group, but within their own extended family.

10   Individualism within the family—i.e., the right to marry whomever you want—is the mother of all individualisms, and it is the denial of this right that allows traditional social structure and culture to be transmitted across the generations. Traditionalist

Muslims are thus more astute than they are given credit for when they insist on marking their daughters with headscarves that signal their sexual unavailability to outsiders. The girls themselves who want to wear the headscarf as a symbol of their identity do not understand the long-term threat to their individual freedom it represents.

11   Americans, looking at Europe, should be glad that they have made their country an assimilation powerhouse. But as the authors of a new volume on assimilation edited by Tamar Jacoby indicate, this is not something that we can take for granted. During the big immigration wave of the late-19th/early-20th centuries, the largely Protestant native-born elites deliberately sought to use the public school system to assimilate the newcomers from southern and eastern Europe to their cultural values. The 1960s and '70s gave rise to multiculturalism, affirmative action, and bilingualism, which sought to reverse course on assimilation. The '90s saw a backlash against this kind of divisive identity politics with the passage of Proposition 227 in California that wiped out public school bilingual programs at a stroke. This was our version of the headscarf ban, one that worked well because it was supported by a great many Hispanic parents themselves who felt their children were being held back in a Spanish language ghetto.

12   It is in this context that we should evaluate President Bush's recent proposal to grant illegal aliens work permits. Many Americans dislike the policy because it rewards breaking the law. This is all true; we should indeed use our newly invigorated controls over foreign nationals to channel future immigrants into strictly legal channels. But since we are not about to expel the nearly seven million people potentially eligible for this program, we need to consider what policies would lead to their most rapid integration into mainstream American society. For the vast majority of illegal aliens, the law they broke on entering the country is likely to be the only important one they will ever violate, and the sooner they can normalize their status, the faster their children are likely to participate fully in American life.

13   It is no exaggeration to say that the assimilation of culturally distinct immigrants will be the greatest social challenge faced by developed democracies over the coming decades. Given the sub-replacement fertility rates of native-born populations, high levels of immigration have become necessary to fund not just current standards of living but future social security benefits. Divergent immigration patterns will unfortunately deepen the wedge that has emerged between America and Europe in foreign policy. We cannot do much to affect European policy, but we can take steps to see that their problems do not become our own.

For Class Discussion

1. How would you summarize Fukuyama's view of the global challenges posed by immigration? What changes does he claim that Europe must make?

2. How has Fukuyama shaped his analytical argument for a general audience yet also for policymakers, business leaders, and journalists? What information about European conflicts and political context does Fukuyama offer?

3. How does Fukuyama interpret the headscarf controversy in France?

4. What connections does Fukuyama see between European responses to the cultural problems of immigration and American responses to these problems?

5. This piece is a short policy statement. How does Fukuyama persuade you that he is authoritative and correct in his views about Europe?

6. How do the terrorist bombings in London in July 2005 and the fires and riots near Paris in fall 2005 relate to Fukuyama's points in this argument? ∎

CHAPTER QUESTIONS FOR REFLECTION AND DISCUSSION

1. How has immigration affected your community, city, or region? List the effects and influences.

2. Where do Jagdish Bhagwati's and Kofi Annan's acceptance and praise of global migration intersect? Where do their arguments differ in rhetorical features and in content?

3. Authorities are in disagreement about whether the volume and patterns of economic immigration the United States is experiencing today are a continuation—albeit a stepped-up one—of earlier immigration trends or a new phenomenon shaped by worldwide political, economic, and technological forces. From your reading of the articles in this chapter, which view do you support?

4. What do the readings in this chapter suggest that the United States can learn from other countries' experiences with guest worker programs and from their problems with cultural conflicts and integrating immigrants? What alternatives to a guest worker program do you think are the most promising and why?

5. How do the views of the following people on the effects of immigration on American workers and immigrant workers agree and disagree: Linda Chavez, John Laughland, Don Melvin, the supporters of the

bumper stickers, and the political cartoonists Clay Bennett and Brian Fairrington? Does a large immigrant labor force lower the wages for native workers? You might want to deepen your discussion of labor by investigating these sources:

Bureau of Labor Statistics (www.bls.gov/) (Check the effect of immigrant labor on the earnings of unskilled American workers.)
Rescue American Jobs (www.rescueamericanjobs.org/)
American Federation of Labor (www.afl-cio.org) (What is the current union response to immigration?)

6. A number of the articles in this chapter argue that immigration brings cultural problems as serious and pressing as economic ones. What intersections and differences do you see in the views of Samuel P. Huntington, the two organizations MALDEF and LULAC, Yasmin Alibhai-Brown, and Francis Fukuyama?

7. Which authors suggest connections between immigration's economic and cultural repercussions? In other words, which authors' views provide the most complex and informed approach to immigration issues?

8. One of the main questions regarding immigrants is how to create effective legal channels for immigration. Using the Web, research the kinds of visas that the United States currently grants as well as the "matricula consular" IDs that Linda Chavez mentions in her article "Guest Worker Visas," and answer the following questions about the options for legal status for immigrants. You might find the following Web sites useful:

United States Immigration Support (www.usimmigrationsupport.org/)
United States Citizenship and Immigration Services (uscis.gov/graphics/index.htm.)

- What are the differences between FI student visas, HIB work visas, H2B work visas, and TN NAFTA visas?
- How do "matricula consular" IDs differ from these U.S. visas?
- How would Bush's temporary worker visa differ from the current U.S. visas available for workers?
- What are green cards and how do they differ from visas?

WRITING ASSIGNMENTS

Brief Writing Assignments

1. Write a short narrative recounting (a) some part of your family's immigration story; (b) some part of the immigration story of a friend; or (c) an

experience of acceptance or alienation you had while living in another country.

2. Choose one of the following controversial claims and write for twenty minutes supporting or rebutting the claim. Use examples from the readings, your own background knowledge, and your experiences to develop your view.

   A. Illegal immigation to the United States cannot be stopped.

   B. Immigrants—even undocumented ones—are beneficial to Americans and the United States.

   C. U.S. policy toward immigration, especially illegal immigration, is contradictory and hypocritical.

   D. Immigration problems can be solved only by international institutions and policies.

   E. In the United States (and/or Europe), the effects of immigration on national identity and culture are more urgent and important than immigration's effect on the economy.

3. For you, which reading in this chapter presents the most powerful and illuminating argument on immigration problems? Write a short justification of your choice.

4. Write a short response to this question: How have the readings in this chapter helped you understand the complexity of immigration issues in a globalized world?

Writing Projects

1. Choose one of the articles in this chapter that you think is very effective for a general audience, and write an essay that analyzes this piece and argues for its persuasiveness. In what ways does it make a valuable contribution to the public debates on global immigration? Include a short summary of the piece and an analysis of several of its rhetorical features (for example, the clarity of its claim; the strength of its evidence; its emotional impact; the author's credibility). How has this article changed your views of immigration?

2. Write an editorial for your university or college newspaper in which you construct your own argument for or against guest worker programs based on your synthesis of the ideas in the readings in this chapter. Use your documentation of these ideas in your argument to strengthen your own credibility as a person knowledgeable about this issue.

3. Sometimes the citizens of a country that is experiencing a heavy influx of immigrants feel overwhelmed, irritated, or threatened by foreigners. Imagine that you have a friend who is wrestling with these feelings toward immigrants. Write an argument with this person as your audience. Try to enlarge your friend's understanding of immigration and

arouse sympathy for immigrants as struggling human beings seeking jobs and dignity, and as small pieces in a vast, global political and economic system.

4. From your understanding of U.S. immigration issues, write a letter to your U.S. senator or representative in which you present an argument in favor of or against a guest worker program for the United States. In other words, what national policies on immigration would you like him or her to support and why?

   The following research suggestions can lead to informative or argumentative writing projects.

5. Research the patterns of immigration in your own region of the country, or more locally, your city or community, and write a description of these patterns. If your region is experiencing an influx of immigrants, you could develop your research into an argument in which you first describe those patterns and then claim that immigration is or is not an issue in your community. Based on your research, you might (a) argue for measures that are successfully integrating immigrants into your community; (b) argue against current unsuccessful measures for integrating immigrants; or (c) propose alternative measures that you think would be helpful. Your audience for this piece could be the residents of your community or its decision–makers and political representatives.

6. After doing field research about organizations that seek to integrate immigrants into your community or region, create a brochure that informs the general public of how people can support the work of one or several of these organizations.

7. Both European Union nations and the United States have groups of citizens alarmed about national security and seeking to preserve their countries' traditional cultures. Think of the English Only movement in the United States and organizations such as the Federation for American Immigration Reform (www.fairus.org); Americans for Immigration Control (www.immigrationcontrol.com); Center for Immigration Studies (www.cis.org); and Americans for Better Immigration (www.betterimmigration.org). Research the European Union's controversies over immigration (for instance, the resistance to Turkey's bid to join the EU; concerns over terrorism and crime related to immigration; or the hijab ban controversy) and a corresponding immigration issue in the United States. Write an analysis for your class in which you explain similarities or differences in European and American problems with immigration.

8. This chapter has dealt primarily with U.S. immigrants from Mexico and Latin America. Investigate the current concerns of another U.S. immigrant group such as the Irish or people from Arab or Muslim countries

and propose a way that U.S. immigrant policy could help integrate them into American life. Consider these organizations:

Irish Radio Network in New York
Philadelphia's Irish Immigration and Pastoral Center
Emerald Isle Immigration Center in Queens
Council on American-Islamic Relations
American Muslim Alliance

9. Compose a brief argument for your class, arguing for several key features of an immigration policy that you think would do the most to bolster homeland security. The following government organizations might provide useful information for your argument.

Immigration and Customs Enforcement
Department of Homeland Security
U.S. Customs and Border Protection

10. Many articles and reports about remittances—money earned by immigrants and sent back to their families in their home countries—speak enthusiastically about the way that this money pays for food, health care, housing, and clothing; for establishing businesses such as gas stations and supermarkets; and for building roads. After examining several sources that investigate the role of remittances in developing countries, write an argument for your classmates, asserting that remittances are or are not a positive force for international relations.

11. For many people, the issue of immigration is strongly entangled in issues of race, ethnicity, culture, and values. Three writers who take different stands on the value of immigrants to American society and on immigrants' desire to integrate into American society are these: neoconservative political scientist Samuel P. Huntington of Harvard, author of the book *Who Are We? The Challenges to National Identity* (2004); sociologist Amitai Etzioni, the University Professor at George Washington University and author of the book *Monochrome Society* (2003); and Tamar Jacoby, prolific, well-known conservative journalist, senior fellow at the Manhattan Institute, and author of the book *Reinventing the Melting Pot: The New Immigrants and What It Means to Be American* (2004). Research the ideas of these three writers and write a short argument in support of the writer whose ideas you think are the most realistic and constructive.

12. A number of Latino organizations and advocacy groups are working for the well-being of legal and illegal immigrants. After researching some of these groups' programs and proposals, write an argument for your classmates in which you support a program, proposal, or piece of

legislation as the best solution to a particular problem related to Latino immigrants.

AgJobs Bill
National Council of La Raza
Workplace Project
Hispanic Alliance for Progress
Latino Coalition
Pew Hispanic Center
Labor Council of Latin American Advancement
Urban Institute
Justice for Janitors campaign
California Coalition for Immigration Reform
United Farm Workers Union

CHAPTER 5

Cultural Rights
Global Tensions Over Media, Technology, Music, Film, and Food

QUESTION TO PONDER

The United Nations has declared these practices as cultural rights: digital literacy (the opportunity and ability to access information and communication technologies); linguistic diversity on the Internet; and all cultures' ability to promote their own cultural products digitally. Yet a huge "digital divide" exists between countries with digitally literate societies and those without. According to the International Telecommunication Union Digital Access Index of 2002, the following fifteen countries have the lowest access to digital resources in the world: Eritrea, Congo, Benin, Mozambique, Angola, Burundi, Guinea, Sierra Leone, Central African Republic, Ethiopia, Guinea-Bissau, Chad, Mali, Burkina Faso, and Niger.* Although the United Nations has established a fund to provide computers to developing countries, you are wondering if money and effort should first be invested in cell phones. Should your business club support fund-raising for cell phone service or computers in Niger to encourage this country's economy and culture?

CONTEXT FOR A NETWORK OF ISSUES

Many big disputes about globalization center on culture. Of course, cultural exchange has been going on for millennia, and yet globalization has stepped up cultural contact through business, media, and travel. These contemporary cultural interactions have brought new possibilities and problems.

---

*"ITU Digital Access Index: World's First Global ICT Ranking Education and Affordability Key to Boosting New Technology Adoption." *International Telecommunications Union*, March 19, 2003. www.itu.int/newsarchive/press_releases/2003/30.html (accessed March 29, 2005).

Think of the effect of reality TV on the Arab world, of fast food on Asian countries, of Japanese anime (animation) on American cartoons, and of cell phones on South America. Because culture encompasses the material, intellectual, artistic, and spiritual practices of a society—including food and diet, art, music, literature, traditions and lifestyles, beliefs and values—it is bound up with national identity, preservation of heritage, cultural self-respect, and people's sense of home and belonging.

In discussions about globalization's impact on culture, Marshall McLuhan's concept of the "global village," first articulated in 1964, figures prominently. McLuhan, a historian and prophetic cultural commentator, theorized about the cultural effects of mass communication, especially the impact of television on modern society. He explored how technology has extended—indeed, transformed—the ways that human beings relate to the world:

> After three thousand years of specialist explosion and of increasing specialism and alienation in the technological extensions of our bodies, our world has become compressional by dramatic reversal. As electrically contracted, the globe is no more than a village. Electric speed in bringing all social and political functions together in a sudden implosion has heightened human awareness of responsibility to an intense degree.*

The key words in this quotation—"extensions", "compressional," "contracted," "together," and "implosion"—suggest a double dynamic, a world that is expanding *and* shrinking. The metaphor of global society as a "global village" is problematic, however. The idea of the world's cultures drawn together in a global village raises questions about equal representation, reciprocal sharing, enriched diversity, and mutual understanding.

These complex ideas become more concrete when we look at examples of controversial cultural exchange:

- **The impact of American media and television networks.** In 2004, MTV calculated that around "eighty percent of its viewership is now outside the United States."† MTV executives claim that it adapts to each country by offering a mix of American programming, local versions of American programming, and programming that originates in the local culture. MTV also plans to bring some of the successful programming from MTV China and MTV Korea back to the United States to reach out to ethnic audiences. Yet some people in other countries are voicing concern about the pervasiveness of American television. For example, Ukrainian student Liliya Vovk points out that many viewers in her country are becoming obsessed with American soap operas and that viewers have no control over what is

---

*Marshall McLuhan, *Understanding Media: The Extension of Man* (Cambridge, MA: MIT Press, 1964), 5.
†David Bauder, "MTV Reaches Global Milestone," Associated Press, December 20, 2004.

shown; for example, horror films from the United States are shown any time of day, and children can easily see them.*

- **Global contact and the international popular music scene.** Some music critics say the American music industry is stimulating healthy competition, spurring musicians and performers to create more innovative expressions of their own national cultures. In a 2001 special edition of *TIME Magazine* on global music, Executive Editor Christopher Porterfield claims that the Internet and television have created "a vast electronic bazaar through which South African kwaito music can make pulses pound in Sweden, or Brazilian post-mambo can set feet dancing in Tokyo".† However, other cultural critics point out that major labels and big money are not promoting world music. As Pino di Benedetto, the marketing director for EMI Africa, a main African recording company, has said, "There is a lot of music that comes out of Africa that would be marketable in the States and Europe. . . . Nobody gives us a chance. We just are not seen as hit makers."‡

One global organization that is addressing these tensions and attempting to shape global cultural exchange for the benefit of all countries is the United Nations Educational, Scientific, and Cultural Organization (UNESCO). In 2001, this group, consisting of about two hundred member nations, formed the Convention on Cultural Diversity and wrote the Universal Declaration on Cultural Diversity, grounded in the principles that "cultural diversity is as necessary for humankind as biodiversity" and that "cultural rights are an integral part of human rights."§ However, as any investigation of sites of cultural contact such as media, music, or food reveals, respecting cultural rights is challenging and the stakes in cultural globalization are high.

STAKES AND STAKEHOLDERS

Many stakeholders, including international institutions, nongovernmental organizations, transnational corporations, cultural critics, and citizen groups, are striving to influence the way that globalization affects their own cultures and the cultures of other nations. Here are some of the big issue questions with which these groups are wrestling.

How Is Increasing Global Cultural Contact Affecting Cultural Diversity? Some activists and cultural critics assert that cultural contact is creating uniformity, standardization, homogenization—a global monoculture that

---

*"American Influence on Our Society," *Topics Online Magazine for ESL*, http://www.topics-mag.com/projects/ukraine/liliya.htm.

†"Planet Pop. Music Goes Global," *TIME*, http://www.time.com/time/musicgoesglobal/la/med.html.

‡Sharon LaFraniere, "Africa, and Its Artists Belatedly Get Their MTV," *New York Times*, February 24, 2005.

§UNESCO, Thirty-First Session, "Universal Declaration on Cultural Diversity" (Paris, November 2, 2001).

is sterile, dull, and artificial. For example, some American travelers express their frustration when they find many foreign cities looking like home with Starbucks, Kentucky Fried Chicken, Wal-Mart, Pizza Hut, Taco Bell, the Hard Rock Café, and the most current American films playing. More than monotony and homogenization, the issue for some linguists, anthropologists, activists, and spokespeople for indigenous cultures is the loss of cultural heritage and cultural identity. They are warning that whole cultures are on the brink of vanishing. Anthropologists, environmentalists, and activists are striving to preserve languages that are dying out as some formerly remote cultures are drawn into more contact with the outside world. Scholars and activists like Helena Norberg-Hodge, founder of the International Society for Ecology and Culture, argue that language is bound to culture and that culture is connected to the deep values and structures that hold societies together. Some advocates for indigenous cultures argue that many of the smaller threatened cultural groups—such as the people of Ladakh, an ancient culture nestled next to India, China, and Tibet—possess knowledge of peaceful lifestyles and social cooperation that the world needs. As Norberg-Hodge writes in her book *Ancient Futures* (1991), "There is more than one path into the future."*

In contrast, proponents of free trade, corporate leaders, some cultural analysts, and many citizens around the world applaud the opportunity and cross-fertilization engendered by globalization's stepped-up cultural contact and sharing. To people examining the international music scene like journalist Christopher Porterfield, the world has become a lively, richly stocked "bazaar," not a monoculture. These people contend that cultural globalization has brought new possibilities of pleasing everyone.

What Are the Power Dynamics of Cultural Globalization? Many critics contend that the United States and other rich countries are dominating developing countries through *cultural imperialism.* Just as rich nations imposed political power and economic control on third world countries in earlier centuries (and, indeed, became rich nations partly through this imperialism), many critics, policymakers, activists, and citizens assert that rich nations are imposing their own culture and undermining the cultural diversity and integrity of poor, developing nations. For example, how can poor countries lacking information and communication technologies and the financial resources to support their own domestic music, arts, and film possibly compete with the production and distribution systems of affluent Hollywood? Still other cultural critics and citizen groups in some countries say that it is arrogant and simpleminded to assume that American culture is "conquering" the cultures of countries around the world. Many critics reject sociologist George Ritzer's McDonaldization model and claim instead that "glocalization," whereby local cultures take an active part in adopting and adapting

---

Ancient Futures: Learning from Ladakh, (San Francisco: Sierra Club Books, 1991), 1.

foreign culture, is more accurate.* After all, many McDonald's restaurants are owned and managed by people from those countries, and MTV has incorporated much local programming.

Other critics argue that American and Western culture are mixed, diverse cultures themselves, having been changed by other cultures around the world for centuries. America and Europe have experienced an influx of people from developing countries and have become new composite cultures. Using words like *integration* and *cultural fusion*, these analysts claim that the mixing of cultures is inevitable, healthy, and enriching. Other arguers claim that many countries and groups of people are welcoming American and Western culture, which they see as modernization and progress. The people watching American movies and buying Kentucky Fried Chicken want to be included in the new global society and are embracing the modern Western "good life."

Can Cultural Exchange Be an Instrument for Promoting Global Understanding, Cooperation, and Peace? UNESCO supports the idea that protecting cultural rights and diversity has the potential to promote peaceful international relations. Its Universal Declaration on Cultural Diversity states that "[a]ffirming that respect for the diversity of cultures, tolerance, dialogue and cooperation, in a climate of mutual trust and understanding [is] among the best guarantees of international peace and security."[†] Thomas L. Friedman, well-known American journalist, also posits connections between global cultural and economic exchanges and peaceful relations in his "Golden Arches Theory of Conflict Prevention." Friedman contends that the spreading of McDonald's is closely bound up with the economic development of a strong middle class and that "people in McDonald's countries [don't] like to fight wars anymore," preferring instead "to wait in line for burgers" and not risk their economic and cultural prosperity.[‡] Friedman's critics, however, cite the number of McDonald's in other countries as an example of the United States' cultural imperialistic encroachment. Other analysts argue that because cultural imperialism—or at least, very imbalanced cultural exchanges—is usually the reality, increased cultural contact frequently does not foster peace; instead, it engenders resentment and antipathy, as seen in the Arab world's growing hostility toward American culture.

---

*Sociologist George Ritzer posits the global spread of McDonald's as a business model and a cultural force in *The McDonaldization of Society* (2000). However, sociologist Ronald Robertson speaks of glocalization (a term combining *globalization* and *localization*). He adopted this term from Japanese business, which used it to describe customizing products made for the global market to fit local cultures. See Habibul Haque Khondker, "Glocalization as Globalization: Evolution of a Sociological Concept," *Bangladesh e-Journal of Sociology* 1, no. 2 (July 2004).

[†]UNESCO, Thirty-First Session, "Universal Declaration on Cultural Diversity" (Paris, November 2, 2001).

[‡]*The Lexus and the Olive Tree* (New York: Anchor Books, 2000), 249.

How Can Cultural Contact and the Marketing of Culture Be Regulated to Promote and Preserve Cultural Diversity? Friedman proposes that countries engage in active glocalizing by filtering powerful cultures. He urges cultures to become active agents learning how "to assimilate aspects of globalization into [their] country and culture in a way that adds to [their] growth and diversity, without overwhelming it."* However, Friedman admits that glocalization must be supplemented by other "filters" such as governmental intervention to ensure the preservation of cultural heritage, educational programs, and wise promotion of tourism. UNESCO's international and intercultural agreement, its Universal Declaration on Cultural Diversity, seeks to advance "cultural pluralism" and to prevent culture from being turned into a commodity controlled by transnational corporations. A legal agreement still in progress, the declaration calls on national governments, international governmental and nongovernmental organizations, civil society, and private businesses to work together to prevent consumerism from overrunning culture and to stop the free trade advocates, transnationals, and the WTO from controlling the marketing of culture. The UNESCO supporters of cultural diversity assert that national and local bodies must maintain the power to decide how cultural exchanges will be managed and must preserve the right to create and protect their own cultural industries.

This chapter—first in the "Student Voice," "International Voices," and "Global Hot Spot" sections and then in its readings—explores how the big issues of cultural identity, values, and quality of life are embedded in a variety of global cultural controversies.

 ## STUDENT VOICE: EXPERIENCING INTERCULTURAL EXCHANGE

Many Americans have appreciation of and fondness for food, music, and art forms from other cultures. Student writer Owen Johnson talks about the importance of Japanese anime to him and explains some reasons for its growing popularity in the United States.

Owen Johnson

My adventure started nine years ago with a haircut. Sitting in a barber's chair, I became bored and began looking at the various pictures and drawings posted around my barber's station when an unfamiliar form of cartoon caught my eye. The drawing showed a complaining customer sitting in a barber's chair. The barber, grinning maliciously behind the customer, was holding a giant pair of open scissors, each blade on one side of the customer's neck.

The Lexus and the Olive Tree (New York: Anchor Books, 2000), 295.

I found the drawing humorous, but at the same time it caused me to glance in the mirror at my barber, an Asian fellow in his late twenties. Catching the slightly concerned look on my face, and realizing that I had been observing his drawings, he laughed and said that his friend who drew many of those pictures was an animator, and when I asked why the characters in the drawings had bigger eyes and sharper features than most cartoon characters, he replied that these were done in Japanese animation style, which had not yet become hugely popular in the United States. He explained that anime characters have bigger eyes because in the Japanese culture, the eyes are seen as "windows to the soul." He told me about a Japanese animated show that aired on Sunday (not the usual Saturday morning cartoon time) called *DragonBall Z*. When I turned on the TV the next day, I was exposed for the first time to the wonderful world of anime, forever changing my perspective on cartoons.

Japanese animation has brought a whole new dimension to American cartoon watching and American cartoons, which tend to be children's entertainment—like *Sponge Bob Square Pants*—with pretty colors, slapstick comedy, and hardly any real substance. In contrast, Japanese animated shows such as *One Piece, Naruto,* and *Cowboy Bebop* cross genres—action, adventure, science fiction, and even comedy—and have more meaty plots for even the deepest thinkers. Animes also have good character development. Viewers can easily connect with the characters' misery, joy, sorrow, or fear and with the themes that deal with subjects like boldness and loyalty without being obvious or cheesy. I have always been a fairly imaginative kid, but watching hours of anime has pushed my imagination to new levels of possibility.

As America has become more diverse and open to other cultural influences, Japanese animation has become a regular part of Cartoon Network's (a network dedicated entirely to animation) programming. Anime started out being shown in a two-hour afternoon block and occasionally at midnight, but in the past few years anime has evolved into the most viewed shows on the network, my guess making up forty percent of CN's shows. Japanese animation has also influenced American cartoons. Recently I noticed that the flare of anime style has given one of my favorite childhood shows, *Teenage Mutant Ninja Turtles* (TMNT), new and much needed pizazz. Similarly, in *Batman Beyond*, the new Batman's martial arts seem more . . . well, to put it bluntly, more kick ass like animes' fighting. Clearly, countries learn from those who do an art best, and in the case of animation, that's Japan.

I can't imagine, even with my anime-stimulated imagination, how different my life would have been if I hadn't met that barber and seen *DragonBall Z* years ago. That show was a gateway to even better Japanese animation and to my interest in Japanese culture, which in turn inspired me to take Japanese for four years and to travel all throughout Kyushu (Southern Japan) during one high school summer. My cultural fascination continues, and I am planning to study in Japan during my college career.

INTERNATIONAL VOICES

Cultural contact is an ongoing, daily global occurrence, and citizens of countries everywhere are reflecting on the way that other cultures are changing their lives. In the following statement, posted on *TOPICS Online Magazine for ESL*,* a student from Korea comments on the influence of American fast food on Korean food and habits. As Yeunhwa Jang observes, changes in a culture's food are closely bound up with cultural identity and social relationships.

Yeunhwa Jang from Korea Comments on American Fast Food

American fast food has definitely affected Koreans. You can spot fast food restaurants from America everywhere and many of the younger generation don't like traditional Korean food anymore. Koreans are now using western spices such as ketchup, mayonnaise, and butter to cook regular meals. Salad with western style dressing is also popular now.

In addition, manners in restaurants are not the same as before. Waiters address us in a more westernized manner. We Koreans don't use individual dishes for eating something from main dishes. We have always eaten from one bowl, but now some people think that it is dirty or unsanitary.

Tipping is also new for us. In some luxurious restaurants, we are now supposed to give tips to the waiter. Basically, we have never valued service with money, but now every service is based on money. It's far from our traditional way of doing things.

Finally, new food is being invented. Korean food and American food are combined into fusion food, such as a modified pizza to which Korean spices have been added. These new foods are beginning to appeal to Korean people.

GLOBAL HOT SPOT: THE MIDDLE EAST

The introduction of reality TV to the Middle East has sparked enormous controversy over cultural rights, cultural identity, and cultural survival. This controversy has pitted young people against the older generation, liberals against conservatives, and business leaders against religious leaders, and has intensified animosity between the East and West. While some viewers throughout Syria, Egypt, Kuwait, Yemen, Lebanon, and Saudi Arabia—many of them young—are delighting in Arab versions of *American Idol, Fear Factor,* and *Survivor,* many outraged conservative Muslims are posting blistering responses on the Web. Denouncing *Star Academy,* an imitation of a

---

*http://www.topics-mag.com/globalization/food-korea.htm (accessed March 2, 2005).

French show, one critic wrote, "I am stunned by the corruption and blind imitation [of the West] on the program."*

One recent cultural argument focused on the reality TV show *Big Brother*, filmed in Bahrain's Amwaj Islands. This show featured young people living together in a house, violating Islamic cultural notions of privacy and gender roles, including the rule about veiling women's faces in public. A number of Islamic leaders have denounced this show and all media from the West as a cultural imperialist plot by the United States to take over the Middle East by imposing Western values. In the following excerpt, journalist Samira Ragab challenges her audience to strengthen moderate Islamic values. This excerpt appeared in "Special Dispatch no. 707" for May 6, 2004, on the Web site of the Middle East Media Research Institute (MEMRI, www.memri.org), a nonpartisan organization that translates and analyzes Arabic, Farsi, and Hebrew media. This report gathered and quoted the public statements that led to the banning of *Big Brother*.

> From the Bahraini daily *Akhbar Al-Khaleej*: "The mistake is thinking that the 'Big Brother' program is only a television program that can be handled [merely] by objecting to its airing or filming in Bahrain. . . . [But] it is a media war directed at and planned for the youth, which is targeted in this war strategy. Thus, stimuli and temptations [are directed] at the youth, which perhaps will be unable to absorb them, reject them, or refrain from sinking to them. . . .
>
> "The solutions [to this] are in our hands, and begin with our homes. Educate your sons and daughters to free and logical speech, distant from the burden of traditionalist words within their minds. Let them suckle concepts of nationalism, loyalty, and belonging to this great land and homeland. Let them suckle concepts of Arab culture that emerged and grew under Islam and illuminated proper Islamic thought, not strict and extreme [Islamic thought]. Your children in your home are the weapons by which you will fight the impending Tatar and Crusader attacks."

News commentaries in the United States and Europe have discussed the mixed Arab responses to reality TV, including the support of business leaders, who see reality TV as a source of jobs, investment, and even positive cultural change. The following excerpt from the article "Can Reality TV 'Survive' in the Middle East?" by Samar Farah, correspondent of the *Christian Science Monitor*, appeared in that publication on March 26, 2004.

> Beirut and Adma, Lebanon, and Damascus, Syria–. . . It's Friday night, or "Prime" time for "Star Academy," one of the hottest incarnations of reality TV in the Arab world. There's no sex, no alcohol, and no swearing, but that hasn't diminished the enthusiasm of fans. . . . "There's no one in Lebanon who hasn't heard of ['Star Academy']," says Maythem Shamesdine, a Beirut college student. . . .
>
> For Arab producers, certain changes to the Western formats were a given. When water is involved on "Fear Factor," females don full-body wet suits.

---

*Zeina Karam, "Reality TV a Hit in Arab World, to the Horror of Conservatives," *Seattle Times* March 4, 2004.

Cameras were removed from bathrooms, and bedrooms were segregated on "Star Academy." Arab "Big Brother" went further, providing separate common rooms and separate prayer rooms for men and women and forbidding candidates to enter bedrooms of the opposite sex. For the rest, many producers rely on the participants' common sense.

"They've all grown up in Middle Eastern homes," says Roula Saad, producer and director of "Star Academy." "They know what is acceptable."

But both "Big Brother" and "Star Academy" still required single men and women to live together under the same roof—a notion new to most viewers and illegal in many Arab countries. Three girls leaving a trendy store in Damascus say that, initially, the idea of a coed house bugged them. . . .

According to some viewers, even the older generation is coming around. Yasmina Fayad, an assistant producer at Future Television, says her father is no longer protesting the living arrangements on "Star Academy." But she's quick to add, "If I were to tell my dad that I wanted to live with a guy—never!"

Can cultural exchange through reality TV improve international relations in the Middle East? In 2003, tens of thousands of Israeli teenagers voted twenty-one-year-old Firas Khoury the winner of the fifteen contestants who had been housed together and required to sing and dance to show their talent. Firas Khoury, the only Arab to participate in a reality TV show on Israeli satellite television, remarked that many of the Israeli contestants had never had an Arab friend. He hopes "to have an influence on Arab and Jewish youth . . ." and believes that "[s]ometimes you just need to close your eyes, and try to understand we are all human beings and we should love each other and there is nothing to fight for at the end."*

The readings in this chapter examine various cultural pressure points around the world by looking at cultural exchanges in the areas of media, technology, film, music, and food.

READINGS

When Here Sees There
George Packer

George Packer is an award-winning journalist for the *New York Times*. He has written many articles, works of nonfiction, and novels, including *Blood of the Liberals* (2001), *The Village of Waiting* (2001), the anthology *The Fight for Democracy* (2003), and *The Assassin's Gate: America in Iraq* (2005), all of which support liberal views regarding world issues. This editorial appeared in the *New York Times* on April 21, 2002.

What does George Packer claim is wrong with "the global communication system" and its effects on the world?

---

*David Chazan, "Arab Wins Israeli Reality TV Show," *BBC News*, November 28, 2003.

1   An Arab intellectual named Abdel Monem Said recently surveyed the massive anti-Israel and anti-American protests by Egyptian students and said: "They are galvanized by the images that they see on television. They want to be like the rock-throwers." By now everyone knows that satellite TV has helped deepen divisions in the Middle East. But it's worth remembering that it wasn't supposed to be this way.

2   The globalization of the media was supposed to knit the world together. The more information we receive about one another, the thinking went, the more international understanding will prevail. An injustice in Thailand will be instantly known and ultimately remedied by people in London or San Francisco. The father of worldwide television, Ted Turner, once said, "My main concern is to be a benefit to the world, to build up a global communications system that helps humanity come together." These days we are living with the results—a young man in Somalia watches the attack on the south tower live, while Americans can hear more, and sooner, about Kandahar or Ramallah than the county next to theirs.

3   But this technological togetherness has not created the human bonds that were promised. In some ways, global satellite TV and Internet access have actually made the world a less understanding, less tolerant place. What the media provide is superficial familiarity—images without context, indignation without remedy. The problem isn't just the content of the media, but the fact that while images become international, people's lives remain parochial—in the Arab world and everywhere else, including here.

4   "I think what's best about my country is not exportable," says Frank Holliwell, the American anthropologist in *A Flag for Sunrise,* Robert Stone's 1981 novel about Central America. The line kept playing in my mind recently as I traveled through Africa and watched, on television screens from Butare, Rwanda, to Burao, Somalia, CNN's coverage of the war on terrorism, which was shown like a mini-series, complete with the ominous score.

5   Three months after the World Trade Center attacks, I found myself sitting in a hotel lobby by Lake Victoria watching Larry King preside over a special commemoration with a montage of grief-stricken American faces and flags while Melissa Etheridge sang "Heal Me." Back home, I would have had the requisite tears in my eyes. But I was in Africa, and I wanted us to stop talking about ourselves in front of strangers. Worse, the Ugandans watching with me seemed to expect to hear nothing else. Like a dinner guest who realizes he has been the subject of all the talk, I wanted to turn to one of them: "But enough about me—anything momentous happening to you?" In CNN's global village, everyone has to overhear one family's conversation.

6   What America exports to poor countries through the ubiquitous media—pictures of glittering abundance and national

self-absorption—enrages those whom it doesn't depress. In Sierra Leone, a teenage rebel in a disarmament camp tried to explain to me why he had joined one of the modern world's most brutal insurgencies: "I see on television you have motorbikes, cars. I see some of your children on TV this high"—he held his hand up to his waist—"they have bikes for themselves, but we in Sierra Leone have nothing." Unable to possess what he saw in images beamed from halfway around the world, the teenager picked up an automatic rifle and turned his anger on his countrymen. On generator-powered VCR's in rebel jungle camps, the fantasies of such boy fighters were stoked with Rambo movies. To most of the world, America looks like a cross between a heavily armed action hero and a Lexus ad.

7   Meanwhile, in this country the aperture for news from elsewhere has widened considerably since Sept. 11. And how does the world look to Americans? Like a nonstop series of human outrages. Just as what's best about America can't be exported, our imports in the global-image trade hardly represent the best from other countries either. Of course, the world is a nonstop series of human outrages, and you can argue that it's a good thing for Americans, with all our power, to know. But what interests me is the psychological effect of knowing. One day, you read that 600 Nigerians have been killed in a munitions explosion at an army barracks. The next day, you read that the number has risen to a thousand. The next day, you read nothing. The story has disappeared—except something remains, a thousand dead Nigerians are lodged in some dim region of the mind, where they exact a toll. You've been exposed to one corner of human misery, but you've done nothing about it. Nor will you. You feel—perhaps without being conscious of it—an impotent guilt, and your helplessness makes you irritated and resentful, almost as if it's the fault of those thousand Nigerians for becoming your burden. We carry around the mental residue of millions of suffering human beings for whom we've done nothing.

8   It is possible, of course, for media attention to galvanize action. Because of a newspaper photo, ordinary citizens send checks or pick up rocks. On the whole, knowing is better than not knowing; in any case, there's no going back. But at this halfway point between mutual ignorance and true understanding, the "global village" actually resembles a real one—in my experience, not the utopian community promised by the boosters of globalization but a parochial place of manifold suspicions, rumors, resentments and half-truths. If the world seems to be growing more, rather than less, nasty these days, it might have something to do with the images all of us now carry around in our heads.

For Class Discussion

1. What assumptions about the benefits of technology might Packer's audience have? How does he challenge these assumptions?

2. According to Packer, how has the goal of "technological togetherness" failed? What reasons and evidence does Packer offer to support his claim?

3. Part of the rhetorical power of this piece derives from Packer's skillful use of language. List as many memorable phrases like "technological togetherness" and "the global-image trade" as you can and explain what ideas these phrases capture and why they are rhetorically effective.

4. Where and how does Packer acknowledge alternative views?

5. What has this article contributed to your thinking about the idea of a global village? ∎

Behind the Digital Divide
The *Economist*

The *Economist* is a London-based, weekly generalist magazine that analyzes international political and business concerns and advocates "free markets and free trade" (www.economist.com). Its target audience is British and international business leaders and political decision makers, and it is written by anonymous authors with the intention of creating a collective voice. This piece was first published on March 12, 2005.

> According to this article, why is it so difficult for economists and policymakers to determine how to integrate information and communication technologies (computers with Internet access) into the lives of citizens of developing countries?

1 Development: Much is made of the "digital divide" between rich and poor. What do people on the ground think about it?

2 In the village of Embalam in southern India, about 15 miles outside the town of Pondicherry, Arumugam and his wife, Thillan, sit on the red earth in front of their thatch hut. She is 50 years old; he is not sure, but thinks he is around 75. Arumugam is unemployed. He used to work as a drum-beater at funerals, but then he was injured, and now he has trouble walking. Thillan makes a little money as a part-time agricultural labourer—about 30 rupees ($0.70) a day, ten days a month. Other than that, they get by on meager (and sporadic) government disability payments.

3   In the new India of cybercafes and software tycoons, Arumugam and Thillan, and the millions of other villagers around the country like them, seem like anachronisms. But just a few steps outside their section of the village—a section known as the "colony", where the untouchables traditionally live—the sheen of India's technology boom is more evident in a green room equipped with five computers, state-of-the-art solar cells and a wireless connection to the Internet. This is the village's Knowledge Centre, one of 12 in the region set up by a local non-profit organisation, the M. S. Swaminathan Research Foundation (MSSRF). The centres, established with the aid of international donor agencies and local government support, offer villagers a range of information, including market prices for crops, job listings, details of government welfare schemes, and health advice.

4   A conservative estimate of the cost of the equipment in the Embalam centre is 200,000 rupees ($4,500), or around 55 years' earnings for Thillan. Annual running costs are extra. When asked about the centre, Thillan laughs. "I don't know anything about that," she says. "It has no connection to my life. We're just sitting here in our house trying to survive."

5   Scenes like these, played out around the developing world, have led to something of a backlash against rural deployments of new information and communications technologies, or ICTs, as they are known in the jargon of development experts. In the 1990s, at the height of the technology boom, rural ICTs were heralded as catalysts for "leapfrog development", "information societies" and a host of other digital-age panaceas for poverty. Now they have largely fallen out of favour: none other than Bill Gates, the chairman of Microsoft, derides them as distractions from the real problems of development. "Do people have a clear view of what it means to live on $1 a day?" he asked at a conference on the digital divide in 2000. "About 99% of the benefits of having a PC come when you've provided reasonable health and literacy to the person who's going to sit down and use it." That is why, even though Mr. Gates made his fortune from computers, the Bill & Melinda Gates Foundation, now the richest charity in the world, concentrates on improving health in poor countries.

6   The backlash against ICTs is understandable. Set alongside the medieval living conditions in much of the developing world, it seems foolhardy to throw money at fancy computers and Internet links. Far better, it would appear, to spend scarce resources on combating AIDS, say, or on better sanitation facilities. Indeed, this was the conclusion reached by the recently concluded Copenhagen Consensus project, which brought together a group of leading economists to prioritise how the world's development resources should be spent. The panel came up with 17 priorities: spending more on ICTs was not even on the list.

7   Still, it may be somewhat hasty to write off rural technology altogether. Charles Kenny, a senior economist at the World Bank who has studied the role of ICTs in development, says that traditional cost-benefit calculations are in the best of cases "an art, not a science". With ICTs, he adds, the picture is further muddied by the newness of the technologies; economists simply do not know how to quantify the benefits of the Internet.

THE VIEW FROM THE GROUND

8   Given the paucity of data, then, and even of sound methodologies for collecting the data, an alternative way to evaluate the role of ICTs in development is simply to ask rural residents what they think. Applied in rural India, in the villages served by the MSSRF, this approach reveals a more nuanced picture than that suggested by the skeptics, though not an entirely contradictory one.

9   Villagers like Arumugam and Thillan—older, illiterate and lower caste—appear to have little enthusiasm for technology. Indeed, Thillan, who lives barely a five-minute walk from the village's Knowledge Centre, says she did not even know about its existence until two months ago (even though the centre has been open for several years). When Thillan and a group of eight neighbours are asked for their development priorities—a common man's version of the Copenhagen Consensus—they list sanitation, land, health, education, transport, jobs—the list goes on and on, but it does not include computers, or even telephones. They are not so much sceptical of ICTs as oblivious; ICTs are irrelevant to their lives. This attitude is echoed by many villagers at the bottom of the social and economic ladder. In the fishing community of Veerapatinam, the site of another MSSRF centre, Thuradi, aged 45, sits on the beach sorting through his catch. "I'm illiterate," he says, when asked about the centre. "I don't know how to use a computer, and I have to fish all day."

10   But surely technology can provide information for the likes of Thuradi, even if he does not sit down in front of the computers himself? Among other things, the centre in this village offers information on wave heights and weather patterns (information that Thuradi says is already available on television). Some years ago, the centre also used satellites to map the movements of large schools of fish in the ocean. But according to another fisherman, this only benefited the rich: poor fishermen, lacking motorboats and navigation equipment, could not travel far enough, or determine their location precisely enough, to use the maps.

11   Such stories bring to mind the uneven results of earlier technology-led development efforts. Development experts are familiar with the notion of "rusting tractors"—a semi-apocryphal reference to imported agricultural technologies that littered poor countries in the 1960s and 1970s. Mr Kenny says he similarly

anticipates "a fair number of dusty rooms with old computers piled up in them around the countryside."

12   That may well be true, but it does not mean that the money being channeled to rural technology is going entirely unappreciated. Rural ICTs appear particularly useful to the literate, to the wealthier and to the younger—those, in other words, who sit at the top of the socio-economic hierarchy. In the 12 villages surrounding Pondicherry, students are among the most frequent users of the Knowledge Centres; they look up exam results, learn computer skills and look for jobs. Farmers who own land or cattle, and who are therefore relatively well-off, get veterinary information and data on crop prices.

13   Outside the Embalam colony, at a village teashop up the road from the temple, Kumar, the 35-year-old shop owner, speaks glowingly about the centre's role in disseminating crop prices and information on government welfare schemes, and says the Knowledge Centre has made his village "famous". He cites the dignitaries from development organisations and governments who have visited; he also points to the fact that people from 25 surrounding villages come to use the centre, transforming Embalam into something of a local information hub.

14   At the centre itself, Kasthuri, a female volunteer who helps run the place, says that the status of women in Embalam has improved as a result of using the computers. "Before, we were just sitting at home," she says. "Now we feel empowered and more in control." Some economists might dismiss such sentiments as woolly headed. But they are indicators of a sense of civic pride and social inclusiveness that less conventional economists might term human development or well-being.

A QUESTION OF PRIORITIES

15   Given the mixed opinions on the ground, then, the real issue is not whether investing in ICTs can help development (it can, in some cases, and for some people), but whether the overall benefits of doing so outweigh those of investing in, say, education or health. Leonard Waverman of the London Business School has compared the impact on GDP of increases in teledensity (the number of telephones per 100 people) and the primary-school completion rate. He found that an increase of 100 basis points in teledensity raised GDP by about twice as much as the same increase in primary-school completion. As Dr. Waverman acknowledges, however, his calculations do not take into account the respective investment costs—and it is the cost of ICTs that makes people such as Mr. Gates so sceptical of their applicability to the developing world.

16   Indeed, Ashok Jhunjhunwala, a professor at the Indian Institute of Technology in Chennai (formerly Madras), argues that cost is the

"deciding factor" in determining whether the digital divide will ever be bridged. To that end, Dr. Jhunjhunwala and his colleagues are working on a number of low-cost devices, including a remote banking machine and a fixed wireless system that cuts the cost of access by more than half. But such innovation takes time and is itself expensive.

17   Perhaps a more immediate way of addressing the cost of technology is to rely on older, more proven means of delivering information. Radios, for example, are already being used by many development organisations; their cost (under $10) is a fraction of the investment (at least $800) required for a telephone line. In Embalam and Veerapatinam, few people actually ever sit at a computer; they receive much of their information from loudspeakers on top of the Knowledge Centre, or from a newsletter printed at the centre and delivered around the village. Such old-fashioned methods of communication can be connected to an Internet hub located further upstream; these hybrid networks may well represent the future of technology in the developing world.

18   But for now, it seems that the most cost-effective way of providing information over the proverbial "last mile" is often decidedly low-tech. On December 26th 2004, villagers in Veerapatinam had occasion to marvel at the reliability of a truly old-fashioned source of information. As the Asian tsunami swept towards the south Indian shoreline, over a thousand villagers were gathered safely inland around the temple well. About an hour and a half before the tsunami, the waters in the well had started bubbling and rising to the surface; by the time the wave hit, a whirlpool had formed and the villagers had left the beach to watch this strange phenomenon.

19   Nearby villages suffered heavy casualties, but in Veerapatinam only one person died out of a total population of 6,200. The villagers attribute their fortuitous escape to divine intervention, not technology. Ravi, a well-dressed man standing outside the Knowledge Centre, says the villagers received no warning over the speakers. "We owe everything to Her," he says, referring to the temple deity. "I'm telling you honestly," he says. "The information came from Her."

"I'm illiterate," says one fisherman. "I don't know how to use a computer, and I have to fish all day."

For Class Discussion

1. This article grows out of an effort to investigate how rural residents of India think and feel about computer centers (information and communications technologies, or ICTs) in their communities. What views emerge from informal surveys?

2. On the argument spectrum—from argument as inquiry and problem solving on one end to argument as hard-sell persuasion on the other

end—where would you place this piece? In other words, what specifically is its purpose and how does it hope to affect its audience's views?

3. What views against providing computers for communities in developing countries does this article acknowledge?

4. What is the rhetorical effect on readers of the short narrative that
concludes this article?

FIGURE 5.1   Cover Image from the *Economist* (© *Chris Sattlberger/Panos Pictures*)

Cover Image from the *Economist*

This photo (p. 208) appeared on the cover of the *Economist*, a weekly London-based political and economic news commentary magazine with a pro-free trade perspective, on March 12, 2005, the same issue that featured the article "Behind the Digital Divide."

> What features of this cover photo are especially intended to appeal to this magazine's audience of business executives and political leaders?

For Class Discussion

1. What makes this image arresting? What are some implications viewers might draw from this image?

2. What is rhetorically effective about having the cell phone be made out of mud? About the smiling boy?

3. From your interpretation of this cover image, what audience assumptions will the articles in this magazine challenge?

4. What ways could this image be used in arguments about cultural rights and digital literacy?   ∎

In Defense of Globalization: Why Cultural Exchange Is Still an Overwhelming Force for Good Globalization

Philippe Legrain

Formerly a special advisor in the World Trade Organization, Philippe Legrain is now the chief economist of Britain in Europe, a pressure group that advocates a Europe united by culture, economy, the military, and politics. He has been published in the *Times*, *Financial Times*, the *Wall Street Journal Europe*, the *Guardian*, the *Independent*, *Foreign Policy*, and many other leading political and economic news commentary journals. This article appeared in the *International Economy*, a magazine about global policy, trade, and trends that is aimed at financial professionals and politicians, in summer 2003.

> Legrain is an economist who is directing his argument to readers who live in countries that are part of the European Union. Where do you see evidence of the influence of his profession on his views and evidence of his primary audience?

1   Fears that globalization is imposing a deadening cultural uniformity are as ubiquitous as Coca-Cola, McDonald's, and Mickey

Mouse. Many people dread that local cultures and national identities are dissolving into a crass all-American consumerism. That cultural imperialism is said to impose American values as well as products, promote the commercial at the expense of the authentic, and substitute shallow gratification for deeper satisfaction.

2   Thomas Friedman, columnist for the *New York Times* and author of *The Lexus and the Olive Tree*, believes that globalization is "globalizing American culture and American cultural icons." Naomi Klein, a Canadian journalist and author of *No Logo*, argues that "Despite the embrace of polyethnic imagery, market-driven globalization doesn't want diversity; quite the opposite. Its enemies are national habits, local brands, and distinctive regional tastes."

3   But it is a myth that globalization involves the imposition of Americanized uniformity, rather than an explosion of cultural exchange. And although—as with any change—it can have downsides, this cross-fertilization is overwhelmingly a force for good.

4   The beauty of globalization is that it can free people from the tyranny of geography. Just because someone was born in France does not mean they can only aspire to speak French, eat French food, read French books, and so on. That we are increasingly free to choose our cultural experiences enriches our lives immeasurably. We could not always enjoy the best the world has to offer.

5   Globalization not only increases individual freedom, but also revitalizes cultures and cultural artifacts through foreign influences, technologies, and markets. Many of the best things come from cultures mixing: Paul Gauguin painting in Polynesia, the African rhythms in rock 'n' roll, the great British curry. Admire the many-colored faces of France's World Cup-winning soccer team, the ferment of ideas that came from Eastern Europe's Jewish diaspora, and the cosmopolitan cities of London and New York.

6   Fears about an Americanized uniformity are overblown. For a start, many "American" products are not as all-American as they seem; MTV in Asia promotes Thai pop stars and plays rock music sung in Mandarin. Nor are American products all-conquering. Coke accounts for less than two of the 64 fluid ounces that the typical person drinks a day. France imported a mere $620 million in food from the United States in 2000, while exporting to America three times that. Worldwide, pizzas are more popular than burgers and Chinese restaurants sprout up everywhere.

7   In fashion, the ne plus ultra is Italian or French. Nike shoes are given a run for their money by Germany's Adidas, Britain's Reebok, and Italy's Fila. American pop stars do not have the stage to themselves. According to the IFPI, the record-industry bible, local acts accounted for 68 percent of music sales in 2000, up from 58 percent in 1991. And although nearly three-quarters of television

drama exported worldwide comes from the United States, most countries' favorite shows are homegrown.

8   Nor are Americans the only players in the global media industry. Of the seven market leaders, one is German, one French, and one Japanese. What they distribute comes from all quarters: Germany's Bertelsmann publishes books by American writers; America's News Corporation broadcasts Asian news; Japan's Sony sells Brazilian music.

9   In some ways, America is an outlier, not a global leader. Baseball and American football have not traveled well; most prefer soccer. Most of the world has adopted the (French) metric system; America persists with antiquated British Imperial measurements. Most developed countries have become intensely secular, but many Americans burn with fundamentalist fervor—like Muslims in the Middle East.

10   Admittedly, Hollywood dominates the global movie market and swamps local products in most countries. American fare accounts for more than half the market in Japan and nearly two-thirds in Europe. Yet Hollywood is less American than it seems. Top actors and directors are often from outside America. Some studios are foreign-owned. To some extent, Hollywood is a global industry that just happens to be in America. Rather than exporting Americana, it serves up pap to appeal to a global audience.

11   Hollywood's dominance is in part due to economics: Movies cost a lot to make and so need a big audience to be profitable; Hollywood has used America's huge and relatively uniform domestic market as a platform to expand overseas. So there could be a case for stuffing subsidies into a rival European film industry, just as Airbus was created to challenge Boeing's near-monopoly. But France's subsidies have created a vicious circle whereby European film producers fail in global markets because they serve domestic demand and the wishes of politicians and cinematic bureaucrats.

12   Another American export is also conquering the globe: English. By 2050, it is reckoned, half the world will be more or less proficient in it. A common global language would certainly be a big plus—for businessmen, scientists, and tourists—but a single one seems far less desirable. Language is often at the heart of national culture, yet English may usurp other languages not because it is what people prefer to speak, but because, like Microsoft software, there are compelling advantages to using it if everyone else does.

13   But although many languages are becoming extinct, English is rarely to blame. People are learning English as well as—not instead of—their native tongue, and often many more languages besides. Where local languages are dying, it is typically national rivals that are stamping them out. So although, within the United States, English is displacing American Indian tongues, it is not doing away with Swahili or Norwegian.

14   Even though American consumer culture is widespread, its significance is often exaggerated. You can choose to drink Coke and eat at McDonald's without becoming American in any meaningful sense. One newspaper photo of Taliban fighters in Afghanistan showed them toting Kalashnikovs—as well as a sports bag with Nike's trademark swoosh. People's culture—in the sense of their shared ideas, beliefs, knowledge, inherited traditions, and art— may scarcely be eroded by mere commercial artifacts that, despite all the furious branding, embody at best flimsy values.

15   The really profound cultural changes have little to do with Coca-Cola. Western ideas about liberalism and science are taking root almost everywhere, while Europe and North America are becoming multicultural societies through immigration, mainly from developing countries. Technology is reshaping culture: Just think of the Internet. Individual choice is fragmenting the imposed uniformity of national cultures. New hybrid cultures are emerging, and regional ones re-emerging. National identity is not disappearing, but the bonds of nationality are loosening.

16   Cross-border cultural exchange increases diversity within societies—but at the expense of making them more alike. People everywhere have more choice, but they often choose similar things. That worries cultural pessimists, even though the right to choose to be the same is an essential part of freedom.

17   Cross-cultural exchange can spread greater diversity as well as greater similarity: more gourmet restaurants as well as more McDonald's outlets. And just as a big city can support a wider spread of restaurants than a small town, so a global market for cultural products allows a wider range of artists to thrive. If all the new customers are ignorant, a wider market may drive down the quality of cultural products: Think of tourist souvenirs. But as long as some customers are well informed (or have "good taste"), a general "dumbing down" is unlikely. Hobbyists, fans, artistic pride, and professional critics also help maintain (and raise) standards.

18   A bigger worry is that greater individual freedom may undermine national identity. The French fret that by individually choosing to watch Hollywood films they might unwittingly lose their collective Frenchness. Yet such fears are overdone. Natural cultures are much stronger than people seem to think. They can embrace some foreign influences and resist others. Foreign influences can rapidly become domesticated, changing national culture, but not destroying it. Clearly, though, there is a limit to how many foreign influences a culture can absorb before being swamped. Traditional cultures in the developing world that have until now evolved (or failed to evolve) in isolation may be particularly vulnerable.

19   In *The Silent Takeover*, Noreena Hertz describes the supposed spiritual Eden that was the isolated kingdom of Bhutan in the

Himalayas as being defiled by such awful imports as basketball and Spice Girls T-shirts. But is that such a bad thing? It is odd, to put it mildly, that many on the left support multiculturalism in the West but advocate cultural purity in the developing world—an attitude they would tar as fascist if proposed for the United States. Hertz appears to want people outside the industrialized West preserved in unchanging but supposedly pure poverty. Yet the Westerners who want this supposed paradise preserved in aspic rarely feel like settling there. Nor do most people in developing countries want to lead an "authentic" unspoiled life of isolated poverty.

20   In truth, cultural pessimists are typically not attached to diversity per se but to designated manifestations of diversity, determined by their preferences. Cultural pessimists want to freeze things as they were. But if diversity at any point in time is desirable, why isn't diversity across time? Certainly, it is often a shame if ancient cultural traditions are lost. We should do our best to preserve them and keep them alive where possible. Foreigners can often help, by providing the new customers and technologies that have enabled reggae music, Haitian art, and Persian carpet making, for instance, to thrive and reach new markets. But people cannot be made to live in a museum. We in the West are forever casting off old customs when we feel they are no longer relevant. Nobody argues that Americans should ban nightclubs to force people back to line dancing. People in poor countries have a right to change, too.

21   Moreover, some losses of diversity are a good thing. Who laments that the world is now almost universally rid of slavery? More generally, Western ideas are reshaping the way people everywhere view themselves and the world. Like nationalism and socialism before it, liberalism is a European philosophy that has swept the world. Even people who resist liberal ideas, in the name of religion (Islamic and Christian fundamentalists), group identity (communitarians), authoritarianism (advocates of "Asian values") or tradition (cultural conservatives), now define themselves partly by their opposition to them.

22   Faith in science and technology is even more widespread. Even those who hate the West make use of its technologies. Osama bin Laden plots terrorism on a cellphone and crashes planes into skyscrapers. Antiglobalization protesters organize by e-mail and over the Internet. China no longer turns its nose up at Western technology: It tries to beat the West at its own game.

23   Yet globalization is not a one-way street. Although Europe's former colonial powers have left their stamp on much of the world, the recent flow of migration has been in the opposite direction. There are Algerian suburbs in Paris, but not French ones in Algiers. Whereas Muslims are a growing minority in Europe, Christians are a disappearing one in the Middle East.

24   Foreigners are changing America even as they adopt its ways. A million or so immigrants arrive each year, most of them Latino or Asian. Since 1990, the number of foreign-born American residents has risen by 6 million to just over 25 million, the biggest immigration wave since the turn of the 20th century. English may be all-conquering outside America, but in some parts of the United States, it is now second to Spanish.

25   The upshot is that national cultures are fragmenting into a kaleidoscope of different ones. New hybrid cultures are emerging. In "Amexica" people speak Spanglish. Regional cultures are reviving. The Scots and Welsh break with British monoculture. Estonia is reborn from the Soviet Union. Voices that were silent dare to speak again.

26   Individuals are forming new communities, linked by shared interests and passions, that cut across national borders. Friendships with foreigners met on holiday. Scientists sharing ideas over the Internet. Environmentalists campaigning together using e-mail. Greater individualism does not spell the end of community. The new communities are simply chosen rather than coerced, unlike the older ones that communitarians hark back to.

27   So is national identity dead? Hardly. People who speak the same language, were born and live near each other, face similar problems, have a common experience, and vote in the same elections still have plenty in common. For all our awareness of the world as a single place, we are not citizens of the world but citizens of a state. But if people now wear the bonds of nationality more loosely, is that such a bad thing? People may lament the passing of old ways. Indeed, many of the worries about globalization echo age-old fears about decline, a lost golden age, and so on. But by and large, people choose the new ways because they are more relevant to their current needs and offer new opportunities.

28   The truth is that we increasingly define ourselves rather than let others define us. Being British or American does not define who you are: It is part of who you are. You can like foreign things and still have strong bonds to your fellow citizens. As Mario Vargas Llosa, the Peruvian author, has written: "Seeking to impose a cultural identity on a people is equivalent to locking them in a prison and denying them the most precious of liberties—that of choosing what, how, and who they want to be."

For Class Discussion

1. Legrain's piece provides an overview of the controversies over globalization's effects on cultures around the world. According to this article, what is the range of topics encompassed by this controversy over culture?

2. What opposing views does Legrain confront in this piece? How does he particularly criticize liberal views?

3. What defense does Legrain offer against the charges of the cultural domination of American consumerism? While acknowledging that cultural contact changes national identity, what does Legrain see as positive about cultural globalization?

4. This piece throws example after example at the reader. If you were creating a paragraph summary of this piece, what key points would you include? What examples would you include and why?

■

Brave New McWorld; *Creative Destruction: How Globalization Is Changing the World's Cultures*
Benjamin Barber

Benjamin Barber is a professor and political theorist at the University of Maryland and the author of several best-selling books, including *Strong Democracy* (1984) and *Jihad vs. McWorld* (1995). This piece is an example of a common genre of public argument in which a scholar or expert reviews a book by another expert and includes his or her own argument on the book's thesis. In this piece, Barber is reviewing Tyler Cowen's book *Creative Destruction: How Globalization Is Changing the World's Cultures* (2002) and critiquing and rebutting Cowen's libertarian argument in favor of more free trade and less government interference in cultural exchanges. This argumentative book review was published on February 2, 2003, in the *Los Angeles Times*.

> How does Barber situate Tyler Cowen's book within the big-picture controversy over globalization, free trade, and the homogenization of the world's cultures? In other words, how does Barber sketch out different views of cultural exchange and free trade in his opening paragraph?

1 Critics of imperialism have long insisted that international exchange and free trade are screens for the colonization of one culture by another. In my *Jihad vs. McWorld*, for example, I argued that the dominant pop culture of the United States, embedded in fast food, fast music and fast computers, not only erodes the particularity of foreign cultures but also promotes a radical homogenization of taste and mores within American society as well as around

the world. The homogenization thesis does, however, have challengers. They are mostly anthropologists such as David Howes, Constance Classen or Jean Comaroff who, reporting from the field on the reception of global markets, have been at pains to show how complex and multifaceted cultural interaction can actually be. Using terms like "hybridization" and "creolization," such scholars have noted that culture is constructed by consumption as well as by production and that through the "creativity of consumption" imperial homogenization can be turned back into cultural particularity or even into a kind of counter-colonization. Classen cites the surreal artist Leonora Carrington's charmingly ironic story about how "in the Mexico of the future one would find tins of Norwegian enchiladas from Japan and bottles of the 'rare old Indian drink called Coca-Cola.'"

2   Economists, though dispositionally inclined to champion cultural exchange as a facet of free trade, are not usually such anthropological sophisticates. But Tyler Cowen, an unapologetic neoliberal who teaches at that busy hive of free market economics, George Mason University, prides himself on his cultural cosmopolitanism. As Chris Mooney notes in a recent profile of Cowen in the *Boston Globe*, Cowen is not only the author of the not-so-subtle and altogether revealing laissez-faire celebration *In Praise of Commercial Culture* (1998) but also a gourmand sophisticate who writes an online restaurant guide whose motto is "restaurants manifest the spirit of capitalist multiculturalism." He describes himself as a devoted "cultural consumer," suggesting just how rooted in the language of consumption his free trade approach to cultural exchange is. Yet he admits to tastes that run the gamut from Vietnamese cuisine to Taco Bell. He likes Beethoven but listens to Smashing Pumpkins as well. According to Mooney, Cowen collects Haitian art, has traveled to more than 60 countries and drinks French wines. A rather different breed of economist.

3   Once we know something about Cowen's predilections, we can be sure that in his new book, *Creative Destruction,* he is doing something more than merely sharing a student's academic library research. When he opens this short work, subtitled "How Globalization Is Changing the World's Cultures," with a comment on the cultural complexity of Haitian music and closes it with a remark about how a visit to a Wal-Mart in Mexico will prove that America's export commercialism brings diversity rather than uniformity to other lands, we figure he's probably got a Haitian music collection and has walked the aisles of Wal-Marts in places other than Virginia. As it turns out, Cowen actually does bring the knowledge of a traveler and the love of a collector to the mixed cultural artifacts he uses as evidence for his defense of globalization and free trade.

This gives to what otherwise might seem merely an ideological tract a certain experiential authenticity that enhances the persuasiveness of its sometimes dubious arguments.

4   At its best, *Creative Destruction*—its title is drawn from economist Joseph Schumpeter's classic description of the dialectic in which capitalism destroys as it evolves—offers good reasons to treat with several grains of salt the claims of critics, like this reviewer, that McWorld is homogenizing the planet and leaving in its wake a trail of devastated local cultures. That is especially true because in this work (unlike in his *In Praise of Commercial Culture*) Cowen displays some ideological balance, acknowledging, for example, that while international trade can enhance diversity, it can also lead to what he calls "the tragedy of cultural loss."

5   Cowen's case for the pluralizing effect of global cultural trade is most effectively argued in the chapters written while he is wearing his amateur anthropologist's travel-wear rather than his economist's library bowtie, for this is where he substantiates his position from his own experience with the cultures about which he writes. His argument is twofold: "Culture" is itself an evolving category rather than a fixed signifier of some unchanging "original" essence. What critics worry may be altered and perverted by confrontation with "foreign" or "outside" influences is in fact from the outset a product of ongoing cultural interaction and exchange. There is no such thing as an original culture, no wholly other "alterity," only phases in cultural development that become embedded in time and hence regarded (inaccurately) as fixed and indigenous. As historians such as Michael Kammen would agree, cultures are all invented and hence to be viewed as collective artifacts of many different earlier historical and cultural streams.

6   Second, Cowen argues, even when a particular culture that is relatively insular encounters a relatively cosmopolitan "colonizing" culture, the local culture usually does as much to transform the encroaching culture as the encroaching culture does to transform it. The outcome is not homogeneity but new forms of diversity: "fusion" music or "fusion" art that, like "fusion" cuisine, is genuinely innovative in ways not limited to the cultural parts being conjoined.

7   It is on his first point that Cowen is most convincing. He shows, for example, that the "indigenous" music of Zaire, which dominates much of Africa today and—critics fear—is in danger of being lost in the din of MTV's international music, was itself actually a product of the electric guitar, saxophone, trumpet, clarinet and flute, "none of which are indigenous to Africa." Indeed, "Cuban influences, especially the Son, Mambo, Cha-Cha, Biguine

and Bolero, entered Zaire by the time of the Second World War." These foreign influences accelerated in the 1950s with the visits of cruise ships, the introduction of radio and phonograph technology and with them American rhythm and blues styles. For those like me who worry about the corrupting effect of MTV on "local" African music from, say, Kinshasa, Cowen's message is "not to worry." The music was never pure but was "corrupted" long ago in ways that created its fresh and powerful hold on African and, in time, foreign audiences. That "ancient traditional culture" that cosmopolitan worrywarts anxiously try to protect from the corruption of today's new foreign influences is actually yesterday's corruption made over into tradition by time and cultural propaganda.

8   Take Trinidad's steel bands, among its greatest "indigenous" tourist attractions but in fact a relatively recent creation of Trinidad's interaction with the global energy market that led in the late 1930s to the replacement of truly indigenous bamboo instruments with the byproducts of the world oil trade. Steel drums cut from oil barrels not only lent themselves to interesting and varied new tonalities (Trinidadians had experimented with various other imported metal objects from the Machine Age) but were far more resilient and enduring than traditional instruments.

9   Or take those storied "indigenous" Navajo designs and colors—above all the deep red serape patterns with their serrated zigzag lines—that distinguish their traditional blankets from all others. Stunning, yes, but indigenous? Hardly. The designs reflected a pattern borrowed from "the ponchos and clothing of Spanish shepherds in Mexico, which in turn drew upon Moorish influences in Spain," though of course the Navajos altered them and made them their own. And that distinctive Navajo "bayeta" red? Drawn from threads "unraveled from Spanish cloth, which was in turn imported by the Spanish from England (English baize)."

10   And so it goes, from "threatened" culture to "threatened" culture, with Cowen retelling a seeming story of colonization as something quite different and far less threatening: redrawing, for example, Gandhi's campaign to protect indigenous Indian hand-weaving crafts from the colonizing influence of foreign mechanization as something of a protectionist exercise in the name of cheap local cloth that was actually made not by hand but in Indian mills. Indeed, Cowen suggests, quality foreign cloth made in technologically advanced mills in England in time forced hand-weavers (of whom 6 million survive today in India) to up the quality of their goods and develop a handicraft worth defending. Why, Cowen asks, should poorer societies in any case "be required to serve as diversity slaves," their quaint distinctiveness used as an excuse to obstruct their path to modernization?

11   Cowen's second more economic argument, while not without truth, is less persuasive and ends up revealing the primary defect of his overall position. In suggesting that in an open market there is a confrontation of two cultures—in which the colonizing culture is itself as equally colonized as the society it thinks it is colonizing—Cowen makes a mistake common to anthropologists and economists alike. He ignores the role of power: the relative political and cultural coerciveness the stronger party brings to the table. Anthropologists treat cultural exchange in a vacuum. Culture confronts culture, they posit; each borrows from the other, both emerge changed and enriched but more different than ever. Economists treat exchange within the mythic frame of perfect market freedom, where it is the result of two equally free, equally voluntary, equally powerful contractees who sit down as gentlemen and make a deal. You get our technology, which will transform your cultural goods; we get your cultural goods, which will transform our technology. You look more like us, and we look more like you.

12   Once the relative power of the intersecting cultures is factored in, however, the happy reciprocity of cultural hybridization is trumped by the unhappy preeminence of the dominant culture. One McDonald's in Tiananmen Square may enhance diversity in China, just as the first Starbucks in Berlin diversifies its cuisine. But the market corporations of McWorld aspire not just to penetrate but also to permeate markets, and their ultimate objective is monopoly. The tenth McDonald's is a different story than the first, and No. 100 begins to force out the competition. When the franchises break the 1,000 mark, homogenization is more salient than diversification. Pluralism is not only diminished within a given culture (Cowen admits as much), it is diminished among cultures as well, with one looking more and more like the next (the claim Cowen wants to rebut).

13   With a Starbucks on every corner in traditional coffeehouse Vienna, the city loses its distinctive Viennese coffeehouse culture. Competition inside the United States withers too, with delis and coffee shops being put out of business in favor of a bland global Starbucks culture. In the 1992 Coca-Cola corporate report, when Coke was going into the Indian market, it identified "Indian tea culture" as a rival that would have to be overcome if Coke was to prosper on the subcontinent. Film industries in Mexico, India and Hong Kong may still be flourishing, as Cowen says, but the percentage of world screens devoted to American-made product continues to grow in ways that make it hard to believe that Hollywood's global muscle is good for cultural diversity.

14   Then, finally, there is the question of the authenticity of origins, the integrity of the cultures that produce diverse goods. As Cowen

himself finally acknowledges, in reproducing and commodifying cultural goods, their character is put at risk. "Cosmopolitan attitudes," Cowen agrees, "if held fully and consistently, would defeat the cosmopolitan end of diversity and freedom of choice." As cultures are borrowed from, encroached upon, altered and sold to, they may continue to affect those doing the borrowing, encroaching, altering and selling, but the sources of their authenticity upon which their own distinctive cultures are founded gradually are eroded away. Take a (fictional) recipe for Grandma's Maryland crab cakes, developed over generations by families who live and work the Maryland eastern shore: When its success as a subcultural taste icon turns it into a national brand that is sold back to Grandma's kids living in Baltimore and then to Grandma herself, who no longer bothers to cook, cultural capital is being exploited and exhausted in ways that will ultimately vitiate Grandma's disappearing culture and with it the crab cake recipe. At this point, cultural diversity is reduced to a plastic theme-park variety show that resembles the wild West shows of the turn of the century that marked the end both of frontier life and native American society as a living and evolving culture.

15   When anthropologists talk about hybridization, I am reminded of the sorts of exchanges "negotiated" by hares and pythons. "Oh, yes," exclaim the relatives of the hare, "you may think our cousin has been consumed, but look at the snake! There our cousin is, his profile distending the shape of the serpent! Each has transformed the other! Neither is gone, both are transformed." But wait a week or two and, as the python's relatives know very well, the hare will have vanished and the serpent will slither on in search of new prey in the false name of voluntary market exchange. Cultural exchange may be a form of "creative destruction," but over time dialectic is trumped by power, and destruction merely destroys, leaving the Panglossian Cowens of the world with neither new cultural creation nor genuine diversity but a handful of Disney souvenirs that in their shallow mimicry mock true pluralism.

For Class Discussion

1. In his summarizing of Tyler Cowen's book *Creative Destruction: How Globalization Is Changing the World's Cultures*, what does Barber say are Cowen's main points?

2. What features of Cowen's book does Barber praise?

3. In the eleventh paragraph of this article, Barber shifts the focus to refuting Cowen's argument. What counterreasoning and counterexamples does Barber offer?

4. What does Barber mean by these terms: "homogenization thesis," "ideological balance," "cultural hybridization," "authenticity," "theme-park variety show," and "Panglossian Cowens"? (Dr. Pangloss is a character in Voltaire's novel *Candide* who is known for his foolish optimism and belief that the existing world is the best possible.)

5. The book review-critique-argument is a common academic genre that appears frequently in scholarly journals and sophisticated journalistic publications such as the *Atlantic Monthly*, *Harper's*, and the *New York Times Book Review*. How does Barber try to make this piece interesting and understandable to the general readership of the *Los Angeles Times*?

6. How does Barber's analogy comparing cultural exchanges to the python's eating of the hare function rhetorically in his argument?

Learning from One Another
Jane Poynter

Jane Poynter has lived in Biosphere 2, an enclosed ecological system, for two years. She is president of Paragon Space Development Corporation, an aerospace engineering service in Tucson, Arizona, that specializes in supporting cutting-edge technology. This article was first published in the *Seattle Times* on December 19, 2004. Ladakh, the subject of this article, is a part of India located in the Himalayas.

> In this article, what vision of the high cultural stakes in the cultural globalization controversy does Poynter introduce?

1 I was sitting on a rickety bench in Little Tibet, chatting, when a young woman stumbled into the room. Her sightless white eyes rolled in large sockets, underlined by protruding cheekbones and slack lips. As she bent to sit next to me, her scrawny frame grazed mine, and she sat on my left leg, feeling my face and arms to introduce herself.

2 As almost any American might have been, I was repulsed and uncomfortable. But then she began to sing a lilting ballad, and the strength, control and emotion in her pitch-perfect voice filled the small kitchen, transfixing everyone.

3 Thukjay Dolma turned out to be one of the most famous singers in Ladakh, a remote patch of India perched high in the Himalayas, where a millennium-old culture struggles to survive. But Dolma's songs are not about old things and old ways. They are about the importance of education, of saving the Ladakhis' sense of

community and unique traditions, of the need to raise their standard of living and to meet environmental and social challenges.

4   That's Ladakh in a nutshell—one of the highest inhabited spots on Earth, home to 200,000 people and a deep commitment to Tibetan Buddhism. But Ladakh is also a land struggling with modern dilemmas: lack of water, new cultures pouring in, the continual threat of religious strife, even how to handle the adventuresome tourists eager to visit this remote and gorgeous land. (Hint: Bring cash. Ladakh doesn't do credit cards.)

5   Today, an influential core of Ladakhis is struggling to retain the best of traditional culture—community, art and history—while embracing the many benefits development would bring. Tsering Samphel, director of the oldest non-government agency in Ladakh, the Leh Nutrition Project, puts it this way: "Change is no problem, it is inevitable. But community and values should not degrade, that is a challenge."

6   They want prosperity, education and a higher standard of living but not at the cost of a way of life that has so far saved Ladakh from being sucked into the religious and cultural warfare that surrounds it on the borders of Pakistan, Afghanistan and China.

7   Whether they succeed in their struggles is important to all of us, and to every developing country around the globe.

8   One of the amazing things about Ladakh is just how remote it still is. It takes at least 48 hours and four flights to reach the capital city of Leh from the West Coast of the United States. Although Ladakh has been part of India since 1947, eight of 10 Ladakhis practice Tibetan Buddhism, which has flourished in this section of the Himalayas since the 10th century. The other 20 percent of inhabitants are Muslim.

9   Around 20,000 Ladakhis—10 percent of the population—live in Leh. The rest inhabit villages and tiny hamlets with as few as three or four households; they're strewn across a rugged desert, cut off from the rest of the world by snow and ice during the eight-month winter.

10   During the four months of summer, valleys turn green with the barely that Ladakhis have grown in these fields for more than 1,000 years, using the same primitive, but effective, technologies. Dzos, a cross between a yak and a cow, pull wooden ploughs and carry loads of manure to the fields from the family outhouses; each is a two-story breezy building with the facilities on the top floor and manure collection on the ground floor.

11   Narrow canals run alongside every field, turning grinding wheels to make flour. Nomadic tribes herd goats between pastures. Women spin yarn made from the fleece of goats and sheep.

12   Tsering Dorjay, president of Ladakh's only political party, recalls guiding the first foreigners allowed into the area in 1974. "In

one village they were so scared that they did not come out. Everyone was hiding. They saw funny people."

13   For much of the last 50 years, it looked as if predominantly Hindu India would simply swallow whole this agrarian outpost. Schools taught in Hindi and Urdu and the Ladakhi language was dying. Many young men left their farms and joined the Indian army, which offered better salaries and benefits than any local employer. Subsidized rice flooded the markets from southern India and cost less than locally grown barley.

14   Ladakhis came to believe that they were backward, their rich culture an embarrassing anachronism, as heavy as the turquoise-studded heirloom headdresses worn by traditional brides.

15   Today, Ladakh is fighting back.

16   Surprisingly, tourism is proving to be one of the Ladakhis' most important weapons.

17   Buddhist devotees and the simply curious are pouring into the country. Guesthouses are springing up; Tsering Dorjay himself runs one. Internet cafes serve locals and foreigners. Monasteries are using donations from visitors to refurbish centuries-old buildings. This year Leh held the first exhibit of Thangkas, intricate religious paintings, created by local artists.

18   All the favorable attention is fueling a resurgence of the Ladakhi language, festivals and architecture. "It is compulsory that hotels be made in the traditional way, and people are building new homes with traditional architecture now," says Dorjay. The local radio station broadcasts in pure Ladakhi, so the young are learning their native language undiluted by Hindi.

19   The Women's Alliance of Ladakh boasts members in almost every village and hamlet. The alliance trains women in spinning, weaving and other handiwork to sell to eager tourists in Leh and has helped women open restaurants that serve traditional Ladakhi food. "It is the women who carry the tradition and the values. They are the ones that raise the children, and are left at home when the men go to find jobs in Leh or in the Army," says Dolma Tsering, executive director of the alliance.

20   The Students' Educational and Cultural Movement of Ladakh spearheaded revamping local schools to make them more applicable to Ladakhi life. Young children learn in Ladakhi and English. They no longer read about elephants and camels prancing around Hindu temples that they have never seen, but of yaks and dzos cavorting in a Himalayan landscape.

21   Unfortunately, many Westerners who want to help Ladakh oppose most modernization. They view Ladakh with romantic eyes and see only happy, peaceful people living a simple, ecologically sustainable life. Neighbors take turns watching over each other's

cattle and donkeys; they help build each other's houses; young and old work, sing and dance together.

22   Some of these Western NGOs fear that the independence a cash economy brings will break the bonds of community that have been the hallmark of Ladakhi culture. The International Society for Ecology and Culture, an NGO with headquarters in England, promotes what it calls "counterdevelopment" in Ladakh. ISEC has done much to help the Ladakhi people, such as introducing solar heating. However, the group would not have done so "had not other less sustainable heating methods—like coal and oil—already begun to disrupt traditional practices," as Helena Norberg-Hodge, the NGO's founder, wrote in her acclaimed book, *Ancient Futures*.

23   But Ladakhis like Tsering Dorjay say the romanticizers are wrong. They see Ladakh only in the summer. He describes winter, with families running out of food and going hungry, freezing winds howling through poorly insulated houses with little heat, no running water and electricity for only an hour or two in the evenings.

24   Many Ladakhis suffered from the nutritional deficiencies of a diet made up mostly of barley until the local Leh Nutrition Project taught farmers how to grow various vegetables. LNP has provided the nomadic tribes with smokeless stoves, replacing open fires in tents that caused rampant respiratory problems.

25   Hydroelectricity now provides almost half the power. Glaciers are receding all over Ladakh, providing less water in the spring for irrigation. So, the Ladakhis are making artificial glaciers during the winter from the water that trickles from the shrinking natural glaciers. Ladakhis have also begun to gain political power, with the ultimate goal of forming their own state within India.

26   Whether traditional Ladakh survives these developments matters to all of us, even in the comfort of the United States. Cultures matter, and it matters when cultures die. Beyond the beauty and exotic adventures a Ladakh offers, we humans need cultural diversity as a storehouse of human resources, just as the Earth needs species diversity as a bank of genetic material we can draw on to meet new challenges.

27   Although Western culture is sweeping the globe, here in the West we worry about loss of community, about social isolation, about children growing up without any strong sense of family and place. We desperately need to find ways to live together in a world where religion, suburbanization and social mobility are tearing us apart.

28   Ladakh has a lot to teach us. Even as Amnesty International reports that racial profiling in America has risen to one in nine people, mostly Muslims, Buddhist and Muslim Ladakhis live together

in peace. When a deadly uprising exploded in Kashmir in the 1980s, it threatened to infect Ladakh. But the Buddhist live-and-let-live attitude won out, and the Muslim and Buddhist communities learned to get along.

29   On July 24, 2004, suspected Muslim militants opened fire on counterinsurgency police in a busy Kashmir market place, killing two police officers and wounding two civilians. But, 150 miles away in a Ladakh monastery, 15,000 Buddhists crowded on the roofs and in a tiny courtyard to celebrate the birthday of Padmasambhava, who brought Buddhism to the Tibetan plateau more than 1,200 years ago. Many of the attendees arrived in taxis driven by Muslims. The chanting and swirling prayer wheels seemed a world away from the fighting just across the snow-capped mountains.

For Class Discussion

1. What are the cultural conflicts facing the small region and ancient culture of Ladakh near Nepal, India, and China?

2. What is Jane Poynter's claim in this argument?

3. How does Poynter use analogy, reasoning, and examples to support her claim?

4. How does she use description and narrative—techniques of creative nonfiction—to appeal to readers' emotions and values and to develop her argument?

5. How successful is Poynter in persuading you that remote places such as Ladakh could be very important to Americans? ∎

Global Media
Benjamin Compaine

Besides being a research consultant for MIT's Internet and Telecoms Convergence, Benjamin Compaine is a strong proponent of media globalization and the author or coauthor of twelve books including *Who Owns the Media?* (published originally in 1979 and updated in July 2000). This article appeared in the November–December 2002 edition of *Foreign Policy*, a politically nonbiased magazine about international politics and economics that is "dedicated to reaching a broad, nonspecialized audience who recognizes that what happens 'there' matters 'here,' and vice versa" (www.foreignpolicy.com).

Why do you think that Benjamin Compaine has chosen this debate forum in the magazine *Foreign Policy* to present his views on global media domination?

"A FEW BIG COMPANIES ARE TAKING OVER THE WORLD'S MEDIA"

1   **No.** Much of the debate on media structure is too black-and-white. A merger of Time Inc. with Warner Communications and then with America Online dominates headlines, but the incremental growth of smaller companies from the bottom does not. Breakups and divestitures do not generally receive front-page treatment, nor do the arrival and rapid growth of new players or the shrinkage of once influential players.

2   In the United States, today's top 50 largest media companies account for little more of total media revenue than did the companies that made up the top 50 in 1986. CBS Inc., for example, was then the largest media company in the United States. In the 1990s, it sold off its magazines, divested its book publishing, and was not even among the 10 largest U.S. media companies by the time it agreed to be acquired by Viacom, which was a second tier player in 1986. Conversely, Bertelsmann, though a major player in Germany in 1986, was barely visible in the United States. By 1997, it was the third largest player in the United States, where it owns book publisher Random House. Companies such as Amazon.com, Books-A-Million, Comcast, and C-Net were nowhere to be found on a list of the largest media companies in 1980. Others, such as Allied Artists, Macmillan, and Playboy Enterprises, either folded or grew so slowly as to fall out of the top ranks.

3   Indeed, media merger activity is more like rearranging the furniture: In the past 15 years, MCA with its Universal Pictures was sold by its U.S. owners to Matsushita (Japan), who sold to Seagram's (Canada), who sold to Vivendi (France). Vivendi has already announced that it will divest some major media assets, including textbook publisher Houghton-Mifflin. Bertelsmann also has had difficulty maintaining all the parts of its global enterprise: It recently fired its top executive and is planning to shed its online bookstore. There is an ebb as well as a flow among even the largest media companies.

4   The notion of the rise of a handful of all-powerful transnational media giants is also vastly overstated. Some media companies own properties internationally or provide some content across borders (for example, Vivendi's Canal+ distributes movies internationally), but no large media conglomerate owns newspapers, book publishers, radio stations, cable companies, or television licenses in all the major world markets. News Corp. comes closest to being a global media enterprise in both content and distribution, but on a global scale it is still a minor presence—that is, minor as a percentage of global media revenue, global audience, and in the number of markets it covers.

5   Media companies have indeed grown over the past 15 years, but this growth should be understood in context. Developed economies have grown, so expanding enterprises are often simply standing still in relative terms. Or their growth looks less weighty. For example, measured by revenue, Gannett was the largest U.S. newspaper publisher in 1986, its sales accounting for 3.4 percent of all media revenue that year. In 1997, it accounted for less than 2 percent of total media revenue. Helped by major acquisitions, Gannett's revenue had actually increased by 69 percent, but the U.S. economy had grown 86 percent. The media industry itself had grown 188 percent, making a "bigger" Gannett smaller in relative terms. Similar examples abound.

"U.S. COMPANIES DOMINATE THE MEDIA"

6   **No.** Long before liberalization of ownership in television in the 1980s, critics around the world were obsessed by the reach of U.S. programming, which cultural elites often considered too mass market and too infused with American cultural values. However, in most of the world, decisions of what programming to buy traditionally lay in the hands of managers who worked for government-owned or government-controlled broadcasters. Then, as now, no nation's media companies could require a programmer to buy their offerings or force consumers to watch them. As the market becomes more competitive, with content providers such as Canal+ and the BBC marketing their products globally, it is even more important that media enterprises offer programming that people want to watch.

7   While Viacom, Disney, and AOL Time Warner are U.S. owned, many non-U.S.-owned companies dominate the roster of the largest media groups: News Corp. (Australia), Bertelsmann (Germany), Reed-Elsevier (Britain/Netherlands), Vivendi and Lagadere-Hachette (France), and Sony Corp. (Japan).

8   The pervasiveness of a handful of media companies looks even less relevant when one looks at media ownership across countries. The United Nations' "Human Development Report 2002" examined ownership of the five largest newspaper and broadcast enterprises in 97 countries. It found that 29 percent of the world's largest newspapers are state owned and another 57 percent are family owned. Only 8 percent are owned by employees or the public. For radio stations, 72 percent are state owned and 24 percent family owned. For television stations, 60 percent are state owned, 34 percent family owned. These data suggest there is little foreign direct investment in the media sectors of most countries.

9   News media can tap wire services from around the globe such as Reuters, Agence France-Presse, the Associated Press, Kyodo

News, Xinhua News Agency, and Itar-Tass. TV news editors can use video feeds from sources as diverse as U.S.-based CNN to the Qatar-based Al Jazeera. The variety and ownership of TV content in general has substantially increased—a reality media critics ignore. From two state-owned channels in many European countries and from three U.S. networks plus the Public Broadcasting Service, there are now dozens, often hundreds, of video options via terrestrial, cable, and satellite transmission, not to mention the offline variety of videocassettes and DVDs and the online availability of music and movies. In addition, book and magazine publishing continues to be robust worldwide. Encouraged by relatively low start-up costs, new publishers are popping up constantly.

"CORPORATE OWNERSHIP IS KILLING HARD-HITTING JOURNALISM"

10   **A bright red herring.** When exactly was this golden age of hard-hitting journalism? One might call to mind brief periods: the muckrakers in the early 20th century or Watergate reporting in the 1970s. But across countries and centuries, journalism typically has not been "hard-hitting." With more news outlets and competition today, there is a greater range of journalism than was typical in the past. Further, a 2000 comparison of 186 countries by Freedom House, a nonprofit devoted to promoting democracy, suggests that press independence, including journalists' freedom from economic influence, remained high in all but two members (Mexico and Turkey) of the Organisation for Economic Co-operation and Development, where global media's markets are concentrated.

11   Also underlying the complaint that news has been "dumbed down" is an assumption that the media ought to be providing a big dose of policy-relevant content. Japan's dominant public broadcaster, NHK, does so, yet is Japan a more vibrant democracy as a result? More to the point, with so many media outlets today, readers and viewers can get more and better news from more diverse perspectives, if that is what they want. Or they can avoid it altogether. The alternative is to limit the number of outlets and impose content requirements on those remaining.

12   The third problem with this notion of corporations killing journalism is that it assumes ownership matters. In the old days of media moguls it may have: William Randolph Hearst, William Loeb, and Robert McCormick were attracted to the media because they each had political agendas, which permeated their newspapers. Nearly a century before Italian media owner Silvio Berlusconi rose to the top of Italian politics, Hearst, whose newspapers dominated in the United States, was elected to the U.S. Congress and harbored presidential aspirations. But Hearst's dual roles did not affect U.S.

politics or democracy in any lasting way. The jury is still out on the effect of Berlusconi's dual roles.

13   Corporate-owned newspapers may actually provide better products than those that are family owned: Research suggests that large, chain-owned newspapers devote more space to editorial material than papers owned by small firms. In many parts of South America, where regulation has restricted or prevented corporate ownership, family-run enterprises have often been closely identified with ideological biases or even with using political influence to benefit other businesses. Brazilian media enterprise Globo, owned by the politically involved Marinho family, encompasses a TV network, radio, cable, and magazines. Yet Globo no longer opposes recent moves to liberalize Brazilian media ownership because then it could gain access to desirable foreign investment. As Latin American media shift from family-owned, partisan media to corporations, observes Latin American media scholar Silvio Waisbord, the media become less the "public avenues for the many ambitions of their owners," and their coverage of government corruption "is more likely to be informed by marketing calculations and the professional aspirations of reporters." This trade-off may not be bad.

14   Global media will not necessarily introduce aggressive journalism in places where press freedom has traditionally been constricted. For instance, News Corp. was criticized for dropping BBC news programming from Star TV presumably to mollify Chinese leaders in the mid-1990s. Yet satellite broadcaster Phoenix TV (in which News Corp.'s Star TV maintains a 37.6 percent stake, alongside that of the local Chinese owners) sometimes pushes the envelope in China, as when it reported on the election of Chen Shui-bian as president in Taiwan.

"GLOBAL MEDIA DROWN OUT LOCAL CONTENT"

15   **Absolutely not.** Most media—like politics—are inherently local. Global firms peddle wholly homogeneous content across markets at their peril. Thus, MTV in Brazil plays a mix of music videos and other programming determined by local producers, even though it shares a recognizable format with MTV stations elsewhere. News Corp.'s newspapers in the United Kingdom look and read differently from those in the United States. When Star TV, an Asian subsidiary of News Corp., began broadcasting satellite television into India, few tuned in to *Dallas* and *The Bold and the Beautiful* dubbed in Hindi. The network only succeeded in India once it hired an executive with experience in Indian programming to create Indian soap operas and when an Indian production house took over news and current affairs programming.

16   Often viewed as a negative, consolidation may have considerable social benefits. It took the deep pockets of News Corp. to create and sustain a long-awaited fourth broadcast network in the United States. And the 1990 merger in the United Kingdom of Sky Channel and BSB created a viable television competitor from two money-losing satellite services.

"THE INTERNET HAS LEVELED THE PLAYING FIELD"

17   **Yes.** Or more accurately, it's helping to level the terrain because it is a relatively low-cost conduit for all content providers. As the old adage goes, "Freedom of the press is guaranteed only to those who own one." Make no mistake: an activist with a dial-up Internet connection and 10 megabytes of Web server space cannot easily challenge Disney for audiences. But an individual or a small group can reach the whole world and, with a little work and less money, can actually find an audience.

18   Worldwide, an estimated 581 million people were online by 2002, more than one third of whom lived outside North America and Europe. Yet the Internet is in its infancy. The number of users is still growing and will continue to expand to the literate population as access costs decrease.

19   Once online, Internet users have access to thousands of information providers. Some are the same old players—Disney with its stable of cartoon icons, Infinity with its familiar music and talk-radio broadcasting, and old government-run stations still operating in much of the world. But these coexist with newer, Internet-only options such as those found at Realguide.com, which links to 2,500 real-time audio streams from around the world, or NetRadio, which outdraws many traditional stations. These Internet-only "broadcasters" have not had to invest in government-sanctioned licenses and generally have no limits on their speech.

20   In countries where governments strictly control print and broadcast media, governments also can try to restrict Internet access, as China does. But some may choose not to do so: In Malaysia, the government pledged not to censor the Internet to promote its version of Silicon Valley to foreign investors. As a consequence, Malaysian cyberspace media are free of the restrictions their print and broadcast brethren face.

"PROLIFERATING MEDIA OUTLETS BALKANIZE PUBLIC OPINION"

21   **No.** The flip side of concerns that media concentration has limited available information is the concern that technology has made it possible to access so many voices that people in democratic societies can and will seek only information that supports their

prejudices. A fragmented public, tuning in only to select cable channels or specific Web sites, could thus wall itself off from healthy public debate.

22   Recent U.S. studies show that as users gain experience with the Internet, they use it not to replace other sources of information but for more practical applications. They perform work-related tasks, make purchases and other financial transactions, write e-mail messages, and seek information that is important to their everyday lives.

23   Although news is low on the list of its uses, the Internet functions in much the same way as older news media: offering opportunities for both those who directly seek news sites and those who chance upon news links serendipitously. The Pew Internet and American Life Project reports that 42 percent of those who read news on the Web typically find news while they are doing other things online. This picture is not consistent with the notion that Web audiences routinely tune out information with which they disagree.

"MEDIA COVERAGE DRIVES FOREIGN POLICY"

24   **Probably not often.** Analyzing media coverage is often a chicken-and-egg dilemma: What stimulated the media to cover an event or issue? And if public policy responds to an event the news media cover, does that mean the media (or those who run the media) set the agenda?

25   The idea that media coverage of international crises can spark a response from politicians is termed the "CNN effect." The classic case is the coverage of starving children in Somalia in the early 1990s, which was followed by U.S. military involvement in humanitarian relief efforts. But even in the case of Somalia, some administration officials actually used the media to get the attention of other officials, and the majority of the coverage in Somalia followed rather than preceded official action.

26   In many places, governments are even more likely to be driving media coverage rather than the other way around, although it may suit governments to appear as if they have bowed to public opinion. The Chinese government delayed release of the crew of the U.S. EP-3 spy plane that made an emergency landing on Hainan Island in 2001, claiming that an embittered Chinese public demanded it. Angry Web comments did precede and were then reflected in media coverage of the incident. But at the same time, the government had been fanning the flames, cultivating nationalistic sentiment through the selection and treatment of stories in the news. At other times, the Chinese government both censors Web comments and withholds information from the media when it needs to preserve its foreign policy options.

"STRICTER REGULATION OF MEDIA
IS IN THE PUBLIC INTEREST"

27   **Just the opposite.** Beware when someone claims to be speaking for the "public interest." In most cases, those who invoke the term really mean "interested publics." For example, advertisers' sense of which policies on media ownership are in their interest may differ from that of regular newspaper readers or that of satellite TV subscribers.

28   Fostering competition has long been a central tenet of U.S. media regulation. What if preventing two newspapers from merging results in both having to trim news budgets or pages, neither having the resources to engage in investigative reporting, or worse yet, one closing shop? Media concentration may be in the public interest if it provides a publisher with greater profit margins and the wherewithal to spend some of that on editorial content, and research in fact shows this is the case.

29   Licensing acts as an entry barrier to new players, and antitrust laws often lag behind reality. In the market for video program distribution, for instance, terrestrial broadcast licensees compete with cable operators and networks, who in turn compete with satellite providers. Regulation and policy limits will always be necessary, but having different regulatory frameworks for each media segment makes less sense today.

30   Governments that give can also take. Japanese law makes public broadcaster NHK one of the world's most autonomous public broadcasters, yet the ruling Liberal Democratic Party (LDP) strongly influences the agencies that control media licenses and that select NHK 's governing board. Not coincidentally, NHK provides neutral, policy-relevant news but avoids controversial topics and investigative reporting. Where Japanese commercial television has tried to fill this gap, LDP politicians have reacted: in one case, asking an advertiser to withdraw sponsorship and in another, seeking the withdrawal of a broadcasting license.

31   Paradoxically, relaxing broadcast regulation may expand competition. When News Corp. put together a fourth network in the United States in 1986, the timing was not random. It followed two regulatory decisions: the Federal Communications Commission raised the limit on local licenses that a single firm could own from seven to twelve and waived a rule that kept TV networks from owning their programming. The first change allowed News Corp. to assemble a core of stations in larger markets that gave it a viable base audience, and the second sanctioned News Corp.'s purchase of 20th Century Fox, with its television production studio. Fox was thus able to launch the first successful alternative to the Big Three

in 30 years. Its success also paved the way for three other large media players to initiate networks.

For Class Discussion

1. Benjamin Compaine structures his argument in response to critical views of a dominant media. What views does Compaine refute?
2. Compaine's main argumentative strategy is to offer counterevidence. Where in his argument does this strategy work particularly well?
3. Compaine attempts to offer a positive outlook on media and globalization. What points does he make that are hopeful and encouraging?
4. To rebut Compaine's argument, what counterevidence would you need? One of Compaine's most well-known and respected opponents is Robert McChesney, a professor of communications at the University of Illinois at Urbana-Champaign and author of seven books, most recently *Rich Media, Poor Democracy: Communication Politics in Dubious Times* (2000). Investigate Robert McChesney on the Web. How does he challenge Compaine's views?
5. How has this article influenced your view of cultural globalization? ■

Great Mall of China
Henry Payne

Henry Payne is an editorial cartoonist for the *Detroit News*. His work has been published in the *New York Times*, the *National Review*, and *USA Today*, and he is a contributing cartoonist to *Reason*. This cartoon (p.234) was originally published in the *Detroit News* and later reprinted in *Reason*.

What knowledge of the Great Wall of China does the cartoonist assume that his audience has?

For Class Discussion

1. Which controversy over cultural exchange does this cartoon examine?
2. What claim does the cartoon support?
3. What questions about culture, free trade, and globalization does this cartoon raise? Whom does it appear to be satirizing?
4. What readings in this chapter would this cartoon agree with or support? ■

"THINGS HAVEN'T BEEN THE SAME SINCE WE OPENED OUR MARKETS..."

FIGURE 5.2 Great Mall of China *(Henry Payne: © Detroit News/Dist. By United Feature Syndicate, Inc.)*

Culture Goes Global

Henry Jenkins

Henry Jenkins is a professor of literature and comparative media studies at the Massachusetts Institute of Technology. He has written several books, among them *Textual Poachers: Television Fans and Participatory Culture* (1992), and articles on popular culture, most recently on *Star Trek*, Nintendo, Dr. Seuss, and WWF Wrestling. This article first appeared in the July–August 2001 issue of *Technology Review*, which is MIT's magazine dedicated to promoting "the understanding of emerging technologies and their impact on business and society" and aimed at business leaders around the world (www.technologyreview.com).

> How has Jenkins tailored his argument for the main audience of *Technology Review?*

1   Pounding drums, throaty voices and electronic pulses rock my CD player. I have entered the world of Oceania, a remarkable musical collaboration between Maori poet and singer Hinewehi Mohi and Jaz Coleman, lead singer of the British post-punk band Killing Joke. Although Mohi characterizes the Maori as "precious feathers" blown about by global forces, her music, which sets traditional chants to a techno soundtrack, celebrates their ability to surf the winds of change.

2   We often imagine peoples like the Maori as existing pristine and timeless, within a display case at a natural-history museum. Yet cultures have never remained static or isolated; even in ancient times, war, trade and migration made their marks. Now, rapid transportation and global communication and commerce accelerate change. The anthropologist Renata Rosaldo compares the high-speed transformations of cultures to a garage sale, where "cultural artifacts flow between unlikely places, and nothing is sacred, permanent or sealed off." We need to recognize the richness, diversity and creativity of this garage-sale culture. Hinewehi Mohi sings in her people's traditional language, yet to a techno beat, enabling her songs to escape national boundaries and enter the global marketplace.

3   For decades, critics have depicted the international circulation of American goods as cultural imperialism. The United States, for example, produces nine of the top ten box office films screened in Europe each year, undercutting local culture industries. Living off their domestic grosses, the big studios can offer lower rates, maintain higher production values and spend more on marketing than local competition, while the American market remains largely closed to imports.

4   Those days are numbered. We are no longer the world's only powerful media-producing nation. African consumers are more apt to be fans of Hindi musicals than MTV. And even American childhood has increasingly been shaped by Asian cultural imports. Most parents now know about the Power Rangers, Tamagotchi and Pokémon, Sega and Nintendo. For the moment, English remains cyberspace's dominant language, and having Web access often means that Third-World youth have greater exposure to American popular culture. Yet these same technologies enable Balkan students studying in the United States to hear webcast news and music from Serbia or Bosnia. Thanks to broadband communication, foreign media producers will distribute films and television programs directly to American consumers without having to pass by U.S. gatekeepers.

5   And they may be assisted in their conquest of the U.S. market by American teens who have developed more cosmopolitan tastes through travel or online chatting. Some fans now teach themselves Japanese in order to do grass-roots translation and subtitling of animated films (anime) or comics (manga). They scan Japanese television guides for hot properties and post their own ratings to help parents filter the often mature content. These fans have become key niche marketers, promoting U.S. awareness and acceptance of Asian popular culture.

6   For signs of this coming cultural revolution, look in the world-music section of your local record shop. The lower production costs and smaller shelf-space requirements of CDs have dramatically expanded the diversity of today's music store. Older consumers may find this totally alien. But contemporary college students now sample the once-exotic sounds of African pennywhistle, Tuvian throat singing or Scandinavian mandolin as casually as they choose between tacos, pizza and sushi. Seeking broader circulation, non-Western artists like Mohi often attach themselves to trends inspired by American artists. Madonna's *Ray of Light*, for example, borrowed from bhangra, an Indian-inflected dance music that previously circulated mainly on dub tapes in ethnic grocery stores. Through such exchanges, global music enters the mainstream.

7   In some cases, international performers return to their musical roots, appealing to the nostalgia of their country folk now scattered worldwide. Yet just as often, they mix and match once-distinctive styles to create music unlike anything we've heard. Sheila Chandra's aptly titled *Weaving My Ancestors' Voices*, for example, fuses Indian and Celtic traditions. These hybrid sounds express the experience of "third-culture" youths who may be of mixed racial, national or linguistic backgrounds, and who have spent their early years moving between countries.

8   Some fear that globalization will destroy cultural diversity, resulting in a world ruled by American exports. Yet the world-music scene suggests an alternative, where global popular culture enters our marketplace with help from American youth, audiences demand new forms of diversity and performers fuse traditions to create novel forms that express a widespread experience of dislocation. Call it global fusion, the Third World's answer to Walt Disney and Coca-Cola.

For Class Discussion

1. Key phrases in Jenkins's article are "cultural revolution" and "global fusion." How does he explain these terms, and how does he support his claim of reciprocal exchanges between the United States and the rest of the world?

2. According to Henry Jenkins, how has culture become global without becoming a monoculture?

3. Jenkins cites anthropologist Renata Rosaldo's metaphor of cultural transformation as a garage sale. How does this image work to describe global cultural exchange?

4. What alternative views does Jenkins address? What views does he *not* consider?

■

The Bland Play On

John Harris

John Harris is an esteemed British journalist whose work has regularly appeared in *NME*, *Mojo*, *Q Magazine*, *Select*, the *New Statesman*, and the *Independent*. He is the author of *The Last Party: Britpop, Blair and the Demise of English Rock* (2004), a book relating the rise and fall of British rock to politics. This article appeared in the May 8, 2004, edition of the *Guardian*, a United Kingdom-based newspaper committed to "editorial and political independence" (www.guardian.co.uk).

> What irony does Harris say underlies the fate of oppositional rock music, and how does this irony relate to the globalization of popular music?

1   A few years ago, I travelled to Brazil to watch the American rock band REM perform at Rock In Rio, an outdoor festival of unimaginable vastness. It was quite a spectacle: close to a million people, a stage seemingly the size of an aircraft carrier, and a stifling heat that led to the odd breakdown of pop etiquette—this was the festival at which the then virginal Britney Spears left her microphone switched on and unwittingly regaled the crowd with the f-word.

2   Twenty-plus years into their career, REM are among the few surviving standard-bearers for a transatlantic subculture that took root in the wake of punk, founded on the notion—vague, but usually palpable—that rock music should express some kind of dissent. Staunchly anti-Republican, proudly eco-conscious, and with a record of playing benefits for liberal causes, they used their trip to South America to issue at least one attention-grabbing soundbite: "George W. Bush is not my president," their vocalist, Michael Stipe, told the local press.

3   On the night of their show, unfortunately, none of that counted for very much. Rock In Rio was sponsored by AOL, who were using the event to launch their Brazilian operation. The visual language was globalisation's semiotic trickery in excelsis: lest anyone fear that AOL's arrival represented any kind of online imperialism, their logo had been resprayed in the heartwarmingly Brazilian colour scheme of green and yellow. The presence of some of the USA's biggest musicians, however, drove the most important message home: opening AOL accounts could, it seemed, induct the Brazilians into the same spangled world as Britney, Guns'n'Roses and—oh, yes—REM.

4   For musicians whose sensitivity to such chicanery places them a few notches up the evolutionary chain from Busted and Avril Lavigne, the implied contradictions can be pretty hard to swallow. Put bluntly, Anglo-American popular music is among

globalisation's most useful props. Never mind the nitpicking fixations with interview rhetoric and stylistic nuance that concern its hardcore enthusiasts—away from its home turf, mainstream music, whether it's metal, rap, teen-pop or indie-rock, cannot help but stand for a depressingly conservative set of values: conspicuous consumption, the primacy of the English language, the implicit acknowledgement that America is probably best.

5   Even the most well-intentioned artist can't escape: once you have run onstage, plugged in your guitar and yelped "Hello, Tokyo!", your allegiances have surely been established. I once saw Radiohead's neurotically ethical Thom Yorke address a crowd in Modena as follows: "Sorry, we don't speak Italian. We're sad fucks." Even a clumsy "grazie mille" might have underwritten his public fretting about the effects of corporate power—but no. This, after all, was rock.

6   To make things worse, though the output of MTV, VH1 and the snowballing number of radio stations owned by Clear Channel might be dressed up in pop's customary language of diversity and individualism, the music they pump out is now standardised to the point of tedium. As the record industry's corporate structure has hardened into an immovable oligarchy—EMI, Time-Warner, BMG, Sony and Universal—so the range of musical options on offer has been dramatically scythed down. In 2004, there were but a handful of international musical superstars: Beyoncé, 50 Cent, Justin Timberlake, Eminem, Norah Jones, Coldplay. To characterise the process behind their global success as top-down is something of an understatement. MTV may have initially been marketed with the superficially empowering slogan, "I want my MTV"; more recently, with billions gladly hooked up, it has used the flatly sinister, "One planet, one music". Those four words beg one question: who decides?

7   In the context of the music's historical roots, this a surreally topsy-turvy outcome. Never mind those arcane debates about the true origins of rock'n'roll: it's surely instructive to understand modern pop as the endpoint of a centuries-long lineage of people's music; stuff that originated outside the patronage of church and court, and took in a mind-boggling diversity of voices. Come the 20th century, its endlessly variegated textures might have seemed under threat; and yet, through the appearance of the blues, country music, R&B, rockabilly and rock'n'roll—not to mention the first stirrings of the modern music industry—the devolved, uncontrollable ways of folk culture remained in place.

8   The resulting commerce, split between an ever-changing array of record labels, was often as anarchic as the music itself. Hit American records usually took root as word slowly spread from state to state. By the time British musicians worked up the confidence

to join in, the transatlantic traffic must surely have confounded any sensible predictions. Who would have seen that four-head monster emerging from Liverpool, or have anticipated the likes of Ray Davies and Pete Townshend so consummately blending an American form with their own unmistakably British experiences—let alone selling such a collision back to the States?

9   Two factors hardened pop into the hegemonic monolith it is today. Firstly, though the transatlantic cultural exchange brought pop a new artistic richness, it failed to repeat the trick elsewhere. With a few notable exceptions, continental Europe has long been barred from offsetting an ongoing deluge of Anglo-American imports with any lasting worldwide successes of its own; even the popular music of Africa, where the fusion of regional styles with western pop has long been inspirational, seems unable to snare our attention. And then there is the aforementioned domination of a once chaotic industry by those lumbering corporations. Wither such examples of creative autonomy as Chess, Tamla Motown, Island and Creation? Long since gobbled up, like so many of the western world's more interesting elements.

10   Underlying that picture is a tragic irony indeed: music founded in a spirit of spontaneity and self-expression ending up at the core of an ever-more standardised planet (those Pepsi ads starring Pink, Beyoncé and Britney speak volumes). Moreover, as the music industry shrinks, pop's increasing dearth of diversity is starting to impact on the UK. Each year, the odds against British acts making inroads in the US seem slimmer than ever; in music, too, there is but one superpower.

11   Such, to use a phrase beloved of the Bush White House, is the cultural aspect of the New American Century. How long, I wonder, before Halliburton and Exxon start sponsoring festivals?

For Class Discussion

1. How would you sum up John Harris's claim in this article? What model of intercultural exchange does Harris assert that pop music has followed?

2. What evidence does Harris offer for his position? How knowledgeable and credible is Harris as a music expert? How does his identity as a British citizen influence his views?

3. What assumptions does Harris make about his British audience's view of American rock recording artists?

4. How does the tone of this piece differ from proglobalization articles in this chapter?

5. How could a reader challenge Harris's argument?   ■

Why Is Bollywood Obsessed with Producing "Crossover Films"?

Rajal Pitroda

Bollywood, the subject of this article, is India's equivalent of America's Hollywood. This center of the Indian film industry produces over seven hundred films a year that are popular throughout Africa, Asia, and the Middle East. Typical Bollywood films are musicals that feature singing and elaborate choreography and cinematography. Bollywood films such as *Lagaan* (2001) are beginning to get attention from American audiences. While *Lagaan* is strictly an Indian film, *Bride and Prejudice* (2004)—called a "crossover film"—was intended to blend film cultures and to introduce America to Bollywood features. In this piece, Rajal Pitroda, a Chicago-based writer and knowledgeable critic of the Indian entertainment industry, questions the value and cultural impact of such crossover films. This piece appeared in the *News India-Times*, published in New York, on March 11, 2005.

> What audience does Pitroda particularly want to reach with this proposal argument and what features appeal to that audience?

1   Gurinder Chadha's *Bride and Prejudice,* which opened last month in the U.S., is mainstream America's first exposure to India's singing and dancing tradition of cinema. Distributed in North America by Miramax Films, the publicity of *Bride and Prejudice* centered largely on its lead actress, Aishwarya Rai. Although a household name in India and other parts of the world familiar with Bollywood, Aishwarya was introduced to America through a series of television appearances, namely on *60 Minutes, Nightline* and *The Late Show with David Letterman.*

2   Almost immediately after each of the interviews was aired, Indians around America, and even at home in India, took to an analysis of her performance. Around dinner tables, on the Internet and in newspapers, we scrutinized her giggles, her grammar and the eternal question of what substance, if any, lay behind her looks. Headlines in India heralded 'Ash Does Fine,' while Internet interviews decreed her lack of sound judgment in choosing to wear a skirt over a sari. Almost all of us found some way to comment on Aishwarya's ability (or inability) to truly "crossover" into America. But why?

3   The reason, most likely, is that Aishwarya Rai is largely symbolic, a torchbearer of a larger revolution—one that takes Indian entertainment beyond the developing world, and into America.

4   However, instead of merely criticizing and evaluating her, we should be asking ourselves larger questions prompted by her presence—why, as a culture of global Indians, are we so obsessed with a marriage of Bollywood into the West? Why are so many of our filmmakers at home in India seeking to make the next big "crossover" film? And why—when we say that Bollywood is the largest film industry in the world, making movies for a global audience of nearly three billion—when one actress arrives in Hollywood, do we turn our entire focus on her? Are we just seeking appreciation and acceptance from the West? And what about our industry at home? What is actually happening to Bollywood in Mumbai?

5   Aishwarya's arrival in Hollywood, and its surrounding media blitz, needs to be viewed beyond the individual. She is cultural capital, a symbol of the Indian ethos, the Indian entertainment industry and a larger possibility. The challenge is to translate this into economic growth, and that is where the industry at home becomes critical.

6   India, and much of the world, is fixated on Hollywood because, despite making less than half the number of films as the Indian industry, it is the largest moneymaking film industry in the world. *Titanic*, released in 1997, earned $1.8 billion dollars at the global box office, more than the nearly 1,000 films combined released by the Indian industry in that year.

7   Hollywood, through its years, has built itself into this industry—it has created and shaped institutions that support talent, recognize achievement and respect the creative process.

8   Aishwarya offers India an entry point into Hollywood, and the global film industry. However, without the proper attention to our own processes, institutions and policies, the opportunity for global expansion may not materialize.

9   Recognized as an official "industry" by the government in 2001, the Indian film industry finally became eligible for bank finance and opened up to foreign investment, and thus, increased credibility. Despite these changes, it continues to operate much as it has in the past, with illegitimate sources of financing still rampant. The industry has not adequately studied its audiences with market surveys, and it is typical for films in India to not fully recoup their investment. These numbers, however, are difficult to monitor, as there is no single reputable source of box office receipt information. On any given week, all of the film trade journals may report different information on collections for a particular film, as producers, distributors and exhibitors do not fully disclose their particular cut of a deal.

10   In addition to financing and monitoring of funds, the Indian industry suffers from a severe lack in training institutions for creative talent. The once highly regarded Film and Television Institute of India is severely under-funded and understaffed, with equipment that has not been updated for over a decade. There are few other training schools for actors, writers, directors and more, contributing both to stale content and an ingrained lack of respect for creative pursuits, as they seemingly do not require a degree.

11   India has not cultivated institutions that support creative professionals either—there is no Directors Guild or Writers Guild to work with individuals on their rights and support them in their professions, within an Indian context.

12   All of these issues prevent India from creating and sustaining a stronger film industry at home, and one that is exportable beyond its borders.

13   Government institutions that support the entertainment industry are nearly defunct in their financing and international marketing abilities. Authorities are ineffective and uninterested in communicating with Western counterparts, and regulatory policies are altered on a whim, making it difficult for U.S. studios and distribution companies to keep up with policy changes that affect their interaction with India. Piracy is still rampant, high rates of entertainment tax plague distributors and exhibitors, and co-production treaties with countries such as Canada and Italy have been stalled for upward of three years.

14   Aishwarya Rai, whether giggling or not, draws interest and attention to our industry, and is paving the way for a greater international audience. The globalization of the Indian entertainment industry may begin with one actress, but it cannot be sustained by her alone. India requires a movement that develops its own talent while drawing production to its borders, much like the software industry did in the 1990s, supported by institutions like the IITs, and organizations like Nasscom and TiE. In order to create a truly international industry, one that not only moves West but also builds East, we must first cultivate Bollywood at home, and continue to entertain billions of people as only we do best.

For Class Discussion

1. What cultural interaction and what Bollywood conditions is Pitroda protesting in this piece?

2. What proposal does she put forth?

3. How does she persuade readers of her knowledge and of the importance of her proposal?

4. How rhetorically effective is Pitroda's conclusion in wrapping up her argument and persuading her audience?

5. What theories or principles of cultural globalization discussed in the introduction to this chapter does Pitroda's argument support?

Marvel Comics and Manifest Destiny
David Adesnik

David Adesnik is a fellow in Public Affairs at the University of Virginia and is in the process of finishing his doctorate in international relations at Oxford University as a Rhodes Scholar. This piece was posted January 28, 2005, on the Web site of the *Daily Standard* (www.weeklystandard.com), a British daily online publication affiliated with the *Weekly Standard*, a news commentary magazine.

> This piece is more exploratory than argumentative. What claims does it make about comic superheroes? What questions does it raise about popular culture and cross-cultural exchanges?

1   Devarajan's aspirations are noble, yet it's interesting to wonder if American audiences will recognize this Spider-Man after his translation into the local idiom. Or, conversely, if Devarajan, born in New York to parents from India, will preserve too much of Spider-Man's American heritage and wind-up with a character that won't resonate with Indian audiences.

2   In short, Devarajan's attempt to transform Peter Parker into Pavitr Prabhakar forces him to confront the age-old challenge of separating the universal aspects of human nature from the particular characteristics of a specific culture. The success (or failure) of Devarajan's effort matters, because it may tell us something important about the validity of Americans' faith in the universality of our most cherished ideals.

3   The first issue of *Spider-Man: India* demonstrates that Devarajan was dead serious when he spoke of preserving the Spider-mantra that "with great power comes great responsibility." In 1962, Spider-Man learned this enduring lesson when a security guard asked him to stop an armed robber in the midst of making his get-away. At that time, Peter Parker was an embittered teenager with no sense of obligation to the greater good. He refused to apprehend the robber.

4   Later that same night, Peter returns home to find out that his beloved Uncle Ben has been murdered. Enraged, Peter hunts down the murderer, only to discover that it is the tough he let go. This tragic coincidence provokes his epiphany.

5   In *Spider-Man: India*, young Pavitr Prabhakar learns his lesson in an almost identical manner. While swinging across Mumbai, Pavitr hears the cries of a young woman surrounded by a gang of thugs. He does nothing and swings away. Moments later, Pavitr's beloved Uncle Bhim hears the cries of the same young woman and decides to confront her assailants. They warn Uncle Bhim that they will hurt him if he does not walk away. Bhim stays. He is murdered. Later that night, Pavitr learns of his uncle's death, hunts down the murderers, and experiences an epiphany of his own.

6   Although its innovations seem trivial, *India*'s reworking of the Spider-myth brilliantly enhances the painful irony of the American original. Whereas Ben's murder is a matter of pure coincidence, Bhim dies because he had the courage to confront precisely the same evil that his nephew wouldn't. In both instances, the punishment for selfishness is the death of a loved one. Yet in *India*, that loved one is also a martyr whose death becomes the embodiment of the ethos to which Spider-Man must aspire.

7   The counterpoint to *India*'s subtle reworking of the death of Uncle Ben is its ambitious recasting of Spider-Man's powers as the worldly incarnation of a purposeful, mystical force rather than the accidental outgrowth of a scientific experiment. In a recent interview, Devarajan observed that the diametrically opposed forces of science and magic represent the fundamental contrast between Eastern and Western culture.

8   At a time when IBM is outsourcing thousands of high-tech jobs to Bangalore, it may seem strange to hear an Indian-American insist that magic is the essence of Eastern culture. Nonetheless, Devarajan's decision to build his story on a mythological foundation provides a much better testing ground for the hypothesis that the superhero ethic is part of a "universal psyche" rather than an American one.

9   As a literary device, the replacement of science with magic functions smoothly. In both accounts of Spider-Man's origins, there is a seamless integration of plot and metaphor. Although Peter Parker is now a married man in his thirties, he was a bespectacled teenage bookworm when Spider-Man debuted in the 1960s. A friendless outcast, Parker devoted all of his time to academic pursuits, such as the public science exhibit at which he was bitten by a radioactive spider. Although nominally an accident, the spider bite

is a metaphorical expression of the American faith that knowledge is power and that science is the engine of progress. Initially taunted because of his devotion to science, Parker ultimately becomes all the more powerful because of it.

10   In *Spider-Man: India*, Pavitr Prabhakar is an outcast not because of his academic talent, but because of the traditional clothing that he wears to an expensive private school in cosmopolitan Mumbai. As a scholarship student from a small village in the countryside, it is all Pavitr can afford. One day, while being chased by the bullies who taunt him for wearing harem pants reminiscent of the glory days of MC Hammer, Pavitr stumbles upon an ancient mystic who warns him of an impending battle between ancient forces of good and evil. The old man endows Pavitr with the power of the spider and tells him "This is your destiny, young Pavitr Prabhakar. Rise to the challenge . . . fulfill your karma." In the same manner that Parker embodies the ideals of modern America, Prabhakar embodies those of traditional India.

11   At first, the suggestion that Pavitr has a destiny that he must fulfill may strike some readers as un-American. In the land of opportunity, we reject out of hand the notion that individuals must resign themselves to their fate. Instead, we believe that there are no limits to what can be achieved by a combination of hard work and ingenuity.

12   Yet is the concept of destiny really so foreign? Was it not under the banner of Manifest Destiny that the young United States claimed for itself the Great Plains and the northern reaches of Mexico? Was it not Ronald Reagan who constantly reminded the citizens of the United States that they had a "rendezvous with destiny"? To what else did George W. Bush refer to in his second inaugural address when he stated that "History has an ebb and flow of justice, but history also has a visible direction, set by liberty and the author of liberty"?

13   The most important difference Spider-fans will notice between the Indian and American notions of destiny is the Indian belief that tyranny and evil are primal forces no less powerful than freedom and good. Yet there is also a considerable measure of doubt embedded in the American vision of progress. Although one scientific accident gave Spider-Man his powers, other scientific accidents were responsible for the creation of his arch-nemeses, Dr. Octopus and the Green Goblin. In the final analysis, that which makes Pavitr Prabhakar authentically Indian does not make him in any way un-American.

14   Today the Republic of India is the most populous democracy on the face of the Earth. Someday, it may rival the United States in

terms of wealth and power. Conventional thinking suggests that the emergence of a second superpower would threaten the security of the United States of America. Yet if India's first superhero recognizes that with great power there also comes great responsibility, perhaps we should look forward to the emergence of an Indian superpower.

For Class Discussion

1. What are the main changes that Devarajan has made in translating Spider-Man into an Indian comic book superhero?

2. What does this article suggest are the important connections between nations' popular heroes and their values and identities?

3. What is the rhetorical effect of the title of this article? How does Adesnik use the concept of "Manifest Destiny"?

4. Do you think the *Spider-Man: India* comic exemplifies a positive or a negative cultural exchange? Why? ∎

Image from *Spider-Man: India*
Jeevan J. Kang

This image is part of the Gotham Comics press release of a new series coming out in India, drawn by famous Indian artist Jeevan J. Kang. Gotham Studios Asia is a new company committed to creating comics for a global audience. In this new comic, Pavitr Prabhakar, a poor Indian boy from the country and the counterpart of Peter Parker, discovers his karma and embraces the fight against evil. For more images from the comic, see the Web site www.gothamcomics.com/spiderman_india/.

As an American reader, what is your spontaneous response to the drawing of this character?

For Class Discussion

1. In its press release, Gotham Comics calls *Spider-Man: India* a "transcreation," by which it means an Indian retelling of the American superhero's story. What signs of adaptation and cultural contextualizing do you see in this image?

2. Can you think of any other characters from popular U.S. culture who have crossed cultures in this way?

SPIDER-MAN © 2004 Marvel Characters Inc.

FIGURE 5.3 Image from *Spider-Man: India*
*(Spider-Man:™ and © 2005 Marvel Characters, Inc. Used
with permission. Illustration by Gotham Studios Asia)*

3. Based on what you have read in David Adesnik's article, do you
   think these kinds of cultural transpositions are effective, creative,
   and interesting? Why? Why do you think American audiences
   would or would not enjoy this new comic?

4. How could you make a case that "transcreation" is an example of
   "glocalizing" rather than an example of cultural imperialism? ∎

Special Report on Slow Food
Eric Schlosser

Journalist Eric Schlosser is the author of the nationwide best seller, *Fast Food Nation* (2001), a book that explores the far-reaching effects of the fast-food industry on the world. This piece was published in the April 2004 issue of the *Ecologist*. The *Ecologist*, centered in London and "published in four continents," is "the world's most widely-read environmental magazine." It seeks to influence "environmental and political agendas across the world" (from its "About Us" link, www.theecologist.org/).

How does Schlosser tailor this argument about fast food's global spread to the liberal proenvironment audience of the *Ecologist*?

1   In February a report by George W. Bush's Council of Economic Advisers (CEA) suggested that fast food workers might in the future be classified as manufacturing workers. A CEA report asked: 'When a fast-food restaurant sells a hamburger, for example, is it providing a "service", or is it combining inputs to "manufacture" a product?'

2   Reclassifying fast-food restaurants as 'factories' would have a number of benefits for the Bush administration. It would, in a single stroke, add about 3.5 million manufacturing jobs to the US economy, at a time when such jobs are rapidly being exported overseas. From a statistical point of view, it would make the U.S. seem like an industrial powerhouse once again, instead of an ageing superpower threatened by low-cost competitors. And it would allow the fast-food industry, a strong backer of the Republican Party, to enjoy the tax breaks provided to U.S. manufacturers.

3   The CEA's chairman N. Gregory Mankiw was derided and ridiculed in the press for making the proposal, and his plan is likely to go nowhere. Yet there was an underlying logic to it. Fast food is indeed factory food, perhaps the most heavily processed food on the planet, and the low-paid workers who defrost, reheat and reconstitute it have jobs as boring, highly regimented and strictly supervised as the workers in a 19th century textile mill would have had. Moreover, the founding fathers of the industry probably wouldn't have minded the manufacturing label at all. Bringing the philosophy of the assembly line to the commercial restaurant kitchen was the simple innovation responsible for Ronald McDonald's global conquest.

4   The fast-food industry began in 1948. Richard and Maurice McDonald were growing tired of running their successful drive-in restaurant in San Bernardino, California. They were tired of constantly hiring new car-hops, the teenaged girls who took food to

customers waiting in parked automobiles. They were tired of replacing the dishes and glasses broken by their adolescent customers. But most of all, they were tired of paying the high wages demanded by skilled short-order cooks.

5   So the McDonalds decided to shut down their drive-in and replace it with a revolutionary new form of restaurant. The McDonald brothers started by firing all their car-hops and short-order cooks. They simplified the menu, hired unskilled workers and made each worker perform the same task again and again. One person only made French fries. Another only made shakes. Another only flipped burgers. By getting rid of skilled workers, by serving food and drinks in paper cups and plates, by demanding that customers wait on line for their own meals, the new 'Speedee Service System' allowed the brothers to serve fast, cheap food.

6   The new restaurant was an instant success. It fitted perfectly with the new culture emerging in post-war southern California—a car culture that worshipped speed, convenience and the latest technology. Ray Kroc, the milk shake machine salesman who bought out the McDonald brothers in the early 1960s and later exported their Speedee system around the world, embraced a blind faith in science: a Disneyesque vision of society transformed through chemistry and families living happily in plastic homes and travelling in sleek, nuclear-powered cars.

7   Kroc also believed fervently in the ethic of mass production. A philosophy of uniformity, conformity and total control that had long dictated the manufacture of steel wire was now applied not only to food, but to the people who prepared the food. 'We have found out . . . that we cannot trust some people who are non-conformists,' Kroc declared. 'We will make conformists out of them in a hurry . . . The organisation cannot trust the individual; the individual must trust the organisation.'

8   For the first two decades of its existence, the McDonald's operating system had little impact on the way people lived and ate. In 1968 there were only 1,000 McDonald's restaurants, all of them in the United States. The chain bought fresh ground beef and potatoes from hundreds of local suppliers. But the desire for rapid growth—and the desire for everything to taste exactly the same at thousands of different locations—transformed not only the McDonald's supply system, but also the agricultural economy of the entire United States.

9   McDonald's switched entirely to frozen hamburger patties and frozen fries, relying on a handful of large companies to manufacture them. Other fast food chains spread nationwide at the same time, helping to drive local restaurants, small suppliers, independent ranchers and farmers out of business. And by the 1970s

McDonald's began to expand overseas, taking with it a mentality perfectly expressed years later in one of the company's slogans—'one taste worldwide'.

10   Half a century after Richard and Maurice McDonald decided to fire their carhops, the world's food supply is dominated by an agro-industrial complex in which the fast-food chains occupy the highest rung. Monsanto developed genetically-modified potatoes to supply McDonald's with perfectly uniform French fries—and then halted production of the 'New Leaf' GM potato when McDonald's decided, for publicity reasons, not to buy it. When the fast-food industry wants something, the major food processors rush to supply it.

11   Although many of the foods we eat look the same as the ones we ate a generation ago, they have been fundamentally changed. They have become industrial commodities, with various components (flavour, colour, fats) manufactured and assembled at different facilities. If you bought a hamburger in the United States 30 years ago, it would most probably have contained meat from one steer or cow, which would have been processed at a local butcher shop or small meat-packing plant. Today a typical fast-food hamburger patty contains meat from more than 1,000 different cattle, raised in as many as five different countries. It looks like an old-fashioned hamburger, but is a fundamentally different thing.

12   Here is a partial list of what fast food and the fast-food mentality have recently brought us: the homogenisation of culture, both regionally and worldwide; the malling and sprawling of the landscape; the feeling that everywhere looks and feels the same; a low-wage, alienated service-sector workforce; a low-wage, terribly exploited meat-packing workforce; a widening gap between rich and poor; concentration of economic power; the control of local and national governments by agribusiness; an eagerness to aim sophisticated mass marketing at children; a view of farm animals as industrial commodities; unspeakable cruelty toward those animals; the spread of factory farms; extraordinary air and water pollution; the rise of food-borne illnesses; antibiotic resistance; BSE; soaring obesity rates that have caused soaring rates of asthma, heart disease and early-onset diabetes; reduced life-expectancy; a cloying, fake, manipulative, disposable, plastic worldview, the sole aim of which is to make a buck.

13   None of this was inevitable. The triumph of the fast-food system was aided at almost every step by government subsidies, lack of proper regulation, misleading advertisements, and a widespread ignorance of how fast, cheap food is actually produced. This system is not sustainable. In less than three decades it has already done extraordinary harm. When the fast-food industry is made to bear the

costs it is now imposing on the rest of society, it will collapse. The alternative to fast food now seems obvious: slow food.

14   By 'slow food' I do not mean precious, gourmet food, sold by celebrity chefs and prepared according to recipes in glossy cookbooks. I mean food that is authentic, that has been grown and prepared using methods that are local, organic and sustainable. Most slow foods are peasant foods. Somehow mankind existed for thousands of years without Chicken McNuggets. And I'd argue that our future survival depends on living without them.

For Class Discussion

1. In the first part of his article, Eric Schlosser develops a definitional claim for fast food as a manufacturing industry. How does he support this reclassifying of fast food?
2. Schlosser connects fast food to environmental and health issues. How does he also argue for its cultural influence?
3. How does he define slow food?
4. Which of his criticisms of fast food and McDonald's in particular does Schlosser support?
5. This article is partly an ad for Schlosser's book *Fast Food Nation*. What would be a better title for this article?
6. Which pattern of intercultural relations (pluralism, imperialism, fusion) does he claim American fast food follows? What assumptions do you have to accept to agree with Schlosser?   ∎

China's Big Mac Attack
James L. Watson

James L. Watson is a professor of anthropology and Chinese society at Harvard University. He is also the editor of *Golden Arches East: McDonald's in East Asia* (1997), an anthropologic study of the influence of fast food on five East Asian cities. This article was published in the May–June 2000 issue of *Foreign Affairs*, a leading publication on international policy. *Foreign Affairs* is published by the Council on Foreign Relations, a nonprofit organization of past U.S. presidents and officials as well as scholars and other nongovernmental leaders.

What reasons does Watson offer for McDonald's success as a fast-food restaurant chain in China? Why would these be persuasive to an educated audience?

RONALD McDONALD GOES TO CHINA

1   Looming over Beijing's choking, bumper-to-bumper traffic, every tenth building seems to sport a giant neon sign advertising American wares: Xerox, Mobil, Kinko's, Northwest Airlines, IBM, Jeep, Gerber, even the Jolly Green Giant. American food chains and beverages are everywhere in central Beijing: Coca-Cola, Starbucks, Kentucky Fried Chicken, Häagen-Dazs, Dunkin' Donuts, Baskin-Robbins, Pepsi, TCBY, Pizza Hut, and of course McDonald's. As of June 1999, McDonald's had opened 235 restaurants in China. Hong Kong alone now boasts 158 McDonald's franchises, one for every 42,000 residents (compared to one for every 30,000 Americans).

2   Fast food can even trump hard politics. After NATO accidentally bombed the Chinese embassy in Belgrade during the war in Kosovo, Beijing students tried to organize a boycott of American companies in protest. Coca-Cola and McDonald's were at the top of their hit list, but the message seemed not to have reached Beijing's busy consumers: the three McDonald's I visited last July were packed with Chinese tourists, local yuppies, and grandparents treating their "little emperors and empresses" to Happy Meals. The only departure from the familiar American setting was the menu board (which was in Chinese, with English in smaller print) and the jarring sound of Mandarin shouted over cellular phones. People were downing burgers, fries, and Cokes. It was, as Yogi Berra said, déjà vu all over again; I had seen this scene a hundred times before in a dozen countries. Is globalism—and its cultural variant, McDonaldization—the face of the future?

IMPERIALISM AND A SIDE OF FRIES

3   American academe is teeming with theorists who argue that transnational corporations like McDonald's provide the shock troops for a new form of imperialism that is far more successful, and therefore more insidious, than its militarist antecedents. Young people everywhere, the argument goes, are avid consumers of soap operas, music videos, cartoons, electronic games, martial-arts books, celebrity posters, trendy clothing, and faddish hairstyles. To cater to them, shopping malls, supermarkets, amusement parks, and fast-food restaurants are popping up everywhere. Younger consumers are forging transnational bonds of empathy and shared interests that will, it is claimed, transform political alignments in ways that most world leaders—old men who do not read *Wired*—cannot begin to comprehend, let alone control. Government efforts to stop the march of American (and Japanese) pop culture are futile; censorship and trade barriers succeed only in making forbidden films, music, and Web sites irresistible to local youth.

4   One of the clearest expressions of the "cultural imperialism" hypothesis appeared in a 1996 *New York Times* op-ed by Ronald Steel: "It was never the Soviet Union, but the United States itself that is the true revolutionary power. . . . We purvey a culture based on mass entertainment and mass gratification. . . . The cultural message we transmit through Hollywood and McDonald's goes out across the world to capture, and also to undermine, other societies. . . . Unlike traditional conquerors, we are not content merely to subdue others: We insist that they be like us." In his recent book, *The Lexus and the Olive Tree*, Thomas Friedman presents a more benign view of the global influence of McDonald's. Friedman has long argued in his *New York Times* column that McDonald's and other manifestations of global culture serve the interests of middle classes that are emerging in autocratic, undemocratic societies. Furthermore, he notes, countries that have a McDonald's within their borders have never gone to war against each other. (The NATO war against Serbia would seem to shatter Friedman's Big Mac Law, but he does not give up easily. In his July 2, 1999, column, he argued that the shutdown and rapid reopening of Belgrade's six McDonald's actually prove his point.)

5   If Steel and his ideological allies are correct, McDonald's should be the poster child of cultural imperialism. McDonald's today has more than 25,000 outlets in 119 countries. Most of the corporation's revenues now come from operations outside the United States, and a new restaurant opens somewhere in the world every 17 hours.

6   McDonald's makes heroic efforts to ensure that its food looks, feels, and tastes the same everywhere. A Big Mac in Beijing tastes virtually identical to a Big Mac in Boston. Menus vary only when the local market is deemed mature enough to expand beyond burgers and fries. Consumers can enjoy Spicy Wings (red-pepper-laced chicken) in Beijing, kosher Big Macs (minus the cheese) in Jerusalem, vegetable McNuggets in New Delhi, or a McHuevo (a burger with fried egg) in Montevideo. Nonetheless, wherever McDonald's takes root, the core product—at least during the initial phase of operation—is not really the food but the experience of eating in a cheerful, air-conditioned, child-friendly restaurant that offers the revolutionary innovation of clean toilets.

7   Critics claim that the rapid spread of McDonald's and its fast-food rivals undermines indigenous cuisines and helps create a homogeneous, global culture. Beijing and Hong Kong thus make excellent test cases since they are the dual epicenters of China's haute cuisine (with apologies to Hunan, Sichuan, and Shanghai loyalists). If McDonald's can make inroads in these two markets, it

must surely be an unstoppable force that levels cultures. But the truth of this parable of globalization is subtler than that.

THE SECRET OF MY SUCCESS

8   How did McDonald's do it? How did a hamburger chain become so prominent in a cultural zone dominated by rice, noodles, fish, and pork? In China, adult consumers often report that they find the taste of fried beef patties strange and unappealing. Why, then, do they come back to McDonald's? And more to the point, why do they encourage their children to eat there?

9   The history of McDonald's in Hong Kong offers good clues about the mystery of the company's worldwide appeal. When Daniel Ng, an American-trained engineer, opened Hong Kong's first McDonald's in 1975, his local food-industry competitors dismissed the venture as a nonstarter: "Selling hamburgers to Cantonese? You must be joking!" Ng credits his boldness to the fact that he did not have an M.B.A. and had never taken a course in business theory.

10   During the early years of his franchise, Ng promoted McDonald's as an outpost of American culture, offering authentic hamburgers to "with-it" young people eager to forget that they lived in a tiny colony on the rim of Maoist China. Those who experienced what passed for hamburgers in British Hong Kong during the 1960s and 1970s will appreciate the innovation. Ng made the fateful decision not to compete with Chinese-style fast-food chains that had started a few years earlier (the largest of which, Café de Coral, was established in 1969). The signs outside his first restaurants were in English; the Chinese characters for McDonald's (Cantonese *Mak-dong-lou*, Mandarin *Mai-dang-lao*) did not appear until the business was safely established. Over a period of 20 years, McDonald's gradually became a mainstay of Hong Kong's middle-class culture. Today the restaurants are packed wall-to-wall with busy commuters, students, and retirees who treat them as homes away from home. A 1997 survey I conducted among Hong Kong university students revealed that few were even aware of the company's American origins. For Hong Kong youth, McDonald's is a familiar institution that offers comfort foods that they have eaten since early childhood.

11   Yunxiang Yan, a UCLA anthropologist, hints that a similar localization process may be underway in Beijing. McDonald's there is still a pricey venue that most Chinese treat as a tourist stop: you haven't really "done" Beijing unless you have visited the Forbidden City, walked around Tiananmen Square, and eaten at the "Golden Arches." Many visitors from the countryside take Big Mac boxes, Coke cups, and napkins home with them as proof that they did

it right. Yan also discovered that working-class Beijing residents save up to take their kids to McDonald's and hover over them as they munch. (Later the adults eat in a cheaper, Chinese-style restaurant.) Parents told Yan that they wanted their children to "connect" with the world outside China. To them, McDonald's was an important stop on the way to Harvard Business School or the MIT labs. Yan has since discovered that local yuppies are beginning to eat Big Macs regularly. In 20 years, he predicts, young people in Beijing (like their counterparts in Hong Kong today) will not even care about the foreign origin of McDonald's, which will be serving ordinary food to people more interested in getting a quick meal than in having a cultural experience. The key to this process of localization is China's changing family system and the emergence of a "singleton" (only-child) subculture.

THE LITTLE EMPERORS

12   In China, as in other parts of East Asia, the startup date for McDonald's corresponds to the emergence of a new class of consumers with money to spend on family entertainment. Rising incomes are dramatically changing lifestyles, especially among younger couples in China's major cities. Decisions about jobs and purchases no longer require consultations with an extended network of parents, grandparents, adult siblings, and other kin. More married women in Hong Kong, Beijing, and Shanghai work outside the home, which in turn affects child-rearing practices, residence patterns, and gender relations. At least in the larger cities, men no longer rule the roost. One of China's most popular television shows features a search for the "ideal husband," a man who does the shopping, washes the dishes, and changes the baby's diapers—behavior inconceivable in Mao's heyday.

13   Most Chinese newlyweds are choosing to create their own homes, thereby separating themselves from parents and in-laws. The traditional system of living with the groom's parents is dying out fast, even in the Chinese countryside. Recent research in Shanghai and Dalian (and Taipei) shows that professional couples prefer to live near the wife's mother, often in the same apartment complex. The crucial consideration is household labor—child care, cooking, shopping, washing, and cleaning. With both husband and wife working full time, someone has to do it, and the wife's mother is considered more reliable (and less trouble) than the husband's mother, who would expect her daughter-in-law to be subservient.

14   In response to these social and economic changes, a new Chinese family system is emerging that focuses on the needs and aspirations of the married couple—the conjugal unit. Conjugality

brings with it a package of attitudes and practices that undermine traditional Chinese views regarding filial piety and Confucianism. Should younger couples strive, irrespective of personal cost, to promote the welfare of the larger kin group and support their aging parents? Or should they concentrate on building a comfortable life for themselves and their offspring? Increasingly, the balance is shifting toward conjugality and away from the Confucian norms that guided earlier generations.

15   The shift also coincides with a dramatic decline in China's birth rate and a rise in the amount of money and attention lavished on children. The Communist Party's single-child family policy has helped produce a generation of "little emperors and empresses," each commanding the undivided affection and economic support of two parents and (if lucky) four grandparents. The Chinese press is awash with articles bemoaning the rise of singletons who are selfish, maladjusted, and spoiled beyond repair—although psychologists working on China's singletons find them little different from their American or European counterparts.

16   McDonald's opened in Beijing in 1992, a time when changes in family values were matched by a sustained economic boom. The startup date also coincided with a public "fever" for all things American—sports, clothing, films, food, and so on. American-style birthday parties became key to the company's expansion strategy. Prior to the arrival of McDonald's, festivities marking youngsters' specific birth dates were unknown in most of East Asia. In Hong Kong, for instance, lunar-calendar dates of birth were recorded for use in later life—to help match prospective marriage partners' horoscopes or choose an auspicious burial date. Until the late 1970s and early 1980s, most people paid little attention to their calendar birth date if they remembered it at all. McDonald's and its rivals now promote the birthday party—complete with cake, candles, and silly hats—in television advertising aimed directly at kids.

17   McDonald's also introduced other localized innovations that appeal to younger customers. In Beijing, Ronald McDonald (a.k.a. Uncle McDonald) is paired with an Aunt McDonald whose job is to entertain children and help flustered parents. All over East Asia, McDonald's offers a party package that includes food, cake, gifts, toys, and the exclusive use of a children's enclosure sometimes known as the Ronald Room. Birthday parties are all the rage for upwardly mobile youngsters in Hong Kong, Beijing, and Shanghai. Given that most people in these cities live in tiny, overcrowded flats, the local Kentucky Fried Chicken or McDonald's is a convenient and welcoming place for family celebrations.

18   For the first time in Chinese history, children matter not simply as future providers but as full-scale consumers who command respect in today's economy. Until the 1980s, kids rarely ate outside the home. When they did, they were expected to eat what was put in front of them. The idea that children might actually order their own food would have shocked most adults; only foreign youngsters were permitted to make their opinions known in public, which scandalized everyone within earshot. Today children have money in their pockets, most of which they spend on snacks. New industries and a specialized service sector have emerged to feed this category of consumers, as the anthropologist Jun Jing has noted in his new book, *Feeding China's Little Emperors*. In effect, the fast-food industry helped start a consumer revolution by encouraging children as young as three or four to march up to the counter, slap down their money, and choose their own food.

19   In Hong Kong, McDonald's has become so popular that parents use visits to their neighborhood outlet as a reward for good behavior or academic achievement. An old friend told me that withholding McDonald's visits was the only threat that registered with his wayward son. "It is my nuclear deterrent," he said.

20   McDonald's could not have succeeded in East Asia without appealing to new generations of consumers—children from 3 to 13 and their harried, stressed-out parents. No amount of stealth advertising or brilliant promotions could have done the trick alone. The fast-food industry did not create a market where none existed; it responded to an opportunity presented by the collapse of an outdated Confucian family system. In effect, McDonald's tailgated the family revolution as it swept through East Asia, first in Japan and Hong Kong (1970s), then in Taiwan and South Korea (1980s), and finally in China (1990s). There is no great mystery here, unless one is predisposed to seeing imperialist plots behind every successful business.

GRIMACE

21   In 1994 students protesting against California's Proposition 187, which restricted state services to immigrants, ransacked a McDonald's in Mexico City, scrawling "Yankee go home" on the windows. In August 1999 French farmers dumped tons of manure and rotting apricots in front of their local McDonald's to protest U.S. sanctions on European food imports. During the past five years, McDonald's restaurants have been the targets of violent protests—including bombings—in over 50 countries, in cities including Rome, Macao, Rio de Janeiro, Prague, London, and Jakarta.

22   Why McDonald's? Other transnationals—notably Coca-Cola, Disney, and Pepsi—also draw the ire of anti-American demonstrators, but no other company can compete with the "Golden Arches." McDonald's is often the preferred site for anti-American demonstrations even in places where the local embassies are easy to get at. McDonald's is more than a purveyor of food; it is a saturated symbol for everything that environmentalists, protectionists, and anticapitalist activists find objectionable about American culture. McDonald's even stands out in the physical landscape, marked by its distinctive double-arched logo and characteristic design. Like the Stars and Stripes, the Big Mac stands for America.

23   Despite the symbolic load it carries, McDonald's can hardly be held responsible for the wholesale subversion of local cuisines, as its many critics claim. In China's larger cities, traditional specialties are supported by middle-class connoisseurs who treat eating out as a hobby and a diversion. Beijing's food scene today is a gourmet's paradise compared to the grim days of Maoist egalitarianism, when China's public canteens gave real meaning to the term "industrialized food." Party leaders may have enjoyed haute cuisine on the sly, but for most people, eating extravagantly was a counterrevolutionary crime. During the 1960s, refugee chefs kept microregional specialties alive in the back streets of Hong Kong and Taipei, where Panyu-style seafood, Shandong noodles, and Shunde vegetarian delights could be had at less than a dollar a head. Today, many Cantonese and Taiwanese lament the old refugees' retirement and complain that no one has carried on their culinary traditions; the chefs' own children, of course, have become brokers, lawyers, and professors.

24   Meanwhile, there has been an explosion of exotic new cuisines in China's cities: Thai, Malaysian, Indonesian, French, Spanish, Nepali, Mexican, and Hong Kong's latest hit, Louisiana creole. Chinese-style restaurants must now compete with these "ethnic" newcomers in a vast smorgasbord. The arrival of fast food is only one dimension of a much larger Chinese trend toward the culinary adventurism associated with rising affluence.

25   McDonald's has not been entirely passive, as demonstrated by its successful promotion of American-style birthday parties. Some try to tag McDonald's as a polluter and exploiter, but most Chinese consumers see the company as a force for the improvement of urban life. Clean toilets were a welcome development in cities where, until recently, a visit to a public restroom could be harrowing. The chain's preoccupation with cleanliness has raised consumer expectations and forced competitors to provide equally clean facilities. Ray Kroc, the legendary founder of McDonald's, was once asked if he had actually scrubbed out toilets during the

early years of his franchise: "You're damn right I did," he shot back, "and I'd clean one today if it needed it." In a 1993 interview, Daniel Ng described his early efforts to import the Kroc ethos to his Hong Kong franchise. After an ineffectual first try, one new employee was ordered to clean the restrooms again. The startled worker replied that the toilets were already cleaner than the collective facilities he used at home. Ng told him that standards at McDonald's were higher and ordered him to do it again.

26   Another innovation is the line, a social institution that is seldom appreciated until it collapses. When McDonald's opened in Hong Kong, customers clumped around the cash registers, pushing their money over the heads of the people ahead of them—standard procedure in local train stations, banks, and cinemas. McDonald's management appointed an employee (usually a young woman) to act as queue monitor, and within a few months, regular consumers began to enforce the system themselves by glaring at newcomers who had the effrontery to jump ahead. Today the line is an accepted feature of Hong Kong's middle-class culture, and it is making headway in Beijing and Shanghai. Whether or not McDonald's deserves the credit for this particular innovation, many East Asian consumers associate the "Golden Arches" with public civility.

HAVE IT YOUR WAY

27   At first glance, McDonald's appears to be the quintessential transnational, with its own corporate culture nurtured at Hamburger University in Oak Brook, Illinois. But James Cantalupo, the president of McDonald's Corporation, maintains that his strategy is to become as much a part of local culture as possible and protests when people call McDonald's a multinational or a transnational. "I like to call us multilocal," he told *The Christian Science Monitor* in 1991. McDonald's goes out of its way to find local suppliers whenever it enters a new market. In China, for instance, the company nurtures its own network of russet-potato growers to provide french fries of the requisite length. McDonald's has also learned to rely on self-starters like Daniel Ng to run its foreign franchises—with minimal interference from Oak Brook. Another winning strategy, evident everywhere in East Asia, is promoting promising young "crew" (behind-the-counter) workers into management's ranks. Surprisingly few managers are dispatched from the Illinois headquarters. Yan found only one American, a Chinese-speaker, on McDonald's Beijing management team.

28   Critics of the fast-food industry assume that corporations always call the shots and that consumers have little choice but to

accept what is presented to them. In fact, the process of localization is a two-way street, involving changes in the local culture as well as modifications of the company's standard mode of operation.

29   The hallmark of the American fast-food business is the displacement of labor costs from the corporation to consumers. For the system to work, consumers must be educated—or "disciplined"—so that they voluntarily fulfill their side of an implicit bargain: we (the corporation) will provide cheap, fast service if you (the customer) carry your own tray, seat yourself, eat quickly, help clean up afterward, and depart promptly to make room for others. Try breaking this contract in Boston or Pittsburgh by spreading out your newspaper and starting to work on a crossword puzzle in McDonald's. You will soon be ousted—politely in Pittsburgh, less so in Boston.

30   Key elements of McDonald's pan-national system—notably lining up and self-seating—have been readily accepted by consumers throughout East Asia. Other aspects of the Oak Brook model have been rejected, especially those relating to time and space. In Hong Kong, Taipei, and Beijing, consumers have turned their neighborhood restaurants into leisure centers for seniors and after-school clubs for students. Here, "fast" refers to the delivery of food, not its consumption.

31   Between 3:00 and 5:30 p.m. on Hong Kong weekdays, McDonald's restaurants are invaded by armies of young people in school uniforms. They buy a few fries, pour them out on a tray for communal snacking, and sit for at least an hour—gossiping, studying, and flirting. During the midmorning hours, the restaurants are packed with white-haired retirees who stay even longer, drinking tea or coffee (free refills for senior citizens) and lingering over pancake breakfasts. Many sit alone, reading newspapers provided by the management. Both retirees and students are attracted by the roomy tables, good light, and air-conditioning—a combination not easily found in Hong Kong, Beijing, or Shanghai. In effect, local citizens have appropriated private property and converted it into public space.

32   The process of localization correlates closely to the maturation of a generation of local people who grew up eating fast food. By the time the children of these pioneer consumers entered the scene, McDonald's was an unremarkable feature of the local landscape. Parents see the restaurants as havens for their school-age children: smoking is banned and (in China and Hong Kong) no alcohol is served, effectively eliminating drugs and gangs. McDonald's has become so local that Hong Kong's youth cannot imagine life without it.

33   Everyone has heard the story: Japanese little leaguers tour California and spot a McDonald's, whereupon they marvel that America also has Japanese food. Such anecdotes are not apocryphal. The children of visiting colleagues from Taiwan and South Korea were overjoyed when they saw a McDonald's near their temporary homes in the Boston suburbs: "Look! They have our kind of food here," one eight-year-old Korean exclaimed. The stories also work within East Asia: last year, Joe Bosco, an anthropologist at the Chinese University of Hong Kong, took several of his students to Taipei for a study tour. After a week of eating Taiwanese restaurant food, Bosco's charges began to complain that they missed home-style cooking. "Okay," Bosco said, "where do you want to eat tonight?" The students all said, "McDonald's!"

NEXT TO GODLINESS

34   In China's increasingly affluent cities, parents now worry more about what their children eat outside the home. Rumors frequently sweep through Beijing and Shanghai with the same story line: migrants from the countryside set up a roadside stall selling *youtiar*, deep-fried dough sticks eaten with rice gruel for breakfast. To expand the batter, they add industrial detergent to the mix, creating a powerful poison that kills everyone who eats it. Families of the deceased rush back to the scene to discover that the stall has disappeared; the local police are more interested in silencing the survivors than pursuing the culprits. Such stories are, of course, unverifiable, but they carry a "truth" that resists official denials, much like urban legends in the United States. Last summer's food scare in Belgium over dioxin-laced eggs and the recent British mad-cow fiasco were well covered in the Chinese media, feeding the anxieties of urbanities with no reliable system of consumer protection.

35   McDonald's appeals to China's new elites because its food is safe, clean, and reliable. Western intellectuals may scoff at McDonald's for its unrelenting monotony, but in many parts of the world (including China) this is precisely what consumers find so attractive. Why else would competitors go to such extremes to imitate McDonald's? In Beijing one can find fast-food restaurants with names such as McDucks, Mcdonald's, and Mordornal. In Shanghai a local chain called Nancy's Express used a sign with one leg of the double arches missing, forming an "N." Another popular chain of noodle shops, called Honggaoliang (Red sorghum), advertises itself with a large "H" that bears an uncanny resemblance to the "Golden Arches." All over China, competitors dress their staff in McDonald's-style uniforms and decorate their restaurants in yellow. Corporate mascots inspired by Ronald McDonald—clowns, ducks, cowboys,

cats, hamburger figures, mythic heroes, and chickens—parade along the sidewalks of Chinese cities. Local fast-food chains frequently engage in public exhibitions of cleanliness: one worker mops the floors and polishes the windows, all day long, every day. The cleaners usually restrict their efforts to the entryway, where the performance can best be seen by passersby.

SO LONELY

36   During McDonald's first three years in China, Communist Party officials could barely restrain their enthusiasm over this new model of modernization, hygiene, and responsible management. By 1996, however, media enthusiasm cooled as state authorities began to promote an indigenous fast-food industry based on noodles, barbecued meats, soups, and rice pots. Now that McDonald's, Kentucky Fried Chicken, and Pizza Hut had shown the way, party officials reasoned, local chains should take over the mass market. (No such chain has seriously challenged McDonald's, but a Shanghai-based restaurateur has fought a much-reported "battle of the chickens" with KFC.)

37   Meanwhile, China faces yet another family revolution, this one caused by the graying of the population. In 1998, 10 percent of China's people were over 60; by 2020, the figure is expected to rise to approximately 16 percent. In 2025, there will be 274 million people over 60 in China—more than the entire 1998 U.S. population. Since Beijing has made few provisions for a modern social-security system, the implications are profound. The locus of consumer power will soon shift generations as the parents of today's little emperors retire. Unlike the current generation of retirees—the survivors of Maoism—China's boomers will not be content with 1950s-level pensions, and they cannot expect their children to support them. Like their counterparts in the American Association of Retired Persons, future retirees in China are likely to be a vociferous, aggressive lot who will demand more state resources.

38   So what will happen to child-centered industries? If its experience in Hong Kong is any guide, McDonald's will survive quite handily as a welcoming retreat from the isolation and loneliness of urban life. The full ramifications of China's single-child policy will not be felt for another 20 years. Having one grandchild for every four grandparents is a recipe for social anomie on a truly massive scale. The consequences of China's demographic time bomb can already be seen on the streets of Hong Kong, where the family began to shrink decades ago. Tens of thousands of retirees roam Hong Kong's air-conditioned shopping malls, congregate in the handful of overcrowded parks, and turn their local McDonald's during the midmorning hours into a substitute for the public gardens, opera

theaters, and ancestral halls that sheltered their parents. What stands out at McDonald's is the isolation among Hong Kong elders as they try to entertain themselves. Americans may be bowling alone and worrying about the decline of family life, but in early 21st-century Hong Kong, no one even seems concerned about the emergence of a civil society that ignores the elderly.

WHOSE CULTURE IS IT, ANYWAY?

39 Is McDonald's leading a crusade to create a homogenous, global culture that suits the needs of an advanced capitalist world order? Not really. Today's economic and social realities demand an entirely new approach to global issues that takes consumers' perspectives into account. The explanatory device of "cultural imperialism" is little more than a warmed-over version of the neo-Marxist dependency theories that were popular in the 1960s and 1970s—approaches that do not begin to capture the complexity of today's emerging transnational systems.

40   The deeper one digs into the personal lives of consumers anywhere, the more complex matters become. People are not the automatons many theorists make them out to be. Hong Kong's discerning consumers have most assuredly not been stripped of their cultural heritage, nor have they become the uncomprehending dupes of transnational corporations.

41   In places like Hong Kong, it is increasingly difficult to see where the transnational ends and the local begins. Fast food is an excellent case in point: for the children who flock to weekend birthday parties, McDonald's is self-evidently local. Similarly, the Hong Kong elders who use McDonald's as a retreat from the loneliness of urban life could care less about the company's foreign origin. Hong Kong's consumers have made the "Golden Arches" their own.

42   One might also turn the lens around and take a close look at American society as it enters a new millennium. Chinese food is everywhere, giving McDonald's and KFC a run for their money in such unlikely settings as Moline and Memphis. Mandarin is fast becoming a dominant language in American research laboratories, and Chinese films draw ever more enthusiastic audiences. Last Halloween, every other kid in my Cambridge neighborhood appeared in (Japanese-inspired) Power Ranger costumes, striking poses that owe more to Bruce Lee than to Batman. Whose culture is it, anyway? If you have to ask, you have already missed the boat.

For Class Discussion

1. What does Watson mean by "a localization process" and how does he show that China's embrace of McDonald's exemplifies this process?

2. What changes in China's cultural patterns help to explain the acceptance of McDonald's?

3. What positive societal changes does Watson credit McDonald's with introducing?

4. What alternative views of McDonald's and globalization does Watson address? How does he refute charges of cultural imperialism?

5. Watson devotes the last part of his argument to a full statement of his overriding claim. How does this rhetorical move affect the argument's impact on readers?

6. How has this article influenced your view of positive and negative intercultural interactions?   ∎

Photos of Cultural Contact in China: Fast Food and Advertising

These photographs of American-brand advertisements were taken by William Lalicker, a scholar of rhetoric and Chinese culture, in China in the summer of 2004. The first photo shows a billboard of a Kentucky Fried Chicken sandwich with popular bicycle carts and bicycles passing. The second is of a café in the city of Zhouzhuang, Jiangsu Province, in the south-central section of the east coast of China. One of several centuries-old "water cities," like a Chinese Venice, Zhouzhuang is a major tourist attraction, offering canal boat rides, open markets, and beautiful traditional canal-side cafés.

What features of these photos support or contradict the points that James Watson makes about China's embrace of McDonald's and Western culture?

For Class Discussion

1. What details are striking or surprising about these photos? Consider these points:
   - The "XXL" in the billboard sandwich photo (Why would "extra extra large" be a concept the Chinese would include?)
   - The Budweiser umbrella next to a centuries-old canal (Why would an American brand name appear in this historical setting?)

2. If you were an American tourist in China encountering these scenes, what would your response be?

3. Which of the models of intercultural interaction—cultural imperialism, cultural pluralism, cultural protectionism, cultural fusion, or some other—do you think these photos illustrate and why?   ∎

FIGURE 5.4 Photo of KFC Sandwich in China

FIGURE 5.5 Photo of China Canal Café

CHAPTER QUESTIONS FOR REFLECTION AND DISCUSSION

1. Several of the readings in this chapter focus on problems with the way that media are shaping people's perceptions of other cultures. What problems do George Packer and Benjamin Compaine identify? How do these writers interpret, support, or attack the idea of the global village?

2. The main perspectives on global cultural exchanges discussed in the readings in this chapter can be summarized by these labels: cultural loss, cultural survival of the fittest, cultural superiority, cultural imperialism, cultural homogenization, cultural assimilation, cultural fusion, preservation of cultural rights, cultural diversity, and cultural pluralism. In your own words, how would you describe each of these views of intercultural exchange? From the readings and your own experience, find examples to illustrate these views. For instance, what is an example of cultural fusion?

3. A number of articles in this chapter argue that cultural homogenization and Western domination are endangering other cultures around the world. Drawing on the articles by Benjamin Barber, Jane Poynter, Eric Schlosser, and John Harris, what do you see as the strongest reasons and examples to support this claim?

4. Using the articles by Philippe Legrain and Henry Jenkins, how would you build a case to support the claim that globalization is nurturing cultural diversity and reciprocal cultural exchanges?

5. Many of the arguments in these readings turn on the quality and quantity of their examples. From a logical, philosophical, and ethical perspective, why is this "arguing by example" problematic? Can you illustrate your response with particular readings?

6. Which reading or readings in this chapter do you think make the most effective and persuasive use of appeals to readers' values, imaginations, and emotions? Which examples, narratives, and quotations appeal most powerfully to the writer's target audience? Which authors are the most knowledgeable, credible, reliable, and reasonable?

7. Choose one of the following pairs of authors and map out their points of agreement and disagreement. Consider their target audiences, their assumptions and values, their main claims and reasons, and the points that each overlooks or ignores.

   - Eric Schlosser and James Watson
   - Benjamin Barber and James Watson, Philippe Legrain, or Henry Jenkins
   - Henry Jenkins and John Harris
   - Rajal Pitroda and David Adesnik
   - George Packer and Benjamin Compaine

- Philippe Legrain and Jane Poynter
- The *Economist* and Benjamin Compaine

8. How are these concepts similar: "glocalization" explained in the introduction to this chapter; Watson's "localization process"; and Jenkins's "cultural fusion"?

9. Both the film industry and the comic book industry are thriving in the United States, yet other countries are developing strong industries or have the potential to develop strong industries. Research Bollywood or the film industry in Europe or Africa, or anime or the comic book industry in the Philippines, Egypt, or India. If you look at Bollywood, you might also consider the recent crossover film by British writer/director Gurinder Chadha *Bride and Prejudice* (2004) and this director's other popular film, *Bend It Like Beckham* (2002). If you look at comic book industries, you might explore the local comic book industries in the Philippines (Mango Comics, Summit Publishing, and Culture Crash), anime in Japan, AK Comics from Cairo, or the new *Spider-Man: India* and other Indian comics.

WRITING ASSIGNMENTS

Brief Writing Assignments

1. Thinking about your own identity, personal style, and cultural choices, briefly explain what part of foreign or international culture is most important to you. You could focus on food, music, clothing, sports, film, animation, language, television programming, religion, art, philosophy, or literature.

2. Write a brief essay that informally describes or explains how your own region of the country reflects a mix of cultures and racial backgrounds. Consider the settlement history, place-names, ethnic communities and districts of cities, and distinctive local food. You might mention historical influences or current contemporary cultural influences, for example, the increase in the number of ethnic restaurants in your region. (You might also develop this assignment into a community project and create a tourist brochure for students new to your region.)

3. Write freely and informally for twenty minutes in response to this question: From this chapter, which article on the impact of globalization on culture surprised, intrigued, disturbed, or persuaded you the most and why?

4. Choose one of the following claims and write for twenty minutes in support of it. Use evidence from the readings and from your own experience to develop your claim persuasively.

   A. Americans can't get away from home because home—the American way of life—is everywhere.

B. Countries and regions should have complete control of what culture they export and import.

C. The marketing, buying, and selling of culture is inevitable and mostly benefits everyone.

D. Media have increased global understanding and cooperation.

E. Cultural exchanges can fuel peaceful relations among countries.

5. Write out a short list of questions concerning cultural globalization and cultural rights that most interest or disturb you or that you would most like to investigate.

Writing Projects

1. Synthesizing the arguments in this chapter with your own experiences and ideas, construct the best case you can to argue that globalization threatens the cultural rights and identities of less-powerful countries or, conversely, that globalization enriches and enlarges all countries' cultural repertoires. Write for your university community.

2. Joenia Wapixana, staff attorney for the Roraima Indigenous Council in Brazil, is the first Indian from the Amazon to become a lawyer in Brazil. She ascribes some of her success as a lawyer and an advocate for her people to her strong sense of cultural identity: "Why have we as a people been able to continue to exist? Because we know where we come from. By having roots, you can see the direction in which you want to go."* As the readings in this chapter show, "roots" are closely connected to culture. Although many people place cultural issues in the category of entertainment, the readings in this chapter explore how culture is a very weighty matter, especially in this age of global cultural bombardment. Write an argument addressed to a neutral, indifferent, or uninformed audience of your peers. Your purpose is to persuade your audience to see the importance of cultural identity—and similarly, cultural rights and cultural pluralism—in this period of increased global contact. Use specific examples and evidence from personal experience where it is relevant.

3. Writing for an uninformed audience, build a strong case that one of the cultural forms below—or one you know from your own experience—has had a profound, transformative influence on American life:

A. Anime (from Japan)

B. Music from Africa, Latin America, or the Caribbean

C. Food from Asia

---

*Larry Rohter, "Using Courts in Brazil to Strengthen an Indian Identity," *New York Times*, November 13, 2004.

D. Film from India or Europe

E. Television programs from Britain

F. Dance from Africa

G. Soccer from Europe or South America

You might write an argument as a feature story for your university or local newspaper.

4. Investigate the contemporary music scene of some country such as Brazil, Mexico, South Africa, or Japan—perhaps focusing on a particular style of music (such as hip-hop, punk rock, folk). You might think of Jamaican reggae artists Bob Marley and his son Ziggy; Nigeria's Femi Kuti; Brazil's samba and hip-hopper Max de Castro and Marisa Monte of samba and art-pop fame; diva Brenda Fassie from South Africa; Shakira from Colombia; Thalia from Mexico; and Charlotte Church from Wales. Argue that that country's music has had an important effect on world music. Or you could argue that this music/music style/recording artist should receive world attention. You will need to provide criteria to evaluate the importance of this music or artist.

5. Tourism can be a force for good, inspiring cultures to spend money to preserve their own cultural heritages and enabling people from other countries to experience these cultures. On the other hand, tourism can also speed up the destruction of cultural heritages by fueling rampant development and foreign investment and control. Choose a remote country with an especially old culture (such as Ladakh, Bhutan, Indonesia, or Ecuador) and research the tourism in that country and the impact it is having on the culture. Depending on the information that your research yields, argue that tourism needs to be curtailed, better controlled, or encouraged. Write your argument for a tourist magazine that caters to well-educated, wealthy Americans.

6. Do some research on the status of languages in the world today. Construct an argument in which you support a proposal (a) to raise money to help preserve a particular language or (b) to require students in your major at your university to study a language of a country that is currently a cultural hot spot, such as a Middle Eastern language, Chinese, Korean, or an African language.

7. Research the status of information and communication technology in a developing country in Africa, South America, or Asia, and write a brief policy proposal arguing what a local business, university club, or nongovernmental organization could do to provide more cell phones and/or computers and Internet access to this country.

8. Explore the connection between free trade and the preservation of cultural rights and argue whether you think the global free trade system is nurturing or threatening cultural diversity. You will need to choose a

specific region of the world and a specific cultural practice (for example, diet and eating habits, the music industry, reality TV programming, sports, the film industry). Some of the ideas in Chapter 2 on free trade and consumerism and in Chapter 4 on immigration might relate to your focus. You also may want to investigate these organizations:

The International Network on Cultural Diversity (INCD)
Communication Rights in the Information Society (CRIS)
Media Trade Monitor
UNESCO and the Universal Declaration on Cultural Diversity
American Library Association (which is interested in public access to cultural diversity)

You could direct this argument to UNESCO or to an audience of your peers.

9. Investigate the global importance and presence of some sport (for example, basketball, soccer, or NASCAR). Research the controversies surrounding this sport and write to persuade your American peers to share your views. For example, you might argue that American sports fans should care about soccer as an international sport.

Human Rights

Trafficking of Women and Children and Forced Child Labor

QUESTION TO PONDER

Estimates are that "more than 27 million people are enslaved" around the world and that more than fifteen thousand people are forcibly brought to the United States yearly.* These people are trafficked—moved across national borders against their will, intimidated by the loss of their visas and passports and by threats to their families, and coerced through violence to work for minimal or no pay. Often they are mistaken for illegal immigrants. Recently in Illinois, Governor Rod Blagojevich signed a bill to support "outreach and training to local social service organizations, law enforcement and health care professionals" to help in identifying trafficking victims and to aid these people in "rebuilding their lives."† You are wondering whether your state has made trafficking a state crime and what can U.S. citizens do to stop human trafficking?

CONTEXT FOR A NETWORK OF ISSUES

Many people think all slavery ended several centuries ago. Britain's Abolition Act of 1833 launched the abolition of slavery throughout its empire; the United States banned the importation of slaves in 1808 and abolished slavery with the Thirteenth Amendment in 1865; and Brazil ended slavery

---

*Free the Slaves & Human Rights Center, University of California–Berkeley, "Hidden Slaves: Forced Labor in the United States," September 2004, http://www .freetheslaves.net/.

†"Illinois Adopts Plans for Human Trafficking," *Crime Control Digest* 39, no. 29 (July 22, 2005): 6.

in 1888. Yet a new form of slavery—human trafficking—is illicitly thriving around the globe despite progress with human rights.

Since World War II, the United Nations and advocacy groups have brought human rights to the attention of the world. The Universal Declaration of Rights, adopted by the General Assembly of the United Nations on December 10, 1948, declares that "recognition of the inherent dignity and of the equal and inalienable rights of all members of the human family is the foundation of freedom, justice, and peace in the world" (www.un.org/ Overview/rights.html). Humanitarian advocacy groups such as Amnesty International, founded in 1961 to defend prisoners of conscience, have turned a spotlight on human rights violations. Today, human rights encompasses basic rights: the political freedoms of speech, assembly, and suffrage, and the right to religion, work, welfare, and health. However, the trafficking of women and children and forced labor represent serious violations of these rights.

The illegal business of trafficking of human beings, involving the buying and selling of people who are forced to work for the profit of others, is a problem affecting most countries, including European Union nations, Canada, and the United States. Girls and boys as well as men and women are "trafficked": that is, transported within countries or across national borders, traded for money, and kept subjugated by violence and brutality. The United Nations defines trafficking as

> the recruitment, transportation, transfer, harbouring or receipt of persons, by means of the threat or use of force or other forms of coercion, of abduction, of fraud, of deception, of the abuse of power or of a position of vulnerability or of the giving or receiving of payments or benefits to achieve the consent of a person having control over another person, for the purpose of exploitation. Exploitation shall include, at a minimum, the exploitation or the prostitution of others or other forms of sexual exploitation, forced labour or services, slavery or practices similar to slavery, servitude or the removal of organs.*

Although the exact number of persons trafficked is difficult to pin down because this trade is criminal, Human Rights Watch, a leading human rights organization, estimates that between 700,000 and four million persons are trafficked annually (www.hrw.org). The International Labor Organization reports that about "8.4 million children are caught in 'unconditional' worst forms of child labour, including slavery, trafficking, debt bondage, and other forms of coerced labour, forced recruitment for armed conflict, prostitution, pornography, and other illicit activities."† These large numbers of

---

*Protocol to Prevent, Suppress, and Punish Trafficking in Persons, Especially Women and Children, Supplementing the United Nations Convention Against Transnational Organized Crime (2000).

†"Child Labor Remains 'Massive Problem,'" *World of Work*, no. 43 (June 2002): 4–5.

adults and children become caught in trafficking through abduction; through their vulnerability in orphanages, refugee camps, street life, poverty, and unemployment; or through the abuse of their earnest desires for a better life.

Shocking statistics only begin to convey the depth of human suffering that trafficking inflicts. For example, one of the main trafficking patterns involves the removal of women and girls from the former Soviet Union republics for sale and exploitation in Europe, the Middle East, and Japan. Lured and deceived by false job offers, women are sold for $2,500, raped and beaten into submission, and forced to service ten to thirty men a night, making between $75,000 and $250,000 a year for their "owners."* Terrorized into submission, these women are exposed to psychological abuse, rape, torture, and sexually transmitted diseases, including HIV/AIDS. When they are not working, they are often kept locked up, sometimes in filthy conditions. Similar exploitation is present in the burgeoning sex tourism industry in Southeast Asia, where girls as young as twelve are trafficked from Burma to Thailand, from Nepal to India, and from Vietnam to Cambodia.

Children, officially anyone under age eighteen, are also being sold and held in hopeless, dehumanizing labor. Activists distinguish between child labor, which is customary in some developing countries to supplement family income, and bondage. While the former can involve dangerous conditions, long hours, and low pay, the latter involves the abduction of children from their homes and entrapment in harmful, degrading work in other parts of their countries or outside their countries. Anti-Slavery International notes that only a small percentage of child labor is involved in manufacturing items for export. However, hundreds of thousands of children in Sri Lanka, Cambodia, India, Pakistan, Nepal, and African nations are trapped in bleak, arduous, isolated work as domestic laborers, and are often exploited sexually as well.

While this human suffering should arouse our compassion, these violations of human rights should also concern us because human trafficking feeds crime domestically and contributes to the political and social destabilization of many regions of the world. The global trafficking of women and girls in the sex trade has fueled the AIDS pandemic, which in turn advances social disintegration, political instability, and potential terrorism. Currently, sex trafficking, the spread of AIDS, and subsequent social unraveling are threatening India, Nepal, and China.[†] Human trafficking also fuels organized crime and the growth of corruption; the huge potential profits attract

---

*Victor Malarek, *The Natashas: Inside the New Global Sex Trade* (New York: Arcade Publishing, 2003): 4–5.

[†]Chapter 9, "The Spread of Disease in the Global Community," examines the social and economic damage caused by AIDS and the connections among trafficking, prostitution, and AIDS.

organized crime, and wealthy traffickers can easily bribe local government officials and police. After trade in drugs and weapons, the traffic of women and children is the most lucrative criminal business. Often the drug trade and the sex trade nurture each other by using the same routes and contacts. In addition, forced child labor jeopardizes the future of societies and perpetuates countries' cycles of poverty as worn-down children are denied education and opportunities to acquire skills that could help them improve their economic status.

The United Nations, the United States and many other countries, and numerous nongovernmental organizations (NGOs) are trying to address these human rights problems. The United Nations has formally proscribed trafficking and forced labor in Article 4 of its Universal Declaration of Rights: "No one shall be held in slavery or servitude; slavery and the slave trade shall be prohibited in all their forms" (www.un.org/Overview/rights.html). Similarly, Article 32 of the UN Convention on the Rights of the Child adopted by the United Nations General Assembly on Nov. 20, 1989, declares, "State Parties recognize the right of the child to be protected from economic exploitation and from performing any work that is likely to be hazardous or to interfere with the child's education or to be harmful to the child's health or physical, mental, spiritual, moral, or social development." In 2000, the U.S. Congress passed the Trafficking Victims Protection Act that established the Tier System for measuring countries' efforts to combat human trafficking. Tier 1 includes the most cooperative countries and Tier 3 includes the least diligent in fighting trafficking. This approach is intended to work by using shame and economic pressure to compel countries to confront their human trafficking problems. The United States has banned sex tourism involving children in the PROTECT Act of 2003 and has called on other nations to criminalize such behavior. Numerous organizations are working with governments on preventative strategies, detection and prosecution of traffickers, and rehabilitation of victims. For example, the Angel Coalition of the Moscow Trafficking Assistance Center has begun educational programs in orphanages and schools warning of trafficking, and has established a free telephone helpline for Russian-speaking women and girls trafficked to Europe. As this chapter shows, the immensity and complexity of the human trafficking problems necessitate local and regional efforts as well as international cooperation.

STAKES AND STAKEHOLDERS

Many stakeholders such as national governments, international advocacy groups, and civil society organizations around the world are struggling to grasp the causes and extent of human trafficking and are investigating solutions to this global problem. In addressing this problem, they are focusing on a number of subcontroversies.

How Has Globalization Affected the Trafficking of Women and Children? Free trade proponents believe that many of the current violations of human rights, especially in developing countries, are part of the temporary conditions of economic development. They argue that global trade and growing prosperity will bring new freedoms and improve the societal and economic conditions that make people vulnerable to human trafficking. These advocates object to using economic sanctions to penalize countries for their human rights violations and trafficking problems. Some free trade supporters and governments and businesses in developing countries themselves argue that making money from their women and children, although harsh and unpleasant, is a practical way of dealing with economic needs, of paying their countries' debts, and of entering the global market.

In opposition, social activists and critics of economic globalization hold multinational corporations and free trade accountable for forcing rapid economic change, for undermining the social order and traditional societies in these countries, and for creating ready global markets for trafficked people. Kevin Bales, author of *Disposable People: New Slavery in the Global Economy* (1999) and activist in Anti-Slavery International, asserts that the emphasis on profits and speedy modernization has nurtured these countries' tolerance of human trafficking and that the lure of big money has fostered corruption in developing countries. Many critics also fault multinationals for indifference to human rights violations in developing countries.

Some analysts and critics stress the role of global communication and connections in facilitating the smuggling of slaves across national borders and the falsifying of passports, airline tickets, visas, and work contracts. Investigative journalist Victor Malarek, in his book *The Natashas: Inside the New Global Sex Trade* (2003), argues that the Internet is fueling the sex trade. Malarek calls the Internet "the biggest whorehouse on the planet,"* and claims that "in no time porn kings, pimps and traffickers were online promoting their products and services. Indeed, many observers believe that the Net is singularly responsible for the incredible explosion in the trafficking of women and girls worldwide."†

Who Should Be Protecting Human Rights? Despite various treaties and agreements, the global community is in conflict about who should enforce them. NGOs, activists, and some policymakers are calling for more UN and U.S. involvement in establishing laws to catch and punish traffickers and those who benefit from trafficked persons. Some advocacy groups and NGOs want the U.S. Department of State to emphasize human rights in applying its Tier System more rigorously. These activists and analysts criticize multinational corporations, trade agreements, institutions such as the World Trade

---

*Malarek, p. 80.
†Malarek, p. 81.

Organization, and governments for valuing property over human lives, and they challenge them to make human trafficking unprofitable and, therefore, unattractive. These activists contend that protecting human rights is a good business practice that creates political and economic stability beneficial for investment.

How Big Is the Human Trafficking Problem and What Are the Motives of Activists? Some critics and public health officials argue that NGOs are exaggerating the problem in order to gain more governmental aid. The human trafficking issue has brought together conservative Protestants, Catholics, Jews, Buddhists, and feminists in the cause of international human rights; yet some politicians and critics suggest that these social activists are using the sex trade issue to fuel their campaign against prostitution. Some researchers, politicians, and analysts also contest the idea that certain groups of child laborers and sex workers are being trafficked, disagreeing over who are victims and who are willing workers using prostitution and servitude knowingly as solutions to their economic problems.

How Can We End Trafficking and Help Current and Potential Victims? Controversies swirl around whether we need more legislation or better enforcement of the legislation we have. Many stakeholders are asking, How can countries be held to their commitment to treaties such as the Convention on the Rights of the Child and their own laws? Some NGOs, politicians, and activists point out that the people who have the highest stakes in human trafficking, the victims themselves, are first silenced by coercion and then by the legal processes that criminalize them or penalize them as illegal migrants. These activists are campaigning for new laws and procedures for victims to have access to greater protection and aid. Trafficking Programme Officer of Anti-Slavery International Elaine Pearson recommends "increased employment and migration opportunities; protection and support for those trafficked, including temporary or permanent residence in countries of destination; and opportunities for legal redress and compensation."*

NGOs, researchers, and policymakers disagree about what strategies and solutions to pursue. Some target root causes, prevention, and the connection between trafficking and poverty, noting that the dominant global patterns of trafficking are from east to west and south to north, from poorer countries to richer ones. Kevin Bales asserts that the trafficking victims and the poor need to own their own lives; he recommends that we "give them access to credit, let them choose their work, get rid of corruption, offer rehabilitation programs, and provide education."† Some activists focus on the global market, for example, challenging sex work as an industry, promoting the curbing of sex tourism, or asking consumers to buy or not buy

---

*"Trapped in Traffic," *New Internationalist*, no. 337 (August 2001): 26.
†*Disposable People* (Berkeley: University of California Press, 1999): 257.

items produced by child workers. Other analysts, activists, and policymakers call for public support of local in-the-field groups who are in tune with specific regional conditions. Still others demand a rethinking of human trafficking in terms of migration patterns or global health problems.

The three sections that follow—"Student Voice," "International Voices," and "Global Hot Spot"—take you deeper into local and global, personal and social connections to the trafficking of women and children.

 ## STUDENT VOICE: EXPERIENCING HUMAN RIGHTS PROBLEMS

In the following reflection, student writer Spencer Jones recounts his experience trying to come to grips with the suffering of girls around the world who are being forced into child labor and prostitution.

Spencer Jones

When I went home for vacation after my first quarter of college, I looked at my family through different eyes, as if I had gotten new glasses. What had changed my vision most was my seminar on world poverty and human rights. Who had changed most were my sisters, ages twelve and fourteen. They looked taller and older to me. Amused, annoyed, surprised, I wondered, Who are they? Little girls or young women? Who are they becoming?

During my vacation at home, there they were: flopped on the rug in the family room, watching *American Idol*; racing out the door for school in jeans, pastel sweatshirts, and layers of lip gloss; laughing with their friends at the movie complex; lean and strong, running laps for soccer; lugging home backpacks heavy with textbooks and homework; typing essays on the computer; and dancing in *The Nutcracker Suite*, slender figures in satin and glitter.

But in my mind, other pictures from my world poverty class haunted me, photos from human rights advocacy groups: of the bony, hollow-eyed little girls, domestic slaves in West Africa, working with baskets of laundry bigger than they were; the skinny-legged, twelve-year-old girl in the Congo who had been raped by a UN soldier; the scarred and deformed feet of the eleven-year-old girl who had worked in vats of boiling water preparing silk thread in India; the fourteen-year-old prostitute in a brothel in Thailand who had been beaten and forced to have unprotected sex; and the cigarette-burned fifteen-year-old, abducted off the street in the Czech Republic and sold into the sex trade in Israel.

These girls, too, are someone's sisters.

INTERNATIONAL VOICES

Among the many ongoing global conversations about forced child labor are the research contributions of scholars who are trying to determine how widespread and how detrimental forced child labor is. The passage that follows is a case study from a research project funded by the United Nations Children's Fund (UNICEF) in September 2000. Omolar Dakore Oyaide, from the department of gender studies at the University of Zambia, investigated child workers in Zambia, Africa. This passage comes from her published study "Child Domestic Labour in Lusaka: A Gender Perspective."

Testimony of a Child Domestic Worker in Zambia

This case study describes a thirteen-year-old orphaned girl worker, who didn't have money to go to school. At the time of this interview, she had been paid two months' wages for four months of work. She described her daily duties in these terms:

"I wake up at 0500 hours [5 A.M.]. I sweep the house and prepare breakfast for all the members of the house. I wash the dishes. I bathe the children and get them ready for school. I take them to school. I sweep the surrounding of the house. Then I wash the blankets of the young ones because they wet their bed and [wash] the clothes of everybody. I prepare lunch after this and serve lunch to everybody. I wash dishes and clean the dishes and then I iron clothes for the children and their parents. Then I start preparing dinner and after everyone has eaten, I wash up and tidy the kitchen. I prepare packed lunch for school for the children for the following day. I lock the door after everybody has gone to bed before I can sleep. I go to bed at 23 hours [11 P.M.] and sleep on the floor of the living room. My employer likes to shout at and insult [me] and is very rude. My employer's younger brother takes advantage of me sexually. If I refuse, he threatens me that he will tell them that I went out of the yard instead of working."

While child domestic workers are silenced by their youth; by social, economic, and often racial discrimination; and by their isolation, the girls and women entangled in sex trafficking experience these repressions as well as the power of the criminal forces that ensnared them and that continue to subjugate them. Consequently, only a few of these victims have shared their horrendous personal experiences. The following testimony is from the U.S. House of Representatives, Committee on International Relations Hearing on the Implementation of the Trafficking Victims Protection Act, November 8, 2001. It appeared on the Protection Project Organization's Web site on its "Survivor Story" link (www.protectionproject.org). This testimony reveals that the United States is also involved in sex trafficking.

Testimony of a Trafficked Woman in the Sex Trade

My name is "Maria." I am in disguise today because I am in fear that my captors would recognize me and place my life and that of my family in danger.

My story begins in May of 1997 in Veracruz, Mexico when I was approached by an acquaintance about some jobs in the United States. She told me that there were jobs available in restaurants and that I would earn enough money to support my daughter and my parents in Mexico. I accepted the offer and a "coyote" brought me to Texas.

I was transported to Florida and there, one of the bosses told me I would be working in a brothel as a prostitute. I told him he was mistaken and that I was going to be working in a restaurant, not a brothel. He said I owed him a smuggling debt and the sooner I paid it off the sooner I could leave. I was eighteen years old and had never been far from home and had no money or way to return.

I was constantly guarded and abused. If any of the girls refused to be with a customer, we were beaten. If we adamantly refused, the bosses would show us a lesson by raping us brutally. We worked six days a week, twelve hours a day.

. . . I never knew where I was. We were transported every fifteen days to different cities. I knew if I tried to escape I would not get far because everything was unfamiliar. The bosses said that if we escaped they would get their money from our families. . . .

GLOBAL HOT SPOT: THE BALKANS AND EASTERN EUROPE

The sex trafficking of women is a global problem; recently, however, prime trafficking sites with the greatest number of women involved have been the states that were formerly part of the Soviet Union: Ukraine, Belarus, Moldova, Armenia, Georgia, Azerbaijan, Kyrgyzstan, and Kazakhstan. Girls and women trafficked from these impoverished countries end up most frequently in Europe and the Balkans and sometimes in the Middle East, Japan, the United States, and Canada. The following report was written by Mara Radovanovic, head of Lara, a women's organization devoted to helping women who have been trafficked from the former Soviet Union republics to Bosnia and Herzegovina. This report appeared on the Web site of Kvinna till Kvinna, a women's support foundation (www.iktk.se/english/news/2002/021018_lara.htm) in October 2002.

. . . . We contacted our local police station and the police at the border to inform them about the importance of paying attention to girls or boys that could be victims of trafficking. It worked out well. The police started to contact us so that we could take care of those affected and give them a secure place to stay while trying to help them. Our goal is to help them return to their countries, but they also need access to food, clothes, medical and psychological assistance. It is also very important that they have interpreters present so the victims can give a testimony of their experiences. So far we have helped 60 persons, and we have listened to their stories, one worse than the other.

Many people mix up trafficking with prostitution. Consequently, they claim those affected should not be treated as victims, since they have made a choice. Even the police and the authorities sometimes regard those affected by trafficking as prostitutes who have come to Bosnia and Herzegovina to make money. But we know how trafficking works, how the dealers do it.

They reach out to poor girls from the east, for example Ukraine, Moldavia or Romania and they promise them a good job in Bosnia and Herzegovina. Already when they cross the border, they are sold for the first time to professional traffickers, and after that they are sold again at every border, each time at a higher price. . . . They are then transported to trafficking centers, for example in Belgrade and Serbia, where trafficked women from many countries are gathered. There the women are deprived of their identity. Their passports are taken from them, and they are given false names, birth dates and sometimes even a new country of origin. We helped two twin sisters who looked exactly the same, but one of them had a Ukrainian passport while the other had a Romanian one. . . .

We have done research to get all the details and now we struggle to spread information and raise awareness of the situation with as many people as possible. In Bijeljina we have succeeded to build opinion against the slave trade and both politicians and the public support us. As a result, all the bars involved in such activities have had to close down. But a lot of work remains to be done and we continue the struggle, both locally and internationally. We co-operate with several women's organizations in the Balkans and the rest of Europe, since the traffickers work in a similar way everywhere.

Mara Radovanovic's account gives insight into the governmental, legal, and social channels that need to be enlisted to combat human trafficking. However, testimonies of sex trafficked girls and women, like those posted on the Protection Project Organization Web site (www.protectionproject. org), reveal the huge obstacles to solving this problem. The arguments in this chapter, which present policy statements, scholarly research, and calls to action, will introduce you to the political, economic, social, and ethical dimensions of human trafficking and will help you formulate your own views.

READINGS

Human Trafficking
David A. Feingold

David A. Feingold is an anthropologist, author, filmmaker, and director of the Ophidian Research Institute, a nongovernmental organization focused on human trafficking. He has worked for UNESCO Bangkok as international coordinator for HIV/AIDS and Trafficking Projects. His documentary film *Trading Women* (2003) exposes the complexities of trafficking in Southeast Asia. In his film and writing, Feingold calls for more research and more accurate statistics. He says that trafficking involves two main elements, "migration and coercion," and that "trafficking is like a disease" that is constantly mutating and needs responses that are continuously being adjusted and refined in order to get at the underlying factors and to find an effective solution.* He favors work with local NGOs to improve the status and job opportunities of potential victims. This article appeared in the September–October 2005 edition of *Foreign Policy,* a politically nonbiased magazine about international politics and economics that is "dedicated to reaching a broad, nonspecialized audience who recognizes that what happens 'there' matters 'here,' and vice versa" (www.foreignpolicy.com).

How does Feingold show his double purpose of clarifying and complicating his audience's understanding of human trafficking?

1   Judging by news headlines, human trafficking is a recent phenomenon. In fact, the coerced movement of people across borders is as old as the laws of supply and demand. What is new is the volume of the traffic—and the realization that we have done little to stem the tide. We must look beyond our raw emotions if we are ever to stop those who trade in human lives.

"MOST VICTIMS ARE TRAFFICKED INTO THE SEX INDUSTRY"

2   No. Trafficking of women and children (and, more rarely, young men) for prostitution is a vile and heinous violation of human rights, but labor trafficking is probably more widespread. Evidence can be found in field studies of trafficking victims across the world and in the simple fact that the worldwide market for labor is far greater than that for sex. Statistics on the "end use" of trafficked people are often unreliable because they tend to overrepresent the sex trade. For example, men are excluded from the trafficking statistics gathered in Thailand because, according to its national law, men cannot qualify as trafficking victims. However, a detailed 2005 study by the International Labour Organization (ILO) found that, of the estimated 9.5 million victims of forced labor in Asia, less than 10 percent are trafficked for commercial sexual exploitation. Worldwide, less than half of all trafficking victims are part of the sex trade, according to the same report.

3   Labor trafficking, however, is hardly benign. A study of Burmese domestic workers in Thailand by Mahidol University's Institute for Population and Social Research found beatings, sexual assault,

---

*Vicki Silverman, "*Trading Women* Shatters Myths about Human Trafficking," USINFO.STATE.GOV, September 11, 2003, http://usinfo.state.gov/gi/Archive/2003/Sep/11-2240.html (accessed December 30, 2005).

forced labor without pay, sleep deprivation, and rape to be common. Another study, by the German Agency for Technical Cooperation (GTZ), looked at East African girls trafficked to the Middle East and found that most were bound for oppressive domestic work, and often raped and beaten along the way. Boys from Cambodia and Burma are also frequently trafficked onto deep-sea commercial fishing boats, some of which stay at sea for up to two years. Preliminary research suggests 10 percent of these young crews never return, and boys that become ill are frequently thrown overboard.

4   The focus on the sex industry may galvanize action through moral outrage, but it can also cloud reason. A recent example is the unsubstantiated press reports that tsunami orphans in Indonesia's Aceh province were being abducted by organized gangs of traffickers. How such gangs could operate in an area bereft of roads and airstrips remains unclear, but that did not stop some U.S. organizations from appealing for funds to send "trained investigators" to track down the criminals. Although the devastation wrought by the tsunami certainly rendered people vulnerable—mostly through economic disruption—investigations by the United Nations have yet to identify a single confirmed case of sex trafficking.

"TIGHTENING BORDERS WILL STOP TRAFFICKING"

5   Wrong. The trafficking issue is often used—some would say hijacked—to support policies limiting immigration. In fact, the recent global tightening of asylum admissions has increased trafficking by forcing many desperate people to turn to smugglers. In southeast Europe, a GTZ study found that more stringent border controls have led to an increase in trafficking, as people turned to third parties to smuggle them out of the country.

6   Similarly, other legal efforts to protect women from trafficking have had the perverse effect of making them more vulnerable. For example, Burmese law precludes women under the age of 26 from visiting border areas unless accompanied by a husband or parent. Although Burmese officials say the law demonstrates the government's concern with the issue, many women believe it only increases the cost of travel (particularly from bribe-seeking police) and decreases their safety by making them dependent on "facilitators" to move them across the border. These women incur greater debt for their passage, thus making them even more vulnerable to exploitation along the way.

"TRAFFICKING IS A BIG BUSINESS CONTROLLED BY ORGANIZED CRIME"

7   False. Trafficking is big business, but in many regions of the world, such as Southeast Asia, trafficking involves mostly "disorganized

crime": individuals or small groups linked on an ad hoc basis. There is no standard profile of traffickers. They range from truck drivers and village "aunties" to labor brokers and police officers. Traffickers are as varied as the circumstances of their victims. Although some trafficking victims are literally kidnapped, most leave their homes voluntarily and become trafficked on their journey.

8   Trafficking "kingpins," along the lines of the late cocaine boss Pablo Escobar, are rare. Japanese mafia, or yakuza, do control many of the venues in Japan where trafficked girls end up, but they are more likely to purchase people than transport them. Doing research in Thailand in 1997, I located the Luk Moo ("Piglet") network, which was responsible for about 50 percent of the women and girls smuggled into Thailand from Burma, China, and Laos to work in brothels. There were also other networks, such as the Kabuankam Loy Fah ("Floating in the Sky") network that specialized in girls for restaurants and karaoke bars. However, these networks have since faded in importance, owing to changes in the structure of the sex industry.

9   The worldwide trade in persons has been estimated by the United Nations Office on Drugs and Crime at $7 billion annually, and by the United Nations Children's Fund at $10 billion—but, of course, no one really knows. The ILO estimates the total illicit profits produced by trafficked forced laborers in one year to be just short of $32 billion. Although that is hardly an insignificant amount, it is a small business compared to the more than $320 billion international trade in illicit drugs.

"LEGALIZING PROSTITUTION WILL INCREASE TRAFFICKING"

10   It depends on how it's done. The intersection of the highly emotive issues of sex work and human trafficking generates a lot more heat than light. Some antitrafficking activists equate "prostitution" with trafficking and vice versa, despite evidence to the contrary. The U.S. government leaves no doubt as to where it stands: According to the State Department Web site, "Where prostitution is legalized or tolerated, there is a greater demand for human trafficking victims and nearly always an increase in the number of women and children trafficked into commercial sex slavery." By this logic, the state of Nevada should be awash in foreign sex slaves, leading one to wonder what steps the Justice Department is taking to free them. Oddly, the Netherlands, Australia, and Germany—all of whom have legalized prostitution—received top marks from the Bush administration in the most recent Trafficking in Persons Report.

11   Moreover, some efforts to prohibit prostitution have increased sex workers' risk to the dangers of trafficking, though largely

because lawmakers neglected to consult the people the laws were designed to protect. Sweden, for example, is much praised by antiprostitution activists for a 1998 law that aimed to protect sex workers by criminalizing their customers. But several independent studies, including one conducted by the Swedish police, showed that it exposed prostitutes to more dangerous clients and less safe-sex practices.

12   Others argue that giving sex workers a measure of legitimacy short of legalization would actually discourage trafficking. In Thailand, many opposed to the commercial sex industry support extending labor and social security laws to sex workers. Such a move could hamper trafficking by opening establishments to inspection, allowing labor organization, and exposing underage prostitution.

"PROSECUTION WILL STOP TRAFFICKERS"

13 Not likely. In the United States, an odd but effective coalition of liberal Democrats, conservative Republicans, committed feminists, and evangelical Christians pushed a law through congress in 2000 that aimed to prosecute traffickers and protect victims at home, while pressuring other countries to take action abroad. The Victims of Trafficking and Violence Protection Act recognized trafficking as a federal crime for the first time and provided a definition of victims in need of protection and services.

14   Despite the political energies expended on human trafficking, there is little evidence that prosecutions have any significant impact on aggregate levels of trafficking. For example, U.S. government figures indicate the presence of some 200,000 trafficked victims in the United States. But even with a well-trained law enforcement and prosecutorial system, less than 500 people have been awarded T visas, the special visas given to victims in return for cooperation with federal prosecutors. In fact, between 2001 and 2003, only 110 traffickers were prosecuted by the Justice Department. Of these, 77 were convicted or pled guilty.

15   Given the nature of the trafficking business, so few convictions will have little effect. Convicting a local recruiter or transporter has no significant impact on the overall scale of trafficking. If the incentives are right, he or she is instantly replaced, and the flow of people is hardly interrupted.

"SANCTIONS WILL STOP TRAFFICKING"

16 Wrong. The same U.S. law that made trafficking a federal crime also gave the United States the right to punish other states that do not crack down on human trafficking. The State Department is required to send a report to congress each year ranking countries

according to their success in combating trafficking and threatening sanctions for those with the worst records.

17   But international humanitarian agencies see the threat of U.S. sanctions against foreign governments as largely counterproductive. Practically speaking, sanctions will likely be applied only against countries already subject to sanctions, such as Burma or North Korea. Threatening moderately unresponsive countries— such as China, Nigeria, or Saudi Arabia—would likely backfire, causing these countries to become less open to dialogue and limiting the flow of information necessary for effective cooperation.

18   Although some countries certainly lack candor and create false fronts of activity, others actively seek Uncle Sam's seal of approval (and the resources that often follow) with genuine efforts to combat trafficking. Bangladesh, for example, received higher marks from the State Department this year by taking significant steps against trafficking, despite the country's poverty and limited resources. Incentives, instead of sanctions, might encourage others to do the same.

"TRAFFICKING VICTIMS SHOULD BE SENT HOME"

19   Not always. Sending victims home may simply place them back in the same conditions that endangered them in the first place, particularly in situations of armed conflict or political unrest. If criminal gangs were involved in the trafficking, they will likely threaten the safety of victims and their families.

20   To complicate matters, people may have no "home" to which they can return. Lack of legal status is a major risk factor in trafficking, impeding and often precluding victims' return and reintegration. That problem is particularly true for minorities, indigenous peoples, and informal migrants who often have no way to prove their nationality. In Thailand, for example, studies by the United Nations Educational, Scientific and Cultural Organization have demonstrated that a lack of proof of citizenship is the single greatest risk factor for a hill tribe girl or woman to be trafficked or otherwise exploited. Without citizenship, she cannot get a school diploma, register her marriage, own land, or work outside her home district without special permission. Lack of legal status prevents a woman from finding alternate means of income, rendering her vulnerable to trafficking for sex work or the most abusive forms of labor.

21   In developing countries, one's lack of legal status usually begins at birth. Without a birth certificate, a child typically has no legal identity: That is why international laws such as the Convention on the Rights of the Child stress that children have the right to be registered at birth. Many activists have never considered that a fix

as simple as promoting birth registration in developing countries is one of the most cost-effective means to combat human trafficking.

"TRAFFICKING IS DRIVEN BY POVERTY"

22 Too simple. Trafficking is often migration gone terribly wrong. In addition to the push of poverty or political and social instability, trafficking is influenced by the expanded world views of the victims—the draw of bright lights and big cities. The lure of urban centers helps to account for why, in parts of Africa, girls from medium-sized towns are more vulnerable to trafficking than those in rural villages.

23   To fill the demand for ever cheaper labor, many victims are trafficked within the same economic class or even within a single country. In Brazil, for example, girls may be trafficked for sex work from rural to urban areas, whereas males may be sold to work in the gold mines of the Amazon jungle. In the Ivory Coast, children are frequently sold into slavery to work on cocoa plantations. In China, girls are trafficked as brides in impoverished rural areas, which are devoid of marriage-age females as a result of China's one-child policy and families' preference for baby boys.

24   Does this mean that "destination" countries or cities are the beneficiaries of trafficking? Not necessarily. What one area or industry may gain in cheap, docile labor, others—especially those situated near national borders—often pay for in terms of security, health costs, and, sometimes, political unrest. Trafficking may answer a demand, but the cost is too steep for this ever shrinking world to bear.

For Class Discussion

1. What common views of human trafficking is Feingold criticizing?
2. What is his main claim about human trafficking?
3. What evidence strikes you as the most effective and persuasive?
4. How well does Feingold convince you of his knowledge and authority and of the reliability of his evidence?
5. This piece has been structured to fit *Foreign Policy*'s "Forum," a regular feature that presents a loose, informal debate. If Feingold were to rewrite this piece as another kind of argument genre (for example, an op-ed piece, policy brief, or open letter to a public official), what claims, reasons, and evidence would you suggest he include? Think of the audience he would be trying to reach and the length and depth of the article.
6. How has Feingold influenced your view of human trafficking? What questions do you have after reading this article? ∎

Fair Trade Chocolate and Cocoa: The Sweet Solution to Abusive Child Labor and Poverty
Global Exchange

On its Web site, Global Exchange, founded in 1988, describes itself as "an international human rights organization dedicated to promoting political, social, and environmental justice globally" (www.globalexchange.org). Based in San Francisco, California, this organization works to involve Americans in global issues, to foster international connections, and to promote fair trade. This policy statement about its chocolate campaign was accessed on its Web site October 24, 2004.

> This argument plays on the irony of a delicious, pleasurable product—chocolate—and the misery involved in its production. How have the writers used this irony to make this piece persuasive to a general audience?

1   While chocolate is sweet for us, it is heartbreaking for cocoa producers and their families. In 2001, the US State Department and the ILO reported child slavery on Ivory Coast cocoa farms, the origin of 43 percent of the world's cocoa. Subsequent research by the International Institute of Tropical Agriculture indicated that though child slavery is thankfully very limited, other egregious forms of child labor are unfortunately widespread. Hundreds of thousands of children work in dangerous tasks on cocoa farms. At least 12,000 child cocoa workers have come to their present situation through trafficking. Most child cocoa workers in the Ivory Coast do not have the opportunity to attend school. The same investigation identified poverty as the cause—West African cocoa revenues average $30–$108 per year per household member. These impoverished producers have no choice but to keep their kids out of school to work in dangerous tasks on cocoa farms, or even use child slaves.

2   Producer poverty comes at the hands of large chocolate corporations, such as M&M/Mars and other members of the Chocolate Manufacturers Association of America, that manipulate the market to keep profits high while producer incomes stay low. The industry has developed a Protocol to end abusive child labor, but it doesn't guarantee the minimum price producers need to meet their costs and thus cease needing child labor. Without a stable and sufficient income, producers will remain trapped in poverty and forced to rely on child labor against their heartfelt wishes to do otherwise. The Protocol also unjustly lays the blame on producers and

their strapped governments instead of admitting the role and responsibility of the industry in exacerbating poverty and child labor problems.

3   The solution is FAIR TRADE (denoted by the "Fair Trade Certified" or Fair Trade Federation labels), which ensures that producers earn enough to send their kids to school and pay their workers. Since 2002, Global Exchange has been demanding that the US chocolate industry solve this crisis by selling Fair Trade chocolate. M&M/Mars and its industry partners have refused the demands of over 200 organizations, thousands of K–12 students, and thousands of concerned adults who have contacted them to demand Fair Trade.

4   We need to come together in even larger numbers [to] make it clear that we will accept nothing less than Fair Trade from M&M/Mars and the US chocolate industry. We also need to work to make existing Fair Trade chocolate and cocoa products available in our communities through school/youth-club fundraisers, stores, campuses, community groups, faith-based groups, and more. Join us today to make chocolate as sweet for cocoa producers as it is for you. You can get involved wherever you are.

For Class Discussion

1. This proposal argument uses causal reasoning to assess the problem and propose a solution. What economic forces have led to the exploitation of child laborers? What actions and policies would lead to improved conditions for these children?

2. Focusing on the phrases "egregious forms of child labor" and "dangerous tasks on cocoa farms," how do you think Global Exchange could make this call for action even more vivid and compelling?

3. How has this piece affected your view of the connections between the food products you enjoy and human rights?   ■

Chinese Children and Harry Potter
Mike Lester

Mike Lester is a conservative editorial cartoonist for the *Rome News—Tribune* in Georgia. This cartoon from June 19, 2003, is archived with his others on www.caglecartoons.com.

What background information do readers need to have in order to understand this political cartoon?

FIGURE 6.1   Chinese Children and Harry Potter *(© Mike Lester, 2003)*

For Class Discussion

1. What story does this political cartoon tell? Who are the characters?
2. This cartoon is built on a number of ironies. What are they?
3. How does this cartoon link economic issues in developing countries, human rights, free trade, and child labor?　■

Put Your Money Where Their Mouths Are

Nicholas D. Kristof

Nicholas D. Kristof holds degrees from Harvard College and Oxford University and is the winner of a Pulitzer Prize in international reporting (along with his wife, Sheryl Wudunn). With her, he has written *China Wakes* (1995) and *Thunder from the East* (2001) about China's economic and political transformation. He has worked as the *New York Times* bureau chief in Hong Kong, Beijing, and Tokyo, and in the last five years, he has written numerous provocative editorials on sweatshop labor and prostitution in the developing world. This op-ed piece appeared in the April 3, 2004, issue of the *New York Times*.

> What general audience and what specific audience does Kristof address in this op-ed piece? What relationship does he establish with his dual audiences?

1 With Democrats on the warpath over trade, there's pressure for tougher international labor standards that would try to put Abakr Adoud out of work.

2 Abakr lives with his family in the desert near this oasis in eastern Chad. He has never been to school and roams the desert all day with his brothers, searching for sticks that can be made into doors for mud huts. He is 10 years old.

3 It's appalling that Abakr, like tens of millions of other children abroad, is working instead of attending school. But prohibiting child labor wouldn't do him any good, for there's no school in the area for him to attend. If child labor hawks manage to keep Abakr from working, without giving him a school to attend, he and his family will simply be poorer than ever.

4 And that's the problem when Americans get on their high horses about child labor, without understanding the cruel third world economics that cause it. The push by Democrats like John Kerry for international labor standards is well intentioned, but it is also oblivious to third world realities.

5 Look, I feel like Scrooge when I speak out against bans on sweatshops or on child labor. In the West, it's hard to find anyone outside a university economics department who agrees with me. But the basic Western attitude particularly among Democrats and warm-and-fuzzy humanitarians sometimes ends up making things worse. Consider the results of two major American efforts to ban imports produced by child labor.

6 In 1993, when Congress proposed the U.S. Child Labor Deterrence Act, which would have blocked imports made by children (if it had passed), garment factories in Bangladesh fired 50,000 children. Many ended up in worse jobs, like prostitution.

7 Then there was the hue and cry beginning in 1996 against soccer balls stitched by children in their homes (mostly after school) in Sialkot, Pakistan. As a result, the balls are now stitched by adults, often in factories under international monitoring.

8 But many women are worse off. Conservative Pakistanis believe that women shouldn't work outside the home, so stitching soccer balls is now off limits for many of them. Moreover, bad publicity about Pakistan led China to grab market share with machine-stitched balls; over the next two years, Pakistan's share of the U.S. soccer ball market dropped to 45 percent from 65 percent.

9 So poor Pakistani families who depended on earnings from women or children who stitched soccer balls are now further impoverished.

10 I'm not arguing that child labor is a good thing. It isn't. But as Jagdish Bhagwati, the eminent trade economist, notes in his new book, *In Defense of Globalization*, thundering against child labor doesn't address the poverty that causes it.

11   In the village of Toukoultoukouli in Chad, I visited the 17 girls and 31 boys in the two-room school. Many children, especially girls, never attend school, which ends after the fourth grade.

12   So a 12-year-old boy working in Toukoultoukouli has gotten all the education he can. Instead of keeping him from working, Westerners should channel their indignation into getting all children into school for at least those four years and there is one way that could perhaps be achieved.

13   It's bribery. The U.N. World Food Program runs a model foreign aid effort called the school feeding program. It offers free meals to children in poor schools (and an extra bribe of grain for girl students to take home to their families). Almost everywhere, providing food raises school attendance, particularly for girls. "If there were meals here, parents would send their kids," said Muhammad Adam, a teacher in Toukoultoukouli.

14   School feeding costs just 19 cents per day per child.

15   So here's my challenge to university students: Instead of spending your energy boycotting Nike or pressing for barriers against child labor, why not sponsor school meals in places like Toukoultoukouli?

16   I spoke with officials at the World Food Program, and they'd be thrilled to have private groups or individuals help sponsor school feedings. (See www.nytimes.com/kristofresponds for details.) Children in Africa will be much better off with a hot meal and an education than with your self-righteous indignation.

For Class Discussion

1. What is Nicholas Kristof's main claim in this proposal argument?

2. In this piece, Kristof is criticizing humanitarians, liberals, and activists for their approach to child labor. What does he say is wrong with their approach? How does he defend his criticism of them and support his own view?

3. How has this piece influenced your thinking about the connections among child labor, poverty, and the citizens of rich nations? ∎

A World Fit for Us
Children's Forum (Special Session on Children—UNICEF)

The three-day Children's Forum sponsored by UNICEF took place during May 2002 in New York City. Its purpose was to involve children in influencing their governments and NGOs in implementing programs to benefit children. Two children per government and NGO were invited to participate. This speech, "A World Fit for Us," was written by the Children's Forum and delivered to the United Nations General Assembly Special Session on Children on May 8, 2002, by two child delegates: thirteen-year-old Gabriela Azurduy Arrieta from Bolivia and seventeen-year-old Audrey Cheynut from Monaco. This speech is printed on the Special Sessions link of UNICEF (www.unicef.org/specialsession/documentation/childrens-statement.htm).

> How does this speech, with its special occasion, speakers, and audience, seek to establish children as primary stakeholders in human rights issues?

1   We are the world's children.
We are the victims of exploitation and abuse.
We are street children.
We are the children of war.
We are the victims and orphans of HIV/AIDS.
We are denied good-quality education and health care.
We are victims of political, economic, cultural, religious and environmental discrimination.
We are children whose voices are not being heard: it is time we are taken into account.

2   We want a world fit for children, because a world fit for us is a world fit for everyone.

3   In this world, we see respect for the rights of the child:
   • governments and adults having a real and effective commitment to the principle of children's rights and applying the Convention on the Rights of the Child to all children,
   • safe, secure and healthy environments for children in families, communities, and nations.

4   We see an end to exploitation, abuse and violence:
   • laws that protect children from exploitation and abuse being implemented and respected by all,
   • centres, and programmes that help to rebuild the lives of victimized children.

5   We see an end to war:
   • world leaders resolving conflict through peaceful dialogue instead of by using force,
   • child refugees and child victims of war protected in every way and having the same opportunities as all other children,
   • disarmament, elimination of the arms trade and an end to the use of child soldiers.

6   We see the provision of health care:
   • affordable and accessible life-saving drugs and treatment for all children,

- strong and accountable partnerships established among all to promote better health for children.

7   We see the eradication of HIV/AIDS:
- educational systems that include HIV prevention programmes,
- free testing and counselling centres,
- information about HIV/AIDS freely available to the public,
- orphans of AIDS and children living with HIV/AIDS cared for and enjoying the same opportunities as all other children.

8   We see the protection of the environment:
- conservation and rescue of natural resources,
- awareness of the need to live in environments that are healthy and favourable to our development,
- accessible surroundings for children with special needs.

9   We see an end to the vicious cycle of poverty:
- anti-poverty committees that bring about transparency in expenditure and give attention to the needs of all children,
- cancellation of the debt that impedes progress for children.

10   We see the provision of education:
- equal opportunities and access to quality education that is free and compulsory,
- school environments in which children feel happy about learning,
- education for life that goes beyond the academic and includes lessons in understanding, human rights, peace, acceptance and active citizenship.

11   We see the active participation of children:
- raised awareness and respect among people of all ages about every child's right to full and meaningful participation, in the spirit of the Convention on the Rights of the Child,
- children actively involved in decision-making at all levels and in planning, implementing, monitoring and evaluating all matters affecting the rights of the child.

12   We pledge an equal partnership in this fight for children's rights. And while we promise to support the actions you take on behalf of children, we also ask for your commitment and support in the actions we are taking, because the children of the world are misunderstood.

13   We are not the sources of problems; we are the resources that are needed to solve them.
We are not expenses; we are investments.
We are not just young people; we are people and citizens of this world.

14   Until others accept their responsibility to us, we will fight for our rights.

We have the will, the knowledge, the sensitivity and the dedication.

We promise that as adults we will defend children's rights with the same passion that we have now as children.

We promise to treat each other with dignity and respect.

We promise to be open and sensitive to our differences.

15   We are the children of the world, and despite our different backgrounds, we share a common reality.

We are united by our struggle to make the world a better place for all.

You call us the future, but we are also the present.

For Class Discussion

1. What image of children does this speech seek to convey?

2. Repetition, antithesis (contrasting statements), and the use of examples are the main rhetorical devices employed most prominently in this speech. Why are these effective in a speech? What effects do you think these devices had on the immediate listeners?

3. What words would you use to describe the tone of this speech?

4. How has this piece influenced your view of the violation of children's rights discussed in this chapter? ■

Chadian Eight-Year-Old Soldier Smoking
Luc Novovitch

Advocacy organizations believe that around 300,000 children from more than thirty countries are fighting in wars around the world. Many of these children—both boys and girls—have been abducted or coerced into military service, tortured, sexually abused, forced to participate in violence, and compelled to witness terrible atrocities. These children are fighting in armies in Nepal, Sri Lanka, Indonesia, Colombia, Guatemala, Burma, Peru, Sudan, Uganda, Sierra Leone, and Liberia, among other countries. Many countries have signed the UN protocol of 2002 to stop the military recruitment of children; however, Asian and African signatories who have violated the protocol have not been brought before the International Criminal Court. This photo, one of many taken by news agencies reporting the problem of child soldiers, shows an eight-year-old soldier in Chad.

The more readers know about the horrors experienced by child soldiers, the more disturbing photos of these children are. What details of this photo stand out for you?

FIGURE 6.2   Chadian Eight-Year-Old Soldier Smoking *(© Luc Novovitch/Reuters/Corbis)*

For Class Discussion

1. What features of this photo suggest that this boy has suffered?

2. With this photo in mind, list some of the psychological problems that child soldiers may have while they are serving in these armies and when they are liberated.

3. Investigate the problem of child soldiers by consulting the Web sites for such advocacy organizations as Human Rights Watch (www.hrw.org/), the Anti-Slavery Society (www.anti-slaverysociety .addr.com), and Save the Children (www.savethechildren.org/). What key facts from these sources would you use in a report for your peers on this human rights issue? What makes a photo rhetorically effective to protest child soldiers?

4. How has this photo influenced your thinking about forced child labor?   ■

Trafficking and Health
Joanna Busza, Sarah Castle, and Aisse Diarra

Joanna Busza and Sarah Castle are lecturers at the Center for Population Studies at the London School of Hygiene and Tropical Medicine. Busza has researched reproductive and sexual health issues in Southeast Asia, and from 1997 to 2001, she focused on HIV prevention with migrant sex workers. Sarah Castle spent fifteen years in Mali, Africa, working with out-migration. Aisse Diarra, an independent consultant, has extensive experience with women's health and women's rights issues in Mali. This research article appeared in the scholarly publication the *British Medical Journal* on June 5, 2004.

This article follows a surprising-reversal format in that it sets up a common view of the trafficking of women and children and then argues that this view is erroneous and misinformed. What is the common view that Joanna Busza, Sarah Castle, and Aisse Diarra challenge? What is the new, surprising view that they seek to establish?

1 Trafficking in women and children is now recognised as a global public health issue as well as a violation of human rights. The *UN Protocol to Prevent, Suppress, and Punish Trafficking in Persons, especially Women and Children* states that trafficking involves force, threat, or fraud and intent to exploit individuals.[1] Intermediaries often smuggle victims across international borders into illegal or unsafe occupations, including agriculture, construction, domestic labour, and sex work. A recent study identified trafficking to be associated with health risks such as psychological trauma, injuries from violence, sexually transmitted infections, HIV and AIDS, other adverse reproductive health outcomes, and substance misuse.[2] These risks are shaped by lack of access to services in a foreign country, language barriers, isolation, and exploitative working conditions. However, as this article shows, efforts to reduce trafficking may be making conditions worse for voluntary migrants.

RESPONSE TO TRAFFICKING

2   Multinational, governmental, and non-governmental groups working to counter trafficking sometimes misinterpret the cultural context in which migration occurs.[3] They often seek to eradicate labour migration rather than target specific instances of exploitation and abuse.[4,5] Regulatory measures, such as introducing new requirements for documentation and strengthening of border controls, criminalise and marginalise all migrants, whether trafficked or not. This exacerbates their health risks and vulnerability by reducing access to appropriate services and social care. Such approaches do not adequately distinguish between forced and voluntary migrants, as it is extremely difficult to identify the motivations of migrants and their intermediaries before travel.[6]

3   We illustrate these concerns with evidence from research conducted among child migrants in Mali who had been returned from the Ivory Coast and Vietnamese sex workers in Cambodia. The evidence draws from studies conducted between 2000 and 2002.[7,8] In both settings, the international media has reported emotively on the existence of "child slaves," "sex slaves," and "trafficking" and oriented donors and nongovernmental organisations to this agenda.[9–11]

CHILD MIGRANTS IN MALI

4   Although no substantiated figures exist, an estimated 15,000 Malian children have been "trafficked" to the cocoa plantations in the Ivory Coast.[12] This study responded to a demand from several international non-governmental organisations that wanted to improve their understanding of the situation.[7] We compiled a sampling frame with the assistance of nongovernmental organisations working with children and their governmental partners. It included young people from communities deemed to be at high risk of trafficking, as well as intercepted or repatriated children thought to have been trafficked. However, a survey of nearly 1000 young people from this list found that only four could be classified as having been deceived, exploited, or not paid at all for their labour. Rather, young people voluntarily sought employment abroad, which represented an opportunity to experience urban lifestyles, learn new languages, and accumulate possessions. For both boys and girls, the experience provided a rite of passage with cultural as well as financial importance.

5   For many of these migrants, movement across international borders depended on assistance from intermediaries, often family members. In Mali there is a longstanding tradition of using intermediaries to facilitate a range of social and economic activities, such as looking for employment, negotiating purchases, handling disputes, and even seeking a spouse. Our research found that

intermediaries could protect the migrants during their journey and help them search for work. In destination areas, they advocated for young people in cases of non-payment of salary or abrupt termination of employment. Migrants also relied on intermediaries to negotiate with corrupt authorities that demanded bribes at international borders. Classifying such assistance as "trafficking" simplifies a much deeper cultural reality.

6   Local anti-trafficking policies and interventions, however, have not acknowledged these complex dynamics and have instead posed obstacles to safe, assisted migration. For example, interviews with Malian legal experts showed that new legislative measures do not enable them to distinguish between a trafficker with intent to exploit and an intermediary who, for a fee, facilitates a young migrant's journey and search for housing and employment. Local anti-trafficking surveillance committees have been established; these have come to view all migration as negative and local leaders seem to seek to arrest children if they attempt to leave. At the national level, a new child's passport is required for all children under the age of 18 who wish to travel. In reality, young people find the document difficult to obtain, and failure to possess it provides an easy excuse for law enforcement officers to extort additional bribes at borders.

7   These measures discourage community members from assisting in traditional labour migration and have the potential to force migrants to rely increasingly on corrupt officials to waive travel documents or provide forgeries. Clandestine migrants are generally more difficult to reach at destination points, as they may be reluctant to seek health care or other help if they fear being forcibly repatriated or detained. Child migrants who left home of their own free will report being returned home against their wishes by nongovernmental organisations, only to leave for the border again a few days later.

8   The study found that rehabilitation centres for trafficked children run by two non-governmental organisations in the Malian town of Sikasso were usually empty. Such interventions are neither appropriate nor cost effective and do not tackle the exploitative conditions encountered by children in the Ivory Coast. Children would be better served through services offered in the Ivory Coast or support through protective networks of intermediaries and community members.

VIETNAMESE SEX WORKERS IN CAMBODIA

9   As with Malians in the Ivory Coast, it is difficult to obtain accurate data on the number of Vietnamese migrants in Cambodia. Some estimates suggest that up to 10,000 Vietnamese women are sex

workers in Cambodia.[13] The research presented here was conducted in collaboration with a local non-governmental organisation as part of a wider investigation of sex workers' perceptions, motivations, and experiences.[8] The study formed one component of a service delivery programme to about 300 brothel based Vietnamese sex workers in Svay Pak district, Phnom Penh. Before the research, medical services, outreach, and counselling had been provided to sex workers for over five years, and a trusting relationship had been established between non-governmental organisation staff and both sex workers and brothel managers. Young, female, Vietnamese speaking project staff familiar to the sex workers conducted in-depth interviews with 28 women and focus group discussions with 72 participants to explore patterns of entry into sex work.

10   Most women knew before they left Vietnam that they would be engaged in sex work under a system of "debt bondage" to a brothel. The work would repay loans made to them or their families. Some women showed clear ambition in their choices to travel to Cambodia for sex work, citing economic incentives, desire for an independent lifestyle, and dissatisfaction with rural life and agricultural labour. As in Mali, intermediaries from home communities were instrumental in facilitating safe migration. Many women were accompanied by a parent, aunt, or neighbour who provided transport, paid bribes to border patrols, and negotiated the contract with brothel managers.

11   Of the 100 participants in this qualitative study, six women reported having been "tricked" into sex work or betrayed by an intermediary. Many sex workers, however, expressed dissatisfaction with their work conditions or stated that they had not fully appreciated the risks they would face, such as clients who refused to use condoms, coercion from brothel owners, and violence from both clients and local police.

12   A policy focus on combating "trafficking" again seemed to threaten rather than safeguard migrants' health and rights. Local and international non-governmental organisations conducted raids on brothels during which sex workers were taken to "rehabilitation centres," often against their will. Police sometimes assisted in these raids, although they also conducted arrests independently.

13   Our research found that "rescued" women usually returned to their brothel as quickly as possible, having secured their release through bribes or by summoning relatives from Vietnam to collect them. Furthermore, police presence in the raids scared off custom[ers], thus reducing earnings, increasing competition for clients, and further limiting sex workers' power in negotiating improved work conditions. Bribes and other costs were added to sex workers' debts, increasing their tenure in the brothel and

adding pressure to take on additional customers or agree to condom-free sex to maximise income. Raids and rescues could also damage the relationship between service providers and brothel managers, who restricted sex workers' mobility, including access to health care, to avoid arrest. These findings mirror recent reports from other sex worker communities throughout the region.[14–16]

THE WAY FORWARD

14 Our research in Mali and Cambodia shows disturbing parallels in ways that anti-trafficking measures can contribute to adverse health outcomes. Without wanting to minimise the issue of trafficking, these studies show that a more flexible and realistic approach to labour migration among young people is required. The needs of vulnerable young migrants, whether trafficked or not, can be met only through comprehensive understanding of their motivations and of the cultural and economic contexts in which their movements occur. Criminalising migrants or the industries they work in simply forces them "underground," making them more difficult to reach with appropriate services and increasing the likelihood of exploitation.

15 We do not dispute that in both settings migrants have suffered hardship and abuse, but current "anti-trafficking" approaches do not help their problems. The agendas need to be redrawn so that they reflect the needs of the populations they aim to serve, rather than emotive reactions to sensationalised media coverage. This requires deeper investigation at both local and regional levels, including participatory research to inform interventions from the experiences of the migrants and their communities. From the research that we have conducted in Mali and Cambodia, we recommend the following:

- Policy makers need to recognise that migration has sociocultural as well as economic motivations and seeking to stop it will simply cause migrants to leave in a clandestine and potentially more dangerous manner. Facilitating safe, assisted migration may be more effective than relying on corrupt officials to enforce restrictive border controls.
- Instead of seeking to repatriate migrants, often against their will, interventions should consider ways to provide appropriate services at destination points, taking into consideration specific occupational hazards, language barriers, and ability to access health and social care facilities.
- Programmes aimed at improving migrants' health and welfare should not assume that all intermediaries are "traffickers"

intending to exploit migrants. Efforts to reach migrants in destination areas could use intermediaries.

- Organisations that have established good rapport with migrant
communities should document cases of abuse and advocate for
improved labour conditions. In the case of sex work, however,
this can be politically difficult. For example, the United States
Agency for International Development recently announced its
intention to stop funding organisations that do not explicitly
support the eradication of all sex work.

16   Ultimately, trafficking and other forms of exploitation will cease
only with sustainable development in sending areas combined
with a reduction in demand for cheap, undocumented labour in
receiving countries. Non-governmental organisations and government partners therefore need to focus on the root causes of rural
poverty and exploitation of labour as well as mitigating the health
risks of current migrants. At the moment, trafficking is big business
not just for traffickers but also for the international development
community, which can access funds relatively easily to tackle the
issue without investing in a more comprehensive understanding of
the wider dynamics shaping labour migration.

References

1. United Nations. *Protocol to prevent, suppress and punish trafficking in persons, especially women and children, supplementing the United National Convention Against Transnational Organized Crime.* New York: United Nations, 2000.

2. Zimmerman C, Yun K, Shvab I, Watts C, Trappolin L, Treppete M, et al. *The health risks and consequences of trafficking in women and adolescents. Findings from a European study.* London: London School of Hygiene and Tropical Medicine, 2003.

3. Butcher K. Confusion between prostitution and sex trafficking. *Lancet* 2003;361: 1983. [CrossRef][ISI][Medline]

4. Marshall P. *Globalization, migration and trafficking: some thoughts from the South-East Asian region.* Bangkok: UN Inter-Agency Project on Trafficking in Women and Children in the Mekong Sub-region, 2001. (Occasional paper No 1.)

5. Taran PA, Moreno-Fontes G. *Getting at the roots.* UN Inter-Agency Project Newsletter 2002;7: 1–5.

6. Coomaraswamy R. *Integration of the human right of women and the gender perspective: violence against women: report of the special rapporteur on violence against women, its causes and consequences.* New York: UN Economic and Social Council, 2000.

7. Castle S, Diarra A. *The international migration of young Malians: tradition, necessity or rite of passage?* London: London School of Hygiene and Tropical Medicine, 2003.

8. Busza J, Schunter BT. From competition to community: participatory learning and action among young, debt-bonded Vietnamese sex workers in Cambodia. *Reprod Health Matters* 2001;9: 72–81. [CrossRef][ISI][Medline]

9. Bobak L. For sale: the innocence of Cambodia. *Ottawa Sun* 1996 Oct 24.

10. Chocolate slaves carry many scars. *Daily Telegraph* 2001 Apr 24.

11. Child slavery: Africa's growing problem. *CNN* 2001 Apr 17.

12. United States Agency for International Development. *Trafficking in persons: USAID's response.* Washington, DC: USAID Office of Women in Development, 2001: 10–6.

13. Unicef. Unicef supports national seminar on human trafficking. www.unicef.org/vietnam/new080.htm (accessed 11 Nov 2003).

14. Jones M. Thailand's brothel busters. *Mother Jones* 2003 Nov/Dec.

15. Phal S. *Survey on police human rights violations in Toul Kork.* Phnom Penh: Cambodia Women's Development Association, 2002.

16. Sutees R. Brothel raids in Indonesia—ideal solution or further violation? *Research for Sex Work* 2003;6: 5–7.

For Class Discussion

1. This article addresses the complexities of child labor in Mali, Africa, and of Vietnamese sex workers (many of them young girls) in Cambodia, and it also exposes the conflicting agendas of stakeholders on the trafficking controversy. What complexities does it want readers to understand?

2. What claims do these writers make about stakeholders' conflicting agendas for dealing with global child labor and the sex trade?

3. In this researched policy proposal, how do the writers establish their credibility and authority? What makes their use of evidence effective and persuasive?

4. How has this article influenced your view of the trafficking of children and women? In what ways do you think free trade advocates would agree with the writers of this article?   ■

The Horrors of the International Sex Trade

The *Independent*

This anonymously written article appeared in the popular British news publication the *Independent* on December 23, 2003.

> How is this article trying to change the attitudes and perspectives of the British public and government toward victims of the sex trade?

1   According to the UN, about 700,000 women are being illegally trafficked around the world to supply the sex trade. Yesterday in the British courts, seven of them did what none ever expected to do, and testified against the man who had enslaved them.

2   An Albanian-born British citizen, Luan Plakici, has been found guilty of 15 charges of kidnap, living off prostitution, procuring a girl for unlawful sex, incitement to rape and facilitating the illegal

entry of immigrants. He denied all but the final charge, and admitted to bringing around 50 to 60 women into Britain illegally. About half of them, he claimed, were prostitutes anyway. All he had done, he said, was smuggle them in.

3   But seven women knew differently, and were not afraid to tell the police about it. This case is unusual, because it is rare for women caught up in the international sex trade to give evidence to the police.

4   Typically, they are fearful because they are beaten, raped and imprisoned by their tormentors, who justify their behaviour by insisting that the women must work as prostitutes in order to pay the costs of their travel. They are also trapped by their position as illegal immigrants and intimidated by threats against their relatives back home, usually in Eastern Europe. They are often told, as well, that the police will not listen to them, because they, too, are involved in the sex trade.

5   What seems to have made the crucial difference in this is that a 25-year-old Romanian, who managed to escape from a flat she was being held in, had left her 17-year-old sister behind. She immediately flagged down a police car, and asked the police to help save her sister and a 16-year-old being held with them.

6   All three of these women testified against Plakici, as did another woman who was married to him. This girl, a teenager, found herself forced into prostitution within hours of a registry office wedding to Plakici. She had been forced to have two abortions and to return to work within hours of the terminations. She estimates that she handed about £140,000* to him in the two years of her enslavement.

7   The stories told by the women inveigled into coming to Britain by Plakici are familiar. Living in some of the most impoverished parts of Europe, they were promised work as waitresses or barmaids in London, which in their naive and desperate optimism they believed to be the truth. These particular young women are all from rural parts of Romania or Moldavia, the latter a state so degraded that 90 per cent of its young people declare themselves desperate to leave.

8   It is such desperation that is exploited by the traffickers, a fact that the West understands pretty well. One of the most horrific things about the international sex trade is that we all know who [is involved] and why it works, yet seem entirely unable to do anything at all about it.

9   *Lilya 4-Ever*, the film by Swedish director Lucas Moodysson, which told in harrowing detail the story of one young girl plucked from her miserable home by the sort of promises these seven girls

---

*£140,000 is about $263,200 in U.S. dollars.

were lured with, served to bring the mechanics of the sex trade to international attention. For those who have seen the film, the memory of Lilya's dead eyes as she is forced to submit to impersonal sex-act after impersonal sex-act is unforgettably horrific. Yet while the film has been rightly lauded worldwide for the unflinching story of utter exploitation and dehumanisation it tells, it failed to stimulate debate about how the pervasive and unspeakably cruel trade can be tackled.

10   It is not clear what will happen to the seven young women who testified. It may be that they are happy to return to their home countries now that their ordeal is over. This would make sense, because one thing that European governments tend to avoid doing, however much they wish to tackle the sex trade, is offer sanctuary to women who are willing to give evidence against traffickers. The argument is that if such measures are undertaken, then there will be more of a "pull-factor" for women wishing to escape from their old lives.

11   In one tiny project, in which a charity has been offered grants to offer a safe haven to women escaping from the sex trade, government stipulations about what the women must be prepared to do in order that the charity can achieve funding were impossibly unwieldly. Despite the fact that it can accept no asylum seekers, no women who will not co-operate with the police, and no one [who] will not agree to return home, the project has still managed to help 22 women to escape from bondage. It will have its £700,000 grant renewed next year.

12   Clearly, this single pilot project is nothing like adequate as a response to the burgeoning sex trade. But elsewhere, the pattern is the same. Only recently was it announced that funding for tackling people-trafficking as [a] whole would be increased by two thirds from a modest £20m. Yet while there is a police unit that specialises in sex-trafficking, there are only 14 people in the squad. They reckon that with a team of 200, they might begin to be able to do some useful work.

13   This case, despite its desirable outcome, is unlikely to change things for the better. In fact, it is more likely to harden attitudes, since Mr Plakici is himself a spectacular example of all the worst fears people have about the idea of Britain as a soft touch for villainous immigrants. The 26-year-old first came to Britain seven years ago as an asylum seeker. He was granted political asylum and later British citizenship after claiming he was Kosovan. (The police now want this fictitious claim to be investigated by the Home Office).

14   A talented linguist, his determination to play the system had made him something of an immigration expert. He had a legitimate career as a much sought-after translator for law companies specialis[ing] in immigration cases, and even took part in a BBC

documentary about the subject. In reality though, his expertise had allowed him fraudulently to get himself a British passport. He then used this to travel widely in Europe, seeking recruits for his empire.

15   Using his excellent connections among law firms, he arranged for the women he smuggled to apply for asylum-seeker status themselves. Meanwhile, using the money he raised from the women's activities, he proceeded to build himself luxurious homes in Italy and Albania. He is estimated to have made more than £1m in the four years he has been trafficking women.

16   It may seem to make sense for a top-down policy to concentrate on rooting out the people who are heading up the criminal gangs, even if this makes life difficult for genuine refugees and honest economic migrants as well. But, in reality, it is easier to catch the people running these organisations by making it less difficult for those who can provide evidence against them. In this way, the trade's untouchable illegality is broken down, and it becomes more dangerous for traffickers to operate because there is more danger of them being caught.

17   The Home Office promises that it is looking at ways of making it easier for women in the bonded sex trade to come forward. It must do so as a matter of urgency, because the lack of policy has done nothing but allow this illegal trade to boom.

18   That women are living in Britain effectively as bonded sexual slaves is repulsive and vile. That so far it has been considered wise to ignore this burgeoning trade because any mercy shown to women thus imprisoned and tortured may encourage others is almost as repulsive. These women are victims not just of the traffickers who prey on them, but of the cruel vagaries of the global economic system under which Britain prospers. The upholding of their human rights must come before all other considerations.

For Class Discussion

1. What is the implicit and delayed main claim of this argument? What supporting reasons can you reconstruct?

2. Most of this article is devoted to conveying the problems experienced by women who have been trafficked to Britain. List as many of these problems as you can, including the ways that the laws favor traffickers over their victims.

3. This article gives details of a particular case and then builds to a point. Try to imagine another structure or organization for this article. Using the same points and evidence, how could you make the article more clear and persuasive for a general newspaper audience?

FIGURE 6.3 For Sale *(© International Organization for Migration (IOM), taken from the Southern African Counter-Trafficking Assistance Programme. www.iom.org.za/ CounterTrafficking.html)*

For Sale
International Organization for Migration

The International Organization for Migration is a fifty-year-old global organization that seeks to "assist in meeting the growing operational challenges of migration management; advance understanding of migration issues; encourage social and economic development through migration; and uphold the human dignity and well-being of migrants" (from its mission statement, www.iom.org). IOM works with governments and civil society on every continent. Its countertrafficking projects focus on information campaigns, counseling services, research, safe conduct and assistance for victims, and working with governments on their legal systems to stop trafficking.

What are your first impressions of this poster?

For Class Discussion

1. How would you describe the girl on this poster?
2. What is the emotional effect of the combination of the photo of the girl, the words "FOR SALE," and the placement of the words?
3. What primary and secondary audiences do you think this poster is attempting to reach?
4. Examine the "What We Do" link of the Web site of this organization (www.iom.int/). How does this organization on its Web site and in this poster establish the connections between migration and human trafficking? What are some of those connections?
5. What readings in this chapter does this poster support?   ∎

Confusion Between Prostitution and Sex Trafficking
Kate Butcher

Kate Butcher is a public health consultant with John Snow Research International and Training, a leading provider of consultation on public health based in the United Kingdom. She has worked extensively with HIV/AIDS programs in Africa and Asia, and she has written much about combating AIDS, including her 2001 article "Danger and Opportunity: Responding to HIV with Vision," published in the journal *Gender and Development*. Her article here was originally published in the *Lancet* on June 7, 2003. The *Lancet*, a well-known and highly reputable British medical journal dating from 1823, is "an independent and authoritative voice in global medicine." It has always sought to "combine publication of the best medical science with a zeal to counter the forces that undermine the values of medicine, be they political, social, or commercial" (from "About *The Lancet*" at www.thelancet.com/about).

How does the thesis of Butcher's article suit the reformist purpose of this medical journal?

1   In May, 2003, the US government passed the Leadership Against HIV/AIDS, Tuberculosis and Malaria Act of 2003, which outlines the areas and support that the US administration is prepared to endorse in the fight against these diseases. The act includes the limitation that

"No funds made available to carry out this Act . . . may be used to provide assistance to any group or organization that does not have a policy explicitly opposing prostitution and sex trafficking."[1]

2   This statement might go unnoticed, but it deserves attention. The juxtaposition of the terms prostitution and sex trafficking demonstrates a belief that both share similar characteristics, and thus reflects moral ideology rather than objective reality.

3   The distinction between trafficking and prostitution is important because it pivots on individual agency. Trafficking, though variously defined,[2] covers coercion, forced labour, and slavery. Prostitution describes the sale of sex, by no means necessarily without consent or with coercion. At a time when trafficking is increasing, as are international efforts to tackle it, it is critical to clarify the differences between the issues.[3]

4   The merging of these issues is not new, nor confined to the USA. In Asia, where human trafficking (both for prostitution and for bonded labour) has a longer history than in Europe, responses by governments and feminist groups alike have often been to call for eradication of prostitution, and therefore trafficking.

5   But this approach overlooks an important fact; millions of women have made the decision to sell sex, usually but not always, on economic grounds. Selling sex is a pragmatic response to a limited range of options. If you can earn the equivalent of UK £100 in a night, why knit sweaters or sweep floors to earn the same money in a month?

6   When women's groups call for rehabilitation and rescue of trafficked and prostituted women they argue from their own moral perspective and not that of the women they are seeking to save. The situation is complex, in that a spectrum can exist between trafficking and prostitution, with trafficked girls at one end and women who have decided to work as prostitutes at the other. Some women who have been trafficked may eventually begin to define themselves as sex workers. The longer a woman is involved in the sex industry the more likely this is to be the case; 6 years after being trafficked to India a Nepalese woman told me: "Why would I want to return to Nepal? I have friends here, I make good money. In Nepal what would I do? Look after goats and have no money! I'm good at my job and I know it. I don't want to return to Nepal."

7   Of course there will be other women and men who may wish to leave the sex industry. The responsibility of public health, development, and human rights workers is to ensure that individuals enjoy the same level of human rights whatever their involvement in the sex industry.

8   The prominence of debate about sex work and trafficking has grown largely as a result of the HIV epidemic.[4] Sex workers, initially identified as a public health threat, embodied in phrases such as

"pools of infection" and "vectors of disease", were recruited to promote safer sex. Sex workers around the world have been practising safer sex and educated many of their clients to do the same.[5] Their importance in responding to the HIV epidemic is evident, but evidence of improved rights for these men and women is harder to find.

9   Key rights listed in the UNAIDS handbook for legislators on HIV, law, and human rights include:

- Non-discrimination and equality before the law
- Freedom from inhuman or degrading treatment or punishment
- Autonomy, liberty, and security of the person

10   All over the world these basic entitlements are violated in the context of sex work. It is rare to read of a successful lawsuit made by a sex worker against a rapist, violation from a policeman, or unlawful arrest.

11   By merging trafficking and prostitution, the agency of sex workers is overlooked. Rather than promoting opposition to prostitution we would do better to promote human rights. The right to resist being drawn into prostitution by trafficking certainly, but so too the right to work with the law's protection from harm, be it rape, violence, robbery, or other violations.

12   We can expect sex workers to continue contributing to the fight against HIV and thus to public health: it is after all in everyone's interest including their own. We should also expect public health and development professionals to support their so doing without fear for their lives or their safety—in sum, by advocating for the human rights of sex workers.

1. HR 1298 US leadership against HIV/AIDS, tuberculosis and malaria act of 2003. http://www.thebody.com/govt/global_aids.html (accessed May, 2003).
2. Luckoo F, Tzvetkova M. Combating trafficking in persons: a directory of organisations. London: Change, 2002.
3. Human Rights Caucus. UN trafficking protocol: lost opportunity to protect the rights of trafficked persons. December, 2000. http://www.unodc.un.or.th/factsheet/fact2001_trafficking.htm (accessed May, 2003).
4. Kotiswaran P. Preparing for civil disobedience: Indian sex workers and the law. *21 Boston College Third World Law J,* no 2, Spring, 2001.
5. Network of Sex Work Projects. Making sex work safe. http://www.nswp.org/safety/msws/ (accessed May, 2003).

For Class Discussion

1. According to Butcher, what is the complex relationship between sex trafficking, prostitution, human rights, and the AIDS epidemic? Why does Butcher claim it is important to distinguish between prostitution and sex trafficking?
2. Whom is Butcher criticizing and rebutting in this article?

3. What reasoning and evidence does Butcher offer to support her views?

4. What assumptions do readers have to accept in order to agree with Butcher's argument?

5. Butcher has worked extensively in global public health and in combating AIDS around the world. How does knowledge of her background influence your response to this article? ■

Letter to Colin Powell on the Trafficking in Persons Report 2003

Human Rights Watch, LaShawn R. Jefferson

Human Rights Watch is an independent, nongovernmental organization supported by independent contributors, not the government. It is the largest organization for human rights based in the United States (New York). A staff of lawyers, journalists, researchers, people with knowledge of particular countries, and volunteers work "with victims and activists to prevent discrimination, to uphold political freedom, to protect people from inhumane conduct in wartime, and to bring offenders to justice" (www.hrw.org/about/). Human Rights Watch investigates and publicizes human rights violations, bringing public pressure to bear on governments. This 2003 open letter, signed by LaShawn R. Jefferson, Executive Director of the Women's Rights Division, was retrieved from the Human Rights Watch Web site on October 28, 2004.

How is this open letter tailored to its immediate audience, Colin L. Powell, secretary of state during President George W. Bush's first term?

The Honorable Colin L. Powell
Secretary of State
U.S. Department of State
2201 C Street, N.W.
Washington, D.C. 20520

June 27, 2003

Dear Secretary Powell:

1   We write to share some concerns about the U.S. State Department's third annual Trafficking in Persons Report (Trafficking Report). The Trafficking Report has the potential to become a powerful tool to address trafficking worldwide. However, persistent shortcomings seriously undermine its effectiveness. We urge the State Department to remedy those shortcomings in future reports.

2   As you know, trafficking in persons threatens the lives, health, dignity, and security of millions of people throughout the world, with women and children suffering the brunt of the abuses. Trafficking is a blatant violation of human rights and is almost universally condemned, yet many countries are failing to address this problem seriously.

3   Human Rights Watch has documented and monitored trafficking in persons for more than a decade. We have advocated for increased respect for the human rights of victims of trafficking and for greater accountability of traffickers. For example, we have investigated trafficking of persons from Eastern Europe to Bosnia and Herzegovina; in West African countries such as Togo, Gabon, Benin, Nigeria, Niger, Ghana, and Côte d'Ivoire; from Bangladesh to Pakistan; from Burma to Thailand; from Nepal to India; from Thailand to Japan; and from North Korea to China.

4   Based on our experience and consultations with nongovernmental and other organizations working to end trafficking around the world, we have the following concerns about the Trafficking Report:

• The report does not meaningfully evaluate anti-trafficking efforts. The Trafficking Report lauds governments' efforts to combat trafficking, such as initiating information campaigns, setting up victim service programs, and proposing draft legislation, but generally does not evaluate the content or effectiveness of such measures. For example, some country chapters note that legal services are provided to victims, but do not assess the quality of the services. Other chapters indicate that governments have established inter-ministerial task forces to combat trafficking in persons, but do not evaluate their work. Draft trafficking legislation is mentioned in some chapters without assessing the adequacy of the draft legislation. To maximize its usefulness, the Trafficking Report must do more than superficially list anti-trafficking measures. It must assess the quality of those measures. For example, it should answer questions such as: Are the victim service programs appropriately designed and funded, and are they effectively assisting victims in practice? What are the inter-ministerial task forces mandated to do, and have they succeeded? Does draft legislation cover trafficking into all forms of forced labor and provide adequate victim services and witness protections?

• The report inconsistently uses statistics. Statistical data are spotty in the Trafficking Report. While some chapters provide basic data on the numbers of trafficking victims, arrests, prosecutions and convictions, many more do not. The Trafficking Report should explain the absence of such data. It should also urge governments to compile and publish statistics on trafficking in persons disaggregated by age, sex, nationality, and the nature of their forced labor.

- The report fails to weigh and condemn harmful immigration policies: The report notes that some countries summarily deport or incarcerate trafficking victims but does not condemn these practices as further victimizing of trafficked people. A country that summarily incarcerates or deports a victim of trafficking essentially punishes the individual for being a victim of a human rights abuse and eliminates any chance for the victim to seek redress or medical or other attention. Such practices call into question a country's commitment to protecting the rights of victims of trafficking and the government's genuine understanding of trafficking as a human rights abuse.
- The report credits countries without trafficking legislation. The Trafficking Report credits many countries for their anti-trafficking efforts even when they have not passed legislation specifically criminalizing trafficking into all forms of forced labor, or when they have failed to ratify the Protocol to Prevent, Suppress, and Punish Trafficking in Persons, Especially Women and Children, which supplements the U.N. Convention against Transnational Organized Crime (Trafficking Protocol). In our view, it should be a minimum requirement for all countries ranking in Tier 1 that they have legislation specifically criminalizing all forms of forced labor as trafficking and providing remedies and assistance to victims. While legislation is just the beginning of providing a legal structure to address trafficking, and laws alone do not guarantee state action, passing legislation is vital to the effective prosecution of traffickers and to ensure that the victims' rights are respected.
- The report lacks specificity. The Trafficking Report is often vague or cursory. For example, some chapters note that prosecutions occurred, but fail to explain whether those prosecutions were completed and their results. At a minimum, the Trafficking Report should specify whether a country's legislation penalizes trafficking into all forms of forced labor (not just forced prostitution), which types of government agents are complicit in trafficking, and what measures have been taken to investigate and prosecute them. The Trafficking Report should include whether the country is failing to investigate and prosecute trafficking offenses vigorously, and what appear to be the reasons for such failure; whether the country has effective government-funded witness protection and victim services programs to which all trafficking victims have access; and whether the country is a party to the Trafficking Protocol.
- The report fails adequately to explain the criteria for Tier movement. The Report does not adequately explain the criteria applied when countries move from one Tier to another. For example, the Report does not explain why Benin was moved from Tier 2 last

year to Tier 1 this year. We believe the decision was inappropriate, given that Benin has not ratified the Trafficking Protocol and has no national legislation criminalizing all forms of trafficking. The Trafficking Report should describe the justification for moving countries from one Tier to another. Failing to do so jeopardizes the credibility of the Trafficking Report's Tier system.

5   Despite our serious concerns, we note that the Trafficking Report has improved since last year, in part by including more countries, better organizing the country narratives, ensuring that the report includes information on trafficking into many forms of forced labor, and including more discussion of domestic (internal) as well as international trafficking. However, this important document still needs significant improvement.

6   To protect the rights of millions of trafficking victims around the world, and prevent others from being trafficked, we ask that you ensure that all future reports evaluate the effectiveness of anti-trafficking efforts; include disaggregated statistics on trafficking victims and prosecutions; urge all countries to enact anti-trafficking legislation and bar any countries that do not have such legislation from Tier 1; provide more specificity on issues such as corruption, prosecutions, and service programs; and better explain the criteria for moving countries from one Tier to another.

7   Absent a deeper and clearer evaluation of governments' anti-trafficking records, the Trafficking Report risks becoming a public relations opportunity for states that inadequately protect trafficking victims and fail to punish traffickers.

8   We thank you for your attention to the concerns raised in this letter and hope to meet you to discuss these issues further.

Sincerely,

LaShawn R. Jefferson
Executive Director
Women's Rights Division

Cc: Mr. John R. Miller, Senior Advisor and Director of the Office to Monitor and Combat Trafficking in Persons
Ms. Paula J. Dobriansky, Under Secretary for Global Affairs
Charlotte Ponticelli, Senior Coordinator for International Women's Issues

For Class Discussion

1. What is the structure of this letter and how does it fit the specific purpose and genre of the official, institutional public letter?

2. How do the claims, reasons, and evidence in this argument convey the knowledge and authority of Human Rights Watch?

3. What specifically does this letter add to your understanding of the official U.S. response to the global trafficking of women and children? (For more information on the Tier System and for the list of countries assigned to Tiers 1, 2, and 3, you can check the Web site for the U.S. Department of State's "Trafficking in Persons Report" for 2005: www.state.gov/g/tip/rls/tiprpt/2005/46610.htm.)   ■

Slavery in 2004
John R. Miller

Ambassador John R. Miller has been a Republican congressman from the state of Washington and is now the director of the State Department's Office to Monitor and Combat Trafficking in Persons. He frequently travels abroad to meet with representatives of other nations to confer on their efforts to combat human trafficking. He is known for his bold, uncompromising stance against human trafficking. This op-ed piece appeared in the *Washington Post* on January 1, 2004.

1   Do U.S. sanctions move other countries toward progress on human rights? Of one thing I am sure: On the emerging human rights issue of the 21st century—modern-day slavery—the threat of cutting U.S. aid has brought forth efforts that will free thousands from bondage.

2   That slavery exists as we enter 2004 may shock many. Nonetheless, slavery in many forms, particularly sex and forced labor, reaches into almost every country. Sex slavery affects thousands of women and children and has caused trafficking in human beings to become the third-largest source of money for organized crime, after the drug and arms trades. That grim reality motivated President Bush this fall to become the first world leader to raise the slavery issue at the U.N. General Assembly. He called for new international efforts to fight the slave trade and pledged to almost double U.S. resources devoted to this cause.

3   The U.S. government estimates that 800,000 to 900,000 men, women and children are trafficked across international borders every year, including 18,000 to 20,000 into the United States. Some estimate total worldwide slavery to be in the millions.

4   In September I visited a number of countries to meet with the human beings behind such numbers. If you talk with Sasha, a former sex slave in Amsterdam, or with Lord, a former factory slave in Bangkok, you quickly understand the toll this takes on individual bodies and spirits. The story that one victim, Maria, told Congress a few years ago is typical. Lured with the hope of a restaurant job from Vera Cruz, Mexico, and trafficked through Texas, Maria was

finally delivered to a brothel in Florida. There she resisted but—frightened, threatened, beaten and raped in a strange land—she succumbed and "worked" to pay off the debts that traffickers claimed she owed them.*

5   Cases such as hers and the urgings of faith-based and feminist organizations led Congress to pass legislation that not only strengthened U.S. prosecution of traffickers and assistance to victims but also mandated the State Department to report on slavery and the slave trade around the world.

6   And here we see how the threat of economic penalties has started to play a crucial role. For the first two years the law was in effect, there were zero consequences. But this year, Congress provided that countries rated by the State Department as having made no significant efforts be faced with the potential loss of U.S. military aid, educational and cultural assistance, and support from the World Bank and International Monetary Fund.

7   In the three months before the slavery report came out this past June, my office saw more progress in some countries than in the previous two years. Laws against trafficking in persons were passed in places from the Philippines to Haiti to Burkina Faso. Victims were rescued and massive arrests of traffickers were made in Cambodia and Serbia.

8   The U.S. law provided that for those countries poorly rated in this year's report, there would be a three-month period to make antislavery efforts. In 10 countries, including military allies of the United States, there was a flurry of activity.

9   Turkey set up and implemented new screening procedures that recognized 200 victims. Georgia appointed special officers with responsibility for trafficking and started broadcasting hotline numbers for victims on national television. The Dominican Republic launched a national educational billboard campaign and set up a national anti-trafficking police unit with special prosecutors. In these and other countries there were numerous arrests and prosecutions.

10   Of course not all these actions resulted from the threat of aid cuts. Many government officials, finally recognizing the enormity of the human crises, wanted to act. Some undoubtedly were embarrassed by the State Department's report. Strenuous efforts by diplomats in many U.S. embassies were crucial.

11   We continue, however, to face the problem that many countries' economies have links to slavery. Corrupt and complicit police pose a challenge in many nations. And there is the difficulty of trying to fight diseases such as HIV-AIDS at the same time we are fighting the sex trafficking that causes so much of that disease.

---

*Maria's story is quoted in the "International Voices" section of this chapter on page 278.

12   To meet these challenges we need support and action at home and an-tislavery allies abroad. But we also need the willingness to impose eco-nomic penalties that give antislavery laws and diplomacy meaning.

For Class Discussion

1. Political conservatives (Republicans) and especially free trade pro-ponents and libertarians oppose economic intervention as a means to pressure foreign governments to attend to their problems with human rights and trafficking. What is John Miller's stance?

2. How does Miller build a case for his main claim?

3. What features of this article show Miller's attempting to bring American citizens into the controversies over human trafficking and to move them to agree with his views?

4. Who do you think opposes John Miller's views and on what basis?

5. Where do Human Rights Watch and John Miller agree in their poli-cies in response to human trafficking?   ∎

Globalization and the Sex Trade: Trafficking and the Commodification of Women and Children

Richard Poulin

This scholarly article was first published in *Canadian Women Studies/Les Cahiers de la Femme* in December 2003 and was posted on the Canadian feminist site *Sisyphe* in February 2004. Richard Poulin, a professor of soci-ology at the University of Ottawa, has published articles on ethnic ques-tions, socialist societies, and pornography and globalization.

According to Poulin, how is the sex trade today in a globalized market "qualitatively different from the prostitution of yesterday"?

1   Capitalist globalization today involves an unprecedented "com-modification" of human beings. In the last 30 years, the rapidly growing sex trade has been massively "industrialized" worldwide (Barry; Jeffreys). This process of industrialization, in both its legal and its illegal forms, generates profits amounting to billions of dol-lars (1). It has created a market of sexual exchanges in which mil-lions of women and children have been converted into sexual com-modities. This sex market has been generated through the massive deployment of prostitution (one of the effects of the presence of military forces engaged in wars and/or territorial occupation)

(Strudevant and Stolzfus) in particular in the emerging economies, the unprecedented expansion of the tourist industry (Truong), the growth and normalization of pornography (Poulin 2000), and the internationalization of arranged marriages (Hughes).

2   The sex industry, previously considered marginal, has come to occupy a strategic and central position in the development of international capitalism. For this reason it is increasingly taking on the guise of an ordinary sector of the economy. This particular aspect of globalization involves an entire range of issues crucial to understanding the world we live in. These include such processes as economic exploitation, sexual oppression, capital accumulation, international migration, and unequal development and such related conditions as racism and poverty.

3   The industrialization of the sex trade has involved the mass production of sexual goods and services structured around a regional and international division of labour. These "goods" are human beings who sell sexual services. The international market in these "goods" simultaneously encompasses local and regional levels, making its economic imperatives impossible to avoid (2). Prostitution and related sexual industries—bars, dancing clubs, massage parlors, pornography producers etc.—depend on a massive subterranean economy controlled by pimps connected to organized crime. At the same time, businesses such as international hotel chains, airline companies, and the tourist industry benefit greatly from the sex industry. In Thailand, trafficking is a 500 billion Bahts annual business (equivalent to approximately 124 million U.S. dollars), which represents a value equal to around 60 per cent of the government budget (CATW). In 1998, the International Labor Organization (ILO) estimated that prostitution represented between two and 14 per cent of the economic activities of Thailand, Indonesia, Malaysia, and Philippines (Jeffreys). According to a study conducted by Ryan Bishop and Lilian Robinson, the tourist industry brings four billion dollars a year to Thailand. It is not without reason, then, that in 1987 the Thai government promoted sexual tourism through advertising "The one fruit of Thailand more delicious than durian [a local fruit], its young women" (Hechler).

GLOBALIZATION AND DEVELOPMENT STRATEGY

4   The industrialization of the sex trade and its globalization are fundamental factors that make contemporary prostitution qualitatively different from the prostitution of yesterday. "Consumers" in the economic North now have access to "exotic" and young, very young bodies worldwide, notably in Brazil, Cuba, Russia, Kenya, Sri Lanka, Philippines, Vietnam, Nicaragua, and, given the trafficking of children, in their own countries. The sex industry is diversified, sophisticated, and specialized: it can meet all types of demands.

5   Another factor, which confers a qualitatively different character on the current sex trade, is the fact that prostitution has become a development strategy for some countries. Under obligations of debt repayment, numerous Asian, Latin American, and African States were encouraged by international organizations such as the International Monetary Fund (IMF) and the World Bank (WB) to develop their tourism and entertainment industries. In each case, the development of these sectors inspired the development of the sex trade (Hechler). In certain cases, as in Nepal, women and children were put directly on regional or international markets (notably in India and in Hong-Kong) without the country experiencing a significant expansion of local prostitution. In other cases, as in Thailand, local, regional, and international markets developed simultaneously (Barry).

6   We can see that, in every case, the "goods" in this market move transcontinentaly and transnationally from regions with weak concentrations of capital toward regions with stronger concentrations.

7   For example, over ten years, 200,000 Bangladeshi women and girls were the object of trafficking to Pakistan (CATW), and we find that between 20,000 to 30,000 Thai prostitutes are from Burma (CATW). A good part of the migratory stream makes its way towards industrialized countries (3). Foreign women are generally at the bottom of the prostitution hierarchy, are socially and culturally isolated, and work in the worst possible conditions.

8   Any political economic analysis of prostitution and trafficking in women and children must take into account structural discrimination, uneven development, and the hierarchical relationships between imperialist and dependent countries and between men and women. In recent years under the impact of structural adjustment and economic liberalization policies in numerous countries of the Third World, as well as in the ex-USSR and Eastern Europe, women and children have become "new raw resources" within the framework of national and international business development. Capitalist globalization is more and more characterized by a feminization of migration (Santos). Women of ethnic minorities and other relatively powerless groups are particularly exploited. So, the internal traffic of Thai females consists mostly of 12–16 year olds from hill tribes of the North and the Northeast. In Taiwan, 40 per cent of young prostitutes in the main red light district are aboriginal girls (Barry 139). At the world level, the customers of the North abuse women of the South and of the East as well as local women from disadvantaged groups. From an economic point of view, these "goods" are doubly valuable because bodies are both a good and a service. More precisely, we have seen a commodification not only of the body, but also of women and children as human beings. This

has led many to see this trafficking in women and children as a form of slavery (CATW).

9   Kidnapping, rape, and violence continue to act as midwives of this industry. They are fundamental not only for the development of markets, but also for the "manufacturing" of these "goods," as they contribute to making them "functional" for an industry that requires a constant supply of bodies. Research has shown that between 75 and 80 per cent of prostitutes were sexually abused in their childhood (Satterfield; Chaleil) (4). More than 90 per cent of prostitutes are controlled by a pimp (Silbert and Pines 1982; Barry). A study of street prostitutes in England established that 87 per cent had been victims of violence during the last 12 months and 43 per cent suffered from grave physical consequences of abuse (Raymond). An American study showed that 78 per cent of prostitutes had been victims of rape by pimps and customers, on average 49 times a year; 49 per cent had been victims of removal and transported from one state to another and 27 per cent had been mutilated (Raymond). The average age of entrance into prostitution in the United States is 14 years (Silbert and Pines 1981; Giobbe).

10   Only 15 per cent of the prostitutes in the United States have never contracted a venereal disease (Leidholdt). Fifty-eight per cent of the prostitutes of Burkina Faso have AIDS, as have, 52 per cent in Kenya, about 50 per cent in Cambodia and 34 per cent in the North of Thailand. In Italy, in 1988, two per cent of the prostitutes had AIDS, compared to 16 per cent ten years later (Leidholdt; see also, Mechtild). One of the reasons customers give for sexually exploiting children is to avoid sexually transmitted diseases. But the data show this is no protection. For example, in Cambodia there are between 50,000 and 70,000 prostitutes. More than a third of them are less than 18 years old and about 50 per cent of these young people are HIV positive (Véran). In the industrialized countries, 70 per cent of female infertility is caused by venereal diseases caught from husbands and partners (Raymond).

11   Given such conditions, it is hard to understand how some researchers can continue to treat "sex work" as a predominantly and simply a freely chosen occupation/activity.

PROSTITUTION AND TRAFFICKING

12   Over the last three decades, most of the countries of the Southern Hemisphere have experienced a phenomenal growth of prostitution. For a decade, this has also been the case for the countries of the ex-USSR and Eastern Europe. Millions of women, teenagers, and children thus live in the red-light districts of the urban metropolises of their own countries or in those of the nearby countries. Two million women prostitute themselves in Thailand (Barry 122),

400,000 to 500,000 in the Philippines (CATW), 650,000 in Indonesia (CATW), about ten million in India (of whom 200,000 are Nepalese) (CATW), 142,000 in Malaysia (CATW), between 60,000 and 70,000 in Vietnam (CATW), one million in the United States, between 50,000 and 70,000 in Italy (of whom half are foreigners, most notably from Nigeria), 30,000 in the Netherlands (CATW), 200,000 in Poland (Oppermann), and between 60,000 (Guéricolas) and, more credibly, 200,000 (Oppermann) in Germany. German prostitutes sell sexual services to 1.2 million "customers" per day (Oppermann; Ackermann and Filter).

13   UNICEF estimates that a million children are brought into the sex industry every year. The industry of child prostitution exploits 400,000 children in India (UNICEF 2003), 100,000 children in the Philippines (CATW), between 200,000 and 300,000 in Thailand (Oppermann), 100,000 in Taiwan (UNICEF 2001) and in Nepal (ECPAT), 500,000 children in Latin America, and from 244,000 to 325,000 children in the United States. If one includes children in all the sex industries, the U.S. figures climb to 2.4 million (UNICEF 2001). In the People's Republic of China, there are between 200,000 and 500,000 prostituted children. In Brazil, estimates vary between 500,000 and two million (UNICEF 2001). About 35 per cent of the prostitutes of Cambodia are less than 17 years old (CATW). Certain studies estimate that during one year, the prostituted "sexual services" of one child are sold to 2,000 men (Robinson).

14   Just as the development of local prostitution is tied up with rural migration towards cities, hundreds of thousands of young women are moving internationally towards the urban areas of Japan, Western Europe, and North America. These rural migrations towards close or distant urban areas show no sign of slowing down (Santos). On the contrary, everything indicates that it is continuing and that traffic in women and children is widespread. The women and children of South and Southeast Asia constitute the most important group: 400,000 persons a year are objects of the afore-mentioned traffic. Russia and independent states from the ex-USSR constitute the second most important group (175,000 persons a year) (UUSC) followed by Latin America and the Caribbean (about 100,000 persons) and Africa (50,000 persons).

15   The number of prostitutes from the Philippines, Taiwan, Thailand, and Russia installed in Japan is estimated at 150,000 (CATW). About 50,000 Dominicans prostitute themselves abroad, notably in the Netherlands, where they were found to make up 70 per cent of the occupants of 400 Amsterdam sex-shop "windows" (Guéricolas 31). About 500,000 women of Eastern Europe and between 150,000 and 200,000 women of the countries of the ex-USSR prostitute themselves in Western Europe. Of these, it is estimated

that 150,000 are in the red-light districts of Germany—a country where 75 per cent of the prostitutes are foreign (Oppermann). About 40 per cent of Zurich's prostitutes are from a Third World country (Oppermann). About 50,000 foreigners arrive each year in the United States to supply the prostitution networks (O'Neill).

16   Every year, nearly a quarter million women and children of Southeast Asia (Burma, Yunnan province in China, Laos and Cambodia) are bought in Thailand, a transit country, for a price varying between 6,000 and 10,000 U.S. dollars (CATW). In Canada, the intermediaries pay 8,000 dollars for a young Asiatic from the Philippines, Thailand or Malaysia whom they resell for 15,000 dollars to a pimp (CATW). In Western Europe, the current price of a European woman from the former "socialist" countries is between 15,000 and 30,000 USD (CATW). On their arrival in Japan, Thai women have a debt of 25,000 USD (CATW). The bought women have to work for years to pay off "expenses" incurred by the pimps.

17   Sex tourists do not limit themselves to poor countries. Hamburg's Reeperbahn, Berlin's Kurfürstendamm and the red-light districts of Amsterdam and Rotterdam are well known destinations. In countries that have legalized prostitution or where it is tolerated, prostitution has become an important tourist draw. NGOs from these countries are actively lobbying at the European and international levels for the recognition of prostitution as simply "sex work," an occupation like any other.

18   The growth of sexual tourism over the last 30 years has entailed the "prostitutionalization" of the societies involved. In Thailand, with 5.1 million sexual tourists a year, 450,000 local customers buy sex every day (Barry 60). The now massive South East Asian sex industry began with the Vietnam war. The U.S. government stationed servicemen not only in Vietnam, but also in Thailand and the Philippines (Jeffreys), these last two countries serving as rear bases in the fight against the Vietminh. The resulting increase in local prostitution established the infrastructure necessary for the development of sexual tourism. The presence of the military created an available work force. More importantly the military presence also provided opportunities for contact with foreigners and the social construction, through pornography, of an exotic sexual image of young South Asian women. Government policies favourable to sex tourism contributed to the explosion of this industry. A decade ago there were 18,000 prostitutes in the service of the 43,000 U.S. servicemen stationed in South Korea (Barry 139). Between 1937 and 1945 the Japanese army of occupation exploited between 100,000 and 200,000 Korean women imprisoned in "comfort stations" (Barry 128). After the Japanese defeat, the Association for the Creation of Special Recreational Facilities, financed indirectly

by the U.S. government, opened a first comfort station for U.S. soldiers. At its height this association exploited 70,000 Japanese prostitutes (Barry 129). Today these numbers have swelled and include women from the Philippines, Russia, and other countries in sex industries around the U.S. bases (Moon).

THE LIBERALIZATION OF THE SEX INDUSTRY

19   In 1995 during the United Nation's Fourth World Women's Congress in Beijing the principle of "forced" prostitution appeared (UN). This was the first time the term "forced prostitution" was used in a UN document. This created a special (presumed minority) category of prostitution that could be opposed without opposing the sex industry as such. Constraint/force was identified as the problem rather than the sex trade itself. The way was opened for the normalization and legalization of the industry.

20   In 1997 at the Hague Ministerial Conference on Private International Law, when the European ministers attempted to draw up guidelines harmonizing the European Union's fight against trafficking for the purposes of sexual exploitation, their definition of trafficked women included only those women who were being trafficked against their will.

21   In 1998, the International Labour Organization (ILO) called for the economic recognition of the sex industry on the grounds that prostitutes would then benefit from workers' rights and protections and improved working conditions that it presumed would follow (Lim). In June 1999, the ILO adopted an agreement on unbearable working conditions for children, the Convention Concerning the Prohibition and Immediate Action for the Elimination of the Worst Forms of Child Labour. The agreement provides a long list of the work children do, including prostitution. This is the first time in an international text that sex work is presented as simply a job. Countries, such a[s] France, although ratifying this Convention, have underlined that their ratification in no way recognizes prostitution as work. The United Nations' Special Raporteur on Violence against women was at pains in her report to the UN Human Rights Committee in April 2000 in Geneva, to distinguish trafficked women from "clandestine migrant sex professionals."

22   All these statements and agreements tend to undermine the struggle against the growing sex industry and the system of prostitution which is at its heart, for they shift opposition from the system itself, to the use of force/constraint within the system. They aim to protect only women who have not agreed to their exploitation and can prove this, placing the burden of proof on already vulnerable women. In attempting to regulate this fast growing area

of the economy these approaches are tending to regularize it. For instance, when the European Union declares its opposition to the illegal traffic in persons, it implies that there is a "legal" traffic. Thus, as Marie-Victoire Louis (131) has pointed out, such initiatives transform the struggle against the commodification of women and girls into its legitimization.

CONCLUSION

23 Over 30 years, we have seen an extremely profitable "sexualization" of many societies based on social domination. We have witnessed the industrialization of prostitution, of the traffic in women and children, of pornography, and of sexual tourism. This once marginal market is an increasingly central aspect of current capitalist globalization. Sex multinationals have become independent economic forces (Barry) quoted on the stock exchange (5), sexual exploitation is more and more considered to be an entertainment industry (Oppermann), and prostitution a legitimate job (Kempadoo; Dorais).

24   The increasing size and centrality of the global sex industry helps explain why so many groups and agencies are adopting normalizing regulatory approaches in their attempts to address its harms. However, this strategy is deeply flawed. The rapidly expanding international sex market exploits above all women and children, especially members of marginal and minority groups in the Third World and in the former "socialist" countries. This "leisure industry" is based on the systematic violation of human rights, for it requires a market in commodified human beings and the complicity of pimps and clients who are prepared to buy and sell women and children.

25   The commodification at the heart of the growing sex industry is only one among many varied instances of the commodification of all of life which is a defining characterization of current neo-liberalism. Patents are now issued on genetic life forms (including human genomes) and all forms of traditional knowledge (Shiva 1997, 2000). Water is being privatized (Barlow). In the name of environmental protection and sustainable development, markets are being created for trade in CO_2 and emissions credits (the right to pollute) (Kyoto Protocol). The apparent "normalcy" of trade in human beings in this period has led to misguided regulatory approaches in some quarters. Yet this very "normalcy" is what makes refusal of the sex industry, as such, so essential. In this context, resisting or struggling against the commodification of women and children in the sex industry becomes a central element in the struggle against capitalist globalization. Anything less is complicity.

Notes

1. According to Chulalungkborn Political Economy Center at the University of Thailand, in 1993 worldwide the sex industry generated incomes of between 20 and 23 billion USD (ECPAT Australia 29). Other estimates put incomes from the legal sex industry at 52 billion dollars (Leidholdt).

2. Kathleen Barry reports that as a result of globalization, complete fishing villages in the Philippines and Thailand have been transformed into service providers (126).

3. For example, the majority of New Zealand's prostitutes are from Asia (CATW).

4. These data confirm the findings of my own research with escort dancers (Poulin 1994).

5. The most important bordello in Melbourne, Australia, "The Daily Planet," is now quoted on the stock exchange (Jeffreys 185).

References

Ackermann L. and C. Filter. *Die Frau nach Katalog.* Freiburg: Herder Verlag, 1994.

Barlow, M. *Blue Gold: The Battle Against the Corporate Theft of the World's Water.* Toronto: Stoddart, 2002.

Barry, Kathleen. *The Prostitution of Sexuality.* New York: New York University Press, 1995.

Bishop, R. and L. Robinson. *Night Market. Sexual Cultures and the Thai Economic Miracle.* New York, Routledge, 1998.

Chaleil, Max. *Prostitution. Le désir mystifié.* Paris: Parangon, 2002.

Coalition Against Trafficking in Women (CATW). *Factbook on Global Sexual Exploitation.* Manila: CATW, 2001. [cited March 2, 2003] Available online: http://catwinternational .org/fb/.

Convention Concerning the Prohibition and Immediate Action for the Elimination of the Worst Forms of Child Labour (ILO No. 182), 38 I.L.M. 1207 (1999), entered into force Nov. 19, 2000.

Dorais, Michel. *Travailleurs du sexe.* Montréal: VLB, 2003.

End Child Prostitution, Child Pornography, and Trafficking of Children for Sexual Purposes (ECPAT) Australia. *ECPAT Development Manual.* Melbourne: ECPAT, 1994.

Giobbe E. "Juvenile Prostitution: Process of Recruitment." *Child Trauma I: Issues and Research.* New York, Garaland Publishing, 1992.

Guéricolas, Pascale. "Géographie de l'inacceptable", *Gazette des femmes* 22(1) (mai–juin 2000): 27–31.

Hechler, David. *Child Sex Tourism.* [online] New York: Don't buy Thai. 1995. [cited May 6, 2001] Online: ftp://members.aol.com/hechler/tourism.html.

Hughes, Donna M. "Rôle des agences matrimoniales dans la traite des femmes". *L'impact de l'utilisation des nouvelles technologies de communication et d'information sur la traite des êtres humains aux fins d'exploitation sexuelle.* Bruxelles: Conseil de l'Europe, 2001. 4–16.

Jeffreys, Sheila. "Globalizing Sexual Exploitation: Sex Tourism and the Traffic in Women." *Leisure Studies* 18 (3) (July 1999): 179–186.

Kempadoo K and J. Doezema. *Global Sex Workers.* New York: Routledge, 1998.

Kyoto Protocol. United Nations Framework Convention on Climate Change. Online: http://unfccc.int/resource/convkp/kpeng.html.

Leidholdt, Dorchen. *Position Paper for the Coalition Against Trafficking in Women.* Eds. Donna M. Hughes and Claire M. Roche. Kingston, Rhode Island: CATW 2001. [cited

September 12, 2002]. Online: http://www.uri.edulartsci/wms/hugues/catw/posit2.htm.

Lim, L. L. *The Sex Sector. The Economic and Social Bases of Prostitution in Southeast Asia.* Geneva: ILO, 1998.

Louis, Marie-Victoire. "Pour construire l'abolitionnisme du XXIe siècle." *Cahiers marxistes* 216 (juin–juillet 2000): 123–151.

Mechtild, M. *Tourisme, prostitution, sida.* Paris/Genève: Harmattan/Cetim, 1992.

Moon, K. *Sex Among Allies: Military Prostitution in U.S.-Korea Relations.* New York: Columbia University Press, 1997.

Oppermann M. "Introduction." *Sex Tourism and Prostitution: Aspects of Leisure, Recreation, and Work.* Ed. M. Oppermann. New York, Cognizant Communication Corporation, 1998. 1–19.

Poulin, Richard. *La violence pornographique, industrie du fantasme et réalités.* Second edition. Yens-sur-Morges: Cabédita, 2000.

Poulin, Richard. *Le sexe spectacle, consommation, main-d'œuvre et pornographie.* Hull/Ottawa: Vents d'Ouest/Vermillion, 1994.

Raymond, Janice. *Health Effects of Prostitution.* Kingston: University of Rhode Island, 1999. [cited March 12, 2001] Online: http://www.uri.edu/artsci/wms/Hugues/mhvhealth.htm.

Report of the Special Raporteur on Violence Against Women. Intergration of the Human Rights of Women and the Gender Perspective: Violence Against Women. Commission on Human Rights, 56th Session. E/CN.4/2000/68: 29 February 2000.

Robinson, L. N. *The Globalization of Female Child Prostitution.* [online] Bloomington: Indiana University, 1998. [cited March 3, 2001] Online: http://www.law.indiana.Edu1glsj/vol5/no1/robinson.html.

Santos, Aida F. *Globalization, Human Rights and Sexual Exploitation.* University of Rhode Island, 1999. [cited March 3, 2001] Online: http://www.uri.edu/artsci/wms/hugues/mhvglo.htm.

Satterfield, S. B. 1981. "Clinical Aspects of Juvenile Prostitution." *Medical Aspects of Human Sexuality.* 15 (9) (1981): 126.

Shiva, V. *Biopiracy: The Plunder of Nature and Knowledge.* Boston, MA: South End Press, 1997.

Shiva, V. *Stolen Harvest: The Hijacking of the Global Food Supply.* Cambridge, MA: South End Press, 2000.

Silbert, M. and A. M. Pines. "Entrance in to Prostitution." *Youth and Society* 13 (4) (1982): 471–500.

Silbert M and A. M. Pines. 1981. "Occupational Hazards of Street Prostitutes." *Criminal Justice Behaviour* 195 (1981): 395.

Strudevant, S. P. and B. Stolzfus. Eds. *Let the Good Times Roll. Prostitution and the U.S. Military in Asia.* New York: The New Press, 1992.

Truong, T. D. *Sex, Money and Morality: Prostitution and Tourism in Southeast Asia.* London: Zed Books, 1990.

United Nations (UN). *Report of the Fourth World Conference on Women.* Beijing 4–15 September 1995. Conf.177/20, 113b.

UNICEF. *Child Trafficking Statistics.* New York: UNICEF, 2003. [cited February 27, 2003] Online: http://www.unicef.org/programme/cprotection/focus/trafficking/stats.htm.

UNICEF. *L'Unicef demande l'élimination de l'exploitation sexuelle des enfants à des fins commerciales.* New York: UNICEF, 2001. [cited May 13, 2002] Online: http://www.unicef.org/french/newsline/pr/2001/01pr97fr.htm.

UUSC. *The Modern International Slave Trade*. Cambridge, MA: UUSC, 2001. [cited May 14, 2001] Online: http://www.uusc.org/programs/index_frames.html?straffic2.html.

O'Neill Richard, Amy. *International Trafficking in Women to the United States: To Contemporary Manifestation of Slavery and Organized Crime*. DCI: Center for the Study of Intelligence, 1999. Véran, Sylvie. 2000. "Cambodge. Vendua à 9 ans, prostituée, séropositive", *Nouvel Observateur*, 3 au 10 août: 10–11.

For Class Discussion

1. In this scholarly article, sociologist Richard Poulin presents a politically leftist economic view of the global sex trafficking of women and children. What is the main thesis of this article and what are the important subclaims and reasons?

2. Poulin relies heavily on quantitative data. How effective is his use of numerical evidence in supporting his claim?

3. Poulin's diction is suited to his field, sociology, and to his academic audience. Using the Glossary in this text, a dictionary, and context, write your own definition of these terms: "capitalist globalization," "commodification of human beings," "industrialization of the sex industry," "development strategy," "structural adjustment," "economic liberalization," "neo-liberalism," and any other important terms you find. How are the concepts represented by these terms central to Poulin's argument? How would you translate these ideas for a general audience? How would you summarize this article in your own words?

4. What alternative views of sex trafficking is Poulin opposing? In other words, with whom does he disagree and how does he challenge and rebut his opposition's views?

5. How rhetorically effective is Poulin's conclusion in this argument?

6. How persuasive did you find Poulin's stand on the sex trade and trafficking of women and children and why?   ∎

Law Enforcement Poster on Sex Trafficking

HumanTrafficking.com

This poster appears on the HumanTrafficking.com Web site under the Anti-Trafficking Toolkits. The HumanTrafficking.com database describes itself as "your one-stop gateway to research and training to combat modern-day slavery, whether you are a professional, a researcher, or a concerned community member" (home page, www.humantrafficking.com/) and "the largest online collection of resources on human trafficking" (Anti-Trafficking

Toolkits link). The Department of Health and Human Services has created this poster for law enforcement as part of its campaign against trafficking.

Even if you had little knowledge of the human trafficking issue and the main problems it poses, what ideas could you glean from this poster?

FIGURE 6.4   Law Enforcement Poster on Sex Trafficking

For Class Discussion

1. One problem in fighting human trafficking is identifying the victims. A number of campaigns are directed at equipping social servants such as law enforcement officers and medical personnel to identify victims. What features of this poster indicate its main target audience?

2. What assumptions is this poster addressing and arguing against?

3. After studying the image, the text, the use of type, and the layout of this poster, reconstruct the thinking of its creators. What creative choices did they make and why?

4. The "Question to Ponder" at the beginning of this chapter mentions the state of Illinois' recent bill to equip "local social service organizations, law enforcement and health care professionals" to fight human trafficking and help victims. If you were part of a design team assigned to create a comparable poster for your state for health care professionals, what image, text, and layout would you choose for your poster and why? ∎

CHAPTER QUESTIONS FOR REFLECTION AND DISCUSSION

1. According to this chapter's readings, what obstacles and problems do trafficked victims face when they try to break free from the people and situations that are controlling them?

2. Where do David Feingold, Nicholas Kristof, Global Exchange, Joanna Busza and her coauthors, and the Children's Forum differ in their claims about child labor and in their assumptions, reasons, and use of evidence? Where do the biggest disagreements lie?

3. Where do David Feingold, the *Independent*, Kate Butcher, the International Organization for Migration, Joanna Busza and her coauthors, and Richard Poulin differ in their claims about sex trafficking and in their assumptions, reasons, interpretation of facts, and use of evidence? What are the major disagreements?

4. What do this chapter's readings suggest are the main economic and legal issues related to forced child labor and the trafficking of women and children for sexual exploitation?

5. Which readings do each of the visual arguments in this chapter support?

6. The human rights violations discussed in this chapter suggest many questions for further investigation. Choose one of the questions below and do some research to help you formulate an informed answer.

    A. Many policymakers discourage the boycotting of companies and products as a way to combat human rights violations; however, consumer power was successful in the Rugmark Campaign in improving the treatment of child workers in the rug and carpet industry in India. How did this campaign achieve its success?

B. A number of NGOs have decided to involve children in their search for ways to stop the exploitation of children. Choose one of the following organizations and examine its Web site. What are some of the ways that this organization is including children and working to help them?

Global Movement for Children (www.unicef.org/gmfc/)
Child Workers of Asia (CWA) (www.cwa.tnet.co.th/)
Save the Children (www.savethechildren.net/)
South Asian Coalition on Child Servitude (Bachpan Bachao Andolan) (www.bbasaccs.org/)

C. While the United Nations is a leader in working for human rights, in some cases peacekeeping troops have taken advantage of women and children refugees in war-torn regions. Research the "sex for food" problems and the cases of brutality in Congo, Sudan, or another African country. How do these situations complicate the global community's responsibility to protect the human rights of women and children?

D. Research Nicholas Kristof's numerous columns about the sex trade written for the *New York Times* throughout 2003 and 2005. Summarize Kristof's main views. Prepare to share with your class both his main points and some of his most moving emotional appeals.

E. Children are being abducted and forced to be camel jockeys, soldiers, and domestic and agricultural workers. Research one of these abusive practices and the efforts to stop them. What strategies offer the most hope?

7. What connections do you see among free trade, immigration, and the trafficking of women and children? You might consult Chapters 2 and 3.

WRITING ASSIGNMENTS

Brief Writing Assignments

1. Write for twenty minutes informally about what surprised, shocked, or disturbed you the most about the trafficking of women and children and which reading had the most impact on you.

2. After considering the readings in this chapter, use one of the following prompts to begin sorting out your own thinking on the views of human rights you encountered in this chapter:

A. Before reading I thought _____, but now I think _____.

B. Although these readings, or one specific reading, have persuaded me that _____, I still have doubts about _____.

C. After reading these articles (fill in titles), I have major questions about _____.

3. In your own words, answer one of the following questions:

A. What is the relationship between the international flesh trade and free trade?

B. How is globalization affecting human trafficking?

C. What can consumers in rich nations do to end human rights violations such as forced child labor?

4. Which article do you think presents the strongest argument and why?

Writing Projects

1. Write an analysis and synthesis essay in which you analyze two readings from this chapter and then explain how these pieces have changed or shaped your view of the trafficking of women and children. The arguments in this chapter take different approaches to the trafficking of women and children, to their interpretation of the problem, and to the solutions they propose. Choose one of the following pairs of authors and map out their points of agreement and disagreement. Consider their target audiences, their assumptions and values, their interpretation of the problem, their proposed solutions, and the points that each overlooks or ignores. In your synthesis section of your paper, show how both authors have contributed to your informed view.

   - David Feingold and John Miller or Richard Poulin
   - Kate Butcher and Richard Poulin
   - The *Independent* and Kate Butcher
   - Global Exchange and Nicholas Kristof
   - David Feingold and LaShawn R. Jefferson
   - Joanna Busza, Sarah Castle, and Aisse Diarra and Richard Poulin
   - Nicholas Kristof and the Children's Forum

2. Suppose a friend said to you, "Okay, I am sickened by the horrible treatment of women and children in Russia, Cambodia, and Bosnia, and I hate the idea of people being bought and sold, but I don't see how the sex trade in Bosnia or children's debt bondage in Southeast Asia affects me or how I could influence these issues." Use ideas and information from the readings in this chapter to write a short, specific argumentative letter to your friend to change his/her view of the issue. Avoid vague generalizations, and make your letter as focused and persuasive as you can.

3. Investigate the status of antitrafficking legislation and programs in your state and determine if trafficking is a state crime and if your state has an

antitrafficking task force. What social services resources are available to help trafficking victims? You might also consult the brochure produced by the U.S. Department of State Bureau for International Narcotics and Law Enforcement entitled "Be Smart, Be Safe . . .," found at the www .HumanTrafficking.com site, and the preparation of other states. Consider your state's geographical location, borders, ports, and waterways; main sources of revenue such as agriculture; and major cities. Based on your fieldwork and research, write a letter to your state legislator proposing a bill to create antitrafficking resources for your state or to implement ideas that have been successful in other states and communities.

4. Identify a major controversy within the human trafficking issue such as (a) which methods of combating human trafficking within Eastern Europe or Southeast Asia are the most promising; (b) how effective economic sanctions are in motivating countries to fight human trafficking; or (c) whether legalizing prostitution helps or hinders NGOs' and governments' fight against sex trafficking. Based on your reading and thinking about this issue, formulate a claim that articulates your position, and construct an argument developing this claim. Write your argument for an uninformed, neutral audience of your peers.

5. Sometimes when issues are as complex as human trafficking, we become overwhelmed and discouraged. However, at that point, we need to think about activists such as Don Cesare Lo Deserto and his home for rescued victims of the sex trade in Italy; Mara Radovanovic of the Lara organization in Bosnia; politician Linda Smith and Shared Hope, her organization to help women and children; Ambassador John Miller and the antitrafficking legislation he has sponsored; and Brazilian mother Pureza Lopes Loyola and her courageous search for her trafficked son. Investigate and research one of these activists or one you discover on your own, and write a short report explaining what you found impressive and inspirational about this person's contribution to the fight against trafficking violations of human rights.

6. Unless people pressure their governments to call for stricter laws and more enforcement of laws to punish traffickers, human trafficking will continue to grow. A number of Web sites of advocacy groups and NGOs are committed to educating the public about the horrors of the trafficking of women and children and enlisting support. Among some of the most active ones are these:

Human Rights Watch (www.hrw.org)
Anti-Slavery International (www.antislavery.org)
Save the Children (www.savethechildren.org)
The Protection Project (www.protectionproject.org)
Global Movement for Children (www.unicef.org/gmfc/)
United Nations Children's Fund (UNICEF) (www.unicef.org)

Using three or four of the following criteria or some you develop on your own, write an evaluation argument about the effectiveness of the public appeal of the Web site of one of these organizations:

A. Functional and attractive layout and design of the site

B. Clear explanation of the problem

C. Strong appeal to readers' emotions, sympathies, and values

D. Good credibility or currency of the information presented

E. Clear requests and directives indicating what the organization wants readers to do

Argue that this organization's site does or does not measure up to your criteria. In your evaluation argument, show why you would or would not recommend this site to someone who is seeking to understand trafficking of women and children.

7. Write a letter to your U.S. representative or senator arguing that the United States (a) should take a tougher stand on the trafficking of women and children; (b) should focus more on helping countries tackle the root causes of human trafficking; (c) should allocate more money to provide education in developing countries; or (d) should adopt some other proposal of your choice to combat this new slavery. Make your letter clear, focused, and specific, and show that you are knowledgeable about this issue by accurately citing any sources that you use. As an alternative, you might write a policy proposal intended to motivate voters in your state to support your perspective on combating human trafficking.

Environmental Resources and Rights

Global Conflicts Over Water and Climate Change

QUESTION TO PONDER

You have recently read an article that claimed that the world spends around thirty billion dollars a year on bottled water and that many of these consumers reside in developed countries that have good, safe tap water. Furthermore, you've heard that bottling water wastes water, energy, and plastic and that bottled water is not necessarily more pure than tap water. You are wondering if you and your friends should promote the use of tap water over bottled water and spend your money instead on environmental causes or on helping global organizations provide safe water in developing countries.*

CONTEXT FOR A NETWORK OF ISSUES

The global community is wrestling with conflicting views of the earth's natural resources. These are classified as *renewable resources*, which includes renewable energy (solar, wind, and geothermal power), and *nonrenewable resources* such as minerals and fossil fuels (coal, oil, and natural gas). Whereas some corporations envision the earth as an expansive space with vast, lucrative resources to be tapped and marketed, other groups see the earth as our life-support system that has finite resources that need careful

---

*Tom Standage argues for this course of action in his article "Bad to the Last Drop," *New York Times*, August 1, 2005.

management. Recently, scientists have been wondering whether some renewable resources—trees, fertile soil, and water—are being depleted or contaminated at a rate that exceeds their replenishment and have been warning that the world's population growth over the next fifty years will only increase this threat to the environment. In addition, greenhouse gas emissions and changes in climate may very well be affecting the availability of resources.

Two concepts that regularly appear in controversies over natural resources, human dependence on the environment, and global interdependence are "sustainable development" and "the commons." In 1987, the World Commission on Environment and Development (often called the "Brundtland Commission" after its chairwoman Gro Harlem Brundtland) articulated this now widely accepted definition of "sustainable development" as "development that meets the needs of the present without compromising the ability of future generations to meet their own needs."* The concept of "the commons" asks people to think of the earth's resources as belonging equally to all nations and peoples of the world. The commons include "the air we breathe, the freshwater we drink, the oceans and the diverse wildlife and plant biodiversity of the world, . . . and among indigenous peoples, communal lands that have been worked cooperatively for thousands of years."† Clearly, the ideas of sharing environmental resources with future generations and with all peoples directly oppose the practices of environmental overuse and competition.

Freshwater is a prime example of a finite natural resource that is subject to global competition. The award-winning musical *Urinetown* depicts a fictional city where one company owns the water system and manipulates accessibility and cost according to its own whims. The poor must pay a fee to use the restrooms, and it is illegal *not* to use the facilities. The penalty for breaking the law is banishment to Urinetown, a death sentence. Although *Urinetown* is a melodramatic postmodern self-parody, its main conflict between "the people" and a powerful corporation who controls the water imitates real-world conflicts over water. For example, recently in Cochabamba, Bolivia, hundreds of thousands of poor people protested against a group of corporations (among them, the Bechtel Corporation) that controlled the city's water distribution system. Rallying behind the slogans "Water is God's gift and not merchandise" and "Water is life," the Citizen Alliance compelled the government to regain control of the water system. The Bolivian crisis and the musical raise serious environmental, political, and economic questions about the scarcity of usable water; the privatizing of water

---

*1987: Brundtland Report," http://www.are.admin.ch/are/en/nachhaltig/definition/index.html.

†The International Forum on Globalization, *Alternatives to Economic Globalization: A Better World Is Possible* (San Francisco: Berrett-Koehler Publishers, Inc., 2002), 81.

supplies; the money and technology required to manage water systems; and the consequences of corporate control of environmental resources.

What is the global status of water? The following facts give some idea of global problems with water:

Water: A Limited Resource

- 97.5 percent of earth's water is saltwater and undrinkable.
- Polar snow and ice hold most of the freshwater.
- Less than 1 percent of freshwater is usable, amounting to only 0.01 percent of the earth's total water.
- 70 percent of water goes to agricultural use; 22 percent to industrial use; 8 percent to domestic use.*
- "Across the world, 1.1 billion people have no access to clean drinking water. More than 2.6 billion people lack basic sanitation."
- "Each year, diseases related to inadequate water and sanitation kill between 2 and 5 million people and cause an estimated 80 percent of all sicknesses in the developing world."[†]
- Water is wasted through misuse, inefficiency, leakage, evaporation, and allocation of pure water to tasks that don't need it.
- It is projected that in twenty years, the demand for water will increase by 50 percent and two-thirds of the world population will be water-stressed.[‡]

Clearly, water is a precious global resource that requires efficient, equitable management worldwide.

Present and future equitable treatment of the environment is also at issue in the global controversies over atmospheric pollution and climate change. Climate change is affecting rainfall patterns, the intensity and frequency of storms, and the longevity of droughts. Many scientists think that pollution from greenhouse gases (mostly carbon dioxide caused by the burning of fossil fuels) that trap the earth's heat like a greenhouse is playing a role in raising average surface temperatures, and that changes in temperatures are causing changes in the earth's climate. According to scientists, "[c]arbon emissions from burning fossil fuel now stand at 6.5 billion tons a year (four times 1950 levels), resulting in atmospheric carbon dioxide concentrations 33 percent greater than pre-industrial levels."[§] Furthermore,

---

*"Water the Facts," *New Internationalist*, March 2003.
[†]"I Thirst," Water Advocates Advertisement, *New York Times*, March 22, 2005.
[‡]Richard Steiner, "The Real Clear and Present Danger," *Seattle Post-Intelligencer*, May 30, 2004.
[§]Ibid.

countries have unequally contributed to this atmospheric pollution: each American emits about 5.99 tons of carbon dioxide a year compared with 0.31 ton emitted by each resident of India and 0.05 ton by each Bangladeshi.* Most climatologists believe that the growing population and industrialization of third world countries will magnify problems with greenhouse gases and their effect on the earth's atmosphere and climate.

This chapter explores water scarcity and climate change as global environmental problems.

STAKES AND STAKEHOLDERS

Because all humans need fresh air, safe water, and predictable weather, we are all prime stakeholders in global environmental issues, along with governments and corporations, who often control citizens/consumers' access to natural resources, and scientists, who analyze environmental conditions and make predictions and recommendations about human impacts. These and other stakeholders are debating issues related to the following key questions.

What Are Some of the World's Major Problems with Environmental Resources? As stakeholders battle over defining the problems, many scientists are now saying that the amount of environmental resources humans consume and the damage to the earth we do (our "ecological footprint") is 20 percent over Earth's carrying capacity; we are overusing the earth's resources at too great a rate. Conservation specialist Richard Steiner, a professor at the University of Alaska–Fairbanks, describes this overuse in these terms:

> Conspicuous consumption has become a homogenizing force across the developed world. Just since 1950, we have consumed more goods and services than all previous generations combined. The consumption of energy, steel and timber more than doubled; fossil fuel use and car ownership increased four-fold; meat production and fish catch increased five-fold; paper use increased six-fold, and air travel increased 100-fold.†

Furthermore, ecologists point out that about 20 percent of the world's population, those from developed countries, consume between 70 and 80 percent of the planet's resources, a level of use that cannot continue.‡ Considering the excessive consumption of developed countries, environmentalists and social justice activists are now worried about the increasing drain on environmental resources as giants China and India as well as third world

---

*Maria Woolf and Colin Brown, "Beckett Exposes G8 Rift on Global Warming" and "Global Warming: The US Contribution in Figures," *Independent,* June 13, 2005.
†"The Real and Clear Present Danger," *Seattle Post-Intelligencer,* March 30, 2004.
‡Thomas Pugh and Erik Assadourian, "What Is Sustainability, Anyway?" *World-Watch,* September–October, 2003, 17.

countries adopt the developmental pattern of Europe and the United States in their effort to industrialize and advance economically. Studies have projected that if people in the developing world were to take on the American lifestyle, the world would need the resources of five or six Earths to maintain that level of consumption. In contrast, many political leaders, policy-makers, economists, and businesses acknowledge the increasing pressures on the environment caused by population growth and the economic development of third world countries, but they disagree about the severity and urgency of the problem.

Perhaps the fiercest battles raging over environmental issues involve global warming and climate change. Stakeholders disagree about the extent and causes of global warming. Are natural causes creating global warming or are human-produced high emissions of carbon dioxide from the burning of fossil fuels (for industry, agriculture, energy, and cars) a major contributor to rising temperatures on Earth? Or are both natural and human causes involved? The reputable Intergovernmental Panel on Climate Change* thinks of global warming in terms of climate change and is focusing on critical temperature changes such as those that cause the warming of the oceans and the melting of the polar ice caps. These scientists cite erratic weather, more intense storms, earlier blooming of plants, changes in animals' seasonal ranges, and cooling of the Northern Hemisphere as signs of climate change. They also speak in terms of the complex, cumulative interplay among many factors (such as ocean currents, ocean warming, snowfall, etc.) and regard climate change as not fully understood or calculable. For many, climate change is a human rights and social justice issue because rising sea levels and coastal flooding as well as changes in rainfall and violent storms hit hardest the most vulnerable, climate-dependent people—the poor.

In opposition, a small number of scientists, the fossil fuel industry, some corporate leaders, some American political leaders, especially in the Bush administration, and some outspoken public figures like novelist Michael Crichton (in his recent novel on global warming and ecoterrorism, *State of Fear* [2004]), maintain that human influence on the global climate is insignificant, that we are seeing mostly natural climate fluctuations and changes, and that computer climate models are inaccurate.

Questions about environmental problems and climate change also involve conflicts among scientists, politics, and the way the media represent environmental issues to the public. Both environmentalists and global

---

*The Intergovernmental Panel on Climate Change, established in 1988 by the World Meteorological Organization (WMO) and the United Nations Environment Programme (UNEP), focuses on evaluating "scientific, technical and socio-economic information relevant for the understanding of climate change, its potential impacts and options for adaptation and mitigation." The IPCC issues regular reports (1990, 1995, 2001, and 2007) to provide "an assessment of the state of knowledge on climate change" (www.ipcc.ch/about/about.htm).

warming skeptics accuse the other side of violating principles of science, of oversimplifying causes and effects, and of pursuing a political agenda; both groups claim the media are biased. Arguments about what science can deliver in the way of certainty and predictions are entangled with scientists' government funding and affiliations with the fossil fuel industry and environmental organizations.

As Third World Countries Develop and the Global Population Increases, How Can Environmental Resources Be Conserved and Fairly and Wisely Managed? Many nongovernmental organizations (NGOs), governments, indigenous peoples, and activist groups call for respect for the environmental commons and an environmental ethic of sustainable development. They advocate immediate changes in consumption patterns and the adoption of alternative clean energy sources, such as wind and solar power and hybrid and hydrogen-fueled cars. These stakeholders want voluntary limits on the production of greenhouse gases through international controls like the Kyoto Protocol. This global agreement, which went into effect in February 2005 and has been ratified by 153 countries as of summer 2005, compels thirty-five developed nations, by 2008–2012, to reduce their greenhouse gas emissions by 5.2 percent compared to 1990. Some people see the Kyoto Protocol as more symbolic than instrumental and argue for much more radical changes and reductions in emissions, beyond 50 percent and even 70 percent over the next few years in order to return to preindustrial levels of greenhouse gas emissions.

In contrast, some economists, corporate leaders, and politicians claim that major shifts in energy use would be too economically disruptive and damaging. Contending that climate changes are natural and cyclical over millennia and that global warming is not human-induced, these people argue that reducing greenhouse gas emissions, especially as called for by the Kyoto Protocol's proposal, will have no positive impact on the earth's atmosphere and will be excessively costly to industries, consumers, and workers.*

What Is the Role of Economics and the Market in Managing Environmental Resources? Many environmental and anticorporate advocates argue that multinational corporations' pursuit of short-term profits leads to the exploitation of natural resources with little concern for the long-term good of the environment or for the lives of the local people most affected by these corporations' use of resources. For example, advocates maintain that when water is privatized, the public loses access to information about its quality. Social justice advocates emphasize that free trade agreements and institutions

---

*S. Fred Singer, atmospheric physicist and president of the Science and Environmental Policy Project, is a strong spokesperson for this view.

like the World Trade Organization, the World Bank, and the International Monetary Fund grant corporations the freedom to act without accountability, promote the privatization of resources, and enable corporations to override national governments' efforts to protect resources. The biggest water corporations, Vivendi Environment and Suez-Lyonnaise des Eaux, hold water interests in 120 countries. Vandana Shiva, an Indian physicist and environmental and political activist, claims that big corporations in India can easily take advantage of the scarcity of environmental resources:

> Privatization will aggravate the water crisis, because . . . water markets will take the water from the poor to the rich, from impoverished rural areas to affluent urban enclaves. It will also lead to overexploitation of water, because when access to water is determined by the market and not by limits of renewability, the water cycle will be systematically violated and the water crisis will deepen. Local community management is a precondition for both consumption and equitable use.*

Arguing that these resources are the commons belonging to everyone, environmental advocates insist that governments should regulate and protect these resources for the public interest. Many social justice activists believe that access to safe water should be declared a human right so that water cannot be sold for profit.

In contrast, many corporate leaders and economists think that *more* market involvement in natural resources will foster good stewardship. They claim that government subsidies encourage waste and that the task of managing environmental resources is so huge and expensive that only capital-rich companies can take on the job. Richard L. Sandor, chairman and CEO of Chicago Climate Exchange, which enables companies to trade, sell, or buy credits in carbon dioxide emissions, explains his view of markets:

> Nobody owns the atmosphere, so nobody takes account. Respectfully treating it as the limited resource it really is requires limiting consumption, and instituting a process for treating it responsibly. The zero price now being charged for its use means there is no direct reward for those who might . . . [try to conserve]. Private capital is not being mobilized. The market is missing.[†]

In the absence of a clear governmental policy for environmental protection, some businesses have decided that embracing limits on their own is shrewd. Anticipating the need to meet European Union emissions standards, companies such as Dupont, IBM, General Electric, United Technologies, Baxter International, and International Paper are embracing the Kyoto restrictions on

---

*Vandana Shiva, "World Bank, WTO, and Corporate Control over Water," *International Socialist Review* (August–September 2001).

[†]Richard L. Sandor. "Climate and Action: Trading Gases," *Our Planet Magazine,* 9.6 (November 1998), http://www.ourplanet.com/imgversn/96/sandor.html.

their own. Some American companies, along with EU and Chinese companies, are using these restrictions to spur innovation with low-carbon technologies and clean energy. Policymakers and analysts point to Brazil as an example of how fruitful collaboration between government and the market can help the environment *and* the economy. After the oil crisis in the 1970s, the Brazilian government financially encouraged its new ethanol industry (ethanol is a clean burning fuel consisting of alcohol from sugarcane), which has been thriving since the 1980s.

What International Organizations Should Regulate Conflicts Between Nations Over Natural Resources and Encourage Global Cooperation in Establishing Sustainable Practices? In the 1970s, when scientists began to understand that most environmental problems are global and interrelated (for example, weather patterns, rainfall, and growing seasons), the need for global institutions to tackle these problems became apparent. Conflicts over resources can be politically destabilizing, weakening poor countries and making them vulnerable to terrorists and dangerous political forces; indeed, environmental problems are security problems requiring global solutions. Still, people disagree about how to measure sustainability and what goals and timetables to establish.

Nations are also realizing that dependence on foreign countries for natural resources can lead to political instability. To prevent takeover by multinational companies and to ensure that domestic businesses stay competitive with foreign businesses, many analysts, policymakers, and businesses are calling for strong, clear national water and energy policies.

In particular, many developing nations are turning to the United Nations and its various programs and agencies to help them protect the environmental rights of their people. By designating water a human right, the United Nations could further global cooperation and help ward off water wars. Because approximately 260 rivers flow through two or more countries and numerous bodies of water are bounded by multiple countries, intergovernmental organizations are needed to regulate the rights to and use of this water. On the global warming issue, advocates of global cooperation such as Europe and Japan are pleased that industrialized nations have accepted the Kyoto Protocol's legal restraint and have established a mutually beneficial exchange, the first "international trading system allowing countries to earn credits toward their treaty targets by investing in emissions cleanups outside their borders."* Some people are arguing that countries should have legal recourse when they suffer from global warming damages and water exploitation. For example, developing countries should be able to seek reparations from multinationals in world courts; perhaps the International Court of Justice should mandate that rich polluting countries pay poorer developing countries for damages to their environment.

---

*Larry Rohter and Andrew C. Revkin. "Cheers, and Concern, for New Climate Pact," *New York Times*, December 13, 2004.

Finally, many NGOs and policymakers are calling for global strategies for water conservation, reclamation, and efficiency, and for equitable, sustainable environmental practices to prepare for the world's population growth.

What Can Technology Contribute to Encouraging Sustainability and to Solving Problems with Environmental Resources? Some more radical ecologists (deep ecologists) would argue that humans have created environmental problems by interfering with nature and that more technology represents more interference. Some ecofeminists like Vandana Shiva argue that we must consider power relationships: Who owns the technology? Who decides how it will be used? Will it harm nature? Many environmentalists would say that wise investment in technology—for example, to find renewable energy alternatives—should supplement a drastic reprogramming of our habits. Some environmentalists call for completely new designs for energy systems, cars, insulation, lighting, household appliances, and water systems. Many corporate leaders believe in technology and have embraced environmental problems as incentives and business opportunities. They cite the improvement in car fuel economy from 1977–1985, the advance in energy-efficient refrigerators and air conditioners, and the current work with desalination of water. And on the far protechnology extreme, some people assume that technology will be able to solve our environmental problems, remedy all our mistakes, and renew the environment; therefore, they see no need for new habits of consumption or energy use.

The three sections that follow—"Student Voice" "International Voices," and "Global Hot Spot"—take you deeper into the network of environmental issues connected to water resources and climate change that we as global citizens need to address.

 ## STUDENT VOICE: EXPERIENCING WATER SCARCITY

For some Americans like Malia Burns-Rozycki, experiencing the great need for water elsewhere in the world—in this case, in rural Benin, West Africa—has led to a deeper awareness of how Americans take water for granted.

Malia Burns-Rozycki

The dash board read 43 degrees Centigrade. Reaching for my second bottle of water I calculated the temperature to be around 110 Fahrenheit. It was almost unbearable, even inside the air-conditioned SUV. It was during times like these that I questioned what I was doing in Benin, West Africa. Why hadn't I found an internship in Washington DC like all my other friends? And yet here I was, camera in hand, bumping over winding dirt roads, miles from the nearest flushing toilet.

Stepping out of the car, I was blasted in the face by the heat. The sun seared the barren landscape, preventing grass from growing. A few brave trees seemed to stand in defiance of the elements saying "look at me, I can survive the heat." I was amazed at how flat and monochromatic everything was. Even the huts in the village were made out of red dirt, making them disappear into the horizon.

Fifty people were gazing intently at a large piece of machinery. I cannot imagine what this kind of technology would have looked like to a community where not one person owns a car, women walk miles to sell their goods at market, and few speak the national language. For a brief moment all villagers had put down their work to witness this momentous event, the drilling of a community well.

The project coordinator explained to me that the nearest well was in the next village, more than two hours on foot, I estimated. Each morning women from the village set out with large metal bowls on their heads, returning in time to prepare the morning meal. Four hours a day is spent on this commute. Village life is not easy. Indicators can be seen everywhere, on the weathered faces, in the tired eyes, the muscular arms. A little girl who barely reached my hip carried an infant on her back and twigs on her head, proving that literally everyone who was capable, worked.

I wondered how Catholic Relief Services even found this village, when so many of these northern communities need water. In Benin only 23% of the population has access to improved sanitation and only 63% have sustainable access to an improved water source. Catholic Relief Services funded the drilling as part of their education program, conceptualizing water as a prerequisite for formal education. The village is in no way unique; it is one of many that need water, though I never found out why this one had been chosen.

The drilling had already been going for a few hours and the drillers were not yet pleased with their soil samples; they were still too dry. Yet with the superior technology and expertise, they had no doubt that water would soon be reached.

It wasn't until I got home and looked at the photos that I really understood. Looking through the lens I missed the magic of the moment, the marvel on their faces, and the true importance of what was taking place. I am constantly humbled by how much I take for granted. The showers, the laundry, the dishes—all the water—this valuable resource goes down the drain without a second thought. And yet this hole in the ground will fundamentally alter the way of life in the village. For most of the women there will be more hours in the day. The crops will have a much larger chance of survival during the two dry seasons. Hygiene could improve dramatically if people are able to wash their hands after they use the latrine. Sanitation in food preparation can prevent the spread of illness-causing bacteria. Life will change because the village now has water.

INTERNATIONAL VOICES

The disparity between developed and developing countries' access to safe water is pronounced: "The average American uses 90 gallons of water a day, says the EPA. A European uses only 53 gallons; a sub-Saharan African, 5 gallons."* Recognizing these disparities and the centrality of water in sustaining and improving life, the United Nations General Assembly in 2003 declared that 2005–2015 would be the International Decade for Action, "Water for Life," and it targeted Africa as a special focus. The Millennium Development Goals for water include halving the "proportion of people without access to safe drinking water," halting "unsustainable exploitation of water resources," and creating "integrated water resource management and efficiency plans."† Africa, which has some 288 million people without access to safe drinking water and 36 percent of the population without access to basic sanitation,‡ is particularly in need of water. However, Africans' problems with water are entangled in complex economic, political, and environmental conditions as shown in the news story "Swaziland: Coping with Diminishing Water Resources" from *Africa News*, March 22, 2005. (Swaziland is a tiny country surrounded by South Africa and Mozambique.)

Comments from Water Authorities in Swaziland

Rivers that were once perennial have now begun to run dry during the winter months, from June to September, when little or no rain falls. Dams throughout the country were below their usual level for this time of year. The largest of these, the Maguga dam in the mountainous northern Hhohho region, a joint venture between Swaziland and South Africa, had not reached even half its capacity since it opened two years ago.

---

*Micah Morrison, "Will We Run Dry?" *Parade*, August 24, 2005, 4.

†"International Decade for Action: Water for Life, 2005–2015," http://www.un.org/waterforlifedecade/.

‡Inter Press Service, "PanAfrica; Water, Water Everywhere . . .," *Africa News*, August 23, 2005. "The eight Millennium Development Goals include a 50 percent reduction in poverty and hunger; universal primary education; reduction of child mortality by two-thirds; cutbacks in maternal mortality by three-quarters; the promotion of gender equality; the reversal of the spread of HIV/AIDS, malaria and other diseases; environmental sustainability, including access to safe drinking water; and a North-South global partnership for development."

Melvin Mayisela, senior water engineer in the rural water supply department, said, "We encourage communities to use boreholes and streams instead of rivers—if a river is used, it would mean qualified technicians would have to monitor the project to ensure a safe water supply."

He recently denied the residents of rural Hosea community permission to use water from the Ngwavuma river in southern Swaziland, due to its high level of toxic pollutants. River pollution is a lethal byproduct of Swaziland's push for industrialisation, and has further compromised the nation's water supply.

GLOBAL HOT SPOT: AFRICA

African countries are engaged in numerous strategies to solve their water problems. These countries are seeking both big solutions involving large investments of foreign capital and technological equipment and small, community-based solutions that nurture independence and sustainable development. In the following excerpt from the news article "PanAfrica: Water, Water Everywhere . . ." from the August 23, 2005, issue of the *Africa News*, South Africa's minister of water affairs and forestry gives a big-picture sketch of Africa's water problems and reaches toward solutions.

. . . . "In spite of a few large rivers like the Congo and the Nile, 21 of the world's most arid countries, in terms of water per person, are located in Africa," South Africa's Minister of Water Affairs and Forestry told a symposium marking "World Water Week" in the Swedish capital.

The Nile and its tributaries flow through nine countries: Egypt, Uganda, Sudan, Ethiopia, Democratic Republic of Congo (DRC), Kenya, Tanzania, Rwanda and Burundi. The Congo, the world's fifth longest river, flows primarily through DRC, People's Republic of Congo, Central African Republic, and partially through Zambia, Angola, Cameroon and Tanzania.

Addressing over 1,400 water experts and representatives of nongovernmental organizations, Buyelwa Sonjica said that in arid and semiarid countries, rivers only flow for short periods in the rainy season, "and you need dams to store water for dry periods."

"The need for water resource infrastructure in Africa is clear. The same arguments are also applicable to many countries in the developing world," she added.

But she warned that the construction of dams should be conditioned on two factors: first, people affected or displaced by a dam should be guaranteed benefits of some nature—"and they should also be better off after the construction of the dam than they were before." Secondly, she said, the impacts on aquatic and terrestrial ecosystems should be mitigated. . . .

The state of Jigawa, Nigeria, in West Africa has achieved success through the government's commitment to the "Water for All" project, involving boreholes (open wells) and hand pumps. To supply water for households and irrigation, the government has constructed 1,420 open wells. Appreciative citizens of Jigawa have supported the governor for his follow-through on his promises, and international organizations and other countries are hoping to imitate Jigawa's success. The following excerpt from the news story "Nigeria; Jigawa: When Governance Overrides Politics" from the August 18, 2005, issue of *Africa News* recounts this achievement.

> Nigeria—[The State Commissioner for Water Resources Alhaji Yusuf Shitu] Galambi said to ensure a more organized approach to the provision of water, the state government set up the State Water Initiative Committee (SWIC), at a time [when] about 38 wild cart drilling rigs purchased from Texas, USA had just arrived [in] the state. According to him, "the committee was inaugurated on August 22, 2003 to drill 900 boreholes in a month in the 30 constituencies of the state. . . ."
>
> Galambi said his ministry had introduced a proven medium, tagged the "Peoples Forum" of sensitizing the local communities on water hygiene and standard practices with respect to water treatment in the state. He explained that the programme involved the selection of qualified community leaders to oversee the monitoring of government water projects in the state. . . .

As you read the articles in this chapter, think about the interconnection of environmental, political, and economic issues and note how assumptions about the environment and science operate in these arguments' interpretations of problems and proposed solutions.

READINGS

Water Wars: Bottling Up the World's Supply of H₂O

Joshua Ortega

Joshua Ortega is a journalist and author who has written for major comic book companies, among them DC Comics, Marvel, and Dark Horse. His fiction includes a novel, *Frequencies*, and its sequel, *Vibrations*. This piece exposing the problems and dangers of bottled water appeared in the Opinion section of the *Seattle Times* on March 20, 2005.

> How does Joshua Ortega interest his audience in the environmental, health, and political problems related to the availability of safe drinking water?

1   Clean, unpolluted, affordable water. There is nothing more important in the world—but it's in serious danger.

2   From health and environmental concerns to the very question of who should control the Earth's water supply, the issue can be distilled into a simple, opening proposition: tap, or bottled water?

3   As Americans, we are all fortunate enough to live in a country where clean, drinkable tap water is a reality, making bottled water a "luxury" rather than a necessity.

4   However, there is a perception among many people that bottled water is somehow more healthy or pure than water from their tap. This is simply an illusion of marketing.

5   A four-year study by the National Resources Defense Council (NRDC), released in 1999, found that one-fifth of the sampled bottled waters contained known neurotoxins and carcinogens such as styrene, toluene and xylene. Another NRDC study found that, out of 103 brands of bottled water, one-third contained traces of arsenic and E. coli. This means that out of a sample of 1,000 bottles sold in the U.S., at least 300 would have some level of chemical contamination.

6   But how can bottled water be contaminated and still be sold in the U.S.? The answer is simple.

7   Bottled water is one of the world's least-regulated industries, and is usually held to less-stringent standards than tap water. Since tap water is a public resource, extensive documentation on its quality and content must be made available to the consumer. There is no such accountability for bottled water, which is regulated more like a soft drink than a public resource.

8   Bottled water gives the pre-packaged impression of safety—if it's in a bottle, it must be safe and clean. Unfortunately, this is not always the case, as evidenced by the worldwide recall of Perrier in the early 1990s, in which the bottled water was found to have benzene, a poison that has produced cancer in lab animals.

9   When you factor in the devastating environmental costs associated with bottling a public, natural resource, the difference between bottled and tap becomes even clearer.

10   The most common plastic used in water bottle manufacturing is PET (polyethylene terephthalate), an environmentally unfriendly substance that actually requires 17.5 kilograms of water to produce only 1 kilogram of PET. In fact, more water is used to make PET bottles than is actually put into them.

11   The production of the plastic also produces numerous byproducts that are extremely harmful to the environment. The Container Recycling Institute reported that 14 billion water bottles were sold in the U.S. in 2002, yet only 10 percent of these bottles were recycled—90 percent ended up in the trash. That's an extra 12.6 billion plastic bottles for the landfills; bottles that contained water that was no more—and often less—healthy than tap water.

12   Granted, there are many places in the world where bottled water is the only source of drinkable water, and thus it becomes much more than a luxury item. However, bottled water is ultimately a Band-Aid

solution. Rather than actually solving the problem—making public water clean, affordable and environmentally friendly—the citizens of these countries are forced to pay exorbitant prices for water that comes in an environmentally unfriendly delivery system.

13   Whether in America or less-developed countries, the evidence is as clear as the plastic it's sold in—bottled water, compared to good tap water, is not worth the costs, whether they be environmental, health-related or economic.

14   But bottled water is not the only danger to clean, affordable tap water—it is simply one part of a much larger issue.

15   *Fortune* magazine has touted water as the "best investment sector for the century." The European Bank for Reconstruction and Development has said that "water is the last infrastructure frontier for private investors." The Toronto Globe & Mail has stated that "water is fast becoming a globalized corporate industry." This news should send shivers down the spine of any concerned American.

16   Currently, the privatized water market is led by two French multinational corporations, Suez Lyonnaise des Eaux (builders of the Suez Canal) and Veolia Environnement, though many other multinationals are also now in the market, including American companies such as General Electric and Bechtel.

17   In the United States, recent laws have paved the way for a larger private-sector presence in America's water supply. Whereas small or local public-sector operators, such as city or county utility companies, used to control the market, now the big players of world business are getting involved.

18   For example, Veolia (formerly owned by Vivendi) bought U.S. Filter Corporation for $6 billion, and it also owns a large portion of Air and Water Technologies. Suez once purchased two of the largest producers of water-treatment chemicals, Calgon and Nalco, and also owns United Water Resources. So much fuss was made about France's opposition to the war in Iraq, yet there was little or no public outcry over the selling of U.S. water companies to foreign interests.

19   Many people will argue that the privatization of water will not affect U.S. consumers, but the facts unfortunately say otherwise. When the French privatized their water services, customer rates went up 150 percent within a few years. In Britain, water corporations have had a terrible track record. In an eight-year period, from 1989 to 1997, four large corporations, including Wessex (a former subsidiary of Enron), were prosecuted 128 times for various infractions.

20   One of the main problems with water privatization is that the public no longer has the right to access information or data about water quality and standards. In 1998, the water supply of Sydney,

Australia, currently controlled by Suez, was contaminated with cryptosporidium and giardia, yet the public had not been informed when the parasites were first discovered.

21   When the government of Ontario, Canada, deregulated its water-protection infrastructure and privatized water-testing labs, the results were disastrous for many communities. In the small Canadian town of Walkerton, seven people died and more than 200 were sickened from drinking E. coli-contaminated water in 2000.

22   The situation is even worse in Third World nations, where large financial institutions such as the IMF (International Monetary Fund) and the World Bank are actively promoting water privatization as a solution to the world's water problems. In many instances, the privatization of a nation's water supply is a requirement for debt relief or a loan. Out of 40 IMF loans that were granted in 2000, at least 12 were contingent upon water privatization.

23   The danger here is that when anything is privatized, it is then subject to pricing as decided by the open market. Many have argued that water is a basic human right, and if this is the case, as with all human rights, it should never be sold on the open market to the highest bidder. Otherwise, water will be subject to the same whims of business as any other commodity.

24   An energy crisis was bad enough—just imagine if the Enron scenario happened with water. In the words of a former director of Suez, "We are here to make money. Sooner or later the company that invests recoups its investment, which means the customer has to pay for it." These are not the people you want to be in control of your water.

25   Water corporations exist to make profits—not to preserve water's quality or affordability. Let's say they own all of the world's water, and then start selling it back to you in little plastic bottles. When the prices and the environmental costs of bottled water get too high, you may find yourself going to war over your water.

26   "The wars of the next century will be about water."

27   This is a quote from Ismail Serageldin, former vice president of the World Bank, in 1999. This is the same World Bank that encourages the privatization of the world's water supply. The same World Bank whose members have financial ties to multinational corporations such as General Electric and Enron.

28   These same multinational corporations also have stakes in the biggest industry of them all—defense and warfare. Indeed, it is a strange day when the same corporation that makes bombs and missiles also owns your water, an "industry" that putatively will be the major focus of this century's wars.

29   Some may argue that these companies are an essential part of national defense, and thus are protecting national interests by the

strategic acquisition of the world's major water supplies. However, once a company owns a water supply, it could be in its best financial interest to make the water scarce and hard to afford. Creating a problem, then marketing a solution, is a very profitable business practice—not to mention the additional profits to be gained from defending the supply in a war.

30   History is rife with conflicts over one party or another's control of a limited resource.

31   Most people will agree that the driving economic force behind today's wars is oil. A war over water would be a hundred times worse. Oil is vastly different. No one puts a gun to your head and forces you to drive. No one makes you fill your tank. Gas and oil are ultimately luxuries. Water, however, is a necessity. Taking away your water is the same thing as putting a gun to your head. This is an unacceptable proposition.

32   If there is one cause in the whole world that crosses all social, national, racial and economic lines, it's water. This is the most important issue we will face in our lifetime.

33   Thankfully, there are solutions to the problem. The simplest way to start making a difference is to choose tap water over bottled. If the taste of your local water is unappealing, buy a filter for your tap, or invest the money you would spend on bottled water into public infrastructure or watershed protection. Nothing speaks louder than where you spend your dollar. Bottled water will only be produced if there is a demand for it.

34   If you want to do more than that, then tell your representatives that you will not accept the selling of American water to foreign, multinational or corporate interests. Support public-sector projects and programs that encourage and create long-term, sustainable water solutions. Get involved with groups such as The Blue Planet Project (www.blueplanetproject.net), which is actively finding ways to solve the world's looming water crisis.

35   And above all else, remember that it's not too late. Clean, affordable water is still a reality in this country. It is our patriotic duty as Americans to ensure that it stays that way.

For Class Discussion

1. What surprising claims does Joshua Ortega assert in this article?

2. What evidence does he offer to support these claims? How persuasive is Ortega's use of the current global conflicts over oil as a cautionary precedent for potential wars over water?

3. What advantages might big water companies offer the public? How would including their perspective strengthen Ortega's argument?

4. What solutions does Ortega offer to the problems he exposes?

5. How has this article influenced your view of public-controlled versus market-controlled resources, or put another way, government-regulated resources versus privatized resources? ∎

Private Water Saves Lives

Fredrik Segerfeldt

Fredrik Segerfeldt researches and writes for the Swedish think tank Timbro, founded in 1978 and committed to "an agenda of reform based on our core values—individual liberty, economic freedom, and an open society" (from www.timbro.com). Timbro shares perspectives with its American free market counterpart, the Cato Institute. Segerfeldt authored *Water for Sale: How Business and the Market Can Resolve the World's Water Crisis* (2005), which has been translated and published by the Cato Institute. The following article was originally published by the *Financial Times* on August 25, 2005, and was posted on the Cato Institute Web site on August 29, 2005.

How does this piece, clearly identified with a free market philosophy, appeal to a wider audience than fellow libertarians?

1   Worldwide, 1.1 billion people, mainly in poor countries, do not have access to clean, safe water. The shortage of water helps to perpetuate poverty, disease and early death. However, there is no shortage of water, at least not globally. We use a mere 8 per cent of the water available for human consumption. Instead, bad policies are the main problem. Even Cherrapunji, India, the wettest place on earth, suffers from recurrent water shortages.

2   Ninety-seven per cent of all water distribution in poor countries is managed by the public sector, which is largely responsible for more than a billion people being without water. Some governments of impoverished nations have turned to business for help, usually with good results. In poor countries with private investments in the water sector, more people have access to water than in those without such investments. Moreover, there are many examples of local businesses improving water distribution. Superior competence, better incentives and better access to capital for investment have allowed private distributors to enhance both the quality of the water and the scope of its distribution. Millions of people who lacked water mains within reach are now getting clean and safe water delivered within a convenient distance.

3   The privatization of water distribution has stirred up strong feelings and met with resistance. There have been violent protests

and demonstrations against water privatization all over the world. Western anti-business non-governmental organizations and public employee unions, sometimes together with local protesters, have formed anti-privatization coalitions. However, the movement's criticisms are off base.

4   The main argument of the anti-privatization movement is that privatization increases prices, making water unaffordable for millions of poor people. In some cases, it is true that prices have gone up after privatization; in others not. But the price of water for those already connected to a mains network should not be the immediate concern. Instead, we should focus on those who lack access to mains water, usually the poorest in poor countries. It is primarily those people who die, suffer from disease and are trapped in poverty.

5   They usually purchase their lower-quality water from small-time vendors, paying on average 12 times more than for water from regular mains, and often more than that. When the price of water for those already connected goes up, the distributor gets both the resources to enlarge the network and the incentives to reach as many new customers as possible. When prices are too low to cover the costs of laying new pipes, each new customer entails a loss rather than a profit, which makes the distributor unwilling to extend the network. Therefore, even a doubling of the price of mains water could actually give poor people access to cheaper water than before.

6   There is another, less serious, argument put forward by the anti-privatization movement. Since water is considered a human right and since we die if we do not drink, its distribution must be handled democratically; that is, remain in the hands of the government and not be handed over to private, profit-seeking interests. Here we must allow for a degree of pragmatism. Access to food is also a human right. People also die if they do not eat. And in countries where food is produced and distributed "democratically", there tends to be neither food nor democracy. No one can seriously argue that all food should be produced and distributed by governments.

7   The resistance to giving enterprise and the market a larger scope in water distribution in poor countries has had the effect desired by the protesters. The pace of privatization has slowed. It is therefore vital that we have a serious discussion based on facts and analysis, rather than on anecdotes and dogmas.

8   True, many privatizations have been troublesome. Proper supervision has been missing. Regulatory bodies charged with enforcing contracts have been non-existent, incompetent or too weak. Contracts have been badly designed and bidding processes sloppy. But these mistakes do not make strong arguments against privatizations

as such, but against bad privatizations. Let us, therefore, have a discussion on how to make them work better, instead of rejecting the idea altogether. Greater scope for businesses and the market has already saved many lives in Chile and Argentina, in Cambodia and the Philippines, in Guinea and Gabon. There are millions more to be saved.

For Class Discussion

1. What are Segerfeldt's main reasons in support of his claim?

2. Many countries worldwide are trying to determine who can most efficiently and fairly manage their access to water—the government, private corporations, or public-private partnerships. How does Segerfeldt acknowledge that he is entering a very heated controversy? How does he avoid emotionalism?

3. How does Segerfeldt accommodate and respond to opposing views?

4. What do you see as the strongest points or features of this argument? How has this piece influenced your view of water privatization?

5. In what ways do the Web sites for big water corporations such as Veolia Environnement (www.veoliaenvironnement.com) and Suez (www.suez.com) echo Segerfeldt's defense of privatization? ∎

Blue Gold: An Interview with Maude Barlow
Jeff Fleischer

Maude Barlow is a leading member of the International Forum on Globalization, a well-known Canadian water activist, and an author or coauthor of numerous books critiquing corporate globalization, including *Blue Gold, the Battle Against Corporate Theft of the World's Water* (2002) and *Profit Is Not the Cure* (2002). This interview appeared in the January 14, 2005, issue of *Mother Jones*, a liberal news commentary magazine devoted to "social justice implemented through first rate investigative reporting" (from www.motherjones.com). Jeff Fleischer works as an editorial fellow at MotherJones.com.

> According to Maude Barlow, what are the political and economic stakes in defining water as a "good" or commodity, rather than as a "human right"?

1   In 1995, a vice president of the World Bank famously declared that, as the wars of the 20th century were fought over oil, so the wars of

the 21st would be fought over water. In the decade since, potable water, scarce even then, has become even more so thanks to pollution, industrial development in nations like China—and especially the process whereby giant firms like Vivendi, Suez and Bechtel increasingly buy up impoverished nations' water supplies, taking sorely needed water and selling it at a profit, all with the blessing of transnational organizations like the World Bank and World Trade Organization.

2   As Maude Barlow explains, this process isn't sustainable. Barlow is national chairperson of The Council of Canadians, a non-partisan public watchdog group working to fight against global trends in privatization and deregulation, and co-founder of the organization's Blue Planet Project. She's also the co-author, with Tony Clarke, of *Blue Gold*, a 2002 international best-seller about the world's growing water crisis. While in San Francisco recently, Barlow spoke with MotherJones.com about how governments are ceding control of their water supplies to the private sector and what can be done before the public's water supply dries up for good.

3   MOTHERJONES.COM: How have international trade agreements encouraged the privatization and commercialization of the world's water?

4   MAUDE BARLOW: Water was included, as a good and later as an investment, in the very first trade agreement in the world, when Canada and the U.S. signed a free-trade agreement that later morphed into NAFTA. The GATT definition of a good includes water. There's now negotiations to put water, as a *service*, into the General Agreement on Trade and Services, which is a proposed international agreement on services. So the World Trade Organization and NAFTA—and bilateral agreements, because water is also included in a lot of bilateral agreements—are ways to enforce a corporate discipline, if you will, over governments that want to maintain public control of their water. Basically, once you privatize it, it's very, very hard to turn back. And once you've started the sale of commercial water, both the receiving country—if it's in a trade agreement with you—and the corporations involved have inherent rights in these agreements that don't exist if you don't sign them.

5   MJ.COM: Besides trade agreements, what other factors caused commercialization to grow so rapidly?

6   MB: Well, I think the reality of the scarcity and the pollution of the world's surface water has just suddenly become real to people. And whereas 20 years ago you couldn't imagine getting most of your water from bottles, it's just become an accepted part of people's lives now. On planes, in restaurants, everybody drinks

bottled water; you carry it around in your pocket. So it came first from scarcity, people needing access to clean water in their lives. And then the view that it was an okay thing to start commodifying water and using it in this way. Of course, behind all this are the big corporations. They've been aggressively promoting and marketing their water as better, as cleaner, as purer, as safer—which it is not. And it is to their advantage to let the public systems of the world's water deteriorate while they get to make huge amounts of money off people's need for clean water.

7   MJ.COM: Historically, how were corporations able to change the perception of water from a basic right to a commodity?

8   MB: This started with the privatization of municipal water services. It was encouraged when water was declared a commodity or a good in the trade agreements. It started to be considered and talked about as a good and a need—not a human right—by the World Water Council when it was founded in 1997. The World Water Council is basically the World Bank, the other regional development banks and the development agencies of the northern governments. It set itself up as a global high command of water existing for its own benefit, to commercialize and commodify water. They have a big forum every three years, where they invite governments to come and observe, and the governments pick up this language of water as a commodity, such that governments really didn't think about this language 10 or 20 years ago, now they're getting together and saying, "There's this U.N. millennium plan and we have to be helping the developing countries bring on water, and how do we do that?" They're all buying into this commodification notion, which is all very new and has happened very quickly—and, I believe, has been driven by corporate interests. It's important to remember that it's a very small, incestuous circle—these water companies, the World Water Council, the World Bank, the World Trade Organization, the IMF. There's a lot of money to be made from the commodification of water, and these people know that whoever controls water is going to be both very rich and very powerful.

9   MJ.COM: So why do governments cede control to this privatization system instead of, say, selling their water to the public themselves?

10 MB: Really, the same reasons that governments have bought into the whole concept of neoliberalism. Governments that used to protect their citizens and provide them with health care and water services and education no longer are allowed to do that if they're poor and owe a debt to the developed world. Through structural adjustment programs, the IMF and the World Bank

basically forced developing countries to abandon those relationships with their people, whether it's health care or energy or state enterprises, because the funding was going to be cut if they didn't. It's been to the advantage of the powerful in northern countries, who are more and more controlled by their own big-business communities, to adopt this language. So it didn't start with water, but water just kind of fell in there when they started talking about everything as a commodity. When you start commodifying things like social services, energy, forests, fish and even air—because you're now trading air-pollution credits and so on—it's not a big step to say "why is water different?" One of the first questions I often get asked in hostile interviews is why water is different than forests or fish. And one of my answers is well, actually, we should be protecting our forests and fish, too. However, we can restock fish, we can find alternatives to energy, and we can even replant trees. But there's only so much water, and the more we destroy, the less access we have to potable water and the more desperate the situation becomes.

11   MJ.COM: How does third-world debt play into this conflict?

12   MB: Of course, if the third-world countries didn't have a debt to the north—and as you know, they send more as debt payment to the north than we send them in trade and aid together—they would be in a position to start delivering not-for-profit services, including water, health care and other services. But as long as they remain in that desperate situation, having to pay even just the interest on the debt payment, they are totally at the mercy of the IMF, the World Bank, the United States, Canada and Europe. A few years ago, the World Bank was [merely] encouraging water privatization, but now they're saying it's a condition of any aid that you privatize water, and we're going to negotiate the agreement and tell you the company you're going to use. So countries are forced to take the conditions under which they can get the money to deliver water to their people.

13   MJ.COM: Would eliminating third-world debt necessarily solve this problem?

14   MB: It would be a huge step toward it, either canceling or at least seriously renegotiating the debt. If the first world was really interested in delivering water to the poor of the world, we would also have a tax on financial speculation. If the World Bank can afford to pay these great big water companies to come in and run a water service—because it's their money; the companies aren't investing—if they can afford to bring a private company in to do this, they can afford to train public-sector workers to deliver water on a not-for-profit basis.

15   I look at Japan and the Philippines. Japan has a highly skilled public workforce delivering clean water, on an island, to millions of people. Tokyo itself is nearly the population of Canada, so it's amazing what they do. But the World Bank goes to the Philippines, so close to Japan, and says, "You're going to have to take these private companies" instead of saying, "Let's bring a bloc of these wonderful public-sector experts from Japan over and transfer this technology on a not-for-profit basis." It would be cheaper. It would have a longer-lasting effect. It would mean water would get delivered to everyone on a not-for-profit basis, which means you could deliver it to way more people. And we could start to really move toward solving the world's crisis. Then that extra money could go into rebuilding infrastructure, because 90 percent of all the wastewater in the developing world goes untreated into rivers and lakes and streams and wetlands. So the infrastructure to stop that pollution is desperately needed.

16   MJ.COM: What are some examples of governments in the developing world that have tried to break free from this system?

17   MB: Well, Uruguay's a good example. A country that just had an election, brought in a center-left government, and just had a vote Oct. 31 about their water. They voted two-thirds to say that water is a fundamental human right, which requires a constitutional amendment. Their government's position now is that it's required to deliver water on a not-for-profit basis, but they've got these corporations there. So this is going to be a really interesting test of what they can do. Will they kick the company out, as Bolivia did when they kicked Bechtel out? You get governments like that of South Africa, where when they amended the constitution after apartheid ended, they brought water in as a basic human right. But then they brought Suez [a private firm] in to deliver it, so it was only a human right if you could pay for it. I think the government there is under tremendous pressure now to reconcile their constitutional amendment that says it's a basic right and the fact they were forced to bring in a for-profit company.

18   There are other governments, Suharto's in Indonesia was one of them, that worked very closely with some private water companies to skim off money from the people the way the water companies did. There's no question there's collusion. But let's face it, it's often collusion that's watched and condoned by the World Bank, by the American government, by our government in Canada. Certainly by the government of France, which promotes its water companies in the most outrageous venues and situations. So there's no question that there's sometimes a

symbiotic relationship between corrupt governments, these companies and the World Bank.

19   MJ.COM: We've talked about the developing world, but how much control do the governments of industrialized countries—the U.S., Canada, Europe—have over their own water supplies?

20   MB: Much less than they think they do. For one thing, the pollution is taking place at such an accelerated rate that we're all mining our groundwater, and the actual water systems are being mined far faster than they can be replenished. Our prairies are going to be experiencing really deep drought, as are yours, within the next 10–20 years; a permanent kind of drought, so our scientists tell us. So it's not just a so-called third-world problem. Confronted with this reality, our governments are starting to ask questions about who should have access to water and who should pay for it and all that. They've bought into the ideology of neoliberalism or economic globalization or market capitalism.

21   When you take a new problem—you always had all the air and water you needed; it was never a problem—and suddenly you're confronted with a water-scarcity problem, and the thinking and ideology you already have starts to fit itself around this. So I don't think it's a big jump for governments in industrialized countries to start to see reasons to commodify and privatize water. And as soon as you take water out of its natural state—bidding on it, trading it for commercial purposes or selling it—it is then a commodity clearly defined under these trade agreements and that's it—you've lost control over it. So governments in the developing world have been forced into privatization by the World Bank, regional development banks and the IMF. Countries in the northern, industrialized world are coming at it through another door. I've always said free trade is to the north what structural adjustment is to the south, and water is getting caught in that web.

22   MJ.COM: Are there positive steps the industrialized nations could take at this stage that could then spread to the rest of the world?

23   MB: Absolutely. We're calling in Canada for a national water act, which would outline the protections needed environmentally, really put limits on the use and abuse of our water from industry, remove water from the trade agreements and exempt water from all future trade agreements. We also believe that if we can get water defined as a human right—which it is, but if we can get it recognized—in some kind of binding treaty at the United Nations, it would be a strong challenge to the existing situation in these trade agreements.

24   It would be a very powerful tool for people to be able to say to their governments, "You've signed an agreement saying that water is our human right, so therefore you can't charge us." It's not a semantic question, this human need or human right. If it's a human need, it can be delivered by the private sector on a for-profit basis. If it's a human right, that's different. You can't really charge for a human right; you can't trade it or deny it to someone because they don't have money. And we need laws at every level of government, from the most local to international, on the current abuse of water. All of us are going to have to change our relationship with water.

For Class Discussion

1. What role does Barlow assign to these parties in the increasing commercialization of water: national governments, global free trade agreements like NAFTA (North American Free Trade Agreement), organizations like the World Bank, and citizens/consumers? Which party does she criticize the most?

2. What examples does Barlow offer of successfully public sector-run water systems? What political solutions does she offer to the problem of privatized water?

3. According to Barlow, what is the argument for declaring water a human right and not a human need?

4. What assumptions and values underlie Barlow's criticism of big business?

5. How does this interview clarify, support, and/or expand the understanding you gained from Joshua Ortega of global problems with water?   ■

Technology and Water: Looking for the Workaround

Robert L. Ayers

Robert L. Ayers is former senior vice president of ITT Industries and president of ITT Fluid Technology. ITT Industries describes itself as "the world's largest provider of water and wastewater treatment solutions, and a leading provider of pumps and related technologies for industrial, chemical and commercial customers" (from www.itt.com/profile). Ayers gave this speech at a workshop in Washington, D.C., on global water management sponsored by the Center for Strategic and International Studies Global Strategy Institute and Sandia National Laboratories on March 9, 2005.

What features of this piece are tailored to the speech genre and to its audience—members of a nonpartisan, interdisciplinary think tank involved in developing national and international public policy?

1   Not very long ago in the youth of the internet, if you wanted to find specific information you were in trouble. Either you couldn't find what you wanted on the web because of the immensity of the listings and the primitive search functions, or you depended on a search operation manned by groups of librarians/cybrarians trying to get you to the data manually. Everyone looking for data was following the traditional library model: books on shelves, Dewey Decimal.

2   Then Larry Page and Sergey Brin came up with the concept of the Google search engine, and the rest is history. They "worked around" the need for manpower and made the power of internet design, the power of their engine. Their search formulas tapped into the very structure of the web.

3   Google is now part of an international information infrastructure, an infrastructure "like the power grid, sewer lines, and the internet itself."

4   Google now answers 200 million queries a day and deals with more content on the young internet than even Gutenberg and all of the publishers after him could have imagined.

5   The presence of Google is such that when Google became unavailable to Chinese citizens, the outcry was so great that the service was back in full force 10 days later. Quite a workaround, and quite an international infrastructure.[1] For its next "workaround," Google is tackling the inefficiencies of many libraries in many places—by housing all great libraries digitally. . . .

6   Then there is the cell phone. Yes, a simple amenity for those of us in a well-wired country like the U.S. but for the Chinese, Indians, and Russians the cell phone is a workaround for the expense and inefficiencies of stringing telephone wire over huge countries trying to develop modern economies.

7   In 1992 China had 10 million wired phones and was adding up to 20 million new lines annually. Yet at the end of 1998 less than 7% of the Chinese had phone numbers of their own, compared to 50% for Singapore. With the government's active encouragement of cell phones, the Chinese today have 310 million users, about 25% of its total population, with more to come. Developing countries now account for 56% of all mobile subscribers world-wide.[2]

8   Skip the wires, don't think of the traditional infrastructure, and you have a remarkably successful and cost-effective workaround.

9   You can see where I am going with this. We need equally innovative and effective breakthroughs, workarounds, and technology assists, for water to meet the needs of our water century.

10   So where are we and how do we get farther in meeting the challenge of enough safe and healthful water? Today, I would like to look at available and needed technology and available and needed workarounds, to meet the challenges of sustainable development, water scarcity, and water purity.

SUSTAINABLE DEVELOPMENT

11   We should begin with an agreement and understanding of the sine qua non to succeed in meeting the challenges of our water century. That is sustainable development.

12   Medieval scientist, Hanns Carl von Carlowitz, observed that the thriving business of mining copper and iron was taking a huge number of logs to support mining shafts. He saw that there soon would not be enough trees for the mines and wrote a paper in 1713 where he coined the phrase "nachhaltige Entwicklung" or sustainable development.

13   He observed that the number of trees cut had to be less than those grown in any period of time. The assumption was and has developed in our time to be that a society lives in prosperity only, if "economic, social, and environmental affairs are kept in balance" and can be on-going rather than event-driven in the present-tense only.

14   Water is a critical unit for sustainable development in every society and economy. Consider if all of the world's water were compressed into one gallon jug. From that gallon, the fresh water available for us would equal about one tablespoon. That image should give you as much pause as it does me.

15   If you have any doubt about this, consider these questions and facts.

16   Three hundred million people now live in areas of serious to severe water shortages. In 25 years that number will be 3 billion. But, less than one percent is the amount of fresh water available for use. That's the tablespoon from the gallon.

17   Two million tons of human waste is released into streams and rivers of the world every day. Maintaining clean, safe water and disposing of our waste is paramount for sustainable development. Hubert Humphrey was correct when he said our affluent society was also our effluent society. Victor Hugo was equally correct when he said that a city's sewers are its conscience.

18   Great rivers of the world, including the Nile of Egypt, the Ganges of India, the Yellow River of China, and the Colorado of the U.S. do not reach their destinations for significant periods of time. The Yellow River has gone dry on average 70 days a year in each of the last 10 years.[3] Again, bad decisions and over-use are the culprits. We may say, "Oh, back when we were making decisions about the Colorado River and water dispersal for the west, we had

no idea of the long-term implications." But let me quote John W. Powell, geologist and explorer of the Grand Canyon and Colorado River, from an 1893 speech: "I wish to make it clear to you, there is not sufficient water to irrigate all the lands which could be irrigated, and only a small portion can be irrigated. . . . I tell you, gentlemen, you are piling up a heritage of conflict!"

19   This is an appropriate place to suggest another problem of sustainable development: it has been said that "water runs uphill—to money in the American west." Shortsightedness and short-term gain have stood in the way of sustainable development in the past, and of course, our west is just an easy, close-to-home example of the problems.

20   Agriculture uses 70% of all of the world's available fresh water. Many governments, including our own, subsidize irrigation thereby encouraging waste. What sense does it make that farmers in the Imperial Valley of California pay $15.50 an acre foot while residential water in southern California costs $431 an acre foot? . . .

21   And finally as we assess our sustainable development position, we need only to look at the purity of water and its effect on health to be truly discouraged.

22   At least 90% of the diseases of the world are and have been water related. This means that 5–7 million people die every year because of contaminated water. This is a problem for both developing and developed countries.

23   Consider, for example, the cholera epidemic in South America in the early 1990s. It resulted in 11,000 deaths, a million or more sick, and an economic impact beyond calculation for the entire continent.

24   And lest we think that such things don't affect us, for example, in the United States, let's look back to the 1993 cryptosporidiosis contamination in Milwaukee. It caused 58 deaths and [cost] $96 million. Contaminated water is no longer the problem of developing countries only.

IT IS A GLOBAL PROBLEM

25 India, for example, lost 73 million working days because of water illnesses, costing the economy $600 million.

26   Internationally, in human costs, one child dies every 8 seconds from water-born disease! Whether India or Milwaukee, the human and economic costs are not acceptable!

27   I think we all can agree sustainable development should be our guide; indeed I think we can do and must do better! We need to reach higher! With our technology and knowledge we can hand over our planet to our offspring in better condition than it was given to us.

SCARCITY

28 Let's look next at the scarcity issue. The amount of freshwater avail-able to us is not going to change. Huge engineering projects are no longer the answer to get that water to more people. The days of enormous dams are over because of the few remaining appropriate locations, environmental issues, and cost.

29   Building extensive infrastructures of pipes, wastewater treat-ment plants, and pumping stations is not possible for the mega cities developing across the world. These cities already have seri-ous and expensive problems of housing, food, and jobs, as well as major problems of adequate, safe water for their citizens. We need workarounds and technology to help us succeed in this challenging water century. . . .

30   **Conservation, re-use,** and **desalination** coupled with small scale solutions are three routes I would like to propose.

31   Conservation of course can come in many ways. I'll briefly look at the greatest waterwaste, that is, irrigation. (Remember that 90% of water consumption is related in some way to food produc-tion.) Typically, in developing countries, the efficiencies of irriga-tion range from 25–45 per cent. Even the highest success rates of efficiencies internationally are only 50–60 percent. If we line canals, stop broadcast spraying, laser level fields, and use drip irrigation, the savings would be enormous. Only 1% of the world's irrigated land now has any kind of improved, precision irrigation. This has to change everywhere. It has to change in the American west as we look at boom cities like Las Vegas and Phoenix where farmers still grow water-intensive crops with subsidized water. It has to change in countries where there may be only 79,000 gallons (300 cubic meters) of water per capita, areas where the shortage is so severe that agricultural efficiencies can mean the difference between life and death.

32   Policy and will, however, are as important as practice in ad-dressing need. A major effort has been made by South Africa, for example, to address both availability and conservation via national policy. South Africa has made a commitment to having a tap within 650 feet (200 meters) of every household and to providing the first 1,600 gallons (6000 liters) of water per month per family for free. After that amount is used, there is a charge. An important point to observe here is that there has to be a political will and national pol-icy for water problems to be fully addressed. The U.S. without any national water policy must certainly consider its priorities in these most serious times of shortage and need world-wide.

33   Dual piping is another way that scarcity is being addressed. One piping system carries potable water at a higher price, while another carries non-potable water with a clear price advantage.

The non-potable water can be used for landscaping, agriculture, and manufacturing. Places as diverse as Bangalore, India; Singapore; Florida; and California are using dual piping to conserve water.

34   Re-use is a major opportunity for water to be a part of sustainable development in addressing scarcity. Professor Takashi Asano, winner of the Stockholm Water Prize, is considered the father of water re-use. He has shown us the way which is more and more our future.

35   But, if we look at manufacturing, the current picture is not encouraging. The world manufacturing systems are largely open, meaning water is drawn in for production and then discarded at the end of the process. More often than not, we are discarding a valuable "recyclable."

36   The manufacture of a car and its four tires requires 39,000 gallons of water for production. One barrel of crude oil takes 1,800 gallons, a ton of steel 62,000 gallons, and just one semi-conductor 3,000 gallons.

37   Industrial re-cycling of water dramatically alters the intake of water and the quality of discharge. A decade ago it was standard procedure for water to be "run through" a manufacturing process just once and then discharged. This was a major cause of pollution and shortage.

38   Now, more and more companies are looking at self-contained systems where the same water is used, cleaned, and used again.

39   Note the savings of self-contained systems. Our ITT Defense/ Avionics plant is a totally self-contained system that re-uses the water it has, rather than regularly taking in new water and then discarding it. Through this totally contained water system, it saves 160,000 gallons of water per day.

40   From 1962–75, Israel moved from using 5,300 gallons (20 cubic meters) of water to manufacture $100 worth of goods to using only 2,000 gallons (7.8 cubic meters) per $100 of goods. This conservation is a three-fold increase in water efficiency. This efficiency, of course, cuts costs, never mind creating a better environment. This total wastewater re-use has been so successful that it has become Israeli national policy.

41   Intel reports that strict water management and re-use policies have enabled it to lessen its global water requirements by a third— from over 9 billion to just over 6 billion gallons annually.

42   Singapore has embraced the Newater technology. This technology reclaims wastewater. That is, it turns sewage into drinking water or industrial use water by taking it through two different membrane filtering processes, then subjecting it to UV (ultra-violet) disinfection. Singapore's first two Newater factories supply about 10 million gallons of re-cycled wastewater each day.

43   Another simple, promising re-use solution to water shortages is water harvesting. In south and Southeast Asia 80% of the rainfall may come in under 20 days during the monsoon season.

44   Or think of Los Angeles with its recent storms. How often did we hear, "If only L.A. had that water when it needed it!" There is now interest in harvesting this kind of water. Water collection and aquifer re-charging are in their infancies, but it takes little imagination to understand the potential. If we can pave over land and remove wetlands which increased runoff by huge amounts, surely we can also devise effective means of collection, renewing aquifers, and re-use.

45   Despite such creative approaches, and success stories of re-use, re-cycling is still very much the exception rather than the rule for water. Re-cycling of paper and plastic are now a part of our economy and culture. Water cannot be far behind.

46   **"Irrigation of the land with seawater desalinated by fusion power is ancient.** It's called rain." But desalination is an old technology with a big future. Its future is big because costs are steadily dropping due to advances. As we know, however, there is not enough rain in the right places. So we must desalinate by technology. Reverse osmosis and less energy-intensive new technologies have resulted in steadily decreasing costs for desalinated water.

47   Florida, Texas, California, China, Caribbean, Massachusetts, and several Middle Eastern countries are among participants in the desalination movement. If you look at the costs from 1991 to 2003, the savings are dramatic: from $6.00 per 1000 gallons in Santa Barbara to $1.50 in Singapore.

48   New technologies have offset the cost of energy. The goal is to continue making desalination as energy-efficient as possible by continuing improvements. Unlike dams and larger engineering projects, desalination is also responsive to issues of scale. It can effectively serve small communities as well as large cities at proportional investment rates. . . .

WATER SANITATION

49   Water purity is literally a matter of life and death. One child dying every 8 seconds world-wide is more than enough motivation to break current patterns and find new workarounds.

50   It is hard for us to realize that money is not the answer, that traditional engineering is not the answer. That, however, is the truth.

51   If new pipelines and mega delivery and processing plants are not the answer, what to do, where to start?

52   One way is to look at the "point of use" for water, rather than looking for a central location to process and pump water. Point of

use, or POU, is an important concept in finding solutions to our current untenable positions.

53   An important perspective on sanitation and re-use is offered by professor Wilderer, winner of the Stockholm Water Prize in 2003 and a strong proponent of re-use of water and of finding the workarounds from conventional pipe, pump, and treatment systems. His influential work has emphasized the importance of decentralized, small scale treatment and re-use of water. He developed the important concept and reality of DESA, decentralized sanitation and re-use. He emphasizes, and I certainly agree, that the traditional approaches of the West to water availability and purity cannot be applied globally. . . .

54   At ITT we are particularly excited by our POU system, one originally created for the British army, namely, the ST1. Portable ST1 water treatment units are capable of treating more than 1800 gallons of water every hour. The units are diesel powered—enabling them to operate in the many areas that are without electricity—and simple to operate and maintain.

55   ITT sent these ST1 units to the tsunami victims in Sri Lanka to help provide clean water quickly. These treatment pumps, which are portable and relatively inexpensive, proved the difference between life and death after the devastating tidal wave. An application, which had been developed originally to support our troops in the field, proved to be a remarkable success in this moment of tragedy. No pipes, no infrastructure, just water where you need it!

56   A POU example that we are particularly proud of is one pump given by ITT to the Malawi children's village in Africa. This village for orphans had no dependable source of clean water. One pump made that water possible. It became the difference between life and death for several hundred orphans. It also became a "model" for nearby villages and an economic incentive. Freedom from the labor of finding water and from the sickness from dirty water is the means to a whole new quality of life for individuals and their communities.

57   No discussion of clean, safe water can ignore the problem of human waste!

58   There are problems of scale, processing options, and public understanding in treating wastewater and in dealing with the sludge or bio-solids that remain after treatment. Large processing plants are not possible for rural villages. They are also not feasible for the mega cities which would have to have every street dug up and repaved to install prohibitively expensive systems.

59   The result? Too much raw sewage goes into rivers and seas around the world. We must redefine our view of waste treatment. It must be smaller, more local, and manageable in technology and execution. European Union regulations and the European commitment

are providing leadership in this area requiring all populations over 5,000 to have wastewater treatment processes in effect. . . .

60   The cities of the world that lack wastewater treatment will have to consider a series of localized treatment areas within their cities, rather than one enormous facility for the entire municipality. Big is definitely not better in wastewater treatment. . . .

61   There are many small technology advances, many new understandings of the challenge and needs of our water century. But there is no amazing equation like that which makes Google work. There is no Fred Smith of water to turn an industry on its head. But there are many options like the cell phone transforming China, Russia, and Japan. By that I mean there are many small technologies, often created for other reasons, which can transform water availability and quality. I have suggested how some of these workarounds may help us move beyond the capital intensive, traditional infrastructure approaches—approaches which demand a workaround just like Google jumping past the library model or the cell phones jumping over stringing wires across a country.

62   We need many more workarounds and innovations to get where we need to be in our water century. That will happen only when water is fully understood by the public as a critical issue of our time. This will not happen when the U.S. for example, has no national water policy, when our own water usage and technology are a hodgepodge of problems, applications, waste, and "sometime" solutions. Our government must move water to a top priority, no less important than energy. The congress must examine current practices and critical needs at home and then look to ways to help our neighbors on the globe.

63   There must be private and public cooperation to continue to investigate the challenges of water. The people in this room reflect this opportunity, but this is far from enough in the face of such a severe challenge. More industries and more NGOs must work together on water issues. And there must be ways for the government to spur water research into new technologies. The Russian launching of the Sputnik satellite resulted in an education initiative that created a generation of scientists and engineers. That generation of scientists did everything from getting us to the moon to creating the internet. We can not wait for a water disaster to cause our government to move to action sponsoring research via grants and tax incentives. The disaster is occurring now as a child dies every 8 seconds. The time to act is now. . . .

1. Evans, Harold. *They Made America*. (New York, 2004) pp.458–463.
2. Andrew Tanzer, "China Goes Wireless." *Forbes*, July 26, 1999.
3. Sandra Postel, *Last Oasis* (W.W. Norton, New York, 1997), xix.

For Class Discussion

1. How does Robert L. Ayers establish the water scarcity and pollution problems that he is proposing to solve?

2. Ayers bases his proposal argument on the concept of a "work-around," a business/engineering innovation that solves a problem, saves money, and opens up a whole new realm of business efficiency and capability. How does Ayers propose to solve the problems he presents?

3. How does Ayers use precedents, extended examples, and analogies in this speech?

4. What does Ayers mean by "sustainable development"? What assumptions and values underlie his claims? What role does cost-effectiveness play in his solution?

5. How has this speech, written by an engineer and businessman, contributed to your idea of the role of technology and business in responding to problems with environmental resources?   ∎

Water Is a Human Right
Council of Canadians' Blue Planet Project

The Council of Canadians is a nonpartisan citizens' watchdog organization that lists as some of its main goals "promoting economic justice, renewing our democracy, asserting Canadian sovereignty, advancing alternatives to corporate-style free trade, and preserving our environment" (www .canadians.org). The Council began the Blue Planet Project "to protect the world's fresh water from the growing threats of trade and privatization" (www.blueplanet.project.net/). One of the Blue Planet Project's specific action groups is the Friends of the Right to Water, which is dedicated to affirming the universal right to water through international compaigns. This handbill, posted on the Blue Planet Project Web site, is an advocacy ad for an international campaign.

> What features of the writing, layout, and image in this handbill seek to create its immediate, urgent, emotional appeal?

For Class Discussion

1. This proposal argument presents a problem and calls for action to address it. In your own words, what is the problem that this handbill highlights and what are its economic, political, and social dimensions?

2. What connections between national governments and global institutions like the United Nations does this piece seek to foster, and according to this campaign, why are they important?

WATER IS A HUMAN RIGHT

An international campaign to enshrine water as a human right at the United Nations

The Right to Water is the Right to Life

When the United Nations' Universal Declaration of Human Rights was drafted over 50 years ago, water was not included in the list of protected rights. The rationale was simple. Water, like air, was considered so fundamental to life that naming a right to it would have been redundant.

Times have changed.

Despite everyday dependence we have on water, access to fresh water is far from equal or guaranteed. Of the world's population of 6 billion, at least 1.5 billion people do not have access to clean drinking water and another 4 billion lack adequate sanitation services. In parts of the developing world, a child dies every 15 seconds due to easily preventable water-related diseases.

Global water corporations, international financial institutions, trade agreements, governments and even parts of the United Nations have been promoting privatization and commodification of water as a way to deal with this crisis.

But the evidence shows that privatization leads to rising water rates, unclean water—and of course, soaring corporate profits. Water should be safe, affordable, and accessible to everyone—not just those who can afford to pay.

Time for Action

Without action, inequality and human suffering will only worsen. The UN predicts that by 2025, the number of people deprived of water will climb to over 3 billion. Such disparity is an affront to the world's shared humanity and threatens our future security. Water scarcity is a common source of conflict in this new century and promises to become more so. And for many developing nations, the lack of proper infrastructure to deliver clean water only perpetuates and worsens poverty.

The only way to solve this crisis is to ensure that water remains under public control. Governments must enshrine the human right to water and protect the ecosystems that people and nature rely upon.

Water belongs to the earth and all species and is an inalienable human right that must not be appropriated for profit.

– Maude Barlow, National Chairperson,
The Council of Canadians

Friends of the Right to Water

In recognition that water is the essence of life, a group known as "The Friends of the Right to Water" (FRW) has begun an international campaign seeking to affirm the universal right to water. Building upon General Comment No. 15 (GC 15) adopted in November 2002 by the UN Committee on Economic, Social and Cultural Rights, the FRW is inviting organizations to join in the effort to secure the right to water.

General Comment 15 notes that the right to water has already been established in a wide range of international documents and underscores the fundamental importance that water plays in the realization of all other human rights.

As it stands, all 144 signatories to the UN Covenant on Economic, Social and Cultural rights are bound by the pronouncements of GC 15. The problem is that countries can ignore their responsibilities because there is no effective means of holding them to account. The campaign proposed by the Friends of the Right to Water is working to create a binding means to hold these states accountable.

FIGURE 7.1 Water Is a Human Right *(photo © Howard Davies/CORBIS)*

Uruguay Victory an Inspiration to the Water Movement

On October 31, 2004, the people of Uruguay made history by being the first people in the world to vote on the human right to water.

By almost two-thirds majority, the people of Uruguay voted to amend their constitution to ensure not only that access to piped water and sanitation is a fundamental human right available to everyone, but also that in the creation of water policies social considerations take precedence over economic considerations. Further, the constitution must now reflect that the "public service of water supply for human consumption will be served exclusively and directly by state legal persons"—that is to say, not by for-profit companies.

This referendum is a historic development and will form the basis of our campaign for a United Nations treaty on the right to water. The referendum in Uruguay was the result of a two-year grassroots fight led by a network called the National Commission for the Defence of Water and Life. It was composed of trade unions, human rights groups, and environmental organizations, including Friends of the Earth Uruguay. This fight also brought unprecedented support from the international civil society water movement, which provided funding, resource materials, a massive number of e-mails and letters of support, and visiting delegations who then took the story of this struggle back to their home countries. People in Argentina are now organizing to promote a similar constitutional amendment on the right to water.

Maude Barlow, the Council of Canadians' National Chairperson, was in Uruguay to witness this historical moment:

"The night before I left I spoke to hundreds of people at a big public forum, assuring them that their work had been worth it and that we would take their constitutional amendment and use it as the basis of an international campaign. But the standing ovation and tears came when I ended my speech with the words affirming that on October 31 *"Todos somos uruguayos"* —we are all Uruguayans."

The Right to Water Campaign

The Friends of the Right to Water is promoting a two-tiered strategy. We are encouraging our international partners to work with the UN to adopt a convention or treaty on the right to water. We are also encouraging local groups to push their governments and courts to recognize the human right to water. This 'inside-outside' strategy will be the most effective way to accomplish our goals.

The Uruguay constitutional amendment is a good example of how a grassroots initiative can press for and secure our rights. Where the rules exist for similar initiatives, we use them, where they don't we must find other ways to ensure the right to water. In some countries the strategy may need to be more localized, or focus on the court system.

On local, national and international levels, we must assert our right to water and demand recognition in the courts and parliaments of the world.

We are encouraging like-minded organizations to join us. The adoption of a strong treaty or convention on water is crucial to the international water justice campaign. Pro-privatization groups are already developing their own water convention. The time to act is now!

Take Action!

The Right to Water Campaign is being led by a network of international organizations, including the Council of Canadians' Blue Planet Project.

To get involved in the Right to Water Campaign, check out <u>www.blueplanetproject.net</u>, or email us at <u>blueplanet@canadians.org</u>.

3. What solution is being advocated and how is this solution justified?

4. What alternative views and solutions might corporate leaders and global institutions like the World Bank offer?

5. How does the selection and condensation of information, layout, and use of a photo, headings, and type suit the genre of the hand-bill and contribute to the effectiveness of this advocacy piece?

6. How has this piece contributed to your understanding of the global conflicts over water? ∎

Learning from China: Why the Western Economic Model Will Not Work for the World

Lester R. Brown

Lester R. Brown is a renowned environmental leader and writer. He holds a master of science from the University of Maryland and a master of public administration from Harvard University. In 1974, he founded the World-watch Institute, the first of its kind to focus on global economic issues, and began *World Watch* magazine, along with the annual reports *State of the World* and *Vital Signs: The Trends That Are Shaping Our Future*. In 2001, he launched the Earth Policy Institute, devoted to "achieving an environmentally sustainable economy" (www.earth-policy.org/About/Lester_bio.htm). He has won many awards for his environmental leadership. Of his fifty books, the most recent are *Eco-Economy: Building an Economy for the Earth* (2001), *Plan B: Rescuing a Planet Under Stress and a Civilization in Trouble* (2003), and *Outgrowing the Earth: The Food Security Challenge in an Age of Falling Water Tables and Rising Temperatures* (2005). This "Eco-Economy Update" was posted on the Earth Policy Institute Web site on March 9, 2005.

> Lester Brown devotes most of his article to presenting economic and environmental predictions about China. What is his rhetorical strategy and what effect do you think he wants it to have on his readers?

1   Could the American dream in China become a nightmare for the world? For China's 1.3 billion people, the American dream is fast becoming the Chinese dream. Already millions of Chinese are living like Americans—eating more meat, driving cars, traveling abroad, and otherwise spending their fast-rising incomes much as Americans do. Although these U.S.-style consumers are only a small fraction of the population, China's claims on the earth's resources are already becoming highly visible.

2   In an Eco-Economy Update released in February, we pointed out that China has replaced the United States as the world's leading consumer of most basic commodities, like grain, coal, and steel. Now the question is, What if consumption per person of these resources in China one day reaches the current U.S. level? And, closely related, how long will it take for China's annual income per person of $5,300 to reach the 2004 U.S. figure of $38,000?

3   During the 26 years since the far-reaching economic reforms of 1978, China's economy has been growing at a breakneck pace of 9.5 percent a year. If it were now to grow at 8 percent per year, doubling every nine years, income per person in 2031 for China's projected population of 1.45 billion would reach $38,000. (At a more conservative 6 percent annual growth rate, the economy would double every 12 years, overtaking the current U.S. income per person in 2040.)

4   For this exercise we will assume an 8 percent annual economic growth rate. If the Chinese consume resources in 2031 as voraciously as Americans do now, grain consumption per person there would climb from 291 kilograms today to the 935 kilograms needed to sustain a U.S.-style diet rich in meat, milk, and eggs. In 2031 China would consume 1,352 million tons of grain, far above the 382 million tons used in 2004. This is equal to two thirds of the entire 2004 world grain harvest of just over 2 billion tons.

5   Given the limited potential for further raising the productivity of the world's existing cropland, producing an additional 1 billion tons of grain for consumption in China would require converting a large part of Brazil's remaining rainforests to grain production. This assumes, of course, that once they are cleared these soils could sustain crop production.

6   To reach the U.S. 2004 meat intake of 125 kilograms per person, China's meat consumption would rise from the current 64 million tons to 181 million tons in 2031, or roughly four fifths of current world meat production of 239 million tons.

7   With energy, the numbers are even more startling. If the Chinese use oil at the same rate as Americans now do, by 2031 China would need 99 million barrels of oil a day. The world currently produces 79 million barrels per day and may never produce much more than that.

8   Similarly with coal. If China's coal burning were to reach the current U.S. level of nearly 2 tons per person, the country would use 2.8 billion tons annually—more than the current world production of 2.5 billion tons.

9   Apart from the unbreathable air that such coal burning would create, carbon emissions from fossil fuel burning in China alone would rival those of the entire world today. Climate change could

spiral out of control, undermining food security and inundating coastal cities.

10   If steel consumption per person in China were to climb to the U.S. level, it would mean that China's aggregate steel use would jump from 258 million tons today to 511 million tons, more than the current consumption of the entire Western industrialized world.

11   Or consider the use of paper, another hallmark of modernization. If China's meager annual consumption of 27 kilograms of paper per person were to rise in 2031 to the current U.S. level of 210 kilograms, China would need 303 million tons of paper, roughly double the current world production of 157 million tons. There go the world's forests.

12   And what about cars? If automobile ownership in China were to reach the U.S. level of 0.77 cars per person (three cars for every four people), China would have a fleet of 1.1 billion cars in 2031— well beyond the current world fleet of 795 million. The paving of land for roads, highways, and parking lots for such a fleet would approach the area now planted [for] rice in China. The competition between automobile owners and farmers for productive cropland would be intense.

13   The point of this exercise of projections is not to blame China for consuming so much, but rather to learn what happens when a large segment of humanity moves quickly up the global economic ladder. What we learn is that the economic model that evolved in the West—the fossil-fuel-based, auto-centered, throwaway economy— will not work for China simply because there are not enough resources.

14   If it does not work for China, it will not work for India, which has an economy growing at 7 percent per year and a population projected to surpass China's in 2030. Nor will it work for the other 3 billion people in the developing world who also want to consume like Americans. Perhaps most important, in an increasingly integrated global economy where all countries are competing for the same dwindling resources it will not continue to work for the 1.2 billion who currently live in the affluent industrial societies either.

15   The sooner we recognize that our existing economic model cannot sustain economic progress, the better it will be for the entire world. The claims on the earth by the existing model at current consumption levels are such that we are fast depleting the energy and mineral resources on which our modern industrial economy depends. We are also consuming beyond the sustainable yield of the earth's natural systems. As we overcut, overplow, overpump, overgraze, and overfish, we are consuming not only the interest from our natural endowment, we are devouring the endowment itself. In ecology, as in economics, this leads to bankruptcy.

16   China is teaching us that we need a new economic model, one that is based not on fossil fuels but that instead harnesses renewable sources of energy, including wind power, hydropower, geothermal energy, solar cells, solar thermal power plants, and biofuels. In the search for new energy, wind meteorologists will replace petroleum geologists. Energy architects will be centrally involved in the design of buildings.

17   In the new economy, the transport system will be designed to maximize mobility rather than automobile use. This new economy comprehensively reuses and recycles materials of all kinds. The goal in designing industrial processes and products is zero emissions and zero waste.

18   Plan A, business as usual, is no longer a viable option. We need to turn quickly to Plan B before the geopolitics of oil, grain, and raw material scarcity lead to political conflict and disruption of the social order on which economic progress depends.

For Class Discussion

1. What is Brown's main claim behind his extended focus on China? What implicit argument does he suggest about the inequalities in the consumption of Earth's resources?

2. How does Brown's perspective remain compelling even if his projections and extrapolations are speculative?

3. How effective is the proposal with which he concludes?

4. Where might this argument be vulnerable to criticism?

5. How has this article influenced the way you think about your and the world's consumption of resources?   ∎

Acceptance Speech for the Nobel Peace Prize for 2004
Wangari Muta Maathai

Wangari Muta Maathai of Kenya is an internationally known political and environmental leader and one of the foremost women of our time. She holds a doctorate in veterinary anatomy and served as chair of the department of veterinary anatomy at the University of Nairobi, the first woman in East and Central Africa to attain this professional stature. She was chairwoman of the National Council of Women in Kenya from 1976–1987. In 1977, she founded the Green Belt Movement, a grassroots NGO, involved in "planting trees with women groups in order to conserve the environment and improve their quality of life." The GBM describes its values as "volunteerism, love for environmental conservation, pro-action for self-betterment, accountability, transparency, and empowerment" (www.greenbeltmovement. org). In 1986, this movement developed a Pan African Green Belt Network. Maathai has won numerous prestigious awards for her activism, was elected to the Kenya parliament in 2002, and now serves as the asssistant minister for environment, natural resources, and wildlife. She delivered her acceptance speech for the Nobel Peace Prize on December 10, 2004, in Oslo, Norway.

> How does Wangari Muta Maathai use the convention of award acceptance speeches—the traditional tributes and acknowledgments— to reach out to her larger audience (fellow Africans and global citizens) and build community?

Your Majesties
Your Royal Highnesses
Honourable Members of the Norwegian Nobel Committee
Excellencies
Ladies and Gentlemen

1   I stand before you and the world humbled by this recognition and uplifted by the honour of being the 2004 Nobel Peace Laureate.

2   As the first African woman to receive this prize, I accept it on behalf of the people of Kenya and Africa, and indeed the world. I am especially mindful of women and the girl child. I hope it will encourage them to raise their voices and take more space for leadership. I know the honour also gives a deep sense of pride to our men, both old and young. As a mother, I appreciate the inspiration this brings to the youth and urge them to use it to pursue their dreams.

3   Although this prize comes to me, it acknowledges the work of countless individuals and groups across the globe. They work quietly and often without recognition to protect the environment, promote democracy, defend human rights and ensure equality between women and men. By so doing, they plant seeds of peace. I know they, too, are proud today. To all who feel represented by this prize I say use it to advance your mission and meet the high expectations the world will place on us.

4   This honour is also for my family, friends, partners and supporters throughout the world. All of them helped shape the vision and sustain our work, which was often accomplished under hostile conditions. I am also grateful to the people of Kenya—who remained stubbornly hopeful that democracy could be realized and their environment managed sustainably. Because of this support, I am here today to accept this great honour.

5   I am immensely privileged to join my fellow African Peace laureates, Presidents Nelson Mandela and F.W. de Klerk, Archbishop

Desmond Tutu, the late Chief Albert Luthuli, the late Anwar el-Sadat and the UN Secretary General, Kofi Annan.

6   I know that African people everywhere are encouraged by this news. My fellow Africans, as we embrace this recognition, let us use it to intensify our commitment to our people, to reduce conflicts and poverty and thereby improve their quality of life. Let us embrace democratic governance, protect human rights and protect our environment. I am confident that we shall rise to the occasion. I have always believed that solutions to most of our problems must come from us.

7   In this year's prize, the Norwegian Nobel Committee has placed the critical issue of environment and its linkage to democracy and peace before the world. For their visionary action, I am profoundly grateful. Recognizing that sustainable development, democracy and peace are indivisible is an idea whose time has come. Our work over the past 30 years has always appreciated and engaged these linkages.

8   My inspiration partly comes from my childhood experiences and observations of Nature in rural Kenya. It has been influenced and nurtured by the formal education I was privileged to receive in Kenya, the United States and Germany. As I was growing up, I witnessed forests being cleared and replaced by commercial plantations, which destroyed local biodiversity and the capacity of the forests to conserve water.

9   Excellencies, ladies and gentlemen,

10   In 1977, when we started the Green Belt Movement, I was partly responding to needs identified by rural women, namely lack of firewood, clean drinking water, balanced diets, shelter and income.

11   Throughout Africa, women are the primary caretakers, holding significant responsibility for tilling the land and feeding their families. As a result, they are often the first to become aware of environmental damage as resources become scarce and incapable of sustaining their families.

12   The women we worked with recounted that unlike in the past, they were unable to meet their basic needs. This was due to the degradation of their immediate environment as well as the introduction of commercial farming, which replaced the growing of household food crops. But international trade controlled the price of the exports from these small-scale farmers and a reasonable and just income could not be guaranteed. I came to understand that when the environment is destroyed, plundered or mismanaged, we undermine our quality of life and that of future generations.

13   Tree planting became a natural choice to address some of the initial basic needs identified by women. Also, tree planting is simple,

attainable and guarantees quick, successful results within a reasonable amount [of] time. This sustains interest and commitment.

14   So, together, we have planted over 30 million trees that provide fuel, food, shelter, and income to support their children's education and household needs. The activity also creates employment and improves soils and watersheds. Through their involvement, women gain some degree of power over their lives, especially their social and economic position and relevance in the family. This work continues.

15   Initially, the work was difficult because historically our people have been persuaded to believe that because they are poor, they lack not only capital, but also knowledge and skills to address their challenges. Instead they are conditioned to believe that solutions to their problems must come from 'outside'. Further, women did not realize that meeting their needs depended on their environment being healthy and well managed. They were also unaware that a degraded environment leads to a scramble for scarce resources and may culminate in poverty and even conflict. They were also unaware of the injustices of international economic arrangements.

16   In order to assist communities to understand these linkages, we developed a citizen education program, during which people identify their problems, the causes and possible solutions. They then make connections between their own personal actions and the problems they witness in the environment and in society. They learn that our world is confronted with a litany of woes: corruption, violence against women and children, disruption and breakdown of families, and disintegration of cultures and communities. They also identify the abuse of drugs and chemical substances, especially among young people. There are also devastating diseases that are defying cures or occurring in epidemic proportions. Of particular concern are HIV/AIDS, malaria and diseases associated with malnutrition.

17   On the environment front, they are exposed to many human activities that are devastating to the environment and societies. These include widespread destruction of ecosystems, especially through deforestation, climatic instability, and contamination in the soils and waters that all contribute to excruciating poverty.

18   In the process, the participants discover that they must be part of the solutions. They realize their hidden potential and are empowered to overcome inertia and take action. They come to recognize that they are the primary custodians and beneficiaries of the environment that sustains them.

19   Entire communities also come to understand that while it is necessary to hold their governments accountable, it is equally important that in their own relationships with each other, they exemplify the leadership values they wish to see in their own leaders, namely justice, integrity and trust.

20   Although initially the Green Belt Movement's tree planting activities did not address issues of democracy and peace, it soon became clear that responsible governance of the environment was impossible without democratic space. Therefore, the tree became a symbol for the democratic struggle in Kenya. Citizens were mobilised to challenge widespread abuses of power, corruption and environmental mismanagement. In Nairobi's Uhuru Park, at Freedom Corner, and in many parts of the country, trees of peace were planted to demand the release of prisoners of conscience and a peaceful transition to democracy.

21   Through the Green Belt Movement, thousands of ordinary citizens were mobilised and empowered to take action and effect change. They learned to overcome fear and a sense of helplessness and moved to defend democratic rights.

22   In time, the tree also became a symbol for peace and conflict resolution, especially during ethnic conflicts in Kenya when the Green Belt Movement used peace trees to reconcile disputing communities. During the ongoing re-writing of the Kenyan constitution, similar trees of peace were planted in many parts of the country to promote a culture of peace. Using trees as a symbol of peace is in keeping with a widespread African tradition. For example, the elders of the Kikuyu carried a staff from the thigi tree that, when placed between two disputing sides, caused them to stop fighting and seek reconciliation. Many communities in Africa have these traditions.

23   Such practices are part of an extensive cultural heritage, which contributes both to the conservation of habitats and to cultures of peace. With the destruction of these cultures and the introduction of new values, local biodiversity is no longer valued or protected and as a result, it is quickly degraded and disappears. For this reason, The Green Belt Movement explores the concept of cultural biodiversity, especially with respect to indigenous seeds and medicinal plants.

24   As we progressively understood the causes of environmental degradation, we saw the need for good governance. Indeed, the state of any country's environment is a reflection of the kind of governance in place, and without good governance there can be no peace. Many countries, which have poor governance systems, are also likely to have conflicts and poor laws protecting the environment.

25   In 2002, the courage, resilience, patience and commitment of members of the Green Belt Movement, other civil society organizations, and the Kenyan public culminated in the peaceful transition to a democratic government and laid the foundation for a more stable society.

26   Excellencies, friends, ladies and gentlemen,

27   It is 30 years since we started this work. Activities that devastate the environment and societies continue unabated. Today we

are faced with a challenge that calls for a shift in our thinking, so that humanity stops threatening its life-support system. We are called to assist the Earth to heal her wounds and in the process heal our own—indeed, to embrace the whole creation in all its diversity, beauty and wonder. This will happen if we see the need to revive our sense of belonging to a larger family of life, with which we have shared our evolutionary process.

28   In the course of history, there comes a time when humanity is called to shift to a new level of consciousness, to reach a higher moral ground. A time when we have to shed our fear and give hope to each other.

29   That time is now.

30   The Norwegian Nobel Committee has challenged the world to broaden the understanding of peace: there can be no peace without equitable development; and there can be no development without sustainable management of the environment in a democratic and peaceful space. This shift is an idea whose time has come.

31   I call on leaders, especially from Africa, to expand democratic space and build fair and just societies that allow the creativity and energy of their citizens to flourish. Those of us who have been privileged to receive education, skills, and experiences and even power must be role models for the next generation of leadership. In this regard, I would also like to appeal for the freedom of my fellow laureate Aung San Suu Kyi so that she can continue her work for peace and democracy for the people of Burma and the world at large.

32   Culture plays a central role in the political, economic and social life of communities. Indeed, culture may be the missing link in the development of Africa. Culture is dynamic and evolves over time, consciously discarding retrogressive traditions, like female genital mutilation (FGM), and embracing aspects that are good and useful.

33   Africans, especially, should re-discover positive aspects of their culture. In accepting them, they would give themselves a sense of belonging, identity and self-confidence.

34   Ladies and Gentlemen,

35   There is also need to galvanize civil society and grassroots movements to catalyse change. I call upon governments to recognize the role of these social movements in building a critical mass of responsible citizens, who help maintain checks and balances in society. On their part, civil society should embrace not only their rights but also their responsibilities.

36   Further, industry and global institutions must appreciate that ensuring economic justice, equity and ecological integrity are of greater value than profits at any cost. The extreme global inequities and prevailing consumption patterns continue at the expense of the environment and peaceful co-existence. The choice is ours.

37   I would like to call on young people to commit themselves to activities that contribute toward achieving their long-term dreams. They have the energy and creativity to shape a sustainable future. To the young people I say, you are a gift to your communities and indeed the world You are our hope and our future.

38   The holistic approach to development, as exemplified by the Green Belt Movement, could be embraced and replicated in more parts of Africa and beyond. It is for this reason that I have established the Wangari Maathai Foundation to ensure the continuation and expansion of these activities. Although a lot has been achieved, much remains to be done.

39   Excellencies, ladies and gentlemen,

40   As I conclude I reflect on my childhood experience when I would visit a stream next to our home to fetch water for my mother. I would drink water straight from the stream. Playing among the arrowroot leaves I tried in vain to pick up the strands of frogs' eggs, believing they were beads. But every time I put my little fingers under them they would break. Later, I saw thousands of tadpoles: black, energetic and wriggling through the clear water against the background of the brown earth. This is the world I inherited from my parents.

41   Today, over 50 years later, the stream has dried up, women walk long distances for water, which is not always clean, and children will never know what they have lost. The challenge is to restore the home of the tadpoles and give back to our children a world of beauty and wonder.

42   Thank you very much.

For Class Discussion

1. Wangari Muta Maathai articulates a philosophy of environmental and political activism as much as she outlines a proposed course of action. What are the main points of her philosophy and how does she underscore the connections among "sustainable development, democracy and peace"?

2. What global organizations and people constitute the larger audience for this talk? How does Maathai seek to inspire and move her audience through appeals to their values, imaginations, and emotions? What actions is she calling on them to take?

3. What many meanings and values do trees have for Maathai?

4. How does this speech convey her authority and credibility?

5. What important connections does Maathai establish between women and the environment?

6. How has this speech affected your view of Africa, environmental resources, and successful environmental practices? ∎

FIGURE 7.2 United Nations Environment Programme Poster *(This poster has been reproduced by kind permission of the United Nations Environment Programme. This poster on "poverty and the environment" can be found at www.unep.org/wssd/Pictures/Posters/POVERTY.1.jpg)*

Health and Environment
United Nations Environment Programme

This poster is one of a series sponsored by the United Nations Environment Programme for an exhibition at the World Summit on Sustainable Development, held August 26–September 3, 2002, in Johannesburg, South Africa. The United Nations Environment Programme's mission is "to provide leadership and encourage partnership in caring for the environment by inspiring, informing, and enabling nations and peoples to improve their quality of life without compromising that of future generations" ("About UNEP," www.unep.org). The posters in this series have a dual educational and persuasive aim.

> If you look only at the title of the poster, "Health and Environment," and the photo, what connections between environmental, economic, and social problems can you see? What background knowledge does it expect of its audience?

For Class Discussion

1. What are the impressions and ideas that this poster conveys?
2. In your own words, how would you state the main claim of this poster? What evidence does it offer in support of its claim?
3. What ideas about water, sanitation, and health does this poster convey?
4. How does this poster appeal to the emotions and values of a global audience, especially people living in developed countries?
5. In what ways does this poster argue causes and consequences? In what way does it make a proposal and support it? How effective is it in communicating its argument? ■

Why We Owe So Much to Victims of Disaster
Andrew Simms

Andrew Simms has been an environmental activist with Greenpeace UK, Oxfam, and the Energy and Resources Institute Europe. As policy director, he heads the Climate Change program of the New Economics Foundation, an independent UK think tank that aims to "improve the quality of life by promoting innovative solutions that challenge mainstream thinking on economic, environment and social issues" and by putting "people and the planet first" (from its "About Us" link, www.neweconomics.org). Simms's book *Ecological Debt: The Health of the Planet and the Wealth of Nations* was published in 2005. This article appeared in the *New Statesman* on May 16, 2005. A British magazine, the *New Statesman* was founded in 1913 as an organ of socialist ideas; it has a reputation for high-quality writing and appeals to "bright thinkers everywhere" (www.newstatesman.com).

> What rhetorical features of this argument suggest that Andrew Simms is writing for an audience who shares his views? What assumptions about climate-related disasters underlie this argument?

1   If you want to know how to tackle global warming, try the simple wisdom of Wilkins Micawber in Dickens's David Copperfield. "Annual income twenty pounds, annual expenditure nineteen pounds nineteen and six, result happiness," he said. "Annual income twenty pounds, annual expenditure twenty pounds ought and six, result misery."

2   It is rarely understood this way, but climate change is really a problem of debt. Not a cash debt, but an ecological one. Environmentally, we're living way beyond our means, spending more than the bank of the earth and the atmosphere can replace in our accounts. It is this debt—not the hole in the nation's public spending plans—that ought to have been the subject of the election campaign. And it is this debt—not the financial debts of poor nations to rich—that should guide the thinking of the Chancellor and other western leaders as they approach the G8 summit in July.

3   Gordon Brown and Tony Blair have set Africa and global warming as the summit's key themes. Yet newly released documents reveal one of the government's more embarrassing oversights. It was agreed at an international summit, more than three years ago, to create a special pot of money to help poor countries cope with climate change. Britain, alone among major European aid donors, has failed to contribute to the "Least Developed Countries Fund".

4   For years, we have been pilfering from the natural resource accounts of the rest of the world. When the people of Asia, Africa and Latin America decide they want to spend their fair share of nature's equity, either it won't be there or we could be on the verge of a crash in its already overstretched banking system. If the whole world wanted to live like people in the UK, we would need the natural resources of three more planets. If the US were the model, we would need five.

5   It's not just that we owe these countries for our profligate use of the planet's resources. It is also that they suffer the worst effects of our overuse. The most vulnerable people in the poorest countries—particularly children and women—are in effect paying the interest on our ecological debts. According to the World Disasters Report, the number of mostly climate-related disasters rose from just over

400 a year in 1994–98 to more than 700 a year in 1999–2003, with the biggest rise in the poorest countries.

6   The sight of a Mozambican woman giving birth in a tree during the great storms of 2000 is seared into the world's consciousness. Mozambique was desperately poor and burdened with debt payments. The floods were the worst for 150 years. Not only had its potential to develop been mismanaged by western creditors, Mozambique was left more vulnerable because it had to choose between preparing for disasters or spending its meager resources on health and education. Now, in a warming world, Africa's rainfall, so crucial to its farming, is about to become even more erratic.

7   The story is similar outside Africa. In the mid- to late 1990s, at the height of the Jubilee 2000 debt cancellation campaign, nearly half the Jamaican government's spending went on debt service. The island is rich in natural resources, but it was getting harder for it to earn a living from exporting crops such as sugar and bananas. Yet, under pressure from the IMF and the World Bank, the money available for social programmes in Jamaica was halved.

8   Angela Stultz-Crawle, a local woman who ran a project in Bennetlands, Kingston to provide basic health and education services, saw the consequences at first hand: reductions in health programmes, in education, in road repairs, in lights. "Just walking around," she said, "you see people living in dirt yards, scrap-board houses. It is repaying. Every day you hear the government come out and say, 'Oh, we have met our IMF deadlines, we have paid,' and everyone claps." Again, Jamaica is particularly vulnerable to the extreme weather that climate change will make more frequent. Last year alone, two major hurricanes, Ivan and Charley, skirted its shores.

9   So across the developing world, the poorest people suffer from two crises, to neither of which they contributed: financial debt (which their governments are repaying) and ecological debt (which our governments aren't repaying).

10   In case after case—the IMF-approved kleptocracy of Mobutu's Zaire, the collusion with corruption, asset-stripping and violence in Nigeria's oilfields—the responsibility for financial debts lies at least as much in western capitals as in developing countries in the south. Yet, to win paltry debt relief, poor countries had to swallow the economic-policy equivalent of horse pills. Even the Financial Times commented that the IMF "probably ruined as many economies as they have saved". Yet we still expect poor countries to repay most of their debts, despite the effects on their people's lifestyles. Rich countries, faced with ecological debt, will not even give up the four-wheel-drive school run.

11   The widening global gap in wealth was built on ecological debts. And today's economic superpowers soon became as successful in

their disproportionate occupation of the atmosphere with carbon emissions as they were in colonial times with their military occupation of the terrestrial world. Until the Second World War, they managed this atmospheric occupation largely through exploiting their own fossil-fuel reserves. But from around 1950 they became increasingly dependent on energy imports. By 1998, the wealthiest fifth of the world was consuming 68 per cent of commercially produced energy; the poorest fifth, 2 per cent.

12   In 2002, many rich countries were pumping out more carbon dioxide per person than they were a decade earlier, when they signed the UN Framework Convention on Climate Change. Now, with Africa and climate change at the top of the G8 summit agenda, there couldn't be a better time for a little paradigm shift. If Blair and Brown want to show leadership, they could relabel the G8 as the inaugural meeting of the ecological debtors' club, and start discussing how to pay back their creditors down south.

13   But is there any chance that the advanced industrial economies could make the cuts in consumption needed to clear their debts? Perhaps we should ask the women recently seen reminiscing about VE Day, women who during the world war had to keep house under severe constraints. After all, global warming is now described as a threat more serious than war or terrorism. Drawing on articles in Good Housekeeping, and on guides with such titles as Feeding Cats and Dogs in Wartime or Sew and Save, they enormously reduced household consumption—use of electrical appliances, for example, dropped 82 per cent—while at the same time dramatically improving the nation's health.

14   The ecological debt problem of climate change, if it is to be solved, will still require a proper global framework, eventually giving everybody on the planet an equal entitlement to emit greenhouse gases, and allowing those who under-emit to trade with those who wish to over-emit. But such efforts will be hollow unless the argument to cut consumption can be won at household level.

15   To refuse the challenge would be the deepest hypocrisy. We have demanded that the world's poorest countries reshape their economies to pay service on dodgy foreign debts. It would be an appalling double standard now to suggest that we couldn't afford either to help developing countries adapt to climate change, or to cut our emissions by the 80–90 per cent considered necessary.

16   The language of restraint on public spending permeates our public discourse, yet the concept of living within our environmental means still escapes mainstream economics. That will have to change. "Balancing nature's books" could be the simple language that enables the green movement to resonate with the public. Imagine opening a letter from the bank over breakfast to learn that,

instead of your usual overdraft, you had an ecological debt that threatened the planet. I wouldn't want to be there when the bailiffs called for that one.

For Class Discussion

1. What analogy underlies this argument?
2. What are Andrew Simms's claims about ecological debt and what evidence does he offer?
3. How does Simms use historical precedents and other appeals to his readers' imaginations and emotions? What proposal and challenge does he offer citizens/consumers?
4. What objections might opponents raise to this argument?
5. How emotionally and intellectually effective is Simms's main analogy? What are its rhetorical strengths and weaknesses?   ■

Himalayan Snow Job
Patrick J. Michaels

Patrick J. Michaels, a senior fellow in environmental studies at the libertarian Cato Institute, has authored three books debunking global warming: *Sound and Fury: The Science and Politics of Global Warming* (1992), *The Satanic Gases: Clearing the Air about Global Warming* (2000), and *Meltdown: The Predictable Distortion of Global Warming by Scientists, Politicians, and the Media* (2004). Michaels is a climatologist, a research professor of environmental sciences at the University of Virginia, and a well-known dissenting voice on the Intergovernmental Panel of Climate Change, established by the World Meteorological Organization (WMO) and the United Nations Environment Programme in 1988 to "assess on a comprehensive, objective, and open and transparent basis the scientific, technical and socio-economic information relevant to understanding the scientific basis of risk of human-induced climate change" (www.ipcc.ch/about/about.htm). This op-ed piece first appeared in the *Washington Times*, a right-leaning newspaper, on April 1, 2005.

Patrick J. Michaels wrote this piece to counter what environmental advocacy groups are saying about global warming's damage. To what cause does Michaels attribute glacial melting? Whom do you see as the most receptive audience for Michaels's argument in this piece?

1   Recently, a World Wildlife Fund press release was picked up by Reuters. "Himalayan glaciers are among the fastest-retreating glaciers globally due to the effects of global warming," the advocacy group announced.

2   WWF timed its press release for a two-day Energy and Environmental Ministerial conference in London, where the United States was (predictably) criticized because it won't commit economic suicide by adopting the Kyoto Protocol on global warming.

3   This is one of those repeating news stories, like "Strife in Haiti" or "Irish unrest." It goes like this. "The (glaciers, polar bears, butterflies) of (anywhere) are in dramatic decline because of global warming. Unless the (U.S., U.S., U.S.) signs on to the Kyoto Protocol, their continued decline is assured."

4   Here's another broken record. "It appears that the (U.N., World Wildlife Fund, New York Times) forgot to check the temperature histories where the (ice, polar bears, butterflies) are in decline, and the (U.S., U.S., U.S.) isn't going along with counterfactual nonsense produced by agenda-driven environmentalists."

5   We offer this evidence. WWF is especially interested in the Gangotri glacier, in the Indian Himalayas. The glacier is retreating an average 75 feet yearly.

6   Glaciers are in steady state when the annual snowfall and summer melting rate are roughly in balance. Actually, this is rare. When glaciers melt too much in the summer, they retreat. And if it snows more in the winter than normal, they advance.

7   The United Nations Intergovernmental Panel on Climate Change (IPCC) publishes historical temperature records around the planet. They are averages for 5×5 degree latitude/longitude rectangles. They used these somewhat large areas so that, in general, many local records are averaged up to form a reliable regional picture. The Gangotri Glacier, which feeds the Ganges River, is in the 30–35N, 75–80E box.

8   High-altitude glaciers melt during the summer. The IPCC has June–August temperatures for the Gangotri region back [to] 1875. The net decline in temperature over the last 130 years is striking. In fact, at 1.2 degrees (C), it is one of the largest summer coolings on Earth. That's right: cooling. In contrast, the temperature for the Northern Hemisphere as a whole increased 0.8 degrees during the same period.

9   Still, no one doubts the Gangotri glacier is receding. It was expanded far beyond where it is today when the cooling was first noted more than a century ago. Temperatures reached their low in 1990 and have popped up a bit, to the long-term average for the last 130 years. Perhaps this has something to do with Gangotri's recent more rapid retreat.

10   But that it has been in such a decline as overall century-scale temperatures have cooled tells us much about the long-term fate of glaciers away from polar regions: They are relics of the Ice Age, destined to melt.

11   Another place with an ice history that resembles Gangotri is our own Glacier National Park in Montana. There were 147 glaciers in the park 150 years ago, near the start of the Gangotri temperature record. Today there are only 37. What happened to summer temperatures? Unlike Gangotri, they didn't cool. But temperatures remained fairly constant, with no significant warming since records began in 1895.

12   Most scientists think the mid-19th century marks the end of a multicentury period known as the "Little Ice Age," though a small but vocal core of skeptics maintain a view known as the "Hockey Stick" history—one in which temperatures do not change for nearly a millennium and then shoot up in the last 100 years, producing a graph that indeed resembles a hockey stick. This view has been pretty much marginalized in a number of papers in scientific literature over the last year.

13   Indeed, glaciers went into retreat at the end of this cold period. Gangotri is even more tenuous, receding even as local temperatures continued declining.

14   Incidentally, the Northern Hemisphere's largest ice mass—the Greenland icecap—is in retreat in the southern part of the island, where temperatures also show a substantial net cooling for the last 75 years.

15   All this leads to an obvious conclusion. Southern Greenland, Glacier National Park and the Himalayan glaciers are on their way out, with little or no nudging needed from people. They're relics of the Big Ice Age that ended 11,000 years ago. It's too bad, though, that in the fight to hype global warming, the truth is also rapidly becoming another relic.

For Class Discussion

1. What evidence does Patrick J. Michaels use to refute his opponents and to support his view?

2. What might the World Wildlife Fund say in response to Michaels's criticisms? Does anything besides temperatures affect glaciers' advance and retreat?

3. What rhetorical effect does Michaels's word choice and tone in these phrases have: "Himalayan Snow Job," "commit economic suicide," "broken record," "counterfactual nonsense produced by agenda-driven environmentalists," and "fight to hype global warming"?

4. Some of Michaels's opponents have asserted that he has received financial support from coal and oil companies. These opponents might say that Michaels also has an "agenda." What other weaknesses do you see in this argument?

5. To make an informed evaluation of Michaels's views, what questions and ideas might you want to research? ■

Gentlemen, We Have a Dilemma
John Morris

John Morris is an artist, graphic designer, and political cartoonist in the United Kingdom. He regularly publishes business cartoons featured on his Web site, Morris Business Cartoons (www.businesscartoons.co.uk). This cartoon was posted on the cartoon database www.cartoonstock.com.

How might business executives respond to this cartoon?

For Class Discussion

1. How would you describe the setting and story line of this cartoon?
2. What is the conflict and who are the opposing characters depicted directly or indirectly in this cartoon?
3. How might these authors of readings in this chapter—Fredrik Segerfeldt, Robert L. Ayers, Joshua Ortega, Maude Barlow, and Ross Gelbspan—respond to this cartoon?
4. What is this cartoon's contribution to the global controversies over the environment? ■

"Gentlemen, we have a dilemma. Pollution scientists say it'll destroy the ozone - however, Market Research predict it'll sell like hot cakes."

FIGURE 7.3 "Gentlemen, We Have a Dilemma" *(© www.Cartoonstock.com)*

False Prophets, Bad Economics
Bjorn Lomborg

Bjorn Lomborg, a Danish economist and former associate professor of statistics in the department of political science at the University of Aarhus, Denmark, is one of the most prominent figures in the international controversy over global warming and climate change. He wrote his controversial book *The Skeptical Environmentalist: Measuring the Real State of the World* (2001) to rebut the reports of environmentalist think tanks and advocacy groups such as Worldwatch Institute and its yearly *State of the World* analysis of environmental problems. Lomborg's main thesis in this book is that economical and statistical analysis of the data reveals that the environment and ecosystems are not deteriorating; that natural resources aren't disastrously dwindling; that air and water aren't increasingly polluted; and that global warming cannot be feasibly and economically countered by reducing greenhouse gas emissions. Recently, Lomborg assembled a panel of eight eminent economists as the Copenhagen Consensus to create a "rational prioritization" of global problems and the "costs and benefits" of global investment in trying to solve or treat these problems. Lomborg's book *Global Crises, Global Solutions* (2004) reports how this group ranked ten global challenges (www.copenhagenconsensus.com). This op-ed piece appeared in *Newsweek International* on December 13, 2004, and also on the MSNBC.com Web site.

> What rhetorical strategies for handling opposing views and using data in support of his own claim has Bjorn Lomborg employed in this op-ed piece for a general readership?

1   Global warming gets more scary by the minute. The European Union calls it "one of the most threatening issues that we are facing today." Britain's chief scientist considers it "more serious even than the threat of terrorism." His boss, Tony Blair, sees it as "the single most important issue," and plans to use his dual EU and G8 presidency next year to make the battle against global warming the industrial world's top priority. This message will resound at the U.N. climate-change summit starting this week in Buenos Aires: strong action, built around the Kyoto Protocol, is not only urgent. It is the moral test of our time.

2   This is a counterproductive exaggeration. Global warming is happening and is very important, no question, but its negative impacts are vastly overblown. Headlines warn of intense hurricanes and a deluging ocean, the Gulf Stream's shutting down, megadroughts and famine, ending in the extinction of the human race, or its confinement to Antarctica. This is fiction, the stuff of Hollywood imaginations. There is also no question that climate change will hit hardest

in the Third World, but the hype has impaired our ability to ask where our money can do the most good for the poor. A group of the world's top economists, gathered by the Copenhagen Consensus project this May, asked that very question: where can we do the most good? Global warming ended up at the bottom of the priority list.

3   The sloppy logic of the Kyoto advocates is surprising. The protocol would demand the biggest international financial commitment in history, yet it rests on an elementary fallacy: it compares the *total* costs of potential damage with the *marginal* costs of slightly ameliorating the problem. Even if every industrial country met the Kyoto goals of reducing carbon emissions 30 percent by 2010, the impact would be tiny. By 2100 that would have postponed global warming by a mere six years. The guy in Bangladesh driven from his home by rising sea levels would have to move in 2106, instead of 2100.

4   This makes little sense. The best estimates of the cost of implementing Kyoto run between $150 billion and $350 billion a year. The best estimates of the damage from global warming reach about $500 billion annually in 2100. Proponents argue that paying $150 billion to avoid $500 billion in damages is a good deal. But that's not what's on offer. We still have to pay the $500 billion, only six years later. So the real offer is: we pay $150 billion each year for 100 years to postpone payment of $500 billion annually, starting in 2100. *All* economic models show this to be, as the Copenhagen Consensus put it, a "bad" deal.

5   The fearmongers assume a static world that will do nothing to protect itself. Citing Poland, the U.N. Climate Panel figures the cost of flooding could be $46 billion, although they assume twice the likely rise in sea levels and that Poland will not spend just $6.1 billion to avoid it. A similar assumption underlies the theory that malaria outbreaks will rise with the temperature. Malaria has disappeared as a major epidemic disease in the West, despite rising temperatures, because rising wealth brought better health care and infrastructure. As the developing world gets more wealthy, malaria is likely to decrease.

6   There are many better ways to help the poor than by fighting global warming. Directly addressing the most pressing issues of disease, hunger and polluted water will not only do obvious good, it will make the poor less vulnerable to climate change.

7   And poverty is a huge problem *now*. The United Nations projects that the average person in the developing world in 2100 will be at least as rich as we are today, and more likely two to four times richer. When Bangladesh faces those elevated seas in 2100, it will be a rich Netherlands. The real question is whether we spend money to do a little good in a rich Netherlands far into the future, or a lot of good in a poor Bangladesh now.

8   The world can't (or won't) pay for everything, so we have a moral obligation to set priorities. This was the starting point of the Copenhagen Consensus project, which found that problems like AIDS, hunger and malaria could be fought very cost-efficiently, but climate change could not. We can prevent HIV by handing out condoms and improving health education. We can prevent millions from dying of malnutrition with simple vitamin supplements. This does not mean we should ignore climate change. We should, for example, look at the right mix of incentives and regulations to encourage investment in renewable energy. But it does mean that there are far better ways to spend $150 billion a year. World leaders would be well advised to let go of their obsession with the distant and exaggerated threat of climate change in order to start doing some real good for the world, now.

For Class Discussion

1. What policy proposal does Bjorn Lomborg sketch out in this op-ed piece?

2. What assumptions has Lomborg made about economics that he does not discuss or defend in this argument?

3. What questions is Lomborg *not* asking, or put another way, what gaps do you see in Lomborg's reasoning that you would want to investigate in order to take your own stand on the issue of economics and global warming?

4. What is persuasive about Lomborg's argument and what is weak?

Boiling Point: Nature Doesn't Compromise on Global Climate Change; Activists Must Not Either

Ross Gelbspan

A bold, eminent environmental journalist, Ross Gelbspan has worked as an editor and reporter for such prominent news publications as the *Boston Globe*, the *Philadelphia Bulletin*, the *Washington Post*, and the *Village Voice*. Gelbspan has covered several UN conferences on the environment. He has written for *Harper's* and the *Nation* and has authored two books on climate change: *The Heat Is On: The Climate Crisis, the Cover-Up, the Prescription* (1998) and *Boiling Point: How Politicians, Big Oil and Coal, Journalists and Activists Are Fueling the Climate Crisis—And What We Can Do to Avert Disaster* (2004). This article is an excerpt from *Boiling Point,* published in the *Nation,* a liberal news commentary magazine focused on social justice, on August 16, 2004.

> What groups and organizations does Gelbspan target in this argument and what case does he make against each? What makes this article particularly suitable for publication in the *Nation?*

1   Climate change is not just another issue. It is the overriding threat facing human civilization in the twenty-first century, and so far our institutions are doing dangerously little to address it. Americans in particular are still in denial, thanks largely to the efforts of the fossil-fuel industry and its allies in the Bush Administration. But the nation's biggest environmental organizations and opposition politicians have also displayed a disturbing lack of leadership on this crucial challenge.

2   They are by no means the only roadblocks to meaningful action on climate change. In addition to the Bush Administration and the fossil-fuel lobby, the failure of the press to cover the climate crisis has left the United States ten years behind the rest of the world in addressing this issue. Given this background, the failure of environmentalists to fill the informational and political vacuum is especially distressing.

3   Over the past decade, the arguments against the reality of climate change by the carbon lobby have been as inconsistent as the weather itself. During the early years of the 1990s, the fossil-fuel lobby insisted that global warming was not happening. In the face of incontrovertible findings by the scientific community, the industry then conceded that climate change is happening but is so inconsequential as to be negligible. When new findings indicated that the warming is indeed significant, the spokesmen for the coal and oil industries then put forth the argument that global warming is good for us.

4   But the central argument that big coal and big oil have spent millions of dollars to amplify over the past decade is that the warming is a natural phenomenon on which human beings have little or no impact. That argument has been repeatedly discredited by the world's leading climate scientists. Under the auspices of the United Nations, more than 2,000 scientists from 100 countries have participated over the past fifteen years in what is most likely the largest, most rigorously peer-reviewed scientific collaboration in history. In 1995 the UN-sponsored panel found a "discernible human influence" on the planet's warming climate. The scientists subsequently concluded that to stabilize our climate requires humanity to cut its use of coal and oil by 70 percent in a very short time.

5   The Kyoto Protocol, by contrast, calls for industrial countries to cut aggregate emissions by just 5.2 percent by 2012. That is a woefully inadequate response; as British Prime Minister Tony Blair admitted in 2002, "Even if we deliver on Kyoto, it will at best mean a reduction of one percent in global emissions. . . . In truth, Kyoto is not radical enough."

6   Nevertheless, the current low goals of the Protocol are championed by many Americans who should know better, including leading Democrats like John Kerry and virtually every national environmental organization. Confronted by the steel wall of resistance of the fossil-fuel lobby and their political allies, most climate activists and sympathetic politicians have retreated into approaches that are dismally inadequate to the magnitude of the challenge.

7   Around the country, advocates are working to get people to drive less, turn down their thermostats and reduce their energy use. Unfortunately, while many environmental problems are susceptible to lifestyle changes, climate change is not one of them.

8   Several of the country's leading national environmental groups are promoting limits for future atmospheric carbon levels that are the best they think they can negotiate. But while those limits may be politically realistic, they would likely be environmentally catastrophic. Most advocates, moreover, are relying on goals and mechanisms that were proposed about a decade ago, before the true urgency of the climate crisis became apparent. In 2000, researchers at the Hadley Center, Britain's main climate research institute, found that the climate will change 50 percent more quickly than was previously assumed. Their projections show that many of the world's forests will begin to turn from sinks (vegetation that absorbs carbon dioxide) to sources (which release it)—dying off and emitting carbon—by about 2050. In 1998 a team of researchers reported in the journal *Nature* that unless the world is getting half its energy from noncarbon sources by 2018, we will see an inevitable doubling—and possible tripling—of atmospheric carbon levels later in this century.

9   Virtually all the approaches by activists in the United States, moreover, are domestic in nature. They ignore both the world's developing countries and, equally important from the standpoint of national security, the oil-producing nations of the Middle East. Ultimately, even if the United States, Europe, Canada, Australia and Japan were to cut emissions dramatically, those cuts would be overwhelmed by the coming increase of carbon from India, China, Mexico, Nigeria and all the other developing countries struggling to stay ahead of poverty.

10   Many alternative approaches rely on market-based solutions because their proponents believe that, in an age of market fundamentalism, no other approach can gain political traction.

Unfortunately, nature's laws are not about supply and demand; they are about limits, thresholds and surprises. The progress of the Dow does not seem to influence the increasing rate of melting of the Greenland ice sheet; the collapse of the ecosystems of the North Sea will not be arrested by an upswing in consumer confidence.

11   Many groups justify the minimalist goals of making people more energy efficient as the first phase in building a political base for more aggressive action. In the past, that pattern has been successful in developing various movements. In the case of climate change, however, nature's timetable is very different from that of political organizers. Unfortunately, the signals from the planet tell us we do not have the luxury of waiting another generation to allow for the orderly maturation of a movement.

12   Finally, the environmental establishment insists on casting the climate crisis as an environmental problem. But climate change is no longer the exclusive franchise of the environmental movement. Any successful movement must include horizontal alliances with groups involved in international relief and development, campaign finance reform, public health, corporate accountability, labor, human rights and environmental justice. The real dimensions of climate change directly affect the agendas of a wide spectrum of activist organizations.

13   The environmental movement has proved it cannot accomplish large-scale change by itself. Despite occasional spasms of cooperation, the major environmental groups have been unwilling to join together around a unified climate agenda, pool resources and mobilize a united campaign on the climate. Even as the major funders of climate and energy-oriented groups hold summit meetings in search of a common vision, they shy away from the most obvious of imperatives: using their combined influence and outreach to focus attention—and demand action—on the climate crisis. As the major national groups insist on promoting exclusive agendas and protecting carefully defined turfs (in the process, squandering both talent and donor dollars on internecine fighting), the climate movement is spinning its wheels.

14   Take the critical issue of climate stabilization—the level at which the world agrees to cap the buildup of carbon concentrations in the atmosphere. The major national environmental groups focusing on climate—groups like the Natural Resources Defense Council, the Union of Concerned Scientists and the WWF (World Wildlife Fund)—have agreed to accept what they see as a politically feasible target of 450 parts per million of carbon dioxide. While the 450 goal may be politically realistic, it would likely be environmentally catastrophic. With carbon levels having risen by only 90 parts per million (from their pre-industrial level of 280 ppm to more than 370 ppm today), glaciers are now melting into puddles, sea levels

are rising, violent weather is increasing and the timing of the seasons has changed—all from a 1-degree Fahrenheit rise in the past century. Carbon concentrations of 450 ppm will most likely result in a deeply fractured and chaotic world.

15   The major national environmental groups, moreover, are trapped in a Beltway mentality that measures progress in small, incremental victories. They are operating in a Washington environment that is at best indifferent and at worst actively antagonistic. And too often these organizations are at the mercy of fickle funders whose agendas range from protecting wetlands to keeping disposable diapers out of landfills.

16   The fossil-fuel lobby has hijacked America's energy and climate policies. One appropriate response might involve environmental leaders' forging a coalition of corporate and financial institutions of equivalent force and influence to counteract the carbon industry's stranglehold on Congress and the White House.

17   The vast majority of climate groups shun confrontation and work instead to get people to reduce their personal energy footprints. That can certainly help spread awareness of the issue. But by persuading concerned citizens to cut back on their personal energy use, these groups are promoting the implicit message that climate change can be solved by individual resolve. It cannot. Moreover, this message blames the victim: People are made to feel guilty if they own a gas guzzler or live in a poorly insulated home. In fact, people should be outraged that the government does not require automakers to sell cars that run on clean fuels, that building codes do not reduce heating and cooling energy requirements by 70 percent and that government energy policies do not mandate decentralized, home-based or regional sources of clean electricity.

18   What many groups offer their followers instead is the consolation of a personal sense of righteousness that comes from living one's life a bit more frugally. That feeling of righteousness, coincidentally, is largely reserved for wealthier people who can afford to exercise some control over their housing and transportation expenditures. Many poorer people—who cannot afford to trade in their 1990 gas guzzlers for shiny new Toyota Priuses—are deprived of the chance to enjoy the same sense of righteousness, illusory though it may be.

19   Given the lock on Congress and the White House by the carbon lobby, there is no way the US government will pursue a rapid global energy transition without a massive uprising of popular will. Environmentalists should therefore be forging alliances with other activists who focus on international development, campaign finance reform, corporate accountability, public health, labor, environmental justice and human rights—not to mention with

communities of faith—to mobilize a broad, inclusive constituency around the issue.

20   The tragedy underlying the failure of the environmental community lies in the fact that so many talented, dedicated and underpaid people are putting their lives on the line in ways that will make little difference to the climate crisis. They are outspoken in their despair about what is happening to the planet. They are candid about their acceptance of a self-defeating political realism that requires relentless accommodation. What is missing is an expression of the rage they all feel.

21   The United States did not withdraw from Vietnam because a few individuals moved to Canada or Sweden to avoid military service or because the leaders of the antiwar movement negotiated a reduction of the bombing runs over Vietnam. The United States left Vietnam because a sustained uprising of popular will forced one President of the United States to drop his plans for reelection and pressured his successor to scramble until he had achieved something he could call "peace with honor."

22   These comparisons to the climate movement may be seen as too harsh until one considers the most fundamental fact about the climate crisis: Activists compromise. Nature does not.

For Class Discussion

1. What reasons and evidence does Ross Gelbspan employ to expose the fossil fuel industry?

2. Gelbspan argues a radical view of global warming. By what reasoning and with what evidence does he justify his urgency and intensity?

3. This article includes a number of passages like this one:

   Unfortunately, nature's laws are not about supply and demand; they are about limits, thresholds and surprises. The progress of the Dow does not seem to influence the increasing rate of melting of the Greenland ice sheet; the collapse of the ecosystems of the North Sea will not be arrested by an upswing in consumer confidence.

   What is the tone of this passage? How does Gelbspan use language and sentence style for rhetorical effect? What other sentences or passages are similarly forceful?

4. Gelbspan concludes this impassioned piece with a historical precedent. How does he hope to tap his readers' values and emotions with this example?

5. What surprised or disturbed you about Gelbspan's view of global warming? What do you imagine was Gelbspan's response to the hurricane damage in New Orleans, Louisiana, in August 2005? ■

FIGURE 7.4 Environmental Hourglass *(© www.Cartoonstock.com)*

Environmental Hourglass
Bill Greenhead

British animator and cartoonist Bill Greenhead, who often signs his work "Stik," has published cartoons in *Punch*, *Daily Express*, *Daily Mirror*, the *Times*, *News of the World*, and the *Telegraph*, as well as in many major American publications. He has worked on advertising campaigns, including Safeway's healthy foods for kids, and has illustrated children's books. This political cartoon was posted on the CartoonStock database (www.cartoonstock.com).

What are the connotations of an hourglass?

For Class Discussion

1. This cartoon is highly symbolic. What perspective of time and the earth does this cartoon convey? What features of the cartoon speak to environmental issues?

2. What thoughts and emotions does it seek to evoke in readers?

3. Which writers of articles in this chapter might choose this cartoon to illustrate or reinforce their view of global environmental problems? What writers would object to this cartoon and why?

4. How can you imagine other stakeholders using this cartoon? What rhetorical effect would they be trying to achieve? ■

CHAPTER QUESTIONS FOR REFLECTION AND DISCUSSION

1. What are your perceptions of bottled water and how often do you drink it? How have the articles in this chapter influenced your views on bottled water?

2. What reasons have you encountered in these articles that support the argument that water should be a human right? A good or service?

3. According to environmentalists, why isn't corporate trade in water or emissions futures a good solution to environmental shortages and problems?

4. Choose a pair of writers from the following list and analyze where they agree and disagree about effective and ethical approaches to natural resources. Specifically examine their assumptions, reasoning, and interpretation of facts, and where their use of language reveals their values and challenges alternative views.

   A. Robert L. Ayers and Joshua Ortega or Maude Barlow

   B. Fredrik Segerfeldt and Maude Barlow or Wangari Muta Maathai

   C. Lester R. Brown and Patrick J. Michaels or Bjorn Lomborg

   D. Ross Gelbspan and Bjorn Lomborg

   E. Patrick J. Michaels and Andrew Simms

   F. Council of Canadians' Blue Planet Project and Fredrik Segerfeldt or Wangari Muta Maathai

   G. "Health and Environment" poster and Wangari Muta Maathai

   H. Patrick J. Michaels and Ross Gelbspan or Bjorn Lomborg

5. Choose one of the readings in this chapter that argues for important connections between economics and environmental problems. What connections does the reading make and how persuasive is its approach or solution?

6. Having read the articles on global warming, what would you say is the most reasonable and compelling view of global warming and why?

7. A number of the writers in this chapter (Maude Barlow, Wangari Muta Maathai, Lester R. Brown, and Bjorn Lomborg) have international

reputations as spokespersons for particular stances in global environmental debates. Select one of these writers' arguments and examine it rhetorically. How directly and explicitly does the writer present his or her claim? How specific, relevant, and effective is his or her evidence? How does this writer use emotional and imaginative appeals to the audience and treat alternative views? How well do these features confirm the writer's knowledge and expertise?

8. Working in groups or individually, investigate and take the environmental quiz "The Good Stuff? Quiz" posted on the Worldwatch Institute site (www.worldwatch.org/pubs/goodstuff/quiz/). What has this quiz shown you about your use of environmental resources?

9. Research and report to your class on one of the following topics:

   A. China, in its rapid industrialization, is experiencing serious problems with water pollution, growing energy needs, and conflicts over damming its major rivers. Research the recent crises related to these problems. How is China dealing with these problems? What is the response of the global community?

   B. If you wanted to invest ten thousand dollars in an ecofriendly, socially responsible company known for its commitment to sustainable development, which companies would you consider?

   C. A number of the world's rivers cross national borders. In Africa, the Nile and Congo Rivers are potential sites of international conflict. What countries are competing for the water from these rivers? What intergovernmental agreements for equitable use of this water exist?

   D. Water privatization is an issue in the United States also. Research the Mesa Water Project's plan to supply water to the Texas Panhandle by tapping the Ogallala Aquifer (an aquifer is a geologic formation of porous rock that naturally stores water underground). What other companies, including multinationals, have financial investments in water systems in the United States?

   E. Indigenous peoples, citizens of developing countries, and the poor everywhere are the most vulnerable to environmental disasters. Research the concept of "environmental refugees." What events like the December 2004 tsunami, Hurricane Katrina in August 2005, and other floods or droughts have exposed this vulnerability?

   F. Some people committed to saving the environment have decided to reduce their "ecological footprint" by using only renewable energy or radically changing their lifestyles. Research communities such as Beddington Zero (fossil) Energy Development, an ecovillage in the United Kingdom sponsored by One Planet Living, and the global green cities movement. What changes are these people making to help the environment and how are these changes working?

G. Much water is wasted. What are ways that individuals, agriculture, and industry can use water more efficiently? What methods hold promise for global use?

WRITING ASSIGNMENTS

Brief Writing Assignments

1. Briefly describe how the readings in this chapter have influenced your thinking about your own use of water and energy.

2. Which article in this chapter about environmental problems did you find the most eye-opening, disturbing, or inspirational? What features of the argument affected you?

3. Based on your reading of the articles in this chapter, write a brief statement in which you discuss what you see as the main problems with the way that scientists, journalists, and political figures are writing about global warming. In other words, where do these articles become unclear, illogical, confusing, or destructive of their own cases?

4. Explain and discuss how sensational versions of climate change like that depicted in the film *The Day After Tomorrow* (2004) or the novel *State of Fear* (2004) have influenced your understanding of global warming. What is problematic about popular science?

5. Freewrite for twenty or more minutes on one of these propositions using ideas and examples from the readings in this chapter. To force yourself to think from different perspectives, you might try writing in agreement with the statement and then writing against it:

   A. Water should be a human right, not a commodity for sale.

   B. Technology is more important than conservation in finding solutions to water shortages and global warming.

   C. Governments, not businesses, should control and manage environmental resources.

   D. Climate change calls for radical national and international government solutions, not just individual conservation.

   E. We should reduce greenhouse gases now rather than wait until we have incontrovertible evidence of human impact.

   F. Developing countries need corporations with their capital and technological know-how to help solve their water problems.

   G. Developing countries such as China and India need to reject Western patterns of industrial and economic advancement and find a sustainable development pattern of their own.

6. In her 2004 Nobel Prize acceptance speech, Wangari Muta Maathai writes, ". . . there can be no peace without equitable development; and

there can be no development without sustainable management of the environment in a democratic and peaceful space." Using ideas from the readings in this chapter, write in support of this claim by briefly discussing the connections among equitable and sustainable management of environmental resources, social well-being, and political stability.

Writing Projects

1. Write a synthesis paper in which you explain how the readings in this chapter have shaped your view of problems related to water or climate. You might sketch out your view (for example, on the need for more government or business control of water in Africa or on the need for the public to have a better understanding of global warming) or simply present your view as a series of key questions you think individuals and countries need to address. Use ideas from the arguments in this chapter to support your view or questions, and document these sources.

2. Make an advocacy poster for your residence, community, or university similar to the United Nations Environment Programme poster on page 380 supporting use of the environment that aids the poor. Your poster might urge people to use water or energy more efficiently. Think in terms of a powerful main image/photo and a small amount of text that reinforces or interprets the image and that calls people to action.

3. Using fieldwork and research, investigate the water system in your area: What is the source of your water? Who owns it? Are the records regarding the quality of water available to the public? Who sets the standards for safety? How efficient and sustainable is this system? Then write an argument addressed to your community in which you either (a) support or criticize this water management system or (b) propose strategies for individual and communal conservation of water.

4. The role of corporations and businesses in managing environmental resources is a key controversy that many writers in this chapter address. In addition, corporate leaders such as Robert L. Ayers and Richard Sandor and environmentalists such as Vandana Shiva and Maude Barlow write and speak extensively on corporate involvement, sustainable development, public benefit, and human rights. Based on the readings in this chapter, take your own stand on this controversy over privatizing water or greater engagement of corporations in solving environmental problems. Write your argument for an audience of your peers who have only a basic knowledge of this controversy. You might want to research these relevant global issues: the Friends of the Earth's campaign to stop the privatization of water in Bolivia; Chile's recent water management successes; or engineering advances in Africa such as water purifiers, nonelectrical water pumps, and desalination procedures.

5. In his books, op-ed pieces, and interviews, Danish economist Bjørn Lomborg uses cost-benefit analysis to argue against developed countries'

investment in reducing greenhouse gas emissions. However, many organizations, scientists, and individuals disagree with Lomborg. Write an argument directed toward policymakers in your state or in the U.S. House of Representatives or Senate in which you either (a) support and extend Lomborg's position or (b) rebut his position with reasoning and evidence that curbing greenhouse gas emissions is necessary and will be cost-effective. You may want to research the policy statements and recommendations of Lomborg's Copenhagen Consensus and of some of Lomborg's most vocal opponents such as Lester R. Brown at the Worldwatch Institute, Ross Gelbspan in his recent publications, and Patricia Glick's "Global Warming: The High Costs of Inaction," found on the Sierra Club site (www.sierraclub.org).

6. Argue that water management or energy efficiency is a political issue that calls for political solutions in the form of national policies that promote government-business collaboration. You might research one of the following examples: France has had good results through taxing gasoline, encouraging industries to shift from oil to other fuels, and promoting diesel-powered cars. In the 1970s, Brazil financially motivated farmers, investors in distilleries, and automakers to develop a domestic ethanol fuel industry. Responding to the 1970s oil embargo, the United States supported the building of a clean coal-burning plant in Tampa, Florida, lowered the speed limit to 55 miles per hour, and promoted the manufacture of small cars with high gas mileage. South Africa has instituted a two-tier pricing system for water that provides 25 litres per day free but charges users beyond that amount. Australia has instigated a new system of government ownership of water and of pricing and trading. Make the case, directed toward a political representative, that political power can help solve environmental problems.

7. In the absence of a national policy that sets and enforces emissions controls, some regions and cities have committed to supporting the Kyoto Protocol on their own. Investigate the nine northeastern states (Connecticut, Delaware, Maine, Massachusetts, New Hampshire, New Jersey, New York, Rhode Island, and Vermont) participating in the Regional Greenhouse Gas Initiative (RGGI), a state-level emissions capping and trading program (www.rggi.org/), or the cities that have agreed to abide by the Protocol (U.S. Mayors Climate Protection Agreement, www.ci.seattle.wa.us/mayor/climate/). After researching your state or city's position, write an argument for your city, promoting or questioning the value of this state-level or city-level involvement in a clean energy economy (for example, clean cars, solar energy, reduction of power plant emissions).

8. Ecotourism that aims to preserve the environment and local culture while educating tourists is growing in Guatemala, Belize, Ecuador, Peru, Bolivia, Kenya, and elsewhere in the developing world so much that the

UN World Tourism Organization and the UN Environment Programme have produced the publication *Making Tourism More Sustainable: A Guide for Policy Makers* (a link is at www.unep.org). After researching this publication or ecotourist sites like Kapawi, Ecuador, that are using ecotourism for environmental protection, write an editorial for your local or university newspaper that supports or challenges the idea that ecotourism can promote sustainable development.

9. Suppose a friend says to you, "Okay, I recycle all my plastics, newspapers, and cans. I carpool once a week to campus and take a bus once a week; I keep the heater in the apartment at sixty-two degrees; and I turn off all lights and electrical appliances when I am not using them. But some analysts, both liberals and conservatives, tell me that these individual efforts are pretty useless in saving energy and affecting environmental issues like global warming." What argument would you make to your friend, affirming or rebutting this claim that individual efforts to change energy consumption are insignificant?

10. Research one of the following organizations and prepare a short speech in which you argue for the importance of this organization to global management of environmental issues. Try to recruit supporters.

Natural Resource Defense Council
Intergovernmental Panel on Climate Change (IPCC)
Global Water Policy Project
The Blue Planet Project
UN Global Alliance for Water Security
International Rivers Network
Electric Power Research Institute
Water Aid
Water for People
Global Strategy Institute
Water Partners International
Center for Global Safe Water
Global H_2O Resources
Earth Summit
New Economics Organization
Natural Capitalism
Rocky Mountain Institute

CHAPTER

Feeding Global Populations

QUESTION TO PONDER

In newspapers, you have seen the photos of gaunt African children with stick-thin limbs in countries such as Sudan, Niger, and Malawi, which have experienced devastating famines recently. According to Sophia Murphy, director of the Trade Program at the Institute for Agriculture and Trade Policy in Minneapolis, when droughts and shortages in the agricultural areas add to the inadequate food production in these countries, the death rate for children under age five threatens to rise above one in four.* Murphy claims that U.S. food aid is not substantially helping these starving people. You are wondering, Should developed countries give aid in the form of money, not food, as Murphy suggests? And how can individuals contribute to finding solutions to the problem of world hunger—through changes in our eating habits, voting, donations?

CONTEXT FOR A NETWORK OF ISSUES

Between the 1940s and 1970s, the Green Revolution transformed agriculture, industrializing it in part by applying scientific and technological advances such as pesticides, herbicides, chemical fertilizers, hybrid seeds, and animal antibiotics. These new approaches dramatically increased crop yields of rice, wheat, and other basic foods. Favoring agribusinesses, or corporate farming, over smaller farmers who were less likely to be able to afford them, these capital-intensive changes led to a reduction in the number of small farms in the United States and around the world. At the same time, agribusinesses, growing single crops for export, came to dominate the global food system and global trade. In the last ten years, a second Green Revolution—scientific advances with gene splicing or bioengineering of crops—has offered possibilities for increased food production.

---

*"Feeding More for Less in Niger," *New York Times*, August 19, 2005.

404

How have these technological advances in agriculture affected the world's hunger problems? According to a UN study in 2004, although the portion of the world's population who is hungry or undernourished has dropped from one-fifth to one-sixth, this one-sixth involves 852 million people. According to UN figures, 221 million people in India, 204 million in sub-Saharan Africa, 156 million in Asia and the Pacific, 142 million in China, 53 million in Latin America and the Caribbean, 39 million in the Near East and North Africa, and 37 million in industrialized countries are undernourished.* In a statement of its Millennium Development Goals, the United Nations reports these facts: "Extreme poverty remains a daily reality for more than 1 billion people who subsist on less than $1 a day"; "every year, almost 11 million children die—that is, 30,000 children a day—before their fifth birthday"; and "malnutrition contributes to over half these deaths."† While famines, droughts, environmental disasters such as the tsunami of December 2004, and political strife create hunger crises that contribute to starvation and malnutrition, chronic hunger is a systemic problem related to what food is grown, who grows it, and how it is priced, sold, and traded. A UN report from 2004 shows that 50 percent of the people suffering from hunger are people working the land who should have direct access to nourishing food, while 20 percent are the landless poor. These numerical data suggest that we need to look beyond population growth to understand the complex relationship among global trade, poverty, and hunger to figure out how the global standard of living and advances in agriculture have left one-sixth of the world underfed. To focus on this hunger and poverty problem, the United Nations has chosen as the first of its Millennium Development Goals to call the global community to "[e]radicate extreme poverty and hunger"; "reduce by half the proportion of people living on less than a dollar a day"; and "reduce by half the proportion of people who suffer from hunger."‡

Other parts of the global food picture reflect problematic benefits. Global food trade is prospering, having tripled in the last forty years. Although some of this food travels from rural agricultural areas to cities, some trade involves countries' importing food they produce themselves, raising questions about fossil fuel use, its costs, and its eventual impact on food prices. Furthermore, the Green Revolution's emphasis on industrialized farming and the production of single crops (monocultures) for export has left many countries dependent on other parts of the world for their food. This dependence weakens *food security*, or the ability of countries independently

---

*These numerical data appear in a pie chart in *UN Millennium Project 2005. Halving Hunger: It Can Be Done*, produced by the Task Force on Hunger. The lead authors are Pedro Sanchez, M. S. Swaminathan, Philip Dobie, and Nalan Yuksel.

†*The United Nations Millennium Development Report 2005*; the 191 member states of the United Nations have pledged to meet the Millennium Development Goals by 2015. This document is posted on the UN Millennium Development Goal Web site, www.un.org/millenniumgoals/index.html.

‡http://www.un.org/millenniumgoals/index.html.

to provide regular, adequate, and reliable food at a reasonable cost for their own people. In addition, tests of soil and water and even of animal and human blood indicate an accumulation of pesticides and chemical residues from industrialized farming. Finally, although supermarkets in rich countries display a good assortment of fruits and vegetables year-round and have low prices, the freshness of these fruits and vegetables is questionable when they have traveled over one thousand miles to the store. Also, ten multinational food and beverage companies control the production of about half of the 300,000 or so items in our supermarkets.* These troubling points are motivating more people to explore the connections among this consolidated, long-distance, global food system, overabundance in developed countries, starvation and malnutrition for millions in developing countries, and the environment. This chapter investigates issues of available, affordable, sustainable, safe, and healthy food for both developed and developing countries.

STAKES AND STAKEHOLDERS

All of us are immediate stakeholders in world food issues. Also, governments, multinationals, global trade organizations, scientific research institutes, indigenous peoples, NGOs, environmental and human rights activists, and many civil society groups are invested in the production and distribution of food. To understand what economic, political, and environmental conflicts these stakeholders are arguing about, we can start with the following major issue questions.

What Is Causing World Hunger? Some people claim that the world simply isn't producing enough food: low and inefficient production causes shortages. Corporate leaders, proponents of free trade, economists, and some political leaders and scientists cite lack of financial resources and technology and ineffective farming methods coupled with poor or exhausted soil, poor irrigation, weak crops that can't resist harsh weather or pests, and unstable, often corrupt, governments as the root causes of cycles of poverty and starvation.

In contrast, many social justice activists, NGOs, indigenous peoples, and civil society groups maintain that economic and political control of food production and trade, not food shortage, is the primary contributor to poverty and starvation around the world. These people contend that together, the Green Revolution and the global free trade system† have favored agribusiness and multinationals. This global free trade system has forced small farmers in developing countries to grow export crops such as bananas, cotton, coffee, and sugar that have to compete in volatile global markets. To produce these crops in this volume, small farmers in developing

---

*Brian Halweil, "The Argument for Local Food," *Worldwatch*, May–June 2003, 22.
†For a discussion of the history and main principles of free trade, see the introduction in Chapter 2, "Consumerism, Free Trade, and Sweatshops."

countries have turned to expensive Green Revolution technology such as tractors, special fertilizers, pesticides, and now, genetically modified seeds that have made these farmers increasingly debt-ridden and dependent on the prosperous corporations that make these products. As world-renowned economist Amartya Sen asserts, "Hunger has increased . . . because the poor's entitlement to food has been eroded by technological developments that displaced farmers and reduced the production of staple foods. . . ."* When displaced small farmers try to survive by farming marginal lands, by becoming landless workers, or by moving to cities, they are often left with little means to produce or buy food.

Some people say that global institutions, rich countries, and corporate domination are contributing to world hunger in other ways as well. These activists and analysts emphasize that when the World Bank forces third world countries to pay off their debts, these countries have to reduce their financial help to their own farmers. When wealthy countries "dump" their surplus crops in third world markets, selling their food far below the prices that farmers in developing countries can meet, these low-cost surpluses weaken the domestic markets of developing countries and often drive small farmers out of business. In addition, these analysts and activists protest the way that global free trade agreements have constrained national governments' abilities to protect the interests of their own people from the will of multinational corporations and the fluctuations in trade.

Some environmentalists and ecologists are framing problems with food production as a large-scale environmental crisis. They believe exhaustion of the earth's ecosystem threatens the earth's ability to continue to feed its growing population. According to Lester Brown of the Earth First Institute, "mega-threats" to the earth's potential to support adequate food production include (1) overuse of the world's underground water supplies (aquifers); (2) erosion of soil and desertification; (3) the depletion of fisheries; and (4) climate changes bringing extremes such as heat waves.[†] Brown and others believe that the earth will not be able to sustain production for a larger world population of meat eaters and that the collapsing environment will have a domino effect, creating economic conflicts and eventually political conflicts over food.[‡]

How Can We End World Hunger Now and Meet the World's Food Needs in the Future? Most stakeholders emphasize that sustainable agricultural practices and environmental conservation are their goals. Green Revolution supporters believe that science and technology hold answers for

---

*Quoted in Robert K. Schaeffer's *Understanding Globalization: The Social Consequences of Political, Economic, and Environmental Change* (Oxford, England: Rowman & Littlefield Publishers, Inc., 1997), 168.

[†]Lester Brown, "Rescuing a Planet Under Stress," *Humanist*, November–December 2003.

[‡]The readings in Chapter 7, "Environmental Resources and Rights," discuss problems with water shortages and climate change.

continued high-yield production and for environmental preservation. These agriculturalists, economists, and researchers like the Consultative Group on International Agricultural Research (CGIAR) advocate the following solutions to increase agricultural efficiency and productivity: better food policies; investment in roads, communication, and management of resources like water; more strategic investment in technology to develop new farming methods; and the application of innovative science, particularly biotechnology. Some corporations, research groups, and scientists believe that biotechnology—the genetic modification of plants (also called "gene splicing" and "transgenic crops")—offers the best solution to the world's food needs. They claim that biotech crops will cut soil erosion, reduce the use of pesticides, enable crops to grow in poor or dry soil, and provide important nutrients and vitamins. However, some environmentalists warn that biotech crops could destroy the valuable genetic diversity inherent in wild and traditional plants. Anticorporate advocates, indigenous peoples, and civil society groups believe that multinationals such as Monsanto and Syngenta are largely economically motivated and are fostering small farmers' dependence on these large corporations' patented, genetically modified seeds. Other moderate voices in the biotech crop controversy also object to corporate control of this technology but believe that some research into plant genetics holds promise for bigger and better crop yields.

In opposition to agribusinesses' use of biotech seeds, chemicals, and large one-crop farms, many people are proposing an organic small-farm model of food production to maximize a sustainable food supply and environmental preservation. Environmental activist Vandana Shiva asserts that agribusiness calculates crop yields in terms of volume of individual crops produced instead of in terms of "total output of food" and that "small biodiverse farms can produce thousands of times more food than large, industrial monocultures": "In Java, small farmers cultivate 607 species in their home gardens. In sub-Saharan Africa, women cultivate as many as 120 different plants in the spaces left alongside the cash crops."* Proponents of organic food argue that pests, weeds, and soil quality, fertility, and productivity can be managed with intercropping (planting mixed crops together), crop rotation, and human care for the land.

Focusing on the big picture of saving the earth and preventing further environmental deterioration, environmentalists and ecologists are calling for population reduction, a change in countries' diets away from meat and processed junk food, and global regulation of damaging practices such as fossil fuel emissions and polluting of water.

Can Global Free Trade Help Solve World Hunger? Free trade proponents say that developing countries will become more prosperous and

---

*Vandana Shiva, "Globalization and Poverty," *Resurgence*, no. 202, http://www.resurgence .gn.apc.org/issues/shiva202.htm.

advanced when they participate more fully in free trade through such agreements as the Central American Free Trade Agreement (CAFTA), voted into law in 2005 by the U.S. Congress. At the 2005 meeting of the World Trade Organization in Hong Kong, developing countries fought for and won more access to markets in rich countries. To help developing countries compete, rich countries finally agreed to phase out their agricultural export subsidies and their tariffs and quotas on agricultural imports—all of which have hurt small farmers in poor countries. Meanwhile, fair trade advocates want a different model of agricultural trade that places the farmer-producer in more direct contact with consumers and restores power to these farmers through fair, guaranteed prices.*

In contrast, some stakeholders insist that food be removed from the global free trade system and are campaigning for *food sovereignty* with land reform as the first major step to returning control of food to citizens everywhere. Agricultural ecologist Peter Rosset defines food sovereignty as "being able to feed yourself as a people or nation," free from the economic and political power of other countries; "[f]ood sovereignty says that every nation and people should have the right to define their own kind of agriculture with their own culinary and historic and agrarian traditions."† Groups around the world—particularly in Brazil, Bolivia, Venezuela, and Mexico—have embraced the cause of food sovereignty and land reform to redistribute land and return to family farms: among the most active are Via Campesina, the global alliance of peasant organizations representing roughly 200 million people; the Land Research Action Network; the Landless Social Movement; and the Center for the Study of Change in the Mexican Countryside. These groups also call for national governments to provide realistic, fair subsidies to support domestic agriculture through roads, credit, or regulation of market prices. In addition, they are campaigning for agroecology that involves preservation of local varieties of plants and farmers' control of native seeds. A number of NGOs and other groups see hope in working directly with third world governments, the landless, and small farmers by making it possible through microcredit loans and microplots of home and garden land for the poor to be able to grow their own food and support themselves.

Would a Return to a Local Food System Be a Good Global Food Policy? Multinationals and large supermarket chains continue to emphasize their ability to supply food cheaply. Supporters of global free trade stress the magnitude of the global food system and the logistical and financial unfeasibility of returning to dismantled local food systems, asking how

---

*See the discussion of fair trade in Chapter 2, "Consumerism, Free Trade, and Sweatshops."
†"Interview with Peter Rosset of CECCAM and Land Research Action Network, San Felipe, Yaracuy, Venezuela," *In Motion Magazine*, July 4, 2005, http://www.inmotionmagazine .com/global/p_rosset_int.html.

local agriculture could produce the volume and crop diversity needed to feed regional cities and surrounding areas. These skeptics point out that many communities and regions also no longer have food processing systems such as dairies, slaughterhouses, canneries, and mills for grain as well as marketing systems.

Still, many people argue that reconstructing local food systems would enhance regional and national security, boost local economies, and encourage direct ties between farmers and consumers. Supporters of local food systems are actively promoting farmers markets, food delivery subscription schemes, farmers' marketing cooperatives, and connections among local farmers and school cafeterias.

The local food movement intersects with the advocates for food sovereignty, small farmers, and cultural rights by pushing for developing countries' independence from global markets. Nonprofit organizations such as the International Society for Ecology and Culture work to preserve ancestral diets and the uniqueness of regions and cultures.

How Can Food Be Made Safer to Eat, Less Contaminated with Chemicals, and Less Destructive of the Environment? Environmentalists point out that returning to a local food system would help the environment by reducing the amount of fossil fuel expended on transporting food and would foster more accountability from food producers who would be less likely to use toxic chemicals. In addition, ecologists claim that rebuilding local food systems would counteract the soil-depleting overcultivation of single crops and encourage biodiversity. Groups like Via Campesina want to replace large-scale, chemical-intensive farming with agroecology—organic farming, native wisdom, and traditional environmentally friendly practices.

Health advocates argue that a return to local food systems would enable people to regain control over what they eat. Other countries may have lower environmental standards for chemical toxins; and food that travels long distances has more potential for bacterial contamination and more need for preservatives. Nutritionists point out that people's health suffers when they abandon local diets and begin eating imported foods, as seen in developing countries where consumption of Western food has led to Western illnesses such as heart disease and diabetes.

The three sections that follow—"Student Voice," "International Voices," and "Global Hot Spot"—take a closer look at problems with hunger and food.

 ## STUDENT VOICE: EXPERIENCING PROBLEMS WITH FOOD PRODUCTION

In the following narrative, student writer Kevin Uhl contrasts his experience with organic farming in the United States with his experience observing the consequences of industrial agriculture in Nicaragua.

Kevin Uhl

The best food I have ever tasted is the food I grew myself on an organic farm in Carnation, Washington, where I worked for a season. This farm, part of community supported agriculture, raised potatoes of all colors including purple, apples, lettuce, cabbage, carrots, tomatoes, and the craziest melons, which for some reason grew incredibly well next to the river. All these crops grew without synthetic chemicals, and when I ate a plump tomato or purple potato, it tasted delicious and "pure."

The environment abounded with trees, animals, and birds: the land itself was full of life. Sometimes I would stop and watch the birds fly by or close my eyes and simply listen to the symphonies of the returning birds in spring. After rainstorms, the farm breathed, and I felt more alive.

This cooperative farm ran on volunteer labor with participants receiving fresh fruits and vegetables. There were always at least four of us working together, talking and building our own little community. We put our hands in the rich soil and it gave us life. I felt a connection with these people and the earth.

When I visited Nicaragua, however, I saw a different world of farming. In Managua, coffee workers and banana farmers were camping out in front of the government building because they had no money and nothing to eat. They were farmers with no land and no access to unused portions. Many were sick from the chemicals they used while farming and hungry because the crops they grew, mostly nonfood, were for export. The market had failed them.

In Chinandega, Nicaragua, I noticed the farmland itself—deforested and stripped to grow bananas and cotton. The land was dying. Growing one crop drains the land while growing many crops restores and nurtures it. Here to pressure the land to keep producing, many synthetic fertilizers were used and many poisons employed to fight weeds and pests. I was warned about chemical residues, soil contamination, and poisoned water. This land could kill as it was dying.

Indeed, this farming system seemed to be promoting death. I saw many people drinking water from visibly contaminated places and eating foods that would make them sick later. Almost all of the dogs were mangy, and they were definitely not pets. Burning garbage left a foul smell and toxic air. Everything seemed to be poisoned and poisonous.

Despite all this pain, I did see hope. People worked together, cooperative and generous. They wanted a better life through participation, not pity. I took these impressions back with me to the United States.

I have seen two farming styles. The deadly one prevails, not just in Nicaragua, but throughout this country and the world. The terms of land tenure leave a few with much and many with so little. If more people could participate in farming and growing their own food, working with the land, not against it, this understanding of ecology would nurture healthful, tasty food, singing birds, and living land.

INTERNATIONAL VOICES

As the UN data on page 405 show, there are many global sites of hunger and malnutrition. India's agricultural and hunger problems are particularly controversial. India has experienced both the Green Revolution and the current biotech crop revolution. Yet recently thousands of farmers, burdened by drought and debts from the cost of fertilizers and high interest rates, have committed suicide, especially in the state of Andhra Pradesh. Shamed by their debts, these small farmers—growers of rice, sunflowers, peanuts, and cotton—have resorted to swallowing pesticides to escape despair.

The Oral Testimony Programme of the Panos Institute believes that the global community should consult disadvantaged and marginalized people, who are often the ones most affected by development policies in which they have little say. This organization has collected over three hundred interviews with poor farmers in rural mountain communities throughout the world. The following excerpts from interviews with farmers in the Himalaya, the mountainous regions of northern India, reveal how these small farmers have struggled with Green Revolution technology.

Excerpts from Interviews with Farmers and Activists in Northern India

Sudesha, a fifty-year-old woman, farmer, and activist:

"Yes, in the first year, I thought [chemical fertilizer] was really wonderful. But in the second year the yield began to fall, and in the third year it fell even lower. In the fourth year it was exactly where it was before I started using fertilizer. The money that I spent on buying the fertilizer is a separate matter. Our land was harmed in exactly the same way that a man's body [is] harmed when he drinks liquor. That was the effect the fertilizer had upon my land. . . ."

Vijay, a forty-one-year-old man, farmer, and activist:

"Our traditional agriculture was fully self-reliant. The seeds, the manure and the bullock, everything was personal. Only seeds were exchanged by farmers. But the farmer today is totally dependent on the government machinery. It would not be an exaggeration to say that he has become a slave to multinational seeds and fertilizer.

". . . the government and the scientists are telling us not to grow [the traditional crops of] mandua and jhangora, but to grow soya bean, as oil and milk can be produced from it, and it is rich in proteins. But who can extract oil and milk out of it? It is not possible for local men to do this. Earlier, when people cultivated mandua and jhangora, they had enough food grain for the cattle. Soya bean is useless for fodder but good only for big factories.*

GLOBAL HOT SPOT: INDIA

India has the largest population of hungry, malnourished people; however, India is also the site of a variety of efforts to solve these problems. The Rural Development Institute (RDI) is an American legal institution committed to using its knowledge of international land law to combat "one of the chief structural causes of global poverty—rural landlessness." For the last thirty-six years, this institute has worked with over forty governments of developing countries and foreign aid agencies to create microcredit loans to enable poor people to buy microplots to grow food. This case study from the RDI Web site reveals how help of this kind leads to better nutrition and health, self-sufficiency, and economic and social progress.

42 teak trees on 1/10 of an acre plus 12 mango, 8 neem, 4 bamboo, 1 sandalwood, 2 jambu, pomegranate, gooseberry, custard apple, guava, papaya, date palm, lime, almond, areca, field beans, bitter gourds, onions, curry leaf, ginger, greens, sweet potatoes, eggplant, passion fruit, roses, jasmine, and chrysanthemums are the trees, fruits, nuts, vegetables, herbs and medicinals grown by Jiyappa and his family on a 5,400 square foot house-and-garden plot they have owned since 1993 in the Indian state of Andhra Pradesh.

Jiyappa is a former "bonded laborer"—an indentured servant who lived and worked in his master's house and farm fields in exchange for basic food, a primitive shelter, and 700 Rupees (US $16) per year. That was before he was hired by the Deccan Development Society (DDS), a local NGO working to economically empower the poorest of the rural poor. In 1993, the DDS employee's association helped Jiyappa and fellow DDS workers purchase small house-and-garden plots of about 1/10 of an acre.

Today, Jiyappa, his wife Sukkammaa, and three of their six children live in a small house they have constructed on the plot. The plot is producing 90% of the family's annual vegetable and fruit needs, plus 6,000 Rupees (US $133) a year from the sale of what they can't eat themselves. The 20 chickens they keep on the plot are used for family consumption, plus provide 3,000 Rupees (US $67) a year from the sale of poultry and eggs. And ten years from now, when the teak trees begin to reach maturity, the wood from each tree will fetch at least 25,000 Rupees (US $556), giving the 42 trees a total value of roughly 1,050,000 Rupees (US $23,333) in today's Rupees/dollars—an enormous sum for a poor rural family in India.†

---

*http://www.mountainvoices.org.
†"Rural Development Institute—Lives Changed," http://www.rdiland.org/OURWORK/OurWork_LivesChanged03.html.

Despite some hopeful movements to restore land to the landless, India's farmers are struggling to grow export crops using genetically modified seeds. Crop failures point to flaws in the system and are fueling poverty and suicide. The following news story, "Approval for New Modified Cotton Planting Stirs Alarm" by Ranjit Devraj, published in New Delhi on April 22, 2005, shows how decisions influenced by corporations, politics, and global trade affect farmers' lives.

> Environmentalists are alarmed that the Indian government has given approval for more areas to be planted with new varieties of genetically modified Bt cotton, despite farmers suffering huge losses in the past from growing the transgenic crop.
>
> Bt cotton is genetically modified to include a pest-killing gene borrowed from a soil bacterium called "bacillus thuringiensis." While Bt cotton is sold as pest resistant seed in India, it has proved to be more vulnerable to pests and diseases than the traditional and conventional varieties. . . .
>
> Approvals of three cotton hybrids developed by Mahyco-Monsanto Biotech Ltd expired in March but the Genetic Engineering Approval Committee could not grant extensions on their licenses because of adverse reports coming in not only from leading voluntary agencies but also from the state government of Andhra Pradesh.
>
> In fact, local authorities in the Warangal district of Andhra Pradesh have been demanding that Mahyco-Monsanto compensate the Andhra Pradesh farmers after crop losses last year drove scores of them to commit suicide.
>
> "The problems of the peasants started with rampant supply of spurious seeds and pesticides which continued with every stage of crop production up to the marketing stage," wrote the *Deccan Herald* newspaper. . . .
>
> The main idea behind approving genetically engineered Bt cotton as a commercial crop was that this would increase farmers' income by reducing expenditure on chemical pesticides. However, studies indicate that in the past few years the amounts spent on pesticides by Indian farmers growing the crop have actually increased by two-to-three fold, because of the growing resistance of pests—especially the bollworm—to chemical pesticides.

The articles in this chapter will help you further explore the complexities of global food production, hunger, and poverty.

READINGS

Why You Can't Sit Down to Eat Without Making a Statement

Scott Canon

Scott Canon is a national correspondent for Knight Ridder Newspapers, which publishes over thirty daily newspapers including the *Kansas City Star*, where this piece first appeared. Recently, he has covered conflicts involving food and markets, including food aid to Africa and Anheuser-Busch's rejection of biotech crops. This piece was reprinted in the *Seattle Times* on June 25, 2005.

> Written for a general newspaper audience, this article seeks to sketch out the main conflicts among the parties involved in the global food market. Who are these stakeholders and how do they wield power?

1   Whether consumers care or not, just about everything they eat is spiked with implications for the environment, international trade, health and the American economy.

2   Some people talk of how buying some foods undermines the world's rain forests or coastlines. Others campaign to save the American family farm or improve conditions for foreign laborers. Some call for the American system of big farms and companies to get bigger and deliver ever-cheaper food. Box labels and grocery shelves don't mention the federal fights over tariffs and subsidies, but they're there.

3   In the global village of 21st-century food production, what you eat makes a political statement.

BIG AG

4   For many, purchasing McNuggets is a tacit endorsement of Big Agriculture—from genetically engineered crops that make for cheaper feed, to concentrated poultry barns where manure can spoil the local groundwater, to a system of production that leaves little room for smaller farms.

5   At the same time, however, McDonald's has responded to public pressure. The fast-food chain uses its substantial buying power to insist that suppliers not dose their chickens with antibiotics to promote growth. The company has also been commended by animal-rights groups for pressuring slaughterhouses into using more humane methods—imposing its standards by surprise audits at packing houses.

6   Granola stands as the iconic organic snack—that healthful mix of grains and dried fruit. When certified organic, the nibbler can chow down knowing the food was grown without pesticides.

7   But most oats in this country are imported—new short-season varieties of more heavily subsidized soybeans have elbowed oats out of acres in the upper Midwest. So if that granola isn't certified organic, its oats were probably grown in countries with less stringent labor standards and are more likely to carry traces of pesticides outlawed in the U.S.

IMPORTS JUMP

8   In fact, there's hardly a meal that doesn't relate in some way to legislative food fights in Washington pitting home-grown lobbies against foreign-interest groups, one region opposite another, or crop-versus-crop. Even as America ships its meat and grain around the planet, the country imports 13 percent of its food—56 percent more than two decades ago.

9   As food crosses borders, so do trade squabbles such as those between the United States and Europe over wine and cheese.

10   Still, picky eaters are every bit as influential in such matters as politicians.

11   Consumer pressure changed fishing practices so now countries that don't properly monitor dolphin-free tuna catches face U.S. import restrictions. Starbucks and others hold on to consumers by making their suppliers deliver "shade-grown" coffee raised below the rain-forest canopy rather than on land razed to make way for farming. A generation ago boycotts of grapes gave bargaining leverage to California farmworkers.

12   Today the debate over the best way to stock pantries churns on.

13   "This global food system has been a great benefit to agribusiness, but it has not been a benefit at all for farmers," said Ben Lilliston of the Institute for Agriculture and Trade Policy, a group that sees itself as the champion of small family farms. "Both here and in the developing world, there are fewer farmers every day."

THE VIRTUES OF YIELD

14   Go organic if you want, say others, but big-scale farming feeds the world.

15   "We haven't given high-yield farming enough credit for the high yield," said Dennis Avery, director of the agribusiness-supported Center for Global Food Issues and author of *Saving the Planet with Pesticides and Plastic*.

16   Avery and other defenders of conventional large-scale agriculture say it makes food cheap. Government research shows that in 1930 Americans spent an average of 21.2 percent of their family income on food. Today, that portion is 6.1 percent—the lowest in the world.

17   What's more, American food is typically safer than that consumed by the rest of the developed world. And incidences of foodborne illness caused by listeria, salmonella and E. coli continue to decline.

18   "We spend less than anyone else," said American Meat Institute spokeswoman Janet Riley, "and we get the safest food."

19   Even as the market explodes for fresh and organic foods, the amount of processed food consumed by Americans continues to

grow—a market eating up $500 billion of the national annual grocery bill.

20   "American consumers are concerned about what they're eating, but they put a priority on making it work with their lifestyle," said Stephanie Childs of the Grocery Manufacturers of America. "They want to know: How convenient is it? Will it fit into their family's budget? Will their kids even eat it?"

21   Still, advocates for various trade, environmental or labor standards say food's path to market matters.

THE SALMON DEBATE

22   Consider salmon, chock full of heart-healthy omega 3 fatty acids. Demand is up, but natural fisheries are dwindling.

23   "Farm-raised" salmon has grown popular as depleted fisheries have made wild salmon harder to find and even harder to afford. But farmed salmon have been found in repeated studies to contain higher levels of PCBs, contaminants that pregnant women and nursing mothers have been advised to avoid. Critics also complain about the excessive use of antibiotics with aquaculture.

24   The author of *Dwellers in the Land*, environmentalist Kirkpatrick Sale, is a fierce advocate for buying seasonally and regionally. He said that when people attempt to bring global variety to their diet, they end up supporting the reckless use of natural resources and corporations he says have little financial incentive to protect the environment.

25   Yet the federal government and the Food and Agricultural Organization of the United Nations estimate that fishing open waters can meet only half the global demand for seafood as commercial fish stocks decline worldwide.

26   "Aquaculture is a sustainable alternative," said Stacey Felzenberg, a spokeswoman for the National Fisheries Institute, which represents fishermen, processors and restaurants.

BIG ON SHRIMP

27   Americans have yet to develop much farm-raised shrimp, but they eat plenty of it. The environmental group Worldwatch Institute estimates that as much as 35 percent of the world's coastal mangrove forests have been destroyed in the past 20 years, mostly for shrimp farms. Even with tariffs used to discourage dumping—importing below cost to capture the market—more than 85 percent of the shrimp consumed in the United States is imported, chiefly from Thailand and China. Meantime, the number of American shrimpers trawling the Gulf of Mexico has fallen by half in the past five years.

28   "We can compete on taste," said Ewell Smith of the Louisiana Seafood Promotion and Marketing Board. "We can't compete on price."

29   The global market of vegetables doesn't offer such a price break, but rather cherries and pineapples in the Midwest in winter. Much of America's whole fruits and vegetables are harvested green in another country and ripen on the way to market.

30   That gives Americans a variety of food once unimagined. But those who advocate buying locally say such imports reduce the incentive of U.S. farmers to grow produce and encourage them to turn to more subsidized commodity grains.

31   In 1997, an outbreak of potentially fatal hepatitis A from frozen strawberries shipped from Mexico sickened 270 people in five states, 130 Michigan schoolchildren among them. The U.S. Food and Drug Administration says imported food is three times more likely than U.S.-grown food to be contaminated with illegal pesticide residues.

32   The Environmental Working Group found those chemicals on 18.4 percent of strawberries, 15.6 percent of head lettuce and 12.3 percent of carrots imported from Mexico. Whether that poses a health risk is controversial.

33   FDA inspections of imported food dropped from about 8 percent before the 1994 North American Free Trade Agreement to less than 2 percent five years later as import volume ballooned.

34   Now comes the Central American Free Trade Agreement, or CAFTA, pending before Congress. This country's sugar industry, in which strict quotas limiting production prop up U.S. sugar costs to nearly three times the world market, fears the agreement.

35   Government farm subsidies in the United States and Europe draw criticism from groups who say such policies keep crop prices artificially low. That, in turn, discourages farmers in poor countries from trying to compete.

36   Buy chocolate and you risk supporting Ivory Coast plantations notorious for using child slave labor to grow and harvest cocoa. Drink java, and unless it's shade-grown, you could be accused of encouraging destruction of South American rain forests to make room for your coffee beans. Even your table's floral centerpiece carries implications. Half the cut flowers sold in the United States are grown in Colombia, where human-rights groups say farmworkers are exposed to dangerous amounts of pesticides.

37   Kate Van Ummersen, who sells cheese made by dairies that shun antibiotics and hormones, tried briefly and largely in vain to peddle organic flowers in the Pacific Northwest. She touted them as more people- and planet-friendly than imported flowers.

38   "People would say, 'Why should I care? I don't eat flowers,'" she said. "They just weren't willing to pay a premium for organic flowers."

For Class Discussion

1. What is Scott Canon's main purpose in this piece?

2. Canon quotes a number of stakeholders as authoritative representatives of their respective groups. How well do these quotations contribute to the ideas and persuasiveness of this piece?

3. How has this article influenced the way that you view global food production and the food you eat?   ■

Health and Environment

United Nations Environment Programme

Part of a series of posters on the environment, poverty, energy, food, water, and health, this poster (p. 420), sponsored by the United Nations Environment Programme, appeared in an exhibition at the World Summit on Sustainable Development held August 26–September 3, 2002, in Johannesburg, South Africa. The United Nations Environment Programme's mission is "to provide leadership and encourage partnership in caring for the environment by inspiring, informing, and enabling nations and peoples to improve their quality of life without compromising that of future generations" ("About UNEP," www.unep.org). This poster refers to the recent studies showing that pesticides, chemical fertilizers, and other industrial wastes have contaminated soil, water, and the entire food chain. In the Arctic countries, the Inuits, the Aleuts, the Inupiats, the Siberian tribes, and the Saami—indigenous peoples who are dependent on whales and seafood—show high levels of toxins in their blood and breast milk.

What are your first impressions of and responses to this poster?

For Class Discussion

1. How does this poster reveal its dual purpose of educating and persuading?

2. How do the use of light/dark, the images, the type, and the layout contribute to the rhetorical power of this poster? What effect were its designers trying to achieve?

3. What views sketched in the introduction of this chapter does this poster illustrate and support?

4. What does this poster contribute to the controversy over how to provide safe and adequate food for the world's 6.3 billion people?

■

FIGURE 8.1 Health and Environment *(This poster has been reproduced by kind permission of the United Nations Environment Programme. This poster on "health and the environment" can be found at http://www.unep.org/wssd/wssdpageposters.asp?poster=HEALTH.3.jpg)*

Technology That Will Save Billions from Starvation

C. S. Prakash and Gregory Conko

Gregory Conko is vice president of the AgBioWorld Foundation and a senior fellow and director of food safety policy at the Competitive Enterprise Institute, a policy think tank devoted to "free enterprise and limited government" ("About CEI," www.cei.org). He has published extensively on the safety of pharmaceutical drugs and bioengineered foods, including the book *The Frankenfood Myth: How Protest and Politics Threaten the Biotech Revolution* (coauthored with Henry I. Miller). C. S. Prakash started AgBioWorld Foundation, a nonprofit organization that does not accept financial support from biotech corporations and that seeks to "provide information to teachers, journalists, policymakers, and the general public about developments in plant science biotechnology, and sustainable agriculture" (www.agbioworld.org). Prakash is a world-renowned scientific researcher, professor, scholar, and director of the Center for Plant Biotechnology Research at Tuskegee University, Alabama. Known for promoting biotechnology research in developing countries and training students and scholars from these countries, he has written prolifically to gain the public's acceptance of plant biotechnology. This policy argument was published by *The American Enterprise* on March 1, 2004, and posted on the AgBioWorld Foundation site.

> What features of this article (its claim, structure, treatment of scientific ideas and terms) indicate that this piece is designed to reach both people well versed in biotechnology and a less-informed general public?

1   Today, most people around the world have access to a greater variety of nutritious and affordable foods than ever before, thanks mainly to developments in agricultural science and technology. The average human life span—arguably the most important indicator of quality of life—has increased steadily in the past century in almost every country. Even in many less developed countries, life spans have doubled over the past few decades. Despite massive population growth, from 3 billion to more than 6 billion people since 1950, the global malnutrition rate decreased in that period from 38 percent to 18 percent. India and China, two of the world's most populous and rapidly industrializing countries, have quadrupled their grain production.

2   The record of agricultural progress during the past century speaks for itself. Countries that embraced superior agricultural

technologies have brought unprecedented prosperity to their people, made food vastly more affordable and abundant, helped stabilize farm yields, and reduced the destruction of wild lands. The productivity gains from G.M. crops, as well as improved use of synthetic fertilizers and pesticides, allowed the world's farmers to double global food output during the last 50 years, on roughly the same amount of land, at a time when global population rose more than 80 percent. Without these improvements in plant and animal genetics and other scientific developments, known as the Green Revolution, we would today be farming on every square inch of arable land to produce the same amount of food, destroying hundreds of millions of acres of pristine wilderness in the process.

3   Many less developed countries in Latin America and Asia benefited tremendously from the Green Revolution. But due to a variety of reasons, both natural and human, agricultural technologies were not spread equally across the globe. Many people in sub-Saharan Africa and parts of South Asia continue to suffer from abject rural poverty driven by poor farm productivity. Some 740 million people go to bed daily on an empty stomach, and nearly 40,000 people— half of them children—die every day of starvation or malnutrition. Unless trends change soon, the number of undernourished could well surpass 1 billion by 2020.

4   The U.N. Food and Agriculture Organization (FAO) expects the world's population to grow to more than 8 billion by 2030. The FAO projects that global food production must increase by 60 percent to accommodate the estimated population growth, close nutrition gaps, and allow for dietary changes over the next three decades. Food charity alone simply cannot eradicate hunger. Increased supply—with the help of tools like bioengineering—is crucial.

5   Although better farm machinery and development of fertilizers, insecticides, and herbicides have been extremely useful, an improved understanding of genetic principles has been the most important factor in improving food production. Every crop is a product of repeated genetic editing by humans over the past few millennia. Our ancestors chose a few once-wild plants and gradually modified them simply by selecting those with the largest, tastiest, or most robust offspring for propagation. Organisms have been altered over the millennia so greatly that traits present in existing populations of cultivated rice, wheat, corn, soy, potatoes, tomatoes and many others have very little in common with their ancestors. Wild tomatoes and potatoes contain very potent toxins, for example. Today's cultivated varieties have been modified to produce healthy and nutritious food.

6   Hybridization, the mating of different plants of the same species, has helped us assimilate desirable traits from several varieties into elite specimens. And when desired characteristics were unavailable in cultivated plants, genes were liberally borrowed from wild relatives and introduced into crop varieties, often of different but related species. Wheat, rye, and barley are regularly mated with wild grass species to introduce new traits. Commercial tomato plants are commonly bred with wild tomatoes to introduce improved resistance to pathogens, nematodes, and fungi. Successive generations then have to be carefully backcrossed into the commercial cultivars to eliminate any unwanted traits accidentally transferred from the wild plants, such as toxins common in the wild species.

7   Even when crop and wild varieties refuse to mate, various tricks can be used to produce "wide crosses" between two plants that are otherwise sexually incompatible. Often, though, the embryos created by wide crosses die before they mature, so they must be "rescued" and cultured in a laboratory. Even then, the rescued embryos typically produce sterile offspring. They can only be made fertile again by using chemicals that cause the plants to mutate and produce a duplicate set of chromosomes. The plant triticale, an artificial hybrid of wheat and rye, is one such example of a wide-cross hybrid made possible solely by the existence of embryo rescue and chromosome doubling techniques. Triticale is now grown on over 3 million acres worldwide, and dozens of other products of wide-cross hybridization are common.

8   When a desired trait cannot be found within the existing gene pool, breeders can create new variants by intentionally mutating plants with radiation, with chemicals, or simply by culturing clumps of cells in a Petri dish and leaving them to mutate spontaneously during cell division. Mutation breeding has been in common use since the 1950s, and more than 2,250 known mutant varieties have been bred in at least 50 countries, including France, Germany, Italy, the United Kingdom, and the United States. A relatively new mutant wheat variety, made to be resistant to a commercial herbicide, was put on the market in the U.S. as recently as July 2003.

9   Recombinant DNA (rDNA) methods are a recent extension of the myriad techniques that have been employed to modify and improve crops. The primary difference is that modern bioengineered crops involve a precise transfer of one or two known genes into plant DNA—a surgical alteration of a tiny part of the crop's genome compared to the traditional sledgehammer approaches, which bring about gross genetic changes, many of which are unknown and unpredictable.

10   Leading scientists around the world have attested to the health and environmental safety of agricultural biotechnology, and they

have called for bioengineered crops to be extended to those who need them most—hungry people in the developing world. Dozens of scientific and health associations, including the U.S. National Academy of Sciences, the American Medical Association, the U.K.'s Royal Society, and the United Nations Development Programme, have endorsed the technology. Nearly 3,500 eminent scientists from all around the world, including 24 Nobel laureates, have signed a declaration supporting the use of agricultural biotechnology. And a review of 81 separate research projects conducted over 15 years— all funded by the European Union—found that bioengineered crops and foods are at least as safe for the environment and for human consumption as conventional crops, and in some cases even safer.

11 Crops enhanced through modern biotechnology are now grown on nearly 143 million acres in 16 countries. More important, more than three quarters of the 5.5 million growers who benefit from bioengineered crops are resource-poor farmers in the developing world. Unremarkably, most commercially available biotech plants were designed for farmers in the industrialized world. They include varieties of corn, soybean, potato, and cotton modified to resist insect pests, plant diseases, and to make weed control easier. However, the increasing adoption of bioengineered varieties by farmers in developing countries over the past few years has shown that they can benefit at least as much as, if not more than, their industrialized counterparts. The productivity of farmers everywhere is limited by crop pests and diseases—and these are often far worse in tropical and subtropical regions than the temperate zones.

12 About 20 percent of plant productivity in the industrialized world, and up to 40 percent in Africa and Asia, is lost to insects and pathogens, despite the ongoing use of copious amounts of pesticides. The European corn borer destroys approximately 7 percent, or 40 million tons, of the world's corn crop each year—equivalent to the annual food supply for 60 million people. So it comes as no surprise that, when they are permitted to grow bioengineered varieties, poor farmers in less developed nations have eagerly snapped them up. According to the International Service for the Acquisition of Agri-Biotech Applications, farmers in less developed countries now grow nearly one quarter of the world's bioengineered crops on more than 26 million acres.

13 Bioengineered plants have also had other important benefits for farmers in less developed countries. In China, where pesticides are typically sprayed on crops by hand, some 400 to 500 cotton farmers die every year from acute pesticide poisoning. Researchers at Rutgers University and the Chinese Academy of Sciences found that using bioengineered cotton in China has lowered the amount

of pesticides by more than 75 percent and reduced the number of pesticide poisonings by an equivalent amount. Another study by economists at the University of Reading in Britain found that South African cotton farmers have seen similar benefits.

14   The reduction in pesticide spraying also means that fewer natural resources are consumed to manufacture and transport the chemicals. In 2000 alone, U.S. farmers growing bioengineered cotton used 2.4 million fewer gallons of fuel and 93 million fewer gallons of water, and were spared some 41,000 ten hour days needed to apply pesticide.

15   Soon, many bioengineered varieties that have been created specifically for use in underdeveloped countries will be ready for commercialization. Examples include insect resistant rice for Asia, virus-resistant sweet potato for Africa, and virus-resistant papaya for Caribbean nations. The next generation of bioengineered crops now in research labs around the world is poised to bring even further improvements for the poor soils and harsh climates that are characteristic of impoverished regions. Scientists have already identified genes resistant to environmental stresses common in tropical nations, including tolerance to soils with high salinity and to those that are particularly acidic or alkaline.

16   The primary reason why Africa never benefited from the Green Revolution is that plant breeders focused on improving crops such as rice, wheat, and corn, which are not widely grown in Africa. Also, much of the African dry lands have little rainfall and no potential for irrigation, both of which played essential roles in the success stories for crops such as Asian rice. Furthermore, the remoteness of many African villages and the poor transportation infrastructure in landlocked African countries make it difficult for African farmers to obtain agricultural chemical inputs such as fertilizers, insecticides, and herbicides—even if they could be donated by charities, or if they had the money to purchase them. But, by packaging technological inputs within seeds, biotechnology can provide the same, or better, productivity advantage as chemical or mechanical inputs, and in a much more user-friendly manner. Farmers would be able to control insects, viral or bacterial pathogens, extremes of heat or drought, and poor soil quality, just by planting these crops.

17   Still, anti-biotechnology activists like Vandana Shiva of the New Delhi-based Research Foundation for Science, Technology and Ecology, and Miguel Altieri of the University of California at Berkeley, argue that poor farmers in less developed nations will never benefit from biotechnology because it is controlled by multinational corporations. According to Altieri, "Most innovations in agricultural biotechnology have been profit-driven rather than need-driven. The real thrust of the genetic engineering industry is not to make

Third World agriculture more productive, but rather to generate profits."

18   That sentiment is not shared by the thousands of academic and public sector researchers actually working on biotech applications in those countries. Cyrus Ndiritu, former director of the Kenyan Agricultural Research Institute, argues, "It is not the multinationals that have a stranglehold on Africa. It is hunger, poverty and deprivation. And if Africa is going to get out of that, it has got to embrace" biotechnology.

19   Biotechnology also offers hope of improving the nutritional benefits of many foods. The next generation of bioengineered products now in development is poised to bring direct health benefits to consumers through enhanced nutritive qualities that include more and higher-quality protein, lower levels of saturated fat, increased vitamins and minerals, and many others. Bioengineering can also reduce the level of natural toxins (such as in cassava and kidney beans) and eliminate certain allergens from foods like peanuts, wheat, and milk. Many of these products are being developed primarily or even exclusively for subsistence farmers and consumers in poor countries.

20   Among the most well known is Golden Rice—genetically enhanced with added beta carotene, which is converted to Vitamin A in the human body. Another variety developed by the same research team has elevated levels of digestible iron. The diet of more than 3 billion people worldwide includes inadequate levels of essential vitamins and minerals, such as Vitamin A and iron. Deficiency in just these two micronutrients can result in severe anemia, impaired intellectual development, blindness, and even death. Even though charities and aid agencies such as the United Nations Children's Fund and the World Health Organization have made important strides in reducing Vitamin A and iron deficiency, success has been fleeting. No permanent effective strategy has yet been devised, but Golden Rice may finally provide one.

21   The Golden Rice project is a prime example of the value of extensive public sector and charitable research. The rice's development was funded mainly by the New York-based Rockefeller Foundation, which has promised to make the rice available to poor farmers at little or no cost. Scientists at public universities in Switzerland and Germany created it with assistance from the Philippines-based International Rice Research Institute and from several multinational corporations. Scientists at publicly funded, charitable, and corporate research centers are developing many other similar crops. Indian scientists, for example, have recently announced that they would soon make a new high-protein potato variety available for commercial cultivation.

22   Research is already under way on fruits and vegetables that could one day deliver life-saving vaccines—such as a banana with the vaccine for Hepatitis B, and a potato that provides immunization against diarrheal diseases.

23   It is true that certain aspects of modern farming have had a negative impact on biodiversity and on air, soil, and water quality. But biotechnology has proven safer for the environment than anything since the invention of the plow. The risk of cross-pollination from crops to wild relatives has always existed, and such "gene flow" occurs whenever crops grow in close proximity to sexually compatible wild relatives. Yet, breeders have continuously introduced genes for disease and pest resistance through conventional breeding into all of our crops. Traits, such as stress tolerance and herbicide resistance, have also been introduced in some crops with conventional techniques, and the growth habits of every crop have been altered. Thus, not only is gene modification a common phenomenon, but so are many of the specific kinds of changes made with rDNA techniques.

24   Naturally, with both conventional and rDNA-enhanced breeding, we must be vigilant to ensure that newly introduced plants do not become invasive and that weeds do not become noxious because of genetic modification. Similarly, we must ensure that target genes are safe for human and animal consumption before they are transferred. But, while modern genetic modification expands the range of new traits that can be added to crop plants, it also ensures that more will be known about those traits and that the behavior of the modified plants will be, in many ways, easier to predict.

25   The biggest threats that hungry populations currently face are restrictive policies stemming from unwarranted public fears. Although most Americans tend to support agricultural biotechnology, many Europeans and Asians have been far more cautious. Anti-biotechnology campaigners in both industrialized and less developed nations are feeding this ambivalence with scare stories that have led to the adoption of restrictive policies. Those fears are simply not supported by the scores of peer reviewed scientific reports or the data from tens of thousands of individual field trials.

26   In the end, over-cautious rules result in hyper-inflated research and development costs and make it harder for poorer countries to share in the benefits of biotechnology. No one argues that we should not proceed with caution, but needless restrictions on agricultural biotechnology could dramatically slow the pace of progress and keep important advances out of the hands of people who need them. This is the tragic side effect of unwarranted concern.

27   In 2002, Zambian President Levy Mwanawasa rejected some 23,000 metric tons of food aid in the midst of a two-year-long drought that threatened the lives of over 2 million Zambians. President Mwanawasa's public explanation was that the bioengineered corn from the United States was "poisonous." Other Zambian government officials conceded that the bigger concern was for future corn exports to the European Union, which observes a moratorium on new G.M. foods.

28   Zambia is not unique. European biotechnology restrictions have had other, similar consequences throughout the developing world. Thai government officials have been reluctant to authorize any bioengineered rice varieties, even though it has spent heavily on biotechnology research. Uganda has stopped research on bioengineered bananas and postponed their introduction indefinitely. Argentina has limited its approvals to the two bioengineered crop varieties that are already permitted in European markets.

29   Even China, which has spent hundreds of millions of dollars funding advanced biotechnology research, has refused to authorize any new bioengineered food crops since the European Union's moratorium on bioengineered crop approvals began in 1998. More recently, the International Rice Research Institute, which has been assigned the task of field-testing Golden Rice, has indefinitely postponed its plans for environmental release in the Philippines, fearing backlash from European-funded NGO protestors. Still, the E.U. moratorium continues to persist after five long years, despite copious evidence, including from the E.U.'s own researchers, that biotech modification does not pose any risks that aren't also present in other crop-breeding methods.

30   Of course, hunger and malnutrition are not solely caused by a shortage of food. The primary causes of hunger in some countries have been political unrest and corrupt governments, poor transportation and infrastructure and, of course, poverty. All of these problems must be addressed if we are to ensure real, worldwide food security.

31   But during the next 50 years, the global population is expected to rise by 50 percent—to 9 billion people, almost entirely in the poorest regions of the world. And producing enough to feed these people will require the use of the invaluable gift of biotechnology.

For Class Discussion

1. What is the core claim of Prakash and Conko's case in favor of food biotechnology? What are their reasons?

2. Prakash and Conko are very conscious of arguing against opponents of plant biotechnology. How do they summarize these views?

How do they seek to refute them? Where do Prakash and Conko make concessions?

3. Golden rice is a favorite example of biotech proponents. How do Prakash and Conko use golden rice in this argument?

4. What assumptions have Prakash and Conko made about the process and products of plant bioengineering? How do the assumptions of their opponents differ?

5. What are this piece's strongest points? How has it influenced your understanding of biotechnology's potential to combat world hunger?   ■

Transgenic Crops to Address Third World Hunger? A Critical Analysis

Peter M. Rosset

Peter M. Rosset holds a doctorate in agricultural ecology from the University of Michigan. He has served as executive director of the Institute for Food and Development Policy in Oakland, California. His current affiliations include research positions with the Center for the Study of the Americas in Berkeley, California, and with the Center for the Study of Change in the Mexican Countryside at Oaxaca, Mexico—an organization active in the land reform movement for peasants. He has published numerous articles on genetic engineering of crops, agricultural sustainability, poverty, and land reform. This scholarly article was published in August 2005 in the *Bulletin of Science, Technology & Society*, a publication that seeks to reach a wide audience: "faculty and students from sciences, engineering, the humanities, and social science," "professionals in government, industry, and universities," and journalists and public interest groups (www.sagepub.com/journal .aspx?pid=159). In this piece, Rosset uses the phrase "transgenic crops," a term that refers to genetic modification through gene splicing, instead of the more casual *biotech food, GM crops*, or *bioengineered crops*.

What do the structure of this article, the introduction that maps out the piece, the use of headings, the documentation of sources, and the use of terms from agriculture indicate about the target audience and contribute to Rosset's informative, analytical, and persuasive purposes?

1   In this analysis, I take very seriously the oft-repeated claim that genetic engineering of crop seeds could be an important way to attack hunger in the nations of the south, submitting it to a rigorous critical

analysis. Industry and mainstream research and policy institutions often suggest that transgenic crop varieties can raise the productivity of poor third world farmers, feed the hungry, and reduce poverty (e.g., http://www.whybiotech.com; McGloughlin, 1999a, 1999b; Pinstrup-Andersen, 1999). To address these propositions critically, we must examine the assumptions and claims that lie behind them. To do so, I first briefly review the notion that hunger is due to a scarcity of food and, thus, that it could be remedied by producing more. I then look into the situation faced by poor farmers in the third world, including the issue of their productivity. I close by examining some of the special risks that genetic engineering for agriculture may pose for peasant farmers.

FOOD AVAILABILITY AND HUNGER

2   Global data show that there is no relationship between the prevalence of hunger and our ability to produce enough food. In fact, per-capita food production increases during the past 4 decades have far out-stripped human population growth. The world today produces more food per inhabitant than ever before. Enough is available to provide 4.3 pounds for every person every day, including 2.5 pounds of grain, beans, and nuts; about a pound of meat, milk, and eggs; and another pound of fruits and vegetables—more than enough for a healthy, active life. The real causes of hunger are poverty, inequality, and lack of access to readily available food— food that can only be obtained with money—by people who are cash poor. Too many people are too poor to buy the food that is available (but often poorly distributed) or lack the land and resources to grow it themselves (Lappé, Moore, Collins, Rosset, & Esparza, 1998). In fact, farmers around the world, both north and south, believe that overproduction—and consequent low crop prices—is one of the most persistent problems generating poverty (and thus hunger) in rural areas (McMichael, 2004).

3   At this level of macroanalysis, then, it should be clear that we most definitely do not need more food to end hunger. Thus, at a global scale, improved crop-production technology of any kind is unlikely to help.

4   However, this may not be true in all cases of individual countries, or regions within countries, where per-capita food production figures and food availability may lag behind global averages. Thus we must take seriously the notion that in some cases (i.e., parts of sub-Saharan Africa) we may have to address the productivity of poor farmers who grow foodstuffs for consumption in regional and national markets to effectively combat hunger (de Grassi & Rosset, in press).

5   When we speak of these national markets, we find that small and peasant farmers, despite their disadvantaged position in society,

are the primary producers of staple foods, accounting for very high percentages of national production in most third world countries. This sector, which is so important for food production, is itself characterized by poverty and hunger and, in some cases, lagging agricultural productivity. If these problems are to be addressed by a proposed solution—transgenic crop varieties in this case—we must begin with a clear understanding of their causes. If the causes lie in inadequate technology, then a technological solution is at least a theoretical possibility. Thus let me begin by examining the conditions faced by peasant producers of staple foods in most of the third world.

HISTORICAL BACKGROUND

6   The history of the third world since the beginning of colonialism has been a history of unsustainable development. Colonial land grabs pushed rural food-producing societies off the best lands most suitable for farming: the relatively flat alluvial or volcanic soils with ample, but not excessive, rainfall (or water for irrigation). These lands were converted to production for export in the new global economy dominated by the colonial powers. Instead of producing staple foods for local populations, they became extensive cattle ranches or plantations of indigo, cocoa, copra, rubber, sugar, cotton, and other highly valued products. Where traditional food producers had utilized agricultural and pastoral practices developed over thousands of years to be in tune with local soil and environmental conditions, colonial plantations took a decidedly short-term view toward extracting the maximum benefit at minimal costs, often using slave labor and production practices that neglected the long-term sustainability of production (for further development of the arguments put forth in this section see Lappé et al., 1998; Ross, 1998).

7   Meanwhile, local food producers were either enslaved as plantation labor or displaced into habitats that were marginal for production. Precolonial societies had used arid areas and desert margins only for low-intensity, nomadic pastoralism; steep slopes only for low population density, long-fallow shifting cultivation (or sophisticated terracing in some cases); and rain forests primarily for hunting and gathering (with some agroforestry)—all practices that are ecologically sustainable over the long term. But colonialism drove farming peoples—accustomed to the continuous production of annual crops on fertile, well-drained soils with good access to water—en masse into these marginal areas. Whereas precolonial cultures had never considered these regions to be suitable for high population densities or intensive annual cropping, in many cases they were henceforth to be subject to both. As a result, forests were felled, and many fragile habitats were subject to unsustainable

production practices—in this case by poor, newly destitute and displaced farmers—just as the favored lands were being degraded by continuous export cropping at the hands of Europeans.

8   National liberation from colonialism did little to alleviate the environmental and social problems generated by this dynamic because the situation, in fact, worsened in much of the third world. Postcolonial national elites came to power with strong linkages to the global export-oriented economy often, indeed, connected to former colonial powers. The period of national liberation, extending for more than a century, corresponded with the rise of capitalist market and production relations on a global scale and, in particular, with their penetration of third world economies and rural areas. New exports came to the fore—including coffee, bananas, ground nuts, soy beans, oil palm, and others—together with new, more capitalistic (as opposed to feudal or mercantile) agroexport elites. This was the era of modernization, whose dominant ideology was that bigger is better. In rural areas, that meant the consolidation of farmland into large holdings that could be mechanized and the notion that the so-called backwards and inefficient peasantry should abandon farming and migrate to the cities where they would provide the labor force for industrialization. This ushered in a new era of land concentration in the hands of the wealthy and drove the growing problem of landlessness in rural areas. The landless rapidly became the poorest of the poor, subsisting as part-time, seasonal agricultural or day laborers and share croppers or migrating to the agricultural frontier to fell forests for homesteads. Also among the poor were the land poor: sharecroppers, renters of small plots, squatters, or legal owners of parcels too small or too infertile to adequately support their families.

9   Thus rural areas in the third world are, today, characterized by extreme inequities in access to land, security of land tenure, and the quality of the land farmed. These inequities underlie equally extreme inequities in wealth, income, and living standards. The poor majority are marginalized from national economic life because their meager incomes make their purchasing power insignificant. This creates a vicious circle.

10   The marginalization of the majority leads to narrow and shallow domestic markets, so landowning elites orient their production to export markets where consumers do have purchasing power. By doing so, elites have ever less interest in the well-being or purchasing power of the poor at home because the poor are not a market for them but, rather, a cost in terms of wages to be kept as low as possible. By keeping wages and living standards low, elites guarantee that healthy domestic markets will never emerge, reinforcing export orientation. The result is a downward spiral

into deeper poverty and marginalization even as national exports become more competitive in the global economy. One irony of our world, then, is that food and other farm products flow from areas of hunger and need to areas were money is concentrated: northern countries.

11   The same dynamic drives environmental degradation. On one hand, rural populations have historically been relocated from areas suitable for farming to those less suitable, leading to deforestation, desertification, and soil erosion in fragile habitats. This process continues today as the newly landless continuously migrate to the agricultural frontier.

12   On the other hand, the situation is no better in the more favorable lands. Here the better soils of most nations have been concentrated into large holdings used for mechanized, pesticide and chemical fertilizer intensive, monocultural production for export. Many of our planet's best soils—which had earlier been managed sustainably for millennia by precolonial, traditional agriculturalists—are today being rapidly degraded and, in some cases, abandoned completely in the short-term pursuit of export profits and competitiveness. The productive capacity of these soils is dropping rapidly because of soil compaction, erosion, waterlogging, and fertility loss together with growing resistance of pests to pesticides and the loss of in-soil and above-ground functional biodiversity. The growing problem of yield decline in these areas has recently been recognized as a looming threat to global food production by a number of international agencies (see also Lappé et al., 1998).

STRUCTURAL ADJUSTMENT AND OTHER MACROPOLICIES

13   As if that were not enough, the past 3 decades of world history have seen a series of changes in national and global governance mechanisms, which have, in their sum, eroded the ability of governments in southern nations to manage national development trajectories with a view to the broad-based human security of their citizens. Their ability has been critically weakened to ensure the social welfare of poor and vulnerable people, achieve social justice, guarantee human rights, and protect and sustainably manage their natural resources. These changes in governance mechanisms have been made within a paradigm that sees international trade as the key resource for promoting economic growth in national economies and sees that growth as the solution to all ills (Lappé et al., 1998).

14   To make way for increased import/export activity and export-promoting foreign investment, structural adjustment programs (SAPs), and regional and bilateral trade agreements, GATT and WTO negotiations have all shifted the balance of governance over

national economies away from governments and toward market mechanisms and global regulatory bodies like the WTO. Southern governments have progressively lost the majority of the management tools in their macroeconomic policy toolboxes. They have been forced to drastically cut government investment through deficit-slashing requirements, unify exchange rates, devalue and then float currencies, virtually eliminate tariff and nontariff import barriers, privatize state banks and other enterprises, and slash or eliminate subsidies of all kinds, including social services and price supports for small farmers. In most cases—either in preparation for entering trade agreements or with international financial institution funding and/or guidance—governance over land tenure arrangements has followed suit with privatization, land markets, and market mechanisms coming to the fore in search of greater investment in agricultural sectors (Bello, Cunningham, & Rau, 1999; Rosset, 2004).

15   Although such changes have, in some cases, created new opportunities for poor people to exploit new niche markets in the global economy (organic coffee, for example), they have, for the most part, undercut both government-provided social safety nets and guarantees and traditional community management of resources and cooperation in the face of crises. The majority of the poor still live in rural areas, and these changes have driven many of them to new depths of crisis in their ability to sustain their livelihoods. Increasingly, they have been plunged into an environment dominated by global economic forces where the terms of participation have been set to meet the interests of the most powerful. Small farmers find the prices of the staple foods they produce dropping below the cost of production in the face of cheap imports freed from tariffs and quotas. They are increasingly without the subsidized credit, marketing, and prices that once helped support their production and with communal land tenure arrangements under attack from legal reforms and private-sector investors. The result is the declining productivity of small farmers who produce food for domestic consumption, especially in regions like sub-Saharan Africa (de Grassi & Rosset, in press; Lappé et al., 1998).

LAGGING PRODUCTIVITY

16   Third World food producers demonstrate lagging productivity not because they lack so-called miracle seeds that contain their own insecticide or tolerate massive doses of herbicide but because they have been displaced onto marginal, rain-fed lands and face structures and macroeconomic policies that are increasingly inimical to food production by small farmers. When development banks are privatized by SAPs, credit is withdrawn from small farmers. When SAPs cancel subsidies for inputs, small farmers stop using them.

When price supports end and domestic markets are opened to surplus food dumped by northern countries, prices drop and local food production becomes unprofitable. When state marketing agencies for staple foods are replaced by private traders, who prefer cheap imports or buying from large, wealthy farmers, small farmers find there are no longer any buyers for what they produce. These, then, are the true causes of low productivity. In fact, in many parts of the third world, especially Africa, farmers today produce far less than they could with presently available know-how and technology because there is no incentive for them to do so—there are only low prices and few buyers. No new seed, good or bad, can change that. Thus it is extremely unlikely that, in the absence of urgently needed structural changes in access to land and in agricultural and trade policies, genetic engineering could make any dent in food production by the world's poorer farmers (de Grassi & Rosset, in press; Lappé et al., 1998).

17   When seen in this light, it should be clear that genetic engineering is tangential, at best, to the conditions and needs of the farmers we are told it will help: It in no way addresses the principal constraints they face. But tangential is a far cry from bad. Now I turn to the question of whether genetically engineered crops are simply irrelevant to the poor or if they might actually pose a threat to them. First we must ask about the actual circumstances of peasant farming.

A COMPLEX, DIVERSE, AND RISK-PRONE AGRICULTURE

18   Because peasant farmers have historically been displaced, as described above, into marginal zones characterized by broken terrain, slopes, irregular rainfall, little irrigation, and/or low soil fertility and because they are poor and victimized by pervasive antipoor and antismall-farmer biases in national and global economic policies, their agriculture is best characterized as complex, diverse, and risk prone (Chambers, 1990, 1993).

19   To survive under such circumstances and improve their standard of living they must be able to tailor agricultural technologies to their variable but unique circumstances in terms of local climate, topography, soils, biodiversity, cropping systems, market insertion, resources, etc. For this reason, such farmers have for millennia evolved complex farming and livelihood systems that balance risks of drought, market failure, pests, etc. with factors such as labor needs versus availability, investment needed, nutritional needs, seasonal variability, etc. Typically, their cropping systems involve multiple annual and perennial crops, animals, fodder, even fish, and a variety of foraged wild products (Chambers, 1990, 1993; de Grassi & Rosset, 2003, in press).

REPEATING THE ERRORS OF TOP-DOWN RESEARCH

20 Such farmers have rarely benefited from top-down, formal institution research and green revolution technologies. Any new strategy to truly address productivity and poverty concerns will have to meet their needs for multiple suitable varieties. Peasant farmers typically plant several different varieties on their land, tailoring their choice to the characteristics of each patch—whether it has good drainage or bad, is more or less fertile than the rest, etc. However, such varieties cannot be easily developed with current research and extension structures and methods, the same structures that biotech proponents use for genetically engineered varieties (the arguments in this section are developed in Chambers, 1990, 1993; de Grassi & Rosset, 2003, in press).

21   Formal research methods are not able to handle the vast complexity of physical and socioeconomic conditions in most third world agriculture. This stems from the discrepancy between hierarchical research and extension systems that value monocultural yield above all else and complex rural realities. The result of the mismatch is that numerous variables important to farmers have to be reduced to produce new technologies. Measured in a few variables, new seeds are perceived by researchers to be better than old ones. Therefore, researchers are puzzled when farmers fail to adopt new seeds widely.

22   In reality, seeds have multiple characteristics that cannot be captured by a single yield measure—as important as this measure may be—and farmers have multiple site-specific requirements for their seeds, not just controlled condition high yields. These interconnections stand in direct contrast to formal breeding procedures where varieties are selected individually for discrete traits then crossed to combine these individual traits. According to Jiggins, Reijnjets, and Lightfoot (1996), high-yielding variety trials in sub-Saharan Africa show

> larger variations, for both "traditional" and "improved," *among* farmers and *between* years, than the mean differences between "traditional" and "improved" yields in a single year. There is indeed overwhelming evidence throughout SSA that the yield response to fertilizer and improved varieties, soil management and other practices is highly site-, soil-, season-, and farmer-specific.

23   Given such conditions, the inescapable conclusion is that a different approach—participatory breeding by organized farmers themselves—which takes into account the multiple characteristics of both seed varieties and farmers, is essential: Miracle seeds will not just be developed in laboratories and on research stations and then

be effortlessly distributed to farmers. Yet genetic engineering is the very antithesis of participatory, farmer-led research. Proponents of genetically engineered varieties are repeating the very top-down errors that led first-generation green-revolution crop varieties to have low adoption rates among poorer farmers.

24   Yet many would argue that the possibility of delivering enhanced nutrition to the poor should outweigh such concerns, for example in the case of the famous golden rice, which has been engineered to contain additional beta-carotene, the precursor of vitamin A.

ENHANCED NUTRITION?

25 The suggestion that genetically altered rice is the proper way to address the condition of 2 million children at risk of vitamin A deficiency-induced blindness reveals a tremendous naiveté about the reality and causes of vitamin and micronutrient malnutrition. If one reflects on patterns of development and nutrition, one must quickly realize that vitamin A deficiency is not best characterized as a problem but, rather, as a symptom, a warning sign if you will. It warns us of broader dietary inadequacies associated with both poverty and agricultural change from diverse cropping systems toward rice monoculture. People do not present vitamin A deficiency because rice contains too little vitamin A or beta-carotene but, rather, because their diet has been reduced to rice and almost nothing else, and they suffer many other dietary illnesses that cannot be addressed by beta-carotene but could be addressed, together with vitamin A deficiency, by a more varied diet. A magic-bullet solution that places beta-carotene into rice—with potential health and ecological hazards—while leaving poverty, poor diets, and extensive monoculture intact is unlikely to make any durable contribution to well-being. In fact, there are many readily available solutions to vitamin A deficiency-induced blindness, including many ubiquitous leafy plants that when introduced (or reintroduced) into the diet provide both needed beta-carotene and other missing vitamins and micronutrients (ActionAid, 1999; Altieri & Rosset, 1999a, 1999b; Ho, 2000).

26   Yet it is clear that the genetic engineering juggernaut is moving ahead at full speed. What then are the risks associated with forcing transgenic (genetically engineered) varieties into complex, diverse, and risk-prone circumstances?

RISKS FOR POOR FARMERS

27 When transgenic varieties are used in such cropping systems, the risks are much greater than in green-revolution, large, wealthy farmer systems or farming systems in northern countries. The widespread crop failures reported for transgenics because of stem

splitting, boll drop, etc. (e.g., Eckardt, McHenry, & Guiltinan, 1998; Gertz, Vencill, & Hill, 1999; Hagedorn, 1997) pose economic risks that can affect poor farmers much more severely than wealthy farmers. If consumers reject their products, the economic risks are higher the poorer one is. Also, the high costs of transgenics introduce an additional antipoor bias into the system (Altieri & Rosset, 1999a, 1999b).

28   The most common transgenic varieties available today are those that tolerate proprietary brands of herbicides and those that contain insecticide genes. Herbicide-tolerant crops make little sense to peasant farmers who plant diverse mixtures of crop and fodder species because such chemicals would destroy key components of their cropping systems (Altieri & Rosset, 1999a, 1999b).

29   Transgenic plants that produce their own insecticides—usually using the Bt gene—closely follow the pesticide paradigm, which is itself rapidly failing because of pest resistance to insecticides. Instead of the failed one pest, one chemical model, genetic engineering emphasizes a one pest, one gene approach, shown over and over again in laboratory trials to fail because pest species rapidly adapt and develop resistance to the insecticide present in the plant. Bt crops violate the basic and widely accepted principle of integrated pest management (IPM), which is that reliance on any single pest-management technology tends to trigger shifts in pest species or the evolution of resistance through one or more mechanisms. In general, the greater the selection pressure across time and space, the quicker and more profound the pests' evolutionary response. Thus IPM approaches employ multiple pest-control mechanisms and use pesticides minimally and only in cases of last resort. An obvious reason for adopting this principle is that it reduces pest exposure to pesticides, retarding the evolution of resistance. But when the product is engineered into the plant itself, pest exposure leaps from minimal and occasional to massive and continuous, dramatically accelerating resistance. Most entomologists agree that Bt will rapidly become useless both as a feature of the new seeds and as an old standby natural insecticide sprayed when needed by farmers that want out of the pesticide treadmill. In the United States, the EPA has mandated that farmers set aside a certain proportion of their area as a refuge where non-Bt varieties are to be planted to slow down the rate of evolution by insects of resistance. Yet it is unlikely that poor, small farmers in the third world will plant such refuges, meaning that resistance to Bt could occur much more rapidly under such circumstances (Altieri & Rosset, 1999a, 1999b).

30   At the same time, the use of Bt crops affects nontarget organisms and ecological processes. Recent evidence shows that the Bt toxin can affect beneficial insect predators that feed on insect pests

present on Bt crops and that windblown pollen from Bt crops found on natural vegetation surrounding transgenic fields can kill nontarget insects. Small farmers rely, for insect pest control, on the rich complex of predators and parasites associated with their mixed cropping systems. But the effect on natural enemies raises serious concerns about the potential of the disruption of natural pest control because polyphagous predators that move within and between mixed crop cultivars will encounter Bt-containing, nontarget prey throughout the crop season. Disrupted biocontrol mechanisms may result in increased crop losses because of pests or the increased use of pesticides by farmers with consequent health and environmental hazards (Altieri & Rosset, 1999a, 1999b; Dutton, Klein, Romeis, & Bigler, 2002; Hillbeck, Baumgartner, Fried, & Bigler, 1998).

31   The fact that Bt retains its insecticidal properties after crop residues have been plowed into the soil and is protected against microbial degradation by being bound to soil particles, persisting in various soils for at least 234 days, is of serious concern for poor farmers who cannot purchase expensive chemical fertilizers and who, instead, rely on local residues, organic matter, and soil microorganisms (key invertebrate, fungal, or bacterial species) for soil fertility, which can be negatively affected by the soil-bound toxin (Altieri & Rosset, 1999a, 1999b; Donnegan et al., 1995; Zwahlen, Hilbeck, Gugerli, & Nentwig, 2003).

32   When the Bt genes fail, what would poor farmers be left with? It is entirely possible that they would face the serious rebound of pest populations freed of natural control by the impact Bt had on predators and parasites, and reduced soil fertility because of the impacts of Bt crop residues plowed into the ground. These are farmers who are already risk-prone, and Bt crops would likely increase that risk.

33   In the third world, there will typically be more sexually compatible wild relatives of crops present, making pollen transfer to weed populations of insecticidal properties, virus resistance, and other genetically engineered traits more likely with possible food chain and superweed consequences. With massive releases of transgenic crops, these impacts are expected to scale up in those developing countries that constitute centers of genetic diversity. In such biodiverse agricultural environments, the transfer of coding traits from transgenic crops to wild or weedy populations of these taxa and their close relatives is expected to be higher. Genetic exchange between crops and their wild relatives is common in traditional agroecosystems, and transgenic crops are bound to frequently encounter sexually compatible plant relatives; therefore, the potential for genetic pollution in such settings is inevitable (Altieri & Rosset, 1999b).

34   Perhaps of greater concern to peasant farmers is the possibility that their locally adapted crop varieties will be contaminated with transgenes via cross-pollination from transgenic varieties planted by other farmers. This concern was recently highlighted by the contamination with transgenes of local maize varieties in Mexico. It is in Mexico that maize was domesticated by indigenous peoples, and the region remains the present-day center of genetic diversity for this staple food crop so critical to global food security. The thousands of local varieties still cultivated by peasant farmers contain untold genetic diversity on which crop breeders and farmers worldwide depend as a source of novel traits for their breeding programs. Recognizing that this constitutes a critical biological heritage for all of humanity, the Mexican Environment Ministry in 1996 prohibited the import of transgenic maize seed for fear of contaminating this resource. Unfortunately, transgenic maize grain was still imported for human consumption and is sometimes planted by the poor in lieu of maize sold specifically as seed. Thus in 2001 scientists discovered alarmingly high rates of contamination of local maize races, presumably via wind-borne pollination from such plants (Quist & Chapela, 2001). Because of molecular promoters of gene expression incorporated into transgenic varieties, contamination poses a threat to the genetic integrity of local landraces because these promoters can potentially scramble the genomes of contaminated varieties (Ho et al., 2003; Wilson, Latham, & Steinbrecher, 2004). Thus peasant farmers could lose the locally adapted varieties that they depend on, and the world could lose germplasm that is critical to future food security.

35   There is also potential for vector recombination to generate new virulent strains of viruses, especially in transgenic plants engineered for viral resistance with viral genes. In plants containing coat protein genes, there is a possibility that such genes will be taken up by unrelated viruses infecting the plant. In such situations, the foreign gene changes the coat structure of the viruses and may confer properties such as changed method of transmission between plants. The second potential risk is that recombination between RNA virus and a viral RNA inside the transgenic crop could produce a new pathogen leading to more severe disease problems. Some researchers have shown that recombination occurs in transgenic plants and that under certain conditions it produces a new viral strain with altered host range (Steinbrecher, 1996). Crop losses caused by new viral pathogens could have a more significant impact on the livelihoods of poor farmers than they would for wealthier farmers who have ample resources to survive poor harvests.

36   In sum, these and other risks seem to outweigh the potential benefits for peasant farmers, especially when we consider the factors that currently limit their ability to improve their livelihoods, which are largely structural in nature—and thus political—rather than technological. Furthermore, to the extent that so-called better technologies are needed to improve farmer livelihoods and/or productivity, there is a wealth of proven agroecological, participatory, and empowering alternatives available to them (for an introduction to these alternatives see Altieri, Rosset, & Thrupp, 1998; Ho et al., 2003; Pretty, Morison, & Hine, 2003).

References

ActionAid. (1999). *AstraZeneca and its genetic research: Feeding the world or fueling hunger?* London: Author.

Altieri, M. A., & Rosset, P. (1999a). Strengthening the case for why biotechnology will not help the developing world: Response to McGloughlin. *AgBioForum, 2,* 226–236.

Altieri, M. A., & Rosset, P. (1999b). Ten reasons why biotechnology will not ensure food security, protect the environment and reduce poverty in the developing world. *AgBioForum, 2,* 155–162.

Altieri, M., Rosset, P., & Thrupp, L. A. (1998). *The potential of agroecology to combat hunger in the developing world* (Food First Policy Brief No. 2). Oakland, CA: Institute for Food and Development Policy.

Bello, W., Cunningham, S., & Rau, B. (1999). *Dark victory: The United States and global poverty* (2nd ed.). London: Pluto and Food First Books.

Chambers, R. (1990). Farmer-first: A practical paradigm for the third agriculture. In M. A. Altieri & S. B. Hecht (Eds.), *Agroecology and small farm development* (pp. 237–244). Ann Arbor, MI: CRC Press.

Chambers, R. (1993). *Challenging the professions: Frontiers for rural development.* London: Intermediate Technology Publications.

de Grassi, A., & Rosset, P. (2003, July). Public research: Which public is that? *Seedling,* pp. 18–22.

de Grassi, A., & Rosset, P. (in press). *A new green revolution for Africa? Myths and realities of agriculture, technology and development,* Oakland, CA: Food First Books.

Donnegan, K. K., Palm, C. J., Fieland, V. J. Porteous, L. A., Ganis, L. M., Scheller, D. L., et al. (1995). Changes in levels, species, and DNA fingerprints of soil microorganisms associated with cotton expressing the *Bacillus thuringiensis* var. Kurstaki endotoxin. *Applied Soil Ecology, 2,* 111–124.

Dutton, A., Klein, H., Romeis, J., & Bigler, F. (2002). Uptake of Bt-toxin by herbivores feeding on transgenic maize and consequences for the predator *Chrysoperla carnea. Ecological Entomology, 27*(4), 441–447.

Eckardt, N. A., McHenry, L., & Guiltinan, M. J. (1998). Overexpression of EmBP, a truncated dominant negative version of the wheat G-box binding protein EmBP-1, alters vegetative development in transgenic tobacco. *Plant Molecular Biology, 38*(4), 539–549.

Gertz, J. M., Vencill, W. K., & Hill, N. S. (1999, November). Tolerance of transgenic soybean (Glycine max) to heat stress. *Proceedings of an International Conference,* British Crop Protection Conference, Weeds, Brighton, *3,* 835–840.

Hagedorn, C. (1997, December). *Boll drop problems in Roundup-resistant cotton.* Retrieved from http://www.ext.vt.edu/news/periodicals/cses/1997-12/1997-12-04.html

Hillbeck, A., Baumgartner, M., Fried, P. M., & Bigler, F. (1998). Effects of transgenic Bt corn-fed prey on mortality and development time of immature *Chrysoperla carnea* (Neuroptera: Chrysopidae). *Environmental Entomology, 27*(2), 480–487.

Ho, M.-W. (2000). The "golden rice": An exercise in how not to do science. *Third World Resurgence, 118/119,* 22–26.

Ho, M.-W., Li-Ching, L., Cummins, J., Hooper, M., Altieri, M., Rosset, P., et al. (2003). *The Case for a GM-free sustainable world: Report of the Independent Science Panel.* London: Institute of Science in Society.

Jiggins, J., Reijnjets, C., & Lightfoot, C. (1996). Mobilising science and technology to get agriculture moving in Africa: A response to Borlaug and Dowswell. *Development Policy Review, 14*(1), 89–103.

Lappé, F. M., Collins, J., Rosset, P., & Esparza, L. (1998). *World hunger: Twelve myths* (2nd ed.). New York: Grove Press/Earthscan.

McGloughlin, M. (1999a). Ten reasons why biotechnology will be important to the developing world. *AgBioForum, 2,* 163–174.

McGloughlin, M. (1999b, November 1). Without biotechnology, we'll starve. *Los Angeles Times.*

McMichael, P. (2004, July). *Global development and the corporate food regime.* Paper presented at the Symposium on New Directions in the Sociology of Global Development, XI World Congress of Rural Sociology, Trondheim, Norway.

Pingali, P. L., Hossain, M., & Gerpacio, R. V. (1997). *Asian rice bowls: The returning crisis.* Wallingford, UK: CAB International.

Pinstrup-Andersen, P. (1999, October 27). Biotech and the poor. *Washington Post.*

Pretty, J. N., Morison, J. I. L., & Hine, R. E. (2003). Reducing food poverty by increasing agricultural sustainability in developing countries. *Agriculture, Ecosystems and Environment, 95,* 217–234.

Quist, D., & Chapela, I. (2001). Transgenic DNA introgressed into traditional maize landraces in Oaxaca, Mexico. *Nature, 414,* 541–543.

Ross, E. B. (1998). *The Malthus factor: Poverty, politics and population in capitalist development.* London: Zed.

Rosset, P. M. (2004). *Agricultural subsidies and trade issues: The key alternatives.* New York: Global Policy Innovations Project, Carnegie Council on Ethics and International Affairs.

Steinbrecher, R. A. (1996). From green to gene revolution: The environmental genetically engineered crops. *The Ecologist, 26,* 273–282.

Wilson, A., Latham, J., & Steinbrecher, R. (2004, October). *Genome scrambling—myth or reality? Transformation-induced mutations in transgenic crop plants.* Retrieved from www.econexus.info/pdf/ENx-Genome-Scrambling-Summary.pdf

Zwahlen, C., Hilbeck, A., Gugerli, P., & Nentwig, W. (2003). Degradation of the Cry1Ab protein within transgenic *Bacillus thuringiensis* corn tissue in the field. *Molecular Ecology, 12*(3), 765–775.

For Class Discussion

1. How and where does Peter Rosset summarize the protransgenic crops view and talk back to Conko and Prakash? How does his treatment of this opposing view contribute to readers' impressions of his knowledge of the field and the reliability of his claims and evidence?

2. What causal argument does Rosset make connecting colonial history, landlessness, and third world poverty? How does this explanation for third world poverty differ from that of supporters of transgenic crops?

3. Rosset identifies connections among economic, environmental, and social problems. What argument does Rosset make against global free trade organizations like the WTO?

4. This article includes many agricultural and technical terms: "hierarchical research and extension systems" versus "complex rural realities"; "site-specific requirements"; "monocultural yield"; "single yield measure"; "top-down research"; "pesticide paradigm"; "integrated pest management"; "polyphagous predators"; "biocontrol mechanisms"; "soil-bound toxin"; "structural adjustment programs"; "genetic integrity of local landraces"; and others. How does Rosset try to make these ideas accessible to audiences outside the agricultural field? How would you define these terms in your own words?

5. How does Rosset argue against the favorite biotech example of golden rice? What common arguments against biotech crops does Rosset *not* develop in this article?

6. What have the depth and thoroughness of this argument contributed to your understanding of global hunger problems? ∎

Organic Farming: Making an Informed Choice
Syngenta

Syngenta, a Swiss company, is a "world-leading agribusiness" "committed to sustainable agriculture, through innovative research and technology" ("Position Statement," www.syngenta.com). In its Web site link on "Sustainable Agriculture," Syngenta asserts that "[I]n the last decade food safety crises, revelations of unethical working conditions for farmers, increasing attention to symptoms of imbalance such as pollution and decline of biodiversity have dramatically demonstrated the needs for a sustainable approach to agriculture" ("About Syngenta"). As a European-based corporation, Syngenta is aware that the European Union has much higher standards against transgenic crops than other countries. The label "organic food" is a technical one that applies to food that is grown without the use of toxic chemicals and without genetic modification. The following Syngenta brochure takes part in this controversy over organic versus industrial-grown and bioengineered crops. (To see this brochure's use of color and design, go to Syngenta's Web site.)

In its opening approach to organic farming and its self-description, how does Syngenta seek to build a bridge of values and understanding to its audience, the public concerned about food production?

INTRODUCTION

1   Advances in agriculture have become increasingly successful in meeting the global demand for food. Over the past 50 years, the world's total food production has doubled, while many consumers have seen their food expenditure halved.

2   Organic farming has grown in popularity in recent years, especially in Europe, although it still represents less than five per cent of the total crop area. Organic agriculture only uses naturally occurring chemicals or traditional remedies to control pests and diseases. For this reason, the best control technologies are not always available to the organic farmer and yields can be 30–40 per cent lower than with other farming methods. Consequently, the cost of organically grown produce tends to be higher.

3   Syngenta promotes the concept of sustainable agriculture, which aims to optimize the use of resources, while protecting the long-term economic viability of farming. This is achieved through modern crop protection technologies and advanced plant varieties, including those developed using biotechnology. It results in sustainable production of healthier, stronger crops and contributes to abundant, high quality food and animal feed.

4   Accordingly, Syngenta believes that the judicious and targeted use of modern crop protection technologies plays a vital role in food production. However, a choice for both farmers and consumers is also important and organic farming has a role to play in providing this choice.

5   Some consumers choose organic food on the basis of claims that it is healthier and safer to humans and the environment. In many countries, organic farming even receives special government support in the form of subsidies and there is a move to increase this as agricultural policies come up for review.

6   As a science-based company, Syngenta is convinced that some of the claims made about organic crops cannot be scientifically supported. It is essential for consumers to make informed choices about the food they eat, with claims being scientifically proven and the same rules and regulations applied to organic food production that apply to food produced with the aid of modern, sustainable agriculture technologies.

7   Here, some of the popular claims about organic food will be addressed.

WHAT ARE THE MAIN CLAIMS ABOUT ORGANIC FOOD?

Claim—**Organic food is healthier and safer than food produced conventionally. This belief is largely based on the fact that no synthetic fertilizers or pesticides are used in its production, and therefore, there is an assumption that there are no pesticide residues in organic food**

8   First, the truth is that organic farmers are allowed to use certain pesticides. The difference between pesticides used in organic farming and other crop protection technologies is not their toxicity, only their origin. Pesticides used in organic farming are extracted from natural plants, insects, or mineral ores and not by chemical synthesis. In fact, two of the most popular organic-approved pesticides, oil and sulfur, are used more than any other pesticide, by volume, in the USA.

9   Second, it is important to understand that manufacturers of synthetic crop protection products must generate enormous amounts of detailed experimental study information to be able to register a product for sale. They have to demonstrate extensive margins of safety before approval is granted by governments. Therefore, within such margins, no consumers are exposed to harmful levels of residues in food. In fact, government monitoring programs indicate that the residue levels in food that consumers are exposed to are only a fraction of the established safety levels. The European Commission's report for 2000 found that 61 percent of food samples tested contained no detectable residue at all and a further 35 percent contained residues at levels below the set legal limits.

10   It is important to note that governments have been hesitant to tout the health benefits of organic produce because there is no conclusive scientific evidence to show any significant difference between food produced organically and that produced conventionally.

> *USDA makes no claims that organically produced food is safer or more nutritious than conventionally produced food. Organic food differs from conventionally produced food in the way it is grown, handled, and processed.*
>
> —US Department of Agriculture

> *On the basis of current evidence, the Agency's assessment is that organic food is not significantly different in terms of food safety and nutrition from food produced conventionally.*
>
> —UK Food Standards Agency

An extensive literature review of over 150 studies comparing organically and conventionally grown foods found no evidence of better tasting properties or improved nutritional value. In fact, organic produce often had a lower nitrate and protein content.

—Woese, K, *et al.*
J. Sci Food Agric, 74, 1997

Claim—**Organic farming is more friendly to the environment**

11 There is a widespread belief that organic farming is more environmentally friendly and more sustainable than conventional systems. It is argued that biodiversity is promoted and higher levels of plants, insects and birds are found and soil health is improved.

12 In reality, every kind of agriculture has an impact on the environment, so it is important that any kind of farming is carried out in the most environmentally sustainable way. For example, the use of herbicides has enabled "no-till" practices, which reduce disruption of the soil and minimize soil erosion. With organic farming, most weed control is done by mechanical cultivation methods. Mechanical cultivation disrupts the soil structure, releases carbon into the atmosphere, removes valuable moisture, damages earthworms and soil wildlife, and increases soil erosion.

It is true that organic systems tend to produce a greater biodiversity than conventional agriculture, but this is not always the case. For example, organic farmers keep their fields clear of weeds by frequent mechanical cultivation, which can damage nesting birds, worms and insects, and actually damage soil structure.

—Trewavas A, 2001

Conservation or reduced tillage (one or no cultivation together with one application of herbicide) is often used in integrated systems, which greatly benefits wildlife. In addition, integrated farming methods can produce more food from less land than an organic system, hence land can be taken out of cultivation and used to encourage wildlife.

—Holland *et al*, 1994

Claim—**Crop yields from organic farms can be similar to those from conventional farms**

13 In certain rare environments where there are few pests, similar crop yields can be obtained without the use of synthetic pesticides. However, in the vast majority of cases where crops are at risk from pests and diseases, crop protection technologies significantly boost yields.

14 Indeed, organic agriculture cannot, on a large scale, be adopted in a sustainable way and still be expected to produce enough, high quality food at a reasonable price. For Europe to feed itself organically, it has been estimated that an extra 28 million hectares would

have to be ploughed up—equal to the entire forest cover of France, Germany, Denmark and Britain. On a global scale, if all food production in the world were to go organic, an estimated two billion people could be at additional risk of starvation.

> *In Europe the relative yield in organic systems compared to conventional ones averaged 68% for cereals and 73% for potatoes. However, for individual countries these figures can range from 55–78% and 45–100% respectively.*
>
> —Zanoli R, 1999

Claim—Organic farming is better because it does not allow the use of genetically enhanced crops

15 Over the seven years in which they have been widely grown, genetically enhanced crops have proven their safety and worth, in terms of contributing to more efficient and sustainable agriculture. Genetically enhanced crops able to protect themselves from pests and diseases can increase productivity and enable more efficient and targeted use of synthetic pesticides. Food derived from these crops have to go through rigorous safety testing and approval processes.

16 Despite the benefits and proven safety record, the principles set out by organic farming organizations call for zero tolerance of genetically enhanced material found in organic crops.

17 While this "zero tolerance" approach may appear to present a choice for consumers who wish to avoid these products, such an absolute threshold presents practical difficulties for farmers and the food supply chain.

18 In fact, the difficulty of achieving 100 per cent purity has been recognized when setting organic standards, some of which have allowed for many years up to a five per cent content of "non-organic" food.

19 To maintain a choice for farmers and consumers, high purity levels are achievable using existing management systems. These provide a proven balance between practical, realistic thresholds and cost to the consumer.

> *The available information on GM foods and feeds already on the market indicates that they can be considered as safe as conventionally bred crop plants.*
>
> —Noteborn H J P M et al Department of Food Safety and Health, The Netherlands, 2001.

FOOD PRODUCTION FOR THE FUTURE: THE CHOICES

20 Thanks to advances in agricultural technology, total food production has largely been able to keep up with global demand. However,

maintaining this balance will be extremely challenging, as population growth outstrips land and water availability.

21   Whilst organic farming offers consumers in affluent countries an additional choice, it is not a viable solution for feeding an ever-increasing world population. At the same time, it is also clear that the over-use of chemicals is not acceptable in sustainable farming systems.

22   Therefore, many agriculturalists and environmentalists are promoting systems of Integrated Pest Management (IPM) to provide the best social, economical, and environmentally sustainable solution for crop production globally.

23   This involves the management of the whole farming system to produce economic yields of high quality produce in an environmentally sustainable way. The overall principle for the judicious use of synthetic crop protection products within IPM is: "as little as possible and as much as necessary". In IPM, pests are managed using the most appropriate techniques, including cultural, biological, biotechnological, mechanical and chemical measures.

24   Syngenta firmly believes that a truly sustainable agriculture can be achieved through such a system, using the most appropriate technologies, both old and new. This kind of integrated system has significant advantages over organic agriculture.

For Class Discussion

1. "Sustainable agriculture" is a main concern of environmentalists and social activists. How does Syngenta define it and argue that Syngenta's farming methods, and not organic farming, are successful at promoting it?

2. What evidence does Syngenta offer to support its claims in favor of conventional and biotech farming and against organic food?

3. What assumptions does Syngenta make about world hunger, crop yields, and technology and about the importance of efficiency and productivity?

4. What questions or objections would environmentalists and advocates for small organic farms like Peter Rosset and Vandana Shiva have in response to this brochure?

5. What adjectives would you use to describe the corporate image that Syngenta seeks to project in this brochure? (You might examine the brochure on the Web site.) As a public relations tool, how rhetorically effective is this brochure?

6. What is persuasive and what is questionable about this brochure and its argument?

The Next Green Revolution

Pedro Sanchez

Pedro Sanchez from Cuba holds a master's degree and a doctorate from Cornell University. Sanchez's research on managing natural resources to promote food security and reduce poverty has taken him to the Philippines, Peru, Colombia, and Kenya. In 2003, he won a prestigious MacArthur Foundation Fellowship for outstanding scholarship. He is currently director of tropical agriculture and senior research scholar at the Earth Institute of Columbia University and cochair of the Hunger Task Force of the Millennium Project of the United Nations. This op-ed piece appeared in the *New York Times* on October 6, 2004.

> What primary audience does Pedro Sanchez appeal to in this brief policy proposal addressing Africa's hunger problem?

1   Africa is hungry and Americans would like to help. But we've been helping the wrong way—by providing emergency food aid rather than enabling African farmers to produce more food. Last year the United States generously gave $500 million of emergency food aid to Ethiopia to help people survive the drought year. And how much did we provide to African farmers to help them be more productive over the long run? A small fraction of that amount—$4 million.

2   As a result of the Green Revolution in the 1960's, 70's and 80's, crop yields soared in India, China and Latin America, enabling them to break free of extreme hunger and recurrent famine. Indeed, these agricultural changes allowed countries like China and India to become the emerging markets they are today.

3   Tropical Africa—which stretches from the southern edge of the Sahara to the Limpopo River on the border of South Africa—is finally ready for its own Green Revolution. Crop yields there are miniscule, an average of 1,500 pounds of cereals per acre compared with 2,300 pounds in India and 4,900 pounds in China.

4   For better harvests, Africa's farmers need four things: nutrients for the soil, which can be provided by both mineral and organic fertilizers; small-scale irrigation and technologies for collecting rainwater; sturdier, higher-yield seeds; and a corps of master farmers, trained in up-to-date agricultural techniques, who could be posted in villages and would be able to provide advice. By introducing these measures, Africans could triple food production by 2015.

5   Unlike the Green Revolution of the 60's, an African Green Revolution doesn't have to be based on technologies and practices that hurt the environment. Land can be reclaimed not only through appropriate fertilization but through more environmentally sensitive

techniques. For starters, there's agro-forestry, which involves planting trees that replenish the soil with nutrients like nitrogen. Farmers could also learn low-till or no-till farming techniques and be encouraged to plant pest-tolerant crops, which would cut down on insecticide and pesticide use.

6   What's more, small-scale irrigation projects like ones under way in northern Ethiopia can bring water to parched areas more effectively and economically than the large, expensive dam projects of old. Finally, after soil and water are taken care of, biotechnology can help, by fortifying African food crops against droughts and pests, and by increasing the nutritional content of staple foods.

7   A rise in crop yields would do more than end hunger. Raising the productivity of Africa's villages would also raise the status of the women on the continent. Women do much of the farming in Africa today, growing 80 percent of the food there—and they work mostly without tools or modern technologies. If farming was easier, women would be freer to find work off the farm, more girls would be able to stay in school and children would have better food to eat. History has shown that women's empowerment in turn leads to lower population growth and to advances in children's health and education. In addition, using locally grown foods in feeding programs for infants and children will generate additional demand, helping African agriculture to strengthen itself.

8   Given the possible rewards of African renewal, the price tag is small. Key investments on the order of $50 per person per year in tropical African villages would put the continent on the path to long-term sustainable development. Additional annual aid from the developed world might therefore be around $25 billion, a small fraction of what we spend over the long run on emergency food aid, disease epidemics and fighting terrorism and violence in failed states.

9   If we take these simple steps—and promote good governance in African countries—the continent has the potential to go from basket case to trading partner. A sign I saw at a Florida bait shop says it all: "Give people a fish and they will eat for a day; teach people how to fish and they will eat for their lifetime and . . . they will buy fishing equipment."

For Class Discussion

1. What is the core of this policy proposal?

2. How does it represent a middle ground between the strong advocates of biotechnology as a solution to hunger and anticorporate farmers and citizens from around the world who are calling for food sovereignty and local solutions?

3. How does Sanchez use cost-benefit analysis in this argument?

4. How does Sanchez's direct manner and concise treatment of a big issue contribute to the persuasiveness of this piece?

5. Op-ed pieces are too short for fully developed ideas. Which points in this piece would you need to investigate more in order to agree with Sanchez's proposal?

Gift of Food: How to Solve the Agricultural Crisis, the Health Crisis and the Crisis of Poverty
Vandana Shiva

Vandana Shiva, who has a doctorate in physics, is an internationally known environmentalist, social activist, feminist, and vocal opponent of corporate globalization. She has authored several books about the corporate takeover of agriculture in India and other developing countries: *The Violence of the Green Revolution* (1992), *The Plunder of Nature and Knowledge* (1997), and *Stolen Harvest: The Hijacking of the Global Food Supply* (2000). She is director of the Research Foundation for Science, Technology, and Natural Resource Policy and of Bija Vidyapeeth, the International College for Sustainable Living in Dehra Dun, India. In 1993, she won the Alternative Nobel Peace Prize (the Right Livelihood Award). She writes political/economic/environmental commentaries regularly, frequently for *Resurgence*, a magazine devoted to "connecting you to a world of ecology, art and culture" (www.resurgence.org). This article was published in the August 2005 issue of *Resurgence*.

What features of this article indicate that Shiva is writing for people who share her values?

1   The first thing to recognise about food is that it is the very basis of life. Food is alive: it is not just pieces of carbohydrate, protein and nutrient, it is a being, a sacred being. Not only is food sacred, not only is it living, but it is the Creator itself, and that is why in the poorest of Indian huts you find the little earthen stove being worshipped; the first piece of bread is given to the cow, then you are required to find out who else is hungry in your area. In the words of the sacred texts of India, "The giver of food is the giver of life," and indeed of everything else. Therefore, one who desires wellbeing in this world and beyond should especially endeavour to give food.

2   Because food is the very basis of creation, food is creation, and it is the Creator. There are all kinds of duties that we should be

performing with respect to food. If people have food it is because society has not forgotten those duties. If people are hungry, society has rejected the ethical duties related to food.

3   The very possibility of our being alive is based on the lives of all kinds of beings that have gone before us—our parents, the soil, the earthworm—and that is why the giving of food in Indian thought has been treated as everyday sacrifice that we have to perform. It is a ritual embodied in every meal, reflecting the recognition that giving is the condition of our very being. We do not give as an extra, we give because of our interdependence with all of life.

4   One of my favourite images in India is the kolam, a design which a woman makes in front of her house. In the days of Pongal, which is the rice harvest festival in South India, I have seen women get up before dawn to make the most beautiful art work outside their houses, and it is always made with rice. The real reason is to feed the ants, but it is also a beautiful art form that has gone on from mother to daughter, and at festival time everyone tries to make the best kolam as their offering. Thus, feeding the ants and works of art are integrated.

5   The indica rice variety's homeland is a tribal area called Chattisgarh in India. It must be about fifteen years ago that I first went there. The people there weave beautiful designs of paddy, which they then hang outside their houses. I thought that this must be related to a particular festival, and I asked, "What festival is it for?" They said, "No, no, this is for the season when the birds cannot get rice grain in the fields." They were putting rice out for other species, in very beautiful offerings of art work.

6   Because we owe the conditions of our life to all other beings and all other creatures, giving—to humans and to non-human species—has inspired annadana, the gift of food. All other ethical arrangements in society get looked after if everyone is engaging in annadana on a daily basis. According to an ancient Indian saying: "There is no gift greater than annadana, the giving of food." Or again, in the words of the sacred texts: "Do not send away anyone who comes to your door without offering him or her food and hospitality. This is the inviolable discipline of humankind; therefore have a great abundance of food and exert all your efforts towards ensuring such abundance, and announce to the world that this abundance of food is ready to be partaken by all."

7   Thus from the culture of giving you have the conditions of abundance, and the sharing by all.

8   If we really look at what is happening in the world, we seem to have more and more food surpluses, while 820 million people still go hungry every day. As an ecologist, I see these surpluses as

pseudo-surpluses. They are pseudo-surpluses because the over-flowing stocks and packed supermarket shelves are the result of production and distribution systems which take food away from the weak and marginalized, and from non-human species.

9   I went through the food department of Marks & Spencer the other day, and I went dizzy seeing all the food there, because I knew that, for example, a peasant's rice field would have been converted into a banana plantation to get luscious bananas to the world's markets. Each time I see a supermarket, I see how every community and ecosystem's capacity to meet its food needs is being undermined, so that a few people in the world can experience food "surpluses".

10   But these are pseudo-surpluses leading to 820 million mal-nourished people, while many others eat too much and get ill or obese.

11   Let us see how food is produced. To have sustainable food sup-plies we need our soils to function as living systems: we need all those millions of soil organisms that make fertility. And that fertility gives us healthy foods. In industrial cultures we forget that it is the earthworm that creates soil fertility; we believe that soil fertility can come from nitrates—the surplus of explosives factories; that pest-control does not come out of the balance of different crops hosting different species, but from poisons. When you have the right balance, living organisms never become pests: they all coexist, and none of them destroys your crop.

12   The recently released report of the Food and Agriculture Orga-nization has chart after chart to show how in the last century we increased food productivity. But all they really calculated is labour displacement. They only looked at labour productivity—as how much food a human being produces by using technologies that are labour-displacing, species-displacing and resource-destroying. It does not mean that you have more food per acre; it does not mean that you have more food per unit used of water; it does not mean that you have more food for all the other species that need food. All of these diverse needs are being destroyed as we define productiv-ity on the basis of food production per unit of labour.

13   We are now working on technologies, based on genetic engi-neering, which accelerate this violence towards other beings. On my recent trip to Punjab, it suddenly hit me that they no longer have pollinators. Those technologically obsessed people are manip-ulating crops to put genes from the Bt toxin (the soil bacterium Bacillus thuringiensis) into plants, so that the plant releases toxins at every moment and in every cell: in its leaves, its roots, its pollen. These toxins are being eaten by ladybirds and butterflies which then die.

14   We do not see the web of life that we are rupturing. We can only see the interconnections if we are sensitive to them. And when we are aware of them we immediately recognise what we owe to other beings: to the pollinators, to the farmers who have produced the food, and to the people who have nourished us when we could not nourish ourselves.

15   The giving of food is related to the idea that every one of us is born in debt to other beings: our very condition of being born depends on this debt. So we come with a debt and for the rest of our lives we are paying back that debt—to the bees and the butterflies that pollinate our crops, to the earthworms and the fungi and the microbes and the bacteria in the soil that are constantly working away to create the fertility that our chemical fertilisers can never, never replenish.

16   We are born and live in debt to all Creation, and it becomes our duty to recognise this. The gift of food is merely a recognition of the need for constantly paying back that obligation, that responsibility. It is merely a matter of accepting and endeavouring to repay our debts to Creation, and to the communities of which we are a part. And that is why most cultures that have seen ecology as a sacred trust have always spoken of responsibility. Rights have flowed out of responsibility: once I ensure that everyone in my sphere of influence is fed, someone in that sphere is also ensuring that I am fed.

17   When I left university teaching in 1982, everyone said, "How will you manage without a salary?" I replied by saying that if ninety per cent of India manages without a salary, all I have to do is put my life in the kind of relationships of trust that they live through. If you give, then you will receive. You do not have to calculate the receiving: what you have to be conscious of is the giving.

18   In modern economic systems we also have debts, but they are financial debts. A child born in any Third World country already has millions of dollars of debt on her or his head owed to the World Bank, which has every power to tell you and your country that you should not be producing food for the earthworms and the birds, or even for the people of the land: you should be growing shrimps and flowers for export, because that earns money.

19   It does not earn very much money, either. I have made calculations that show that one dollar of trading by international business, in terms of profit, leads to $10 of ecological and economic destruction in local ecosystems. Now if for every dollar being traded we have a $10 shadow-cost in terms of how we are literally robbing food from those who need it most, we can understand why, as growth happens and as international trade becomes more "productive", there is, inevitably, more hunger: because the people who needed that food most are the ones who are being denied access to it by this new

system of trading. This so-called free trade is taking away from them any way of looking after others' needs, or their own.

20 People ask me: "How can we protect biodiversity if we are to meet growing human needs?" My reply is that the only way to meet growing human needs is to protect biodiversity, because unless we are looking after the earthworms and the birds and the butterflies we are not going to be able to look after people either. This idea that somehow the human species can only meet its needs by wiping out all other species is a wrong assumption: it is based on not seeing how the web of life connects us all, and how much we live in interaction and in interdependence.

21 Monocultures produce more monocultures, but they do not produce more nutrition. If you take a field and plant it with twenty crops, it will have a lot of food output, but if any one of those individual yields—say of corn or wheat—is measured in comparison with that of a monoculture field, of course you will have less, because the field is not all corn. So just by shifting from a diversity-based system into a monoculture industrially supported with chemicals and machines, you automatically define it as more, even though you are getting less! Less species, less output, less nutrition, less farmers, less food, less nourishment. And yet we have been absolutely brainwashed into believing that when we are producing less we are producing more. It is an illusion of the deepest kind.

22 Trade today is no longer about the exchange of things which we need and which we cannot produce ourselves. Trade is an obligation to stop producing what we need, to stop looking after each other, and to buy from somewhere else.

23 In trade today there are four grain giants. The biggest of them, Cargill, controls seventy per cent of the food traded in the world; and they fix the prices. They sell the inputs, they tell the farmer what to grow, they buy cheaply from the farmer, then they sell it at high cost to consumers. In the process they poison every bit of the food chain. Instead of giving, they are thinking of how they can take out that last bit, from ecosystems, other species, the poor, the Third World.

24 In the early 1990s Cargill said, "Oh, these Indian peasants are stupid. They do not realise that our seeds are smart: we have found new technologies that prevent the bees from usurping the pollen." Now the concept of "the gift of food" tells us that pollen is the gift that we must maintain for pollinators, and therefore we must grow open-pollinated crops that bees and butterflies can pollinate. That is their food and it is their ecological space. And we have to make sure that we do not eat into their space.

25 Instead, Cargill says that the bees usurp the pollen—because Cargill has defined every piece of pollen as their property. And in a

similar way, Monsanto said: "Through the use of Roundup we are preventing weeds from stealing the sunshine." The entire planet is energised by the life-giving force of the sun, and now Monsanto has basically said that it is Monsanto and the farmers in contract with Monsanto that, alone on the planet, have the right to sunshine— the rest of it is theft.

26   So what we are getting is a world which is absolutely the opposite to the "giving of food". Instead, it is the taking of food from the food chain and the web of life. Instead of gift we have profit and greed as the highest organizing principle. Unfortunately, the more the profit, the more hunger, illness, destruction of Nature, of soil, of water, of biodiversity, the more non-sustainable our food systems become. We then actually become surrounded by deepening debt: not the ecological debt to Nature, to the Earth and to other species, but the financial debt to the money-lenders and to the agents of chemicals and seeds. The ecological debt is in fact replaced by this financial debt: the giving of nourishment and food is replaced by the making of more and more profits.

27   What we need to do now is to find ways of detaching ourselves from these destructive arrangements. It is not just replacing free trade with fair trade: unless we see how the whole is leading to the poisoning and polluting of our very beings, of our very consciousness, we will not be able to make the deeper shifts that allow us to create abundance again. In taking all from nature, without giving, we are not creating abundance; we are creating scarcity.

28   Growing world hunger is part of that scarcity. And the growing diseases of affluence are a part of that scarcity too. If we relocate ourselves again in the sacred trust of ecology, and recognise our debt to all human and non-human beings, then the protection of the rights of all species simply becomes part of our ethical norm and our ethical duty. And as a result of that, those who depend on others for feeding them and for bringing them food will get the right kind of food and the right kind of nourishment. So, if we begin with the nourishment of the web of life, we actually solve the agricultural crisis of small farms, the health crisis of consumers, and the economic crisis of Third World poverty.

For Class Discussion

1. In this article, what principles of the spiritual and ethical view of food and nature does Vandana Shiva declare are important?

2. What claims about industrial farming and the global food system are central to Shiva's argument? How does she explain poverty and world hunger?

3. How does Shiva appeal to the values, emotions, and imaginations of her target audience?

4. How would readers who don't share Shiva's particular kind of reverence for nature respond to this article? How would she need to rework her argument and approach to reach agribusinesses and biotech scientists?

5. Shiva concludes her piece with a proposal that relates to the subtitle of her article. How persuasive and rhetorically effective is this ending? ∎

Ethiopia
Cam Cardrow

This cartoon, by Canadian editorial cartoonist Cameron Cardrow, appeared on May 14, 2003, in the *Ottawa Citizen*, of which Cardrow is a staff member. His cartoons are syndicated and archived on CagleCartoons.com.

> What story does this cartoon tell about the relationship between developing countries like Ethiopia and developed countries like Canada and the United States?

FIGURE 8.2 Ethiopia *(© Cameron Cardrow, 2003)*

For Class Discussion

1. How do the image and the words in this cartoon make an appeal to readers?

2. Whom is this cartoon criticizing? Is this cartoon criticizing more than one group?

3. This cartoon is entitled "Ethiopia" because that country was the site of a hunger crisis in 2003; however, this cartoon could easily have appeared in newspapers in 2005 with the title "Sudan," "Niger," or "Malawi." What deeper message does this cartoon convey about world hunger and poverty, third world countries, and rich countries?

4. Within this chapter, what new perspective on world hunger does this cartoon present? What arguments does it join, extend, or echo? ■

Think Globally, Eat Locally
Jennifer Wilkins

Jennifer Wilkins holds a doctorate in nutrition and consumer economics from Washington State University. She is currently at Cornell University as a food and society policy fellow in the division of nutritional sciences and directs Cornell's Farm to School Program. She has published numerous articles on nutrition, community-based agriculture, and genetically engineered foods, and her chapter "Eating Right Here: The Role of Dietary Guidance in Remaking Community-Based Food Systems" will be published in the forthcoming book *Remaking the North American Food System*. This op-ed piece appeared in the *New York Times* on December 18, 2004.

How does this piece grow out of and respond to the current national concern about terrorism?

1   When Tommy Thompson, the secretary of health and human services, announced this month that he was resigning, he made an unexpected comment: "For the life of me, I cannot understand why the terrorists have not attacked our food supply, because it is so easy to do." He added, "We are importing a lot of food from the Middle East, and it would be easy to tamper with that."

2   Unexpected, but right. The United States is importing more and more food, and not just from the Middle East (which actually accounts for only 0.4 percent of our food imports). Tomatoes from

Mexico, grapes from Chile and beef from Brazil are standard fare on American tables. The Department of Agriculture reports that in 2005, our nation will fail to record an agricultural surplus for the first time in 50 years, demonstrating our rising dependency on foreign agricultural production and distribution systems that may not be safe.

3   Yet few of these imports are examined to ensure they meet American health and safety standards. This year, the Food and Drug Administration will inspect about 100,000 of the nearly five million shipments of food crossing our borders, and distribution is so rapid that tainted food can reach consumers nationwide before officials realize there is a problem. The increasing control of the global food supply by a few corporations has made such tampering even more tempting for a terrorist who wants to have a big impact.

4   You might think that the solution is obvious: we should rely on our domestic food supply. Unfortunately, when it comes to food security, our vulnerabilities at home rival those we face abroad. The federal government's encouragement of consolidation in agriculture diminishes the security of our food supply.

5   Since the 1950's, American agricultural policies have been grounded in the belief that farms should produce as much food as possible for the least cost. These policies have led to a landscape of fewer but bigger farms that specialize in a decreasing number of commodities that are destined for fewer processors and packers.

6   From 1993 to 2000, 33,000 farms with annual sales of less than $100,000 disappeared. Meanwhile, very large farms play a larger role in the United States: farms generating more than $500,000 a year are only 3.3 percent of all farms but use 20.3 percent of America's farmland and account for 61.9 percent of all sales. The 10 largest food companies account for more than half of all products on supermarket shelves. Imagine what might happen to our food supply if a widespread contamination by a food-borne disease, accidental or intentional, were to strike even one of those megafarms or food companies.

7   The increasing power of food processors means that the farmer no longer controls the quality of the food system. About 85 percent of all vegetables destined for freezing and canning are grown under contract, with processors dictating variety, quantity, quality, delivery date and even price. If American farmers cannot produce the cheapest food, the processors turn to foreign countries, where there is greater potential for contamination, whether because of less strict inspection procedures or because of fewer protections against bioterrorism.

8   The combination of cheap food from overseas and the consolidation of domestic production compromises America's ability to feed
itself. A food system in which control of the critical elements is concentrated in few hands can and will fall victim to terrorism or accidents.

9   The solution to these insecurities is to establish community-
based food systems that include many small farmers and a diversity of products. Such systems make large-scale contamination
impossible, even for determined bioterrorists. Far more people
have contact with the Mexican lettuce at the supermarket, for
example, than with the locally grown lettuce at the farmers' market.

10   But is it possible for farmers' markets to feed a growing country
and provide the range of produce we demand? The answer is yes.
With some exceptions, like coffee and chocolate, American farmers
can easily meet demand. They've also had great success in marketing directly to the consumer: the number of farmers' markets has increased to 3,100 in 2002 from approximately 1,700 in 1994.

11   But creating this system of agriculture would require a shift in
policy. We should encourage smaller, diversified farms, a reallocation of farmland from feed grains to food crops, and local food processing. And the change in the cabinet, at both the department of
health and human services and the department of agriculture, is an
opportune moment for a such a change in policy.

12   It would be reassuring to one day hear a new secretary of health
and human services report that a terrorist attack on our food system
would be next to impossible because it is a complex network of farmers, processors and consumers integrated into communities nationwide. Strengthening local food systems and supporting policies that
shorten the distance between producers and consumers will reduce
the points of vulnerability and make America truly food-secure.

For Class Discussion

1. In this policy proposal argument, how does Jennifer Wilkins persuade her general newspaper audience that a problem exists? What
   is wrong with the global food system?

2. What opposing views or reservations does Wilkins address?

3. What is Wilkins's proposed solution? How does she justify and
   support it?

4. Where might resisting readers attack her views?

5. If Wilkins expanded this op-ed piece into a researched argument,
   policy statement, or white paper, what points would she need to
   develop more fully?

6. What contribution has she made to your understanding of the controversy over global versus local food systems?   ■

Going Local on a Global Scale: Rethinking Food Trade in an Era of Climate Change, Dumping, and Rural Poverty
Kirsten Schwind

Kirsten Schwind is program director of Food First/Institute for Food and Development Policy in Oakland, California. This organization, started in 1975 by Frances Moore Lappé and Joseph Collins, seeks "to eliminate the injustices that cause hunger" through its research into "the root causes of hunger" and its provision of materials to activists, the media, professors, and its supporters "Mission Statement," (www.foodfirst.org/mission). Schwind holds a bachelor's degree in economics and public policy from Swarthmore College, and her graduate work focused on natural resources management. Her work with human rights in Guatemala and her experiences with environmental justice, labor organizing, sustainable agriculture, and fair trade in Latin America have fueled her writing about "the politics of food." This piece was published in Food First's online *Backgrounder* in the spring–summer 2005 volume.

> According to Kirsten Schwind, which stakeholders support local food and which stakeholders support a global food system and why?

1   Fresh, local food is a vision that unites community food security activists, environmentalists, slow food enthusiasts, and small-scale farmers globally. Supporting or rebuilding local food systems to bring fresh and culturally relevant food from local producers to local consumers catalyzes community and regional development in both the global North and the global South. Producing and marketing more food locally can help alleviate both global climate change and rural poverty. Building these local food systems requires rethinking the role of trade and the institutions that promote it.

TRADE FUELS CLIMATE CHANGE

2   Advocating for local food requires reexamining the deeply held economic theory of competitive advantage, which holds that each region should specialize in producing only what it can produce most cheaply, then trade with other regions for everything else. However, traditional economic calculations do not account for the true environmental cost of trade. For example, the potentially cataclysmic impacts of climate change mean that the environmental costs of transporting goods long distances are much higher than previously thought.

3   Most food travels hundreds, even thousands, of miles from farm to plate,[1] and the fossil fuel transportation infrastructure we rely on for all this trade emits greenhouse gasses that are contributing to climate change.[2] Climate change is raising sea temperatures and flooding coastal areas, and has the potential to increase crop failures, cause mass extinctions, and spur more destructive weather patterns such as hurricanes—all with profound implications for agriculture and human habitation.[3] Since the full consequences will not be felt for years after the greenhouse gasses have been emitted, it is exceedingly difficult to predict and price future ecological damage and add it to the energy costs of today's food system. Thus even prices that are adjusted to include current energy subsidies or minor "climate change taxes" are not reliable indicators of the ecological and social price of fossil fuel–driven global trade.

4   Buying local food can make a big difference to the environment. For example, in 1920 Iowa produced a wide variety of fruits and vegetables, but now most of its fruits and vegetables are shipped from elsewhere. If Iowans bought just 10 percent more of their food from within the state, they could collectively save 7.9 million pounds of carbon dioxide emission a year.[4] The Japanese environmental organization Daichi-o-Mamoru Kai (the Association to Preserve the Earth) found that if Japanese families consumed local food instead of imported food, the impact would be equivalent to reducing household energy use by 20 percent; the biggest impact would come from eating tofu products from soy grown in Japan instead of in the US.[5] And researchers in the UK have calculated that purchasing local food has a greater positive impact on the environment than buying organic food that is not local.[6] While some food trade is inevitable, such as tropical products like coffee that are staples in colder climates, a surprising amount of trade is duplicative and ecologically wasteful. For example, Heinz ketchup eaten in California is made with California-grown tomatoes that have been shipped to Canada for processing and returned in bottles. In one year, the port of New York City exported $431,000 worth of California almonds to Italy, and imported $397,000 worth of Italian almonds to the United States.[7] This sort of unnecessary trade mortgages our children's planet for profits today.

GLOBALIZED, CONSOLIDATED FOOD TRADE UNDERMINES LOCAL ECONOMIES

5   Food trade can also undermine rural economies. For those who think that lack of food causes hunger, it's surprising to learn that the world currently has an overproduction of basic food crops,

which results in low prices to farmers and low rural incomes.[8] Overproduction also results in dumping: the selling of imported food at less than it costs to produce it. Developing nations often point to the unfairness of this global food trading system. In response to low prices, many First World farmers receive subsidies, which can allow them to sell their harvests for less than the cost of production. Current trade rules permit this dumping, which can destroy nonsubsidized farmers' ability to compete. For example, rice, one of the world's most universal staple crops and a major US export, is sold on the world market at 20 to 34 percent less than what it costs the average US farmer to grow it—devastating competition for farmers who need to recoup their full production costs to survive.[9] In 2004, Indonesia banned rice imports to protect the livelihoods of its farmers, who produce enough rice to feed Indonesia's population.[10]

6   But if the farmers suffer, do the poor and hungry benefit from floods of cheap food? The surprising truth is that a vast majority of the world's poor make their living off agriculture, and 50 percent of the people who live with hunger globally *are* small-scale farmers.[11] The global overproduction of basic foods is a major factor driving low incomes and poverty in rural areas. Rural poverty drives urban poverty, as desperate economic refugees from failing farms drive down wages in urban areas.[12] Pro-poor development policies need to raise farm incomes for small-scale farmers. Reestablishing small farmers' access to local markets to sell their food is one such policy, and is the proposal put forth by Via Campesina, a network of nearly 100 major small-scale farmer organizations around the world.

7   The expansion of supermarket chains into areas that have long been supplied by local and regional farms through traditional markets is also working against small farmers and local food. From 1992 to 2002, supermarkets have increased their retail market share by 30 percent in East Asia (excluding China) and 45 percent in the South African region.[13] In addition, supermarkets are becoming highly concentrated in a few corporate chains—in South Africa, for example, the top 2 percent of food stores capture 55 percent of retail sales.[14]

8   As supermarket chains grow, they tend to centralize procurement for many stores in a few distribution centers, which buy in bulk from as few producers as possible, including importers of "cheap" commodities and large-scale farms, rather than from brokers that may purchase from smaller farms.[15] In addition to bringing food from farther away, supermarket procurement from a few large-scale suppliers drives a standardization of food that erodes diversity in taste, cultural heritage, and even nutrition.[16]

9   Supermarket concentration allows a few companies to demand ever-lower prices from farmers while driving locally owned food

retail stores out of business. While chain supermarkets may offer lower prices to consumers, local businesses keep money circulating in the community and contribute more to overall community development. A Chicago study found that for every $100 in consumer spending with a local firm, $68 remains in the Chicago economy, versus $43 with a chain firm, and that for every square foot occupied by a local firm, local economic impact is $179, versus $105 for a chain firm.[17]Another study found that union-busting megastores such as Wal-Mart have been found to actually exacerbate poverty in US counties in which they are located, soaking up government subsidies to its stores and to its workers, who are forced to use public benefits to make ends meet.[18] Workers earning a living wage would not need to rely on artificially cheap food sold by Wal-Mart, and could support local farms and businesses instead.

TRADE IS BIG BUSINESS

10   Promoting systems to market food locally for healthier communities and ecosystems requires transforming policies and institutions currently dedicated to promoting ecologically and socially damaging trade. Policies that promote trade liberalization as a global panacea for poverty, hunger, and inequality drive unnecessary trade, but the biggest beneficiaries are large corporations seeking access to markets and greater profits. The International Monetary Fund (IMF) and the World Bank have long promoted rapid trade liberalization with no clear evidence that it helps the poorest populations. Taxpayer-supported export credit agencies spend over $100 billion a year funding loans to developing countries to import goods from corporations in the global North, increasing indebtedness.[19] Powerful countries set global rules in the World Trade Organization (WTO) and agreements such as CAFTA (the Central American Free Trade Agreement) that prevent communities, states, and sovereign nations from nurturing local production and regulating businesses according to the values of their citizens.[20] The US government, advised by a revolving door of big business executives, has demonstrated a willingness to go to war to protect corporate access to markets and trade.[21] These policies open market access for companies like the privately owned Cargill, one of the world's largest global food trading corporations, with profits surpassing $1.3 billion in 2003—almost triple those of 2000.[22]

GLOBAL MOVEMENTS FOR LOCAL FOOD

11   Local food activists in the US and around the world are rising to the challenge to make changes to allow local food systems to thrive.

Citizens are passing innovative laws at the city, county, and state levels, including townships in rural Pennsylvania that are banning corporate ownership of farms.[23] Community builders aren't waiting for supermarkets to come to their neighborhood, but rather are growing or buying food through urban gardens, school gardens, farmer's markets, community supported agriculture, and food purchasing cooperatives. The Community Food Security Coalition is developing programs for schools and hospitals to source fresh, healthier food from local farmers.[24] Environmental groups such as the Sierra Club are hosting locally grown dinners to pressure businesses to sell local food.[25] And the Business Alliance for Local Living Economies (BALLE) network is linking farms with other local businesses to create community networks to support local products.[26] Progressive farm advocates such as the National Family Farm Coalition are promoting agricultural policies to address dumping and reinvigorate family farms, as well as opposing coercive trade agreements.

12   Global movements are also taking action to defend and rebuild local food systems, as a strategy for self-reliance, cultural survival, and pro-poor development. Via Campesina has developed a platform of food sovereignty, "prioritizing local agricultural production in order to feed the people," and is developing new trade rules based on this concept.[27] Small-scale farmers' organizations—Via Campesina members—from nearly fifty countries are uniting their power, lobbying their governments to remove agriculture from WTO negotiations. Before and during the 2003 WTO ministerial meeting in Cancún, grassroots pressure and protests from Via Campesina played a key role in convincing developing country representatives to end the talks rather than sign on to a damaging deal.[28]

13   The local food movement unites community activists, urban gardeners, small-scale farmers, environmentalists, teachers, chefs, nutritionists, local business owners, and eaters of fresh local food. The movement's potential to transform our food system is enormous. The successes of a cornucopia of community food programs have already demonstrated how local food can foster robust local development, improve food security and nutrition, build community, and support productive family farms. Going local can also be a part of the answer to reversing global environmental degradation and greatly reducing rural poverty. It's time to scale up and institutionalize these successes through organizing for policies that promote local food systems globally, and dismantling those that promote ecologically and socially damaging trade.

Notes

1. See Brian Halweil, *Eat Here: Reclaiming Homegrown Pleasures in a Global Supermarket* (New York: Norton, 2004) for an overview of studies on food miles. This very readable book is an excellent overview of the richness of the local food movement in the United States.

2. Hansen, et al., "Earth's Energy Imbalance: Confirmation and Implications." *Science* 2005 0: 11102522.

3. Canadian Department for International Development (DFID), et al., 2002, *Linking Poverty Reduction and Environmental Management: Policy Challenges and Opportunities.*

4. Rich Pirog, Timothy Van Pelt, Kamyar Enshayan, and Ellen Cook, 2001, *Food, Fuel, and Freeways: An Iowa Perspective on How Far Food Travels, Fuel Usage, and Greenhouse Gas Emissions*, Ames. IA: Leopold Center for Sustainable Agriculture, Iowa State University.

5. "Consumption of local food helps cut CO2 emissions," March 2, 2005, *Kyodo News.*

6. J. N. Pretty, A. S. Ball, T. Lang, and J. I. L. Morison, 2005, "Farm Costs and Food Miles: An assessment of the full cost of the UK weekly food basket," *Food Policy* 30:1–19.

7. Katy Mamen, Steve Gorelick, Helena Norberg-Hodge, and Diana Deumling, 2004, *Ripe for Change: Rethinking California's Food Economy*, International Society for Ecology and Culture.

8. Food and Agriculture Organization (FAO), 2004, *The State of Agricultural Commodity Markets 2004.*

9. Institute for Agriculture and Trade Policy (IATP), 2005, *United States Dumping on World Agricultural Markets.*

10. "Imported Rice Ban Could Be Extended Until 2005," September 6, 2004, Jakarta Post; found on the website of the Embassy of Indonesia in Canada, *http://www .indonesia-ottawa.org/information/details.php?type=news&id=83*

11. Food and Agriculture Organization (FAO), 2004, *The State of Food Insecurity in the World 2004.*

12. Maxmilian Eisenburger and Raj Patel, 2003, *Agricultural Liberalization in China: Curbing the State and Creating Cheap Labor*, Food First Policy Brief #9, Oakland, CA: Food First.

13. T. Reardon, P. Timmer, C. Barrett, and J. Berdegué, 2003, "The Rise of Supermarkets in Africa, Asia and Latin America," *American Journal of Agricultural Economics* 85 (5):1140–1146.

14. Dave D. Weatherspoon and Thomas Reardon, 2003, "The Rise of Supermarkets in Africa: Implications for Agrifood Systems and the Rural Poor," *Development Policy Review* 21 (3):333–355.

15. Ibid. Supermarkets don't have to drive smaller farmers out of business or eradicate local food cultures; a few firms do purchase from local producers or producer cooperatives, and many more could. And government policy could promote this choice: an especially innovative government commission in the UK recommended that retailers convert part of their store to a local farmer's market, in exchange for property tax benefits on that portion of their floor space. See Brian Halweil's *Eat Here.*

16. Harriet V. Kuhnlein, 2004, "Karat, Pulque, and Gac: Three Shining Stars in the Traditional Food Galaxy," *Nutrition Review* 62 (11):439–442.

17. Civic Economics, 2004, *Andersonville Study of Retail Economics;* found at *http:// www.civiceconomics.com/Andersonville/html/reports.html*

18. Stephan J. Goetz and Hema Swaminathan, 2004, "Wal-Mart and County-Wide Poverty," Pennsylvania State University Department of Agricultural Economics and Rural Sociology Staff Paper No. 371.

19. Aaron Goldzimer, 2003, "Worse Than the World Bank? Export Credit Agencies—The Secret Engine of Globalization," *Food First Backgrounder* 9(1).

20. CAFTA's chapter on investment, modeled on Chapter 11 of NAFTA, allows corporations to sue local or state governments for passing laws that may cause them to lose profits. This includes basic citizen protections such as environmental and labor laws.

21. Anuradha Mittal, 2003, "Open Fire and Open Markets: Strategy of an Empire," *Food First Backgrounder* 9 (3).

22. *http://www.cargill.com/about/financial/financialhighlights.html#TopOfPage*

23. Adam D. Sacks, 2005, "Rights Fight: Local Democracy vs. Factory Farms in Pennsylvania," *Food First Backgrounder* 11 (1).

24. For more information see the Community Food Security Coalition website, *http://www.foodsecurity.org/* or Christine Ahn, 2004, "Breaking Ground: The Community Food Security Movement," *Food First Backgrounder* 10 (1).

25. See *http://www.sierraclub.org/sustainable_consumption/true-cost/*

26. See *http://www.livingeconomies.org/*

27. See *http://www.viacampesina.org/art_english.php3?id_article=216&PHPSESSID= 3009460 b95082a11b59cb9ce44e880c2*

28. Interview with Ibrahim Coulibaly, farmer organizer from CNOP in Mali, 4/4/05.

For Class Discussion

1. In this meaty researched policy proposal, what connections does Schwind posit among the issues? What rationale does she give for the need to reconstruct local food systems?

2. With what reasons and evidence does Schwind develop her claim that overproduction, not underproduction, is the cause of much world hunger?

3. Who is Schwind's primary audience in this piece? What values does this audience share with her? What assumptions does Schwind *not* explore in her argument?

4. What terms in this piece indicate something about the background knowledge of the target audience?

5. How could Schwind expand or change this argument to reach a neutral or indifferent audience? A hostile audience?

6. The title of this piece works out a new relationship with the words *global* and *local*. What is that relationship? How is it central to Schwind's proposal and part of its appeal?   ■

What If Cows Gave Milk in Peru?
Heifer International

Heifer International describes itself as "a nonprofit organization working to end world hunger by giving cows, goats and other food- and income-producing livestock to impoverished families around the world" ("Fact

Sheet," www.heifer.org). This advocacy group is devoted to training communities in animal husbandry, sustainable agricultural practices, and self-reliance and providing income opportunities especially for women. Launched in 1944, Heifer International has helped four million families and is currently working in forty-seven countries. This poster is part of its media kit on its Web site.

How do the layout and images in this poster seek to appeal to readers?

For Class Discussion

1. The phrase "What if cows gave milk?" is a surprising opening statement. What makes it surprising? What associations with stories, dreams, and goals does it have?

2. What argument for supporting Heifer International is conveyed by this poster? How does the text of this poster work rhetorically? Think about word choice and order, sentence length, and repetition.

3. What features of this poster appeal to children? To adults?

4. Which of the arguments and approaches to world hunger in this chapter does this poster support?

FIGURE 8.3 What If Cows Gave Milk in Peru? *(© Heifer International)*

Factory Farming in the Developing World

Danielle Nierenberg

Danielle Nierenberg holds a bachelor's degree in environmental policy from Monmouth College, Illinois, and a master's degree in agriculture, food, and environment from the School of Nutrition Science and Policy at Tufts University. She is a research associate with the Worldwatch Institute, where she has specialized in investigating and writing about gender and population, sustainable agriculture, food safety, and animal welfare. Her work has appeared in the *International Herald Tribune* and on the BBC *Newshour*. This piece was published in the May–June 2003 issue of *Worldwatch*, the bimonthly magazine published by the Worldwatch Institute, a thirty-year-old research organization founded by Lester Brown and devoted to "an environmentally sustainable and socially just society, in which the needs of all people are met without threatening the health of the natural environment or the well-being of future generations" (www.worldwatch.org/about/).

> How does Danielle Nierenberg employ description and narrative to give readers a sense of the immediacy, significance, and complexity of the dangers of factory farming?

1   Walking through Bobby Inocencio's farm in the hills of Rizal province in the Philippines is like taking a step back to a simpler time. Hundreds of chickens (a cross between native Filipino chickens and a French breed) roam around freely in large, fenced pens. They peck at various indigenous plants, they eat bugs, and they fertilize the soil, just as domesticated chickens have for ages.

2   The scene may be old, but Inocencio's farm is anything but simple. What he has recreated is a complex and successful system of raising chickens that benefits small producers, the environment, and even the chickens. Once a "factory farmer," Inocencio used to raise white chickens for Pure Foods, one of the biggest companies in the Philippines.

3   Thousands of birds were housed in long, enclosed metal sheds that covered his property. Along with the breed stock and feeds he had to import, Inocencio also found himself dealing with a lot of imported diseases and was forced to buy expensive antibiotics to keep the chickens alive long enough to take them to market. Another trick of the trade Inocencio learned was the use of growth promotants that decrease the time it takes for chickens to mature.

4   Eventually he noticed that fewer and fewer of his neighbors were raising chickens, which threatened the community's food security by reducing the locally available supply of chickens and

eggs. As the community dissolved and farms (and farming methods) that had been around for generations went virtually extinct, Inocencio became convinced that there had to be a different way to raise chickens and still compete in a rapidly globalizing marketplace. "The business of the white chicken," he says, "is controlled by the big guys." Not only do small farmers have to compete with the three big companies that control white chickens in the Philippines, but they must also contend with pressure from the World Trade Organization (WTO) to open up trade. In the last two decades the Filipino poultry production system has transitioned from mainly backyard farms to a huge industry. In the 1980s the country produced 50 million birds annually. Today that figure has increased some ten-fold. The large poultry producers have benefited from this population explosion, but average farmers have not. So Inocencio decided to go forward by going back and reviving village-level poultry enterprises that supported traditional family farms and rural communities.

5   Inocencio's farm and others like it show that the Philippines can support indigenous livestock production and stand up to the threat of the factory farming methods now spreading around the world. Since 1997, his Teresa Farms has been raising free range chickens and teaching other farmers how to do the same. He says that the way he used to raise chickens, by concentrating so many of them in a small space, is dangerous. Diseases such as avian flu, leukosis J (avian leukemia), and Newcastle disease are spread from white chickens to the Filipino native chicken populations, in some cases infecting eggs before the chicks are even born. "The white chicken," says Inocencio, "is weak, making the system weak. And if these chickens are weak, why should we be raising them? Limiting their genetic base and using breeds that are not adapted to conditions in the Philippines is like setting up the potential for a potato blight on a global scale." Now Teresa Farms chickens are no longer kept in long, enclosed sheds, but roam freely in large tree-covered areas of his farm that he encloses with recycled fishing nets.

6   Inocencio's chickens also don't do drugs. Antibiotics, he says, are not only expensive but *encourage* disease. He found the answer to the problem of preventing diseases in chickens literally in his own back yard. His chickens eat spices and native plants with antibacterial and other medicinal properties. Chili, for instance, is mixed in grain to treat respiratory problems, stimulate appetite during heat stress, de-worm the birds, and to treat Newcastle disease. Native plants growing on the farm, including *ipil-ipil* and *damong maria*, are also used as low-cost alternatives to antibiotics and other drugs.

7   There was a time when most farms in the Philippines, the United States, and everywhere else functioned much like Bobby Inocencio's. But today the factory model of raising animals in intensive conditions is spreading around the globe.

A NEW JUNGLE

8   Meat once occupied a very different dietary place in most of the world. Beef, pork, and chicken were considered luxuries, and were eaten on special occasions or to enhance the flavor of other foods. But as agriculture became more mechanized, so did animal production. In the United States, livestock raised in the West was herded or transported east to slaughterhouses and packing mills. Upton Sinclair's *The Jungle*, written almost a century ago when the United States lacked many food-safety and labor regulations, described the appalling conditions of slaughterhouses in Chicago in the early 20th century and was a shocking exposé of meat production and the conditions inflicted on both animals and humans by the industry. Workers were treated much like animals themselves, forced to labor long hours for very little pay under dangerous conditions, and with no job security.

9   If *The Jungle* were written today, however, it might not be set in the American Midwest. Today, developing nations like the Philippines are becoming the centers of large-scale livestock production and processing to feed the world's growing appetite for cheap meat and other animal products. But the problems Sinclair pointed to a century ago, including hazardous working conditions, unsanitary processing methods, and environmental contamination, still exist. Many have become even worse. And as environmental regulations in the European Union and the United States become stronger, large agribusinesses are moving their animal production operations to nations with less stringent enforcement of environmental laws.

10   These intensive and environmentally destructive production methods are spreading all over the globe, to Mexico, India, the former Soviet Union, and most rapidly throughout Asia. Wherever they crop up, they create a web of related food safety, animal welfare, and environmental problems. Philip Lymbery, campaign director of the World Society for the Protection of Animals, describes the growth of industrial animal production this way: Imagine traditional livestock production as a beach and factory farms as a tide. In the United States, the tide has completely covered the beach, swallowing up small farms and concentrating production in the hands of a few large companies. In Taiwan, it is almost as high. In the Philippines, however, the tide is just hitting the beach. The industrial, factory-farm methods of raising and slaughtering animals—methods that were

conceived and developed in the United States and Western Europe—have not yet swept over the Philippines, but they are coming fast.

AN APPETITE FOR DESTRUCTION

11   Global meat production has increased more than five-fold since 1950, and factory farming is the fastest growing method of animal production worldwide. Feedlots are responsible for 43 percent of the world's beef, and more than half of the world's pork and poultry are raised in factory farms. Industrialized countries dominate production, but developing countries are rapidly expanding and intensifying their production systems. According to the United Nations Food and Agriculture Organization (FAO), Asia (including the Philippines) has the fastest developing livestock sector. On the islands that make up the Philippines, 500 million chickens and 20 million hogs are slaughtered each year.

12   Despite the fact that many health-conscious people in developed nations are choosing to eat less meat, worldwide meat consumption continues to rise. Consumption is growing fastest in the developing countries. Two-thirds of the gains in meat consumption in 2002 were in the developing world, where urbanization, rising incomes, and globalized trade are changing diets and fueling appetites for meat and animal products. Because eating meat has been perceived as a measure of economic and social development, the Philippines and other poor nations are eager to climb up the animal-protein ladder. People in the Philippines still eat relatively little meat, but their consumption is growing. As recently as 1995, the average Filipino ate 21 kilograms of meat per year. Since then, average consumption has soared to almost 30 kilograms per year, although that is still less than half the amount in Western countries, where per-capita consumption is 80 kilograms per year.

13   This push to increase both production and consumption in the Philippines and other developing nations is coming from a number of different directions. Since the end of World War II, agricultural development has been considered a part of the foreign aid and assistance given to developing nations. The United States and international development agencies have been leaders in promoting the use of pesticides, artificial fertilizers, and other chemicals to boost agricultural production in these countries, often at the expense of the environment. American corporations like Purina Mills and Tyson Foods are also opening up feed mills and farms so they can expand business in the Philippines.

14   But Filipinos are also part of the push to industrialize agriculture. "This is not an idea only coming from the West," says Dr. Abe Agulto, president of the Philippine Society for the Protection of Animals, "but also coming from us." Meat equals wealth in much of

the world and many Filipino businesspeople have taken up large-scale livestock production to supply the growing demand for meat. But small farmers don't get much financial support in the Philippines. It's not farms like Bobby Inocencio's that are likely to get government assistance, but the big production facilities that can crank out thousands of eggs, chicks, or piglets a year.

15   The world's growing appetite for meat is not without its consequences, however. One of the first indications that meat production can be hazardous arises long before animals ever reach the slaughterhouse. Mountains of smelly and toxic manure are created by the billions of animals raised for human consumption in the world each year. In the United States, people in North Carolina know all too well the effects of this liquid and solid waste. Hog production there has increased faster than anywhere else in the nation, from 2 million hogs per year in 1987 to 10 million hogs per year today. Those hogs produce more than 19 million tons of manure each year and most of it gets stored in lagoons, or large uncovered containment pits. Many of those lagoons flooded and burst when Hurricane Floyd swept through the region in 1999. Hundreds of acres of land and miles of waterway were flooded with excrement, resulting in massive fish kills and millions of dollars in cleanup costs. The lagoons' contents are also known to leak out and seep into groundwater.

16   Some of the same effects can now be seen in the Philippines. Not far from Teresa Farms sits another, very different, farm that produces the most frequently eaten meat product in the world. Foremost Farms is the largest piggery, or pig farm, in all of Asia. An estimated 100,000 pigs are produced there every year.

17   High walls surround Foremost and prevent people in the community from getting in or seeing what goes on inside. What they do get a whiff of is the waste. Not only do the neighbors smell the manure created by the 20,000 hogs kept at Foremost or the 10,000 hogs kept at nearby Holly Farms, but their water supply has also been polluted by it. In fact, they've named the river where many of them bathe and get drinking water the River Stink. Apart from the stench, some residents have complained of skin rashes, infections, and other health problems from the water. And instead of keeping the water clean and installing effective waste treatment, the farms are just digging deeper drinking wells and giving residents free access to them. Many in the community are reluctant to complain about the smell because they fear losing their water supply. Even the mayor of Bulacan, the nearby village, has said "we give these farms leeway as much as possible because they provide so much economically."

18   It would be easy to assume that some exploitive foreign corporation owns Foremost, but in fact the owner is Lucia Tan, a Filipino.

Tan is not your average Filipino, however, but the richest man in the Philippines. In addition to Foremost Farms, he owns San Miguel beer and Philippine Airlines. Tan might be increasing his personal wealth, but his farm and others like it are gradually destroying traditional farming methods and threatening indigenous livestock breeds in the Philippines. As a result, many small farmers can no longer afford to produce hogs for sale or for their own consumption, which forces them to become consumers of Tan's pork. Most of the nation's 11 million hogs are still kept in back yards, but because of farms like Foremost, factory farming is growing. Almost one-quarter of the breeding herd is now factory farmed. More than 1 million pigs are raised in factory farms every year in Bulacan alone.

19   Chicken farms in the Philippines are also becoming more intensive. The history of intensive poultry production in the Philippines is not long. Forty years ago, the nation's entire population was fed on native eggs and chickens produced by family farmers. Now, most of those farmers are out of business. They have lost not only their farms, but livestock diversity and a way of life as well.

20   The loss of this way of life to the industrialized farm-to-abattoir system has made the process more callous at every stage. Adopting factory farming methods works to diminish farmers' concern for the welfare of their livestock. Chickens often can't walk properly because they have been pumped full of growth-promoting antibiotics to gain weight as quickly as possible. Pigs are confined to gestation crates where they can't turn around. Cattle are crowded together in feedlots that are seas of manure.

21   Most of the chickens in the country are from imported breed stock and the native Filipino chicken has practically disappeared because of viral diseases spread by foreign breeds. Almost all of the hens farmed commercially for their eggs are confined in wire battery cages that cram three or four hens together, giving each bird an area less than the size of this page to stand on.

22   Unlike laying hens, chickens raised for meat in the Philippines are not housed in cages. But they're not pecking around in back yards, either. Over 90 percent of the meat chickens raised in the Philippines live in long sheds that house thousands of birds. At this time, most Filipino producers allow fowl to have natural ventilation and lighting and some roaming room, but they are under pressure to adopt more "modern" factory-farm standards to increase production.

23   The problems of a system that produces a lot of animals in crowded and unsanitary conditions can also be seen off the farm. The *baranguay* (neighborhood) of Tondo in Manila is best known for the infamous "Smoky Mountain" garbage dump that collapsed on scavengers in 2000, killing at least 200 people. But another hazard

also sits in the heart of Tondo. Surrounded by tin houses, stores, and bars, the largest government-owned slaughtering facility in the country processes more than 3,000 swine, cattle, and *caraboa* (water buffalo) per day, all brought from farms just outside the city limits. The slaughterhouse does have a waste treatment system where the blood and other waste is supposed to be treated before it is released into the city's sewer system and nearby Manila Bay. Unfortunately, that's not what's going on. Instead, what can't be cut up and sold for human consumption is dumped into the sewer.

24   Some 60 men are employed at the plant. They stun, bludgeon, and slaughter animals by hand and at a breakneck pace. They wear little protective gear as they slide around on floors slippery with blood, which makes it hard to stun animals on the first try, or sometimes even the second, or to butcher meat without injuring themselves.

25   The effects of producing meat this way also show up in rising cases of food-borne illness, emerging animal diseases that can spread to humans, and in an increasingly overweight Filipino population that doesn't remember where meat comes from.

26   There are few data on the incidence of food-borne illness in the Philippines or most other developing nations, and even fewer about how much of it might be related to eating unsafe meat. What food safety experts do know is that food-borne illness is one of the most widespread health problems worldwide. And it could be an astounding 300–350 times more frequent than reported, according to the World Health Organization. Developing nations bear the greatest burden because of the presence of a wide range of parasites, toxins, and biological hazards and the lack of surveillance, prevention, and treatment measures—all of which ensnarl the poor in a chronic cycle of infection. According to the FAO, the trend toward increased commercialization and intensification of livestock production is leading to a variety of food safety problems. Crowded, unsanitary conditions and poor waste treatment in factory farms exacerbate the rapid movement of animal diseases and food-borne infections. *E. coli* 0157:H7, for instance, is spread from animals to humans when people eat food contaminated by manure. Animals raised in intensive conditions often arrive at slaughterhouses covered in feces, thus increasing the chance of contamination during slaughtering and processing.

27   Cecilia Ambos is one of the meat inspectors at the Tondo slaughterhouse. Cecilia or another inspector is required to be on site at all times, but she says she rarely has to go to the killing floor. Inspections of carcasses only occur, she said, if one of the workers alerts the inspector. That doesn't happen very often, and not because the animals are all perfectly healthy. Consider that the men

employed at the plant are paid about $5 per day, which is less than half of the cost of living—and are working as fast as they can to slaughter a thousand animals per shift. It's unlikely that they have the time or the knowledge to notice problems with the meat.

28   Since the 1960s, farm-animal health in the United States has depended not on humane farming practices but on the use of antibiotics. Many of the same drugs used to treat human illnesses are also used in animal production, thus reducing the arsenal of drugs available to fight food-borne illnesses and other health problems. Because antibiotics are given to livestock to prevent disease from spreading in crowded conditions and to increase growth, antibiotic resistance has become a global threat. In the Philippines, chicken, eggs, and hog producers use antibiotics not because their birds or hogs are sick, but because drug companies and agricultural extension agents have convinced them that these antibiotics will ensure the health of their birds or pigs and increase their weight.

29   Livestock raised intensively can also spread diseases to humans. Outbreaks of avian flu in Hong Kong during the past five years have led to massive culls of thousands of chickens. When the disease jumped the species barrier for the first time in 1997, six of the eighteen people infected died. Avian flu spread to people living in Hong Kong again this February, killing two. Dr. Gary Smith, of the University of Pennsylvania School of Veterinary Medicine, also warns that "it is not high densities [of animals] that matter, but the increased potential for transmission between farms that we should be concerned about. The nature of the farming nowadays is such that there is much more movement of animals between farms than there used to be, and much more transport of associated materials between farms taking place rapidly. The problem is that the livestock industry is operating on a global, national, and county level." The foot-and-mouth disease epidemic in the United Kingdom is a perfect example of how just a few cows can spread a disease across an entire nation.

MODERN METHODS, MODERN POLICIES?

30   The expansion of factory farming methods in the Philippines is raising the probability that it will become another fast food nation. Factory farms are supplying much of the pork and chicken preferred by fast food restaurants there. American-style fast food was unknown in the Philippines until the 1970s, when Jollibee, the Filipino version of McDonald's, opened its doors. Now, thanks to fast food giants like McDonald's, Kentucky Fried Chicken, Burger King, and others, the traditional diet of rice, vegetables, and a little meat or fish is changing—and so are rates of heart disease, diabetes, and stroke, which have risen to numbers similar to those in the United States and other western nations.

31   The Filipino government doesn't see factory farming as a threat. To the contrary, many officials hope it will be a solution to their country's economic woes, and they're making it easier for large farms to dominate livestock production. For instance, the Department of Agriculture appears to have turned a blind eye when many farms have violated environmental and animal welfare regulations. The government has also encouraged big farms to expand by giving them loans. But as the farms get bigger and produce more, domestic prices for chicken and pork fall, forcing more farmers to scale up their production methods. And because the Philippines (and many other nations) are prevented by the Global Agreement on Tariffs and Trade and the WTO from imposing tariffs on imported products, the Philippines is forced to allow cheap, factory-farmed American pork and poultry into the country. These products are then sold at lower prices than domestic meat.

32   Rafael Mariano, a leader in the Peasant Movement for the Philippines (KMP), has not turned away from the problems caused by factory farming in the Philippines. He and the 800,000 farmers he works with believe that "factory farming is not acceptable, we have our own farming." But farmers, he says, are told by big agribusiness companies that their methods are old fashioned, and that to compete in the global market they must forget what they have learned from generations of farming. Rafael and KMP are working to promote traditional methods of livestock production that benefit small farmers and increase local food security. This means doing what farmers used to do: raising both crops and animals. In mixed crop–livestock farms, animals and crops are parts of a self-sustaining system. Some farmers in the Philippines raise hogs, chickens, tilapia, and rice on the same farm. The manure from the hogs and chickens is used to fertilize the algae in ponds needed for both tilapia and rice to grow. These farms produce little waste, provide a variety of food for the farm, and give farmers social security when prices for poultry, pork, and rice go down.

33   The Philippines is not the only country at risk from the spread of factory farms. Argentina, Brazil, Canada, China, India, Mexico, Pakistan, South Africa, Taiwan, and Thailand are all seeing growth in industrial animal production. As regulations controlling air and water pollution from such farms are strengthened in one country, companies simply pack up and move to countries with more lenient rules. Western European nations now have among the strongest environmental regulations in the world; farmers can only apply manure during certain times of the year and they must follow strict controls on how much ammonia is released from their farms. As a result, a number of companies in the Netherlands and Germany are moving their factory farms—but to the United States,

not to developing countries. According to a recent report in the *Dayton Daily News*, cheap land and less restrictive environmental regulations in Ohio are luring European livestock producers to the Midwest. There, dairies with fewer than 700 cows are not required to obtain permits, which would regulate how they control manure. But 700 cows can produce a lot of manure. In 2001, five Dutch-owned dairies were cited by the Ohio Environmental Protection Agency for manure spills. "Until there are international regulations controlling waste from factory farms," says William Weida, director of the Global Reaction Center for the Environment/Spira Factory Farm project, "it is impossible to prevent farms from moving to places with less regulation."

34 　　Mauricio Rosales of FAO's Livestock, Environment, and Development Project also stresses the need for siting farms where they will benefit both people and the environment. "Zoning," he says, "is necessary to produce livestock in the most economically viable places, but with the least impact." For instance, when livestock live in urban or peri-urban areas, the potential for nutrient imbalances is high. In rural areas, manure can be a valuable resource because it contains nitrogen and phosphorous, which fertilize the soil. In cities, however, manure is a toxic, polluting nuisance.

35 　　The triumph of factory farming is not inevitable. In 2001, the World Bank released a new livestock strategy which, in a surprising reversal of its previous commitment to funding of large-scale livestock projects in developing nations, said that as the livestock sector grows "there is a significant danger that the poor are being crowded out, the environment eroded, and global food safety and security threatened." It promised to use a "people-centered approach" to livestock development projects that will reduce poverty, protect environmental sustainability, ensure food security and welfare, and promote animal welfare. This turnaround happened not because of pressure from environmental or animal welfare activists, but because the large-scale, intensive animal production methods the Bank once advocated are simply too costly. Past policies drove out smallholders because economies of scale for large units do not internalize the environmental costs of producing meat. The Bank's new strategy includes integrating livestock–environment interactions into environmental impact assessments, correcting regulatory distortions that favor large producers, and promoting and developing markets for organic products. These measures are steps in the right direction, but more needs to be done by lending agencies, governments, non-governmental organizations, and individual consumers. Changing the meat economy will require a rethinking of our relationship with livestock and the price we're willing to pay for safe, sustainable, humanely-raised food.

36   Meat is more than a dietary element, it's a symbol of wealth and prosperity. Reversing the factory farm tide will require thinking about farming systems as more than a source of economic wealth. Preserving prosperous family farms and their landscapes, and raising healthy, humanely treated animals, should also be viewed as a form of affluence.

For Class Discussion

1. What does Danielle Nierenberg say are the conditions of factory farming that we should oppose?

2. Nierenberg seeks to establish connections among factory farming, multinational corporations, and the fast-food industry. How does she articulate and support these connections?

3. She presents ways that Filipino farmers can resist the industrial farming model. How persuasive is she in supporting the feasibility of this resistance?

4. How do emotional and logical appeals work in this argument?

5. *Worldwatch* magazine is a publication focused on environmentalism and social justice. How successfully does this article engage readers who do not share these values?

6. How has this article influenced your view of meat production in the global food system? ∎

Confinement Farming a Boon to the Third World

Dennis T. Avery and Tom Elam

Dennis T. Avery is director of and Tom Elam is agricultural agronomist at the Center for Global Food Issues (CGFI), a project of the Hudson Institute, a conservative, nonpartisan research and policy think tank. The Center cites as its goals furthering agricultural free trade, promoting technological innovation as a basis for agricultural sustainability, and connecting agricultural productivity and conservation in the public's mind ("About CGFI," www.cgfi.org/about/about_index.htm). Active in foreign policy, Avery has held numerous governmental appointments, including agricultural analyst for the U.S. Department of State. He writes regularly for the Center, speaks internationally on world food production, and has authored several books, among them *Saving the Planet with Pesticides and Plastic: The Environmental Triumph of High-Yield Farming* (1995, 2000). Dr. Tom Elam has been a professor of economics, the chairman of the Market Research Committee of the U.S. Animal Health Institute, and an agricultural economist for Elanco Products Company, a company that "develops and markets products to improve the health and production of animals" (www.elanco.com). This op-ed piece was published by CGFI on May 13, 2003.

> How does Avery and Elam's use of the term "confinement farming" reflect their professional backgrounds and their audience? What are the connotations of "confinement farming" in contrast to "factory farming" and "industrial farming"?

1   The Worldwatch Institute has a new doom story: the rise of "factory farming" in the Third World. Worldwatch's Danielle Nierenberg writes that the production of low-cost pork and chicken on modern confinement farms overseas is an unmitigated disaster characterized by abused animals and the countryside ruined by the wastes from hog herds and poultry flocks.

2   Worldwatch should start, however, by applauding the improved nutrition available to Third World children because of modern livestock production. The lower-cost feed supplies (generated by today's high-yield seeds and fertilizers), and the healthier birds and animals (protected by indoor facilities and modern veterinary medications) give millions of kids high-quality protein and key micronutrients such as calcium, iron, zinc, and vitamin B-12 from meat, milk, and eggs.

3   Without livestock products, infants are likely to suffer bone deformities, delayed cognitive development, and other nutritional problems. The U.S. Centers for Disease Control recently concluded that two infants raised and breast-fed by vegan mothers suffered retarded development due to serious deficiencies of vitamin B-12.

4   Fortunately for the Third World's kids, meat consumption in the past 20 years increased seven-fold in China, five-fold in Mexico and Brazil, and more than three-fold in the Philippines. This is possible partly because of rising incomes, and partly because modern farms can raise chicken on only 75 percent as much feed and 10 percent as much farmland as is needed by the traditional farmers.

5   Ms. Nierenberg of Worldwatch paints a rosy picture of pastoral family farms raising a few free range chickens and/or outdoor hogs under sunny skies and the careful eye of the peasant farmer. Then, she wails, giant corporations came along and built polluting mega-farms that put the small farmers out of business.

6   She's left out a few things: The backyard farmers expose their birds and animals to predators, parasites, bad weather, and diseases. The confinement farmers don't.

7   The traditional farmers' birds and animals produce manure and urine at the same rates as the birds and animals in confinement. From the small outdoor farms, these wastes wash into the

streams with every storm event. The fact that a million chickens are distributed on 10,000 small farms doesn't make the wastes disappear. But the confinement farms save their wastes and spread them carefully as organic fertilizer to nourish the crops in the fields. The wastes turn from an environmental negative into an eco-asset.

8   Then there's the problem that the peasant farms would need far more land to raise the livestock—land which would have to be taken away from wildlife. If the Third World put all of its 500 million hogs outdoors, at four hogs per acre, the hogs would need another 125 million acres, a land area equal to all the cropland in China.

9   China, in fact, has 430 million hogs, 26 percent of the world's people, and only 7 percent of its arable land. This is why its hogs are kept in small pens. No nation in the world puts hogs out in pastures any more because hogs root and wallow and cause enormous soil erosion and stream bank destruction in addition to their water pollution.

10   The world currently feeds about 150 million tons of grain and oilseeds to its broiler chickens, virtually all of them are raised indoors. Outdoors, the birds suffer more from heat, cold, and stress, which retards their weight gain. Also, we'd need another 50 million tons of feed per year—and might have to clear another 30 million acres of the world's scarce wildlands to raise the extra feed.

11   Of course, if we actually put the birds and animals back on peasant farms, the cost of meat would again become so high that few people could afford it. The price for giving up "factory farms" would be borne by the little kids who didn't get enough meat, milk, or eggs for good health.

12   It's no accident that the criticism of modern farming comes from the best-fed people in the history of the world. They are spoiled by the good fortune that allows them to take their good diets for granted. What would Ms. Nierenberg write if she spent a few years living on one of the outer islands of the Philippines, earning $500 per year, and eating mostly rice and corn?

13   Shame on you, Ms. Nierenberg, and shame on the Worldwatch Institute for publishing your article. If you really want to help the poor of the world, help Third World farmers increase their productivity, not lower it.

For Class Discussion

1. Dennis T. Avery and Tom Elam wrote this piece as a direct rebuttal to Danielle Nierenberg's article against factory farming. How do they refute Nierenberg's points? What counterreasons and evidence do they offer?

2. How many assumptions underlie Avery and Elam's argument? How much do they provide support for these assumptions?

3. How has Avery and Elam's use of language influenced the emotional and logical appeal of this piece? Consider these phrases: "new doom story"; "unmitigated disaster"; "abused animals"; "paints a rosy picture"; "she wails"; and others you notice.

4. With what arguing moves do Avery and Elam end their op-ed piece? How rhetorically effective is this conclusion?

5. How has this piece influenced your view of livestock production in the developing world? ■

CHAPTER QUESTIONS FOR REFLECTION AND DISCUSSION

1. What are five major controversies about feeding the world now and in the future that are discussed in this chapter's readings?

2. What are the major differences among industrialized agriculture, biotech agriculture, organic farming, and small-farm agriculture?

3. The following pairs of writers disagree in major ways about how to provide food for developing nations. Choose one pair and discuss where these writers are most at odds. Are their major differences in their assumptions and values, their interpretations of the problems, their reasoning, or their interpretations of facts and uses of evidence? Why do you think one writer makes a stronger, more persuasive case for his/her view?

   A. Peter Rosset and C. S. Prakash/Gregory Conko

   B. Vandana Shiva and C. S. Prakash/Gregory Conko

   C. Peter Rosset and Pedro Sanchez

   D. Vandana Shiva and Syngenta (brochure)

   E. C. S. Prakash/Gregory Conko and Kirsten Schwind

   F. Danielle Nierenberg and Dennis T. Avery/Tom Elam

4. People embrace the idea of nurturing a local food system for many different reasons. What is the case for local food in each of these views: from the perspective of the environment, food security, social justice, nutrition, and cultural heritage?

5. How do these writers try to open readers' eyes to the conditions under which food is produced and the economic forces that control this production: Scott Canon, Conko/Prakash, Peter Rosset, Kirsten Schwind, Danielle Nierenberg, and Avery/Elam? Which piece had the biggest impact on you and why?

6. Using the introductions to the readings and perhaps doing some brief research on the Web, learn about the background, employment, and institutional affiliations of the following writers. How does this context

appear to inform and shape the writers' views on problems with food systems and hunger?

- C. S. Prakash and Gregory Conko
- Peter Rosset
- Vandana Shiva
- Pedro Sanchez
- Kirsten Schwind
- Dennis T. Avery and Tom Elam

7. Working individually or in groups, research one of the following hunger- and food-related issues and bring your findings and sources back to share with your class.

A. Using Green Revolution advances such as chemical fertilizers, pesticides, herbicides, irrigation, antibiotics for animals, and large one-crop farms, agribusinesses (often called "high-yield farming") have transformed food production. Research what agribusinesses you have in your region and what crops they raise. What have these large farms contributed to the economy of your state and to the nation's food supply?

B. Research the Web sites of the international agribusinesses Monsanto (www.monsanto.com) and Syngenta (www.syngenta.com). How do these companies portray themselves with respect to social responsibility and concern for the environment, farmers, sustainable farming, and developing countries? What is persuasive about their claims? What differences, if any, do you see in their public relations appeals?

C. In December 2005, the Hong Kong World Trade Organization disputes among the United States, the European Union, and the developing nations—most notably India, Brazil, and China—resulted in a free trade agreement in which rich nations would eliminate quotas and tariffs on poor countries' goods by 2008 and all agricultural export subsidies by 2013. Research this agreement and list the major ways it will affect farmers in the United States, European Union countries, and developing countries. How will it affect the agricultural businesses in your region? (For questions exploring food and fair trade, see Chapter 2, pp. 13–18.)

D. José Bové is a French farmer imprisoned for his attack on a McDonald's under construction in Millau, France. Bové has become the folk hero of a global movement against industrial agriculture, junk food, and multinational control over the quality of the food imposed on people throughout the world. Research Bové and his book *The World Is Not for Sale: Farmers Against Junk Food* (2001), written with Gilles Luneau. What is Bové's contribution to the movements for food sovereignty and local food systems?

E. Many people are concerned that a handful of food companies control much of the world's food production and sales. Research one of the following corporations and investigate how many brands and what range of food products each produces: Cargill, Nestlé, Pepsi, Coca-Cola, Philip Morris, Unilever, or ConAgra. Make a list of problems this consolidation could pose for consumers. A good source of information about food processing and food manufacturing companies is the Market Share Matrix (www.marketsharematrix.org).

F. Via Campesina, the global alliance of small farmer organizations, presents a comprehensive policy statement about food sovereignty on its Web site, www.viacampesina.org. Research this statement and others you find on food sovereignty. What are the main principles of this policy? What is food sovereignty *against*? How does it relate to free trade and fair trade? How have outbreaks of mad cow disease, the use of animal antibiotics, and the presence of biotech crops increased global interest in food sovereignty?

WRITING ASSIGNMENTS

Brief Writing Assignments

1. Write a brief informal piece in which you describe and discuss the connections between your eating habits/favorite foods and your family's cultural heritage or the distinctive features of your home region's food.

2. Scott Canon claims that where we shop and the food we buy are political decisions with global consequences. Write a brief self-reflection in which you describe your awareness of food production before and after reading the articles in this chapter. What changes would you consider making in what you eat to help the environment, the laborers who work with food production, and your own health? What challenges face consumers in developed countries who want to focus on socially responsible eating?

3. Using ideas from the arguments you have encountered in this chapter, freewrite an informal defense or refutation of one of the following claims. To expand your thinking or as preparation for writing a formal argument on this food subissue, you might write for twenty or more minutes in support of the claim and then write for twenty or more minutes challenging it.

   A. Small farmers are more likely than corporations to be good stewards of the land and treat the environment well.

   B. The economics and politics of the global free trade system have been a main cause of hunger problems in developing countries.

   C. Individuals can make a substantial difference in the world hunger and poverty picture.

D. Technology and scientific breakthroughs in agriculture offer the best hope to solve the world's need for more food to feed a growing population.

E. The global food system is too powerful and pervasive to change.

4. Many of the articles in this chapter—for example, Vandana Shiva's "Gift of Food," C. S. Prakesh and Gregory Conko's promotion of biotech food, and Danielle Nierenberg's criticism of factory farming—are clearly directed toward audiences receptive to their views. Choose one of these articles and, thinking particularly about opposing views, suggest ways these writers could reshape their arguments more effectively for broader or less sympathetic audiences.

5. Think about the ways that food production and world hunger intersect with other topics in this text such as consumerism and free trade (Chapter 2), immigration (Chapter 4), cultural rights (Chapter 5), environmental problems with water and climate change (Chapter 7), and the spread of AIDS and avian flu (Chapter 9). Then brainstorm a network of issue questions that highlight connected controversies: for example, How has the availability of cheap labor in the form of illegal immigrants encouraged agribusiness in the United States?

Writing Projects

1. Summarize a pair of readings in this chapter, such as those listed in the "Chapter Questions for Reflection and Discussion," that particularly "talk" to each other. Then analyze these pieces rhetorically as effective arguments and contributions to the public conversation, and synthesize these views to create your own informed position. Writing for your classmates, you might discuss how each of these readings has influenced your view on global food production or hunger or how you have concluded that one argument is more persuasive than the other.

2. Many discussions of solving the world's hunger problems include mention of plant biotechnology. Write the most complete argument you can supporting the use of biotechnology in agriculture in third world countries or arguing against the use of biotech crops to combat hunger and poverty in the developing world. Direct your argument at an audience of your peers who may not have studied this issue as much as you have. You may want to do additional research to find your own evidence. Consider, for instance, the interesting claim made by Henry I. Miller and Gregory Conko in their book *The Frankenfood Myth: How Protest and Politics Threaten the Biotech Revolution* (2004): "We find it revealing that when biotech varieties have been made available to farmers in less developed nations, they have been adopted quickly and eagerly" (172). Does your research support or refute this claim?

3. As a child, when you dawdled over eating some vegetable, an adult relative might have said to you, "You should be happy to eat your vegetables; children in Africa are starving and would love that food." In your child's mind, you may have wondered, How would you get that spinach on your plate to Africa? The readings in this chapter have tried to give you a sense of the complex problems causing hunger crises and the challenge of finding a solution. Write an argument directed at fourth and fifth graders in which either (a) you show that what we eat does affect children in Africa or (b) you propose what you believe is the best way to help alleviate hunger and malnutrition in Africa. You might want to include visuals in your argument. Synthesize and document the ideas that you have encountered in this chapter's readings. Tailor your argument to interest and motivate your young audience.

4. Investigate the status of local food in your community by researching and perhaps interviewing local growers and people involved in Community Supported Agriculture (CSA) and subscription farming, farmers markets, urban agriculture, and food co-ops. What is the status of your region's local food system? Shape your research into one of these kinds of writing: (a) a brochure or flier for your community or your city that presents a practical plan for moving toward purchasing a large percentage of vegetables, fruit, and/or dairy products from local growers; (b) an op-ed piece for your university or regional newspaper that argues the problems or advantages of reconstructing your local food system; (c) a policy argument directed toward your state legislators that explores the problems facing a regional food system and a proposal to bolster such a system.

5. As the following excerpt from a news article reveals, many indigenous peoples are powerfully affected by industrial farming, the technology and practices of the Green Revolution, and the movement toward global agribusinesses: "In Brazil in the state of Mato Grosso do Su, over 300 of the 30,000 Kaiowa Indians have killed themselves during the last ten years" in despair over their "landlessness, displacement and unrelenting poverty" (from John Jeter, "Despair Drives Young Brazil Indians to Suicide," *Seattle Times,* April 15, 2004). Research a group of indigenous people in South America or Southeast Asia who have been marginalized by industrial farming and research the way that the global movement in support of food sovereignty is attempting to help these people. You may want to investigate Via Campesina (www.viacampesina .org), the Rural Development Institute (www.rdiland.org), or the Landless Rural Workers' Movement (Movimento dos Trabalhadores Rurias Sem Terra at www.mstbrazil.org). Write a researched argument for your peers in which you propose what you see as the most practical and effective way to combat poverty and restore food sovereignty to the group of indigenous people you have chosen.

6. Investigate the status of organic farming and marketing in your region or city. You might visit farmers markets, supermarkets, specialty food stores, and food co-ops to examine the availability and cost of organic food. Social justice advocates often remark that organic food is an elitest cause because people with low incomes do not have the option to buy organic food, which is usually more expensive and less available. Write an argument for your region in which you focus on the problem of making organic food available to people of all incomes, including those who are dependent on the cheapest food.

7. Research several of the following organizations, exploring how they are involved in the global controversies over food production. Then write an argument directed at your peers in which you advise people from rich nations about the most effective way for individuals to contribute to solving world hunger problems.

Rural Development Institute (www.rdiland.org)
Consultative Group on International Agricultural Research (www.cgiar.org)
International Society for Ecology and Culture (www.isec.org.uk)
Food and Agriculture Organization (www.fao.org)
Food First Institute (www.foodfirst.org)
America's Second Harvest (www.secondharvest.org)
Bread for the World (www.bread.org)
Urban Agriculture Network (www.cityfarmer.org)
Toronto Food Policy Council (www.foodshare.net/train11.htm)
Community Food Security Coalition (www.foodsecurity.org)
AgBioWorld Foundation (www.agbioworld.org)
Heifer International (www.heifer.org)

CHAPTER 9

The Spread of Disease in the Global Community

QUESTION TO PONDER

You have been asked to give your financial support to the global fight against AIDS in developing countries; however, the various newspaper and magazine articles you have read have left you puzzled about the most effective way to fight the AIDS pandemic. Should you support an orphan who has lost his or her parents to AIDS? Should you contribute money to medical research to find a vaccine for HIV? Or should you support antiretroviral* drugs to treat the millions of poor people in Africa and India who cannot afford these life-prolonging drug therapies?

CONTEXT FOR A NETWORK OF ISSUES

Along with global trade, the world has been sharing diseases for centuries; in fact, "pandemics" (infectious diseases spreading rapidly to a high percentage of the populations of several continents simultaneously) often followed trade routes, transmitted from country to country by ships and merchants' overland caravans. One of the most deadly of these pandemics was the Black Death of 1347–1352. It began in China, and then, following trade and shipping routes, spread to central Asia and Asia Minor and to ports in Italy and Egypt. From there, it spread throughout Europe, North Africa, and the Middle East. Although scientists are still debating the exact cause of the Black Death, with many subscribing to the idea that it involved more than one pathogen, scientists and historians agree that it killed around twenty-five million people, or between one-third to one-half of the population of Europe.

---

*HIV is a retrovirus that weakens the immune system. Antiretroviral drugs prevent HIV from replicating and spreading the virus within the body.

Closer to our own time period, the Spanish flu* of 1918–1919, a type of bird flu, swept around the world, attacking the young and vigorous, including soldiers in the trenches in Europe in World War I, and leaving between twenty and fifty million people dead. Between 1957 and 1958, the Asian flu began in East Asia and reached the United States, killing seventy thousand Americans and a million people around the world. In November 2002, SARS (severe acute respiratory syndrome) cropped up in China and spread to Hong Kong, Hanoi, Taiwan, Singapore, and Toronto. By June 2003, over eight thousand people in twenty-seven countries had contracted the virus, and over seven hundred people had died from this disease, which fills up the lungs with fluid. The SARS outbreak particularly disturbed the global community because China tried for a number of months to cover up this virulent disease while it spread within China and was carried beyond China's borders.

Yearly, the influenzas for which many people receive flu shots kill between five hundred thousand and a million people around the world, and three to four times a century these viruses mutate to become influenza pandemics that are beyond the treatment ability of known vaccines and cures. Fearing the onset of one such pandemic, in fall 2005 newspapers began warning of avian flu (bird flu), a disease similar to SARS, which could become a world health crisis. Avian flu often spreads from ducks and wild birds to domestic poultry such as chickens and turkeys. In Vietnam, Thailand, Cambodia, Indonesia, and Turkey, this virus has jumped species, from chickens to humans, and has killed a small number of people in each country. If the virus mutates so that it can spread directly from human to human, it could become a lethal pandemic. In 1997, millions of chickens in Hong Kong had to be killed to prevent the spread of a bird flu, and a similar outbreak in Southeast Asia in 2004 also necessitated a costly killing of poultry.

Globalization has collapsed time and space and heightened the complexity of controlling these influenza outbreaks. As scientists scramble to identify and create medicines and vaccines for mutating and migrating viruses, the global community puzzles over the most efficient ways to collaborate for the benefit of all. Stressing the necessity for increasing cooperation among developed and developing countries, Kofi Annan, secretary-general of the United Nations, has framed disease control as a global security issue:

> . . . the security of developed countries is only as strong as the ability of poor states to respond to and contain a new deadly infectious disease. . . . the incubation period for most infectious diseases is longer than most international air flights. As a result, any one of the 700 million people who travel on airlines in a year could unwittingly carry a lethal virus to an unsuspecting country. The 1918 influenza epidemic killed twice as many

---

*"Flu," or influenza, is a viral infection that involves the lungs and usually brings a fever, a cough, and severe muscle aches. It can involve a secondary bacterial infection.

people in one year as HIV/AIDS has killed in the past 28 years. Today, a
similar virus could kill tens of millions in a fraction of the time.*

Annan exhorts all countries to think as an interdependent global community, to commit to common goals, and to harmonize their efforts against
these diseases.

While specific influenzas suddenly appear, wipe out a percentage of
the population, and then vanish often mysteriously, HIV (human immunodeficiency virus)/AIDS (acquired immunodeficiency syndrome), first officially identified in the United States in 1981, continues to gain momentum
as a pandemic and has grown geometrically, especially in Africa, where it
has reached a critical mass that is battering the social structures of countries. Statistics from the 2005 Joint United Nations Programme on
HIV/AIDS and the World Health Organization show how this pandemic is
affecting different regions of the globe.[†]

Global Statistics on HIV and AIDS for Adults and Children in 2005

Region of the World	Children and Adults Living with HIV at End of 2005	New HIV Infections among Children and Adults in 2005	Child and Adult Deaths from AIDS during 2005
Oceania	74,000	8,200	3,600
Caribbean	300,000	30,000	24,000
North Africa and Middle East	510,000	67,000	58,000
Western /Central Europe	720,000	22,000	12,000
North America	1.2 million	43,000	18,000
East Asia	870,000	140,000	41,000
Eastern Europe and Central Asia	1.6 million	270,000	62,000
Latin America	1.8 million	200,000	66,000
South and Southeast Asia	7.4 million	990,000	480,000
Sub-Saharan Africa	25.8 million	3.2 million	2.4 million
Global Total	40.3 million	4.9 million	3.1 million

---

*Kofi Annan, "Courage to Fulfill Our Responsibilities," *Economist*, December 4, 2004.
[†]The Joint United Nations Programme on HIV/AIDS is involved in organizing world
action to combat the AIDS pandemic by "providing leadership and advocacy; strategic
information and technical support; tracking, monitoring and evaluation; civil society
engagement and the development of strategic partnerships; and mobilization of
resources" (from "UNAIDS in Action," www.unaids.org). These data appear on www
.globalhealthreporting.org and are taken from the AIDS Epidemic Update, UNAIDS/
WHO, December 2005.

As this table shows, the most extensive problems with HIV/AIDS are in South Asia and Southeast Asia, including India, with 990,000 new cases of HIV in 2005 and 480,000 deaths, and sub-Saharan Africa, with 3.2 million new cases and 2.4 million deaths. The compounded problems and seriousness of the AIDS crisis in sub-Saharan Africa can be seen in the way that AIDS is undoing economic and social progress, which is often measured by gain in life expectancy:

> Life expectancy at birth has dropped below 40 years in nine African countries—Botswana, Central African Republic, Lesotho, Malawi, Mozambique, Rwanda, Swaziland, Zambia, and Zimbabwe. All are severely affected by AIDS. In Zimbabwe, life expectancy at birth was 34 years in 2003, compared with 52 years in 1990.*

The expected length of life in this region of the world is dramatically regressing. Furthermore, people whose immune systems are compromised by AIDS are vulnerable to other diseases such as tuberculosis and malaria, which, like AIDS, are fueled by poverty and contribute to poverty.

In the global picture of AIDS, one main problem is that the resources to fight this disease are concentrated in wealthy countries. Although scientists have developed antiretroviral drugs that halt the debilitating advance of AIDS, and even though the cost of these drugs has come down dramatically in the last ten years, they still remain out of reach for the poor in most developing countries, costing from around $250 per patient per year for generic drugs to over $500 per patient per year for brand-name drugs. In addition, these countries lack medical staff to treat AIDS patients, funds for education and prevention programs, and people to implement the programs. As the death toll of the disease cuts deeper into the adult population, taking away parents, teachers, professionals, and workers—striking hardest at women—economies and communities begin to stagger. With inadequate treatment and no vaccine to prevent AIDS even after twenty-five years, this damage threatens to stretch indefinitely into the future.

STAKES AND STAKEHOLDERS

Public health leaders, policymakers, pharmaceutical companies, NGOs, political leaders, health care workers, journalists, and ordinary citizens are seeking to persuade the global community that everyone is a stakeholder in pandemics issues. Many arguments highlight connections: diseases that

---

*UNAIDS Fact Sheet: Africa. UNAIDS frequently updates its fact sheets. For the most recent material, see http://www.unaids.org/en/MediaCentre/PressMaterials/FactSheets.asp. In its March 28, 2006 update, "The Impact of HIV & AIDS on Africa," AVERT reports that average life expectancy in sub-Saharan Africa is forty-seven years (www.avert.org/aidsimpact.htm).

appear to be "over there" in other parts of the world are potentially "right here" in our regions and cities; and diseases today involve not only health issues but also human rights, quality of life, money, and national and global security. The following broad issue questions are the departure points for many of these arguments about diseases and the global community.

What Priorities Should the Global Community and Individual Nations Have in Confronting Influenza Pandemics? Thinking economically, economists, policymakers and businesses argue that it is cost-effective for the private and public sectors to commit funds to prevention and scientific research upfront and to establish global collaboration strategies with emergency health procedures. Still, much debate centers on how this money should be allocated.

Public health and political leaders also seek to mobilize health/science/technology resources proactively. They are calling for national and international plans for vaccinations (for instance, deciding which part of a population should be vaccinated first), for quarantine, and for sharing information and decision-making power among international, national, and local authorities.

Other people argue that influenza viruses pose formidable global security threats and deserve as much attention and funding as military spending. These advocates point out how easily viruses or deadly bacteria such as anthrax could be deployed in bioterrorist attacks and how swiftly such an infectious disease could disrupt transportation systems, manufacturing, businesses, schools, hospitals, and whole countries. These voices insist that nations on their own and through global alliances should institute systems for alerting their populations, for enlisting scientific knowledge, and for activating national control of medical supplies in times of emergency. In contrast, opponents see much less danger and urgency in biological attacks, bird flu, or other influenza pandemics.

Still others target national responsibility and the cultural and political dimensions of pandemics. Citing China's dangerous silence over SARS, they stress that all countries must agree to be open and responsible about reporting virus outbreaks and to share scientific/medical information in timely ways. Much of this debate over epidemics like SARS and avian flu focuses on balancing national and global interests to ensure that countries work fairly and respectfully together on prevention and containment.

What Is the Relationship Between the AIDS Pandemic, Poverty, and Global Security? For the last decade, rich Western countries have tended to regard AIDS as largely a problem of the developing world.* In affluent countries, increasingly convenient and affordable advances in medicine,

---

*Within the United States, the fight against AIDS has been—and still is—embroiled in moral and religious controversy over homosexuality and gay rights.

such as the recent development of one pill to be taken once a day, have given AIDS patients options for longer life. However, in addition to treating the suffering from AIDS in developing countries as a social justice issue, many policymakers and activists believe the devastation of AIDS poses a major global security threat. They underscore the social destruction caused by AIDS in Africa: food production interrupted by the death of farmers; social and governmental institutions weakened by the loss of professionals; children orphaned and left without adult guidance, income, or opportunity for education. These activists warn that desperate people and weakened countries create grounds for terrorism to germinate and destabilize the whole world.

Other humanitarians argue that free trade agreements favoring rich countries have caused poverty, and poverty has nurtured AIDS as well as malaria, tuberculosis, and waterborne diseases. Condemning U.S. negligence, Jeffrey Sachs, the lead economist of the UN Millennium Development Project, recently wrote that poverty in Africa is killing twenty thousand people a day.[*] Advocates like Sachs say that poverty must be addressed directly along with AIDS, in part by ensuring that global trade works for developing countries.

While some activists are calling the United States to follow through on its financial commitment to the Global Fund to Fight HIV/AIDS, others question whether the United States can pour money into the economies and health of developing countries when the United States itself lacks a universal health care system, many Americans have no medical insurance, the child poverty rate (children living in families with incomes 50 percent below the national average) is increasing, and the child mortality rate has edged up to equal Malaysia's.[†] Some political activists want the United States to repeal corporate tax breaks and recent tax cuts for the rich to enable the United States to meet both domestic and global health needs.

Some stakeholders believe that first world countries should tackle the health crises of the AIDS pandemic immediately, before effective solutions to the deeper causes of poverty can be found and implemented. These analysts, activists, public health advocates, and philanthropists want the world to concentrate on achieving scientific breakthroughs and delivering these discoveries and treatments to the poor countries in need.

How and How Much Should Rich Countries Help Developing Countries and How Much Should Developing Countries Take Responsibility for Combating AIDS? Controversy centers on how help should be distributed. Recently, the U.S. government has objected to helping countries

---

[*]"Thousands Died in Africa Yesterday," *New York Times*, February 27, 2005.
[†]Paul Vallely, "UN Hits Back at US in Report Saying Parts of America Are as Poor as Third World," *Independent*, September 8, 2005.

such as Liberia, Zimbabwe, and Swaziland that have corrupt governments, to funding programs that do not emphasize abstinence-only as an AIDS prevention strategy, and to supporting programs that do not denounce prostitution.* However, opponents protest that people suffering under these corrupt governments especially need help; that the abstinence-only strategy is ideological and religious, and not health based; and that antiprostitution policies will prevent NGOs from critical work with groups of people who are especially endangered by HIV/AIDS. A further dispute involves which governments and institutions in the developed world should direct these interventions: global institutions like the United Nations, its agencies, and the Global AIDS Fund; or the United States acting unilaterally or multilaterally?

African countries are also wrestling with their responsibility and ability to confront their AIDS crises. Nelson Mandela, former president of South Africa, asserts the need for collaboration:

> We need, and there is increasing evidence of, African resolve to fight this war. Others will not save us if we do not primarily commit ourselves. Let us, however, not underestimate the resources required to conduct this battle. Partnership with the international community is vital. . . . no government anywhere in the world has sufficient resources on its own to be able to fight and win this battle. Therefore, there must be a partnership between business and the community. . .[†]

However, establishing successful private-public and rich-country–poor-country partnerships is challenging. Brazil and Thailand offer examples of how strong government involvement and commitment coupled with effective public-private partnerships can help countries deal with AIDS. Some African leaders and countries like Mozambique have welcomed Western aid while maintaining their national sovereignty by insisting that they have a major role in managing these global contributions; otherwise, they say, this aid will not strengthen these countries but will become simply a new chapter in a history of Western domination of Africa.

What Prevention and Treatment Offer the Best Ways to Combat AIDS?

Some economic and political conflicts over *how* to prevent and treat AIDS involve who should have control over donated funds for prevention and treatment programs. For example, the United States has tended to promote AIDS

---

*See the President's Emergency Plan for AIDS Relief (PEPFAR), the 2004 bill allocating money for this plan, and the "Anti-Prostitution Pledge." See http://www.state.gov and http://www.usaid.gov/our_work/global_health/aids/pepfar.htm/.

†"Closing Address by Former President Nelson Mandela at the 13th International AIDS Conference, 14 July 2000, Durban." International AIDS Vaccine Initiative, http://www.iavi.org/viewfile.cfm?fid=851.

treatment in the form of brand-name antiretroviral drugs from big-name pharmaceutical companies that have been tested and approved. However, poor African countries have preferred less-expensive and simpler generic drugs from India that are easier for AIDS patients to learn how to take.

Another economic and political issue over prevention and treatment pits many African countries and activists who seek systemic, long-term change against Western benefactors who want to focus on the AIDS crisis only. Advocates for systemic change believe rich countries should help African countries build their own national health systems—a long-term solution that respects national sovereignty and fosters self-determination—instead of only treating AIDS.

One group of stakeholders includes scientists, research institutions, drug companies, and policymakers who emphasize the role of science and technology in combating and conquering AIDS and are pushing for improved drugs and a vaccine.

Many leaders and human rights activists in developing countries endorse holistic approaches that work with cultural values and traditions from within the cultural frames of the people who need help. For instance, Marina Mahathir, president of the Malaysian AIDS Council and daughter of Malaysia's prime minister, rejects generic programs and stresses attuning AIDS prevention and treatment to specific countries, regions, and subgroups of people: "All the responses have to be tailor-made—sometimes even more locally, even to specific communities. . . . There's no way you can talk to women the same way you talk to men about this issue. Talking to young people has to be different than talking to old people."* Many people working with prevention and treatment in Africa stress the need to factor in male social, economic, and sexual dominance, which is seen in polygamy and male reluctance to use condoms. Prevention manuals given to women will not help when women lack sexual autonomy and have few economic rights. Instead, holistic and cultural approaches to the fight against AIDS focus on empowering women. An example of Africans working within their culture for social change is popular Zimbabwean singer Oliver Mtukudzi, who has written songs about the pain of watching loved ones die of AIDS, in the hopes of combating the social shame of this disease. Some African and international organizations have found ways to bring people suffering from AIDS together in communities where social workers can ease psychological and emotional distress while income-generating operations like soap making can help these jobless people provide for themselves and their medicinal needs.

Other stakeholders point out how AIDS prevention is entangled in ethics and religion, for example in the values-laden issue of the use of

---

*Rachel S. Taylor, "Interview: Marina Mahathir," *World Press Review*, November 25, 2002, http://www.worldpress.org/print_article.cfm?article_id=933&don't=yes.

condoms. For some Africans, condoms represent Western individualism and consumerism, which are at odds with African communal values. Meanwhile, faith-based Western organizations, both Protestant and Catholic, and African Catholicism stress abstinence and faithfulness and downplay the use of condoms or reject them entirely. However, many public health workers and activists continue to argue for the value, even necessity, of condoms in the fight against the AIDS pandemic.

The three sections that follow—"Student Voice," "International Voices," and "Global Hot Spot"—make these global controversies over the spread of disease more personal and concrete.

 STUDENT VOICE: EXPERIENCING THE SARS EPIDEMIC

In 2003, SARS unnerved the global community. Seeming to appear from nowhere in China, it was later discovered to have jumped from wild civets (weasel-like creatures eaten as a delicacy) to humans. Especially virulent, it sickened many of the medical staff caring for patients. Epidemiologists discovered that the SARS virus could survive outside the human body for hours, even days, and therefore could be transmitted even without direct contact; and there was no vaccine or cure. Showing how these facts generated social anxiety and triggered governmental restraints, student Mark Merin writes about experiencing this epidemic firsthand. In the following narrative, Mark recounts his effort to complete his senior year of high school in Taiwan while SARS was disrupting and transforming ordinary daily life.

Mark Merin

We were all confident that Taiwan had taken the necessary precautions to prevent the SARS epidemic from reaching us. However, not even the doctors and high tech machinery on standby at the airport were enough to prevent SARS from coming. The numerous businessmen who traveled back and forth weekly from China and Hong Kong to Taiwan must have brought it. Soon enough, we were reading about it in the papers, seeing it on the news, hearing about it on the radio.

I went out every day armed with two essentials, a disposable mask and a small bottle of isopropyl alcohol. Whenever I entered a public area such as a bus or a movie theatre, I put on the mask, and afterwards I sprayed my hands with alcohol. Others around me did the same. Certain pharmaceutical companies soon began to raise the prices on masks. Some companies even developed better and more efficient ones. These disposable masks typically cost from four to twelve dollars apiece, so people were spending anywhere from twenty-eight to eighty-four dollars every week. It was ludicrous, but everyone was afraid. You would see people wearing masks everywhere you went, from restaurants to stores and most especially on airplanes.

Every day I would read in the paper of how several people were quarantined under suspicion of being infected by SARS. People didn't want to get SARS, and people also didn't want to be suspected of having it. They all feared that the government would quarantine them. As the virus infected more people, the government decided to pass a new law: any person with a fever had to report it to the nearest medical facility or be fined several thousand dollars. Thermometers became widely sold in Taiwan after several weeks. The government continually urged people to check their temperature at least three times a day. Fear began to grow and even the slightest feeling of discomfort or sickness would send people into a panic thinking they had SARS. When people sneezed or even coughed on buses or in any public area, those near them would immediately draw away in fear.

While all this was happening in the city, at home I was thinking, "Oh it won't ever affect me that much." I was wrong. My school soon initiated SARS prevention measures. We all had to have our temperatures taken before entering school grounds. Every morning at 7:45, hundreds of students from kindergarten to high school lined up at the doors waiting to get their temperatures taken. Many students were late to class. The school's fears were not unfounded. In fact, one student and the rest of his family were confined in a hospital because they had all been infected by SARS. Unfortunately, a week later I read in the school newspaper that the father had passed away. The school administrators panicked.

Our senior class started worrying about what would happen if SARS got any worse. It would mean an end to senior trips. Maybe colleges would re-evaluate us because we came from countries infected with SARS. Then it hit us. Classes were cancelled a month earlier than planned. A teacher suspected of developing SARS symptoms came into contact with the entire faculty of my school during a conference, and all classes were cancelled because all the teachers were put under quarantine. Advanced placement tests were in question, senior prom was cancelled, and graduation became a maybe.

Several of my friends left the country right away. They didn't care if they weren't there for their exams or for graduation as long as they were safe from the deadly epidemic. Most of us didn't even get to say goodbye. Up to this day, I haven't seen a majority of those friends. The good news, however, was that the school contacted various substitute teachers to sit in while we took our exams. Graduation was thankfully also not cancelled. However, before entering the graduation grounds, temperatures had to be taken.

By the time I had to leave for college, the SARS epidemic had been controlled. Occasionally, I still hear news of SARS resurfacing, but so far those reports have quickly faded away. I think the Taiwan government, having learned through this experience, would now be more efficient in dealing with the threat of SARS.

INTERNATIONAL VOICES

Many African leaders whose families have been touched by AIDS have shared their losses publicly in an effort to foster public acceptance of AIDS. In January 2005, Nelson Mandela, winner of the Nobel Peace Prize for his fight against apartheid and president of South Africa from 1994 to 1999, told the press that his son, age fifty-four, died of AIDS. Mandela believes that in order to halt the destruction of AIDS, people need to confront it openly as a disease rather than treat it as a social stain or spiritual failure. In 2002, Oprah Winfrey interviewed Mandela on her show. The following excerpt from that interview touches on some of Mandela's recurrent themes: the need for education, sexual responsibility, and love, not rejection, of AIDS patients.

Oprah Winfrey's Interview with Nelson Mandela

Nelson: One of the things that is destroying people with AIDS is the stigma which we attach to it. . . . [A person with AIDS feels] . . . I'm shunned by my friend, my parents, I'm a castaway. He or she loses the determination to fight. One thing we must avoid is to allow people to lose hope in the future.

Oprah: Do you think, though, that ignorance prevents healing?

Nelson: There can be no doubt. Now, we must work hard to make sure the stigma about HIV-AIDS is destroyed and give people the love and support. AIDS is killing more people than were killed by all the wars and natural disasters that have occurred . . . during the last two centuries. Let's mobilize everybody to go from village to village to teach people, firstly, about safe sex. Education is the key. Safe sex. And to indicate to them that children, young people, must delay as much as possible before they can have sex. When they do have sex, one partner. And even with one partner, they must use contraceptives. That is how we can mobilize the entire community.*

Bono, the lead singer of U2 and the cofounder of DATA (Debt AIDS Trade Africa), is another public figure trying to change the world's view

---

*"Nelson Mandela: The Epidemic of Aids," *The Oprah Winfrey Show*, http://www2 .oprah.com/tows/pastshows/tows_2002/tows_past_20020509_c.jhtml.

of AIDS. Bono sees the exponential growth of AIDS in Africa as a consequence of poverty. In his commencement address at the University of Pennsylvania on May 17, 2004, he shared the evolution of his own commitment and made an ethical appeal to his audience to tackle the economic conditions that have enabled AIDS to decimate African societies.

Bono's Commencement Address, University of Pennsylvania, May 17, 2004

. . . . Seven thousand Africans dying every day of preventable, treatable disease like AIDS? That's not a cause, that's an emergency. And when the disease gets out of control because most of the population live on less than one dollar a day? That's not a cause, that's an emergency. And when resentment builds because of unfair trade rules and the burden of unfair debt, that are debts by the way that keep Africans poor? That's not a cause, that's an emergency. So—"We Are the World, Live Aid," [a concert in which sixty of the world's biggest rock stars performed for free] . . . was an extraordinary thing and really that event was about charity. But 20 years on I'm not that interested in charity. I'm interested in justice. There's a difference. Africa needs justice as much as it needs charity.

Equality for Africa is a big idea. It's a big expensive idea. I see the Wharton graduates now getting out the math on the back of their programs, numbers are intimidating aren't they, but not to you! But the scale of the suffering and the scope of the commitment they often numb us into a kind of indifference. Wishing for the end of AIDS and extreme poverty in Africa is like wishing that gravity didn't make things so damn heavy. We can wish it, but what the hell can we do about it?

Well, more than we think. We can't fix every problem—corruption, natural calamities are part of the picture here—but the ones we can we must. The debt burden, as I say, unfair trade, as I say, sharing our knowledge, the intellectual copyright for lifesaving drugs in a crisis, we can do that. And because we can, we must.

. . . . The fact is that this generation—yours, my generation—that can look at the poverty, we're the first generation that can look at poverty and disease, look across the ocean to Africa and say with a straight face, *we can be the first to end this sort of stupid extreme poverty, where in the world of plenty, a child can die for lack of food in its belly. . . .*

GLOBAL HOT SPOT: SUB-SARAHAN AFRICA

News reports, interviews, and personal accounts from sub-Saharan African countries show how AIDS has hurt children and women especially. Some of the most disturbing news tells of children who have experienced the death

---

*Bono, "Because We Can, We Must" (commencement address, University of Pennsylvania, May 17, 2004), http://www.upenn.edu/almanac/between/2004/commence-b.html.

of one or both parents (called "double orphans") and who are now forced to live with grandparents or any other remaining relatives or are thrown into the streets to fend for themselves. Women's stories reveal how women's oppression contributes to the spread of AIDS. The following excerpt is from the Ugandan article "Who Violates Women's Rights?", published in *Africa News* on September 14, 2005.

> . . . women in Kenya and Uganda told HRW [Human Rights Watch] they could not reach HIV testing and treatment centers because they had no money to travel or pay for care, were too afraid to ask abusive husbands for funds, or were not allowed to leave the home.
>
> Sules Kiliesa's story [resembles that of many women], as an earlier report by HRW, "Domestic Violence and Women's Vulnerability to HIV-Infection in Uganda," suggests.
>
> Apparently, after her first husband died, Sules was forced to remarry by her father. Her new husband had three wives and 15 children, aside from hers. He beat her and raped her persistently. She is now HIV-positive. . . .
> "He forced me to have sex with him and beat me if I refused. This went for every woman [wife]. Even when he was HIV-positive, he still wanted sex. He refused to use a condom. He said he 'cannot eat sweets with the paper [wrapper] on.'"

Despite the tragedy of women's helplessness in many African societies, there are signs that African countries are taking medical and social initiatives in confronting AIDS. Partly because of its diamond resources, Botswana is a rare and fortunate country in that it is able to provide free antiretroviral drugs for its citizens. The following excerpt from "Botswana Rolls Out ARV Programme" in *Africa News* from September 2, 2005, shows how Botswana has faced the social challenge of treating AIDS.

> . . . . Princess Marina Hospital-based Infectious Diseases Care Clinic is, perhaps, the largest operation of its kind in Africa, with a patient population of more than 11,000 on antiretroviral therapy. . . .
>
> Dr. Ndwapi Ndwapi, co-director of the clinic, enthusiastically notes that people currently on ARV treatment are some of the most courageous.
>
> "The ARVs have, in a way, done a lot to normalise the disease. Stigma is not like it was four to five years ago. The HIV status is no longer regarded as a death sentence. At least 80–90 per cent of patients have either told someone in the family or are actively having someone assisting them with their treatment," he notes.
>
> About 200 to 250 patients are attended to by doctors daily, while 200–350 collect their medication daily. "We also spend most of the time educating them rather than just giving out drugs," Ndwapi says. . . .

The readings in this chapter explore the multiple national and global controversies involved in the 2003 SARS crisis, the spread of bird flu, and the AIDS pandemic.

READINGS

SARS Accelerates Transparency in Government

Huang Xiangyang

Huang Xiangyang has been a copy editor of the Hong Kong edition of the *China Daily*, the country's main English newspaper. When he wrote this piece, he was working at the *Seattle-Post Intelligencer* through the Alfred Friendly Press Fellowship program. This op-ed piece appeared in the *Seattle-Post Intelligencer* on May 8, 2003, in the middle of the furor over the virulence of SARS.

> How does Huang Xiangyang use his knowledge of Chinese history and culture to influence his American audience's perspectives?

1   "We've almost turned our apartment building into a fortress," my father told me on the phone the other day in reference to the quarantine measures his neighborhood has taken against the spread of severe acute respiratory syndrome, or SARS.

2   To ward off possible infected outsiders, admittance is limited to building residents who have to show a special pass at the gate. Inside, every inch of floor space is disinfected on a daily basis. Corridors are permeated with the smell of burning herbal incenses believed to be able to kill "floating virus." Thermometers have been allocated to each household; members are requested to report abnormal body temperatures, one of the disease's symptoms. People are taking extraordinary measures—right or misguided—that they believe will give them an additional layer of protection.

3   "It's always better not to take chances," my father said. After all, the building he lives in is in the Haidian district, which has the highest number of SARS cases in Beijing.

4   I was a little surprised by the attitudinal U-turn toward the virus. In early April, when I called to warn him about the disease that had already wreaked havoc in the southern province of Guangdong and Hong Kong, my father still believed it was nothing more than a health nuisance in a remote corner of the vast country that had been "put under effective control."

5   Ignorance about this new form of coronavirus and its ramifications might have led to the official laxity in preventive efforts in the outbreak's early stage. But the following underreporting and even cover-ups can only be explained by a "never-to-wash-dirty-linen-in-public tradition" and the ingrained bureaucratic penchant for secrecy.

6   The initial delay in responding allowed the epidemic to spread across the country and to the rest of the world. It has, and will continue to, cost China dearly.

7   The economic impact is obvious. Tourism, hotels, airlines and other service sectors are among the hardest hit, as people choose to coop themselves up at home to minimize the threat of infections. Visitors to Beijing have reportedly dropped by 90 percent in April from the same period last year. Economists forecast the epidemic will cut down the country's robust economic growth by at least one percentage point.

8   While economic losses could be temporary—and made up with faster growth in the future—the damage to China's international image will take longer to repair. The sincerity and readiness of the country to further integrate with the global community has been put in doubt. Some have suggested it was a mistake for the International Olympic Committee to award Beijing the Olympic Games. Nothing could be more damaging to China's vow to make it the best Olympics ever than a retarded move to contain a quickly spread and deadly disease.

9   Some 90 countries have imposed entry restrictions of some form on Chinese visitors. In the latest cases, U.S. universities have begun to refuse enrollment of students from the Chinese mainland and Hong Kong. Russia and some central Asian countries have closed their borders with China.

10   I scoff at the notion that these are just another round of "efforts by international hostile forces to demonize China," as some believe. But from a scientific point [of] view, there is no denying that the severity of SARS is out of proportion with the unprecedented attention it has received.

11   For example, Ebola, a virulent viral disease that causes death in up to 90 percent of all clinically ill cases, has rarely, if [ever], been covered with such frequency and intensity by the media. SARS' fatality rate is estimated at 5 percent to 10 percent.

12   In the United States alone, more than 100,000 people are hospitalized with the flu (whose virus is airborne) and at least half of them die from it and its complications each year, according to the U.S. Centers for Disease Control and Prevention. SARS has infected about 7,000 worldwide since last fall, when the first case was detected in Guangdong. Its virus is much less contagious than the flu, experts believe.

13   The less-than-imagined danger posed by SARS by no means justifies the incompetence and deceit by some Chinese government officials in tracking and fighting the disease. Former [Health] Minister Zhang Wenkang, who first insisted SARS had been contained and was later sacked because of negligence of duty, has

become the Chinese version of Al-Sahhaf, the former Iraqi information minister.

14   But it would be a big mistake for the international community to play on China's early inefficiency as well as inexperience in dealing with SARS and turn negative toward the country. As Stephen Roach, chief economist at Morgan Stanley in New York, put it, "at times like this, it is critical to look beyond the shock and focus on the fundamental forces that will shape the (China's) future."

15   The latest reaction of my father's neighborhood to the SARS outbreak epitomizes how quickly the nation at large could mend its ways. Although the public was outraged by early cover-ups, citizens generally appreciated the adaptability of the new government in handling the crisis. "Better late than never" is the common belief.

16   The slogan now is to "take strictest precautions and put up a last-ditch resistance against" the potentially lethal disease. Local officials are shutting down once crowded entertainment facilities such as karaoke bars and Internet cafes for fear of group infections. Health workers are taking temperatures at railway stations and airports. Quarantines are being widened from hospitals to include apartment blocks, universities and construction sites.

17   Problems in China are often not solved because of lack of focus or commitment on the part of the government. But once the colossal machine of mass movement is started, the top-down imposition of order can be achieved with extreme efficiency. The latest example is the construction of a hospital for contagious disease in the northern suburbs of Beijing. The 1,000-bed hospital, claimed to be the largest of its kind in the world, was completed in just eight days to meet the rising demand for treatment of SARS cases.

18   The latest figures suggest that the outbreak in Beijing is showing signs of declining. Based on experience from Guangdong and Hong Kong, experts believe it could peak in a month or two. But changes that have been brought to the country will have an everlasting impact on its future.

19   SARS is a test for China's new leadership, which just took the helm in March. The new leaders have come to realize that in times of globalization, the old method of keeping secret everything deemed ungraceful no longer works. The solutions lie in further openness and facing up to the country's shortcomings. If China wants to become a responsible citizen of the global village, it must undertake due obligations.

20   "I came to face reality and the world. Please have faith in the Chinese government and Chinese people," Premier Wen Jiabao said [when] he arrived in Bangkok for a summit with regional

leaders to find ways to contain the disease. His candidness and frankness were well accepted.

21   On the domestic front, the old bureaucratic system characterized by opaqueness and passivity has been challenged by public demands for greater transparency and accountability.

22   Apart from the health minister and former Beijing Mayor Meng Xuenong, as many as 120 officials have been fired or disciplined for concealing SARS cases, implementing disease control measures slowly and taking leave without approval.

23   The punishment is part of an unprecedented and highly public campaign to ensure that central government directives are implemented at the grass-roots level. It is the first time China has penalized such a wide range of officials for dereliction of duty during an unexpected calamity, and we have good reasons to believe efforts at establishing an accountability system for officials will continue. President Hu Jintao and Premier Wen have warned on many occasions that officials would be held responsible for failing to perform their duties competently and follow central government instructions.

24   It would be unfair to say the Chinese media reports only good news and turns a blind eye to what is considered bad news. In an era of Internet, it is increasingly difficult to ignore the demands from the readership for "nothing but truth." The endeavor by journalists to transform the media from mouthpiece to watchdog, though not smooth, has never ceased. The SARS outbreak has to some extent accelerated that process.

25   "Bad news" about the death tolls and new cases now covers the front pages of almost all newspapers and is transmitted to households nationwide through airwaves. In a country where the demise of more than 20 million people from famine during the Great Leap Forward in the late '50s has never been reported in official print, the current transparency is nothing to be taken lightly.

26   Underlining the change in the media is also the coverage of a submarine accident of Chinese Navy that killed all 70 crew members. The news has come as a surprise to many, as the Chinese armed forces have made it a tradition to keep accidents or mishaps under close wraps. "Even the United States does not report some of its submarine accidents," an American scholar, quoted by a Hong Kong newspaper, observed.

27   There is a Chinese saying that opportunities are hidden inside crisis. SARS, despite all the panic and chaos it has caused, has become a catalyst for China's [striving] to become a more open, free, responsible and rules-based society.

28   In this sense, SARS has changed China in a way no less significant than 9/11 changed the United States.

For Class Discussion

1. What claims about and criticisms of China are driving Huang Xiangyang's argument in this op-ed piece?
2. How does Xiangyang rebut these criticisms?
3. How does personal knowledge contribute to the rhetorical effectiveness of this piece?
4. What features of this argument do you find the most persuasive?
5. What lessons about responding to epidemics could the global community learn from this piece?   ∎

Fighting Human Infection in an Age of Globalization
Ann Marie Kimball

Dr. Ann Marie Kimball is a professor of epidemiology (the science of the causes and controls of epidemics) and health services at the University of Washington School of Public Health. In addition, she directs the Asia Pacific Economic Cooperation Emerging Infections Network. This organization, founded in 1989, promotes cooperation and sharing of information among twenty-one Pacific Rim economies with the goal of using preventive measures to save lives and reduce the cost of fighting infectious diseases. Since fall 2005, this organization has been tracking the cases of avian influenza and fatalities in Indonesia and Vietnam. This op-ed piece was published in the *Seattle Times* on May 2, 2003.

> What does Dr. Ann Marie Kimball want the public to know about advances and challenges in public health? How does she combine informing and persuading in this piece?

1   As the global tally of severe acute respiratory syndrome cases inches over 5,000, it is timely to reflect on what this epidemic tells us. SARS is not the first pandemic to leap continents and infect far-flung populations—and it will not be the last.

2   After the profound reach of HIV/AIDS became clear, we in public health who had been most alarmed by HIV turned our attention to the future. What would be the next great epidemic? What were our vulnerabilities as a human community?

3   Public health is by nature a venture that builds for the future. What could we do to prevent the next incursion of epidemic human infection, or at least slow it down?

4   The pace of commerce and travel is increasing rapidly and inexorably. The community of Asia Pacific economies epitomizes this.

While the events of Sept. 11, 2001, the economic woes of the seven "tiger" economies and the wan recovery of our own economy have had a chilling effect, the human community is bent on trading its goods and visiting. It is our destiny, sooner or later, to be more closely linked with our fellows around the globe than ever in human history.

5   The modern era of trade and travel bears little resemblance to the realities of 12th-century Venice, where the first quarantine laws were coined to keep vessels out of port for 40 days. Survivors could then disembark without fear of bringing plague or yellow fever into port.

6   Despite the snarls caused by airport screening for SARS, we in public health are well aware that these old tools of quarantine and isolation are stopgap measures in halting epidemics.

7   Four innovations hold hope for our continued ability to contain and control new human infections in the era of globalization, but we need to fully deploy them as fast as possible.

8   First, there are amazing advances in molecular diagnostics and microbiology technologies. The ability to sequence viral genomic information reliably has been elegantly demonstrated in the international collaborative effort to identify the SARS agent. While not a magic bullet, these technologies pave the way for new therapies and new vaccines—which hold hope for making such bullets. Seattle hosts some of the leading researchers in this area.

9   Second, the revolution in communication and informatics has arrived. Investment in information technology will have topped $2.6 trillion globally in 2002. This investment is primarily by health-care organizations and governments. So, disease investigations to track the origin of outbreaks can be faster and more accurate than ever before. Information is more quickly and accurately available on a worldwide basis.

10   Investigations will eventually be done collaboratively in real time between centers far distant from one another. All it takes is vision and resources.

11   To assure the public's health, accurate, timely information is pivotal. There are two parts to this strategy. We need the "pipes"— the high-speed Internet linkages—through which to communicate. These we have. We also need a community broadly concerned with the public's health as a core value. In other words, we need the right people, willing to communicate the right stuff at the right time.

12   Strong working relationships with colleagues across borders is the only way to get this done. We have named this dream the "virtual public health department" for the Asia Pacific. For seven years we have been working toward this goal through an industrial science and technology working group of the Asia Pacific Economic Cooperation (APEC).

13   As the fumble of information from Guondong and Beijing points up, we are not there yet. But happily the game is not over; and we are closer than ever before.

14   The third major advance is the increasing appreciation of what globalization means to all of us. The concern for health and welfare is becoming more generalized. This translates to political understanding and facilitation of communications and technology sharing at the highest levels of APEC.

15   The fourth area of innovation is "public-private partnerships" as vehicles for global health. The kind of early warning and response we need in our vital region will take this kind of muscle.

16   Today there is no clear way to fund the kinds of public-health operations we have to have in the Asia Pacific. Each economy finances its own, which means each effort rises and falls with the rhythms of business cycles, currency fluctuations, trade balances and political reverses. Global epidemics tend to keep their own time, without regard to these agendas.

17   Public health must be always vigilant, and always prepared. In the wake of SARS, it seems only prudent to design a public-private partnership for public health in the Asia Pacific to carry us through future epidemics.

For Class Discussion

1. In this op-ed piece, Ann Marie Kimball explores both the problems and the advantages that globalization has brought to public health. What are they?

2. How would you summarize the main points of Kimball's policy proposal in your own words?

3. What does she cite as obstacles to global cooperation on health issues?

4. What response does Kimball hope to elicit from public health officials, policymakers, and the public?   ■

Some Hard Truths About Bird Flu
Henry I. Miller

Henry I. Miller is a physician, a research fellow at the Hoover Institution, and an adjunct scholar at several think tanks. He has served as advisor and medical reviewer with the Food and Drug Administration in the research areas of biotechnology, pharmaceutical development, bioterrorism, new viral diseases, and public policy and regulatory reform for scientific advances in food and medicine. He has authored six books, among them *Public Controversy in Biotechnology: An Insider's View* (1997), *To America's Health: A Model for Reform of the Food and Drug Administration* (2000), and *The Frankenfood Myth: How Protest and Politics Threaten the Biotech Revolution* (2004). He has also written extensively for both scholarly journals and popular science forums. This op-ed piece was published on January 14, 2006, in the *Taipei Times* and posted on the Web site of the Competitive Enterprise Institute, a conservative policy think tank devoted to "free enterprise and limited government" ("About CEI," www.cei.org).

How might readers in Taipei, Southeast Asia, and developing countries respond to Miller's argument?

1   The issues surrounding the possibility of a pandemic of the H5N1 strain of avian flu are extraordinarily complex, encompassing medicine, epidemiology, virology and even politics and ethics. Moreover, there is tremendous uncertainty about exactly when H5N1, which now primarily affects birds, might mutate into a form that is transmissible between humans, and how infectious and lethal it might be.

2   It is thus hardly surprising that commentaries about avian flu often miss the mark. A recent *New York Times* editorial, for example, decried the "me first" attitude of wealthy countries toward a possible H5N1 pandemic, because "[t]he best hope of stopping a pandemic, or at least buying time to respond, is to improve surveillance and health practices in East Africa and Asia, where one would probably begin."

3   To be sure, good surveillance is needed in order to obtain early warning that a strain of H5N1 flu transmissible between humans has been detected, so that nations around the world can rapidly initiate a variety of public health measures, including a program to produce large amounts of vaccine against that strain. But the massive undertaking required to "improve health practices in the poorest countries of the world" plays better on the editorial page than on the ground.

4   Intensive animal husbandry procedures that place billions of poultry and swine in close proximity to humans, combined with unsanitary conditions, poverty and grossly inadequate public health infrastructure of all kinds, make it unlikely that a pandemic can be prevented or contained at the source. It is noteworthy that China's chaotic effort to vaccinate 14 billion chickens has been compromised by counterfeit vaccines and the absence of protective gear for vaccination teams, which might actually spread disease by carrying fecal material on their shoes from one farm to another.

5   In theory, it is possible to contain a flu pandemic in its early stages by performing "ring prophylaxis"—using anti-flu drugs and

quarantine aggressively to isolate relatively small outbreaks of a human-to-human transmissible strain of H5N1. According to Johns Hopkins University virologist Donald Burke, "It may be possible to identify a human outbreak at the earliest stage, while there are fewer than 100 cases, and deploy international resources—such as a WHO stockpile of antiviral drugs—to rapidly quench it. This tipping point strategy is highly cost-effective."

6   However, a strategy can be "cost-effective" only if it is feasible. Although ring prophylaxis might work in Minneapolis, Toronto, or Zurich, in the parts of the world where flu pandemics begin, the probability of success approaches zero. In places like Vietnam, Indonesia and China—where the pandemic strain will likely originate—expertise, coordination, discipline, and infrastructure are lacking.

7   The response in Turkey—where as many as 50 possible cases have appeared in the eastern part of the country—is instructive. Officials in that region warned the government on Dec. 16 of a surge in bird deaths, but it took 12 days for an investigation to begin. When a 14-year-old boy became Turkey's first avian flu mortality last week (soon followed by two siblings), a government spokesman criticized doctors for mentioning the disease because they were "damaging Turkey's reputation." This is ominously reminiscent of China's initial response to SARS in 2003.

8   For now, it seems that all of the human H5N1 infections have been contracted from contact with infected poultry. But the situation in Turkey is what the outbreak of a human to human pandemic could look like at its earliest stages: the rapid spread of confirmed cases (and deaths) from an initial site to nearby villages and cities. We would expect to see a large number of illnesses among both employees and patients in hospitals where the victims are treated, and soon someone [perhaps even a carrier who is not ill] would spread it to Ankara, Istanbul, Tbilisi, Damascus, Baghdad and beyond.

9   The anti-flu drugs Tamiflu and Relenza are extremely expensive and in short supply. History suggests that if we were to make these drugs available to poor countries for ring prophylaxis, they would often be administered improperly—such as in sub-optimal doses—in a way that would promote viral resistance and only intensify a pandemic. Or perhaps they would be sold on the black market to enrich corrupt government officials.

10   A politically incorrect but rational strategy would be for rich countries to devote resources to developing countries primarily for surveillance. They would obtain timely warning of the existence of an H5N1 strain that is transmissible from human to human, but would focus the vast majority of their funding on parallel, low and high-tech approaches—vaccines, drugs and other public health measures—that would primarily benefit themselves.

11   If the pandemic were to begin relatively soon—say, within a year or two—there would be little that could be done to attenuate significantly the first wave of infections. But, if we're ready to rush the pandemic strain into an emergency program to manufacture vaccine, we could possibly blunt the second wave.

12   A flu pandemic will require triage on many levels, including not only decisions about which patients are likely to benefit from scarce commodities such as drugs, vaccines and ventilators, but also broader public policy choices about how best—among, literally, a world of possibilities—to expend resources.

For Class Discussion

1. What alternative views is Henry I. Miller rebutting in this op-ed piece? What concessions to these views does he make?

2. How does Miller refute these views? How persuasive is his counterreasoning and evidence?

3. Why does Miller delay an explicit statement of his main claim until the end of his argument? What is the rhetorical effect of this choice?

4. How do newspaper accounts of superstition, lack of education and health care, and poverty in the developing world relate to Miller's argument? How has this piece shaped your view of global responses to a bird flu pandemic? ∎

Grounding a Pandemic
Barack Obama and Richard Lugar

Barack Obama, a Democrat, and Richard Lugar, a Republican, are both U.S. senators, from Illinois and Indiana, respectively. Both are members of the Senate Foreign Relations Committee, and Lugar is its chairman. This op-ed piece appeared in the *New York Times* on June 6, 2005.

What political and policy measures are these senators proposing? Why is the *New York Times* a good forum for this policy proposal?

1   When we think of the major threats to our national security, the first to come to mind are nuclear proliferation, rogue states and global terrorism. But another kind of threat lurks beyond our shores, one from nature, not humans—an avian flu pandemic. An outbreak could cause millions of deaths, destabilize Southeast Asia (its likely place of origin), and threaten the security of governments around the world.

2   Earlier this year, Dr. Julie L. Gerberding, director of the Centers for Disease Control and Prevention, called the possibility of avian flu spreading from Southeast Asia "a very ominous situation for the globe." A killer flu could spread around the world in days, crippling economies in Southeast Asia and elsewhere. From a public health standpoint, Dr. Gerberding said, an avian flu outbreak is "the most important threat that we are facing right now."

3   International health experts say that two of the three conditions for an avian flu pandemic in Southeast Asia have already been met. First, a new strain of the virus, called A (H5N1), has emerged, and humans have little or no immunity to it. Second, this strain can jump between species. The only remaining obstacle is that A(H5N1) has not yet mutated into a form that is easily transmitted from human to human.

4   However, there have been some alarming developments. In recent months, the virus has been detected in mammals that have never previously been infected, including tigers, leopards and domestic cats. This spread suggests that the virus is mutating and could eventually emerge in a form that is readily transmittable among humans, leading to a full-blown pandemic. In fact, according to government officials, a few cases of human-to-human spread of A(H5N1) have already occurred.

5   The precedent that experts fear is the 1918 flu pandemic, which began in the American Midwest and swept the planet in the era before air travel, killing 20 million to 40 million people. As John M. Barry, author of *The Great Influenza,* has observed, "Influenza killed more people in a year than the Black Death of the Middle Ages killed in a century; it killed more people in 24 weeks than AIDS has killed in 24 years."

6   At the moment, effective responses to an avian flu pandemic are limited and will come far too late for many people in Southeast Asia. Indeed, so far more than 60 percent of those diagnosed with the avian flu have died. There is no proven vaccine for the A(H5N1) strain and it could take months to produce a fully effective one. Moreover, while some antiviral treatments may help flu sufferers, they are not widely available and must be administered to patients within 24 hours after the onset of symptoms.

7   It is essential for the international community, led by the United States, to take decisive action to prevent a pandemic.

8   So what should we do? Recently, the World Health Organization called for more money and attention to be devoted to effective preventive action, appealing for $100 million.

9   Congress responded promptly. A bipartisan group of senators obtained $25 million for prevention efforts (a quarter of the request, the traditional contribution of the United States), allowing the

C.D.C., the Agency for International Development, the Health and Human Services Department and other agencies to improve their ability to act.

10   In addition, the Senate Foreign Relations Committee unanimously approved legislation directing President Bush to form a senior-level task force to put in place an international strategy to deal with the avian flu and coordinate policy among our government agencies. We urge the Bush administration to form this task force immediately without waiting for legislation to be passed.

11   But these are only modest first steps. International health experts believe that Southeast Asia will be an epicenter of influenza for decades. We recommend that this administration work with Congress, public health officials, the pharmaceutical industry, foreign governments and international organizations to create a permanent framework for curtailing the spread of future infectious diseases.

12   Among the parts of that framework could be these:

- Increasing international disease surveillance, response capacity and public education and coordination, especially in Southeast Asia.
- Stockpiling enough antiviral doses to cover high-risk populations and essential workers.
- Ensuring that, here at home, Health and Human Services and state governments put in place plans that address issues of surveillance, medical care, drug and vaccine distribution, communication, protection of the work force and maintenance of core public functions in case of a pandemic.
- Accelerating research into avian flu vaccines and antiviral drugs.
- Establishing incentives to encourage nations to report flu outbreaks quickly and fully.

13   So far, A (H5N1) has not been found in the United States. But in an age when you can board planes in Bangkok or Hong Kong and arrive in Chicago, Indianapolis or New York in hours, we must face the reality that these exotic killer diseases are not isolated health problems half a world away, but direct and immediate threats to security and prosperity here at home.

For Class Discussion

1. How do Obama and Lugar support Dr. Julie L. Gerberding's claim that "'the most important threat that we are facing right now'" is an outbreak of avian flu?

2. What preventive strategies for containing a pandemic like avian flu do Obama and Lugar support?

3. Often the news media heighten the public's fear more than they contribute to helpful public debate. How much do you think this piece feeds public anxiety and how much does it offer constructive, practical measures?

International AIDS Day
Olle Johansson

Swedish editorial cartoonist Olle Johansson publishes his cartoons daily in the northern Swedish newspaper *Norra Vasterbotten*. His cartoons also appear internationally. Johansson created this cartoon for the International AIDS Day, December 1, 2004. It was posted on Daryl Cagle's Professional Cartoon Index, where Johansson's cartoons are archived.

What features of this cartoon stand out for you?

For Class Discussion

1. What story does this cartoon tell? Who are the characters and what is the conflict?
2. How does this cartoon draw on fairy tales and fantasy for its emotional and imaginative appeal?

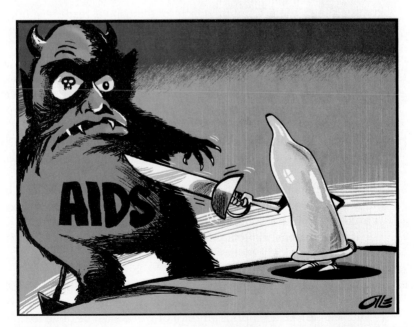

FIGURE 9.1 International AIDS Day *(© Olle Johansson, 2004)*

3. What serious issue question does this cartoon pose? What answer to the question does it suggest?

4. How does this cartoon relate to the articles on AIDS and condoms in this chapter?

AIDS and India
Melinda Gates

Melinda Gates, who has a master of business administration from Duke University, is one of the world's most prominent philanthropists and health and education activists. Her husband, billionaire Bill Gates, is the chairman and chief software architect of Microsoft Corporation, the world's leading software company, which he cofounded in 1975. In 2000, Bill and Melinda created the Bill and Melinda Gates Foundation to act on their belief that "every life has equal value" and "to help reduce inequities" primarily in global health and education ("About Us," www.gatesfoundation.org). Melinda regularly travels around the world and gives speeches to support this foundation's programs to fight AIDS and to develop an AIDS vaccine, to which the Gateses have committed hundreds of millions of dollars. This article, written as a guest column for the *Seattle Times*, appeared on April 11, 2004.

> In this piece, Melinda Gates is writing for the general readership of a major newspaper. In her introductory and concluding paragraphs, how does Gates try to involve her audience and move them to action?

1   India's emergence as one of the world's fastest-growing economies, with a highly skilled workforce and climbing literacy rates, has fueled optimism that the country could one day overcome its crippling poverty.

2   But as I recently saw firsthand, India is on the brink of an AIDS catastrophe that could undermine the country's potential for progress.

3   There are already over 4 million people infected with HIV in India, and the epidemic is on the verge of crossing over from those at highest risk into the general population.

4   If this happens, experts project that as many as 20 million Indians could be infected by the end of the decade—that's more than twice the population of New York City.

5   What I heard during my trip to Calcutta—from AIDS experts, community workers and people affected by the disease— confirmed that a tremendous amount of work must be done to fight AIDS in India. But I am hopeful that the nation can avoid disaster.

A range of HIV-prevention measures are working in India—if expanded to reach all those at risk, these efforts can stem the country's surging AIDS epidemic while there's still time.

6   During my trip, I learned about three urgent priorities for preventing the spread of AIDS in India: the need to empower women; to reach mobile populations, such as truck drivers, with HIV prevention services; and to fight the powerful stigma attached to the disease.

7   I'll never forget a sex worker named Gita, who brought home to me the role that women's empowerment can play in stopping AIDS. Gita has joined with other sex workers in one of Calcutta's poorest districts to educate other women about AIDS. Shockingly, 70 percent of Indian women have never even heard of AIDS.

8   Working together, Gita and her peers have helped to increase condom use from near zero to 70 percent in their district, and to reduce HIV infection rates to 7 percent—compared with rates as high as 66 percent among sex workers elsewhere.

9   I was particularly moved when, during my visit, several sex workers spontaneously started singing "We Shall Overcome." As I listened to their Bengali-accented English, it became clear that the familiar lyrics were not just a dream for them. By taking an active role in educating other sex workers and distributing condoms, these women are playing a vital role in making prevention work.

10   More women must be empowered in the face of AIDS. That means ensuring women a place at the table in planning and implementing HIV-prevention programs, replicating successful programs for sex workers around the country, and accelerating research into new technologies like anti-HIV microbicides that women could use to protect themselves from infection, even if their partners refuse to use condoms.

11   Of course, the best long-term solution is to provide greater economic and educational opportunities so that fewer women enter the sex trade.

12   HIV-prevention services must also be provided to mobile populations in India, such as truck drivers, soldiers and migrant workers, who can be highly vulnerable to HIV and play a key role in the spread of the disease.

13   For example, Indian truck drivers typically spend 80 percent of their time on the road, a majority report having sex with commercial sex workers, and they are 10 times more likely to have HIV than the general population. If infected while on the road, they can easily pass on the virus to their wives or girlfriends when they return home.

14   To learn about prevention efforts targeting mobile populations, I visited a truck stop in Calcutta where, I was told, "lots of sex

happens" between truck drivers and sex workers. But I also saw a sign of progress, in the form of a bamboo hut—a clinic where truck drivers and sex workers receive HIV counseling and testing.

15   Inside the tiny clinic, I had an eye-opening dialogue with six of the truck drivers. They said they had never heard of AIDS before outreach workers talked to them, and they've shared what they have learned about the disease with their friends and teenage sons. The truckers admitted they never use condoms with their wives—it would expose their infidelities—but they do use condoms now with sex workers. Obviously, this is not ideal, but it is an important step in the right direction.

16   Finally, it is critical to end the stigma surrounding AIDS, which often prevents any discussion of sex and keeps people from getting tested for the virus. I was told by the leader of a support group for HIV-positive people that the stigma of AIDS—and the inferior status of women—is so strong that a woman whose husband dies of AIDS is often blamed for his death, and thrown out of the home with her children.

17   AIDS has always raised thorny issues. Many of us are simply not comfortable talking about the behavior that can lead to HIV infection, such as unsafe sex and injection drug use. But every nation that has successfully reduced infection rates has recognized the need to promote open discussion about the disease and reach those populations most at risk.

18   Many of India's leaders see the urgent need for aggressive efforts to stop AIDS—both through prevention programs and recently announced efforts to expand access to treatment—and are taking many of the steps needed to keep the disease from crippling a great nation.

19   Bill and I started our foundation based on the firm belief that every child in our world deserves a chance at good health. But the reality is that more than 10 million children die every year, and two-thirds of them are dying from diseases that could be prevented with low-cost interventions, such as vaccines. Diseases like tuberculosis and malaria are resurging due to neglect, and if nothing is done to change the course of the AIDS epidemic, 100 million people could be infected by the next decade. That is why it is so important that nations with emerging epidemics, like India, act now.

20   Our foundation has committed $200 million to support HIV prevention in India, with a focus on sex workers, truckers and other vulnerable groups. We're hopeful that this initiative will have a major impact, but far more will be needed for the country to turn back its epidemic. India urgently needs more clinics, more condoms,

more testing, more information and more treatment—efforts that require additional resources from rich countries and international agencies.

21   Individuals can make a difference, too—there are things that each of us can do to help stop AIDS around the world. For example, you can educate your friends and family about the disease, volunteer for a local AIDS organization, or ask your lawmakers to increase funding for global AIDS programs. You can also donate to organizations such as the Global Fund to Fight AIDS, TB and Malaria (www.theglobalfund.org), which supports AIDS programs in the hardest-hit countries throughout the world.

22   With the strong support of the international community, I'm confident that India can prevail in its fight against AIDS. If it succeeds, the public health won't be the only benefit—children will thrive, economies will boom, democracies will flourish and women like Gita really shall overcome.

For Class Discussion

1. What is Melinda Gates's main claim in this informal proposal argument?

2. How does she employ evidence from personal experience to develop her proposal?

3. How does she appeal to her readers' emotions and values? What is risky about these appeals?

4. Gates's speech is part of a controversy over effective ways to fight AIDS, to combat human trafficking, and to treat prostitution. John R. Miller, the director of the U.S. State Department's Office to Monitor and Combat Trafficking in Persons, along with the U.S. government, has taken a strong stand against global prostitution. Although Gates's argument does not address alternative views, what questions and objections might John R. Miller raise to Gates's views? (You might investigate Miller's public statements on this controversy, including his response to Gates.)

5. To understand the broader scope of the Gates Foundation's global health work, consult Bill Gates's speech to the World Health Assembly on May 16, 2005, in Geneva, Switzerland, posted on the "Speeches and Commentary" link of the foundation's Web site. How do Bill's four proposals to improve global health relate to Melinda's priorities for combating AIDS in India? In India's efforts to face its AIDS crisis, what role does Melinda assign to medical advances, foreign aid, and social change?

6. What are the strengths and weaknesses of this argument?   ■

Africa's Condom Conundrum: Fighting HIV in Africa

Kingsley Chiedu Moghalu

Kingsley Chiedu Moghalu is an internationally renowned Nigerian diplomat. He graduated from the University of Nigeria, earned his Barrister at Law degree from the Nigerian Law School, and received his doctorate in international relations from the London School of Economics and Political Science. He has appeared on various global media including BBC World Television and CNN, has written as a special correspondent for international newspapers and magazines in Europe and the United States, and is a popular keynote speaker on global issues. As a diplomat with the United Nations, he has worked with UN organizations all over the world. In 1997–2002, he served as counselor to the UN International Criminal Tribunal for Rwanda. Moghalu has written on law and international affairs for scholarly journals and major newspapers and has authored several books, including *Rwanda's Genocide: The Politics of Global Justice* (2005). He has a reputation for strong, active, principled leadership. Since 2002, he has been head of global partnerships at the Global Fund to Fight AIDS, Tuberculosis and Malaria in Geneva, Switzerland. This guest column was posted on the allAfrica.com site on December 1, 2005. AllAfrica Global Media is the "largest electronic distributor of African news and information worldwide" ("Who We Are," www.allafrica.com).

> How does Moghalu shape his argument for both Africans and the larger global audience?

1   A controversy about preventing HIV/AIDS—the most profound strategic threat to Africa's future—has been raging over the past year in Uganda, a country that registered one of the early successes in the fight against the pandemic. Simply put, the debate is about the right mix between sexual abstinence and condom use to prevent and control the spread of AIDS.

2   In all of Africa, and not just in Uganda, the tension between these competing approaches is all too real, with the choice often presented as a dichotomy. Should condoms be promoted, along with an implicit endorsement of sexual freedom, or should they be discouraged in favor of advancing private morality as good public policy?

3   Call it the condom conundrum. The problem arises when, as is often the case, the debate is made into an ideological one that denies the evidence of the scientific benefits of condoms, on the one hand, or the importance of individual moral choices about premarital or extramarital sex as a legitimate response to the pandemic, on

the other. Whatever one may think of the plastic contraption, the reality is that condoms play an important role in the fight against a disease that is spread in Africa mainly through heterosexual sex.

4   The condom conundrum confronts African societies at four main levels—culture, gender, political leadership and religion.

5   The issue of culture embraces technology and its impact on human behavior. Condoms have historically not been a part of sexual relations in African societies. Indigenous African technology never produced a device whose aim was to prevent pregnancy and sexually transmitted diseases at the same time.

6   Natural methods were used for birth control. This situation led to a culture in which condoms, ever since they became part of sexual mores in Africa, have remained an essentially urban phenomenon. Many people in rural Africa have never seen a condom, let alone used one.

7   At the same time, the gender dimension of the fight against AIDS has not been accorded an importance equal to its impact as a cause of the pandemic's spread. The face of AIDS in Africa is mostly female. Sixty per cent of those living with the disease in Africa are women, and the disparity is often even greater among younger age groups.

8   Use of the "c-word" is circumscribed by the history and psychology of how men and women relate in the bedroom and is intrinsically bound in wider issues of gender relations. In many societies, including those of the industrialized global North, women have historically been disempowered—whether by denying them voting rights until well into the 20th century or control over their bodies. African and Islamic societies are not unique in the restrictions they have placed on women, although they have been slower to change. Thus many women, married or unmarried, cannot insist that a man use a condom against his will.

9   This female disempowerment is what has led to the invention of female condoms and microbicides that can help women protect themselves from the HIV virus. But again, few women in Africa know about these things or have access to them.

10   The lack of political leadership is a third factor limiting condom use. The fact that condoms are often seen as a social taboo means that political leaders in Africa do not want to be seen a mile near one—in public at least. As one African leader reportedly told UN Secretary-General Kofi Annan, "I can't utter the word condoms. I'm the father of the nation".

11   That aversion is not universal. When Alpha Konare, the current president of the African Union Commission, was President of Mali, he is reputed to have waved one in public—on television, no less—while talking about sex education and AIDS prevention. Such

political leadership and mobilization at the grassroots level is essential if African countries are to have any chance against HIV/AIDS. It should not be a matter of embarrassment. It is one of life and death.

12   Finally, the tension between religious and social morality and public policy is perhaps the most contentious issue when it comes to condoms. Abstinence, for reasons of spirituality or public health—or both—is a valid approach to fighting AIDS.

13   Posters in Nigeria asking young men and women to "zip up" are not advocating a lifetime ban on close encounters of the intimate kind. They are asking young people to make a choice they can make—to reduce the chance of living with or dying from AIDS by delaying sexual debut, preferably until marriage. Campaigns aimed at delaying sexual debut amongst youth have also emerged in countries like Zambia and South Africa. This campaign is gaining ground even in liberal societies like the United States, where stunningly pretty young women now pop up on television telling their future husbands out there that "you are worth waiting for".

14   What is wrong with this message? Nothing. When we consider that the majority of those living with AIDS are young people in their prime, it becomes clear that their attitudes towards sex affect their health.

15   Many critics of the abstinence message are social libertarians who believe that individual freedom should not be restricted on moral grounds, as was argued among the free sex, marijuana-smoking youth culture of 1960s America. The Nigerian musician Femi Kuti, debunking the United States government's support for abstinence campaigns, recently argued in an interview with the American newsmagazine *Newsweek* that "we were born to have sex". He is entitled to his opinion, but I suspect that is not the advice many parents will be giving their daughters.

16   The political/ideological position that masquerades as a human rights campaign fails to recognize that the public space is often an aggregate of private actions. But the abstinence message runs into difficulties when it is presented as the only acceptable prevention method, especially on religious grounds.

17   The dilemma crops up in the positions of certain influential faiths towards condoms and AIDS. The Catholic Church, for example, has launched a "Marshall Plan" to fight AIDS in Africa, not by joining the condom-distribution chain—it says it will not—but by treating AIDS patients as part of the church's avowed mission to treat the sick.

18   Even here, however, the nagging dilemmas creep in. What of a case where one partner in a Catholic Christian marriage is living

with the virus? Should that partner not use a condom to avoid passing it on to the other?

19   Whatever our personal or religious views about sex outside of marriage, the reality is that not all who wish to abstain succeed in doing so. To preserve their lives—and a chance for a possible latter-day spiritual conversion—they need condoms.

20   Expecting all faith-based organizations to actively encourage the use of condoms may be asking too much. But public health is a legitimate concern and responsibility of governments. They cannot—and should not—discourage or prevent condom use to promote religious doctrine.

21   This is why the "ABC" approach—abstinence, be faithful, and condoms—is the best approach to preventing the spread of HIV/AIDS. Emphasizing one of these three components to the exclusion of the others is not good public health policy. Let the churches and mosques play their role in prevention and treatment. And let the public authorities do their duty to safeguard public health. Neither should stand in the way of the other.

22   But all these methods together have no hope of success in Africa without effective public education about HIV/AIDS. Education, which informs effective prevention, holds the key to breaking the back of AIDS in Africa. When the uninformed man or woman in rural Africa gets to know what this potent virus is, how it is acquired, how to prevent it, and how to live with it when the all-important prevention fails, then he or she will know that the "wasting disease" is often a consequence of preventable behavior. It is not "witchcraft".

For Class Discussion

1. How does Moghalu show that sometimes the way that an issue is framed can contribute to the problem? How does the word "conundrum" serve his purpose?

2. In presenting the African controversy over using condoms in AIDS prevention, what main points does Moghalu make? How does he show his knowledge of African cultures?

3. What various alternative views is Moghalu addressing?

4. Why do you think that Moghalu saves the full statement of his position on AIDS prevention until the end of his article? How rhetorically effective is the structure of this argument?

5. Whom does Moghalu hope to persuade with his argument? How has he influenced your thinking about AIDS prevention in Africa?

African Perspective on AIDS Crisis Differs from West

Raymond Downing

Raymond Downing is an American physician who has practiced family medicine in Sudan, Tanzania, and now Kenya for fifteen years. He writes and speaks on the West's need to see Africa's health problems through African eyes and in a larger cultural, political, and economic context. Downing has authored two books that reflect his experiences and share his insights: *The Wedding Goes on Without Us* (2002) and *As They See It: The Development of the African AIDS Discourse* (2005). This article was published in the *National Catholic Reporter* on January 21, 2005. Valuing high-quality and frank intellectual exchange, this publication "emphasizes solidarity with the oppressed and respect for all. It understands that peace, justice, and integrity of environment are not only goals but also avenues of life" ("About Us," www.natcath.com).

> Raymond Downing begins his article by articulating ideas and misunderstandings that he believes his primary readers, American Catholics, hold about AIDS in Africa. What are these ideas? Why is this rhetorical strategy a good one?

1   Americans sometimes think the main question facing those involved with AIDS in Africa is whether they have access to antiretroviral drugs. For American Catholics, it seems the main question is whether or not to use condoms to prevent AIDS. However, these are not the most pivotal concerns for Africans, including African Catholics. It is more difficult to summarize African perspectives in a single sentence, and partly because of this, most of us don't know what they are.

2   We should. Two-thirds of the world's AIDS burden is in Africa. A careful review of African writings reveals that Africans and Westerners do not always view the world with the same questions, concerns and emphases. Before we suggest—and fund—programs to control AIDS in Africa, we need to be aware of how Africans understand their own epidemic. A good starting place is the writings of three African priests.

3   In 1992, Fr. Laurenti Magesa published "AIDS and Survival in Africa: A Tentative Reflection." This was the last chapter in a collection of essays by African authors titled *Moral and Ethical Issues in African Christianity,* published only in Africa. Fr. Magesa is a Catholic priest and moral theologian, sometimes serving as a parish priest in Tanzanian villages, sometimes teaching in African or U.S. universities.

4   He begins with an observation that is still true 12 years later: "Two distinct tendencies characterize discourse on AIDS in Africa. One tendency caricatures the continent and all but defines Africa in

terms of the epidemic. . . . The other [recognizes] AIDS is a problem 'with social and political causes and hence in theory resoluble.'"

5   He then suggests three ways to understand AIDS in Africa— three "cosmologies." The first is the traditional one, where people see AIDS as a matter of magic and taboo, with the appropriate response being ritual. While this view still clearly influences how people behave, it is "inadequate from the contemporary standpoint. . . . There can be no going back completely to that cosmological view." The third cosmology is the modern view, which sees AIDS as linked to sexual activity, with the appropriate response being sexual continence. While this is clearly a reasonable goal, in 1992 Fr. Magesa doubted that it was the predominant cosmology of most Africans. The number of AIDS cases was—and still is—rising across the continent; the direct link between AIDS and sexual activity, and the response to limit sexual activity, had clearly not yet happened.

6   Between these two cosmologies, Fr. Magesa proposes a second approach, one that sees AIDS as "directly linked to sexual activity," but with people responding in a "confused" or "muddled" way. "In response to the threat of certain death caused by the disease, [their] behavior is not appropriate; it indicates nonchalance or even help- lessness." It is this cosmology, "the confused view," that Fr. Magesa sees as predominating in Africa today.

7   The priest goes on to consider which countries are most affected by AIDS. His discussion of "the AIDS map of Africa" leads back directly to why people might be confused. While "massive sociopo- litical upheavals" and poverty both are important in the spread of AIDS, he says, these factors alone cannot account for why some regions are more heavily affected than others. He then proposes that religion is an important factor: places with low AIDS prevalence "have either a predominantly Muslim or a non-Western (deeply indigenous) Christian influence." In contrast, places with high AIDS prevalence "have a predominantly Western Christian influence."

8   The point is not that the doctrines or practices of Islam are more AIDS-protective than those of Christianity; they are in fact similar. Rather, Islam "adapted itself more readily and much more thor- oughly to significant aspects of African traditional views of sex and sexuality." Christianity, on the other hand, "was overwhelmed by its Western cultural medium, and negated and undermined in real life what it taught in theory. Thus, while not consciously intending it, Western Christianity seems to have encouraged in Africa an unprecedented libertarian sexual behavior. Contrary to the African communitarian, taboo and ritual cosmological approach, sexual rela- tions came to be seen as a private matter of the individuals con- cerned. The consequences of the use of one's sexual powers to the community of the living and the dead faded into the background."

9   Fr. Magesa suggests that behavior modification must be the main focus in the struggle to contain the AIDS epidemic, and that this modification should include two aspects: structural change (economic development, political stability, control of sex tourism, and improved health systems) and a moral or ethical approach. However, this ethical approach must be rooted in "traditional African cosmology"—it is not meant to "resurrect a dead past" but to use "cultural elements still extant in the African social psyche. . . . Completely alien, borrowed solutions will hardly work." He then summarizes, in one sentence, what must be at the core of an African-rooted approach: "Besides the profound sense of God and the hereafter, [there is] the perception of life as the ultimate good and . . . community as the context of the possibility of human existence." Another African theologian who has written about AIDS is Fr. Benezet Bujo, a Congolese Catholic priest who has taught in African universities and is now teaching in Switzerland. In 1993 he published a book in German, which came out in English in 1998 as *The Ethical Dimension of Community: The African Model and the Dialogue Between North and South.* Near the end of this book was his chapter on AIDS: "The Importance of the Community for Ethical Action: The Example of AIDS."

10   For Fr. Bujo, community is foundational in an understanding of African cosmology. "The individual knows him- or herself to be immersed in the community to such an extent that personality can develop only in and through it." Consequently, "because no clan member can live in unrelatedness, in cases of misfortune the cause is looked for within the community itself. According to African wisdom, a disease is always an indication that something in human relations is wrong." Later in the chapter, Fr. Bujo makes it clear that since AIDS is an international disease, it is reasonable to apply these principles internationally: "The problem of this disease is not an individual question alone, but possibly first of all a structural one." The community here is the entire world, and the disordered structures Fr. Bujo sees are ones well-known to NCR readers: unjust economic policies established by the Northern countries, poverty, Third World debt, etc.

11   Naturally, "the reformation of our society is a task which cannot be mastered by the individual alone." Yet "in the discussion concerning AIDS, one often gets the impression that prevention of this epidemic is possible if the individual behaves more carefully." Then, using his own thoughts together with quotes from others, Fr. Bujo shows the inadequacy of an individual behavior-change approach: "'If an information campaign is satisfied with advertising condoms, without exposing the deeper causes and ignoring the ethical questions, then one is merely treating the symptoms.'

Advertising condoms rather promotes the consumer mentality, reducing sexuality to a commodity. . . . Only an ethical conviction is able to fight this consumer mentality efficiently and to restore sexuality its dignity. . . . 'Neither purely technical advice (use condoms, prevent AIDS!) nor moral admonitions (remain faithful!) are sufficient to control the disease. The prevention and stopping of AIDS does not depend solely on the individual but on the quality of our institutions, changes in culture, economy and politics as well.'"

12   Note carefully: Fr. Bujo is not against condoms because the church requires him to be. In fact, neither he nor Fr. Magesa rules out the use of condoms. He is, rather, cautioning against individual approaches to a disease that has communal causes. He is concerned with "condomization" and its effects on Africa. Fr. Bujo puts it this way: "From an African perspective, it is to be stated that an indiscriminate distribution of condoms ultimately wipes out African culture." He is arguing here as an African, not a priest. In fact, mentioning aspects of African tradition which "prepare for sexual self-discipline," he says, "colonial policy and European Christianity have already destroyed this cultural background. . . . If the industrialized nations wish to help Africa, they should offer their support in such a way that the African people can recover their spiritual and moral immunity, which cannot be underestimated even if it does not offer or replace a technical solution for AIDS".

13   Ultimately, this loss of African culture hurts not only Africa but the entire world community. "The African community understands itself as a healing community," but this self-understanding is under threat. When Western medicine was brought to Africa by the colonists, it "was never integrated into people's consciousness; [rather] colonial systems destroyed the African medical tradition which could no longer be effectively applied. For even if the Western type of medicine proved to be more efficient in many cases, the holistic approach to medicine was lost, since the modern method of treatment looked at the person merely from the viewpoint of 'repairing' one's organs."

14   The third African priest is Fr. Emmanuel Katongole, a Ugandan who teaches part time at Uganda Martyrs University and part time at Duke University in the United States. His contribution is the paper "AIDS, Ethics and Society in Africa: Exploring the Limits of an Ethics of Suspicion," which he presented at a conference at Uganda Martyrs University in 2000. He begins with the assumption that Western approaches are now preeminent in the fight against AIDS, and asks how these approaches have affected Africa: "As we make particular decisions and choices what sort of people are we becoming?"

15   He suggests that many Western views of Africa contain misleading and racist attitudes, with the result that the objects of these

views—first the scholars and intellectuals, but eventually all Africans—become suspicious of the West. He sees this suspicion increasing as a result of the AIDS epidemic and the West's narrow approach to it, which "narrowly focuses on 'viral infection' and overlooks the wider economic and political and general health conditions in Africa."

16   Though "we [may] need a certain measure of suspicion as part of the practical wisdom of everyday life and survival," says Fr. Katongole, becoming suspicious has a cost. Africans have not only become suspicious of the West, he says, but they have also been told by the Western approach to AIDS to become suspicious of each other.

17   I remember in the early '80s when, at least in Uganda, billboards warning against the spread of HIV infection carried the picture of what was obviously a married couple with their three young children and bore the caption: "Love Faithfully to Avoid AIDS." This recommendation was soon replaced by the Uganda AIDS Commission with what was seen to be a more potent picture: two young lovers in embrace, with the caption: "Love Carefully." What the Uganda AIDS Commission might not have realized, but what in fact it was confirming was the realization that with AIDS even lovers cannot (or is it, should not) trust each other fully (love faithfully), but must learn the art of loving "carefully," that is, suspiciously. Apparently it did not take a long time to realize that such "careful" love involves regarding the partner as potential danger from which one had to "protect" oneself. Thus, by mid '90s the captions had changed again, this time from "Love Carefully" to "Use a Condom to Avoid AIDS."

18   The West may have long ago adopted this mutual suspicion, but it is new to Africa. This "radical suspicion generated by AIDS gnaws at the very core of our self-understanding, and thus threatens the basic trust on which our individual and societal existence is based," the priest notes.

19   Instead of addressing how Africans can rebuild trust, the West has promoted condoms. One of the leading Western brands is even called Trust. This process of sidestepping the fundamental issues Fr. Katongole calls "condomization": "The issue of course is not whether condoms do or do not protect against the spread of AIDS. . . . The issue is about the sort of culture which 'condomization' promotes, and the sort of people we become as a result." Condomization becomes a "metaphor for the incursion of postmodern culture in Africa."

20   Fr. Katongole, as an African, describes three fundamental problems with that incursion. Condoms are disposable, like so many other aspects of Western culture. But condomization "is not just about the convenience of disposable condoms, but more importantly it is about the popularization of a certain form of sexual activity, i.e., one detached from any serious attachment or stable

commitment. In other words, condomization encourages one to view sex and one's sex partner(s) as essentially disposable, while at the same time parading such lack of attachment as a high mark of freedom and accomplishment."

21   This "freedom" is the second problem with condomization. Using a condom seems to confer immediate freedom—but, of course, "freedom does not come naturally, but is a result of training into the relevant virtues of chastity, fidelity and self-control." That, at least, is the teaching of church and tribal traditions. Without this training, these "free" people become "free-floating individuals who easily become prey to their own whimsical needs and choices."

22   These whimsical choices Fr. Katongole calls "nihilistic playfulness," the third problem with the incursion of postmodern culture into Africa. When people begin to adopt this postmodern worldview, he says, "we lose not only the possibility of locating ourselves within any meaningful material economic practices and history, but even more crucially, we become increasingly prey to the manipulations and misrepresentations of the media and market forces. . . . It may not be a long shot to see a connection between this form of nihilistic playfulness and the various forms of desperate violence with[in] many countries in Africa. Such violence may be just an indication that the extreme form of cynicism, namely fatalism, is, for many Africans, just around the corner."

23   These views, though presented here in an academic form, are broadly reflective of views I have heard during 15 years of medical mission work in Africa. The questions for these scholars, and for most Africans, are not focused on the microbe, or even how to introduce and fund antiretroviral drug programs. They focus on the overall cultural approach to health and disease. Their concern is not whether or not an individual uses a condom, but rather what is ignored when condoms become the essence of prevention. These people, the ones most affected by this epidemic, have a much broader view than we do. Why don't we listen to them?

For Class Discussion

1. Raymond Downing wants to give Westerners—and particularly American Catholics—an African cultural understanding of AIDS. How does he reframe questions about AIDS, especially those that focus on sexuality?

2. A number of terms are important to Downing's views: "African cosmology," "communitarian approach," "libertarian sexual behavior," "condomization," "postmodern culture," "consumer mentality," and "nihilistic playfulness." Use context to help you define these terms.

3. The bulk of the Downing article is a presentation and synthesis of ideas from the writings of three African priests: Father Laurenti

Magesa from Tanzania, Father Benezet Bujo from the Congo, and Father Emmanuel Katongole from Uganda. In your own words, how would you summarize the ideas of these priests?

4. How does this article support the claim that communal, ethical, and global economic/political approaches to AIDS in Africa offer more hope and chance for success than an "individual behavior-change approach"?

5. Where do Kingsley Moghalu's and Raymond Downing's perspectives on AIDS prevention in Africa converge? Where do they differ?

The Global Challenge of HIV/AIDS: Regional Destabilization, State Collapse and Possible New Breeding Grounds for Terrorism

Gayle Smith

For twenty years, Gayle Smith covered military, economic, and political affairs in Africa, writing for the BBC, Associated Press, Reuters, and *Boston Globe,* among other news services. She has been special assistant to President Clinton, senior director for African affairs at the National Security Council from 1998 to 2001, and a member of the Council on Foreign Relations. In 1999 she won the National Security Council's Samuel Nelson Drew Award for Distinguished Contribution to Pursuit of Global Peace. She also coauthored *The Other War: Global Poverty and the Millennium Challenge Account* (2003) at The Brookings Institution and currently is a senior fellow at the Center for American Progress, a nonpartisan think tank committed to seeking "progressive and pragmatic solutions to significant domestic and international problems" and to developing "policy proposals that foster a government 'of the people, by the people, and for the people'" ("About Us," www.americanprogress.org). Smith's presentation, given at the International Film and Television Exchange and Congressional Human Rights Caucus on April 20, 2005, was posted on the Web site for the Center for American Progress. ("PEPFAR" in paragraphs 16 and 17 stands for "President's Emergency Plan for AIDS Relief," a $1.5 billion initiative to combat the global HIV/AIDS pandemic that involves numerous NGOs, community groups, international organizations, and commercial companies.)

What background knowledge of political problems in Africa and of U.S. policies toward fighting AIDS in developing countries does Gayle Smith assume that her audience has?

1   Let me begin by thanking the International Film and Television Exchange and the Congressional Human Rights Caucus for focusing on this critical issue. Five years ago, the Clinton administration declared the global HIV/AIDS pandemic a national security threat, generating new interest in some quarters and disdain from many others. But as the *Washington Post* reported at the time, the threat was real: "Interagency Intelligence Memorandum 91-10005, distributed in classified channels . . . foretold one of the deadliest calamities in human experience. Titled simply, 'The Global AIDS Disaster,' the report projected 45 million infections by 2000—inexorably fatal, the great majority in Africa. The numbers begged comparison. There were not that many combatants killed in World War I, World War II, Korea and Vietnam combined."

2   Today, there is widespread agreement that the HIV/AIDS pandemic does, in fact, threaten the security of countries throughout the developing world and indeed our own. The numbers are staggering, and the resources pledged over the last five years—including through the President's Emergency Program for AIDS Relief—make clear that the world is paying attention.

3   But staggering as they may be, the numbers fail to convey the real and much more horrifying structural dimensions of this crisis. AIDS not only kills people, it also hollows out the core of societies, weakening the ability of communities, states and entire regions to forge and maintain the social, political and economic institutions necessary for peace and security.

4   AIDS kills off the most productive members of society, the able-bodied men and women who work the land and man the factories. It decimates the structure of the extended family by killing off those who care for the young and for the old. It thins the ranks of the lawyers, doctors, nurses, teachers, financial managers and planners who allow states to function.

5   Its impact is even more severe in situations of conflict, where surveillance is uneven if undertaken at all. No one really knows what HIV prevalence rates are in the Democratic Republic of the Congo, and even in post-war Angola, the ravages of conflict continue to undermine surveillance and treatment regimes. In war zones, HIV is spread, unrestricted, by soldiers and the civilian victims forced to flee their homes. Where predatory movements reign, it is impossible to provide sustained and consistent care and treatment, and even in cases where opposing armies might allow AIDS programs, implementation is rendered uneven.

6   In essence, the HIV/AIDS pandemic weakens stable and productive states, and undermines efforts to render weak or post-conflict states more secure.

7   Tackling the structural impact of HIV/AIDS will require more than awareness and an increased budget. This morning I would like to focus on seven key challenges and briefly comment on how we can begin to meet them.

8   First, we need to turn the conventional paradigm on its head. The HIV/AIDS pandemic is rightly regarded as an emergency, but this designation should not cause us to fashion a response that is more characteristic of relief than long-term development. Looking to the world's experience in responding to other "humanitarian" disasters, like famines in Africa, we see that while the international community rallies to provide emergency food aid, water and life-saving medical care, it is less able—or inclined—to make the long-term investments required to reverse structural food deficits. I believe that we are at risk of making the same mistake in dealing with the HIV/AIDS pandemic.

9   It is no coincidence that HIV prevalence is greater in the world's poorest and weakest countries, for it is in these places that there is little with which to counter the spread of the disease—infrastructure is limited in scope and poorly maintained; health services and educational facilities are limited; budgets are constrained by debt, a reliance on primary commodities, and the skewed terms of global trade.

10   If we want to avoid the "relief trap" and prevent the state weakness and insecurity that the HIV/AIDS pandemic can sow, we must be prepared to make major new investments aimed at reducing poverty and strengthening the capacity of governments and communities to manage an epidemic that will, tragically, likely be with us for generations to come. This demands that we consider an increase in the overall aid budget and a redoubling of our efforts to erode the gains of global poverty. In particular, it requires that we invest in infrastructure—a sector that the United States has turned away from over the last 15 years. Infrastructure is expensive, but think of the impact—the same physical infrastructure needed for the delivery of vital medicines also serves local trade, the expansion of health and educational services, the investment that these countries desperately need, the movement of humanitarian goods and services in times of crisis, and the basic supplies upon which people depend. It is expensive, but it is a wise investment.

11   The United States is well placed to take a lead in this regard by endorsing and acting upon the recommendations of the report of Prime Minister Tony Blair's Africa Commission at the G8 Summit in July.

12   Second, we must also avoid looking at and responding to global HIV/AIDS as an isolated issue, for by its very nature, the disease has a direct impact on governance, economic development, security, the provision of social services and even basic food production. At present, the HIV/AIDS pandemic is weakening states and communities faster than we can strengthen them.

13   We are all aware of the threats posed by weak states, as no one can forget that it was from Afghanistan that the al Qaeda network mounted its attack on the United States almost four years ago. And though there are many more Afghanistans out there, few countries are confronting this threat head on, with perhaps the UK's Department for International Development being the primary exception.

14   President Bush rightly pointed to the threat posed to America by weak states in his 2002 National Security Strategy, but three years later we have no plan, no dedicated resources, and no evident political commitment to making the investments necessary to counter this threat. Important as it may be to invest in countries that are functioning well, the new Millennium Challenge Account is not the answer, as we must not only invest in capable states, but also invest in making more states more capable.

15   I would like to here refer you to the report and recommendations of the bipartisan Commission on Weak States and National Security, a project of the Center for Global Development of which I was proud to be a member. As our report demonstrates, the threat is real but the options for tackling it are many.

16   Third, we need to reconsider our enthusiasm for selectivity. Often, because aid budgets are limited and we want to demonstrate impact, we select individual countries to be aid recipients. As well, and particularly in the world's poorest regions, we provide little other than humanitarian aid to countries ruled by authoritarian regimes. Though these choices may reflect a particular logic, however, they contradict the logic of AIDS—a disease that knows no borders and threatens equally democracies and dictatorships. We cannot afford to pursue an AIDS strategy that overlooks countries that may threaten entire regions, and where our failure to respond will only ensure that future democratic change is impeded. In light of this fact, I would strongly recommend that future deliberations on PEPFAR include consideration of an expanded and comprehensive focus rather than a country-specific approach.

17   Fourth, we need to reduce the additional burdens we impose by our failure to coordinate donor assistance, harmonize our policies and standardize our requirements. The Global Fund for AIDS, TB and Malaria was created, in part, to address this problem, and to reduce the management demands of donors upon countries that have limited capacity—and where that capacity is being further eroded by the AIDS crisis. If we really want to help governments tackle the challenges they face, the United States should be doing more, not less, to support the Global Fund, and should use PEPFAR as an instrument for forging greater donor coherence.

18   Fifth, and in countries at war or emerging from conflict, we should incorporate AIDS strategies into our conflict resolution efforts. During the civil war in El Salvador in the 1980s, for example,

UNICEF successfully negotiated "Days of Tranquility" to allow for the implementation of vaccination campaigns. While managing HIV and AIDS requires more than the limited access provided by that model, negotiating "peace corridors" could, for example, allow for AIDS education and treatment along transport routes, within militaries, or among refugee or displaced populations. Similarly, incorporating AIDS programming into immediate post-conflict efforts can allow for the prompt resumption of surveillance efforts while also serving as a non-controversial confidence building measure.

19   Sixth and finally, if we want to have an impact, we need to use as our guide good science and not ideology. I hope that those of you in attendance have read the recent report from Human Rights Watch entitled "The Less They Know, the Better." The report chronicles the extraordinary story of how Uganda—the country that proved to the world that a comprehensive approach to HIV and AIDS could reduce prevalence rates by pursuing what has been called an "ABC" strategy—"Abstinence, Be Faithful, Use Condoms"—has now issued a draft "AB" policy. The report refers to interviews with Ugandan teachers who report that USAID-funded trainers are encouraging them to omit information about condoms from their educational messages. Combined, the policies being pursued by the Ugandan and U.S. governments are likely to result in a national condom shortage.

20   Abstinence is a legitimate moral and personal choice—but it does not constitute a health strategy. And for literally millions of women around the world, it is not even a choice. If we really want to win the war against AIDS, and if we believe that it does pose a threat to our national security, then we must use every means available to conquer it. To do less is to condemn millions to death.

For Class Discussion

1. Gayle Smith's policy proposal follows a typical problem-solution structure. How does she convey the importance and urgency of the problem she is addressing?

2. What is Smith's main claim? What strategies for dealing with the developing world's crisis with AIDS does she sketch out?

3. Identify and explain the following key terms and concepts: "the relief trap," "the logic of AIDS," "donor coherence," and "a health strategy." What other terms are essential to Smith's argument?

4. Where does Smith acknowledge and respond to strong opposing views?

5. Smith's argument is cerebral and abstract rather than vivid and moving. If she were going to give this speech to an audience other

than policymakers and political analysts, what would you suggest she change?

6. After reading this speech, what questions would you like to ask Smith?

7. What contribution does this argument make to the public conversation over the role of developed countries in helping poor countries fight AIDS? ∎

AIDS Prevention Images from Africa

The following three visuals illustrate the efforts of African countries to tackle their AIDS crisis by preventing the spread of HIV.

What details and features stand out for you in the two African posters and the billboard shown in Figures 9.2, 9.3, and 9.4?

Using materials such as this "No Matter How Much You Trust Him" poster (p. 534), the Zambian HEART (Helping Each Other Act Responsibly Together) Campaign seeks "to promote healthy sexual behaviors among young people and reduce HIV transmission among this group" particularly through condom use but also through abstinence.* Its primary target audience is young people ages thirteen through nineteen.

The second poster (p. 535) comes from the small sub-Saharan African country of Lesotho, where around 11 percent of the population has HIV/AIDS. In conjunction with the World Health Organization, the advocacy organization Positive Action has designed a poster and billboard campaign to alert local communities to the dangers of HIV/AIDS and to promote behavioral change and AIDS prevention. Positive Action's posters are drawn by local artists, written in English and Sesotho, and displayed in banks, businesses, and government offices.†

The third image (p. 536) is a photograph of a billboard on the border between Namibia and Botswana taken by Australian Neil Shedden when he visited South Africa, Namibia, Botswana, and Zimbabwe.

For Class Discussion

1. Briefly describe each poster/billboard. What is the style of each (realistic, cartoonish, dramatic, glamorous) and tone (serious, cautionary,

---

*PlusNews Poster Gallery is an archive of anti-AIDS campaigns in Africa, www.irinnews.org/aids/postergallery/.
†Positive Action—HIV/AIDS in Lesotho, www.positive-action.org.

FIGURE 9.2   No Matter How Much You Trust Him *(© PSI, 2005. Used with permission)*

humorous, optimistic)? What do the female and male figures in each poster contribute to the message?

2. What does the text contribute to the rhetorical effect of each poster and billboard?

3. How do these posters and the billboard appeal to viewers' emotions and understanding?

4. How do these posters and the billboard address the African cultural and social issues discussed in the readings in this chapter?

FIGURE 9.3   Being HIV Positive Is Not a Shame!!! *(© Positive Action)*

What response would Kingsley Moghalu, Raymond Downing, and the priests Downing quotes in his article have to these AIDS awareness campaigns? You might want to investigate the PlusNews Poster Gallery (www.irinnews.org/aids/postergallery/) for other AIDS awareness campaigns in Africa. What other strategies and appeals are these organizations using? Which poster campaigns appear to be speaking especially to each of these target groups: men, women, teens, and girls?

FIGURE 9.4 AIDS Prevention Billboard *(© Neil Shedden, 2005. http//home.vicnet.net./au/ ~neils/africa/aids_border.htm.)*

AIDS Has a Woman's Face
Stephen Lewis

Stephen Lewis has been a teacher, politician, diplomat, and human rights advocate. From 1984 to 1988, he was the Canadian ambassador to the United Nations. Lewis was active in drafting the UN Programme on African Economic Recovery, and he currently is serving as the secretary general's special envoy for HIV/AIDS in Africa. Lewis's lifelong commitment to improving the lives of Africans has been institutionalized in the Stephen Lewis Foundation, a grassroots organization devoted to working particularly with women, girls, and children struggling with AIDS and its destruction. This article, an excerpt of a speech Lewis delivered at the Microbicides 2004 conference in London, appeared in the fall 2004 issue of *Ms. Magazine*, a liberal feminist magazine committed to social justice and action. (Microbicides are microbe- or germ-killing topical gels, creams, or suppositories, still in the experimental phase, that would prevent the transmission of HIV and STDs.)

> What features of the article suggest that Lewis is writing to an audience that is well educated and well informed about AIDS as well as highly invested in the welfare of women?

1   There's an amiable irrationality in racing across the ocean for a half-hour speech. But the discovery and availability of microbicides is one of the great causes of this era. Here is where morality and science join.

2   If there's one constant throughout the years I've been U.N. Special Envoy—years spent traversing the African continent—it's the thus-far irreversible vulnerability of women. It goes without saying that the virus has targeted women with a raging, Darwinian ferocity. It goes equally without saying that gender inequality is what sustains and nurtures the virus, causing women to be infected in ever greater, disproportionate numbers. The report issued by UNAIDS on the eve of the 2002 International AIDS Conference identified startling percentages of infected women. UNICEF's Carol Bellamy used a phrase there that would become a mantra: "AIDS has a woman's face."

3   Women's acute vulnerability didn't happen overnight. What should shock us is how long the world took to focus. Why was it only in 2003 that a U.N. Task Force on the plight of women in Southern Africa was appointed? Why did it take until 2004 to form a Global Coalition on Women and AIDS? Why have we allowed a continuing pattern of sexual carnage so grave as to lose an entire generation of women and girls?

4   In 2003, Botswana did a study on HIV prevalence. In urban areas, for women and girls ages 15 to 19, the prevalence rate was 15.4 percent; for men and boys the same age, 1.2 percent. For women between 20 and 24, the rate was 29.7 percent; for men that age, 8.4 percent. For women between 25 and 29, the rate was 54.1 percent, for men, 29.7 percent.

5   The reason we've observed—and still do, without taking decisive action—this wanton attack on women is because it's happening to women. You know it and I know it. African countries, external powers, bilateral donors, even the U.N.—no one shouted from rhetorical rooftops or called an international conference, although in the 1990s it seemed that all we had time for were international conferences.

6   This is the ultimate vindication of the feminist analysis.

7   When the rights of women are involved, the world goes into reverse.

8   For more than 20 years, the numbers of infected women grew exponentially. Now, virtually half the infections in the world are among women—and in Africa the rate is 58 percent, rising to 75 percent between the ages of 15 and 24. This is a cataclysm. Yet while finally (after the doomsday clock passed midnight) we're starting to get agitated, little is changing. Please believe me. On the ground, where women live and die, very little is changing.

9   A few years ago, I visited the prenatal health clinic in Kigali, Rwanda, meeting with women who had decided to take a course of nevirapine. They were excited and hopeful, but asked a poignant question: "We'll do anything to save our babies, but what about us?" Back then, more than four years after antiretrovirals were in widespread use in the West, we simply watched the mothers die.

10   Today, thanks to the Columbia School of Public Health, funded by several foundations and USAID, and working with the Elizabeth Glaser Foundation, UNICEF and governments, the strategy of PMTCT-Plus (Prevention of Mother to Child Transmission Plus) has begun in several countries, where the "Plus" represents treatment of the mothers and partners—indeed, the entire family. But it's a slow, incremental process. In principle, the majority of such women will one day fall under public antiretroviral treatment through their ministries of health. But there's no guarantee of when, or if, that day will dawn. It's entirely possible that men will be at the front of the bus.

11   Everything proceeds at a glacial pace when responding to the needs and rights of women. We deplore patterns of sexual violence against women—violence that transmits the virus—but the malevolent patterns continue. We lament the use of rape as an instrument of war, but in eastern Congo and western Sudan, possibly the worst-known episodes of sexual cruelty and mutilation are occurring, and the world barely notices. We see Rwanda's women survivors, now suffering full-blown AIDS, demonstrating how such stories end. We talk of amending property rights and introducing laws on inheritance rights, but I've yet to see marked progress. We speak of paying women for unacknowledged, uncompensated work; ushering in a cornucopia of income-generating activities. In a few places this is happening, especially where local women's leadership is strong enough to take hold. But mostly, in Churchill's phrase, it's "Jaw, jaw, jaw."

12   For much of my adult life, I've felt the gender-equality struggle is the toughest struggle of all. Never have I felt it more keenly than in the battle against HIV/AIDS. The women of Africa (and elsewhere) run the household, grow the food, assume virtually the entire burden of care, raise the orphans, and do it all with unimaginable stoicism. As recompense for this life of hardship and devotion, they die agonizing deaths. While it's possible that we'll make more progress over the next five years than in the past 20, I can't emphasize enough how the inertia and sexism that plague our response are almost indelibly ingrained.

13   People ask, "What about the men? We have to work with the men." Of course we do. But please recognize that it will take generations to change predatory male sexual behavior. The women of Africa are dying today.

14   Which is where microbicides come in. I'm not pretending they're a magic bullet or vaccine, or that we can forget cultural changes urgently required. But when the landscape is so bleak, the prospect of a microbicide in five to 10 years is intoxicating. That women will have a way to reassert control over their sexuality and

defend their health, have a course of prevention, perhaps have a microbicide that prevents infection but allows for conception; that women can use microbicides without bowing to male dictates—indeed, men won't even know the microbicide is in use—these are ideas whose time has come. Resources of the international community should flow, torrentially, toward this end. Microbicides as a solution would pale if we were making progress on other fronts. But we're not—or we are, but in tiny installments.

15   I don't know how to convey what's happening out there. I travel from country to country, through rural hinterlands, seeing project after project. Everywhere the lives of women are compromised. How do we get governments, international financial institutions and bilateral development donors to understand? It's not changing.

16   Certain incidents sear themselves into the mind.

17   A grandmother, age 73, in Alexandra Township, Johannesburg. She lost all five of her children between 2001 and 2003. She tends four orphans, all HIV-positive. She's one of the legion of African grandmothers who, in a reversal of life's rhythm, bury their children and then, heroically, raise their grandchildren.

18   In Uganda, a child-headed household: a girl of 14, who cares for two sisters, 12 and 10, and two brothers, 11 and 8. This is common across the continent. The mothers are gone.

19   At a clinic in Zambia, where mothers come for testing and the possible use of nevirapine during birth, the women say: "You have drugs in your country to keep your people alive. Why can't we?" I don't know how to answer this question about one of the ugliest chasms between the developing and developed world.

20   In Swaziland, I trek into the bush to visit a small community of women living with AIDS, caring for hordes of orphans. They lead us to the home of a dying woman. I've spent a lot of time in huts where women lie dying. But I've never seen anyone this ill, her face a mask of death: a young woman—they're always in their 20s—valiantly raising her head a few inches to acknowledge visitors. Her children are watching her die. That's what children in Africa do: become orphans while their parents are dying. Then they watch the death itself. Then they attend the funeral.

21   I'm filled with a rage I can barely contain, though I know it reduces my effectiveness. The madness—that what's happening is so unnecessary, that we could subdue this pandemic if the world put its mind to it—renders me almost incoherent.

22   I ask that you see microbicides not merely as one of the great scientific pursuits of the age, but as a significant emancipation for women whose cultural, social and economic inheritance have put them so gravely at risk. Never in human history have so many died for so little reason. It must not continue.

For Class Discussion

1. Stephen Lewis conducts several causal arguments in this article. How would you map out his causal reasoning about the social status of women and the statistics about women and AIDS?

2. How does Lewis try to engage his audience's emotions and make the lives of Africans living with AIDS real to them?

3. How do Lewis's personal experience and conviction contribute to his argument? What image of his own credibility and authority does he convey?

4. What method of combating AIDS does Lewis favor and promote? What is his rationale?

5. What opposing views does he acknowledge and address?

6. How has this article influenced your view of the challenge of fighting AIDS in the developing world? (You might want to investigate the Global Campaign for Microbicides.) ∎

Bad Blood
Jonathan Rauch

Jonathan Rauch, a graduate of Yale University, is a nationally known journalist who writes on wide-ranging subjects, from biotechnology to culture, foreign affairs, and law. He is a columnist for the *National Journal*, a biweekly Washington magazine, and publishes regularly in the *Atlantic*. In addition, his writing frequently appears in the *New Republic, the Economist, Harper's, Reason*, the *New York Times*, and *Slate*, among other prestigious publications. In 2005 he won the National Magazine Award for his columns and commentary. Rauch has written a number of books including *Gay Marriage: Why It Is Good for Gays, Good for Straights, and Good for America* (2004). The following piece was posted on *Reasononline* for January 12, 2004. *Reasononline* is the Web version of *Reason*, a libertarian monthly magazine dedicated to "free minds and free markets" and to "making a principled case for liberty and individual choice in all areas of human activity" ("About Us," www.Reason.com/aboutreason.shtm/).

Why would Rauch's view interest *Reasononline* readers and how does he try to reach these readers emotionally and intellectually in this piece?

1   A year ago, in his 2003 State of the Union message, President Bush announced an unprecedented U.S. effort against the global spread of AIDS. After a slow start, the United States has come to recognize that AIDS, especially in Africa, is not just a humanitarian calamity

but also a threat to international prosperity and stability. The president himself, by various accounts, has become a true believer. "To meet a severe and urgent crisis abroad," he said in that State of the Union speech last year, "tonight I propose the Emergency Plan for AIDS Relief—a work of mercy beyond all current international efforts to help the people of Africa."

2   He called for $15 billion over five years—nearly $10 billion in new money—to prevent 7 million new infections, treat 2 million infected people, and care for 10 million victims and orphans. Though AIDS activists wish for more, even skeptics acknowledge that the scale of this effort makes it a watershed.

3   So listen, people of Africa: Help is on the way. Just one thing. If you have HIV (the virus that causes AIDS), you know those life-saving medicines we'll be sending you? Be sure to hide them, like contraband, when you visit America, because if the immigration authorities discover them in your luggage, you may find yourself on the next plane back home. Better still, never set foot on U.S. soil. If you do get here, make sure the government doesn't find out about your HIV, or you will be deported. American law has a message for you: You have a vile contagion and are not welcome here. Stay out. Go away. Is that clear?

4   As of today, according to the United Nations and the World Health Organization, about one of every 12 adults in sub-Saharan Africa is living with HIV. Counting children as well, almost 30 million Africans have the virus. Unless they are lucky enough to qualify for special waivers, all of these afflicted people are barred from the United States by law. One-quarter of Zimbabwean adults thus cannot come here. One-fifth of South Africans are shut out.

5   The law bars aliens who have HIV whether or not they are sick (not everyone who has HIV gets AIDS) and even if they acquire the virus after they come to America. Of course, many resident aliens have HIV. They just keep their condition out of the sight of the public health authorities—the very people who most need to know about it. After all, if you come from a poor country, being deported with HIV can be a death sentence.

6   Dennis B. Bolt is a 45-year-old Nicaraguan national who has lived in the United States since he was 17 years old. Over the phone from his home in Miami Beach, he talks with a Spanish accent, but his affinities are clearly American. With a vocation as a chef, he has worked in various jobs, and he recently got his associate's degree in hospitality management. He and his partner, an operatic baritone, have been a couple for more than seven years and own their house together.

7   Bolt is HIV-positive. He says he knows for a fact that he was infected in the United States. Nonetheless, his application for legal permanent residence—a green card, as it is popularly known—will

be rejected. His only hope is a long-shot bid for political asylum. If he is deported, could he go to Nicaragua? For HIV, he says, "There is no medical treatment in Nicaragua. It's not available and it's not affordable." Besides, when he goes there, he feels like a stranger. "My home is here," he says. "I've been here for 28 years. I'm going to lose my home and my partner" if forced to leave. He vows to fight to stay "with the last breath I have."

8   Keith (I have changed his name) is a Japanese national in his thirties who has lived in the United States since he arrived for college when he was 18. He found out he had HIV—which he contracted in the United States—while applying for his green card. Unable to stay, he hastily relocated to Canada, leaving behind his long-term partner. Like Bolt, Keith feels the United States is his home. In Japan, he says, "I don't even known how to rent an apartment or open a bank account." And so he lives as an American exile, a thousand miles from the person whom he would rely on if he got AIDS. (He is healthy.)

9   One HIV-positive foreigner who lives here tells of hiding his medications when re-entering after a trip abroad. "People feel like criminals just for having HIV and wanting to visit America," he says. "It's as if it's Iran or something."

10   The ban on aliens with HIV was first imposed administratively, by the Public Health Service, in 1987, when fear of AIDS was at its peak and the disease was effectively untreatable. As therapies became available, public health authorities soon came to believe that the policy merely drove the disease underground and thus was ineffective, if not counterproductive. The first Bush administration and then the Clinton administration tried to revoke it. To no avail: In 1993, Congress wrote the HIV ban into law. No other disease faces such a statutory ban.

11   Even in 1993, the ban made little sense. America was the world's epicenter of AIDS, exporting rather than importing the disease, and so aliens were far more likely to get HIV in America than to bring it in. Anyway, the policy never required an HIV test for entry; only when an alien seeks permanent-resident status, usually after having already been in the country for years, is the blood test routinely required. So the policy, as put into practice, is about kicking people out, not keeping them out.

12   Congress was worried about the costs of welfare and publicly funded care for immigrants with AIDS. A valid concern, but one addressed by the underlying immigration law, which bars aliens deemed likely to become a "public charge," whatever their disease. Today, diabetics and cancer patients can visit and live in the United States on showing they have insurance or resources to keep themselves off the welfare rolls; only people with HIV are barred, whether they are sick or not. This is discrimination, pure and simple.

13   And discrimination—legal discrimination singling out AIDS as an untouchable disease—was in some measure always the point. In the late 1980s and early 1990s, AIDS was a "gay disease," in the public mind if not necessarily in reality. In Senate debate in 1993, then-Sen. Jesse Helms, R-N.C., charged that President Clinton's effort to revoke the HIV ban was a sop "to the AIDS lobby and to the homosexual-rights movement which feeds it." He added, "The Clinton administration's kowtowing to this arrogant and repugnant political group is beyond belief."

14   Times change. In the end, even Helms changed. Now AIDS is ripping through Africa, with parts of Asia and India perhaps not far behind. President Bush is anxious to stop the scourge, which means, above all, fighting the denial, stigma, and discrimination that block prevention and treatment efforts. "The single biggest impediment to fighting AIDS is stigma," says Abner Mason, who chairs the international committee of the Bush administration's Presidential Advisory Commission on HIV/AIDS.

15   In that context, a law singling out and throwing out those with HIV is profoundly unhelpful. "There's no question that we're sending the wrong signal with the ban that is currently in place," says Mason. "The right signal is what President Bush has done, which is, say we're going to spend an enormous amount of money and time and energy getting treatment and care to people who need it in some of the poorest places in the world. The travel ban undermines that signal. We're trying to remove the stigma from having HIV and treat it like any other disease. Now is the time for the United States to get rid of this ban. The only effect of it now is just to create stigma."

16   Moreover, says Mason, some of the best people to provide treatment in Africa are Africans who are themselves infected. In other words, "Some of the best people to implement this program are people we can't bring into this country for training because of the HIV ban."

17   Mason says the AIDS council's international committee favors lifting the ban and will seek the full council's imprimatur, possibly in March. Then the recommendation would go to Bush, who would need to decide whether to take the case to Congress, where being seen as soft on AIDS is never popular.

18   The first Bush administration retreated from its effort to lift the ban at the first sign of political resistance. The Clinton administration tried barely harder, believing, probably correctly, that the cause was lost on Capitol Hill. A decade later, however, AIDS panic has subsided, HIV has become a global threat, and America has a president who promises to lead.

19   "The United States is in a tremendous position to fight this disease," says Mason, "and we need to do everything we can to get unnecessary barriers out of the way." Over to you, President Bush.

For Class Discussion

1. What reasons does Jonathan Rauch give for opposing the U.S. law against aliens with HIV? According to Rauch, why is banning HIV-positive immigrants counterproductive in our fight against AIDS around the world?

2. Why should all Americans know and care about the issue of immigration law and AIDS?

3. What are the reasons behind the discrimination against AIDS?

4. How does Rauch persuade you that he is knowledgeable about this issue?

5. What objections might dissenting readers raise to Rauch's opening examples and his reasons and evidence in this argument?

6. Has Rauch changed your thinking about AIDS and immigrants? Why or why not?

Accelerating Efforts to Achieve Universal Basic Education: A Critical Component of the Global AIDS Response
Global AIDS Alliance

Global AIDS Alliance, founded in 2001, is a nonprofit, Washington-based organization that uses media and education to inspire grassroots participation, to influence policy discussions and campaigns on global AIDS issues, and to ensure that political leaders and their AIDS programs are "advancing a comprehensive, science-based HIV prevention strategy, including condom distribution" ("About Us," www.globalaidsalliance.org). Global AIDS Alliance collaborates with domestic and global HIV/AIDS organizations including UN agencies, human rights advocates, and faith-based groups. This organization directs its attention mainly toward the poor countries most devastated by AIDS and especially concerns itself with AIDS orphans, women, and girls, who suffer in multiple ways from the AIDS pandemic. This advocacy brief was posted on its Web site on May 6, 2005.

The audience for this piece includes policymakers, allied groups, and an interested but general Web readership. How do the layout and format of this policy statement contribute to its rhetorical effectiveness for its readers? Consider the use of headings, sections, and bullets. How does this structure highlight the article's purpose and main ideas?

Global AIDS Alliance

ADVOCACY BRIEF

Accelerating Efforts to Achieve Universal Basic Education:

A Critical Component of the Global AIDS Response

May 6, 2005

"Education is freedom. It provides the tools to affect one's own destiny."—*Oprah Winfrey, November 29, 2004*

"I would like to meet the new President of Kenya. Because he abolished school fees for poor children and a million extra children showed up at school. I think that that's something that's likely to affect more lives positively than almost anything any other political leader will do this year."—*Former President Bill Clinton on ABC's "Primetime Live," November 16, 2004*

"Without achieving gender equality for girls in education, the world has no chance of achieving many of the ambitious health, social and development targets it has set for itself."—*United Nations Secretary-General Kofi Annan, March 3, 2005*

Global AIDS Alliance
1225 Connecticut Avenue, NW, 4th Floor
Washington, DC 20036
www.globalaidsalliance.org

I. SUMMARY

1   In many of the countries hardest hit by the AIDS epidemic, young people ages 15 to 24 now account for 60% of new HIV infections. Almost two-thirds of these newly infected young people are girls, who are highly vulnerable to contracting HIV for a variety of social, cultural, economic, and physiological reasons. Many girls resort to sex with older men, known as "sugar daddies," in order to earn money for themselves and their families to survive and to pay for school-related fees, thereby fostering and accelerating HIV transmission. And they are more likely to be taken out of school to care for sick relatives or to replace family income lost due to AIDS deaths. Orphans are also at higher risk of contracting HIV and much more likely to be forced to leave school.

2   Today, over 113 million children in the world's poorest countries do not attend school, two-thirds of them girls. More than half of the countries that are not on track to reach the goal of universal primary education are also those worst affected by HIV/AIDS. The Global Campaign for Education estimates that if all children received a primary education, as many as 700,000 cases of HIV could be prevented each year. In particular, education is a powerful tool for reducing the social and economic vulnerability that exposes girls and orphans to a high risk of HIV/AIDS. Specifically, girls' education can significantly reduce HIV infection rates by encouraging poverty reduction, gender equality, female empowerment, and awareness of human rights. Education also contributes to female economic independence, delayed marriage, family planning, improved child survival, and work outside the home—all of which can slow and reverse the spread of HIV.

3   In order to expand educational opportunities for girls and orphans and reduce their risk of contracting HIV infection, the Global AIDS Alliance recommends:

- **Eliminate School-Related Fees.** School-related fees prevent millions of children, particularly girls and orphans, from attending school.
- **Mobilize Additional Resources to Achieve Universal Basic Education.** Poor countries need assistance in order to scale up and improve educational systems, as well as to eliminate school fees.
- **Reform Financing and Delivery Mechanisms.** There is an urgent need to reform and accelerate the impact of bilateral education investments and the multilateral Education for All–Fast Track Initiative.

II. POLICY ANALYSIS

4   Health and education drive economic and social progress and are the primary means of reducing the poverty that prevents developing

countries from achieving their full potential. While much remains to be done, important progress is under way to improve health in the world's poorest countries. In particular, the Global Fund to Fight AIDS, TB and Malaria offers a promising new mechanism for mobilizing an expanded response to three of the world's leading killers.

5   The Global AIDS Alliance strongly believes that ensuring universal basic education must be the next major priority toward slowing the spread of AIDS, supporting orphans, and reducing global poverty. Experts agree that basic education ranks among the most effective—and cost-effective—means of HIV prevention. In particular, providing educational opportunities for girls and orphans, who are often excluded from school and at disproportionate risk of HIV infection, will help slow the spread of AIDS.

6   Young people ages 15 to 24 now account for 60% of new HIV infections in many countries. At the same time, AIDS is exacerbating the already desperate situation of children worldwide—devastating families and community support systems, reducing the resources available for basic health, education, and nutrition services, and forcing many youngsters to become caretakers for HIV-infected parents and other family members.

A. Girls Are Especially Vulnerable to HIV/AIDS

7   The physiology of the female genital tract makes women twice as likely to acquire HIV from men as vice versa, and young women are especially vulnerable. Indeed, HIV is spreading faster among teenage girls than in any other group, primarily through sexual relationships with older men who have had much more sexual experience and are more likely to be HIV-infected. In the worst affected areas in sub-Saharan Africa, HIV infection rates among girls ages 15 to 19 are five to six times those of boys in the same age range.

8   Girls' biological vulnerability to HIV is compounded by a host of factors that put them at special risk, including poverty, gender inequality, lack of educational opportunities, and practices such as female genital mutilation. Child-rearing practices and initiation messages encourage girls to be nonassertive and to accept subordinate status in relation to men. And social and cultural norms inhibit girls' discussion of sexual health and accord inferior status to girls. Finally, as parents fall ill and die of AIDS, family burdens shift to children. Students—especially girls—are often forced to leave school and take on adult responsibilities, such as earning income, procuring food, and caring for the ill. In many cases, these

responsibilities can only be fulfilled by selling sex for money. In addition:

- Girls lack the power to protect themselves against sexual violence. In South Africa, 40 to 47% of all rapes involve girls aged 15 or younger.
- Child marriage is another risk factor for girls. Few girls continue to attend school after marrying, and many are exposed to HIV by their husbands. In fact, married adolescent girls tend to have higher HIV infection rates than their sexually active unmarried peers.
- Perversely, poorly monitored schools can pose a danger to girls. In one Ugandan district, 31% of schoolgirls reported being sexually abused, mainly by teachers. And many girls are harassed traveling to and from school.

B. Orphans Are Also at Disproportionate Risk of HIV

9   HIV/AIDS is leaving a generation of orphans in its wake. Over 14 million children have already lost one or both parents to HIV/AIDS—the equivalent of every child under five in America. It is projected that 25 million children will be orphaned by the year 2010. Orphans are more likely than other children to become homeless, to be the victims of sexual violence or trafficking, or to be taken out of school—all of which increase their risk of HIV. Not surprisingly, orphaned girls are particularly vulnerable to HIV. Removed from school, many are forced to survive by providing sex for food or money.

C. A Clear Link Between Increased Education and Reduced HIV Infections

10   Millions of young people lack information or have misconceptions about HIV/AIDS, and girls are generally more poorly informed than boys. But basic education can equip children with the skills and knowledge they need in order to avoid HIV infection. Indeed, education correlates directly to better knowledge, safer behavior, and reduced HIV infection rates. The Global Campaign for Education estimates that if all children received a complete primary education, as many as 700,000 cases of HIV could be prevented each year. In addition, of course, sex education that addresses HIV prevention is essential.

11   Research clearly shows that better educated people have lower rates of infection, especially among younger people. Girls who are enrolled in school are much less likely to be sexually active, and better-educated girls tend to delay having sex and are more likely to require their partners to use condoms. A recent study from rural Uganda shows the positive impact of education on reducing HIV prevalence:

HIV Prevalence by Level of Education
Rural Uganda, 2002—Individuals Aged 18–29

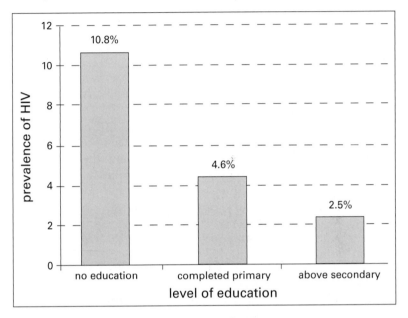

Source: De Walque and J Whitworth, MRC Uganda (2002).

D. Education Empowers Girls

12 Education is critical to helping girls achieve economic independence. A 19-country study by the International Center for Research on Women found that the lower women's social status, the higher their rate of HIV infection. Ultimately, better-educated girls are more likely to delay marriage and childbearing, have fewer children and healthier babies, enjoy better earning potential, and avoid commercial sex.

III. DEFINING AN ADVOCACY AGENDA

13 Today, over 113 million children in the world's poorest countries do not attend school, two-thirds of them girls. UNICEF estimates that international education aid has fallen by 30% over the past decade. And HIV/AIDS is seriously threatening education systems—killing teachers and administrators, increasing absenteeism, and lowering productivity, all of which increase costs to struggling school systems. At least 55 of the poorest countries seem unlikely to achieve the Millennium Development Goal of universal basic education by 2015, and 31 of these countries are also among the 36 worst affected by HIV/AIDS. Clearly, new approaches are needed in order to accelerate progress toward this critically important goal.

A. Eliminate School-Related Fees

14   In the poorest countries, school-related fees keep millions of children out of school. In nearly all countries, separate fees are assessed on various aspects of education, including tuition, textbooks and equipment, uniforms, Parent Teacher Association membership, and community and building services. Many mothers dying from HIV are most concerned with who will pay their children's school fees. And the cost of school fees often prevents people from adopting orphans either formally or informally.

15   Conversely, eliminating such fees dramatically expands school enrollment. When Kenya eliminated primary school fees in 2003, enrollment jumped by 22% in just a few days. In Uganda, school enrollment jumped by 40% after debt relief funds were used to eliminate school fees three years ago. In addition, eliminating school fees is a cost-effective means of dramatically expanding educational access. For example, the total cost of eliminating school fees in Swaziland, the nation with the highest HIV/AIDS rate in the world, would total roughly $20 million. Many other countries that have been heavily impacted by the AIDS epidemic continue to impose school-related fees.

16   Abolition of school fees was recently identified as the first "quick win" priority in The Millennium Project's recent report, "Investing in Development: A Practical Plan to Achieve the Millennium Development Goals," and was included as a specific recommendation in "Our Common Interest," the Blair Commission for Africa's report earlier this year:

> "African governments should undertake to remove school fees for basic education, and donors should fund this until countries can afford these costs themselves. This should be part of a coherent strategy for education, properly sequenced so the quality is not reduced with the massive increase in enrollment likely. The impacts will benefit all children and will be particularly strong for girls—in Uganda when user fees were removed, enrollment of the poorest girls doubled."—*"Our Common Interest," Blair Commission for Africa*

B. Mobilize Additional Resources to Achieve Universal Basic Education

17   The poorest countries need assistance in order to scale up and improve educational systems. Specifically, funds are needed to train teachers, strengthen and expand infrastructure, buy textbooks and equipment, ensure quality, and introduce computer technologies. Additional resources are also needed to leverage the elimination of school fees and underwrite the transitional costs to governments of eliminating fees and meeting increased demand for education.

Importantly, these resources must be channeled to local communities as needed to replace the revenues lost through the elimination of school-related fees.

18   In the few countries that have eliminated school fees, an influx of new students has created serious challenges for the existing educational system. But increased public and political attention to the growing demands on the nation's schools soon catalyzed the resources needed to scale up services and achieve quality improvements.

19   Foreign aid for education totals about $1.5 billion a year, and the Global Campaign for Education estimates that roughly $7 billion per year in external funding will be needed to achieve universal basic education. This sum takes into account the additional resources needed to enhance girls' enrollment, address the impact of AIDS on school systems, and support education in countries experiencing conflicts and other emergencies. A fair-share U.S. contribution of one-third of the amount needed to achieve universal basic education would be roughly $2.34 billion per year.

20   Additional resources will be needed to achieve the goal of establishing schools as community-based centers for the provision of comprehensive services for orphaned and vulnerable children, e.g., food and nutrition, immunization, psychosocial support, etc.

C. Reform Financing and Delivery Mechanisms

21   Countless small-scale projects have proven successful in expanding educational access. To help ramp up these successful models, the Education for All–Fast Track Initiative (FTI) was launched in 2002. Housed at the World Bank, FTI is a partnership of developing countries and donors created to help low-income countries achieve the Millennium Development Goal of universal basic education by 2015. Thirteen countries are now ready to implement FTI, but there is a $1.5 billion funding gap. (Another seven countries are expected to endorse FTI by the end of 2005.)

22   Annual bilateral aid to basic education in Africa has averaged only $419 million in recent years (2000–2003). In addition:

- 60% of bilateral aid to education goes to post-secondary education, which mainly benefits the children of the more affluent.
- 12% of bilateral aid to education reaches the 15 countries with the largest gender gaps in education.
- 70% of aid to education comes in the form of technical cooperation—more than twice the average across all sectors of development assistance. The remaining 30% is heavily biased toward capital investments rather than recurring costs.
- A large share of aid to basic education is project rather than programme funding, leaving governments to juggle dozens of donor-initiated projects that have a relatively small net value.

23 Clearly, existing efforts to achieve universal basic education, including bilateral programs and the multilateral Fast Track Initiative, are not getting the job done. A new approach is needed to take best practices and scale them up dramatically. Specifically, the Global AIDS Alliance recommends advocacy for the reform of these mechanisms and/or the creation of a new financing and delivery mechanism to accelerate access to basic education.

24   Specific reforms should include the acceleration of public-private partnerships, a commitment to locally driven strategic plans, improved monitoring of international standards of accountability, [a] strong civil-society role in governance and monitoring, and expanded use of information technology to achieve results. In particular, the accelerated introduction of new information technologies would help country-level stakeholders "leap frog" progress toward both broader educational access and improved educational quality.

IV. CONCLUSION

25 Providing a basic education to children—while ensuring equal opportunities for girls and orphans—offers a critical window of hope in responding to the AIDS epidemic. In addition, enhancing educational access for girls and orphans will help achieve several of the Millennium Development Goals unanimously adopted by 189 member countries of the United Nations in September 2000, including reducing poverty, achieving universal primary education, improving gender equality, and lowering the prevalence of HIV/AIDS. Finally, getting girls into school matters because educated women improve the health and well-being of families, have fewer children, and do more to educate children.

26   Acceleration of progress toward achieving universal primary education will require results-based advocacy that seeks to achieve real political impact and secure concrete benefits for people in impoverished countries. Policymakers must be persuaded to allocate the necessary resources through reformed financing mechanisms that are held accountable for achieving measurable, on-the-ground impact in terms of enabling more children to secure a basic education.

Bibliography

AIDS Orphans and Vulnerable Children (OVC): Problems, Responses, and Issues for Congress, Congressional Research Service, March 1, 2004 . . . .

Basic Education: A Review of USAID's de facto Basic Education Strategy, RESULTS, December 30, 2004.

Education and HIV/AIDS: A Window of Hope, The World Bank, April 2002.

Education and HIV/AIDS: Ensuring Education Access for Orphans and Vulnerable Children, UNICEF, November 2002.

Education for All–Fast Track Initiative, Country Updates, FTI Secretariat, March 17–19, 2005.

Education in Africa: Obstacles and Opportunities, Basic Education Coalition.

Education: The Best Vaccine Against HIV/AIDS, Basic Education Coalition.

Framework for the Protection, Care and Support of Orphans and Vulnerable Children Living in a World with HIV and AIDS, UNICEF, July 2004.

Investing in Development: A Practical Plan to Achieve the Millennium Development Goals, The Millennium Project, 2005.

Learning to Survive: How Education for All Would Save Millions of Young People from HIV/AIDS, Global Campaign for Education, April 26, 2004.

Our Common Interest, Report of the Commission for Africa, February 2005.

Small Change: An Alternative Progress Report on the Education Fast Track Initiative, Global Campaign for Education, March 2005 (draft).

User Fees in Primary Education, The World Bank, July 2004.

What Works in Girls' Education: Evidence and Policies from the Developing World, Council of Foreign Relations, 2004.

Online Resources:

Education for All–Fast Track Initiative, www.worldbank.org/education/efafti/

Global Campaign for Education, www.campaignforeducation.org/

Joint United Nations Programme on HIV/AIDS (UNAIDS), www.unaids.org

United Nations Children's Fund (UNICEF), www.unicef.org

United Nations Population Fund (UNFPA), www.unfpa.org

For Class Discussion

1. What network of issues does this advocacy brief address? How would you summarize the causal mechanisms that this brief posits and the consequences it believes its proposal will have?

2. How does the Global AIDS Alliance persuade you that it is a knowledgeable, reliable source of information?

3. How well does the Global AIDS Alliance convince you that its policy is practical, significant, and cost-effective?

4. What obstacles to implementing this proposal can you think of?

5. If you were to translate this advocacy statement for a more general audience, how would you do it?

6. What contribution does this piece make to the public debate over stopping the AIDS pandemic? ∎

CHAPTER QUESTIONS FOR REFLECTION AND DISCUSSION

1. From your reading of the articles in this chapter, list three to five problems that the global community is facing in its efforts to control AIDS. How would you rank these problems in terms of seriousness? Which is the greatest obstacle and why?

2. After reading the articles in this chapter, choose one of the following pairs of authors and sketch out their points of agreement and disagreement. What assumptions and values do they share? Where do they differ or clash?

   • Henry I. Miller and Ann Marie Kimball or Obama/Lugar
   • Raymond Downing and Kingsley Moghalu or the African AIDS Prevention Images
   • Melinda Gates and Gayle Smith
   • Raymond Downing and Stephen Lewis
   • Melinda Gates and Raymond Downing or Kingsley Moghalu

3. Which author in this chapter do you think draws most effectively on his/her professional experience and personal convictions to enhance the credibility and persuasiveness of his/her argument?

4. According to the readings in this chapter, what are the most serious problems facing girls and women in developing countries in the struggle against AIDS?

5. In groups or individually, research one of the following topics and bring your information and views back to share with your class. From your research, what have you learned that can deepen the public discussion about fighting diseases in a global community?

   A. In her article "AIDS and India," Melinda Gates mentions approaches to AIDS education and prevention that are having some success in India. Research other culture-based programs in India such as the AIDS Walk for Life, sponsored by Project Concern International in India. How are these programs tailored to Indian society and culture? How effective are they?

   B. Oprah Winfrey, Bono, and other popular figures are using their star appeal and their financial resources to mobilize the global community in the worldwide fight against deadly diseases. Investigate Oprah, Bono, or some other celebrity who is working for global health. Which of the perspectives on diseases presented in the readings in this chapter does this person support? Where is this celebrity investing his or her efforts and resources?

   C. Investigate what kinds of psychological and medical care your state, county, or city is providing for local residents with HIV/AIDS. How many people are receiving health care and what is the cost of treatment?

   D. Imagine that you are going to travel in the rural areas of a country in Latin America, Africa, or Southeast Asia. What is the status of bird flu and other infectious diseases in that region of the world? What shots should you have and what precautions should you take? You might first want to consult the Web site for the Centers for Disease

Control and Prevention (www.cdc.gov) to determine the status of diseases in that country.

E. Jonathan Rauch raises controversial issues about global diseases and immigration. After researching current laws about immigration, comment on what you think is the best way to handle HIV-positive immigrants. What are Rauch's most persuasive points?

F. The stories about AIDS orphans in Africa are heartbreaking and frightening. What programs or approaches are currently being tried in African countries to help these orphans? What approaches look the most promising? If you had the financial resources, which programs would you support?

G. Using the AIDS posters in this chapter as a starting point, research various public awareness and prevention campaigns in sub-Saharan African countries. What kinds of appeals do these campaigns make? You might also investigate posters that have been used in the United States to promote AIDS education. AVERT (www.avert.org), an international AIDS organization, is a good starting point to research the history of AIDS awareness.

H. Research the current controversy between the U.S. government and a group of NGOs over AIDS prevention in developing countries, antitrafficking programs, and the pledge against prostitution. To understand this controversy, you might begin by consulting the advocacy group Human Rights Watch (www.hrw.org).

WRITING ASSIGNMENTS

Brief Writing Assignments

1. Write a brief personal narrative about (a) a time when you had a serious case of the flu or (b) a time when your family, friends, or community experienced an epidemic that made a lot of people around you sick. How did you catch this disease? What was unpleasant or scary about it? How long did it take you or others to get well? How did this experience affect your thinking about diseases?

2. Summarize one of the more complex arguments in this chapter such as the article by Raymond Downing, Stephen Lewis, Gayle Smith, or the Global AIDS Alliance. What are the main points that readers should take away from reading this article?

3. Skimming through the readings in this chapter, find an example of a powerful and rhetorically effective use of numerical data. Briefly explain why it is meaningful and comprehensible. Then write a one-paragraph report about some aspect of the bird flu or AIDS pandemic in which you try your hand at translating a numerical fact into a

rhetorically effective form for your classmates or some specified audience. Be sure to cite your sources.

4. Using ideas from the articles in this chapter, freewrite an informal defense or refutation of one of the following claims. If you might write a formal argument on this issue later, you might write one response in support of this claim and then spend an equal amount of time questioning and refuting it.

   A. Countries experiencing influenza epidemics need to consider the global community as much as their own citizens.

   B. Developed countries should concentrate most of their support for AIDS victims on research to create a vaccine.

   C. The rich countries of the world need to regard AIDS as a global security threat as serious and dangerous as a military threat.

   D. Science and technology are the most powerful tools in the fight against AIDS.

   E. Developed countries need to give third world countries free rein in choosing how they will use financial aid in their battles against AIDS.

5. Write a short response paper in which you explain which article in this chapter had the greatest intellectual and emotional impact on you as a global citizen.

6. Think about how the spread of diseases in the global community is related to other topics in this text such as free trade (Chapter 2), immigration (Chapter 4), the trafficking of women and children (Chapter 6), environmental problems with water and climate change (Chapter 7), and feeding the world (Chapter 8). Brainstorm a network of issue questions that highlight connected controversies: for example, How have free trade agreements between the United States and Africa affected African countries' resources to fight AIDS? How has inadequate and unsafe water in developing countries worsened the AIDS pandemic?

Writing Projects

1. Write an essay that analyzes and critiques the effectiveness of one of the readings in this chapter as an argument. What features of this piece make it particularly rhetorically effective or problematic? Consider its target audience and genre, its claim and use of evidence, its use of emotional appeals, the author's knowledge and reliability, and the contribution of this piece to the public understanding of global health issues. What argumentative strategies are worthy of imitation?

2. Often influenza pandemics such as SARS and bird flu get hyped by the media through alarmist headlines or television news reports that fan people's fear without offering useful information or pragmatic advice. Research the problems of early detection in developing countries and

of having adequate supplies of vaccines and antiviral medicines available. Write an informative and persuasive piece for your university or local newspaper in which you present what you think everyone should know about global and national preparedness. What approaches offer the most hope of reducing the danger of influenza pandemics? How would you like the U.S. government to allocate funds for preparation? You might choose to write an op-ed piece in which you focus on one of these angles.

3. If a flu pandemic were to reach your region or city, it could completely disrupt public life, taking many lives and costing businesses millions of dollars. Investigate the status of your city's emergency preparations by researching and interviewing public health officials and possibly representatives of the largest companies in your area. How would your city handle problems such as workers without sick leave who insist on going to work sick; companies with a large percentage of their employees ill; and interrupted public services such as sanitation, food supply, and public transportation? Write a brief argument in which you praise or criticize the status of preparations in your city. Try to motivate local citizens and businesses to become involved in this issue.

4. The controversy over condoms in Africa is complicated, involving their effectiveness as a prevention strategy and their cultural, spiritual, and moral implications. After researching a variety of perspectives—for example, the views of American Catholics and African Catholics; the results of research studies on the effectiveness of condoms, say, in Uganda; the findings of UNAIDS and other global organizations; views of African leaders; views of African health care workers and other relevant stakeholders—write a policy proposal addressed to your U.S. representatives or senators in which you argue for the role you think condoms should play in the fight against AIDS in Africa.

5. Search for editorial/political cartoons on bird flu or AIDS, and find one that you think is particularly provocative. Write a short paper in which you analyze this cartoon and its contribution to the public conversation over pandemics. What view of bird flu or AIDS does it voice? What readings in this chapter does it support? What readings does it challenge?

6. Some countries such as Brazil and Thailand have been assertive in tackling their domestic problems with AIDS. Research these countries or another country that you have read about to discover what national and/or local approaches to AIDS have been effective. Write a policy proposal for your peers in which you argue in favor of trying this country's programs or policies elsewhere in the world.

7. The controversy over antiretroviral drugs and developing countries brings up the intersection of health issues and medical treatment with politics. After researching AIDS drugs, write a policy proposal in which you

argue (a) that brand-name drugs are better for developing countries; (b) that generic AIDS drugs are just as effective as brand-name drugs; (c) that developing countries should have the right to choose what drugs they will use; or (d) that the global community should pressure the FDA to grant approval of generic drugs manufactured outside the United States. Be sure to consult a range of think tanks such as the Hudson Institute, the Cato Institute, and the Center for American Progress. You could address this argument to a policymaker or to fellow American citizens, who fund AIDS assistance programs with taxes.

8. The names of the following organizations pop up frequently in articles about world health crises. Choose one of these or another global or public health institute or organization and investigate it. Then prepare a short speech for your class in which you explain the role this organization is playing in the world health picture. Summarize and illustrate what you find important about this organization.

Family Health International (www.fhi.org)
Doctors without Borders (www.doctorswithoutborders.org)
World Health Organization (www.who.org)
U.S. Department of Health and Human Services (www.os.dhhs.gov)
National Institutes of Health (www.nih.gov)
Centers for Disease Control and Prevention (www.cdc.gov)
Institute of Medicine of the National Academies (www.iom.edu)
Center for Infectious Disease Research and Policy at the University of Minnesota (www.cidrap.umn.edu)

Glossary of Globalization Terms

agribusiness An industry engaged in the production, processing, manufacture, or distribution of farm goods.

asylum seeker A type of refugee seeking relief from political or religious persecution.

authoritarianism A system of government that favors concentration of power in a dictator or an elite who is not democratically elected.

blog A journal or newsletter that is updated frequently and available on the Internet for public consumption and that provides individual commentary on current events.

blue collar A working-class employee who performs manual labor such as factory work.

call center An office of a company that fields incoming or makes outgoing telephone calls. For example, if you call with questions about your computer program, your call will likely go to a call center.

capital Wealth and durable produced goods that are used in the production of other goods—farm equipment, property, or money, for example.

Central American Free Trade Agreement (CAFTA) A free trade agreement, similar to the North American Free Trade Agreement, between the United States and most Central American countries legalized in 2005.

civil society The public arena between the realm of government and the private arena of family life where people voluntarily interact with one another.

Clean Air Act A set of laws originally passed in 1963 that has since been expanded and revised. These laws aim to improve air quality and focus specifically on the ozone layer, acid rain, and emissions standards for factories and vehicles.

Cold War A period of conflict, roughly from 1940 to 1990, between the political and economic ideological stances of the United States, which promoted capitalism, and those of the former Soviet Union, which promoted communism. Although no direct war took place, it was characterized by a nuclear arms race and conflicts between secondary nations supported by the United States and the former Soviet Union.

colonialism Political, economic, social, and cultural domination and exploitation of a territory by a foreign power. This system was popular among the European powers in the nineteenth century, a notable example being Great Britain's presence in India.

communication technology Technologies used to transmit data or exchange information.

communism A political system in which the government owns the means of production and equitably distributes the common goods among the people.

559

communitarianism   A political philosophy, created in response to the rugged individualism of liberalism, that advocates the preservation and enhancement of the community.

comparative advantage   David Ricardo's theory of economics stating that all countries benefit when each nation specializes in producing and exporting goods it can produce at relatively lower cost, and imports goods it produces at higher cost.

cost-benefit analysis   A method of determining whether the benefits of a proposed policy outweigh the losses.

cultural diversity   Differences in race, ethnicity, language, nationality, or religion among various groups within a community or nation.

cultural homogenization   The act of making a formerly diverse cultural population uniform.

cultural imperialism   Promoting the domination of the culture or language of one nation over another, disregarding cultural diversity.

cultural pluralism   The existence of multiple culturally diverse groups within a larger shared culture.

demographic   A collection of population characteristics used to describe a group of people—for example, fertility, mortality, migration, or density.

dependency theory   A theory of international relations that states that rich countries stay rich and keep poor countries poor by exploiting the resources and wealth of poor countries.

deregulation   The reduction or elimination of government control of private economic activities, usually to the benefit of corporations.

developed countries   The wealthiest nations of the world, which enjoy high levels of education, health standards, and technological advancement.

developing countries   The poorer countries of the world, which are attempting to industrialize or reach the economic level of the developed countries.

diaspora   People settled far from the homelands of their ancestry.

economic development   Usually measured by an increase in a population's standard of living, economic development involves increases in technology, resources, and human capital.

economic growth   An increase in the total output of a nation over time, usually measured in terms of gross domestic product (GDP).

embargo   A legal refusal to sell goods to a disfavored country.

emissions   The release of greenhouse gases into the atmosphere.

Environmental Protection Agency   An agency of the U.S. government created in 1970 to oversee coordinated governmental protection of the environment and natural resources.

epidemic   A widespread disease that affects many individuals in a population in a relatively short period of time.

ethnicity   Cultural characteristics that distinguish one group of people from another.

European Union (EU)   A federation of European states, originally created after World War II to prevent another war through economic integration by means of the establishment of a common currency and free movement of goods across borders. Currently, the EU maintains common economic, foreign, and security policies. The agreement between fifteen countries (Austria, Belgium, Denmark, Finland, France, Germany, Greece, Ireland, Italy, Luxembourg, the Netherlands, Portugal, Spain, Sweden, and the United Kingdom) has expanded to include Cyprus, the Czech Republic, Estonia, Hungary, Latvia, Lithuania, Malta, Poland, Slovakia, and Slovenia.

Export Processing Zone (EPZ) A region within a country aimed at attracting foreign investment from multinational corporations by relaxing tax and labor restrictions. Examples include apparel and textile factories in Saipan and the Philippines, and Motorola and Intel factories in Costa Rica. EPZs are often associated with sweatshops.

fair trade A trade movement characterized by concern for human rights and social responsibility that demands workers and farmers be treated and paid fairly and that works to remove middlemen.

fatwah A statement issued by an Islamic religious figure.

Federal Reserve An institution of the U.S. government responsible for monetary policy, meaning the regulation of banks, adjustments of the money supply, and the control of inflation.

first world Originally used to indicate democratic nations during the Cold War, the term now describes the highly developed, rich nations of the Western world.

food security The ability of countries independently to provide adequate and reliable food at reasonable cost for their own people in socially acceptable ways to sustain healthy living.

food sovereignty The right of people to define their own food and agriculture, free from pressures of the international market.

fossil fuels Fuels formed over millions of years from dead plants and animals; examples include oil, natural gas, and coal.

free trade An economic philosophy of reducing barriers to unrestricted trade, such as tariffs, taxes, subsidies, and quotas, in an effort to move raw materials, goods, and services freely across international borders. This ideology is largely embraced and promoted by the World Trade Organization, the International Monetary Fund, and the World Bank as the best way to benefit both developed countries and developing countries.

Free Trade Area of the Americas (FTAA) A proposed trade agreement that would expand the benefits of the North American Free Trade Agreement to the entire Western Hemisphere.

fundamentalism The belief in strict adherence to certain traditional doctrines and practices of a religion and the tendency to interpret scriptures literally.

General Agreement on Tariffs and Trade (GATT) Created in 1947, GATT is a negotiating framework for international trade aimed at eliminating tariffs and quotas in order to achieve free trade. GATT was absorbed by the WTO.

gene splicing Combining isolated genes from different organisms into the chromosomes of one organism.

genocide Deliberate and systematic annihilation of a racial, political, or cultural group.

global capitalism   The expansion of the system of capitalism (individual and corporate ownership of the means of production) as the primary economic system around the globe.

grassroots   A political movement organized by a network of citizens at the local level.

greenhouse gases   Gases that trap the heat of the sun in the earth's atmosphere, producing the greenhouse effect; examples include carbon dioxide, nitrous oxide, water vapor, and the gases in aerosols.

Green Revolution   A dramatic increase of agricultural production, in both developed and developing countries, between the 1940s and 1970s as a result of the widespread use of pesticides, chemical fertilizers, hybrid seeds, and animal antibiotics.

gross domestic product (GDP)   The total monetary value of goods and services produced by and within a country during a specific period.

gross national product (GNP)   The total monetary value of goods and services produced by a nation at home and abroad during a specific period.

hegemony   The dominance of one power over another and a simultaneous acceptance of the commanding power's right to rule.

ideology   A unifying system of beliefs, values, philosophies, and attitudes that guides a society, particularly in the form of its government.

imperialism   The practice of one country's extending its control over the territory, political system, or economic life of another country.

information technology (IT)   All forms of technology that deal with computers, telecommunications, or the storage, transmission, or retrieval of information.

infrastructure   The system of public works in a country that makes business activities possible—for example, roads, buildings, telephone service, electricity, and public transportation.

International Labor Organization (ILO)   A UN agency created in 1919 to maintain and promote fair and socially just international labor standards.

International Monetary Fund (IMF)   An international organization designed to lend finances to nations with debt problems and provide solutions that will enable international free trade, monetary cooperation, and economic growth. Some people protest IMF policies because membership is undemocratic; the countries that contribute the most money have the most voting power.

Kyoto Protocol   An international agreement negotiated in 1997 in Kyoto, Japan, and effective in 2005, to reduce the rate of fossil fuel emissions to acceptable levels through legally binding commitments. The United States decided not to sign this agreement or adhere to its standards.

land reform   Redistribution of land ownership to small farmers and peasants in order to destroy the concentration of landholdings among a few powerful landowners or corporations.

liberalism   A political philosophy from the nineteenth century that embraces individual rights, civil liberties, and private property.

libertarianism   An economic philosophy that promotes free trade and emphasizes the importance of personal freedom in economic and political affairs and the limitation of government intervention in the lives and choices of individuals.

macroeconomics   Factors that reveal the big picture of a state's economy, including GDP growth, inflation, interest rates, and productivity.

market   A place where buyers and sellers interact and supply and demand control the fluctuation of prices of goods.

Marxism   Marx's theory of socialism that includes class struggle and a dictatorship of the proletariat working toward the eventual realization of a classless society.

microbicide   An antibiotic or chemical that kills microbes, currently being tested to see whether forms of the agent can destroy STDs and HIV.

Millennium Development Goals   Eight goals set by the United Nations to tackle and conquer some of the world's worst problems, including the scarcity of safe water, extreme poverty and hunger, child mortality, HIV/AIDS, and to achieve universal primary education, gender equality, environmental sustainability, and global partnership for development. The proposed time for reaching these goals is 2015.

monocultures   The growing of plants or animals of a single species, absent of biodiversity.

Monroe Doctrine   A declaration made by American President James Monroe in 1823 that stated that European involvement in the territories of North and South America would be viewed as a hostile threat to America's interests.

most favored nation (MFN)   A trade principle utilized by the WTO that states that all of a nation's trading partners must receive the lowest tariff rates the country offers.

multiculturalism   Appreciation for diversity among cultures.

multinational/transnational corporations   Corporations that have divisions in more than two countries.

nationalism   Complete loyalty to and belief in the greatness of one's nation.

nation building   Constructing or structuring a nation using the power of the state, often in the realms of political development, economic growth, and social harmony.

neoliberalism   A political-economic philosophy that encourages deregulation, favors corporations, and suggests that the best way to achieve justice, progress, and growth is through free market economics.

nongovernmental organization (NGO)   A nonprofit agency unconnected to government or corporate or private actors and interests that is devoted to issues of social justice and resource management. Examples include Catholic Relief Services, the International Red Cross, the World Wildlife Fund, and Human Rights Watch.

nonrenewable resources   Natural resources that are finite and exhaustible because of their scarcity or the length of time it takes for them to be replenished; examples include minerals and oil.

North American Free Trade Agreement (NAFTA)   A trade agreement ratified in 1993 and put in effect in 1994 between the United States, Canada, and Mexico created to encourage free trade and investment among the three countries.

organic food   Food grown or raised without the use of man-made fertilizers, pesticides, additives, antibiotics, or growth hormones.

outsourcing/offshore outsourcing   Subcontracting some or all of a business' functions to a foreign company. This term is most often used to describe the movement of jobs to developing countries.

pandemic   A widespread epidemic that crosses international boundaries and affects a large number of people on a number of continents simultaneously.

potable water   Water that is safe for human consumption.

President's Emergency Plan for AIDS Relief (PEPFAR)   President George W. Bush's initiative that proposes a U.S. government fund to allocate fifteen billion dollars in a five-year period to fight AIDS internationally.

privatization   Turning over or selling state-owned industries to the private sector.

productivity   The efficiency with which things are produced, usually with a focus on the amount of labor and time involved.

protectionism   Any policy used to protect domestic industries against competition from imports; tariffs are the most common form of protectionism.

quota   A form of protectionism that limits the total quantity of imports of a good during a set period of time.

rational choice theory   The theory of human nature and interaction that states that people calculate the costs and benefits of any action and rationally decide which course of action would be the best to take.

real politik   A German term describing foreign policy that is based on practical concerns as opposed to theoretical or ethical concerns.

recession   A period of reduced economic activity characterized by rising levels of unemployment, a decline in GDP, and slowed production.

renewable resources   Natural resources such as forests or fisheries that renew themselves through natural processes.

sectarianism   Adherence to a particular form or sect of a religion to the exclusion of other sects.

secularism   A governmental system that embodies the separation of church and state.

Smith, Adam   The founding father of economics and capitalism, most famous for *The Wealth of Nations* (1776), in which he argued that people should be free from government interference to follow their own self-interests in the market, which would regulate economic activity like an "invisible hand." However, Smith believed that government intervention in the economy was at times necessary to provide public works such as roads and schools that would not be profitable for individuals to produce on their own.

socialism   A political and economic system in which a democratic community owns the means of production and distributes the benefits equitably among the community members.

sovereignty   A principle of government that holds that a state exercises absolute power over its territory and population.

Structural Adjustment Programs (SAP)   The package of free market reforms designed to create economic growth and to generate income to pay off a nation's debt. These policies were promoted by the IMF and World Bank. Third world nations agree to SAPs in exchange for debt relief.

subcontracting   To use a third party to complete all or part of the work required for a job.

subsidy   Financial help from the government to the private sector of the economy.

sustainable development   Development that meets the needs of the present while conserving resources so that future generations will be able to meet their own needs.

sweatshop   A factory in which employees work for long hours under unhealthy or dangerous conditions for low pay.

tariff   A tax on each unit of an imported good.

theocracy   A political system in which political organization is based upon religious organization.

third world   Used during the Cold War to describe nations aligned with neither communism nor democracy, this term is now used to describe developing countries.

totalitarianism   A political system characterized by dictatorial, one-party rule. Totalitarian regimes generally do not tolerate political opposition and attempt to control all aspects of citizen life.

trade barriers   Policies utilized by governments to restrict importing and exporting with other countries; tariffs are the most common form of trade barriers.

Trade-Related Intellectual Property Rights (TRIPs)   Laws governing patents, copyrights, and other goods related to information that are hotly disputed in the international trading system; one example is patents in the pharmaceutical industry.

trafficking   An illegal activity involving the international transport of drugs, weapons, or people, the latter by threat, force, or fraud.

transgenic crops   Crops that have been experimentally altered by genetic material from another organism.

United Nations   An international organization created in 1945 by fifty-one countries to preserve peace and security through international cooperation and collective action. Current membership is 191 countries.

Uruguay Round   The final set of trade negotiations under GATT that began in 1986 and closed in 1993. This round created the WTO as a permanent arena to address issues of international free trade.

wastewater   Used water that carries wastes like soap, chemicals, or fertilizers from homes, businesses, or industries.

white collar   Employees who do nonmanual desk work, often for higher compensation than blue-collar workers receive.

World Bank   An international financial institution whose purpose is to lend funds and provide assistance for economic development in poorer countries, often prescribing policies that promote free trade.

World Health Organization (WHO)   An agency of the United Nations, founded in 1948 to promote the attainment of the highest level of human health through research, technical cooperation among countries, international conferences, and various other programs.

World Trade Organization (WTO)   An international organization created in 1994 and active as of 1995, responsible for the legislation and regulation of trade rules and the adjudication of trade disputes, aimed at maintaining free trade in the international trading system.

xenophobia   Fear or hatred of foreigners.

Films on Global Issues

Chapter 1 Introduction: Defining and Exploring Globalization

Being Hmong Means Being Free. Documentary. Produced by Larry Long. 56 min. 2000.

The Corporation. Documentary. Directed by Mark Achbar and Jennifer Abbott. 145 min. 2003.

Granito de Arena. Documentary. Directed by Jill Friedberg. 60 min. 2004.

The New Rulers of the World. Documentary. Directed by Alan Lowery. 53 min. 2001.

Chapter 2 Consumerism, Free Trade, and Sweatshops

Another World Is Possible. Documentary. Directed by Mark Dworkin and Melissa Young. 24 min. 2002.

Behind the Labels: Garment Workers on U.S. Saipan. Documentary. Directed by Tia Lessin. 45 min. 2001.

Cappuccino Trail: The Global Economy in a Cup, a.k.a. *Tales from the Global Economy: The Cappuccino Trail.* Documentary. Directed by Jeremy Newson. 50 min. 2002.

A Struggle (Zheng Zha). Documentary. Directed by Haolun Shu. 50 min. 2001.

Talking to the Wall: The Story of an American Bargain. Documentary. Directed by Steve Alves. 57 min. 2004.

This Is What Democracy Looks Like. Documentary. Directed by Jill Friedberg and Rick Rowley. 72 min. 2000.

Wal-Mart: The High Cost of Low Prices. Documentary. Directed by Robert Greenwald. 95 min. 2005.

Chapter 3 Trading Jobs: Outsourcing and Employment in a Global Economy

American Jobs. Documentary. Directed by Gregg Spotts. 60 min. 2004.

Commanding Heights: The Battle for the World Economy. Documentary miniseries. Directed by William Cran and Greg Barker. 360 min. 2002.

Globalization: Winners and Losers. Documentary. Directed by Keely Purdue. 42 min. 2000.

Legacy of Shame. Documentary. Directed by Maurice Murad. 52 min. 2002.

1-800-INDIA. Documentary. Produced by Anna Carter; directed by Safina Uberoi. 60 min. 2005.

The Seattle Syndrome. Documentary. Directed by Steve Bradshaw. 25 min. 2000.

Chapter 4 Crossing Borders: Immigration

Abandoned: The Betrayal of America's Immigrants. Documentary. Directed by David Belle and Nicholas Wrathall. 55 min. 2000.

The Beautiful Country. Drama. Directed by Hans Petter Moland. 125 min. 2005.

A Day without a Mexican. Comedy. Directed by Sergio Arau. 95 min. 2004.

Death on a Friendly Border. Documentary. Directed by Rachel Antell. 26 min. 2001.

Farmingville. Documentary. Directed by Carlos Sandoval and Catherine Tambini. 72 min. 2003.

Head-On. Drama. Directed by Faith Akin. 118 min. 2004.

In My Own Skin: The Complexity of Living as an Arab in America. Documentary. Directed by Nikki Byrd and Jennifer Jajeh. 16 min. 2001.

Lone Star. Drama. Directed by John Sayles. 134 min. 1996.

The New Americans. Documentary miniseries. Directed by Susana Aikin et al. 408 min. 2004.

New World Border. Documentary. Directed by Jose Palafox and Casey Peek. 28 min. 2001.

Suspino: A Cry for Roma. Documentary. Directed by Gillian Darling Kovanic. 72 min. 2003.

Chapter 5 Cultural Rights: Global Tensions Over Media, Technology, Music, Film, and Food

Akira: The Special Edition, a.k.a. *Akira.* Action animation. Directed by Katsuhiro Otomo. 124 min. 1988.

Bride and Prejudice: The Bollywood Musical. Musical comedy. Directed by Gurinder Chadha. 111 min. 2004.

Howl's Moving Castle. Fantasy animation. Directed by Hayao Miyazaki. 119 min. 2004.

Lagaan: Once Upon a Time in India. Musical. Directed by Ashutosh Gowariker. 225 min. 2001.

Mondovino. Documentary. Directed by Jonathan Nossiter. 135 min. 2004.

Spirited Away. Adventure animation. Directed by Hayao Miyazaki. 125 min. 2001.

Taking Pictures. Documentary. Directed by Les McLaren and Annie Stiven. 56 min. 1996.

Chapter 6 Human Rights: Trafficking of Women and Children and Forced Child Labor

Born into Brothels: Calcutta's Red Light Kids. Documentary. Directed by Zana Briski and Ross Kauffman. 85 min. 2004.

The Garden. Documentary. Directed by Ruthie Shatz and Adi Barash. 85 min. 2004.

Immokalee: A Story of Slavery and Freedom. Documentary. Directed by Jeff Imig. 21 min. 2004.

Stolen Childhoods. Documentary. Directed by Len Morris and Robin Romano. 85 min. 2005.

Trading Women. Documentary. Directed by David A. Feingold. 77 min. 2003.

Chapter 7 Environmental Resources and Rights: Global Conflicts Over Water and Climate Change

Blue Vinyl. Documentary. Directed by Judith Helfand and Daniel B. Gold. 98 min. 2002.

Can Polar Bears Tread Water? Documentary. Produced by Lawrence Moore. 58 min. 1989.

DAM/AGE: A Film with Arundhati Roy. Documentary. Directed by Aradhana Seth. 50 min. 2002.

Extreme Oil. Documentary. Directed by Dominic Allan, Paul Burgess, William Cran, and Rebecca John. 180 min. 2004.

The Next Industrial Revolution: William McDonough, Michael Braungard and the Birth of the Sustainable Economy. Documentary. Directed by Chris Bedford and Shelley Morhaim. 55 min. 2001.

Running Dry. Documentary. Directed by Jim Thebaut. 90 min. 2005.

Sustainable Futures. Documentary. Produced by Unesco-Opeongo Line Co-Production. 39 min. 1999.

Thirst. Documentary. Produced and Directed by Alan Snitow and Deborah Kaufman. 62 min. 2004.

Turning Down the Heat. Documentary. Directed by Jim Hamm. 46 min. 1999.

Chapter 8 Feeding Global Populations

Darwin's Nightmare. Documentary. Directed by Hubert Sauper. 107 min. 2004.

Deconstructing Supper: Is Your Food Safe? Documentary. Directed by Marianne Kaplan. 48 min. 2002.

Fragile Harvest. Documentary. Directed by Robert Lang. 49 min. 1987.

Seeds of Plenty, Seeds of Sorrow. Documentary. Directed by Manjira Datta. 52 min. 1994.

Silent Killer: The Unfinished Campaign Against Hunger. Documentary. Produced by Hana Jindrova and John de Graaf. 57 min. 2005.

Strong Roots: The Landless Workers Movement in Brazil. Documentary. Directed by Aline Sasahara and Marie Luisa Mendoça. 41 min. 2001.

Chapter 9 The Spread of Disease in the Global Community

AIDS Warriors. Documentary. Directed by Andrew Young. 55 min. 2003.

Beware of Time. Documentary. Directed by Ntare Guma Mbaho Mwine. 74 min. 2003.

The Constant Gardner. Drama. Directed by Fernando Meirelles. 129 min. 2005.

46664, The Event—Nelson Mandela's AIDS Day Concert. Documentary. Produced by Bono, Joe Strummer, and Dave A. Stewart. 268 min. 2003.

H5N1-Killer Flu. Documentary. Directed by Steven Silver. 60 min. 2005.

Ithuteng (Never Stop Learning). Documentary. Directed by William Ebersol. 75 min. 2005.

State of Denial. Documentary. Directed by Elaine Epstein. 86 min. 2003.

Yesterday. Drama. Directed by Darrell James Roodt. 96 min. 2004.

Answers to Chapter 1 "Global Pursuit," pp. 3–5

1. Mumbai, India (formerly Bombay); Shanghai, China; Sao Paulo, Brazil
2. Korea
3. Russian vodka
4. Taipei, Taiwan (left); Kuala Lumpur, Malaysia (right)
5. South America
6. Mexico's Presidents
   1982–1988: Miguel de la Madrid Hurtado
   1988–1994: Carlos Salinas de Gortari
   1994–2000: Ernesto Zedillo Ponce de Leon
   2000–   Vincente Fox

   Canada's Prime Ministers
   1984–1993: Brian Mulroney
   1993–2003: Jean Cretien
   2003–2006: Paul Martin
7. Soccer
8. Africa
9. a. Shonen Knife: Japan
   b. Thalia: Mexico
   c. Lebo Mathosa: South Africa
   d. Los Lobos: United States
10. Euro
11. 10 provinces: Alberta, British Columbia, Manitoba, New Brunswick, Newfoundland, Nova Scotia, Ontario, Prince Edward Island, Quebec, and Saskatchewan; 3 territories: Yukon Territory, Northwest Territories, and Nunavut

12. India
13. Leaders of their countries:
    Megawati Sukarnoputri: President of Indonesia, 2001–2004
    Helen Clark: Prime Minister of New Zealand
    Aung San Suu Kyi: Burmese opposition leader, winner of 1991 Nobel Prize for Peace
14. Sex trade/trafficking
15. Indonesia
16. Bollywood in Mumbai is the site of India's huge film industry that produces more than 700 films a year that are shown around the world; Bollywood (blend of "Bombay" and "Hollywood") rivals American Hollywood.
17. Chinese
18. Brazil
19. Asmar, Eritrea
    Harare, Zimbabwe
    Kabul, Afghanistan
    Wellington, New Zealand
    Beijing, China
    Port-au-Prince, Haiti
    Apia, Samoa
    Sofia, Bulgaria
    Colombo, Sri Lanka
    Pyongyang, North Korea
20. Japan

Credits